The Forgotten Bible
Originally Edited by Philip Schaff
Edited by Anthony Uyl

Woodstock, Ontario, Canada 2017

The Forgotten Bible
The Forgotten Bible
Originally Edited by Philip Schaff (1819 - 1893)
Edited by Anthony Uyl

The text of The Forgotten Bible is all in the Public Domain. The layout and Devoted Publishing logo are Copyright ©2017 Devoted Publishing. This edition is published by Devoted Publishing a division of 2165467 Ontario Inc.

What kind of philosophies do you have?
Let us know!

Visit our online store: www.devotedpublishing.com
Contact us at: devotedpub@hotmail.com
Visit us on Facebook: @DevotedPublishing

Published in Woodstock, Ontario, Canada 2017

For bulk educational rates, please contact us at the above email address.

ISBN: 978-1-77356-134-9

Table of Contents

The Testaments of the Twelve Patriarchs 7
   Introductory Notice to The Testaments of the Twelve Patriarchs 7
      Footnotes: 11
   I - The Testament of Reuben Concerning Thoughts 13
      Footnotes: 15
   II - The Testament of Simeon Concerning Envy 16
      Footnotes: 18
   III - The Testament of Levi Concerning the Priesthood and Arrogance 19
      Footnotes: 24
   IV - The Testament of Judah Concerning Fortitude, and Love of Money, and Fornication 26
      Footnotes: 31
   V - The Testament of Issachar Concerning Simplicity 33
      Footnotes: 35
   VI - The Testament of Zebulun Concerning Compassion and Mercy 36
      Footnotes: 38
   VII - The Testament of Dan Concerning Anger and Lying 40
      Footnotes: 42
   VIII - The Testament of Naphtali Concerning Natural Goodness 43
      Footnotes: 45
   IX - The Testament of Gad Concerning Hatred 46
      Footnotes: 48
   X - The Testament of Asher Concerning Two Faces of Vice and Virtue 49
      Footnotes: 51
   XI - The Testament of Joseph Concerning Sobriety 52
      Footnotes: 57
   XII - The Testament of Benjamin Concerning a Pure Mind 58
      Footnotes: 61
Apocrypha of the New Testament 62
   Introductory Notice to Apocrypha of the New Testament 62
      Footnotes: 63
   Translator's Introductory Notice 64
      Footnotes: 67
      Footnotes: 71
   The Protevangelium of James 75
      Footnotes: 83
   The Gospel of Pseudo-Matthew 85
      Footnotes: 86
The Gospel of the Nativity of Mary 108
The History of Joseph the Carpenter 113

The Forgotten Bible

- Footnotes: 121
- The Gospel of Thomas 123
  - First Greek Form 123
    - Footnotes: 127
  - Second Greek Form 129
    - Footnote: 131
  - Latin Form 132
- The Arabic Gospel of the Infancy of the Saviour 138
  - Footnotes: 153
- The Gospel of Nicodemus 154
  - Part I - The Acts of Pilate 154
  - First Greek Form 154
  - Second Greek Form 170
  - Part II - The Descent of Christ into Hell 184
    - Greek Form 184
  - Part I - The Acts of Pilate 189
  - Latin Form 189
  - Part II - Christ's Descent into Hell 203
  - Latin First Version 203
  - Latin Second Version 212
- The Letter of Pontius Pilate, ... 218
- The Narrative of Joseph 225
- The Avenging of the Saviour 230
- Acts of the Holy Apostles Peter and Paul 236
- Acts of Paul and Thecla 250
- The Acts of Barnabus 258
- The Acts of Philip 263
- Acts of Saint Philip the Apostle When He Went to Upper Hellas 271
- Addition to Acts of Philip 277
- Acts and Martyrdom of the Holy Apostle Andrew 282
- Acts of Andrew and Matthias 289
- Acts of Peter and Andrew 301
- Acts and Martyrdom of St. Matthew the Apostle 304
- Acts of the Holy Apostle Thomas 313
  - When He Came into India, and Built the Palace in the Heavens 318
  - About the Dragon and the Young Man 323
  - About the Demon that Dwelt in the Woman 326
  - About the Young Man Who Killed the Maiden. 329
- Consummation of Thomas the Apostle 333
- Martyrdom of the Holy and Glorious Apostle Bartholomew 337
  - Footnotes: 342

Acts of the Holy Apostle Thaddaeus,	343
Footnotes:	344
Acts of the Holy Apostle and Evangelist John the Theologian.	345
Footnotes:	349
Revelation of Moses	351
Footnotes:	357
Revelation of Esdras	359
Footnotes:	364
Revelation of Paul	365
Footnotes:	374
Revelation of John	376
Footnotes:	381
The Book of John Concerning the Falling Asleep of Mary	384
Footnotes:	389
The Passing of Mary	390
First Latin Form	390
Footnotes:	393
Second Latin Form	394
Footnotes:	398
The Gospel of Peter	400
Introduction	400
Footnote:	403
The Gospel According to Peter	404
Footnotes:	406
The Revelation of Peter	407
Introduction	407
Footnote:	410
The Apocalypse of Peter	411
Footnotes:	413
Fragments of the Apocalypse of Peter	415
Footnotes:	415
The Vision of Paul	416
Introduction	416
The Vision of Paul	417
Footnotes:	437
The Apocalypse of the Virgin	439
Introduction	439
Footnote:	439
The Apocalypse of the Holy Mother of God Concerning the Chastisements	440
Footnotes:	448
The Apocalypse of Sedrach	449

The Forgotten Bible
   Introduction 449
      The Apocalypse of Sedrach 450
         Footnotes: 454
The Testament of Abraham 456
   Introduction 456
      The Testament of Abraham 458
         Version I 458
         Version II 468
         Footnotes: 473
The Acts of Xanthippe and Polyxena 474
   Introduction 474
   Life and Conduct of the Holy Women, Xanthippe, Polyxena, and Rebecca 475
   Footnotes: 490
The Narrative of Zosimus 491
   Introduction 491
   The Narrative of Zosimus Concerning the Life of the Blessed 492
      Footnotes: 497

The Testaments of the Twelve Patriarchs
By the Rev. Robert Sinker, M.A., Trinity College, Cambridge.

Introductory Notice to The Testaments of the Twelve Patriarchs

This very curious fragment of antiquity deserves a few words in anticipation of the translator's valuable preface.

Grabe's Spicilegium is there referred to; but it may be well also to consult his citations, in elucidation, of Bull's Defensio Fidei Nicaenae, [1] where he treats the work with respect.

My most valued authority, however, on this subject, is Lardner, [2] who gives a very full account of the work with his usual candor and learning.

He seems to treat the matter with a needless profusion of space and consideration; yet in a much later volume of his great treatise he recurs to the subject [3] with expressions of satisfaction that he had dealt with it so largely before.

Cave placed the composition of the Testaments about a.d. 192, but concedes a much earlier origin to the first portion of the work. Origen quotes from it, and Tertullian is supposed to have borrowed from it one of his expositions, as will be noted in its place.

Lardner clears it from charges of Ebionitism, [4] but thinks the author was so far in accord with that heresy as to use expressions savouring of "Unitarianism."

Of this charge he is not justly susceptible, it appears to me:
quite otherwise.

If we can imagine Trypho coming to the light after his kindly parting with Justin, [5] I can conceive of such a man as the author of this work.

He is a Christian awakening to the real purport of the Old-Testament Scriptures, and anxious to lead rather than drive his brethren after the flesh to the discovery of Him "concerning whom Moses in the law and the prophets did write:"

not a "Judaizing Christian," as Cave imagined, but the reverse,--a Christianizing Jew.

Now, I must think that such a writer would weave into his plan many accepted traditions of the Jews and many Rabbinical expositions of the sacred writers.

He was doubtless acquainted with that remarkable passage in the Revelation in which the patriarchs are so honourably named, [6] and with that corresponding passage which seems to unite the twelve patriarchs with the twelve apostles. [7] St. Paul's claim for the twelve tribes before Agrippa [8] would naturally impress itself on such a mind.

Whether the product of such a character with such a disposition would naturally be such an affectionate and filial attempt as this to identify the religion of the Crucified with the faith of the Jewish fathers, [9] may be judged of by my reader.

It appears to me an ill-advised romance; not more a "pious fraud" than several fictions which have attracted attention in our own times, based on the traditions of the Hebrews.

The legends of the "Wandering Jew" have grown out of corresponding instincts among Christians.

To me they appear like the profane "Passion-plays" lately revived among Christians,--a most unwarrantable form of teaching even truth.

But as to the work itself, seeing it exists, I must acknowledge that it seems to me a valuable relic of antiquity, and an interesting specimen of the feelings and convictions of those believers over whom St. James presided in Jerusalem: [10]"Israelites indeed," but "zealous of the law."

They were now convinced that Abraham and Isaac and Jacob, with Moses and all the prophets, looked for the Messiah who had appeared in Jesus of Nazareth.

The author of this book was anxious to show that the twelve patriarchs were twelve believers in the Paschal Lamb, and that they died in Christian penitence and faith.

He, then, who will read or study the following waif of the olden time, as I have done, will not find it unprofitable reading.

The Forgotten Bible

It really supplies a key to some difficulties in the Scripture narrative.

It suggests what are at least plausible counterparts of what is written. "To the pure all things are pure;" and I see nothing that need defile in any of the details which expose the sins, and magnify the penitence, of the patriarchs.

In fact, Lardner's objection to one of the sections in the beautiful narrative of Joseph strikes me as extraordinary.

It is the story of a heroic conflict with temptation, the like of which was doubtless not uncommon in the days of early Christians living among heathens; [11] and I think it was possibly written to inspire a Joseph-like chastity in Christian youth.

"I do not suppose," says Lardner, "that the virtue of any of these ancient Hebrews was complete according to the Christian rule."

I am amazed at this; I have always supposed the example of Joseph the more glorious because he flourished as the flower of chastity in a gross and carnal age.

Who so pure as he save John the Baptist, that morning star that shone so near the Sun of Righteousness in the transient beauty of his "heliacal rising"?

Surely Joseph was a type of Christ in this as in other particulars, and our author merely enables us to understand the "fiery darts" which he was wont to hurl back at the tempter.

I own (reluctantly, because I dislike this form of teaching) that for me the superlative ode of the dying Jacob receives a reflected lustre from this curious book, especially in the splendid eulogy with which the old patriarch blesses his beloved Joseph.

"The author," says Lardner, "in an indirect manner...bears a large testimony to the Christian religion, to the facts, principles, and books of the New Testament.

He speaks of the nativity of Christ, the meekness and unblameableness of His life, His crucifixion at the instigation of the Jewish priests, the wonderful concomitants of His death, His resurrection, and ascension.

He represents the character of the Messiah as God and man:

the Most High God with men, eating and drinking with them; the Son of God; the Saviour of the world, of the Gentiles and Israel; as Eternal High Priest and King.

He likewise speaks of the effusion of the Holy Spirit upon the Messiah, attended with a voice from heaven; His unrighteous treatment by the Jews; their desolations and the destruction of the Temple upon that account; the call of the Gentiles; the illuminating them generally with new light; the effusion of the Spirit upon believers, but especially, and in a more abundant measure, upon the Gentiles....There are allusions to the Gospels of St. Matthew, St. Luke and St. John, the Acts of the Apostles, and of the Epistles to Ephesians, First Thessalonians, First Timothy, Hebrews, and First St. John, also to the Revelation.

So far as consistent with the assumed character of his work, the author declares the canonical authority of the Acts of the Apostles and the Epistles of St. Paul."

Of which of the minor writers among the Ante-Nicene Fathers can so much be said?

Regarded as a sort of Jewish surrender to Justin's argument with Trypho, this book is interesting, and represents, no doubt, the convictions of thousands of Jewish converts of the first age.

It is, in short, worthy of more attention than it has yet received.

Here follows Mr. Sinker's valuable Introductory Notice:--

The apocryphal work known as the Testaments of the Twelve Patriarchs professes to be, as its name implies, the utterances of the dying patriarchs, the sons of Jacob.

In these they give some account of their lives, embodying particulars not found in the scriptural account, and build thereupon various moral precepts for the guidance of their descendants.

The book partakes also of the nature of an Apocalypse: the patriarchs see in the future their children doing wickedly, stained with the sins of every nation; and thus they foretell the troubles impending on their race.

Still at last God will put an end to their woe, and comfort is found in the promise of a Messiah

There can be little or no doubt that the author was a Jew, who, having been converted to Christianity, sought to win over his countrymen to the same faith, and thus employed the names of the patriarchs as a vehicle for conveying instruction to their descendants, as winning by this means for his teaching at any rate a prima facie welcome in the eyes of the Jewish people.

It does not seem hard to settle approximately the limits of time within which the book was probably written.

It cannot be placed very late in the second century, seeing that it is almost certainly quoted by Tertullian, [12] and that Origen [13] cites the Testaments by name, apparently indeed holding it in considerable respect.

We can, however, approximate much more nearly than this; for the allusions to the destruction of Jerusalem assign to the Testaments a date subsequent to that event.

This will harmonize perfectly with what is the natural inference from several passages,-- namely, that the Gentiles now were a majority in the Church,--as well as with the presence of the many formulae to express the incarnation, and with the apparent collection of the books of the New Testament into a volume. [14]

On the other hand, important evidence as to the posterior limit of the date of writing may be derived from the language used with reference to the priesthood.

Christ is both High Priest and King, and His former office is higher than the latter, and to Him the old priesthood must resign its rights.

Now such language as this would be almost meaningless after Hadrian's destruction of Jerusalem consequent on the revolt of Bar-Cochba (a.d. 135), after which all power of Judaism for acting directly upon Christianity ceased; and, indeed, on the hypothesis of a later date, we should doubtless find allusions to the revolt and its suppression.

On the above grounds, we infer that the writing of the Testaments is to be placed in a period ranging from late in the first century to the revolt of Bar-Cochba; closer than this it is perhaps not safe to draw our limits. [15]

The language in which the Testaments were written was no doubt the Hellenistic Greek in which we now possess them; presenting as they do none of the peculiar marks which characterize a version.

Whether there were a Hebrew work on which the present was modelled--a supposition by no means improbable in itself--we cannot tell, nor is it a matter of much importance.

The phenomena of the book itself may be cited in support of this conclusion:

for instance, the use of the word diatheke in its ordinary classical meaning of "testament," not "covenant" as in Hellenistic Greek, for which former meaning there would be no strictly equivalent word in Hebrew; the numerous instances of paronomasia, such as athetein, nouthetein, [16] aphairesis, anairesis, [17] limos, loimos, [18] en taxei, atakton, [19] taxis, ataxia; [20] the frequent use of the genitive absolute, and of the verb mellein; the use of various expressions pertaining to the Greek philosophy, as diathesis, aisthesis, phusis, telos.

It seems doubtful how far we can attempt with safety to determine accurately the religious standpoint of the writer beyond the obvious fact of his Jewish origin, though some have attempted to show that he was a Nazarene, and others a Jewish Christian of Pauline tendencies. We shall therefore content ourselves with referring those who seek for more specific information on this point to the works mentioned below.

To refer now briefly to the external history of our document, we meet with nothing definite, after its citation by Origen, for many centuries:

there are possible allusions in Jerome [21] and in Procopius Gazaeus; [22] there is also a mention of patriarchai in the Synopsis Sacrae Scripturae found among the writings of Athanasius, as well as in the Stichometria of Nicephorus of Constantinople, on which it is probably based.

Again, in the Canons of the Council of Rome (494 a.d.) under Gelasius, and of the Council of Bracara (563 a.d.), are possible references, though it is far from improbable that in some of the foregoing passages the reference may be to a writing ton trion Patriarchon alluded to in the Apostolic Constitutions, [23] or is even of somewhat loose application.

After this a blank ensues until the middle of the thirteenth century, when it was brought to the knowledge of Western Europe by Robert Grosseteste, Bishop of Lincoln, the earliest of the great English reformers. [24] We cite here the account of the matter given by Matthew Paris, although of course we need not accept all the opinions of the old chronicler respecting the document in question:

"At this same time, Robert, Bishop of Lincoln, a man most deeply versed in Latin and Greek, accurately translated the Testaments of the XII. Patriarchs from Greek into Latin.

These had been for a long time unknown and hidden through the jealousy of the Jews, on account of the prophecies of the Saviour contained in them.

The Greeks, however, the most unwearied investigators of all writings, were the first to come to a knowledge of this document, and translated it from Hebrew into Greek, and have kept it to themselves till our times.

And neither in the time of the blessed Jerome nor of any other holy interpreter could the Christians gain an acquaintance with it, through the malice of the ancient Jews.

This glorious treatise, then, the aforesaid bishop (with the help of Master Nicolaus, a Greek, and a clerk of the Abbey of St. Alban's) translated fully and clearly, and word for word, from Greek into Latin, to the strengthening of the Christian faith, and to the greater confusion of the Jews." [25]

Again, after speaking of the death of "Master John de Basingstokes, Archdeacon of Leicester," a man of very great learning in Latin and Greek, he proceeds: [26] "This Master John had mentioned to Robert, Bishop of Lincoln, that when he was studying at Athens he had seen and heard from learned Greek doctors certain things unknown to the Latins. Among these he found the Testaments of the XII. Patriarchs, that is to say, of the sons of Jacob.

Now it is plain that these really form part of the sacred volume, but have been long hidden through the jealousy of the Jews, on account of the evident prophecies about Christ which are clearly seen in them.

Consequently this same bishop sent into Greece; and when he obtained them, he translated them from Greek into Latin, as well as certain other things."

After this it would seem as though the same fate still pursued our document, for the entire Greek text was not printed until the eve of the eighteenth century, when it was published for the first time by Grabe, whose edition has been several times reprinted. [27]

Four Greek mss. of the Testaments are known to exist:--

1.

The ms. Ff. i. 24 in the University Library of Cambridge, to which it was given by Archbishop Parker, whose autograph it bears on its first page.

It is a quarto on parchment, of 261 leaves (in which the Testaments occupy ff. 203a-261b), double columns, 20 lines in a column, handwriting of the tenth century.

It is furnished with accents and breathings, and a fairly full punctuation.

There are very strong grounds for believing that it was this ms. that Grosseteste's version was made, exhibiting as it does a very large amount of curious verbal coincidence with it. [28]The text of this ms. has been that given in the various editions mentioned below.

2.

The ms. Barocci 133 in the Bodleian Library at Oxford, where it came with the rest of the Barocci collection from Venice, and was presented to the University by its Chancellor, the Earl of Pembroke. It is a quarto volume; and except a leaf or two of parchment, containing writing of an older period, consists of a number of treatises on paper, apparently by several different hands, in the writing of the latter part of the fourteenth century.

The Testaments occupy ff. 179a-203b.

The amount of difference between this ms. and the preceding is considerable, and is sufficient to show that it has had no direct communication with the latter.

A large number of omissions occur in it, in some instances amounting to entire chapters. The variations of this ms. are given more or less fully in the various editions.

3.

A ms. in the Vatican Library at Rome, not yet edited.

It is said to be a small quarto on paper, written in a very distinct hand, though unfortunately some leaves are damaged.

It bears a subscription with the date 1235.

I owe my knowledge of this ms. to an article by Dr. Vorstman in the Godgeleerde Bijdragen for 1866, p. 953 sqq.

4.

A ms. discovered by Tischendorf in the island of Patmos, of which no details have yet been published. [29]

The entire Greek text of the Testaments was first printed by Grabe in his Spicilegium Patrum et Haereticorum, Oxford, 1698, professedly from the Cambridge ms., but in reality from some very inaccurate transcript of it, very possibly from one made by Abednego Seller, also in the Cambridge University Library, Oo. vi. 92.

Grabe also gave a few of the variations of the Oxford ms.

Fabricius, in his Codex Pseudepigraphus Veteris Testamenti, [30] gives little more than a reprint from Grabe. In the second edition of the latter (1714) the true text has been restored in several passages; but in many places Grosseteste's Latin version, which witnessed to the true reading, was altered to suit Grabe's incorrect text.

Fabricius' second edition (1722) is perhaps, on the whole, less accurate than his first.

Since then the text and notes, as given in Grabe's second edition, have been reprinted, with but few additions, by Gallandi, in his Bibliotheca Veterum Patrum, vol. i. p. 193 sqq., Venice, 1765, and in Migne's Patrologia Graeca, vol. ii., Paris, 1857.

The text of the Cambridge ms. with a full statement of the variations of the Oxford ms., has recently been edited directly from the mss. by myself, Cambridge, 1869; from this edition the present translation has been made.

The mss. of Grosseteste's Latin version are numerous, there being no less than twelve in

Cambridge alone and it has been frequently printed, both with the editions of the Greek text and independently. [31]

Besides the Latin version, the Testaments have also been translated into several European languages, in all cases apparently from the Latin.

The English translation made by Arthur Golding was first printed by John Daye in Aldersgate in 1581, and has since been frequently reproduced; the British Museum, which does not possess all the editions, having no less than eleven. [32]

The author of the French translation [33] appears to believe, as the English translator had done, that we have here really the last words of the sons of Jacob.

A German translation has also several times been published, [34] and a German translation in ms. is to be found in the British Museum. [35] We may further mention a Dutch translation (Antwerp, 1570), a Danish translation (1601), and a ms. Icelandic translation of the eighteenth century in the British Museum, add. mss 11,068.

For further information on the subject of the Testaments, reference may be made, in addition to works already mentioned, to the following:--Nitzsch, Commentatio Critica de Testamentis XII. Patriarcharum, libro V. T. Pseudepigrapho (Wittenberg, 1810); Ritschl, Die Entstehung der altkatholischen Kirche (Bonn, 1850; ed. 2, 1857), p. 171 sqq.; Vorstman, Disquisitio de Testamentorum XII. Patriarcharum origine et pretio (Rotterdam, 1857); Kayser in Reuss and Cunitz's Beitraege zu den theol. Wissenschaften for 1851, pp. 107-140; Luecke,Einleitung in die Offenbarung des Joh., vol. i. p. 334 sqq., ed. 2.

R. S.
Trinity College, Cambridge.
February 21, 1871.

Footnotes:

1. Vol. v. p. 176, ed. 1827.
2. Credib., vol. ii. pp. 345-364.
3. Vol. vi. p. 384.
4. The honour done to St. Paul is enough to settle any suspicion of this sort.
5. See vol. i. p. 270, note 2, this series.
6. Rev. vii. 4. v Dxn is excepted.
7. Rev. iv. 4. See vol. vii.
8. Acts xxvi. 7.
9. See The Christ of Jewish History in Stanley Leathes' Bampton Lectures, p. 51, ed. New York, 1874; also Westcott, Introduction to Study of the Gospels, 3d ed., London, Macmillans, 1867. Note, on the Book of Henoch, pp. 9, 93-101; on the Book of Jubilees p. 109. He puts this book into the first century, later than Henoch, earlier than the Twelve Patriarchs. Consult this work on the Alexandrian Fathers, on inspiration of Scripture, etc.; and note the Jewish doctrine of the Messiah, pp. 26, 143, 151, also the apocryphal traditions of words of our Lord, p. 428.
10. Acts xxi. 18-26. To my mind a most touching history, in which it is hard to say whether St. Paul or St. James is exhibited in the more charming light. It suggests the absolute harmony of their Epistles.
11. Vol. i. Elucid. II. p. 57, this series.
12. Adv. Marcionem, v. 1; Scorpiace, 13; cf. Benj. 11.
13. Hom. in Josuam, xv. 6; cf. Reub. 2, 3.
14. Benj. 11.
15. [Compare Westcott, Introduction to Study of the Gospels, p. 132, ed. Boston, 1862.]
16. Benj. 4.
17. Judah 23.
18. Judah 23.
19. Naph. 2.
20. Naph. 3.
21. Adv. Vigilantium, c. 6.
22. Comm. in Genesin, c. 38.
23. vi. 16. [See vol. vii. p. 457, this series.]
24. [Of whom see Lightfoot, Apostolic Fathers, Part II. vol. i. p. 17, ed. London, 1885.]
25. Historia Anglorum, a.d. 1242, p. 801, ed. London, 1571.
26. Op. cit. a.d. 1252, p. 1112.
27. Vide infra.
28. [See, e.g., the curious reading in Levi 18, kai stesei, where the Latin mss. are unanimous in giving stare faciet; also the mistake of 'Iakob for 'Roubem in Issachar 1.

29. See Tischendorf, Aus dem heiligen Lande, p. 341.
30. Hamburgh, 1713.
31. e.g., 1483; Hagenau, 1532; Paris, 1549; and often.
32. This English translation having been made from the Latin, the printed editions of which swarm with inaccuracies (Grosseteste's Latin version itself being a most exact translation), I have been able to make much less use of it than I could have desired. It has, however, been compared throughout.
33. Monsieur Mace, Chefecier, cure de Saint Opportune, Paris, 1713.
34. e.g., Vienna, 1544; Strasburgh, 1596; Hamburgh, 1637.
35. mss. Harl., 1252.

I - The Testament of Reuben Concerning Thoughts

1.

The copy of the Testament of Reuben, what things he charged his sons before he died in the hundred and twenty-fifth year of his life. When he was sick two years after the death of Joseph, his sons and his sons' sons were gathered together to visit him.

And he said to them, My children, I am dying, and go the way of my fathers.

And when he saw there Judah and Gad and Asher, his brethren, he said to them, Raise me up, my brethren, that I may tell to my brethren and to my children what things I have hidden in my heart, for from henceforth my strength faileth me.

And he arose and kissed them, and said, weeping:

Hear, my brethren, give ear to Reuben your father, what things I command you. And, behold, I call to witness against you this day the God of heaven, that ye walk not in the ignorance of youth and fornication wherein I ran greedily, and I defiled the bed of Jacob my father.

For I tell you that He smote me with a sore plague in my loins for seven months; and had not Jacob our father prayed for me to the Lord, surely the Lord would have destroyed me.

For I was thirty years old when I did this evil in the sight of the Lord, and for seven months I was sick even unto death; and I repented for seven years in the set purpose of my soul before the Lord.

Wine and strong drink I drank not, and flesh entered not into my mouth, and I tasted not pleasant food, [1] mourning over my sin, for it was great.

And it shall not so be done in Israel.

2.

And now hear me, my children, what things I saw in my repentance concerning the seven spirits of error.

Seven spirits are given against man from Beliar, and they are chief of the works of youth; and seven spirits are given to him at his creation, that in them should be done every work of man. [2]The first (1) spirit is of life, with which man's whole being is created.

The second (2) spirit is of sight, with which ariseth desire.

The third (3) spirit is of hearing, with which cometh teaching.

The fourth (4) spirit is of smelling, with which taste is given to draw air and breath.

The fifth (5) spirit is of speech, with which cometh knowledge.

The sixth (6) spirit is of taste, with which cometh the eating of meats and drinks; and by them strength is produced, for in food is the foundation of strength.

The seventh (7) spirit is of begetting and sexual intercourse, with which through love of pleasure sin also entereth in:

wherefore it is the last in order of creation, and the first of youth, because it is filled with ignorance, which leadeth the young as a blind man to a pit, and as cattle to a precipice.

3.

Besides all these, there is an eighth (8) spirit of sleep, with which is created entrancement of man's nature, and the image of death. With these spirits are mingled the spirits of error. The first (1), the spirit of fornication, dwelleth in the nature and in the senses; the second (2) spirit of insatiateness in the belly; the third (3) spirit of fighting in the liver and the gall.

The fourth (4) is the spirit of fawning and trickery, that through over-officiousness a man may be fair in seeming.

The fifth (5) is the spirit of arrogance, that a man may be stirred up and become high-minded.

The sixth (6) is the spirit of lying, in perdition and in jealousy to feign words, and to conceal [3] words from kindred and friends.

The seventh (7) is the spirit of injustice, with which are theft and pilferings, that a man may work the desire of his heart; for injustice worketh together with the other spirits by means of craft.

Besides all these, the spirit of sleep, the eighth (8) spirit, is conjoined with error and fantasy.

And so perisheth every young man, darkening his mind from the truth, and not understanding the law of God, nor obeying the admonitions of his fathers, as befell me also in my youth.

And now, children, love the truth, and it shall preserve you.

I counsel you, hear ye Reuben your father.

Pay no heed to the sight of a woman, nor yet associate privately with a female under the authority of a husband, nor meddle with affairs of womankind.

For had I not seen Bilhah bathing in a covered place, I had not fallen into this great iniquity. [4]For my mind, dwelling on the woman's nakedness, suffered me not to sleep until I had done the abominable deed.

For while Jacob our father was absent with Isaac his father, when we were in Gader, near to Ephratha in Bethlehem, Bilhah was drunk, and lay asleep uncovered in her chamber; and when I went in and beheld her nakedness, I wrought that impiety, and leaving her sleeping I departed.

And forthwith an angel of God revealed to my father Jacob concerning my impiety, and he came and mourned over me, and touched her no more. [5]

4.

Pay no heed, therefore, to the beauty of women, and muse not upon their doings; but walk in singleness of heart in the fear of the Lord, and be labouring in works, and roaming in study and among your flocks, until the Lord give to you a wife whom He will, that ye suffer not as I did.

Until my father's death I had not boldness to look stedfastly into the face of Jacob, or to speak to any of my brethren, because of my reproach; and even until now my conscience afflicteth me by reason of my sin.

And my father comforted me; for he prayed for me unto the Lord, that the anger of the Lord might pass away from me, even as the Lord showed me.

From henceforth, then, I was protected, and I sinned not.

Therefore, my children, observe all things whatsoever I command you, and ye shall not sin.

For fornication is the destruction of the soul, separating it from God, and bringing it near to idols, because it deceiveth the mind and understanding, and bringeth down young men into hell before their time.

For many hath fornication destroyed; because, though a man be old or noble, it maketh him a reproach and a laughing-stock with Beliar and the sons of men.

For in that Joseph kept himself from every woman, and purged his thoughts from all fornication, he found favour before the Lord and men.

For the Egyptian woman did many things unto him, and called for magicians, and offered him love potions, and the purpose of his soul admitted no evil desire. Therefore the God of my fathers delivered him from every visible and hidden death.

For if fornication overcome not the mind, neither shall Beliar overcome you.

5.

Hurtful are women, my children; because, since they have no power or strength over the man, they act subtilly through outward guise how they may draw him to themselves; and whom they cannot overcome by strength, him they overcome by craft.

For moreover the angel of God told me concerning them, and taught me that women are overcome by the spirit of fornication more than men, and they devise in their heart against men; and by means of their adornment they deceive first their minds, and instil the poison by the glance of their eye, and then they take them captive by their doings, for a woman cannot overcome a man by force.

Therefore flee fornication, my children, and command your wives and your daughters that they adorn not their heads and their faces; because every woman who acteth deceitfully in these things hath been reserved to everlasting punishment.

For thus they allured the Watchers [6] before the flood; and as these continually beheld them, they fell into desire each of the other, and they conceived the act in their mind, and changed themselves into the shape of men, and appeared to them in their congress with their husbands; and the women, having in their minds desire toward their apparitions, gave birth to giants, for the Watchers appeared to them as reaching even unto heaven. [7]

6.

Beware, therefore, of fornication; and if you wish to be pure in your mind, guard your senses against every woman.

And command them likewise not to company with men, that they also be pure in their mind.

For constant meetings, even though the ungodly deed be not wrought, are to them an irremediable disease, and to us an everlasting reproach of Beliar; for fornication hath neither understanding nor godliness in itself, and all jealousy dwelleth in the desire thereof. Therefore ye will be jealous against the sons of Levi, and will seek to be exalted over them; but ye shall not be able, for God will work their avenging, and ye shall die by an evil death.

For to Levi the Lord gave the sovereignty, and to Judah, [8] and to me also with them, [9] and to Dan and Joseph, that we should be for rulers.

Therefore I command you to hearken to Levi, because he shall know the law of the Lord, and shall give ordinances for judgment and sacrifice for all Israel until the completion of the times of Christ, the High Priest whom the Lord hath declared.

I adjure you by the God of heaven to work truth each one with his neighbour; and draw ye near to Levi in humbleness of heart, that ye may receive a blessing from his mouth.

For he shall bless Israel; and specially Judah, because him hath the Lord chosen to rule over all the peoples.

And worship we his Seed, because He shall die for us in wars visible and invisible, and shall be among you an everlasting king.

7.

And Reuben died after that he had given command to his sons; and they placed him in a coffin until they bore him up from Egypt, and buried him in Hebron in the double [10] cave where his fathers were.

Footnotes:

1. There seems a reminiscence here of the words of Dan. x. 3, LXX. [For proofs of penitence, see p. 11, note 3, infra.]

2. For this use of pneumata as applied to the senses, we may cite Plutarch (De placitis philosophorum, iv. 21), who, speaking with reference to the Stoic philosophy, says, he men horasis esti pneuma diateinon apo tou hegemonikou mechris ophthalmon.

3. This clause is only found in Cd. Oxon.; it seems demanded by the following apo

4. Cf. Gen. xxxv. 22. The Gader mentioned below is the Edar of ver. 21, the Hebrew being reproduced, as often, by g.

5. [This section is censured by Lardner as unsuitable to dying admonitions. He forgets Oriental simplicity.]

6. This name, occurring once again in the Testaments (Naph. 3), is one frequently found applied to the angels as the custodians of the world and of men. Thus, in the Chaldee of Daniel (iv. 10, 14, 20: 13, 17, 23, Eng. Ver.), we find the expression yr, which Aquila and Symmachus render egregoros. The corresponding Ethiopic term is of frequent occurrence in the book of Enoch, not only of the fallen angels (e.g., x. 9, 15, xvi. 1, etc.), but of the good (xii. 2, 3, etc., ed. Dillmann). See also Gesenius, Thesaurus, s.v. yr.

7. [Gen. vi. 4; Revised margin, 1 Cor. xi. 10; Jude 6, 7.]

8. [See Lardner on this root idea of our author, vol. ii. p. 353; but he is wrong as to Levi and Mary. Also Joseph, sec. 19, note 2, infra.]

9. The reading of Cd. Oxon., met' auton, is doubtless to be preferred.

10. i.e., Machpelah, which in Hebrew means double, and is so rendered by the LXX., e.g., Gen. xxiii. 9.

II - The Testament of Simeon Concerning Envy

1.

The copy of the words of Simeon, what things he spake to his sons before he died, in the hundred and twentieth year of his life, in the year in which Joseph died.

For they came to visit him when he was sick, and he strengthened himself and sat up and kissed them, and said to them:--

2.

Hear, O my children, hear Simeon your father, what things I have in my heart.

I was born of Jacob my father, his second son; and my mother Leah called me Simeon, because the Lord heard her prayer. [1]I became strong exceedingly; I shrank from no deed, nor was I afraid of anything.

For my heart was hard, and my mind was unmoveable, and my bowels unfeeling:

because valour also has been given from the Most High to men in soul and in body.

And at that time I was jealous of Joseph because our father loved him; [2] and I set my mind against him to destroy him, because the prince of deceit sent forth the spirit of jealousy and blinded my mind, that I regarded him not as a brother, and spared not Jacob my father.

But his God and the God of his fathers sent forth His angel, and delivered him out of my hands.

For when I went into Shechem to bring ointment for the flocks, and Reuben to Dotham, where were our necessaries and all our stores, Judah our brother sold him to the Ishmaelites.

And when Reuben came he was grieved, for he wished to have restored him safe to his father.
[3] But I was wroth against Judah in that he let him go away alive, and for five months I continued wrathful against him; but God restrained me, and withheld from me all working of my hands, for my right hand was half withered for seven days.

And I knew, my children, that because of Joseph this happened to me, and I repented and wept; and I besought the Lord that He would restore my hand unto me, and that I might be kept from all pollution and envy, and from all folly.

For I knew that I had devised an evil deed before the Lord and Jacob my father, on account of Joseph my brother, in that I envied him.

3.

And now, children, take heed of the spirit of deceit and of envy. For envy ruleth over the whole mind of a man, and suffereth him neither to eat, nor to drink, nor to do any good thing:

it ever suggesteth to him to destroy him that he envieth; and he that is envied ever flourisheth, but he that envieth fades away.

Two years of days I afflicted my soul with fasting in the fear of the Lord, and I learnt that deliverance from envy cometh by the fear of God.

If a man flee to the Lord, the evil spirit runneth away from him, and his mind becometh easy.

And henceforward he sympathizeth with him whom he envied, and condemneth not those who love him, and so ceaseth from his envy.

4.

And my father asked concerning me, because he saw that I was sad; and I said, I am pained in my liver.

For I mourned more than they all, because I was guilty of the selling of Joseph.

And when we went down into Egypt, and he bound me as a spy, I knew that I was suffering justly, and I grieved not.

Now Joseph was a good man, and had the Spirit of God within him:

compassionate and pitiful, he bore not malice against me; nay, he loved me even as the rest of his brothers. Take heed, therefore, my children, of all jealousy and envy, and walk in singleness of soul and with good heart, keeping in mind the brother of your father, that God may give to you also grace and glory, and blessing upon your heads, even as ye saw in him.

All his days he reproached us not concerning this thing, but loved us as his own soul, and beyond his own sons; and he glorified us, and gave riches, and cattle, and fruits freely to us all.

Do ye then also, my beloved children, love each one his brother with a good heart, and remove from you the spirit of envy, for this maketh savage the soul and destroyeth the body; it turneth his purposes into anger and war, and stirreth up unto blood, and leadeth the mind into frenzy, and suffereth not prudence to act in men:

moreover, it taketh away sleep, and causeth tumult to the soul and trembling to the body.

For even in sleep some malicious jealousy, deluding him, gnaweth at his soul, and with wicked spirits disturbeth it, and causeth the body to be troubled, and the mind to awake from sleep in confusion; and as though having a wicked and poisonous spirit, so appeareth it to men.

5.

Therefore was Joseph fair in appearance, and goodly to look upon, because there dwelt not in him any wickedness; for in trouble of the spirit the face declareth it.

And now, my children, make your hearts good before the Lord, and your ways straight before men, and ye shall find grace before God and men.

And take heed not to commit fornication, for fornication is mother of all evils, separating from God, and bringing near to Beliar.

For I have seen it inscribed in the writing of Enoch [4] that your sons shall with you be corrupted in fornication, and shall do wrong against Levi with the sword.

But they shall not prevail against Levi, for he shall wage the war of the Lord, and shall conquer all your hosts; and there shall be a few divided in Levi and Judah, and there shall be none [5] of you for sovereignty, even as also my father Jacob prophesied in his blessings.

6.

Behold, I have foretold you all things, that I may be clear from the sin of your souls.

Now, if ye remove from you your envy, and all your stiffneckedness, as a rose shall my bones flourish in Israel, and as a lily my flesh in Jacob, and my odour shall be as the odour of Libanus; and as cedars shall holy ones be multiplied from me for ever, and their branches shall stretch afar off.

Then shall perish the seed of Canaan, and a remnant shall not be to Amalek, and all the Cappadocians [6] shall perish, and all the Hittites [7] shall be utterly destroyed.

Then shall fail the land of Ham, and every people shall perish.

Then shall all the earth rest from trouble, and all the world under heaven from war.

Then shall Shem be glorified, because the Lord God, the Mighty One of Israel, shall appear upon earth as man, [8] and saved by Him Adam. [9] Then shall all the spirits of deceit be given to be trampled under foot, and men shall rule over the wicked spirits.

Then will I arise in joy, and will bless the Most High because of His marvellous works, because God hath taken a body and eaten with men and saved men.

7.

And now, my children, obey Levi, and in Judah shall ye be redeemed: [10] and be not lifted up against these two tribes, for from them shall arise to you the salvation of God.

For the Lord shall raise up from Levi as it were a Priest, [11] and from Judah as it were a King, God and man. [12] So shall He save all the Gentiles and the race of Israel.

Therefore I command you all things, in order that ye also may command your children, that they may observe them throughout their generations.

8.

And Simeon made an end of commanding his sons, and slept with his fathers, being an hundred and twenty years old.

And they laid him in a coffin of incorruptible wood, to take up his bones to Hebron.

And they carried them up in a war of the Egyptians secretly:

for the bones of Joseph the Egyptians guarded in the treasure-house of the palace; for the sorcerers told them that at the departure of the bones of Joseph there should be throughout the whole of Egypt darkness and gloom, and an exceeding great plague to the Egyptians, so that even with a lamp a man should not recognise his brother.

9.

And the sons of Simeon bewailed their father according to the law of mourning, and they were in Egypt until the day of their departure from Egypt by the hand of Moses.

Footnotes:

1. Gen. xxix. 33.
2. That Simeon was prominent in the hostility to Joseph, is perhaps implied by his detention in Egypt as a surety for the return of the others; and Jewish tradition generally accords with this view. Cf. the Targum of the Pseudo-Jonathan on Gen. xxxvii. 19: "Simeon and Levi, who were brothers in counsel, said one to another, Let us kill him." Also this same Targum on Gen. xlii. 24: "And he took from them Simeon, who had counselled to kill him." Cf. also Breshith Rabba, S: 31.
3. [Gen. xxxvii. 22, 29; xlii. 22.]
4. [See Speaker's Com., N.T., vol. iv. p. 387, ed. Scribners.]
5. The Cam. ms. seems wrongly to omit the negative here. The reference is doubtless to Gen. xlix. 7.
6. The reference seems to be to the Philistines. Cf. Deut. ii. 23; Amos ix. 7, where the LXX. reads Kappadokia.
7. [For modern views of these, see Encyc. Brit., s.v. "Hittites."]
8. [Two of the many passages that leave no room for Lardner's imaginary "Unitarianism" in this author.]
9. The construction here is awkward of the participles after hoti: possibly a clause may have dropped out after 'Adam.
10. [See p. 10, note 5, supra.]
11. John the Baptist. His greatness is declared by Christ Himself.]
12. [Two of the many passages that leave no room for Lardner's imaginary "Unitarianism" in this author.]

III - The Testament of Levi Concerning the Priesthood and Arrogance

1.
 The copy of the words of Levi, what things he appointed to his sons, according to all that they should do, and what things should befall them until the day of judgment.
 He was in sound health when he called them to him, for it had been shown to him that he should die. And when they were gathered together he said to them:--

2.
 I Levi was conceived in Haran and born there, and after that I came with my father to Shechem.
 And I was young, about twenty years of age, when with Simeon I wrought the vengeance on Hamor for our sister Dinah.
 And when we were feeding our flocks in Abel-Maul, a spirit of understanding of the Lord came upon me, [1] and I saw all men corrupting their way, and that unrighteousness had built to itself walls, and iniquity sat upon towers; and I grieved for the race of men, and I prayed to the Lord that I might be saved.
 Then there fell upon me a sleep, and I beheld a high mountain:
 this is the mountain of Aspis [2] in Abel-Maul.
 And behold, the heavens were opened, and an angel of God said to me, Levi, enter.
 And I entered from the first heaven into the second, and I saw there water hanging between the one and the other.
 And I saw a third heaven far brighter than those two, for there was in it a height without bounds.
 And I said to the angel, Wherefore is this?
 And the angel said to me, Marvel not at these, for thou shalt see four other heavens brighter than these, and without comparison, when thou shalt have ascended thither:
 because thou shalt stand near the Lord, and shalt be His minister, and shall declare His mysteries to men, and shalt proclaim concerning Him who shall redeem Israel; [3] and by thee and Judah shall the Lord appear among men, saving in them every race of men; and of the portion of the Lord shall be thy life, and He shall be thy field and vineyard, fruits, gold, silver.

3.
 Hear, then, concerning the seven [4] heavens.
 The lowest is for this cause more gloomy, in that it is near all the iniquities of men. The second hath fire, snow, ice, ready for the day of the ordinance of the Lord, in the righteous judgment of God:
 in it are all the spirits of the retributions for vengeance on the wicked.
 In the third are the hosts of the armies which are ordained for the day of judgment, to work vengeance on the spirits of deceit and of Beliar.
 And the heavens up to the fourth above these are holy, for in the highest of all dwelleth the Great Glory, in the holy of holies, far above all holiness.
 In the heaven next to it are the angels of the presence of the Lord, who minister and make propitiation to the Lord for all the ignorances of the righteous; and they offer to the Lord a reasonable sweet-smelling savour, and a bloodless offering.
 And in the heaven below this are the angels who bear the answers to the angels of the presence of the Lord. And in the heaven next to this are thrones, dominions, in which hymns are ever offered to God.
 Therefore, whenever the Lord looketh upon us, all of us are shaken; yea, the heavens, and the earth, and the abysses, are shaken at the presence of His majesty; but the sons of men, regarding not these things, sin, and provoke the Most High.

The Forgotten Bible

4.

Now, therefore, know that the Lord will execute judgment upon the sons of men; because when the rocks are rent, [5] and the sun quenched, and the waters dried up, and the fire trembling, and all creation troubled, and the invisible spirits melting away, and the grave [6] spoiled in the suffering of the Most High, [7] men unbelieving will abide in their iniquity, therefore with punishment shall they be judged.

Therefore the Most High hath heard thy prayer, to separate thee from iniquity, and that thou shouldest become to Him a son, and a servant, and a minister of His presence.

A shining light of knowledge shalt thou shine in Jacob, and as the sun shalt thou be to all the seed of Israel.

And a blessing shall be given to thee, and to all thy seed, until the Lord shall visit all the heathen in the tender mercies of His Son, even for ever.

Nevertheless thy sons shall lay hands upon Him to crucify Him; and therefore have counsel and understanding been given thee, that thou mightest instruct thy sons concerning Him, because he that blesseth Him shall be blessed, but they that curse Him shall perish.

5.

And the angel opened to me the gates of heaven, and I saw the holy temple, and the Most High upon a throne of glory.

And He said to me, Levi, I have given thee the blessings of the priesthood until that I shall come and sojourn in the midst of Israel.

Then the angel brought me to the earth, and gave me a shield and a sword, and said, Work vengeance on Shechem because of Dinah, and I will be with thee, because the Lord hath sent me.

And I destroyed at that time the sons of Hamor, as it is written in the heavenly tablets. [8] And I said to Him, I pray Thee, O Lord, tell me Thy name, that I may call upon Thee in a day of tribulation.

And He said, I am the angel who intercedeth for the race of Israel, that He smite them not utterly, because every evil spirit attacketh it.

And after these things I was as it were awaked, and blessed the Most High, and the angel that intercedeth for the race of Israel, and for all the righteous. [9]

6.

And when I came to my father I found a brazen shield; [10] wherefore also the name of the mountain is Aspis, which is near Gebal, on the right side of Abila; and I kept these words in my heart.

I took counsel with my father, and with Reuben my brother, that he should bid the sons of Hamor that they should be circumcised; for I was jealous because of the abomination which they had wrought in Israel.

And I slew Shechem at the first, and Simeon slew Hamor.

And after this our brethren came and smote the city with the edge of the sword; and our father heard it and was wroth, and he was grieved in that they had received the circumcision, and after that had been put to death, and in his blessings he dealt otherwise with us.

For we sinned because we had done this thing against his will, and he was sick upon that day.

But I knew that the sentence of God was for evil upon Shechem; for they sought to do to Sarah as they did to Dinah our sister, and the Lord hindered them.

And so they persecuted Abraham our father when he was a stranger, and they harried his flocks when they were multiplied upon him; and Jeblae his servant, born in his house, they shamefully handled.

And thus they did to all strangers, taking away their wives by force, and the men themselves driving into exile.

But the wrath of the Lord came suddenly upon them to the uttermost. [11]

7.

And I said to my father, Be not angry, sir, because by thee will the Lord bring to nought the Canaanites, and will give their land to thee, and to thy seed after thee.

For from this day forward shall Shechem be called a city of them that are without understanding; for as a man mocketh at a fool, so did we mock them, because they wrought folly in Israel to defile our sister.

And we took our sister from thence, and departed, and came to Bethel.

8.

And there I saw a thing again even as the former, after we had passed seventy days.

And I saw seven men in white raiment saying to me, Arise, put on the robe of the priesthood, and the crown of righteousness, and the breastplate of understanding, and the garment of truth, and the diadem of faith, and the tiara of miracle, and the ephod of prophecy. [12]And each one of them bearing each of these things put them on me, and said, From henceforth become a priest of the Lord, thou and thy seed for ever.

And the first anointed me with holy oil, and gave to me the rod of judgment.

The second washed me with pure water, and fed me with bread and wine, the most holy things,[13] and clad me with a holy and glorious robe.

The third clothed me with a linen vestment like to an ephod.

The fourth put round me a girdle like unto purple.

The fifth gave to me a branch of rich olive.

The sixth placed a crown on my head.

The seventh placed on my head a diadem of priesthood, and filled my hands with incense, so that I served as a priest to the Lord.

And they said to me, Levi, thy seed shall be divided into three branches, [14] for a sign of the glory of the Lord who is to come; and first shall he be that hath been faithful; no portion shall be greater than his.

The second shall be in the priesthood.

The third--a new name shall be called over Him, because He shall arise as King from Judah, and shall establish a new priesthood, after the fashion of the Gentiles, to all the Gentiles. [15]And His appearing shall be unutterable, as of an exalted [16] prophet of the seed of Abraham our father.

Every desirable thing in Israel shall be for thee and for thy seed, and everything fair to look upon shall ye eat, and the table of the Lord shall thy seed apportion, and some of them shall be high priests, and judges, and scribes; for by their mouth shall the holy place be guarded.

And when I awoke, I understood that this thing was like unto the former.

And I hid this also in my heart, and told it not to any man upon the earth.

9.

And after two days I and Judah went up to Isaac after [17] our father; and the father of my father blessed me according to all the words of the visions which I had seen:

and he would not come with us to Bethel.

And when we came to Bethel, my father Jacob saw in a vision concerning me, that I should be to them for a priest unto the Lord; and he rose up early in the morning, and paid tithes of all to the Lord through me.

And we came to Hebron to dwell there, and Isaac called me continually to put me in remembrance of the law of the Lord, even as the angel of God showed to me.

And he taught me the law of the priesthood, of sacrifices, whole burnt-offerings, first-fruits, free-will offerings, thank-offerings.

And each day he was instructing me, and was busied for me before the Lord.

And he said to me, Take heed, my child, of the spirit of fornication; for this shall continue, and shall by thy seed pollute the holy things.

Take therefore to thyself, while yet thou art young, a wife, not having blemish, nor yet polluted, nor of the race of the Philistines or Gentiles.

And before entering into the holy place, bathe; [18] and when thou offerest the sacrifice, wash; and again when thou finishest the sacrifice, wash.

Of twelve trees ever having leaves, offer up the fruits to the Lord, as also Abraham taught me; and of every clean beast and clean bird offer a sacrifice to the Lord, and of every firstling and of wine offer first-fruits; and every sacrifice thou shalt salt with salt. [19]

10.

Now, therefore, observe whatsoever I command you, children; for whatsoever things I have heard from my fathers I have made known to you.

I am clear from all your ungodliness and transgression which ye will do in the end of the ages against the Saviour of the world, acting ungodly, deceiving Israel, and raising up against it great evils from the Lord. [20]And ye will deal lawlessly with Israel, so that Jerusalem shall not endure your wickedness; but the veil of the temple shall be rent, so as not to cover your shame.

And ye shall be scattered as captives among the heathen, and shall be for a reproach and for a curse, and for a trampling under foot.

For the house which the Lord shall choose shall be called Jerusalem, as is contained in the book of Enoch the righteous. [21]

11.

Therefore, when I took a wife I was twenty-eight years old, and her name was Melcha.

And she conceived and bare a son, and she called his name Gersham, for we were sojourners in our land:

for Gersham is interpreted sojourning.

And I saw concerning him that he would not be in the first rank.

And Kohath was born in my thirty-fifth year, towards the east.

And I saw in a vision that he was standing on high in the midst of all the congregation.

Therefore I called his name Kohath, which meaneth, beginning of majesty and instruction.

And thirdly, she bare to me Merari, in the fortieth year of my life; and since his mother bare him with difficulty, she called him Merari, which meaneth my bitterness, because he also died.

And Jochebed was born in my sixty-fourth year, in Egypt, for I was renowned then in the midst of my brethren.

12.

And Gersham took a wife, and she bare to him Lomni and Semei.

And the sons of Kohath, Ambram, Isaar, Chebro, and Ozel.

And the sons of Merari, Mooli and Homusi.

And in my ninety-fourth year Ambram took Jochebed my daughter to him to wife, for they were born in one day, he and my daughter.

Eight years old was I when I went into the land of Canaan, and eighteen years when I slew Shechem, and at nineteen years I became priest, and at twenty-eight years I took a wife, and at forty years I went into Egypt.

And behold, ye are my children, my children even of a third generation.

In my hundred and eighteenth year Joseph died.

13.

And now, my children, I command you that ye fear our Lord with your whole heart, and walk in simplicity according to all His [22] law.

And do ye also teach your children learning, that they may have understanding in all their life, reading unceasingly the law of God; for every one who shall know the law of God shall be honoured, and shall not be a stranger wheresoever he goeth.

Yea, many friends shall he gain more than his forefathers; and many men shall desire to serve him, and to hear the law from his mouth.

Work righteousness, my children, upon the earth, that ye may find treasure in the heavens, and sow good things in your souls, that ye may find them in your life.

For if ye sow evil things, ye shall reap all trouble and affliction.

Get wisdom in the fear of God with diligence; for though there shall be a leading into captivity, and cities be destroyed, and lands and gold and silver and every possession shall perish, the wisdom of the wise none can take away, save the blindness of ungodliness and the palsy of sin: for even among his enemies shall it be to him glorious, and in a strange country a home, and in the midst of foes shall it be found a friend.

If a man teach these things and do them, he shall be enthroned with kings, as was also Joseph our brother.

14.

And now, my children, I have learnt from the writing of Enoch that at the last ye will deal ungodly, laying your hands upon the Lord in all malice; and your brethren shall be ashamed because of you, and to all the Gentiles shall it become a mocking.

For our father Israel shall be pure from the ungodliness of the chief priests who shall lay their hands upon the Saviour of the world.

Pure is the heaven above the earth, and ye are the lights of the heaven as the sun and the moon.

What shall all the Gentiles do if ye be darkened in ungodliness?

So shall ye bring a curse upon our race for whom came the light of the world, which was given among you for the lighting up of every man. [23]Him will ye desire to slay, teaching commandments contrary to the ordinances of God.

The offerings of the Lord will ye rob, and from His portion will ye steal; and before ye sacrifice to the Lord, ye will take the choicest parts, in despitefulness eating them with harlots.

Amid excesses [24] will ye teach the commandments of the Lord, the women that have husbands will ye pollute, and the virgins of Jerusalem will ye defile; and with harlots and adulteresses will ye be joined.

The daughters of the Gentiles will ye take for wives, purifying them with an unlawful purification; and your union shall be like unto Sodom and Gomorrah in ungodliness.

And ye will be puffed up because of the priesthood lifting yourselves up against men.

And not only so, but being puffed up also against the commands of God, ye will scoff at the holy things, mocking in despitefulness.

15.

Therefore the temple which the Lord shall choose shall be desolate in uncleanness, and ye shall be captives throughout all nations, and ye shall be an abomination among them, and ye shall receive reproach and everlasting shame from the righteous judgment of God; and all who see you shall flee from you.

And were it not for Abraham, Isaac, and Jacob our fathers, not one from my seed should be left upon the earth.

16.

And now I have learnt in the book of Enoch that for seventy weeks will ye go astray, and will profane the priesthood, and pollute the sacrifices, and corrupt the law, and set at nought the words of the prophets.

In perverseness ye will persecute righteous men, and hate the godly; the words of the faithful will ye abhor, and the man who reneweth the law in the power of the Most High will ye call a deceiver; [25] and at last, as ye suppose, ye will slay Him, not understanding His resurrection, wickedly taking upon your own heads the innocent blood. [26]Because of Him shall your holy places be desolate, polluted even to the ground, and ye shall have no place that is clean; but ye shall be among the Gentiles a curse and a dispersion, until He shall again look upon you, and in pity shall take you to Himself through faith and water. [27]

17.

And because ye have heard concerning the seventy weeks, hear also concerning the priesthood; for in each jubilee there shall be a priesthood.

In the first jubilee, the first who is anointed into the priesthood shall be great, and shall speak to God as to a Father; and his priesthood shall be filled with the fear of the Lord, and in the day of his gladness shall he arise for the salvation of the world.

In the second jubilee, he that is anointed shall be conceived in the sorrow of beloved ones; and his priesthood shall be honoured, and shall be glorified among all.

And the third priest shall be held fast in sorrow; and the fourth shall be in grief, because unrighteousness shall be laid upon him exceedingly, and all Israel shall hate each one his neighbour.

The fifth shall be held fast in darkness, likewise also the sixth and the seventh.

And in the seventh there shall be such pollution as I am not able to express, before the Lord and men, for they shall know it who do these things.

Therefore shall they be in captivity and for a prey, and their land and their substance shall be destroyed.

And in the fifth week they shall return into their desolate country, and shall renew the house of the Lord.

And in the seventh week shall come the priests, worshippers of idols, contentious, lovers of money, proud, lawless, lascivious, abusers of children and beasts.

18.

And after their punishment shall have come from the Lord, then will the Lord raise up to the priesthood a new Priest, to whom all the words of the Lord shall be revealed; and He shall execute a judgment of truth upon the earth, [28] in the fulness of days.

And His star shall arise in heaven, [29] as a king shedding forth the light of knowledge in the sunshine of day, and He shall be magnified in the world until His ascension.

He shall shine forth as the sun in the earth, and shall drive away all darkness from the world under heaven, and there shall be peace in all the earth.

The heavens shall rejoice in His days, and the earth shall be glad, and the clouds shall be joyful, and the knowledge of the Lord shall be poured forth upon the earth, as the water of seas; and the angels of the glory of the presence of the Lord shall be glad in Him.

The heavens shall be opened, and from the temple of glory shall the sanctification come upon Him with the Father's voice, as from Abraham the father of Isaac.

And the glory of the Most High shall be uttered over Him, and the spirit of understanding and of sanctification shall rest upon Him in the water.

He shall give the majesty of the Lord to His sons in truth for evermore; and there shall none succeed Him for all generations, even for ever. [30]And in His priesthood shall all sin come to an end, and the lawless shall rest from evil, and the just shall rest in Him.

And He shall open the gates of paradise, and shall remove [31] the threatening sword against Adam; and He shall give to His saints to eat from the tree of life, [32] and the spirit of holiness shall be on them.

And Beliar shall be bound by Him, and He shall give power to His children to tread upon the evil spirits. [33] And the Lord shall rejoice in His children, and the Lord shall be well pleased in His beloved for ever.

Then shall Abraham and Isaac and Jacob be joyful, and I will be glad, and all the saints shall put on gladness.

19.

And now, my children, ye have heard all; choose therefore for yourselves either the darkness or the light, either the law of the Lord or the works of Beliar.

And we answered our father, saying, Before the Lord will we walk according to His law.

And our father said, The Lord is witness, and His angels are witnesses, and I am witness, and ye are witnesses, concerning the word of your mouth.

And we said, We are witnesses.

And thus Levi ceased giving charge to his sons; and he stretched out his feet, and was gathered to his fathers, after he had lived a hundred and thirty-seven years.

And they laid him in a coffin, and afterwards they buried him in Hebron, by the side of Abraham, and Isaac, and Jacob.

Footnotes:

1. [Isa. xi. 2.]
2. See below, c. 6.
3. Cf. Luke xxiv. 21.
4. For the Jewish idea of seven heavens, cf. Clement of Alexandra, Strom., iv. 7; and Wetstein's note on 2 Cor. xii. 2; [also vol. vii. note 11, this series; and vol. ii. note 7, p. 438, this series].
5. [Matt. xxvii. 51-53.]
6. [Hades, rather.]
7. [epi to pathei tou Upsisou. Compare Tatian, vol. ii. p. 11, this series.]
8. This document, the idea of which is that of a book containing what is fore-ordained in heaven as to the course of the future, is one often appealed to in Apocalyptic literature, when some oracular declaration of weighty import is needed. Thus, in the Book of Enoch, the angel Uriel tells Enoch that the tablets contain all wisdom, the dying Enoch tells his children that the tablets are the source of all understanding, etc. (see, e.g., cc. 21. 1; 93. 2; 106. 19, ed. Dillmann). In the Book of Jubilees, again, it is said that inscribed on the tablets are, e.g., the punishment of the angels who sinned with mortal women, the plan of the division of weeks, the name of Abraham as the friend of God, etc. (cc. 5, 6, 19). See also Test. Asher, 2, 7, infra.
9. [Gen. xlviii. 16. The Jehovah-Angel.]
10. aspis. The Latin version gives the other meaning to aspis here, of asp or viper. The epithet chalken, however, renders "shield" much more probable, as there seems nothing in the context pointing to the "brazen serpent."
11. A quotation from 1 Thess. ii. 16, where the context also is similar to the present. [See Lardner's refutation of the learned Grabe on this quotation, vol. ii. p. 359.]
12. With the whole of this passage we may compare the description of the vestments of Aaron. See especially Ex. xxix. 5, 6 (LXX.). The petalon is the translation of tsyts, the plate of gold on the forehead of the high priest over the mitre. The logion, or logeion, is the breastplate, with the Urim and Thummim. For the poderes, see Ex. xxviii. 27 (LXX.).
13. On the possible reference here to the elements of the Eucharist, see Grabe's note, Spicilegium, in loc.
14. Nitzsch (p. 19, n. 37) explains this division into three archai, as referring to the three orders of the Christian priesthood. This, however, seems improbable. Cf. Kayser, p. 119; Vorstman, p. 41. It is far more probable that the reference is to Moses, Aaron, and Christ. Thus with pisteusas we may compare Num. xii. 7. For this use of arche, cf. Gen. ii. 10. [Isa. lxvi. 21.]
15. [Rom. xvi. 15, 16, 17, Greek. Compare Heb. v. 1.]
16. Or, if we follow the reading of Cd. Oxon., "Prophet of the Most High."
17. Or rather, with Cd. Oxon., "with our father."

18. We constantly find Peter, in the Clementine Homilies and Recognitions, combining with the Agapae the practice of bathing. Cf., e.g., Recog., iv. 3, v. 36.

19. Cf. Hom., xiv. 1. [Lev. ii. 13; Mark ix. 49.]

20. [Annas and Caiaphas. John xix. 11.]

21. This document is frequently quoted in the Testaments: cf. Sim. 5; Levi 14, 16; Judah 18; Dan 5; Naph. 4; Benj. 9. Most of these citations, however, are not to be found in the work as it has come down to us. We must therefore either assume the reference to some other books of Enoch not now extant, or rather perhaps that they are general appeals to the spirit of the book, regarded as a great fount of prophecy.

22. Read autou with Cd. Oxon.

23. [John i. 4-9; viii. 12; ix. 5, etc.]

24. The word pleonxia, like the English "excess," has not unfrequently special reference to sins of sensuality. Cf. 1 Cor. v. 11; Eph. iv. 19; v. 3, 5; Col. iii. 5; 1 Thess. iv. 6, the context in all of which passages points strongly to this conclusion. See Suicer's Thesaurus, s.v.

25. Cf. Matt. xxvii. 3, where ekeinos ho planos is said of our Lord.

26. [Matt. xxvii. 25.]

27. [John iii. 5; Isa. xii. 3; 1 Pet. iii. 20.]

28. [Jer. xxxiii. 15.]

29. [Matt. ii. 2. Constant references to the Gospels proofs of text.]

30. An additional clause occurs here in Cd. Oxon., which generally has a tendency to omit; the copyist of Cd. Cam. having possibly looked on to the same initial words in the next clause: "And in His priesthood shall the Gentiles be multiplied in knowledge on the earth and shall be enlightened through the grace of the Lord; but Israel shall be minished in ignorance, and be darkened in sorrow."

31. The reading of Cd. Oxon. here, apostesei, is to be preferred to Cd. Cam., stesei. Grosseteste's Latin version, in all probability made from the latter, has stare faciet. [See p. 7, note 1, supra.]

32. [Rev. ii. 7.]

33. [Luke x. 18, 19.]

IV - The Testament of Judah Concerning Fortitude, and Love of Money, and Fornication

1.

The copy of the words of Judah, what things he spake to his sons before he died.

They gathered themselves together, and came to him, and he said to them:

I was the fourth son born to my father, and my mother called me Judah, saying, I give thanks to the Lord, because He hath given to me even a fourth son. [1] I was swift and active in my youth, and obedient to my father in everything.

And I honoured my mother and my mother's sister.

And it came to pass, when I became a man, that my father Jacob prayed over me, saying, Thou shalt be a king, and prosperous in all things.

2.

And the Lord showed me favour in all my works both in the field and at home.

When I saw that I could run with the hind, then I caught it, and prepared meat for my father.

I seized upon the roes in the chase, and all that was in the plains I outran.

A wild mare I outran, and I caught it and tamed it; and I slew a lion, and plucked a kid out of its mouth.

I took a bear by its paw, and rolled it over a cliff; and if any beast turned upon me, I rent it like a dog.

I encountered the wild boar, and overtaking it in the chase, I tore it.

A leopard in Hebron leaped upon the dog, and I caught it by the tail, and flung it from me, and it was dashed to pieces in the coasts of Gaza.

A wild ox feeding in the field I seized by the horns; and whirling it round and stunning it, I cast it from me, and slew it.

3.

And when the two kings of the Canaanites came in warlike array against our flocks, and much people with them, I by myself rushed upon King Sur and seized him; and I beat him upon the legs, and dragged him down, and so I slew him.

And the other king, Taphue, [2] I slew as he sat upon his horse, and so I scattered all the people.

Achor the king, a man of giant stature, hurling darts before and behind as he sat on horseback, I slew; for I hurled a stone of sixty pounds weight, and cast it upon his horse, and killed him.

And I fought with Achor for two hours, and I killed him; and I clave his shield into two parts, and I chopped off his feet.

And as I stripped off his breastplate, behold, eight men his companions began to fight with me.

I wound round therefore my garment in my hand; and I slang stones at them, and killed four of them, and the rest fled.

And Jacob my father slew Beelisa, king of all the kings, a giant in strength, twelve cubits high; and fear fell upon them, and they ceased from making war with us. Therefore my father had no care in the wars when I was among my brethren.

For he saw in a vision concerning me, that an angel of might followed me everywhere, that I should not be overcome.

4.

And in the south there befell us a greater war than that in Shechem; and I joined in battle array with my brethren, and pursued a thousand men, and slew of them two hundred men and four kings.

And I went up against them upon the wall, and two other kings I slew; and so we freed Hebron, and took all the captives of the kings.

5.

On the next day we departed to Areta,[3] a city strong and walled and inaccessible, threatening us with death.

Therefore I and Gad approached on the east side of the city, and Reuben and Levi on the west and south.

And they that were upon the wall, thinking that we were alone, charged down upon us; and so our brethren secretly climbed up the wall on both sides by ladders, and entered into the city, while the men knew it not.

And we took it with the edge of the sword; and those who had taken refuge in the tower,--we set fire to the tower, and took both it and them.

And as we were departing the men of Thaffu set upon our captives, and we took it with our sons, and fought with them even to Thaffu; and we slew them, and burnt their city, and spoiled all the things that were therein.

6.

And when I was at the waters of Chuzeba,[4] the men of Jobel came against us to battle, and we fought with them; and their allies from Selom[5] we slew, and we allowed them no means of escaping, and of coming against us.

And the men of Machir[6] came upon us on the fifth day, to carry away our captives; and we attacked them, and overcame them in fierce battle:

for they were a host and mighty in themselves, and we slew them before they had gone up the ascent of the hill.

And when we came to their city, their women rolled upon us stones from the brow of the hill on which the city stood.

And I and Simeon hid ourselves behind the town, and seized upon the heights, and utterly destroyed the whole city.

7.

And the next day it was told us that the cities[7] of the two kings with a great host were coming against us.

I therefore and Dan feigned ourselves to be Amorites, and went as allies into their city. And in the depth of night our brethren came, and we opened to them the gates; and we destroyed all the men and their substance, and we took for a prey all that was theirs, and their three walls we cast down. And we drew near to Thamna,[8] where was all the refuge of the hostile kings.

Then having received hurt I was wroth, and charged upon them to the brow of the hill; and they slang at me with stones and darts; and had not Dan my brother aided me, they would have been able to slay me.

We came upon them therefore with wrath, and they all fled; and passing by another way, they besought my father, and he made peace with them, and we did to them no hurt, but made a truce with them, and restored to them all the captives.

And I built Thamna, and my father built Rhambael. [9]I was twenty years old when this war befell, and the Canaanites feared me and my brethren.

8.

Moreover, I had much cattle, and I had for the chief of my herdsmen Iran[10] the Adullamite.

And when I went to him I saw Barsan, king of Adullam, and he made us a feast; and he entreated me, and gave me his daughter Bathshua to wife.

She bare me Er, and Onan, and Shelah; and the two of them the Lord smote that they died childless:

for Shelah lived, and his children are ye.

9.

Eighteen years we abode at peace, our father and we, with his brother Esau, and his sons with us, after that we came from Mesopotamia, from Laban.

And when eighteen years were fulfilled, in the fortieth year of my life, Esau, the brother of my father, came upon us with much people and strong; and he fell by the bow of Jacob, and was taken up dead in Mount Seir:

even as he went above Iramna[11] was he slain.

And we pursued after the sons of Esau.

Now they had a city with walls of iron and gates of brass; and we could not enter into it, and we encamped around, and besieged them.

And when they opened not to us after twenty days, I set up a ladder in the sight of all, and with my shield upon my head I climbed up, assailed with stones of three talents' weight; and I climbed up, and slew four who were mighty among them.

And the next day Reuben and Gad entered in and slew sixty others.

Then they asked from us terms of peace; and being aware of our father's purpose, we received them as tributaries.

And they gave us two hundred cors of wheat, five hundred baths of oil, fifteen hundred measures of wine, until we went down into Egypt.

10.

After these things, my son Er took to wife Tamar, from Mesopotamia, a daughter of Aram. [12]Now Er was wicked, and he doubted concerning Tamar, because she was not of the land of Canaan. And on the third day an angel of the Lord smote him in the night, and he had not known her, according to the evil craftiness of his mother, for he did not wish to have children from her.

In the days of the wedding-feast I espoused Onan to her; and he also in wickedness knew her not, though he lived with her a year.

And when I threatened him, he lay with her, [13] ...according to the command of his mother, and he also died in his wickedness.

And I wished to give Shelah also to her, but my wife Bathshua suffered it not; for she bore a spite against Tamar, because she was not of the daughters of Canaan, as she herself was.

11.

And I knew that the race of Canaan was wicked, but the thoughts of youth blinded my heart.

And when I saw her pouring out wine, in the drunkenness of wine was I deceived, and I fell before her.

And while I was away, she went and took for Shelah a wife from the land of Caanan. And when I knew what she had done, I cursed her in the anguish of my soul, and she also died in the wickedness of her sons.

12.

And after these things, while Tamar was a widow, she heard after two years that I was going up to shear my sheep; then she decked herself in bridal array, and sat over against the city by the gate. For it is a law of the Amorites, that she who is about to marry sit in fornication seven days by the gate. [14]I therefore, being drunk at the waters of Chozeb, recognised her not by reason of wine; and her beauty deceived me, through the fashion of her adorning.

And I turned aside to her, and said, I would enter in to thee.

And she said to me, What wilt thou give me?

And I gave her my staff, and my girdle, and my royal crown; and I lay with her, and she conceived.

I then, not knowing what she had done, wished to slay her; but she privily sent my pledges, and put me to shame.

And when I called her, I heard also the secret words which I spoke when lying with her in my drunkenness; and I could not slay her, because it was from the Lord.

For I said, Lest haply she did it in subtlety, and received the pledge from another woman: but I came near her no more till my death, because I had done this abomination in all Israel.

Moreover, they who were in the city said that there was no bride in the city, because she came from another place, and sat for awhile in the gate, and she thought that no one knew that I had gone in to her. [15]And after this we came into Egypt to Joseph, because of the famine.

Forty and six years old was I, and seventy and three years lived I there.

13.

And now, my children, in what things so ever I command you hearken to your father, and keep all my sayings to perform the ordinances of the Lord, and to obey the command of the Lord God.

And walk not after your lusts, nor in the thoughts of your imaginations in the haughtiness of your heart; and glory not in the works of the strength of youth, for this also is evil in the eyes of the Lord.

For since I also gloried that in wars the face of no woman of goodly form ever deceived me, and upbraided Reuben my brother concerning Bilhah, the wife of my father, the spirits of jealousy and of fornication arrayed themselves within me, until I fell before Bathshua the Canaanite, and Tamar who was espoused to my sons.

And I said to my father-in-law, I will counsel with my father, and so will I take thy daughter.

And he showed me a boundless store of gold in his daughter's behalf, for he was a king. And he decked her with gold and pearls, and caused her to pour out wine for us at the feast in womanly beauty.

And the wine led my eyes astray, and pleasure blinded my heart; and I loved her, and I fell, and transgressed the commandment of the Lord and the commandment of my fathers, and I took her to wife.

And the Lord rewarded me according to the thought of my heart, insomuch that I had no joy in her children.

14.

And now, my children, be not drunk with wine; for wine turneth the mind away from the truth, and kindleth in it the passion of lust, and leadeth the eyes into error.

For the spirit of fornication hath wine as a minister to give pleasures to the mind; for these two take away the power from a man.

For if a man drink wine to drunkenness, he disturbeth his mind with filthy thoughts to fornication, and exciteth his body to carnal union; and if the cause of the desire be present, he worketh the sin, and is not ashamed.

Such is wine, my children; for he who is drunken revereth no man.

For, lo, it made me also to err, so that I was not ashamed of the multitude in the city, because before the eyes of all I turned aside unto Tamar, and I worked a great sin, and I uncovered the covering of the shame of my sons.

After that I drank wine I reverenced not the commandment of God, and I took a woman of Canaan to wife.

Wherefore, my children, he who drinketh wine needeth discretion; and herein is discretion in drinking wine, that a man should drink as long as he keepeth decency; but if he go beyond this bound, the spirit of deceit attacketh his mind and worketh his will; and it maketh the drunkard to talk filthily, and to transgress and not to be ashamed, but even to exult in his dishonour, accounting himself to do well.

15.

He that committeth fornication, and [16] uncovereth his nakedness, hath become the servant of fornication, and escapeth not [17] from the power thereof, even as I also was uncovered.

For I gave my staff, that is, the stay of my tribe; and my girdle, that is, my power; and my diadem, that is, the glory of my kingdom.

Then I repented for these things, and took no wine or flesh until my old age, nor did I behold any joy.

And the angel of God showed me that for ever do women bear rule over king and beggar alike; and from the king they take away his glory, and from the valiant man his strength, and from the beggar even that little which is the stay of his poverty.

16.

Observe therefore, my children, moderation in wine; for there are in it four evil spirits--of (1) lust, of (2) wrath, of (3) riot, of (4) filthy lucre.

If ye drink wine in gladness, with shamefacedness, with the fear of God, ye shall live.

For if ye drink not with shamefacedness, and the fear of God departeth from you, then cometh drunkenness, and shamelessness stealeth in.

But [18] even if ye drink not at all, take heed lest ye sin in words of outrage, and fighting, and slander, and transgression of the commandments of God; so shall ye perish before your time.

Moreover, wine revealeth the mysteries of God and men to aliens, even as I also revealed the commandments of God and the mysteries of Jacob my father to the Canaanitish Bathshua, to whom God forbade to declare them.

And wine also is a cause of war and confusion.

17.

I charge you, therefore, my children, not to love money, nor to gaze upon the beauty of women; because for the sake of money and beauty I was led astray to Bathshua the Canaanite.

For I know that because of these two things shall ye who are my race fall into wickedness; for even wise men among my sons shall they mar, and shall cause the kingdom of Judah to be diminished, which the Lord gave me because of my obedience to my father. [19]For I never disobeyed a word of Jacob my father, for all things whatsoever he commanded I did.

And Abraham, the father of my father, blessed me that I should be king in Israel, and Isaac further blessed me in like manner.

And I know that from me shall the kingdom be established.

The Forgotten Bible

18.

For I have read also in the books of Enoch the righteous what evils ye shall do in the last days.

Take heed, therefore, my children, of fornication and the love of money; hearken to Judah your father, for these things do withdraw you from the law of God, and blind the understanding of the soul, and teach arrogance, and suffer not a man to have compassion upon his neighbour:

they rob his soul of all goodness, and bind him in toils and troubles, and take away his sleep and devour his flesh, and hinder the sacrifices of God; and he remembereth not blessing, and he hearkeneth not to a prophet when he speaketh, and is vexed at the word of godliness.

For one who serveth two passions contrary to the commandments of God cannot obey God, because they have blinded his soul, and he walketh in the day-time as in the night.

19.

My children, the love of money leadeth to idols; because, when led astray through money, men make mention of those who are no gods, and it causeth him who hath it to fall into madness.

For the sake of money I lost my children, and but for the repentance of my flesh, and the humbling of my soul, and the prayers of Jacob my father, I should have died childless.

But the God of my fathers, who is pitiful and merciful, pardoned me, because I did it in ignorance.[20] For the prince of deceit blinded me, and I was ignorant as a man and as flesh, being corrupted in sins; and I learnt my own weakness while thinking myself unconquerable. [21]

20.

[22] Learn therefore, my children, that two spirits wait upon man--the spirit of truth and the spirit of error; and in the midst is the spirit of the understanding of the mind, to which it belongeth to turn whithersoever it will.

And the works of truth and the works of error are written upon the breast of men, and each one of them the Lord knoweth.

And there is no time at which the works of men can be hid from Him; for on the bones of his breast hath he been written down before the Lord.

And the spirit of truth testifieth all things, and accuseth all; and he who sinneth is burnt up by his own heart, and cannot raise his face unto the Judge.

21.

And now, my children, love Levi, that ye may abide, and exalt not yourselves against him, lest ye be utterly destroyed.

For to me the Lord gave the kingdom, and to him the priesthood, and He set the kingdom beneath the priesthood.

To me He gave the things upon the earth; to him the things in the heavens.

As the heaven is higher than the earth, so is the priesthood of God higher than the kingdom upon the earth.

For the Lord chose him above thee, to draw near to Him, and to eat of His table and first-fruits, even the choice things of the sons of Israel, and thou shalt be to them as a sea.

For as, on the sea, just and unjust are tossed about, some taken into captivity while others are enriched, so also shall every race of men be in thee, some are in jeopardy and taken captive, and others shall grow rich by means of plunder.

For they who rule will be as great sea-monsters, swallowing up men like fishes:

free sons and daughters do they enslave; houses, lands, flocks, money, will they plunder; and with the flesh of many will they wrongfully feed the ravens and the cranes; and they will go on further in evil, advancing on still in covetousness. And there shall be false prophets like tempests, and they shall persecute all righteous men.

22.

And the Lord shall bring upon them divisions one against another, and there shall be continual wars in Israel; and among men of other race shall my kingdom be brought to an end, until the salvation of Israel shall come, until the appearing of the God of righteousness, that Jacob and all the Gentiles may rest in peace. [23] And he shall guard the might of my kingdom for ever:

for the Lord sware to me with an oath that the kingdom should never fail from me, and from my seed for all days, even for ever.

23.

Now I have much grief, my children, because of your lewdness, and witchcrafts, and idolatries, which ye will work against the kingdom, following them that have familiar spirits; ye [24] will make your daughters singing girls [25] and harlots for divinations and demons of error, and ye will be mingled in the pollutions of the Gentiles:

for which things' sake the Lord shall bring upon you famine and pestilence, death and the sword, avenging siege, and dogs for the rending in pieces of enemies, and revilings of friends, destruction and blighting of eyes, children slaughtered, wives carried off, possessions plundered, temple of God in flames, your land desolated, your own selves enslaved among the Gentiles, and they shall make some of you eunuchs for their wives; and whenever ye will return to the Lord with humility of heart, repenting and walking in all the commandments of God, then will the Lord visit you in mercy and in love, bringing you from out of the bondage of your enemies.

24.

And after these things shall a Star arise to you from Jacob in peace, and a Man shall rise from my seed, like the Sun of righteousness, walking with the sons of men [26] in meekness and righteousness, and no sin shall be found in Him.

And the heavens shall be opened above Him, to shed forth the blessing of the Spirit from the Holy Father; and He shall shed forth a spirit of grace upon you, and ye shall be unto Him sons in truth, and ye shall walk in His commandments, the first and the last.

This is the Branch of God Most High, and this the Well-spring unto life for all flesh.

[27] Then shall the sceptre of my kingdom shine forth, and from your root shall arise a stem; and in it shall arise a rod of righteousness to the Gentiles, to judge and to save all that call upon the Lord.

25.

And after these things shall Abraham and Isaac and Jacob arise unto life, and I and my brethren will be chiefs, even your sceptre in Israel:

Levi first, I the second, Joseph third, Benjamin fourth, Simeon fifth, Issachar sixth, and so all in order.

And the Lord blessed Levi; the Angel of the Presence, me; the powers of glory, [28] Simeon; the heaven, Reuben; the earth, Issachar; the sea, Zebulun; the mountains, Joseph; the tabernacle, Benjamin; the lights of heaven, Dan; the fatness of earth, Naphtali; the sun, Gad; the olive, Asher:

and there shall be one people of the Lord, and one tongue; and there shall no more be a spirit of deceit of Beliar, for he shall be cast into the fire for ever.

And they who have died in grief shall arise in joy, and they who have lived in poverty for the Lord's sake shall be made rich, and they who have been in want shall be filled, and they who have been weak shall be made strong, and they who have been put to death for the Lord's sake shall awake in life.[29] And the harts of Jacob shall run in joyfulness, and the eagles of Israel shall fly in gladness; but the ungodly shall lament, and sinners all weep, and all the people shall glorify the Lord for ever.

26.

Observe, therefore, my children, all the law of the Lord, for there is hope for all them who follow His way aright.

And he said to them:

I die before your eyes this day, a hundred and nineteen years old.

Let no one bury me in costly apparel, nor tear open my bowels, [30] for this shall they who are kings do:

and carry me up to Hebron with you.

And Judah, when he had said these things, fell asleep; and his sons did according to all whatsoever he commanded them, and they buried him in Hebron with his fathers.

Footnotes:

1. Gen. xxix. 35. [The name = "Praise". So Gen. xlix. 3.]

2. In c. 5 we find this name, with a slight variety of spelling, as that of a place over which this king may have ruled. It is doubtless equivalent to the Hebrew Tappuah, a name of several cities mentioned in the Old Testament. See Josh. xv. 34; xvi. 8; xvii. 8; 1 Chron. ii. 43. Cf. Thapha, Jubilees, 34.

3. Cd. Oxon. reads heteran; but cf. Aresa, Jubilees, 34.

4. Cf. c. 12; also Chezib (Gen. xxxviii. 5), Chozeba (1 Chron. iv. 22), and Achzib (Josh. xv. 44; Mic. i. 14), all of which are probably different names for the same place, and all connected with

Judah.

5. Cf. Selo, Jubilees, l.c.

6. Cf. 1 Chron. xi. 36. [Here the translator supplies a note of doubt--an interrogation-point.]

7. Cd. Oxon. reads Gaas polis basileon. Cf. Josh. xxiv. 30; Judg. ii. 9; 2 Sam. xxiii. 30. Cf. also "Gaiz," Jubilees, l.c.

8. The Timnah of the Old Testament, which name is, however, borne by several places. Most probably it is the Timnah near Bethshemesh, on the north frontier of Judah, in the neighbourhood, that is, of many of the other localities mentioned in the Testaments. This may be the same as the Timnathah on the Danite frontier (Josh. xix. 43), and with the Timnathah where Samson's wife dwelt (Judg. xiv. 1 sqq). The geographical position of Timnath-serah is against the allusion being to it here. Cf., however, Jubilees, c. 34, where Thamnathares is one of the hostile towns.

9. Cf. Robel, Jubilees, l.c.

10. Cf. Gen. xxxviii. 1.

11. Cd. Oxon. en 'Anoniram, probably per incuriam scribae, for epano 'Iram

12. This seems to arise from the wish to disconnect Israel as far as possible from non-Shemite associations. Cf. the Targum of Onkelos on Gen. xxxviii. 6. "Judah took a wife for Er, his first-born, a daughter of the great Shem, whose name was Tamar."

13. diephtheire de to sperma epi ten gen

14. [Herod. i., cap. 199; Baruch vi. 43.]

15. [To this section Lardner objects. But compare Gen. xxxviii. 12.]

16. Cd. Oxon. here reads the additional clause zemioumenos ouk aisthanetai kai adoxon ouk aischunetai. Kan gar tis basileuse, porneuon--perhaps omitted from Cd. Cant. through the homoeoteleuton.

17. Cd. Oxon. omits the negative. The basileia will then be that from which the man falls by his sin.

18. Cd. Oxon. reads ti de lego; med' holos pinete, which seems much more suitable to the context.

19. [1 Kings xi. 1, and ver. 11.]

20. [Num. xv. 25 and Acts iii. 17.]

21. [See cap. 13, p. 19, supra.]

22. Cd. Oxon. omits the whole of this chapter.

23. [Rom. xi. 26.]

24. The reading of Cd. Oxon. is doubtless to be preferred, which joins kledosi kai daimosi planes to what precedes

25. [Eccles. ii. 8; Ecclus. ix. 4.]

26. [Prov. viii. 31.]

27. Cd. Oxon. omits from here to end of c. 25.

28. [Eph. iii. 10.]

29. [2 Macc. vii. 9-36 and Heb. xi. 35.]

30. i.e., for the purpose of embalmment.

V - The Testament of Issachar Concerning Simplicity

1.
    The record of the words of Issachar.
    He called his sons, and said to them:
    Hearken, my children, to Issachar your father; give ear to my words, ye who are beloved of the Lord.
    I was the fifth son born to Jacob, even the hire of the mandrakes. [1]For Reuben [2] brought in mandrakes from the field, and Rachel met him and took them.
    And Reuben wept, and at his voice Leah my mother came forth.
    Now these mandrakes were sweet-smelling apples which the land of Aram produced on high ground below a ravine of water.
    And Rachel said, I will not give them to thee, for they shall be to me instead of children.
    Now there were two apples; and Leah said, Let it suffice thee that thou hast taken the husband of my virginity:
    wilt thou also take these?
    And she said, Behold, let Jacob be to thee this night instead of the mandrakes of thy son.
    And Leah said to her, Boast not, and vaunt not thyself; for Jacob is mine, and I am the wife of his youth.
    But Rachel said, How so? for to me was he first espoused, and for my sake he served our father fourteen years.
    What shall I do to thee, because the craft and the subtlety of men are increased, and craft prospereth upon the earth?
    And were it not so, thou wouldest not now see the face of Jacob.
    For thou art not his wife, but in craft wert taken to him in my stead.
    And my father deceived me, and removed me on that night, and suffered me not to see him; for had I been there, it had not happened thus.
    And Rachel said, Take one mandrake, and for the other thou shalt hire him from me for one night.
    And Jacob knew Leah, and she conceived and bare me, and on account of the hire [3] I was called Issachar.

2.
    Then appeared to Jacob an angel of the Lord, saying, Two children shall Rachel bear; for she hath refused company with her husband, and hath chosen continency.
    And had not Leah my mother given up the two apples for the sake of his company, she would have borne eight sons; and for this thing she bare six, and Rachel two:
    because on account of the mandrakes the Lord visited her.
    For He knew that for the sake of children she wished to company with Jacob, and not for lust of pleasure. [4]For she went further, and on the morrow too gave up Jacob that she might receive also the other mandrake.
    Therefore the Lord hearkened to Rachel because of the mandrakes:
    for though she desired them, she ate them not, but brought them to the priest of the Most High who was at that time, and offered them up in the house of the Lord.

3.
    When, therefore, I grew up, my children, I walked in uprightness of heart, and I became a husbandman for my parents and my brethren, and I brought in fruits from the field according to their season; and my father blessed me, for he saw that I walked in simplicity.
    And I was not a busybody in my doings, nor malicious and slanderous against my neighbour.
    I never spoke against any one, nor did I censure the life of any man, but walked in the simplicity of my eyes.
    Therefore when I was thirty years old I took to myself a wife, for my labour wore away my

strength, and I never thought upon pleasure with women; but through my labour my sleep sufficed me, and my father always rejoiced in my simplicity.

For on whatever I laboured I offered first to the Lord, by the hands of the priests, of all my produce and all first-fruits; then to my father, and then took for myself.

And the Lord increased twofold His benefits in my hands; and Jacob also knew that God aided my simplicity, for on every poor man and every one in distress I bestowed the good things of the earth in simplicity of heart.

4.

And now hearken to me, my children, and walk in simplicity of heart, for I have seen in it all that is well-pleasing to the Lord. The simple coveteth not gold, defraudeth not his neighbour, longeth not after manifold dainties, delighteth not in varied apparel, doth not picture to himself to live a long life, but only waiteth for the will of God, and the spirits of error have no power against him.

For he cannot allow within his mind a thought of female beauty, that he should not pollute his mind in corruption.

No envy can enter into his thoughts, no jealousy melteth away his soul, nor doth he brood over gain with insatiate desire; for he walketh in uprightness of life, and beholdeth all things in simplicity, not admitting in his eyes malice from the error of the world, lest he should see the perversion of any of the commandments of the Lord.

5.

Keep therefore the law of God, my children, and get simplicity, and walk in guilelessness, not prying over-curiously into the commands of God and the business of your neighbour; but love the Lord and your neighbour, have compassion on the poor and weak.

Bow down your back unto husbandry, and labour in tillage of the ground in all manner of husbandry, offering gifts unto the Lord with thanksgiving; for with the first-fruits of the earth did the Lord bless me, even as He blessed all the saints from Abel even until now.

For no other portion is given to thee than of the fatness of the earth, whose fruits are raised by toil; for our father Jacob blessed me with blessings of the earth and of first-fruits.

And Levi and Judah were glorified by the Lord among the sons of Jacob; for the Lord made choice of them, and to the one He gave the priesthood, to the other the kingdom.

Them therefore obey, and walk in the simplicity of your father; for unto Gad hath it been given to destroy the temptations that are coming upon Israel.

6.

I know, my children, that in the last times your sons will forsake simplicity, and will cleave unto avarice, and leaving guilelessness will draw near to malice, and forsaking the commandments of the Lord will cleave unto Beliar, and leaving husbandry will follow after their wicked devices, and shall be dispersed among the Gentiles, and shall serve their enemies.

And do you therefore command these things to your children, that if they sin they may the more quickly return to the Lord; for He is merciful, and will deliver them even to bring them back into their land.

7.

I am a hundred and twenty-two years old, and I know not against myself a sin unto death.

Except my wife, I have not known any woman. I never committed fornication in the haughtiness of my eyes; I drank not wine, to be led astray thereby; I coveted not any desirable thing that was my neighbour's; guile never entered in my heart; a lie never passed through my lips; if any man grieved, I wept with him, and I shared my bread with the poor.

I never ate alone; I moved no landmark; in all my days I wrought godliness and truth.

I loved the Lord with all my strength; likewise also did I love every man even as my own children.

So ye also do these things, my children, and every spirit of Beliar shall flee from you, and no deed of malicious men shall rule over you; and every wild beast shall ye subdue, having with yourselves the God of heaven walking with men in simplicity of heart.

And he commanded them that they should carry him up to Hebron, and bury him there in the cave with his fathers.

And he stretched out his feet and died, the fifth son of Jacob, in a good old age; and with every limb sound, and with strength unabated, he slept the eternal sleep. [5]

Footnotes:

1. See Gen. xxx. 14 sqq.
2. The Cam. ms. reads 'Iakob by an obvious error.
3. Sachar.
4. [Tobit viii. 7, 8.]
5. [See Dan, note 12, p. 26, infra. "Eternal" ="long."]

VI - The Testament of Zebulun Concerning Compassion and Mercy

1.

The record of Zebulun, which he enjoined his children in the hundred [1] and fourteenth year of his life, thirty-two years after the death of Joseph.

And he said to them:

Hearken to me sons of Zebulun, attend to the words of your father.

I am Zebulun, a good gift [2] to my parents.

For when I was born our father was increased very exceedingly, both in flocks and herds, when with the streaked rods he had his portion.

I know not, my children, that in all my days I have sinned, save only in thought.

Nor do I remember that I have done any iniquity, except the sin of ignorance which I committed against Joseph; for I screened my brethren, not telling to my father what had been done.

And I wept sore in secret, for I feared my brethren, because they had all agreed together, that if any one should declare the secret, he should be slain with the sword.

But when they wished to kill him, I adjured them much with tears not to be guilty of this iniquity.

2.

For Simeon and Gad came against Joseph to kill him.

And Joseph fell upon his face, and said unto them, Pity me, my brethren, have compassion upon the bowels of Jacob our father:

lay not upon me your hands to shed innocent blood, for I have not sinned against you; yea, if I have sinned, with chastening chastise me, but lay not upon me your hand, for the sake of Jacob our father.

And as he spoke these words, I pitied him and began to weep, and my heart melted within me, and all the substance of my bowels was loosened within my soul.

And Joseph also wept, and I too wept with him; and my heart throbbed fast, and the joints of my body trembled, and I was not able to stand.

And when he saw me weeping with him, and them coming against him to slay him, he fled behind me, beseeching them.

And Reuben rose and said, My brethren, let us not slay him, but let us cast him into one of these dry pits which our fathers digged and found no water.

For for this cause the Lord forbade that water should rise up in them, in order that Joseph might be preserved; and the Lord appointed it so, until they sold him to the Ishmaelites.

3.

For in the price of Joseph, my children, I had no share; but Simeon and Gad and six other of our brethren took the price of Joseph, and bought sandals [3] for themselves, their wives, and their children, saying, We will not eat of it, for it is the price of our brother's blood, but will tread it down under foot, because he said that he was king over us, and so let us see what his dreams mean.

Therefore is it written in the writing of the law of Enoch, that whosoever will not raise up seed to his brother, his sandal shall be unloosed, and they shall spit into his face. [4]And the brethren of Joseph wished not that their brother should live, and the Lord loosed unto them the sandal of Joseph.

For when they came into Egypt they were unloosed by the servants of Joseph before the gate, and so made obeisance to Joseph after the fashion of Pharaoh.

And not only did they make obeisance to him, but were spit upon also, falling down before him forthwith, and so they were put to shame before the Egyptians; for after this the Egyptians heard all the evils which we had done to Joseph.

4.

After these things they brought forth food; for I through two days and two nights tasted nothing, through pity for Joseph.

And Judah ate not with them, but watched the pit; for he feared lest Simeon and Gad should run back and slay him.

And when they saw that I also ate not, they set me to watch him until he was sold.

And he remained in the pit three days and three nights, and so was sold famishing.

And when Reuben heard that while he was away Joseph had been sold, he rent his clothes about him, and mourned, saying, How shall I look in the face of Jacob my father?

And he took the money, and ran after the merchants, and found no one; for they had left the main road, and journeyed hastily through rugged byways. [5]And Reuben ate no food on that day.

Dan therefore came to him, and said, Weep not, neither grieve; for I have found what we can say to our father Jacob.

Let us slay a kid of the goats, and dip in it the coat of Joseph; and we will say, Look, if this is the coat of thy son:

for they stripped off from Joseph the coat of our father when they were about to sell him, and put upon him an old garment of a slave.

Now Simeon had the coat, and would not give it up, wishing to rend it with his sword; for he was angry that Joseph lived, and that he had not slain him.

Then we all rose up together against him, and said, If thou give it not up, we will say that thou alone didst this wickedness in Israel; and so he gave it up, and they did even as Dan had said.

5.

And now, my children, I bid you to keep the commands of the Lord, and to show mercy upon your neighbour, and to have compassion towards all, not towards men only, but also towards beasts.

For for this thing's sake the Lord blessed me; and when all my brethren were sick I escaped without sickness, for the Lord knoweth the purposes of each. Have therefore compassion in your hearts, my children, because even as a man doeth to his neighbour, even so also will the Lord do to him. For the sons of my brethren were sickening, were dying on account of Joseph, because they showed not mercy in their hearts; but my sons were preserved without sickness, as ye know.

And when I was in Canaan, by the sea-coast, I caught spoil of fish for Jacob my father; and when many were choked in the sea, I abode unhurt.

6.

I was the first who made a boat to sail upon the sea, for the Lord gave me understanding and wisdom therein; and I let down a rudder behind it, and I stretched a sail on an upright mast in the midst; and sailing therein along the shores, I caught fish for the house of my father until we went into Egypt; and through compassion, I gave of my fish to every stranger.

And if any man were a stranger, or sick, or aged, I boiled the fish and dressed them well, and offered them to all men as every man had need, bringing them together and having compassion upon them.

Wherefore also the Lord granted me to take much fish:

for he that imparteth unto his neighbour, receiveth manifold more from the Lord.

For five years I caught fish, and gave thereof to every man whom I saw, and brought sufficient for all the house of my father.

In the summer I caught fish, and in the winter I kept sheep with my brethren.

7.

Now I will declare unto you what I did, I saw a man in distress and nakedness in wintertime, and had compassion upon him, and stole away [6] a garment secretly from my house, and gave it to him who was in distress.

Do you therefore, my children, from that which God bestoweth upon you, show compassion and mercy impartially to all men, and give to every man with a good heart.

And if ye have not at the time wherewith to give to him that asketh you, have compassion for him in bowels of mercy.

I know that my hand found not at the time wherewith to give to him that asked me, and I walked with him weeping for more than seven furlongs, and my bowels yearned towards him unto compassion.

The Forgotten Bible

8.

Have therefore yourselves also, my children, compassion towards every man with mercy, that the Lord also may have compassion upon you, and have mercy upon you; because also in the last days God sendeth His compassion on the earth, and wheresoever He findeth bowels of mercy, He dwelleth in him.

For how much compassion a man hath upon his neighbours, so much also hath the Lord upon him.

For when we went down into Egypt, Joseph bore no malice against us, and when he saw me he was filled with compassion.

And looking towards him, do ye also, my children, approve yourselves without malice, and love one another; and reckon not each one the evil of his brother, for this breaketh unity, and divideth all kindred, and troubleth the soul:

for he who beareth malice hath not bowels of mercy.

9.

Mark the waters, that they flow together, and sweep along stones, trees, sand; but if they are divided into many streams, the earth sucketh them up, and they become of no account.

So also shall ye be if ye be divided.

Divide not yourselves into two heads, for everything which the Lord made hath but one head; He gave two shoulders, hands, feet, but all the members are subject unto the one head.

I have learnt by the writing of my fathers, that in the last days ye will depart from the Lord, and be divided in Israel, and ye will follow two kings, and will work every abomination, and every idol will ye worship, and your enemies shall lead you captive, and ye shall dwell among the nations with all infirmities and tribulations and anguish of soul.

And after these things ye will remember the Lord, and will repent, and He will lead you back; for He is merciful and full of compassion, not imputing evil to the sons of men, because they are flesh, and the spirits of error deceive them in all their doings.

And after these things shall the Lord Himself arise to you, [7] the Light of righteousness, and healing [8] and compassion shall be upon His wings.

He shall redeem all captivity of the sons of men from Beliar, and every spirit of error shall be trodden down.

And He shall bring back all the nations to zeal for Him, and ye shall see God in the fashion of a man [9] whom the Lord shall choose, Jerusalem is His name.

And again with the wickedness of your words will ye provoke Him to anger, and ye shall be cast away, even unto the time of consummation.

10.

And now, my children, grieve not that I am dying, nor be troubled in that I am passing away from you.

For I shall arise once more in the midst of you, as a ruler in the midst of his sons; and I will rejoice in the midst of my tribe, as many as have kept the law of the Lord, and the commandments of Zebulun their father. [10]But upon the ungodly shall the Lord bring everlasting fire, and will destroy them throughout all generations.

I am hastening away unto my rest, as did my fathers; but do ye fear the Lord your God with all your strength all the days of your life.

And when he had said these things he fell calmly asleep, and his sons laid him in a coffin; and afterwards they carried him up to Hebron, and buried him with his fathers.

Footnotes:

1. The Ox. ms. reads 150, and refers the event to two years after Joseph's death.

The text of the Cam. ms. gives an impossible result here, as it would make Zebulun twenty-eight years younger than Joseph, who died at the age of 110. According to the Ox. ms., Reuben (cf. c. 1) and Zebulun would die in the same year, the former at 125, the latter 150. A comparison of Test. Reub., c. 1 shows the most probable solution to be to give the numerals, rid', b'.

2. The derivation of Zebulun seems to be from zvl, a collateral form of zvr, to give. Hence Leah plays on the double meaning of the former verb, Gen. xxx. 20.

3. Cf. the Targum Ps. Jon. on Gen. xxxvii. 28.

4. [Deut. xxv. 7, 8, 9. See Lardner on the animus of these quotations from Enoch, as it strikes him, vol. ii. p. 350.]

5. Cam. ms. dia traglokolpeton ; Ox. ms. dia trogloduton.

6. ["Finis non determinat probitatem actus."]

7. Mal. iv. 2.

8. The Ox. ms. reads: "And ye shall return from your land, and ye shall see the Lord in Jerusalem for His name's sake." [Heb. vii. 2. At least, Salem is His name.]

9. [Another of those unequivocal passages which refute Lardner's charge of "Unitarianism" in this book.]

10. [Ezek. xlviii. 26, 27. An important example of Hebrew exposition of this prophet.]

VII - The Testament of Dan Concerning Anger and Lying

1.

The record of the words of Dan, which he spake to his sons in his last days.
In the hundred and twenty-fifth year of his life he called together his family, and said:
Hearken to my words, ye sons of Dan; give heed to the words of the mouth of your father.
I have proved in my heart, and in my whole life, that truth with just dealing is good and well-pleasing to God, and that lying and anger are evil, because they teach man all wickedness.
I confess this day to you, my children, that in my heart I rejoiced concerning the death of Joseph, a true and good man; and I rejoiced at the selling of Joseph, because his father loved him more than us.
For the spirit of jealousy and of vainglory said to me, Thou also art his son.
And one of the spirits of Beliar wrought with me, saying, Take this sword, and with it slay Joseph; so shall thy father love thee when he is slain.
This is the spirit of anger that counselled me, that even as a leopard devoureth a kid, so should I devour Joseph.
But the God of Jacob our father gave him not over into my hands that I should find him alone, nor suffered me to work this iniquity, that two tribes should be destroyed in Israel. [1]

2.

And now, my children, I am dying, and I tell you of a truth, that unless ye keep yourselves from the spirit of lying and of anger, and love truth and long-suffering, ye shall perish.
There is blindness in anger, my children, and no wrathful man regardeth any person with truth:
for though it be a father or a mother, he behaveth towards them as enemies; though it be a brother, he knoweth him not; though it be a prophet of the Lord, he disobeyeth him; though a righteous man, he regardeth him not; a friend he doth not acknowledge.
For the spirit of anger encompasseth him with the nets of deceit, and blindeth his natural eyes, and through lying darkeneth his mind, and giveth him a sight of his own making.
And wherewith encompasseth he his eyes?
In hatred of heart; and he giveth him a heart of his own against his brother unto envy.

3.

My children, mischievous is anger, for it becometh as a soul to the soul itself; and the body of the angry man it maketh its own, and over his soul it getteth the mastery, and it bestoweth upon the body its own power, that it may work all iniquity; and whenever the soul doeth aught, it justifieth what has been done, since it seeth not.
Therefore he who is wrathful, if he be a mighty man, hath a treble might in his anger; one by the might and aid of his servants, and a second by his wrath, whereby he persuadeth and overcometh in injustice:
and having a third of the nature of his own body, and of his own self working the evil.
And though the wrathful man be weak, yet hath he a might twofold of that which is by nature; for wrath ever aideth such in mischief. This spirit goeth always with lying at the right hand of Satan, that his works may be wrought with cruelty and lying.

4.

Understand ye therefore the might of wrath, that it is vain.
For it first of all stingeth him in word:
then by deeds it strengtheneth him who is angry, and with bitter punishments disturbeth his mind, and so stirreth up with great wrath his soul.
Therefore, when any one speaketh against you, be not [2] ye moved unto anger.
And if any man praiseth you as good, be not lifted up nor elated, either to the feeling or showing of pleasure. [3] For first it pleaseth the hearing, and so stirreth up the understanding to

understand the grounds for anger; and then, being wrathful, he thinketh that he is justly angry.

If ye fall into any loss or ruin, my children, be not troubled; for this very spirit maketh men desire that which hath perished, in order that they may be inflamed by the desire.

If ye suffer loss willingly, be not vexed, for from vexation he raiseth up wrath with lying.

And wrath with lying is a twofold mischief; [4] and they speak one with another that they may disturb the mind; and when the soul is continually disturbed, the Lord departeth from it, and Beliar ruleth over it.

5.

Observe, therefore, my children, the commandments of the Lord, and keep His law; and depart from wrath, and hate lying, that the Lord may dwell among you, and Beliar may flee from you.

Speak truth each one with his neighbour, so shall ye not fall into lust and confusion; but ye shall be in peace, having the God of peace, so [5] shall no war prevail over you.

Love the Lord through all your life, and one another with a true heart.

For I know that in the last days ye will depart from the Lord, and will provoke Levi unto anger, and will fight against Judah; but ye shall not prevail against them.

For an angel of the Lord shall guide them both; for by them shall Israel stand.

And whensoever ye depart from the Lord, ye will walk in all evil, working the abominations of the Gentiles, going [6] astray with women of them that are ungodly; and the spirits of error shall work in you with all malice.

For I have read in the book of Enoch the righteous, that your prince is Satan, and that all the spirits of fornication and pride shall be subject unto Levi, to lay a snare for the sons of Levi, to cause them to sin before the Lord.

And my sons will draw near unto Levi, and sin with them in all things; and the sons of Judah will be covetous, plundering other men's goods like lions.

Therefore shall ye be led away with them in captivity, and there shall ye receive all the plagues of Egypt, and all the malice of the Gentiles:

and so, when ye return to the Lord, ye shall obtain mercy, and He shall bring you into His sanctuary, calling peace upon you; and there shall arise unto you from the tribe of Judah and of Levi the salvation of the Lord; [7] and He shall make war against Beliar, and He shall give the vengeance of victory to our coasts.

And the captivity shall He take from Beliar, even the souls of the saints, and shall turn disobedient hearts unto the Lord, and shall give to them who call upon Him everlasting peace; and the saints shall rest in Eden, and the righteous shall rejoice in the new Jerusalem, which shall be unto the glory of God for ever and ever.

And no longer shall Jerusalem endure desolation, nor Israel be led captive; for the Lord shall be in the midst of her, dwelling among men, [8] even the Holy One of Israel reigning over them [9] in humility and in poverty; [10] and he who believeth on Him shall reign in truth in the heavens.

6.

And now, my children, fear the Lord, and take heed unto yourselves of Satan and his spirits; and draw near unto God, and to the Angel [11] that intercedeth for you, for He is a Mediator between God and man for the peace of Israel.

He shall stand up against the kingdom of the enemy; therefore is the enemy eager to destroy all that call upon the Lord.

For he knoweth that in the day on which Israel shall believe, [12] the kingdom of the enemy shall be brought to an end; and the very angel of peace shall strengthen Israel, that it fall not into the extremity of evil.

And it shall be in the time of the iniquity of Israel, that the Lord will depart from them, and will go after him that doeth His will, for unto none of His angels shall it be as unto him. And His name shall be in every place of Israel, and among the Gentiles--Saviour.

Keep therefore yourselves, my children, from every evil work, and cast away wrath and all lying, and love truth and long-suffering; and the things which ye have heard from your father, do ye also impart to your children, that the Father of the Gentiles may receive you:

for He is true and long-suffering, meek and lowly, and teacheth by His works the law of God.

Depart, therefore, from all unrighteousness, and cleave unto the righteousness of the law of the Lord:

and bury me near my fathers.

7.

And when he had said these things he kissed them, and slept the long sleep. [13]And his sons buried him, and after that they carried up his bones to the side of Abraham, and Isaac, and Jacob. Nevertheless, as Dan had prophesied unto them that they should forget the law of their God, and should be alienated from the land of their inheritance, and from the race of Israel, and from their kindred, so also it came to pass.

Footnotes:

1. [The tribes of Ephraim and Manasseh.]
2. The reading of the Ox. ms., me kineisthe is to be taken.
3. Cam. ms. eis eidean; Ox. ms. eis aedian.
4. Read kakon
5. The Ox. ms. omits from here to tois ethnesi Soter in c. 6.
6. 'Ekporeuontes may be an error for ekporneuontes, which Grabe wrongly gives as the reading of the Cam. ms.
7. [The root idea, p. 18, notes 5, 6, supra.]
8. [Rev. xxi. 3.]
9. [Here is the Chiliasm of Barnabas, vol. i. p. 146.]
10. [That is, not with the glory of His throne above.]
11. Cf. Dorner, Doctrine of the Person of Christ, Introd., p, 15, Eng. transl.
12. [Rom. xi. 15.]
13. See Zebulun 10, p. 25, supra.]

VIII - The Testament of Naphtali Concerning Natural Goodness

1.

The record of the testament of Naphtali, what things he ordained at the time of his death in the hundred and thirty-second year of his life.

When his sons were gathered together in the seventh month, the fourth day of the month, he, being yet in good health, made them a feast and good cheer.

And after he was awake in the morning, he said to them, I am dying; and they believed him not.

And he blessed the Lord; and affirmed that after yesterday's feast he should die.

He began then to say to his sons:

Hear, my children; ye sons of Naphtali, hear the words of your father.

I was born from Bilhah; and because Rachel dealt craftily, and gave Bilhah in place of herself to Jacob, and she bore me upon Rachel's lap, therefore was I called Naphtali. [1]And Rachel loved me because I was born upon her lap; and when I was of young and tender form, she was wont to kiss me, and say, Would that I might see a brother of thine from my own womb, like unto thee: whence also Joseph was like unto me in all things, according to the prayers of Rachel.

Now my mother was Bilhah, daughter of Rotheus the brother of Deborah, Rebecca's nurse, and she was born on one and the self-same day with Rachel.

And Rotheus was of the family of Abraham, a Chaldean, fearing God, free-born and noble; and he was taken captive, and was bought by Laban; and he gave him Aena his handmaid to wife, and she bore a daughter, and called her Zilpah, after the name of the village in which he had been taken captive.

And next she bore Bilhah, saying, My daughter is eager after what is new, for immediately that she was born she was eager for the breast.

2.

And since I was swift on my feet like a deer, my father Jacob appointed me for all errands and messages, and as a deer [2] did he give me his blessing.

For as the potter knoweth the vessel, what it containeth, and bringeth clay thereto, so also doth the Lord make the body in accordance with the spirit, and according to the capacity of the body doth He implant the spirit, and the one is not deficient from the other by a third part of a hair; for by weight, and measure, and rule is every creature of the Most High. [3]And as the potter knoweth the use of each vessel, whereto it sufficeth, so also doth the Lord know the body, how far it is capable for goodness, and when it beginneth in evil; for there is no created thing and no thought which the Lord knoweth not, for He created every man after His own image.

As man's strength, so also is his work; and as his mind, so also is his work; and as his purpose, so also is his doing; as his heart, so also is his mouth; as his eye, so also is his sleep; as his soul, so also is his word, either in the law of the Lord or in the law of Beliar.

And as there is a division between light and darkness, between seeing and hearing, so also is there a division between man and man, and between woman and woman; neither is it to be said that there is any superiority in anything, either of the face or of other like things. [4]For God made all things good in their order, the five senses in the head, and He joineth on the neck to the head, the hair also for comeliness, the heart moreover for understanding, the belly for the dividing of the stomach, the calamus[5] for health, the liver for wrath, the gall for bitterness. the spleen for laughter, the reins for craftiness, the loins for power, the ribs for containing, the back for strength, and so forth.

So then, my children, be ye orderly unto good things in the fear of God, and do nothing disorderly in scorn or out of its due season.

For if thou bid the eye to hear, it cannot; so neither in darkness can ye do the works of light.

3.

Be ye not therefore eager to corrupt your doings through excess, or with empty words to deceive your souls; because if ye keep silence in purity of heart, ye shall be able to hold fast the will of God, and to cast away the will of the devil.

Sun and moon and stars change not their order; so also ye shall not change the law of God in the disorderliness of your doings.

Nations went astray, and forsook the Lord, and changed their order, and followed stones and stocks, following after spirits of error.

But ye shall not be so, my children, recognising in the firmament, in the earth, and in the sea, and in all created things, the Lord who made them all, that ye become not as Sodom, which changed the order of its nature, in like manner also the Watchers [6] changed the order of their nature, whom also the Lord cursed at the flood, and for their sakes made desolate the earth, that it should be uninhabited and fruitless.

4.

These things I say, my children, for I have read in the holy writing of Enoch that ye yourselves also will depart from the Lord, walking according to all wickedness of the Gentiles, and ye will do according to all the iniquity of Sodom.

And the Lord will bring captivity upon you, and there shall ye serve your enemies, and ye shall be covered with all affliction and tribulation, until the Lord shall have consumed you all.

And after that ye shall have been diminished and made few, ye will return and acknowledge the Lord your God; and He will bring you back into your own land, according to His abundant mercy.

And it shall be, after that they shall come into the land of their fathers, they will again forget the Lord and deal wickedly; and the Lord shall scatter them upon the face of all the earth, until the compassion of the Lord shall come, a Man working righteousness and showing mercy unto all them that are afar off, and them that are near.

5.

For in the fortieth year of my life, I saw in a vision that the sun and the moon were standing still on the Mount of Olives, at the east of Jerusalem.

And behold Isaac, the father of my father, saith to us, Run and lay hold of them, each one according to his strength; and he that seizeth them, his shall be the sun and the moon.

And we all of us ran together, and Levi laid hold of the sun, and Judah outstripped the others and seized the moon, and they were both of them lifted up with them.

And when Levi became as a sun, a certain young man gave to him twelve branches of palm; and Judah was bright as the moon, and under his feet were twelve rays.

And Levi and Judah ran, and laid hold each of the other.

And, lo, a bull upon the earth, having two great horns, and an eagle's wings upon his back; and we wished to seize him, but could not.

For Joseph outstripped us, and took him, and ascended up with him on high.

And I saw, for I was there, and behold a holy writing appeared to us saying:

Assyrians, Medes, Persians, Elamites, Gelachaeans, Chaldeans, Syrians, shall possess in captivity the twelve tribes of Israel.

6.

And again, after seven months, I saw our father Jacob standing by the sea of Jamnia, and we his sons were with him.

And, behold, there came a ship sailing by, full of dried flesh, without sailors or pilot: and there was written upon the ship, Jacob.

And our father saith to us, Let us embark on our ship.

And when we had gone on board, there arose a vehement storm, and a tempest of mighty wind; and our father, who was holding the helm, flew away from us.

And we, being tost with the tempest, were borne along over the sea; and the ship was filled with water and beaten about with a mighty wave, so that it was well-nigh broken in pieces.

And Joseph fled away upon a little boat, and we all were divided upon twelve boards, and Levi and Judah were together.

We therefore all were scattered even unto afar off.

Then Levi, girt about with sackcloth, prayed for us all unto the Lord.

And when the storm ceased, immediately the ship reached the land, as though in peace.

And, lo, Jacob our father came, and we rejoiced with one accord.

7.

These two dreams I told to my father; and he said to me, These things must be fulfilled in their season, after that Israel hath endured many things.

Then my father saith unto me, I believe that Joseph liveth, for I see always that the Lord numbereth him with you. And he said, weeping, Thou livest, Joseph, my child, and I behold thee not, and thou seest not Jacob that begat thee.

And he caused us also to weep at these words of his, and I burned in my heart to declare that he had been sold, but I feared my brethren.

8.

Behold, my children, I have shown unto you the last times, that all shall come to pass in Israel.

Do ye also therefore charge your children that they be united to Levi and to Judah.

For through Judah shall salvation arise unto Israel, and in Him shall Jacob be blessed. For through his tribe shall God be seen dwelling among men on the earth, to save the race of Israel, and He shall gather together the righteous from the Gentiles.

If ye work that which is good, my children, both men and angels will bless you; and God will be glorified through you among the Gentiles, and the devil will flee from you, and the wild beasts will fear you, and the angels will cleave to you.

For as if a man rear up a child well, he hath a kindly remembrance thereof; so also for a good work there is a good remembrance with God.

But him who doeth not that which is good, men and angels shall curse and God will be dishonoured among the heathen through him, and the devil maketh him his own as his peculiar instrument, and every wild beast shall master him, and the Lord will hate him.

For the commandments of the law are twofold, and through prudence must they be fulfilled.

For there is a season for a man to embrace his wife, and a season to abstain therefrom [7] for his prayer.

So then there are two commandments; and unless they be done in due order, they bring about sin.

So also is it with the other commandments.

Be ye therefore wise in God, and prudent, understanding the order of the commandments, and the laws of every work, that the Lord may love you.

9.

And when he had charged them with many such words, he exhorted them that they should remove his bones to Hebron, and should bury him with his fathers.

And when he had eaten and drunken with a merry heart, he covered his face and died.

And his sons did according to all things whatsoever Naphtali their father had charged them.

Footnotes:

1. Gen. xxx. 8. Josephus, Ant., i. 19. 7
2. Gen. xlix. 21.
3. [Wis. xi. 20; Ecclus. xlii. 7.]
4. The Greek text here is obviously corrupt, and doubtless one or two words are wanting. The reading of the Cam. ms. is, ouk estin eipein hoti en to heni tois prosopois e ton homoion. In the Ox. ms. the passage is wanting.
5. It seems very doubtful what is meant by kalamos here.
I have thought it best, therefore, to leave the matter open.
The Ox. ms. punctuates stomachou kal.
6. Cf. Reuben 5 [note 3, p. 10 supra].
7. [Eccles. iii. 5; 1 Cor. vii. 5.]

IX - The Testament of Gad Concerning Hatred

1.

The record of the testament of Gad, what things he spake unto his sons, in the hundred and twenty-seventh year of his life, saying:

I was the seventh son born to Jacob, and I was valiant in keeping the flocks.

I guarded at night the flock; and whenever the lion came, or wolf, or leopard, or bear, or any wild beast against the fold, I pursued it, and with my hand seizing its foot, and whirling it round, I stunned it, and hurled it over two furlongs, and so killed it.

Now Joseph was feeding the flock with us for about thirty days, and being tender, he fell sick by reason of the heat.

And he returned to Hebron to his father, who made him lie down near him, because he loved him. And Joseph told our father that the sons of Zilpah and Bilhah were slaying the best of the beasts, [1] and devouring them without the knowledge of Judah and Reuben.

For he saw that I delivered a lamb out of the mouth of the bear, and I put the bear to death; and the lamb I slew, being grieved concerning it that it could not live, and we ate it, and he told our father.

And I was wroth with Joseph for that thing until the day that he was sold into Egypt.

And the spirit of hatred was in me, and I wished not either to see Joseph or to hear him.

And he rebuked us to our faces for having eaten of the flock without Judah.

And whatsoever things he told our father, he believed him.

2.

I confess now my sin, my children, that oftentimes I wished to kill him, because I hated him to the death, and there were in no wise in me bowels of mercy towards him.

Moreover, I hated him yet more because of his dreams; and I would have devoured him out of the land of the living, even as a calf devoureth the grass from the earth.

Therefore I and Judah sold him to the Ishmaelites for thirty [2] pieces of gold, and ten of them we hid, and showed the twenty to our brethren:

and so through my covetousness I was fully bent on his destruction.

And the God of my fathers delivered him from my hands, that I should not work iniquity in Israel.

3.

And now, my children, hearken to the words of truth to work righteousness, and all the law of the Most High, and not go astray through the spirit of hatred, for it is evil in all the doings of men. Whatsoever a man doeth, that doth the hater abhor:

though he worketh the law of the Lord, he praiseth him not; though he feareth the Lord, and taketh pleasure in that which is righteous, he loveth him not:

he dispraiseth the truth, he envieth him that ordereth his way aright, he delighteth in evil-speaking, he loveth arrogance, for hatred hath blinded his soul; even as I also looked on Joseph.

4.

Take heed therefore, my children, of hatred; for it worketh iniquity against the Lord Himself:

for it will not hear the words of His commandments concerning the loving of one's neighbour, and it sinneth against God.

For if a brother stumble, immediately it wisheth to proclaim it to all men, and is urgent that he should be judged for it, and be punished and slain.

And if it be a servant, it accuseth him to his master, and with all affliction it deviseth against him, if it be possible to slay him.

For hatred worketh in envy, and it ever sickeneth with envy against them that prosper in well-doing, when it seeth or heareth thereof.

For as love would even restore to life the dead, and would call back them that are condemned to die, so hatred would slay the living, and those that have offended in a small matter it would not suffer to live.

For the spirit of hatred worketh together with Satan through hastiness ³ of spirit in all things unto men's death; but the spirit of love worketh together with the law of God in long-suffering unto the salvation of men. ⁴

5.
Hatred is evil, because it continually abideth with lying, speaking against the truth; and it maketh small things to be great, and giveth heed to darkness as to light, and calleth the sweet bitter, and teacheth slander, and war, and violence, and every excess of evil; and it filleth the heart with devilish poison.

And these things I say to you from experience, my children, that ye may flee hatred, and cleave to the love of the Lord.

Righteousness casteth out hatred, humility destroyeth hatred.

For he that is just and humble is ashamed to do wrong, being reproved not of another, but of his own heart, because the Lord vieweth his intent:

he speaketh not against any man, because the fear of the Most High overcometh hatred.

For, fearing lest he should offend the Lord, he will not do any wrong to any man, no, not even in thought.

These things I learnt at last, after that I had repented concerning Joseph.

For true repentance after a godly sort destroyeth unbelief, and driveth away the darkness, and enlighteneth the eyes, and giveth knowledge to the soul, and guideth the mind to salvation; and those things which it hath not learnt from man, it knoweth through repentance.

For God brought upon me a disease of the heart; and had not the prayers of Jacob my father intervened, it had hardly failed that my spirit had departed.

For by what things a man transgresseth, by the same also is he punished. ⁵For in that my heart was set mercilessly against Joseph, in my heart too I suffered mercilessly, and was judged for eleven months, for so long a time as I had been envious against Joseph until he was sold.

6.
And now, my children, love ye each one his brother, and put away hatred from your hearts, loving one another in deed, and in word, and in thought of the soul.

For in the presence of our father I spake peaceably with Joseph; and when I had gone out, the spirit of hatred darkened my mind, and moved my soul to slay him.

⁶ Love ye therefore one another from your hearts; and if a man sin against thee, tell him of it gently, and drive out the poison of hatred, and foster not guile in thy soul.

And if he confess and repent, forgive him; and if he deny it, strive not with him, lest he swear, and thou sin doubly.

Let not a stranger hear your secrets amid your striving, lest he hate and become thy enemy, and work great sin against thee; for ofttimes he will talk guilefully ⁷ with thee, or evilly overreach thee, taking his poison from himself.

Therefore, if he deny it, and is convicted and put to shame, and is silenced, do not tempt him on.

For he who denieth repenteth, so that he no more doeth wrong against thee; yea also, he will honour thee, and fear thee, and be at peace with thee.

But if he be shameless, and abideth in his wrongdoing, even then forgive him from the heart, and give the vengeance to God.

7.
If a man prospereth more than you, be not grieved, but pray also for him, that he may have perfect prosperity.

For perchance it is expedient for you thus; and if he be further exalted, be not envious, remembering that all flesh shall die:

and offer praise to God, who giveth things good and profitable to all men.

Seek out the judgments of the Lord, and so shall thy mind rest and be at peace.

And though a man become rich by evil means, even as Esau the brother of my father, be not jealous; but wait for the end of the Lord.

For either He taketh His benefits away from the wicked, or leaveth them still to the repentant, or to the unrepentant reserveth punishment for ever.

For the poor man who is free from envy, giving thanks to the Lord in all things, is rich among all men, because he hath not evil jealousy of men.

Put away, therefore, hatred from your souls, and love one another with uprightness of heart.

8.

And do ye also tell these things to your children, that they honour Judah and Levi, for from them shall the Lord raise up a Saviour to Israel. ⁸For I know that at the last your children shall depart from them, and shall walk in all wickedness, and mischief, and corruption before the Lord.

And when he had rested for a little while, he said again to them, My children, obey your father, and bury me near to my fathers.

And he drew up his feet, and fell asleep in peace.

And after five years they carried him up, and laid him in Hebron with his fathers.

Footnotes:

1. Cf. Targum Ps. Jon. of Gen. xxxvii. 2.

2. The narrative of Genesis (xxxvii. 28) gives twenty pieces of silver; the LXX. twenty pieces of gold, with which latter agrees Josephus' mnon eikosin (Antiq., ii. 3. 3). [It is worthy of note that Judas took a meaner price for the "Son of Joseph."]

3. For this unusual use of oligopsuchia, cf. Prov. xiv. 29, LXX., where there is the same contrast with makrothumia.

4. [This passage is cited by Lardner as conspicuously fine.]

5. [Wis. xi. 16.]

6. The Ox. ms. omits from here to the last clause of c. 7.

7. For dolophonesai , the reading of the Cam. ms. here, Grabe conjectured dolophonesei. Probably dolophonesei is to be preferred.

8. [The Virgin was the daughter of Judah, but had kinship with Levi. Luke i. 36. Compare Jer. xxxiii. 20-22.]

X - The Testament of Asher Concerning Two Faces of Vice and Virtue

1.

The record of the testament of Asher, what things he spake to his sons in the hundred and twentieth year of his life.

While he was still in health, he said to them:

Hearken, ye children of Asher, to your father, and I will declare to you all that is right in the sight of God.

Two ways [1] hath God given to the sons of men, and two minds, and two doings, and two places, and two ends.

Therefore all things are by twos, one corresponding to the other.

There are two ways of good and evil, with which are the two minds in our breasts distinguishing them.

Therefore if the soul take pleasure in good, all its actions are in righteousness; and though it sin, it straightway repenteth.

For, having his mind set upon righteousness, and casting away maliciousness, he straightway overthroweth the evil, and uprooteth the sin.

But if his mind turn aside in evil, all his doings are in maliciousness, and he driveth away the good, and taketh unto him the evil, and is ruled by Beliar; and even though he work what is good, he perverteth it in evil.

For whenever he beginneth as though to do good, he bringeth the end of his doing to work evil, seeing that the treasure of the devil is filled with the poison of an evil spirit.

2.

There is then, he saith, a soul which speaketh the good for the sake of the evil, and the end of the doing leadeth to mischief. [2] There is a man who showeth no compassion upon him who serveth his turn in evil; and this thing hath two aspects, but the whole is evil.

And there is a man that loveth him that worketh evil; he likewise dwelleth in evil, because he chooseth even to die in an evil cause for his sake:

and concerning this it is clear that it hath two aspects, but the whole is an evil work.

And though there is love, it is but wickedness concealing the evil, even as it beareth a name that seemeth good, but the end of the doing tendeth unto evil.

Another stealeth, worketh unjustly, plundereth, defraudeth, and withal pitieth the poor: this, too, hath a twofold aspect, but the whole is evil.

Defrauding his neighbour he provoketh God, and sweareth falsely against the Most High, and yet pitieth the poor:

the Lord who commandeth the law he setteth at nought and provoketh, and refresheth the poor; he defileth the soul, and maketh gay the body; he killeth many, and he pitieth a few:

and this, too, hath a twofold aspect.

Another committeth adultery and fornication, and abstaineth from meats; yet in his fasting he worketh evil, and by his power and his wealth perverteth many, and out of his excessive wickedness worketh the commandments:

this, too, hath a twofold aspect, but the whole is evil.

Such men are as swine or hares; [3] for they are half clean, but in very deed are unclean. For God in the Heavenly [4] Tablets hath thus declared.

3.

Do not ye therefore, my children, wear two faces like unto them, of goodness and of wickedness; but cleave unto goodness only, for in goodness doth God rest, and men desire it.

From wickedness flee away, destroying the devil by your good works; for they that are double-faced serve not God, but their own lusts, so that they may please Beliar and men like unto themselves.

4.

For good men, even they that are single of face, though they be thought by them that are double-faced to err, are just before God.

For many in killing the wicked do two works, an evil by a good; but the whole is good, because he hath uprooted and destroyed that which is evil.

One man hateth him that showeth mercy, and doeth wrong to the adulterer and the thief:

this, too, is double-faced, but the whole work is good, because he followeth the Lord's example, in that he receiveth not that which seemeth good with that which is really bad. [5]Another desireth not to see good days with them that riot, lest he defile his mouth and pollute his soul:

this, too, is double-faced, but the whole is good, for such men are like to stags and to hinds, because in a wild condition they seem to be unclean, but they are altogether clean; because they walk in a zeal for God, and abstain from what God also hateth and forbiddeth by His commandments, and they ward off the evil from the good.

5.

Ye see therefore, my children, how that there are two in all things, one against the other, and the one is hidden by the other. [6]Death succeedeth to life, dishonour to glory, night to day, and darkness to light; and all things are under the day, and just things under life:

wherefore also everlasting life awaiteth death.

Nor may it be said that truth is a lie, nor right wrong; for all truth is under the light, even as all things are under God.

All these things I proved in my life, and I wandered not from the truth of the Lord, and I searched out the commandments of the Most High, walking with singleness of face according to all my strength unto that which is good.

6.

Take heed therefore ye also, my children, to the commandments of the Lord, following the truth with singleness of face, for they that are double-faced receive twofold punishment.

Hate the spirits of error, which strive against men.

Keep the law of the Lord, and give not heed unto evil as unto good; but look unto the thing that is good indeed, and keep it in all commandments of the Lord, having your conversation unto Him, and resting in Him:

for the ends at which men aim do show their righteousness, and know the angels of the Lord from the angels of Satan.

For if the soul depart troubled, it is tormented by the evil spirit which also it served in lusts and evil works; but if quietly and with joy it hath known the angel of peace, it shall comfort him in life.

7.

Become not, my children, as Sodom, which knew not the angels of the Lord, and perished for ever.

For I know that ye will sin, and ye shall be delivered into the hands of your enemies, and your land shall be made desolate, and ye shall be scattered unto the four corners of the earth.

And ye shall be set at nought in the Dispersion as useless water, until the Most High shall visit the earth; and He shall come as man, with men eating and drinking, and in peace breaking the head of the dragon through water.

He shall save Israel and all nations, God speaking in the person of man.

Therefore tell ye these things to your children, that they disobey Him not.

For I have read in the Heavenly Tablets that in very deed ye will disobey Him, and act ungodly against Him, not giving heed to the law of God, but to the commandments of men.

Therefore shall ye be scattered as Gad and as Dan my brethren, who shall know not their own lands, tribe, and tongue.

But the Lord will gather you together in faith through the hope of His tender mercy, for the sake of Abraham, and Isaac, and Jacob. [7]

8.

And when he had said these things unto them, he charged them, saying:

Bury me in Hebron.

And he fell into a peaceful sleep, and died; and after this his sons did as he had charged them, and they carried him up and buried him with his fathers.

Footnotes:

1. [See the Duae Viae, vol. vii., p. 377, this series.]
2. [This section is commended by Dr. Lardner.]
3. Cf. Lev. xi. 5, 7. [Vol. ii. p. 555 note 6.]
4. Cf. Levi 5. [P. 13, note 8 supra.]
5. [Matt. v. 45. This seems contradictory.]
6. The Ox. ms. adds, en te euphrosune he methe, en to geloti to penthos, en to gamo he akrasia. [Ecclus. xlii. 24.]
7. [The Hebrew triad, father, son, and proceeding.]

XI - The Testament of Joseph Concerning Sobriety

1.

The record of the testament of Joseph.
When he was about to die he called his sons and his brethren together, and said to them:
My children and brethren, hearken to Joseph the beloved of Israel; give ear, my sons, unto your father.
I have seen in my life envy and death, and I wandered not in the truth of the Lord.
These my brethren hated me, and the Lord loved me:
they wished to slay me, and the God of my fathers guarded me:
they let me down into a pit, and the Most High brought me up again:
I was sold for a slave, and the Lord made me free:
I was taken into captivity, and His strong hand succoured me:
I was kept in hunger, and the Lord Himself nourished me:
I was alone, and God comforted me:
I was sick, and the Most High visited me:
I was in prison, and the Saviour showed favour unto me; in bonds, and He released me; amid slanders, and He pleaded my cause; amid bitter words of the Egyptians, and He rescued me; amid envy and guile, and He exalted me.

2.

And thus Potiphar [1] the chief cook [2] of Pharaoh entrusted to me his house, and I struggled against a shameless woman, urging me to transgress with her; but the God of Israel my father guarded me from the burning flame.
I was cast into prison, I was beaten, I was mocked; and the Lord granted me to find pity in the sight of the keeper of the prison.
For He will in no wise forsake them that fear Him, neither in darkness, nor in bonds, nor in tribulations, nor in necessities.
For not as man is God ashamed, nor as the son of man is He afraid, nor as one that is earth-born is He weak, or can He be thrust aside; but in all places is He at hand, and in divers ways doth He comfort, departing for a little to try the purpose of the soul.
In ten temptations He showed me approved, and in all of them I endured; for endurance is a mighty charm, and patience giveth many good things.

3.

How often did the Egyptian threaten me with death!
How often did she give me over to punishment, and then call me back, and threaten me when I would not company with her!
And she said to me, Thou shalt be lord of me, and all that is mine, if thou wilt give thyself unto me, and thou shalt be as our master.
Therefore I remembered the words of the fathers of my father Jacob, and I entered into my chamber [3] and prayed unto the Lord; and I fasted in those seven years, and I appeared to my master as one living delicately, for they that fast for God's sake receive beauty of face. [4]And if one gave me wine, I drank it not; and I fasted for three days, and took my food and gave it to the poor and sick.
And I sought the Lord early, and wept for the Egyptian woman of Memphis, for very unceasingly did she trouble me, and at night she came to me under the pretence of visiting me; and at first, because she had no male child, she feigned to count me as a son.
And I prayed unto the Lord, and she bare a male child; therefore for a time she embraced me as a son, and I knew it not.
Last of all, she sought to draw me into fornication.
And when I perceived it, I sorrowed even unto death; and when she had gone out I came to myself, and I lamented for her many days, because I saw her guile and her deceit.

And I declared unto her the words of the Most High, if haply she would turn from her evil lust.

4.

How often has she fawned upon me with words as a holy man, with guile in her talk, praising my chastity before her husband, while desiring to destroy me when we were alone.

She lauded me openly as chaste, and in secret she said unto me, Fear not my husband; for he is persuaded concerning thy chastity, so that even should one tell him concerning us he would in no wise believe.

For all these things I lay upon the ground in sackcloth, and I besought God that the Lord would deliver me from the Egyptian.

And when she prevailed nothing, she came again to me under the plea of instruction, that she might know the word of the Lord.

And she said unto me, If thou willest that I should leave my idols, be persuaded by me, and I will persuade my husband to depart from his idols, and we will walk in the law of thy Lord.

And I said unto her, The Lord willeth not that those who reverence Him should be in uncleanness, nor doth He take pleasure in them that commit adultery.

And she held her peace, longing to accomplish her evil desire.

And I gave myself yet more to fasting and prayer, that the Lord should deliver me from her.

5.

And again at another time she said unto me, If thou wilt not commit adultery, I will kill my husband, and so will I lawfully take thee to be my husband.

I therefore, when I heard this, rent my garment, and said, Woman, reverence the Lord, and do not this evil deed, lest thou be utterly destroyed; for I will declare thy ungodly thought unto all men.

She therefore, being afraid, besought that I would declare to no one her wickedness.

And she departed, soothing me with gifts, and sending to me every delight of the sons of men.

6.

And she sendeth to me food sprinkled with enchantments.

And when the eunuch who brought it came, I looked up and beheld a terrible man giving me with the dish a sword, and I perceived that her scheme was for the deception of my soul.

And when he had gone out I wept, nor did I taste that or any other of her food.

So then after one day she came to me and observed the food, and said unto me, What is this, that thou hast not eaten of the food?

And I said unto her, It is because thou filledst it with death; and how saidst thou, I come not near to idols but to the Lord alone?

Now therefore know that the God of my father hath revealed unto me by an angel thy wickedness, and I have kept it to convict thee, if haply thou mayest see it and repent.

But that thou mayest learn that the wickedness of the ungodly hath no power over them that reverence God in chastity, I took it and ate it before her, saying, The God of my fathers and the Angel of Abraham shall be with me.

And she fell upon her face at my feet, and wept; and I raised her up and admonished her, and she promised to do this iniquity no more.

7.

But because her heart was set upon me to commit lewdness, she sighed, and her countenance fell.

And when her husband saw her, he said unto her, Why is thy countenance fallen?

And she said, I have a pain at my heart, and the groanings of my spirit do oppress me; and so he comforted her who was not sick.

Then she rushed in to me while her husband was yet without, and said unto me, I will hang myself, or cast myself into a well or over a cliff, if thou wilt not consent unto me. And when I saw the spirit of Beliar was troubling her, I prayed unto the Lord, and said unto her, Why art thou troubled and disturbed, blinded in sins?

Remember that if thou killest thyself, Sethon, the concubine of thy husband, thy rival, will beat thy children, and will destroy thy memorial from off the earth.

And she said unto me, Lo then thou lovest me; this alone is sufficient for me, that thou carest for my life and my children:

I have expectation that I shall enjoy my desire.

And she knew not that because of my God I spake thus, and not because of her.

For if a man hath fallen before the passion of a wicked desire, then by that hath he become enslaved, even as also was she.

And if he hear any good thing with regard to the passion whereby he is vanquished, he receiveth it unto his wicked desire.

8.

I declare unto you, my children, that it was about the sixth hour when she departed from me; and I knelt before the Lord all that day, and continued all the night; and about dawn I rose up weeping, and praying for a release from the Egyptian.

At last, then, she laid hold of my garments, forcibly dragging me to have connection with her. When, therefore, I saw that in her madness she was forcibly holding my garments, I fled away naked.

And she falsely accused me to her husband, and the Egyptian cast me into the prison in his house; and on the morrow, having scourged me, the Egyptian [5] sent me into the prison in his house.

When, therefore, I was in fetters, the Egyptian woman fell sick from her vexation, and listened to me how I sang praises unto the Lord while I was in the abode of darkness, and with glad voice rejoiced and glorified my God only because by a pretext I had been rid of the Egyptian woman.

9.

How often hath she sent unto me, saying, Consent to fulfil my desire, and I will release thee from thy bonds, and I will free time from the darkness!

And not even in thoughts did I incline unto her. For God loveth him who in a den of darkness fasteth with chastity, rather than him who in secret chambers liveth delicately without restraint.

And whosoever liveth in chastity, and desireth also glory, and if the Most High knoweth that it is expedient for him, He bestoweth this also upon him, even as upon me.

How often, though she were sick, did she come down to me at unlooked-for times, and listened to my voice as I prayed!

And when I heard her groanings I held my peace.

For when I was in her house she was wont to bare her arms, and breasts, and legs, that I might fall before her; for she was very beautiful, splendidly adorned for my deception.

And the Lord guarded me from her devices. [6]

10.

Ye see therefore, my children, how great things patience worketh, and prayer with fasting.

And if ye therefore follow after sobriety and purity in patience and humility of heart, the Lord will dwell among you, because He loveth sobriety.

And wheresoever the Most High dwelleth, even though a man fall into envy, or slavery, or slander, the Lord who dwelleth in him, for his sobriety's sake not only delivereth him from evil, but also exalteth and glorifieth him, even as me.

For in every way the man is guarded, whether in deed, or in word, or in thought.

My brethren know how my father loved me, and I was not exalted in my heart; although I was a child, I had the fear of God in my thoughts.

For I knew that all things should pass away, and I kept myself within bounds, and I honoured my brethren; and through fear of them I held my peace when I was sold, and revealed not my family to the Ishmaelites, that I was the son of Jacob, a great man and a mighty.

11.

Do ye also, therefore, have the fear of God in your works, and honour your brethren.

For every one who worketh the law of the Lord shall be loved by Him.

And when I came to the Indocolpitae with the Ishmaelites, they asked me, and I said that I was a slave from their house, that I might not put my brethren to shame.

And the eldest of them said unto me, Thou art not a slave, for even thy appearance doth make it manifest concerning thee.

And he threatened me even unto death.

But I said that I was their slave.

Now when we came into Egypt, they strove concerning me, which of them should buy me and take me.

Therefore it seemed good to all that I should remain in Egypt with a merchant of their trade, until they should return bringing merchandise.

And the Lord gave me favour in the eyes of the merchant, and he entrusted unto me his house.

And the Lord blessed him by my means, and increased him in silver and gold, and I was with him three months and five days.

12.

About that time the Memphian wife of Potiphar passed by with great pomp, and cast her eyes upon me, because her eunuchs told her concerning me.

And she told her husband concerning the merchant, that he had become rich by means of a young Hebrew, saying, And they say that men have indeed stolen him out of the land of Canaan.

Now therefore execute judgment with him, and take away the youth to be thy steward; so shall the God of the Hebrews bless thee, for grace from heaven is upon him.

13.

And Potiphar was persuaded by her words, and commanded the merchant to be brought, and said unto him, What is this that I hear, that thou stealest souls out of the land of the Hebrews, and sellest them for slaves?

The merchant therefore fell upon his face, and besought him, saying, I beseech thee, my lord, I know not what thou sayest.

And he said, Whence then is thy Hebrew servant?

And he said, The Ishmaelites entrusted him to me until they should return.

And he believed him not, but commanded him to be stripped and beaten.

And when he persisted, Potiphar said, Let the youth be brought.

And when I was brought in, I did obeisance to the chief of the eunuchs--for he was third in rank with Pharaoh, being chief of all the eunuchs, and having wives and children and concubines.

And he took me apart from him, and said unto me, Art thou a slave or free?

And I said, A slave.

And he said unto me, Whose slave art thou?

And I said unto him, The Ishmaelites'.

And again he said unto me, How becamest thou their slave?

And I said, They bought me out of the land of Canaan.

And he believed me not, and said, Thou liest:

and he commanded me to be stripped and beaten.

14.

Now the Memphian woman was looking through a window while I was being beaten, and she sent unto her husband, saying, Thy judgment is unjust; for thou dost even punish a free man who hath been stolen, as though he were a transgressor.

And when I gave no other answer though I was beaten, he commanded that we should be kept in guard, until, said he, the owners of the boy shall come.

And his wife said unto him, Wherefore dost thou detain in captivity this noble child, who ought rather to be set at liberty, and wait upon thee?

For she wished to see me in desire of sin, and I was ignorant concerning all these things. Then said he to his wife, It is not the custom of the Egyptians to take away that which belongeth to others before proof is given.

This he said concerning the merchant, and concerning me, that I must be imprisoned.

15.

Now, after four and twenty days came the Ishmaelites; and having heard that Jacob my father was mourning because of me, they said unto me, How is it that thou saidst that thou wert a slave? and lo, we have learnt that thou art the son of a mighty man in the land of Canaan, and thy father grieveth for thee in sackcloth.

And again I would have wept, but I restrained myself, that I should not put my brethren to shame.

And I said, I know not, I am a slave.

Then they take counsel to sell me, that I should not be found in their hands.

For they feared Jacob, lest he should work upon them a deadly vengeance.

For it had been heard that he was mighty with the Lord and with men.

Then said the merchant unto them, Release me from the judgment of Potiphar.

They therefore came and asked for me, saying, He was bought by us with money.

And he sent us away.

16.

Now the Memphian woman pointed me out to her husband, that he should buy me; for I hear, said she, that they are selling him.

And she sent a eunuch to the Ishmaelites, and asked them to sell me; and since he was not willing to traffic with them, he returned.

So when the eunuch had made trial of them, he made known to his mistress that they asked a large price for their slave.

And she sent another eunuch, saying, Even though they demand two minae of gold, take heed not to spare the gold; only buy the boy, and bring him hither.

And he gave them eighty pieces of gold for me, and told his mistress that a hundred had been given for me.

And when I saw it I held my peace, that the eunuch should not be punished.

17.

Ye see, my children, what great things I endured that I should not put my brethren to shame. Do ye also love one another, and with long-suffering hide ye one another's faults.

For God delighteth in the unity of brethren, and in the purpose of a heart approved unto love. And when my brethren came into Egypt, and learnt that I returned their money unto them, and upbraided them not, yea, that I even comforted them, and after the death of Jacob I loved them more abundantly, and all things whatsoever he commanded I did very abundantly, then they marvelled.

For I suffered them not to be afflicted even unto the smallest matter; and all that was in my hand I gave unto them.

Their children were my children, and my children were as their servants; their life was my life, and all their suffering was my suffering, and all their sickness was my infirmity.

My land was their land, my counsel their counsel, and I exalted not myself among them in arrogance because of my worldly glory, but I was among them as one of the least.

18.

If ye also therefore walk in the commandments of the Lord, my children, He will exalt you there, and will bless you with good things for ever and ever.

And if any one seeketh to do evil unto you, do ye by well-doing pray for him, and ye shall be redeemed of the Lord from all evil.

For, behold, ye see that through long-suffering I took unto wife even the daughter of my [7] master.

And a hundred talents of gold were given me with her; for the Lord made them to serve me.

And He gave me also beauty as a flower above the beautiful ones of Israel; and He preserved me unto old age in strength and in beauty, because I was like in all things to Jacob.

19.

Hear ye also, my children, the visions which I saw.

There were twelve deer feeding, and the nine were divided and scattered in the land, likewise also the three.

And I saw that from Judah was born a virgin wearing a linen [8] garment, and from her went forth a Lamb, without spot, and on His left hand there was as it were a lion; and all the beasts rushed against Him, and the lamb overcame them, and destroyed them, and trod them under foot.

And because of Him the angels rejoiced, and men, and all the earth.

And these things shall take place in their season, in the last days.

Do ye therefore, my children, observe the commandments of the Lord, and honour Judah and Levi; for from them shall arise unto you the Lamb of God, by grace saving all the Gentiles and Israel.

For His kingdom is an everlasting kingdom, which shall not be shaken; but my kingdom among you shall come to an end as a watcher's [9] hammock, which after the summer will not appear.

20.

I know that after my death the Egyptians will afflict you, but God will undertake your cause, and will bring you into that which He promised to your fathers.

But carry ye up my bones with you; [10] for when my bones are taken up, the Lord will be with you in light, and Beliar shall be in darkness with the Egyptians.

And carry ye up Zilpah your mother, and lay her near Bilhah, by the hippodrome, by the side of Rachel. [11] And when he had said these things, he stretched out his feet, and slept the long sleep.

And all Israel bewailed him, and all Egypt, with a great lamentation.

For he felt even for the Egyptians even as his own members, and showed them kindness, aiding them in every work, and counsel, and matter.

Footnotes:

1. The Greek spelling here is Photimar, in the later chapters Petephris (Pentephres, Cd. Oxon.). The former is more like the Hebrew, the latter really the LXX. spelling, Petephres. We may perhaps see herein a trace of a double authorship in the Test. Joseph.

2. Cf. Gen. xxxix. 1, LXX., and Josephus (Antiq., ii. 4. 1), who calls Potiphar mageiron ho basileus. The view of the Eng. ver. is most probably correct, though we find tvch used in the sense of cook in 1 Sam. ix. 23.

3. [Matt. vi. 6. He veils the quotation by a fiction, as to authorship, to support the plan of his work.]

4. [Dan. i. 15.]

5. This repetition of a clause seems like the slip of a copyist. The Ox. ms. reads, eis ten heirkten tou Pharao

6. [To this section Lardner takes exception, as unbecoming to the gravity of Joseph.]

7. Another account is given in the Targ. Ps. Jon. of Gen. xli. 45, "And he gave him to wife Asenath, whom Dinah bare to Shechem: and the wife of Potipherah prince of Tanes brought up."

8. This wearing of a linen garment would seem to imply a connection with the priestly tribe. St. Luke (i. 36) indeed calls the Virgin the kinswoman of Elisabeth. On this tendency to associate the old sacerdotal tribe with the new royalty of Messiah, cf., e.g., Protevangel. Jacobi, cc. 6, 7, 9; Augustine, contra Faustum, xxiii. 4; Epiphanius, Haer., lxxviii. 13. [See Reuben, sec. 6, p. 10, supra.]

9. Isa. i. 8; xxiv. 20.

10. Cf. Test. Simeon 8, and Jubilees 46. The account of Joseph's burial in the Targ. Ps. Jon. on Gen. l. 26 is:

"And Joseph died, a hundred and ten years old; and they embalmed him, and placed him in a coffin, and sank him in the middle of the Nile of Egypt."

11. Cf. Gen. xlviii. 7, LXX.

XII - The Testament of Benjamin Concerning a Pure Mind

1.

The record of the words of Benjamin, which he set forth to his sons, after he had lived a hundred and twenty years.

And he kissed them, and said:

As Isaac was born to Abraham in his hundredth year, so also was I to Jacob.

Now since Rachel died in giving me birth, I had no milk; therefore I was suckled by Bilhah her handmaid.

For Rachel remained barren for twelve years after that she had borne Joseph: and she prayed the Lord with fasting twelve days, and she conceived and bare me.

For our father loved Rachel dearly, and prayed that he might see two sons born from her: therefore was I called the son of days, which is Benjamin. [1]

2.

When therefore I went into Egypt, and Joseph my brother recognised me, he said unto me, What did they tell my father in that they sold me?

And I said unto him, They dabbled thy coat with blood and sent it, and said, Look if this is the coat of thy son.

And he said to me, Even so, brother; for when the Ishmaelites took me, one of them stripped off my coat, and gave me a girdle, and scourged me, and bade me run.

And as he went away to hide my garment, a lion met him, and slew him; and so his fellows were afraid, and sold me to their companions.

3.

Do ye also therefore, my children, love the Lord God of heaven, and keep His commandments, and be followers of the good and holy man Joseph; and let your mind be unto good, even as ye know me.

He that hath his mind good seeth all things rightly.

Fear ye the Lord, and love your neighbour; and even though the spirits of Beliar allure you into all troublous wickedness, yet shall no troublous wickedness have dominion over you, even as it had not over Joseph my brother.

How many men wished to slay him, and God shielded him!

For he that feareth God and loveth his neighbour cannot be smitten by Beliar's spirit of the air, being shielded by the fear of God; nor can he be ruled over by the device of men or of beasts, for he is aided by the love of the Lord which he hath towards his neighbour.

For he even besought our father Jacob that he would pray for our brethren, that the Lord would not impute to them the evil that they devised concerning Joseph.

And thus Jacob cried out, My child Joseph, thou hast prevailed over the bowels of thy father Jacob.

And he embraced him, and kissed him for two hours, saying, In thee shall be fulfilled the prophecy of heaven concerning the Lamb of God, even the Saviour of the world, that spotless shall He be delivered up for transgressors, and sinless [2] shall He be put to death for ungodly men in the blood of the covenant, for the salvation [3] of the Gentiles and of Israel, and shall destroy Beliar, and them that serve him.

4.

Know ye, my children, the end of the good man?

Be followers of his compassion in a good mind, that ye also may wear crowns of glory.

The good man hath not a dark eye; for he showeth mercy to all men, even though they be sinners, even though they devise evil concerning him. So he that doeth good overcometh the evil, being shielded by Him that is good; and he loveth the righteous as his own soul.

If any one is glorified, he envieth him not; if any one is enriched, he is not jealous; if any one is valiant, he praiseth him; he trusteth and laudeth him that is sober-minded; he showeth mercy to the poor; he is kindly disposed toward the weak; he singeth the praises of God; as for him who hath the fear of God, he protecteth him as with a shield; him that loveth God he aideth; him that rejecteth the Most High he admonisheth and turneth back; and him that hath the grace of a good spirit, he loveth even as his own soul.

5.
    If ye have a good mind, my children, then will both wicked men be at peace with you, and the profligate will reverence you and turn unto good; and the covetous shall not only cease from their inordinate desire, but shall even give the fruits of their covetousness to them that are afflicted.
    If ye do well, even the unclean spirits shall flee from you; yea, the very beasts shall flee from you in dread.
    For where the reverence for good works is present unto the mind, darkness fleeth away from him.
    For if any one is injurious to a holy man, he repenteth; for the holy man showeth pity on his reviler, and holdeth his peace.
    And if any one betray a righteous soul, and the righteous man, though praying, be humbled for a little while, yet not long after he appeareth far more glorious, even as was Joseph my brother.

6.
    The mind of the good man is not in the power of the deceit of the spirit of Beliar, for the angel of peace guideth his soul.
    He gazeth not passionately on corruptible things, nor gathereth together riches unto desire of pleasure; he delighteth not in pleasure, he hurteth not his neighbour, he pampereth not himself with food, he erreth not in the pride of his eyes, for the Lord is his portion.
    The good mind admitteth not the glory and dishonour of men, neither knoweth it any guile or lie, fighting or reviling; for the Lord dwelleth in him and lighteth up his soul, and he rejoiceth towards all men at every time. The good mind hath not two tongues, of blessing and of cursing, of insult and of honour, of sorrow and of joy, of quietness and of trouble, of hypocrisy and of truth, of poverty and of wealth; but it hath one disposition, pure and uncorrupt, concerning all men.
    It hath no double sight, [4] nor double hearing; for in everything which he doeth, or speaketh, or seeth, he knoweth that the Lord watcheth his soul, and he cleanseth his mind that he be not condemned by God and men.
    But of Beliar every work is twofold, and hath no singleness.

7.
    Flee ye therefore, my children, the evil-doing of Beliar; for it giveth a sword to them that obeyeth, and the sword is the mother of seven evils.
    First the mind conceiveth through Beliar, and first there is envy; secondly, desperation; thirdly, tribulation; fourthly, captivity; fifthly, neediness; sixthly, trouble; seventhly, desolation.
    Therefore also Cain is delivered over to seven vengeances by God, for in every hundred years the Lord brought one plague upon him.
    Two hundred years he suffered, and in the nine hundredth year he was brought to desolation at the flood, for Abel his righteous brother's sake.
    In seven [5] hundred years was Cain judged, and Lamech in seventy times seven; because for ever those who are likened unto Cain in envy unto hatred of brethren shall be judged with the same punishment.

8.
    Do ye also therefore, my children, flee ill-doing, envy, and hatred of brethren, and cleave to goodness and love.
    He that hath a pure mind in love, looketh not after a woman unto fornication; for he hath no defilement in his heart, because the Spirit of God resteth in him.
    For as the sun is not defiled by shining over dung and mire, but rather drieth up both and driveth away the ill smell:
    so also the pure mind, constrained among the defilements of the earth, rather edifieth, and itself suffereth no defilement.

9.

Now I suppose, from the words of the righteous Enoch, that there will be also evil-doings among you:

for ye will commit fornication with the fornication of Sodom, and shall perish all save a few, and will multiply inordinate lusts with women; and the kingdom of the Lord shall not be among you, for forthwith He will take it away. Nevertheless the temple of God shall be built in your portion, and shall be glorious among you.

For He shall take it, and the twelve tribes shall be gathered together there, and all the Gentiles, until the Most High shall send forth His salvation in the visitation of His only-begotten one.

And He shall enter into the front [6] of the temple, and there shall the Lord be treated with outrage, and He shall be lifted up upon a tree.

And the veil of the temple shall be rent, and the Spirit of God shall descend upon the Gentiles as fire poured forth.

And He shall arise from the grave, and shall ascend from earth into heaven:

and I know how lowly He shall be upon the earth, and how glorious in the heaven.

10.

Now when Joseph was in Egypt, I longed to see his visage and the form of his countenance; and through the prayers of Jacob my father I saw him, while awake in the daytime, in his full and perfect shape. Know ye therefore, my children, that I am dying.

Work therefore truth and righteousness each one with his neighbour, and judgment unto faithful doing, and keep the law of the Lord and His commandments; for these things do I teach you instead of all inheritance.

Do ye also therefore give them to your children for an everlasting possession; for so did both Abraham, and Isaac, and Jacob.

All these things they gave us for an inheritance, saying, Keep the commandments of God until the Lord shall reveal His salvation to all nations.

Then shall ye see Enoch, Noah, and Shem, and Abraham, and Isaac, and Jacob, arising on the right hand in gladness.

Then shall we also arise, each one over our tribe, worshipping the King of heaven, who appeared upon the earth in the form of a man of humility.

And as many as believed on Him on the earth shall rejoice with Him; [7] and then shall all men arise, some unto glory and some unto shame.

And the Lord shall judge Israel first, even for the wrong they did unto Him; for when He appeared as a deliverer, God in the flesh, they believed Him not.

And then shall He judge all the Gentiles, as many as believed Him not when He appeared upon earth.

And He shall reprove Israel among the chosen ones of the Gentiles, even as He reproved Esau among the Midianites, who deceived their brethren, so that they fell into fornication and idolatry; and they were alienated from God, and became as they that were no children in the portion of them that fear the Lord.

But if ye walk in holiness in the presence of the Lord, ye shall dwell in hope again in me, and all Israel shall be gathered unto the Lord.

11.

And I shall no longer be called a ravening wolf [8] on account of your ravages, but a worker of the Lord, distributing food to them that work what is good.

And one [9] shall rise up from my seed in the latter times, beloved of the Lord, hearing upon the earth His voice, enlightening with new knowledge all the Gentiles, bursting in upon Israel for salvation with the light of knowledge, and tearing it away from it like a wolf, and giving it to the synagogue of the Gentiles.

And until the consummation of the ages shall he be in the synagogues of the Gentiles, and among their rulers, as a strain of music in the mouth of all; [10] and he shall be inscribed in the holy books, both his work and his word, and he shall be a chosen one of God for ever; and because of him my father Jacob instructed me, saying, He shall fill up that which lacketh of thy tribe.

12.

And when he finished his words, he said:

I charge you, my children, carry up my bones out of Egypt, and bury me at Hebron, near my fathers.

So Benjamin died a hundred and twenty-five years old, in a good old age, and they placed him in a coffin.

And in the ninety-first year of the departure of the children of Israel from Egypt, they and their brethren brought up the bones of their fathers secretly in a place which is called Canaan; and they buried them in Hebron, by the feet of their fathers.

And they returned from the land of Canaan, and dwelt in Egypt until the day of their departing from the land of Egypt.

Footnotes:

1. The ordinary theory as to the meaning of Benjamin is comparatively late, and seems doubtful. The Targum Jerushalmi (on Gen. xxxv. 18), and the Breshith Rabba, S: 82, make Benjamin and Benoni synonymous. Cf. Josephus, Antiq., i. 21. 3; Cyril, Glaph. in Gen., lib. iv. With the view mentioned in the text, cf. Arethas on Rev. vii. 8 (Cramer's Catena, viii. 289).

2. This would seem to be the earliest instance of the application of the word anamartetos to our Lord.

3. [How could any Christian more fully testify to the Nicene Faith? So the Gloria in Excelsis.]

4. [Matt. vi. 22; Luke xi. 34.]

5. For heptakosiois etesin the Ox. ms. reads simply hepta.

6. This would seem to be the meaning of protos naos.

7. [Rev. xx. 5, 6. See p. 25, note 4, supra.]

8. Gen. xlix. 27. This passage, referring to St. Paul (who was of the tribe of Benjamin, Rom. xi. 1; Phil. iii. 5), is quoted by Tertullian, Adversus Marcionem, v. 1. [See vol. iii. p. 430, this series.]

9. Compare Scorpiace, cap. 13 [with reference to Gen. xxv. 34 and xxvii. 25, vol. iii. p. 646, this series. Lardner adds Origen, Hom. in Ezech., iv. tom. iii. p. 731; Theodoret, in Gen. Quaest., cx. tom. i. p. 77; and Augustine, Serm., 279 (and passim), tom. v. ed. Benedict.].

10. ["Mel in ore, melos in aure, melodia in corde."--St. Bernard.]

Apocrypha of the New Testament

Translated by Alexander Walker, Esq., One of Her Majesty's Inspectors of Schools for Scotland.

Introductory Notice to Apocrypha of the New Testament

By Professor M. B. Riddle, D.D.

The translations which follow have been made from the critical edition of Tischendorf (see Bibliography at close of this volume).

The text varies greatly from that of Fabricius.

It was found impossible to introduce the various readings and to cite the manuscript evidence supporting them.

Those who are interested in such study will have recourse to the volumes of Tischendorf.

The general character of the writings here grouped as "Apocrypha of the New Testament" will appear from even a cursory perusal of them.

It did not require any great discernment to distinguish between these and the canonical books of the New Testament.

The negative internal evidence thus furnished in support of the authority of the latter need not be emphasized.

But attention may well be called to certain historical facts in regard to these apocryphal writings:--

1.

No one of them ever obtained any general recognition among Christians; still less, a place in the Canon of the New Testament.

A few so-called Gospels are referred to by early writers; some obtained local recognition; others, written for a purpose, were pressed into notice by the advocates of the tendency they were written to support: but, as a rule, the books were soon rejected, and never obtained extensive circulation.

2.

Though a few of the Apocryphal Gospels are of comparatively early origin (see Translator's Introduction), there is no evidence that any Gospels purporting to be what our four Gospels are, existed in the first century, or that any other than fragmentary literature of this character existed even in the second century.

The Canon of the New Testament was not formed out of a mass of writings possessing some claim to recognition, though there is a popular impression to this effect.

3.

Here the character of the writings comes in as confirmatory evidence.

Of the Apocryphal Gospels in general, R. Hofmann [1] well says:

"The method employed in these compositions is always the same, whether the author intended simply to collect and arrange what was floating in the general tradition, or whether he intended to produce a definite dogmatical effect.

Rarely he threw himself on his own invention; but generally he elaborated what was only hinted at in the Canonical Gospels, or transcribed words of Jesus into action, or described the literal fulfillment of some Jewish expectation concerning the Messiah, or repeated the wonders of the Old Testament in an inhanced form, etc.

The work done, he took care to conceal his own name, and inscribed his book with the name of some apostle or disciple, in order to give it authority."

As a rule, therefore, the Apocryphal Gospels give details regarding those periods of our Lord's life about which the New Testament is wisely silent.

The genesis of much of the literature resembles that of modern "Lives of Christ" written to present a view of the Person of our Lord which is not in accordance with the obvious sense of the New Testament. Probably some of the Apocryphal Gospels and Acts were not intended to be forgeries, but only novels with a purpose. [2]

4.

But while the early Church exercised proper discernment, and the Canon of the New Testament was soon definitely recognised and universally accepted, the apocryphal writings were not without influence.

The sacred legends, the ecclesiastical traditions, all too potent in their effect, are in many cases to be traced to these writings.

Much that Rome inculcates is derived from these books, which the Western Church constantly rejected.

It is, therefore, not strange that modern Protestant scholarship has been most active in the investigation of this literature.

The study of these works furnishes not only a defense of the canonical books of the New Testament, but an effective weapon against that "tradition" which would overbear the authority of Holy Scripture.

No attempt has been made to annotate the various works in illustration of the above positions, although the temptation to do so was very great.

A few notes have been appended, but it was felt that in most cases the intelligent reader would not fail to draw the proper conclusions from the documents themselves. Those who desire to investigate further will find the best helps indicated either in the Introduction of the translator or in the Bibliography which closes this volume and series.

It will be noticed that no Apocryphal Epistles are included in the literature which follows.

Such forgeries were less common, and the Apocryphal Acts furnished a more convenient channel for heretical opinions and argument.

Of the few in existence, some appear, in connection with other works, in the Acts of Thaddaeus, in the Pseudo-Ignatian Epistles, in the Clementine Homilies (Epistles of Peter to James), and in Eusebius.

The forged letters of Paul, to the Laodiceans and a third to the Corinthians, deserve little attention, being made to supply the supposed loss suggested by Col. iv. 16 and I Cor. v. 9.

The correspondence of Paul and Seneca (six letters from the former and eight from the latter) has a certain interest, but scarcely deserves a place even among the apocryphal writings.

Footnotes:

1. Schaff-Herzog, i. p. 105.
2. In most cases the vocabulary of the books furnishes positive evidence of the late origin. A great number of terms can be traced to a particular period of ecclesiastical development, while the dogmatic tendencies which point to a given (and comparatively late) period of controversy are frequent and obvious.

Translator's Introductory Notice

Our aim in these translations has been to give a rendering of the original as literal as possible; and to this we have adhered even in cases--and they are not a few--in which the Latin or the Greek is not in strict accordance with grammatical rule.

It was thought advisable in all cases to give the reader the means of forming an accurate estimate of the style as well as the substance of these curious documents.

Part I - Apocryphal Gospels

The portion of the volume, comprising the Apocryphal Gospels properly so called, consists of twenty-two separate documents, of which ten are written in Greek and twelve in Latin.

These twenty-two may be classed under three heads: (a) those relating to the history of Joseph and of the Virgin Mary, previous to the birth of Christ; (b) those relating to the infancy of the Saviour; and (c) those relating to the history of Pilate.

The origines of the traditions are the Protevangelium of James, the Gospel of Thomas, and the Acts of Pilate.

All or most of the others can be referred to these three, as compilations, modifications, or amplifications.

There is abundant evidence of the existence of many of these traditions in the second century, though it cannot be made out that any of the books were then in existence in their present form.

The greater number of the authorities on the subject, however, seem to agree in assigning to the first four centuries of the Christian era, the following five books:

1. The Protevangelium of James; 2. The Gospel of Pseudo-Matthew; 4. The History of Joseph the Carpenter; 5. The Gospel of Thomas; 9. The Gospel of Nicodemus.

We proceed to give a very brief notice of each of them.

I.

The Protevangelium of James.--The name of Protevangelium was first given to it by Postel, whose Latin version was published in 1552.

The James is usually referred to St. James the Less, the Lord's brother; but the titles vary very much. [1]Origen, in the end of the second century, mentions a book of James, but it is by no means clear that he refers to the book in question.

Justin Martyr, in two passages, refers to the cave in which Christ was born; and from the end of the fourth century down, there are numerous allusions in ecclesiastical writings to statements made in the Protevangelium.

For his edition Tischendorf made use of seventeen mss., one of them belonging to the ninth century.

The Greek is good of the kind, and free from errors and corruptions.

There are translations of it into English by Jones (1722) and Cowper (1867).

II.

The Gospel of Pseudo-Matthew.--The majority of the mss. attribute this book to Matthew, though the titles vary much.

The letters prefixed, professing to be written to and by St. Jerome, exist in several of the mss.; but no one who is acquainted with the style of Jerome's letters will think this one authentic.

There are, however, in his works many allusions to some of the legends mentioned in this book.

Chapter i.-xxiv. were edited by Thilo, chapters xxv. to the end are edited for the first time by Tischendorf.

It is not very clear whether the Latin be original, or a direct translation from the Greek. In most part it seems to be original.

The list of epithets, however, applied to the triangles of the Alpha in chapter xxxi. are pretty obviously mistranslations of Greek technical terms, which it might not be difficult to reproduce.

III.

Gospel of the Nativity of Mary.--This work, which is in substance the same as the earlier part of the preceding, yet differs from it in several important points, indicating a later date and a different author.

It has acquired great celebrity from having been transferred almost entire to the Historia Lombardica or Legenda Aurea in the end of the thirteenth century.

Mediaeval poetry and sacred art have been very much indebted to its pages.

The original is in Latin, and is not a direct translation from the Greek.

In many passages it follows very closely the Vulgate translation.

IV.

The History of Joseph the Carpenter.--The original language of this history is Coptic.

From the Coptic it was translated into Arabic.

The Arabic was published by Wallin in 1722, with a Latin translation and copious notes.

Wallin's version has been republished by Fabricius, and later in a somewhat amended form by Thilo.

This amended form of Wallin's version is the text adopted by Tischendorf. Chapters xiv.-xxiii. have been published in the Sahidic text by Zoega in 1810 with a Latin translation, and more correctly by Dulaurier in 1835 with a French translation.

Tischendorf employs various arguments in support of his opinion that the work belongs to the fourth century.

It is found, he says, in both dialects of the Coptic:

the eschatology of it is not inconsistent with an early date:

the feast of the thousand years of chapter xxvi. had become part of heretical opinion after the third century.

The death of the Virgin Mary in chapter v. is consistent with the doctrine of the assumption, which began to prevail in the fifth century.

V., VI., VII.

The Gospel of Thomas.--Like the Protevangelium of James, the Gospel of Thomas is of undoubted antiquity.

It is mentioned by name by Origen, quoted by Irenaeus and the author of the Philosophumena, who says that it was used by the Nachashenes, a Gnostic sect of the second century.

Cyril of Jerusalem (d. 386) attributes the authorship not to the apostle, but to a Thomas who was one of the three disciples of Manes.

This fact, of course, indicates that Cyril knew nothing of the antiquity of the book he was speaking of.

This Manichaean origin has been adopted by many writers, of whom the best known are in recent times R. Simon and Mingarelli.

The text of the first Greek form is obtained from a Bologna ms. published by Mingarelli with a Latin translation in 1764, a Dresden ms. of the sixteenth century edited by Thilo, a Viennese fragment edited by Lambecius, and a Parisian fragment first brought to light by Coteler in his, edition of the Apostolical Constitutions, and translated into English by Jones.

The second Greek form is published for the first time by Tischendorf, who got the ms., which is on paper, of the fourteenth or fifteenth century, from one of the monasteries on Mount Sinai.

The Latin form is also published for the first time, from a Vatican ms.

There is another Latin text existing in a palimpsest, which Tischendorf assigns to the fifth century, and asserts to be much nearer the ancient Greek copy than any of the other mss.

It seems pretty clear, from the contents of the book, that its author was a Gnostic, a Docetist, and a Marcosian; and it was held in estimation by the Nachashenes and the Manichaeans.

Its bearing upon Christian art, and to some extent Christian dogma, is well known.

The Greek of the original is by no means good, and the Latin translator has in many cases mistaken the meaning of common Greek words

VIII.

Arabic Gospel of the Saviour's Infancy.--Chapters i.-ix. are founded on the Gospels of Luke and Matthew, and on the Protevangelium of James; chapters xxxvi. to the end are compiled from the Gospel of Thomas; the rest of the book, chapters x. to xxxv., is thoroughly Oriental in its character, reminding one of the tales of the Arabian Nights, or of the episodes in the Golden Ass of Apuleius.

It is evident that the work is a compilation, and that the compiler was an Oriental.

Various arguments are adduced to prove that the original language of it was Syriac.

It was first published, with a Latin translation and copious notes, by Professor Sike of Cambridge in 1697, afterwards by Fabricius, Jones, Schmid, and Thilo.

Tischendorf's text is Sike's Latin version amended by Fleischer.

There are not sufficient data for fixing with any accuracy the time at which it was composed or compiled.

IX.-XIV.

The Gospel of Nicodemus. [2] --The six documents inserted under this name are various forms of two books--two in Greek and one in Latin of the Acts of Pilate; one in Greek and two in Latin of the Descent of Christ to the world below.

Of twelve mss., only two or three give the second part consecutively with the first, nor does it so appear in the Coptic translation.

The title of Gospel of Nicodemus does not appear before the thirteenth century.

Justin Martyr mentions a book called the Acts of Pilate, and Eusebius informs us that the Emperor Maximim allowed or ordered a book, composed by the pagans under this title, to be published in a certain portion of the empire, and even to be taught in the schools; but neither of these could have been the work under consideration.

Tischendorf attributes it to the second century, which is probably too early, though without doubt the legend was formed by the end of the second century.

Maury (Mem. de la Societe des Antiq. de France, t. xx.) places it in the beginning of the fifth century, from 405 to 420; and Renan (Etudes d'Hist. Relig., p. 177) concurs in this opinion.

An able writer in the Quarterly Review (vol. cxvi.) assigns it to 439; the author of the article Pilate, in Smith's Bible Dictionary, gives the end of the third century as the probable date.

The author was probably a Hellenistic Jew converted to Christianity, or, as Tischendorf and Maury conclude, a Christian imbued with Judaic and Gnostic beliefs.

The original language was most probably Greek, though, as in the case of Pseudo-Matthew, the History of Joseph the Carpenter, etc., the original language is, in many of the prefaces, stated to have been Hebrew.

Some think that Latin was the original language, on the ground that Pilate would make his report to the Emperor in that, the official, language.

The Latin text we have, however, is obviously a translation, made, moreover, by a man to whom Greek was not very familiar, as is obvious from several instances specified in our notes to the text.

The editio princeps of the Latin text is without place or date, and it has been re-edited by Jones, Birch, Fabricius, Thilo, and others.

The Greek text of Part I., and of a portion of Part II., was first published by Birch, and afterwards in a much improved form, with the addition of copious notes and prolegomena, by Thilo.

The latter part of his prolegomena contains a full account of the English, French, Italian, and German translations.

For his edition Tischendorf consulted thirty-nine ancient documents, of which a full account is given in his Prolegomena, pp. lxxi.-lxxvi.

For an interesting account of these documents, see the introduction to Mr. B. H. Cowper's translation of the Apocryphal Gospels, pp. lxxxv.-cii.

XV.

The Letter of Pontius Pilate.--The text is formed from four authorities, none of them ancient. A translation of the Greek text of the same letter will be found at p. 480.

XVI., XVII.

The Report of Pilate.--The first of these documents was first published by Fabricius with a Latin translation; the second by Birch, and then by Thilo.

Tischendorf has made use of five mss., the earliest of the twelfth century.

It does not seem possible to assign the date.

XVIII.

The Paradosis of Pilate.--It has been well remarked by the author of the article in the Quarterly Review above referred to, that the early Church looked on Pilate with no unfavourable eye; that he is favourably shown in the catacombs; that the early Fathers interpreted him as a figure of the early Church, and held him to be guiltless of Christ's death; that the creeds do not condemn him, and the Coptic Church has even made him a saint.

He remarks also that Dante finds punishments for Caiaphas and Annas, but not for Pilate.

The text was first edited by Birch, and afterwards by Thilo. Tischendorf makes use of five mss., of which the earliest belongs to the twelfth century.

XIX.

The Death of Pilate.--This is published for the first time by Tischendorf from a Latin ms. of the fourteenth century.

The language shows it to be of a late date.

It appears almost entire in the Legenda Aurea.

XX.

The Narrative of Joseph.--This history seems to have been popular in the middle ages, if we may judge from the number of the Greek mss. of it which remain.

It was first published by Birch, and after him by Thilo.

For his edition Tischendorf made use of three mss., of which the oldest belongs to the twelfth century.

XXI.

The Avenging of the Saviour.--This version of the Legend of Veronica is written in very barbarous Latin, probably of the seventh or eighth century.

An Anglo-Saxon version, which Tischendorf concludes to be derived from the Latin, was edited and translated for the Cambridge Antiquarian Society, by C. W. Goodwin, in 1851.

The Anglo-Saxon text is from a ms. in the Cambridge Library, one of a number presented to the Cathedral of Exeter by Bishop Leofric in the beginning of the eleventh century.

The reader will observe that there are in this document two distinct legends, somewhat clumsily joined together--that of Nathan's embassy, and that of Veronica. [3]

Footnotes:

1. [James the Lord's brother, in the earliest Christian literature, is not identified with James the son of Alphaeus, one of the twelve. On the titles, see footnote on first page of text.--R.]

2. [The numbers here correspond with those of Tischendorf in his prolegomena. In his table of contents, however, he gives a separate number to the letter of Pilate, which closes XIII. Hence the enumeration differs from that point.--R.]

3. [For a full list of fragments and titles of other Apocryphal Gospels, see Schaff-Herzog, i. p. 106. Twenty-nine are given, but in some cases the same work probably appears under two titles.--R.]

The Forgotten Bible
Part II - The Apocryphal Acts of the Apostles

This portion of the volume, presents us with documents written in a style considerably different from that of the Apocryphal Gospels properly so called.

There we have without stint the signs that the Jews desired; here we begin to have some glimpses of the wisdom which the Greeks sought after, along with a considerable share of

Quidquid Graecia mendax

Audet in historia.

We have less of miracle, more of elaborate discourse.

The Apocryphal Gospels were suited to the vilis plebecula, from which, as Jerome said, the Church originated; the Apocryphal Acts appeal more to the Academia.

We have in ancient literature, especially Greek literature, a long series of fabulous histories attached to the names of men who made themselves famous either in arts or arms.

This taste for the marvellous became general after the expedition of Alexander; and from that time down we have numerous examples of it in the lives of Alexander, of Pythagoras, of Apollonius of Tyana, of Homer, of Virgil, and others without number; and we all know how much fabulous matter is apt to gather round the names of popular heroes even in modern times.

It is not to be wondered at, then, that round the names of Christ and His apostles, who had brought about social changes greater than those effected by the exploits of any hero of old, there should gather, as the result of the wondering awe of simple-minded men, a growth of the romantic and the fabulous.

These stories came at length to form a sort of apostolic cycle, of which the documents following are portions.

They exist also in a Latin form in the ten books of the Acts of the Apostles, compiled probably in the sixth century, and falsely attributed to Abdias, the first bishop of Babylon, by whom it was, of course, written in Hebrew. [1]

We shall now give a brief account of each of the thirteen documents which make up this part of the volume.

I.

The Acts of Peter and Paul.--This book was first published in a complete form by Thilo in 1837 and 1838.

A portion of it had already been translated into Latin by the famous Greek scholar Constantine Lascaris in 1490, and had been made use of in the celebrated controversy as to the situation of the island Melita, upon which St. Paul was shipwrecked.

For his edition Tischendorf collated six mss., the oldest of the end of the ninth century.

Some portions at least of the book are of an early date.

The Domine quo vadis story, p. 485, is referred to by Origen, and others after him.

A book called the Acts of Peter is condemned in the decree of Pope Gelasius.

II.

Acts of Paul and Thecla.--This book is of undoubted antiquity. There seems reason to accept the account of it given by Tertullian, that it was written by an Asiatic presbyter in glorification of St. Paul (who, however, unquestionably occupies only a secondary place in it), and in support of the heretical opinion that women may teach and baptize.

It is expressly mentioned and quoted by a long line of Latin and Greek Fathers.

The quotations are inserted in Tischendorf's Prolegomena, p. xxiv.

The text was first edited in 1698 by Grabe from a Bodleian ms., republished by Jones in 1726.

A blank in the Bodleian ms. was supplied in 1715 by Thomas Hearne from another Oxford ms.

Tischendorf's text is from a recension of three Paris mss., each of the eleventh century.

III.

Acts of Barnabas.--This book has more an air of truth about it than any of the others.

There is not much extravagance in the details, and the geography is correct, showing that the writer knew Cyprus well.

It seems to have been written at all events before 478, in which year the body of Barnabas is said to have been found in Cyprus.

Papebroche first edited the book in the Acta Sanctorum in 1698, with a Latin translation.

The Vatican ms. which he used was an imperfect one.

Tischendorf's text is from a Parisian ms. of the end of the ninth century.

IV.

Acts of Philip.--A book under this name was condemned in the decree of Pope Gelasius; and that the traditions about Philip were well known from an early date, is evident from the abundant references to them in ancient documents.

The writings of the Hagiographers also, both Greek and Latin, contain epitomes of Philip's life.

The Greek text, now first published, is a recension of two mss.,--a Parisian one of the eleventh century, and a Venetian one.

The latter is noticeable, from being superscribed From the Fifteenth Act to the end, leaving us to infer that we have only a portion of the book.

V.

Acts of Philip in Hellas.--This also is published for the first time by Tischendorf.

It is obviously a later document than the preceding, though composed in the same style.

It is from a Parisian ms. of the eleventh century.

VI.

Acts of Andrew.--In the decree of Pope Gelasius (d. 496), a book under this name is condemned as apocryphal.

Epiphanius (d. 403) states that the Acts of Andrew were in favour with the Encratites, the Apostolics, and the Origenians; Augustine (d. 430) mentions that the Acts of the Apostles written by Leucius Charinus--discipulus diaboli, as Pope Gelasius calls him--were held in estimation by the Manichaeans.

The authorship generally is attributed to Leucius by early writers; Innocentius I. (d. 417), however, says that the Acts of Andrew were composed by the philosophers Nexocharis and Leonidas.

This book is much the same in substance with the celebrated Presbyterorum et Diaconorum Achaiae de martyrio S. Andreae apostoli epistola encyclica, first edited in Greek by Woog in 1749, and by him considered to be a genuine writing of the apostolic age, composed about a.d. 80.

Thilo, while dissenting from this opinion of Woog's, concludes that it is a fragment from the Acts of Leucius, expurgated of most of its heresy, and put into its present shape by an orthodox writer.

Cardinals Baronius and Bellarmine assign the epistle to the apostolic age; Fabricius thinks it much later.

The probability is that the book was written by Leucius, following earlier traditions, and that it was afterwards revised and fitted for general reading by an orthodox hand.

Though some of the traditions mentioned in the book are referred to by authors of the beginning of the fifth century, there does not seem to be any undoubted quotation of it before the eighth and the tenth centuries.

Some portions of Pseudo-Abdias, however, are almost in the words of our Greek Acts.

The text is edited chiefly from two mss.,--the one of the eleventh, the other of the fourteenth century.

The Greek of the original is good of the kind, and exhibits considerable rhetorical skill.

VII.

Acts of Andrew and Matthias.--Thilo assigns the authorship of these Acts also to Leucius, and the use of them to the Gnostics, Manichaeans, and other heretics.

Pseudo-Abdias seems to have derived his account of Andrew and Matthias from the same source.

Epiphanius the monk, who wrote in the tenth century, gives extracts from the history.

There is, besides, an old English--commonly called Anglo-Saxon--poem, Andrew and Helene, published by Jacob Grimm in 1840, the argument of which in great part coincides with that of the Acts of Andrew and Matthias.

There is considerable doubt as to whether it is Matthias or Matthew that is spoken of.

Pseudo-Abdias, followed by all the Latin writers on the subject, calls him Matthew.

The Greek texts hesitate between the two.

Tischendorf edits Matthias, on the authority of his oldest ms. There is also some discrepancy as to the name of the town.

Some mss. say Sinope, others Myrmene or Myrna:

they generally, however, coincide in calling it a town of AEthiopia.

Thilo, and Tischendorf after him, made use chiefly of three mss., only one of which, of the fifteenth century, contains the whole book.

The oldest is an uncial ms. of about the eighth century.

The Acts of Peter and Andrew, from the Bodleian ms., are inserted as an appendix to the Acts of Andrew and Matthias.

VIII.

Acts of Matthew.--This book is edited by Tischendorf for the first time.

It is a much later production than the last, written in bad Greek, and in a style rendered very cumbrous by the use of participial phrases.

On the authority of the oldest ms., Matthew, not Matthias, is the name here.

It is probably owing to this confusion between the names, that there is much uncertainty in the traditions regarding St. Matthew.

Tischendorf gives, in his Prolegomena, a long extract from Nicephorus, which shows that he was acquainted with this book, or something very like it.

The text is edited from two mss.,--a Parisian of the eleventh century, and a Viennese of a later date.

IX.

Acts of Thomas.--The substance of this book is of great antiquity, and in its original form it was held in great estimation by the heretics of the first and second centuries.

The main heresy which it contained was that the Apostle Thomas baptized, not with water, but with oil only.

It is mentioned by Epiphanius, Turribius, and Nicephorus, condemned in the decree of Gelasius, and in the Synopsis of Scripture ascribed to Athanasius, in which it is placed, along with the Acts of Peter, Acts of John, and other books, among the Antilegomena. St. Augustine in three passages refers to the book in such a way as to show that he had it in something very like its present form.

Two centuries later, Pseudo-Abdias made a recension of the book, rejecting the more heretical portions, and adapting it generally to orthodox use.

Photius attributes the authorship of this document, as of many other apocryphal Acts, to Leucius Charinus.

The Greek text was first edited, with copious notes and prolegomena, by Thilo in 1823.

The text from which the present translation is made is a recension of five mss., the oldest of the tenth century.

X.

Consummation of Thomas.--This is properly a portion of the preceding book.

Pseudo-Abdias follows it very closely, but the Greek of some chapters of his translation or compilation has not yet been discovered.

The text, edited by Tischendorf for the first time, is from a ms. of the eleventh century.

XI.

Martyrdom of Bartholomew.--This Greek text, now for the first time edited by Tischendorf, is very similar to the account of Bartholomew in Pseudo-Abdias.

The editor is inclined to believe, not that the Greek text is a translation of Abdias, which it probably is, but that both it and Abdias are derived from the same source.

Tischendorf seems inclined to lay some weight upon the mention made by Abdias of a certain Crato, said to be a disciple of the Apostles Simon and Judas, having written a voluminous history of the apostles, which was translated into Latin by Julius Africanus.

The whole story, however, is absurd.

It is very improbable that Julius Africanus knew any Latin; it is possible, however, that he may have compiled some stories of the apostles, that these may have been translated into Latin, and that Pseudo-Crato and Pseudo-Abdias may have derived some of their materials from this source.

The Greek text is edited from a Venetian ms. of the thirteenth century.

XII.

Acts of Thaddaeus.--This document, of which our text is the editio princeps, is of some consequence, as giving in another form the famous letters of Christ to Abgarus.

Eusebius (H. E., i. 13) says that he found in the archives of Edessa the letters written by their own hands, and that he translated them from the Syriac.

The story of the portrait was a later invention.

It is found in Pseudo-Abdias (x. 1), and with great detail in Nicephorus (H. E., ii. 7).

There is considerable variety in the texts of the letters.

They were probably written in Syriac in the third century by some native of Edessa, who wished to add to the importance of his city and the antiquity of his church.

See the whole subject discussed in Dr. Cureton's Ancient Syriac Documents relative to the earliest establishment of Christianity in Edessa.

The Greek text, which is probably of the sixth or seventh century, seems, from allusions to the synagogue, the hours of prayer, the Sabbath-day, etc., to have been written by a Jew.

It is edited from a Paris ms. of the eleventh century, and a Vienna one of a later date.

XIII.

Acts of John.--A book under this title is mentioned by Eusebius, Epiphanius, Photius, among Greek writers; Augustine, Philastrius, Innocent I., and Turribius among Latin writers.

The two last named and Photius ascribe the authorship to Leucius, discipulus diaboli, who got the credit of all these heretical brochures.

It is not named in the decree of Gelasius.

Augustine (Tractat. 124 in Johannem) relates at length the story of John going down alive into his grave, and of the fact of his being alive being shown by his breath stirring about the dust on the tomb. This story, which has some resemblance to the Teutonic legend of Barbarossa, is repeated by Photius.

There is a Latin document published by Fabricius, Pseudo-Melitonis liber de Passione S. Johannis Evangelistae, which the author professed to write with the original of Leucius before his eyes.

It has considerable resemblances in some passages to the present text.

The only passages in Pseudo-Abdias that appear to have any connection with the present document are those which refer to the apostle's burial.

The text is edited from a Paris ms. of the eleventh century, and a Vienna one, to which no date is assigned.

It is doubtful whether the narrative part of the Acts of John be by the same hand as the discourses.

Footnotes:

1. [That is, this is the tradition. Of such Hebrew original there is no trace.--R.]

The Forgotten Bible
Part III - *Apocryphal Apocalypses*

This portion of the volume, extending from page 565 to page 598, consists of seven documents, four of which are called Apocalypses by their authors.

Of these, the Greek text of the first three is edited for the first time; the fourth, the Apocalypse of John, has appeared before.

The fifth, The Falling Asleep of Mary, appears for the first time in its Greek form, and in the first Latin recension of it.

The mss. of these documents are characterized by extreme variety of readings; and in some of them, especially the earlier portion of the Apocalypse of Esdras, the text is in a very corrupt state.

I.

The Apocalypse of Moses.--This document belongs to the Apocrypha of the Old Testament rather than that of the New.

We have been unable to find in it any reference to any Christian writing.

In its form, too, it appears to be a portion of some larger work.

Parts of it at least are of an ancient date, as it is very likely from this source that the writer of the Gospel of Nicodemus took the celebrated legend of the Tree of Life and the Oil of Mercy.

An account of this legend will be found in Cowper's Apocryphal Gospels, xcix.-cii.; in Maury, Croyances et Legendes de l'Antiquite, p. 294; in Renan's commentary to the Syriac text of the Penitence of Adam, edited and translated by Renan in the Journal Asiatique for 1853.

There appeared a poetical rendering of the legend in Blackwood's Magazine ten or twelve years ago.

Tischendorf's text is made from four mss.:

A, a Venice ms. of the thirteenth century; B and C, Vienna mss. of the thirteenth and twelfth centuries respectively; and D, a Milan ms. of about the eleventh century.

II.

The Apocalypse of Esdras.--This book is a weak imitation of the apocryphal fourth book of Esdras.

Thilo, in his prolegomena to the Acts of Thomas, p. lxxxii., mentions it, and doubts whether it be the fourth book of Esdras or not.

Portions of it were published by Dr. Hase of the Paris Library, and it was then seen that it was a different production.

The ms. is of about the fifteenth century, and in the earlier portions very difficult to read.

III.

The Apocalypse of Paul.--There are two apocryphal books bearing the name of Paul mentioned by ancient writers:

The Ascension of Paul, adopted by the Cainites and the Gnostics; and the Apocalypse of Paul, spoken of by Augustine and Sozomen.

There seems to be no doubt that the present text, discovered by Tischendorf in 1843, and published by him in 1866, is the book mentioned by Augustine and Sozomen.

It is referred to by numerous authorities, one of whom, however, ascribes it to the heretic Paul of Samosata, the founder of the sect of the Paulicians.

There appear to be versions of it in Coptic, Syriac, and Arabic.

One of the Syriac versions, from an Urumiyeh ms., was translated into English by an American missionary in 1864.

This translation, or the greater portion of it, is printed by Tischendorf along with his edition of the text.

Tischendorf, upon what seems to be pretty good evidence, ascribes it to the year 380.

It is from a Milan ms. of not earlier than the fifteenth century.

There is another ms. two centuries older; but they both seem to be copied from the same original.

The Syriac seems to be later than the Greek, and, according to Eastern fashion, fuller in details.

IV.

The Apocalypse of John.--In the scholia to the Grammar of Dionysius the Thracian, ascribed to the ninth century, immediately after the ascription of the Apocalypse of Paul to Paul of Samosata, there occurs the following statement:

And there is another called the Apocalypse of John the Theologian.

We do not speak of that in the island of Patmos, God forbid, for it is most true; but of a supposititious and spurious one.'

This is the oldest reference to this Apocalypse.

Asseman says he found the book in Arabic in three mss.

The document was first edited by Birch in 1804, from a Vatican ms., collated with a Vienna ms.

For his edition Tischendorf collated other five mss., two of Paris, three of Vienna, of from the fourteenth to the sixteenth century.

Of other Apocalypses, Tischendorf in his Prolegomena gives an abstract of the Apocalypse of Peter, the Apocalypse of Bartholomew, the Apocalypse of Mary, and the Apocalypse of Daniel.

The Apocalypse of Peter professes to be written by Clement.

There is an Arabic ms. of it in the Bodleian Library.

It is called the Perfect Book, or the Book of Perfection, and consists of eighty-nine chapters, comprising a history of the world as revealed to Peter, from the foundation of the world to the appearing of Antichrist.

The Apocalypse of Bartholomew, from a ms. in the Paris Library, was edited and translated by Dulaurier in 1835.

The translation appears in Tischendorf's Prolegomena.

The Apocalypse of Mary, containing her descent to the lower world, appears in several Greek mss.

It is of a late date, the work of some monk of the middle ages.

The Apocalypse of Daniel, otherwise called the Revelation of the Prophet Daniel about the consummation of the world, is also of a late date.

About the half of the Greek text is given in the Prolegomena. We have not thought it necessary to translate it.

V., VI., VII.

The Assumption of Mary.--It is somewhat strange that the Greek text of this book, which has been translated into several languages both of the East and the West, is edited by Tischendorf for the first time.

He assigns it to a date not later than the fourth century.

A book under this title is condemned in the decree of Gelasius.

The author of the Second Latin Form (see p. 595, note), writing under the name of Melito, ascribes the authorship of a treatise on the same subject to Leucius.

This, however, cannot be the book so ascribed to Leucius, as Pseudo-Melito affirms that his book, which is in substance the same as the Greek text, was written to condemn Leucius' heresies.

There are translations or recensions of our text in Syriac, Sahidic, and Arabic.

The Syriac was edited and translated by Wright in 1865, in his Contributions to the Apocryphal Literature of the New Testament. Another recension of it was published in the Journal of Sacred Literature for January and April, 1864.

An Arabic version of it, resembling more the Syriac than the Greek or Latin, was edited and translated by Enger in 1854.

The Sahidic recension, published and translated by Zoega and Dulaurier, is considerably different from our present texts.

The numerous Latin recensions also differ considerably from each other, as will be seen from a comparison of the First Latin Form with the Second.

They are all, however, from the same source, and that probably the Greek text which we have translated.

The Greek texts, again, exhibit considerable variations, especially in the latter portions.

In the end of the seventh century, John Archbishop of Thessalonica wrote a discourse on the falling asleep of Mary, mainly derived from the book of Pseudo-John; and in some mss. this treatise of John of Thessalonica is ascribed to John the Apostle.

Epiphanius, however, makes distinctive mention of both treatises.

For his edition of the Greek text, Tischendorf made use of five mss., the oldest of the eleventh century.

The First Latin Form is edited from three Italian mss., the oldest of the thirteenth century.

The Second Latin Form, which has been previously published elsewhere, is from a Venetian

The Forgotten Bible
ms. of the fourteenth century.

We have now concluded our notices, compiled chiefly from Tischendorf's Prolegomena, of the Apocryphal Literature of the New Testament.

While these documents are of considerable interest and value, as giving evidence of a widespread feeling in early times of the importance of the events which form the basis of our belief, and as affording us curious glimpses of the state of the Christian conscience, and of modes of Christian thought, in the first centuries of our era, the predominant impression which they leave on our minds is a profound sense of the immeasurable superiority, the unapproachable simplicity and majesty, of the Canonical Writings.

St. Andrews, 26th March, 1870.

The Protevangelium of James

The Birth of Mary the Holy Mother of God, and Very Glorious Mother of Jesus Christ. [1]

1.

In the records of the twelve tribes of Israel was Joachim, a man rich exceedingly; and he brought his offerings double, [2] saying: There shall be of my superabundance to all the people, and there shall be the offering for my forgiveness [3] to the Lord for a propitiation for me. [4]For the great day of the Lord was at hand, and the sons of Israel were bringing their offerings.

And there stood over against him Rubim, saying:

It is not meet for thee first to bring thine offerings, because thou hast not made seed in Israel.[5]And Joachim was exceedingly grieved, and went away to the registers of the twelve tribes of the people, saying:

I shall see the registers of the twelve tribes of Israel, as to whether I alone have not made seed in Israel.

And he searched, and found that all the righteous had raised up seed in Israel.

And he called to mind the patriarch Abraham, that in the last day [6] God gave him a son Isaac.

And Joachim was exceedingly grieved, and did not come into the presence of his wife; but he retired to the desert, [7] and there pitched his tent, and fasted forty days and forty nights, [8] saying in himself:

I will not go down either for food or for drink until the Lord my God shall look upon me, and prayer shall be my food and drink.

2.

And his wife Anna [9] mourned in two mournings, and lamented in two lamentations, saying: I shall bewail my widowhood; I shall bewail my childlessness.

And the great day of the Lord was at hand; and Judith [10] her maid-servant said:

How long dost thou humiliate thy soul?

Behold, the great day of the Lord is at hand, and it is unlawful for thee to mourn.

But take this head-band, which the woman that made it gave to me; for it is not proper that I should wear it, because I am a maid-servant, and it has a royal appearance. [11]And Anna said: Depart from me; for I have not done such things, and the Lord has brought me very low.

I fear that some wicked person has given it to thee, and thou hast come to make me a sharer in thy sin.

And Judith said:

Why should I curse thee, seeing that [12] the Lord hath shut thy womb, so as not to give thee fruit in Israel?

And Anna was grieved exceedingly, and put off her garments of mourning, and cleaned her head, and put on her wedding garments, and about the ninth hour went down to the garden to walk.

And she saw a laurel, and sat under it, and prayed to the Lord, saying:

O God of our fathers, bless me and hear my prayer, as Thou didst bless the womb of Sarah, and didst give her a son Isaac. [13]

3.

And gazing towards the heaven, she saw a sparrow's nest in the laurel, [14] and made a lamentation in herself, saying:

Alas! who begot me? and what womb produced me? because I have become a curse in the presence of the sons of Israel, and I have been reproached, and they have driven me in derision out of the temple of the Lord.

Alas! to what have I been likened?

I am not like the fowls of the heaven, because even the fowls of the heaven are productive before Thee, O Lord.

Alas! to what have I been likened?

I am not like the beasts of the earth, because even the beasts of the earth are productive before Thee, O Lord.

Alas! to what have I been likened?

I am not like these waters, because even these waters are productive before Thee, O Lord.

Alas! to what have I been likened?

I am not like this earth, because even the earth bringeth forth its fruits in season, and blesseth Thee, O Lord. [15]

4.

And, behold, an angel of the Lord stood by, saying:

Anna, Anna, the Lord hath heard thy prayer, and thou shalt conceive, and shall bring forth; and thy seed shall be spoken of in all the world.

And Anna said:

As the Lord my God liveth, if I beget either male or female, I will bring it as a gift to the Lord my God; and it shall minister to Him in holy things all the days of its life. [16]And, behold, two angels came, saying to her:

Behold, Joachim thy husband is coming with his flocks. [17]For an angel of the Lord went down to him, saying:

Joachim, Joachim, the Lord God hath heard thy prayer.

Go down hence; for, behold, thy wife Anna shall conceive.

And Joachim went down and called his shepherds, saying:

Bring me hither ten she-lambs without spot or blemish, and they shall be for the Lord my God; and bring me twelve tender calves, and they shall be for the priests and the elders; and a hundred goats for all the people.

And, behold, Joachim came with his flocks; and Anna stood by the gate, and saw Joachim coming, and she ran and hung upon his neck, saying:

Now I know that the Lord God hath blessed me exceedingly; for, behold the widow no longer a widow, and I the childless shall conceive.

And Joachim rested the first day in his house.

5.

And on the following day he brought his offerings, saying in himself:

If the Lord God has been rendered gracious to me, the plate [18] on the priest's forehead will make it manifest to me.

And Joachim brought his offerings, and observed attentively the priest's plate when he went up to the altar of the Lord, and he saw no sin in himself.

And Joachim said:

Now I know that the Lord has been gracious unto me, and has remitted all my sins.

And he went down from the temple of the Lord justified, and departed to his own house.

And her months were fulfilled, and in the ninth [19] month Anna brought forth.

And she said to the midwife:

What have I brought forth? and she said:

A girl.

And said Anna:

My soul has been magnified this day.

And she laid her down.

And the days having been fulfilled, Anna was purified, and gave the breast to the child, [20] and called her name Mary.

6.

And the child grew strong day by day; and when she was six [21] months old, her mother set her on the ground to try whether she could stand, and she walked seven steps and came into her bosom; and she snatched her up, saying:

As the Lord my God liveth, thou shalt not walk on this earth until I bring thee into the temple of the Lord.

And she made a sanctuary in her bed-chamber, and allowed nothing common or unclean to pass through her.

And she called the undefiled daughters of the Hebrews, and they led her astray. [22]And when she was a year old, Joachim made a great feast, and invited the priests, and the scribes, and the elders, and all the people of Israel.

And Joachim brought the child to the priests; and they blessed her, saying:

O God of our fathers, bless this child, and give her an everlasting name to be named in all generations.

And all the people said:

So be it, so be it, amen.

And he brought her to the chief priests; and they blessed her, saying:

O God most high, look upon this child, and bless her with the utmost blessing, which shall be for ever.

And her mother snatched her up, and took her into the sanctuary of her bed-chamber, and gave her the breast.

And Anna made a song to the Lord God, saying:

I will sing a song to the Lord my God, for He hath looked upon me, and hath taken away the reproach of mine enemies; and the Lord hath given the fruit of His righteousness, singular in its kind, and richly endowed before Him.

Who will tell the sons of Rubim that Anna gives suck? Hear, hear, ye twelve tribes of Israel, that Anna gives suck.

And she laid her to rest in the bed-chamber of her sanctuary, and went out and ministered unto them.

And when the supper was ended, they went down rejoicing, and glorifying the God of Israel. [23]

7.

And her months were added to the child.

And the child was two years old, and Joachim said:

Let us take her up to the temple of the Lord, that we may pay the vow that we have vowed, lest perchance the Lord send to us, [24] and our offering be not received.

And Anna said:

Let us wait for the third year, in order that the child may not seek for father or mother.

And Joachim said:

So let us wait.

And the child was three years old, and Joachim said:

Invite the daughters of the Hebrews that are undefiled, and let them take each a lamp, and let them stand with the lamps burning, that the child may not turn back, and her heart be captivated from the temple of the Lord.

And they did so until they went up into the temple of the Lord.

And the priest received her, and kissed her, and blessed her, saying:

The Lord has magnified thy name in all generations.

In thee, on the last of the days, the Lord will manifest His redemption to the sons of Israel.

And he set her down upon the third step of the altar, and the Lord God sent grace upon her; and she danced with her feet, and all the house of Israel loved her.

8.

And her parents went down marvelling, and praising the Lord God, because the child had not turned back.

And Mary was in the temple of the Lord as if she were a dove that dwelt there, and she received food from the hand of an angel.

And when she was twelve [25] years old there was held a council of the priests, saying:

Behold, Mary has reached the age of twelve years in the temple of the Lord.

What then shall we do with her, lest perchance she defile the sanctuary of the Lord?

And they said to the high priest:

Thou standest by the altar of the Lord; go in, and pray concerning her; and whatever the Lord shall manifest unto thee, that also will we do.

And the high priest went in, taking the robe [26] with the twelve bells into the holy of holies; and he prayed concerning her.

And behold an angel of the Lord stood by him, saying unto him:

Zacharias, Zacharias, go out and assemble the widowers of the people, and let them bring each his rod; and to whomsoever the Lord shall show a sign, his wife shall she be.

And the heralds went out through all the circuit of Judaea, and the trumpet of the Lord sounded, and all ran.

9.

And Joseph, throwing away his axe, went out to meet them; and when they had assembled, they went away to the high priest, taking with them their rods.

And he, taking the rods of all of them, entered into the temple, and prayed; and having ended his prayer, he took the rods and came out, and gave them to them:

but there was no sign in them, and Joseph took his rod last; and, behold, a dove came out of the rod, and flew upon Joseph's head.

And the priest said to Joseph, Thou hast been chosen by lot to take into thy keeping the virgin

The Forgotten Bible
of the Lord.

But Joseph refused, saying:

I have children, and I am an old man, and she is a young girl.

I am afraid lest I become a laughing-stock to the sons of Israel.

And the priest said to Joseph:

Fear the Lord thy God, and remember what the Lord did to Dathan, and Abiram, and Korah; [27] how the earth opened, and they were swallowed up on account of their contradiction.

And now fear, O Joseph, lest the same things happen in thy house.

And Joseph was afraid, and took her into his keeping.

And Joseph said to Mary:

Behold, I have received thee from the temple of the Lord; and now I leave thee in my house, and go away to build my buildings, and I shall come to thee.
The Lord will protect thee.

10.

And there was a council of the priests, saying:

Let us make a veil for the temple of the Lord.

And the priest said:

Call to me the undefiled virgins of the family of David.

And the officers went away, and sought, and found seven virgins.

And the priest remembered the child Mary, that she was of the family of David, and undefiled before God.

And the officers went away and brought her.

And they brought them into the temple of the Lord.

And the priest said:

Choose for me by lot who shall spin the gold, and the white, [28] and the fine linen, and the silk, and the blue, [29] and the scarlet, and the true purple. [30] And the true purple and the scarlet fell to the lot of Mary, and she took them, and went away to her house.

And at that time Zacharias was dumb, and Samuel was in his place until the time that Zacharias spake.

And Mary took the scarlet, and span it.

11.

And she took the pitcher, and went out to fill it with water. And, behold, a voice saying:

Hail, thou who hast received grace; the Lord is with thee; blessed art thou among women! [31] And she looked round, on the right hand and on the left, to see whence this voice came.

And she went away, trembling, to her house, and put down the pitcher; and taking the purple, she sat down on her seat, and drew it out.

And, behold, an angel of the Lord stood before her, saying: Fear not, Mary; for thou hast found grace before the Lord of all, and thou shalt conceive, according to His word.

And she hearing, reasoned with herself, saying:

Shall I conceive by the Lord, the living God? and shall I bring forth as every woman brings forth?

And the angel of the Lord said:

Not so, Mary; for the power of the Lord shall overshadow thee:
wherefore also that holy thing which shall be born of thee shall be called the Son of the Most High.

And thou shalt call His name Jesus, for He shall save His people from their sins.

And Mary said:

Behold, the servant of the Lord before His face:
let it be unto me according to thy word.

12.

And she made the purple and the scarlet, and took them to the priest.

And the priest blessed her, and said:

Mary, the Lord God hath magnified thy name, and thou shalt be blessed in all the generations of the earth.

And Mary, with great joy, went away to Elizabeth her kinswoman, [32] and knocked at the door.

And when Elizabeth heard her, she threw away the scarlet, [33] and ran to the door, and opened it; and seeing Mary, she blessed her, and said:

Whence is this to me, that the mother of my Lord should come to me? for, behold, that which is in me leaped and blessed thee. [34] But Mary had forgotten the mysteries of which the archangel

Gabriel had spoken, and gazed up into heaven, and said:

Who am I, O Lord, that all the generations of the earth should bless me? [35] And she remained three months with Elizabeth; and day by day she grew bigger.

And Mary being afraid, went away to her own house, and hid herself from the sons of Israel.

And she was sixteen [36] years old when these mysteries happened.

13.

And she was in her sixth month; and, behold, Joseph came back from his building, and, entering into his house, he discovered that she was big with child.

And he smote [37] his face, [38] and threw himself on the ground upon the sackcloth, and wept bitterly, saying:

With what face shall I look upon the Lord my God? and what prayer shall I make about this maiden? because I received her a virgin out of the temple of the Lord, and I have not watched over her.

Who is it that has hunted me [39] down?

Who has done this evil thing in my house, and defiled the virgin?

Has not the history of Adam been repeated in me?

For just as Adam was in the hour of his singing praise, [40] and the serpent came, and found Eve alone, and completely deceived her, so it has happened to me also.

And Joseph stood up from the sackcloth, and called Mary, and said to her:

O thou who hast been cared for by God, why hast thou done this and forgotten the Lord thy God?

Why hast thou brought low thy soul, thou that wast brought up in the holy of holies, and that didst receive food from the hand of an angel?

And she wept bitterly, saying:

I am innocent, and have known no man.

And Joseph said to her:

Whence then is that which is in thy womb?

And she said: As the Lord my God liveth, I do not know whence it is to me.

14.

And Joseph was greatly afraid, and retired from her, and considered what he should do in regard to her. [41] And Joseph said:

If I conceal her sin, I find myself fighting against the law of the Lord; and if I expose her to the sons of Israel, I am afraid lest that which is in her be from an angel, [42] and I shall be found giving up innocent blood to the doom of death.

What then shall I do with her?

I will put her away from me secretly.

And night came upon him; and, behold, an angel of the Lord appears to him in a dream, saying:

Be not afraid for this maiden, for that which is in her is of the Holy Spirit; and she will bring forth a Son, and thou shalt call His name Jesus, for He will save His people from their sins. [43] And Joseph arose from sleep, and glorified the God of Israel, who had given him this grace; and he kept her.

15.

And Annas the scribe came to him, and said:

Why hast thou not appeared in our assembly?

And Joseph said to him:

Because I was weary from my journey, and rested the first day.

And he turned, and saw that Mary was with child.

And he ran away to the priest, [44] and said to him:

Joseph, whom thou didst vouch for, has committed a grievous crime.

And the priest said:

How so?

And he said:

He has defiled the virgin whom he received out of the temple of the Lord, and has married her by stealth, and has not revealed it to the sons of Israel.

And the priest answering, said:

Has Joseph done this?

Then said Annas the scribe:

Send officers, and thou wilt find the virgin with child.

And the officers went away, and found it as he had said; and they brought her along with Joseph to the tribunal.

And the priest said:

Mary, why hast thou done this? and why hast thou brought thy soul low, and forgotten the Lord thy God?

Thou that wast reared in the holy of holies, and that didst receive food from the hand of an angel, and didst hear the hymns, and didst dance before Him, why hast thou done this?

And she wept bitterly, saying:

As the Lord my God liveth, I am pure before Him, and know not a man.

And the priest said to Joseph: Why hast thou done this?

And Joseph said:

As the Lord liveth, I am pure concerning her.

Then said the priest:

Bear not false witness, but speak the truth.

Thou hast married her by stealth, and hast not revealed it to the sons of Israel, and hast not bowed thy head under the strong hand, that thy seed might be blessed.

And Joseph was silent.

16.

And the priest said:

Give up the virgin whom thou didst receive out of the temple of the Lord.

And Joseph burst into tears.

And the priest said:

I will give you to drink of the water of the ordeal of the Lord, [45] and He shall make manifest your sins in your eyes. And the priest took the water, and gave Joseph to drink and sent him away to the hill-country; and he returned unhurt.

And he gave to Mary also to drink, and sent her away to the hill-country; and she returned unhurt.

And all the people wondered that sin did not appear in them. And the priest said:

If the Lord God has not made manifest your sins, neither do I judge you.

And he sent them away.

And Joseph took Mary, and went away to his own house, rejoicing and glorifying the God of Israel.

17.

And there was an order from the Emperor Augustus, that all in Bethlehem of Judaea should be enrolled. [46] And Joseph said:

I shall enrol my sons, but what shall I do with this maiden?

How shall I enrol her?

As my wife?

I am ashamed.

As my daughter then?

But all the sons of Israel know that she is not my daughter.

The day of the Lord shall itself bring it to pass [47] as the Lord will.

And he saddled the ass, and set her upon it; and his son led it, and Joseph followed. [48] And when they had come within three miles, Joseph turned and saw her sorrowful; and he said to himself:

Likely that which is in her distresses her.

And again Joseph turned and saw her laughing.

And he said to her:

Mary, how is it that I see in thy face at one time laughter, at another sorrow?

And Mary said to Joseph: Because I see two peoples with my eyes; the one weeping and lamenting, and the other rejoicing and exulting.

And they came into the middle of the road, and Mary said to him:

Take me down from off the ass, for that which is in me presses to come forth.

And he took her down from off the ass, and said to her:

Whither shall I lead thee, and cover thy disgrace? for the place is desert.

18.

And he found a cave [49] there, and led her into it; and leaving his two sons beside her, he went out to seek a widwife in the district of Bethlehem.

And I Joseph was walking, and was not walking; and I looked up into the sky, and saw the sky astonished; and I looked up to the pole of the heavens, and saw it standing, and the birds of the air keeping still. And I looked down upon the earth, and saw a trough lying, and work-people reclining: and their hands were in the trough.

And those that were eating did not eat, and those that were rising did not carry it up, and those that were conveying anything to their mouths did not convey it; but the faces of all were looking upwards.

And I saw the sheep walking, and the sheep stood still; and the shepherd raised his hand to strike them, and his hand remained up.

And I looked upon the current of the river, and I saw the mouths of the kids resting on the water and not drinking, and all things in a moment were driven from their course.

19.

And I saw a woman coming down from the hill-country, and she said to me:
O man, whither art thou going?
And I said:
I am seeking an Hebrew midwife.
And she answered and said unto me:
Art thou of Israel?
And I said to her:
Yes.
And she said:
And who is it that is bringing forth in the cave?
And I said:
A woman betrothed to me.
And she said to me:
Is she not thy wife?
And I said to her:
It is Mary that was reared in the temple of the Lord, and I obtained her by lot as my wife.
And yet she is not my wife, but has conceived of the Holy Spirit.
And the widwife said to him:
Is this true?
And Joseph said to her: Come and see.
And the midwife went away with him.
And they stood in the place of the cave, and behold a luminous cloud overshadowed the cave.
And the midwife said:
My soul has been magnified this day, because mine eyes have seen strange things--because salvation has been brought forth to Israel.
And immediately the cloud disappeared out of the cave, and a great light shone in the cave, so that the eyes could not bear it.
And in a little that light gradually decreased, until the infant appeared, and went and took the breast from His mother Mary. And the midwife cried out, and said:
This is a great day to me, because I have seen this strange sight.
And the midwife went forth out of the cave, and Salome met her.
And she said to her:
Salome, Salome, I have a strange sight to relate to thee:
a virgin has brought forth--a thing which her nature admits not of.
Then said Salome:
As the Lord my God liveth, unless I thrust in my finger, and search the parts, I will not believe that a virgin has brought forth.

20.

And the midwife went in, and said to Mary:
Show thyself; for no small controversy has arisen about thee.
And Salome put in her finger, and cried out, and said:
Woe is me for mine iniquity and mine unbelief, because I have tempted the living God; and, behold, my hand is dropping off as if burned with fire.
And she bent her knees before the Lord, saying:
O God of my fathers, remember that I am the seed of Abraham, and Isaac, and Jacob; do not make a show of me to the sons of Israel, but restore me to the poor; for Thou knowest, O Lord, that in Thy name I have performed my services, and that I have received my reward at Thy hand.
And, behold, an angel of the Lord stood by her, saying to her:
Salome, Salome, the Lord hath heard thee.

The Forgotten Bible

Put thy hand to the infant, and carry it, and thou wilt have safety and joy.

And Salome went and carried it, saying:

I will worship Him, because a great King has been born to Israel.

And, behold, Salome was immediately cured, and she went forth out of the cave justified.

And behold a voice saying:

Salome, Salome, tell not the strange things thou hast seen, until the child has come into Jerusalem.

21.

And, behold, Joseph was ready to go into Judaea.

And there was a great commotion in Bethlehem of Judaea, for Magi came, saying:

Where is he that is born king of the Jews? for we have seen his star in the east, and have come to worship him.

And when Herod heard, he was much disturbed, and sent officers to the Magi.

And he sent for the priests, and examined them, saying:

How is it written about the Christ? where is He to be born?

And they said:

In Bethlehem of Judaea, for so it is written. [50] And he sent them away.

And he examined the Magi, saying to them:

What sign have you seen in reference to the king that has been born?

And the Magi said:

We have seen a star of great size shining among these stars, and obscuring their light, so that the stars did not appear; and we thus knew that a king has been born to Israel, and we have come to worship him.

And Herod said:

Go and seek him; and if you find him, let me know, in order that I also may go and worship him.

And the Magi went out.

And, behold, the star which they had seen in the east went before them until they came to the cave, and it stood over the top of the cave.

And the Magi saw the infant with His mother Mary; and they brought forth from their bag gold, and frankincense, and myrrh.

And having been warned by the angel not to go into Judaea, they went into their own country by another road. [51]

22.

And when Herod knew that he had been mocked by the Magi, in a rage he sent murderers, saying to them:

Slay the children [52] from two years old and under.

And Mary, having heard that the children were being killed, was afraid, and took the infant and swaddled Him, and put Him into an ox-stall.

And Elizabeth, having heard that they were searching for John, took him and went up into the hill-country, and kept looking where to conceal him.

And there was no place of concealment.

And Elizabeth, groaning with a loud voice, says:

O mountain of God, receive mother and child.

And immediately the mountain was cleft, and received her.

And a light shone about them, for an angel of the Lord was with them, watching over them.

23.

And Herod searched for John, and sent officers to Zacharias, saying:

Where hast thou hid thy son?

And he, answering, said to them:

I am the servant of God in holy things, and I sit constantly in the temple of the Lord:

I do not know where my son is.

And the officers went away, and reported all these things to Herod.

And Herod was enraged, and said:

His son is destined to be king over Israel. And he sent to him again, saying:

Tell the truth; where is thy son? for thou knowest that thy life is in my hand.

And Zacharias said:

I am God's martyr, if thou sheddest my blood; for the Lord will receive my spirit, because thou sheddest innocent blood at the vestibule of the temple of the Lord.

And Zacharias was murdered about daybreak.

And the sons of Israel did not know that he had been murdered.[53]

24.

But at the hour of the salutation the priests went away, and Zacharias did not come forth to meet them with a blessing, according to his custom. [54]And the priests stood waiting for Zacharias to salute him at the prayer, [55] and to glorify the Most High.

And he still delaying, they were all afraid.

But one of them ventured to go in, and he saw clotted blood beside the altar; and he heard a voice saying:

Zacharias has been murdered, and his blood shall not be wiped up until his avenger come.

And hearing this saying, he was afraid, and went out and told it to the priests.

And they ventured in, and saw what had happened; and the fretwork of the temple made a wailing noise, and they rent their clothes [56] from the top even to the bottom. And they found not his body, but they found his blood turned into stone.

And they were afraid, and went out and reported to the people that Zacharias had been murdered.

And all the tribes of the people heard, and mourned, and lamented for him three days and three nights. And after the three days, the priests consulted as to whom they should put in his place; and the lot fell upon Simeon.

For it was he who had been warned by the Holy Spirit that he should not see death until he should see the Christ in the flesh. [57]

And I James that wrote this history in Jerusalem, a commotion having arisen when Herod died, withdrew myself to the wilderness until the commotion in Jerusalem ceased, glorifying the Lord God, who had given me the gift and the wisdom to write this history. [58]And grace shall be with them that fear our Lord Jesus Christ, to whom be glory to ages of ages.

Amen. [59]

Footnotes:

1. [This title is taken by Tischendorf from a manuscript of the eleventh century (Paris). At least seventeen other forms exist. The book is variously named by ancient writers. In the decree of Gelasius (a.d. 495) he condemns it as Evangelium nomine Jacobi minoris apocryphum. The text of Tischendorf, here translated, is somewhat less diffuse than that of Fabricius, and is based on manuscript evidence. The variations are verbal and formal rather than material.--R.]

2. Susanna i. 4.

3. The readings vary, and the sense is doubtful. Thilo thinks that the sense is: What I offer over and above what the law requires is for the benefit of the whole people; but the offering I make for my own forgiveness (according to the law's requirements) shall be to the Lord, that He may be rendered merciful to me.

4. The Church of Rome appoints March 20 as the Feast of St. Joachim. His liberality is commemorated in prayers, and the lessons to be read are Wisd. xxxi. and Matt. i.

5. 1 Sam. i. 6, 7; Hos. ix. 14.

6. Another reading is: In his last days.

7. Another reading is: Into the hill-country.

8. Moses: Ex. xxiv. 18, xxxiv. 28; Deut. ix. 9. Elijah: 1 Kings xix. 8. Christ: Matt. iv. 2.

9. The 26th day of July is the Feast of St. Anna in the Church of Rome.

10. Other forms of the name are Juth, Juthin.

11. Some mss. have: For I am thy maid-servant, and thou hast a regal appearance.

12. Severalmss. insert: Thou hast not listened to my voice; for.

13. Comp. 1 Sam. i. 9-18.

14. Tobit ii. 10.

15. Many of themss. here add: Alas! to what have I been likened? I am not like the waves of the sea, because even the waves of the sea, in calm and storm, and the fishes in them, bless Thee, O Lord.

16. 1 Sam. i. 11.

17. One of themss.: With his shepherds, and sheep, and goats, and oxen.

18. Ex. xxviii. 36-38. For traditions about the petalon, see Euseb., H. E., ii. 23, iii. 31, v. 24; Epiph., Haer., 78.

19. Various readings are: Sixth, seventh, eighth.

20. One of the MSS inserts: On the eighth day.

21. One of themss. has nine.

22. This is the reading of most mss.; but it is difficult to see any sense in it. One ms. reads: They attended on her. Fabricius proposed: They bathed her.

23. Two of themss. add: And they gave her the name of Mary, because her name shall not fade forever. This derivation of the name--from the root mar, fade--is one of a dozen or so.

24. This is taken to mean: Send someone to us to warn us that we have been too long in paying our vow. One ms. reads, lest the Lord depart from us; another, lest the Lord move away from us.

25. Or, fourteen. Postel's Latin version has ten.

26. Ex. xxviii. 28; Sirach xlv. 9; Justin, Tryph., xlii.

27. Num. xvi. 31-33.

28. Lit., undefiled. It is difficult to say what colour is meant, or if it is a colour at all. The word is once used to mean the sea, but with no reference to colour. It is also the name of a stone of a greenish hue.

29. Lit., hyacinth.

30. Ex. xxv. 4.

31. Luke i. 28.

32. Luke i. 39, 40.

33. Other readings are: the wool--what she had in her hand.

34. Luke i. 34, 44.

35. Luke i. 48.

36. Six mss. have sixteen; one, fourteen; two, fifteen; and one, seventeen.

37. The Latin translation has hung down.

38. Ezek. xxi. 12; Jer. xxxi. 19.

39. Two mss.: her.

40. Another reading is: As Adam was in Paradise, and in the hour of the singing of praise (doxology) to God was with the angels, the serpent, etc.

41. Matt. i. 19.

42. Lit., angelic; one ms. has holy; the Latin translation, following a slightly different reading, that it would not be fair to her.

43. Matt. i. 20.

44. Three mss. have high priest.

45. Num. v. 11, ff.

46. Luke ii. 1.

47. Or: On this day of the Lord I will do, etc.

48. Another reading is: And his son Samuel led it, and James and Simon followed.

49. Bethlehem...used to be overshadowed by a grove of Thammuz, i.e., Adonis; and in the cave where Christ formerly wailed as an infant, they used to mourn for the beloved of Venus (Jerome to Paulinus). In his letter to Sabinianus the cave is repeatedly mentioned: "That cave in which the Son of God was born;" "that venerable cave," etc., "within the door of what was once the Lord's manger, now the altar." "Then you run to the place of the shepherds." There appears also to have been above the altar the figure of an angel, or angels. See also Justin, Tryph., 78.

50. Two mss. here add: And thou Bethlehem, etc., from Mic. v. 2.

51. Matt. ii. 1-12. One of the mss. here adds Matt. ii. 13-15, with two or three slight variations.

52. Four mss. have all the male children, as in Matt. ii. 16.

53. Another reading is: And Herod, enraged at this, ordered him to be slain in the midst of the altar before the dawn, that the slaying of him might not be prevented by the people. [This incident was probably suggested by the reference to "Zacharias the son of Barachias" in Matt. xxiii. 35, Luke xi. 51; but comp. 2 Chron. xxiv. 20-22.--R.]

54. Lit., the blessing of Zacharias did not come forth, etc.

55. Or, with prayer.

56. Another reading is: And was rent from the top, etc.

57. Luke ii. 26. One of the mss. here adds Matt. ii. 19-23, with two or three verbal changes.

58. [Assuming that this is among the most ancient of the Apocryphal Gospels, it is noteworthy that the writer abstains from elaborating his stateents on points fully narrated in the Canonical Gospels. The supplementary character of the earliest of these writings is obvious. But what a contrast between the impressive silence of the New Testament narratives, and the garrulity, not to say indelicacy, of these detailed descriptions of the Nativity!--R.]

59. The mss. vary much in the doxology.

The Gospel of Pseudo-Matthew

Here beginneth the book of the Birth of the Blessed Mary and the Infancy of the Saviour. Written in Hebrew by the Blessed Evangelist Matthew, and translated into Latin by the Blessed Presbyter Jerome.

To their well-beloved brother Jerome the Presbyter, Bishops Cromatius and Heliodorus in the Lord, greeting.

The birth of the Virgin Mary, and the nativity and infancy of our Lord Jesus Christ, we find in apocryphal books.

But considering that in them many things contrary to our faith are written, we have believed that they ought all to be rejected, lest perchance we should transfer the joy of Christ to Antichrist.
[1]While, therefore, we were considering these things, there came holy men, Parmenius and Varinus, who said that your Holiness had found a Hebrew volume, written by the hand of the most blessed Evangelist Matthew, in which also the birth of the virgin mother herself, and the infancy of our Saviour, were written.

And accordingly we entreat your affection by our Lord Jesus Christ Himself, to render it from the Hebrew into Latin, [2] not so much for the attainment of those things which are the insignia of Christ, as for the exclusion of the craft of heretics, who, in order to teach bad doctrine, have mingled their own lies with the excellent nativity of Christ, that by the sweetness of life they might hide the bitterness of death.

It will therefore become your purest piety, either to listen to us as your brethren entreating, or to let us have as bishops exacting, the debt of affection which you may deem due.

Reply to Their Letter by Jerome.

To my lords the holy and most blessed Bishops Cromatius and Heliodorus, Jerome, a humble servant of Christ, in the Lord greeting.

He who digs in ground where he knows that there is gold, [3] does not instantly snatch at whatever the uptorn trench may pour forth; but, before the stroke of the quivering spade raises aloft the glittering mass, he meanwhile lingers over the sods to turn them over and lift them up, and especially he who has not added to his gains.

An arduous task is enjoined upon me, since what your Blessedness has commanded me, the holy Apostle and Evangelist Matthew himself did not write for the purpose of publishing.

For if he had not done it somewhat secretly, he would have added it also to his Gospel which he published.

But he composed this book in Hebrew; and so little did he publish it, that at this day the book written in Hebrew by his own hand is in the possession of very religious men, to whom in successive periods of time it has been handed down by those that were before them.

And this book they never at any time gave to any one to translate.

And so it came to pass, that when it was published by a disciple of Manichaeus named Leucius, who also wrote the falsely styled Acts of the Apostles, this book afforded matter, not of edification, but of perdition; and the opinion of the Synod in regard to it was according to its deserts, that the ears of the Church should not be open to it.

Let the snapping of those that bark against us now cease; for we do not add this little book to the canonical writings, but we translate what was written by an Apostle and Evangelist, that we may disclose the falsehood of heresy. In this work, then, we obey the commands of pious bishops as well as oppose impious heretics.

It is the love of Christ, therefore, which we fulfil, believing that they will assist us by their prayers, who through our obedience attain to a knowledge of the holy infancy of our Saviour.

There is extant another letter to the same bishops, attributed to Jerome:--

You ask me to let you know what I think of a book held by some to be about the nativity of St. Mary.

And so I wish you to know that there is much in it that is false.

For one Seleucus, who wrote the Sufferings of the Apostles, composed this book.

But, just as he wrote what was true about their powers, and the miracles they worked, but said a great deal that was false about their doctrine; so here too he has invented many untruths out of his own head.

The Forgotten Bible

I shall take care to render it word for word, exactly as it is in the Hebrew, since it is asserted that it was composed by the holy Evangelist Matthew, and written in Hebrew, and set at the head of his Gospel.

Whether this be true or not, I leave to the author of the preface and the trustworthiness of the writer:

as for myself, I pronounce them doubtful; I do not affirm that they are clearly false.

But this I say freely--and I think none of the faithful will deny it--that, whether these stories be true or inventions, the sacred nativity of St. Mary was preceded by great miracles, and succeeded by the greatest; and so by those who believe that God can do these things, they can be believed and read without damaging their faith or imperilling their souls.

In short, so far as I can, following the sense rather than the words of the writer, and sometimes walking in the same path, though not in the same footsteps, sometimes digressing a little, but still keeping the same road, I shall in this way keep by the style of the narrative, and shall say nothing that is not either written there, or might, following the same train of thought, have been written.

Footnotes:

1. [This introduction is, of itself, an evidence of late origin.--R.]
2. Lit., to Latin ears.
3. Lit., conscious of gold.

Chapter 1 [1]

In those days there was a man in Jerusalem, Joachim by name, of the tribe of Judah.

He was the shepherd of his own sheep, fearing the Lord in integrity and singleness of heart.

He had no other care than that of his herds, from the produce of which he supplied with food all that feared God, offering double gifts in the fear of God to all who laboured in doctrine, and who ministered unto Him.

Therefore his lambs, and his sheep, and his wool, and all things whatsoever he possessed, he used to divide into three portions:

one he gave to the orphans, the widows, the strangers, and the poor; the second to those that worshipped God; and the third he kept for himself and all his house. [2]And as he did so, the Lord multiplied to him his herds, so that there was no man like him in the people of Israel.

This now he began to do when he was fifteen years old.

And at the age of twenty he took to wife Anna, the daughter of Achar, of his own tribe, that is, of the tribe of Judah, of the family of David.

And though they had lived together for twenty years, he had by her neither sons nor daughters. [3]

Footnotes:

1. Two of themss. have this prologue: I James, the son of Joseph, living in the fear of God, have written all that with my own eyes I saw coming to pass in the time of the nativity of the holy virgin Mary, or of the Lord the Saviour: giving thanks to God, who has given me wisdom in the accounts of His Advent, showing His abounding grace to the twelve tribes of Israel.

2. Tobit i. 7.

3. One of themss. has: Only they vowed that, if God should give them offspring, they would devote it to the service of the temple; and because of this, they were wont to go to the temple of the Lord at each of the yearly festivals.

Chapter 2

And it happened that, in the time of the feast, among those who were offering incense to the Lord, Joachim stood getting ready his gifts in the sight of the Lord.

And the priest, Ruben by name, coming to him, said:

It is not lawful for thee to stand among those who are doing sacrifice to God, because God has not blessed thee so as to give thee seed in Israel.

Being therefore put to shame in the sight of the people, he retired from the temple of the Lord weeping, and did not return to his house, but went to his flocks, taking with him his shepherds into the mountains to a far country, so that for five months his wife Anna could hear no tidings of him.

And she prayed with tears, saying:

O Lord, most mighty God of Israel, why hast Thou, seeing that already Thou hast not given me children, taken from me my husband also?

Behold, now five months that I have not seen my husband; and I know not where he is tarrying; [1] nor, if I knew him to be dead, could I bury him.

And while she wept excessively, she entered into the court of His house; and she fell on her face in prayer, and poured out her supplications before the Lord.

After this, rising from her prayer, and lifting her eyes to God, she saw a sparrow's nest in a laurel tree, [2] and uttered her voice to the Lord with groaning, and said:

Lord God Almighty, who hast given offspring to every creature, to beasts wild and tame, to serpents, and birds, and fishes, and they all rejoice over their young ones, Thou hast shut out me alone from the gift of Thy benignity.

For Thou, O God, knowest my heart, that from the beginning of my married life I have vowed that, if Thou, O God, shouldst give me son or daughter, I would offer them to Thee in Thy holy temple.

And while she was thus speaking, suddenly an angel of the Lord appeared before her, saying:

Be not afraid, Anna, for there is seed for thee in the decree of God; and all generations even to the end shall wonder at that which shall be born of thee.

And when he had thus spoken, he vanished out of her sight.

But she, in fear and dread because she had seen such a sight, and heard such words, at length went into her bed-chamber, and threw herself on the bed as if dead.

And for a whole day and night she remained in great trembling and in prayer.

And after these things she called to her her servant, and said to her:

Dost thou see me deceived in my widowhood and in great perplexity, and hast thou been unwilling to come in to me?

Then she, with a slight murmur, thus answered and said:

If God hath shut up thy womb, and hath taken away thy husband from thee, what can I do for thee?

And when Anna heard this, she lifted up her voice, and wept aloud.

Footnotes:

1. Another reading is: Where he has died--reading mortuus for moratus.
2. Comp. Tobit ii. 10.

Chapter 3

At the same time there appeared a young man on the mountains to Joachim while he was feeding his flocks, and said to him:

Why dost thou not return to thy wife?

And Joachim said:

I have had her for twenty years, and it has not been the will of God to give me children by her. I have been driven with shame and reproach from the temple of the Lord:

why should I go back to her, when I have been once cast off and utterly despised?

Here then will I remain with my sheep; and so long as in this life God is willing to grant me light, I shall willingly, by the hands of my servants, bestow their portions upon the poor, and the orphans, and those that fear God.

And when he had thus spoken, the young man said to him:

I am an angel of the Lord, and I have to-day appeared to thy wife when she was weeping and praying, and have consoled her; and know that she has conceived a daughter from thy seed, and thou in thy ignorance of this hast left her.

She will be in the temple of God, and the Holy Spirit shall abide in her; and her blessedness shall be greater than that of all the holy women, so that no one can say that any before her has been like her, or that any after her in this world will be so.

Therefore go down from the mountains, and return to thy wife, whom thou wilt find with child.

For God hath raised up seed in her, and for this thou wilt give God thanks; and her seed shall be blessed, and she herself shall be blessed, and shall be made the mother of eternal blessing.

Then Joachim adored the angel, and said to him:

If I have found favour in thy sight, sit for a little in my tent, and bless thy servant. [1]And the angel said to him: Do not say servant, but fellow-servant; for we are the servants of one Master. [2]But my food is invisible, and my drink cannot be seen by a mortal.

Therefore thou oughtest not to ask me to enter thy tent; but if thou wast about to give me anything, [3] offer it as a burnt-offering to the Lord.

Then Joachim took a lamb without spot, and said to the angel:

I should not have dared to offer a burnt-offering to the Lord, unless thy command had given me the priest's right of offering. [4]And the angel said to him:

I should not have invited thee to offer unless I had known the will of the Lord.

And when Joachim was offering the sacrifice to God, the angel and the odour of the sacrifice went together straight up to heaven with the smoke. [5]

Then Joachim, throwing himself on his face, lay in prayer from the sixth hour of the day even until evening.

And his lads and hired servants who were with him saw him, and not knowing why he was lying down, thought that he was dead; and they came to him, and with difficulty raised him from the ground.

And when he recounted to them the vision of the angel, they were struck with great fear and wonder, and advised him to accomplish the vision of the angel without delay, and to go back with all haste to his wife.

And when Joachim was turning over in his mind whether he should go back or not, it happened that he was overpowered by a deep sleep; and, behold, the angel who had already appeared to him when awake, appeared to him in his sleep, saying:

I am the angel appointed by God as thy guardian:

go down with confidence, and return to Anna, because the deeds of mercy which thou and thy wife Anna have done have been told in the presence of the Most High; and to you will God give such fruit as no prophet or saint has ever had from the beginning, or ever will have.

And when Joachim awoke out of his sleep, he called all his herdsmen to him, and told them his dream.

And they worshipped the Lord, and said to him:

See that thou no further despise the words of the angel.

But rise and let us go hence, and return at a quiet pace, feeding our flocks.

And when, after thirty days occupied in going back, they were now near at hand, behold, the angel of the Lord appeared to Anna, who was standing and praying, and said: [6]Go to the gate which is called Golden, [7] and meet thy husband in the way, for to-day he will come to thee.

She therefore went towards him in haste with her maidens, and, praying to the Lord, she stood a long time in the gate waiting for him.

And when she was wearied with long waiting, she lifted up her eyes and saw Joachim afar off coming with his flocks; and she ran to him and hung on his neck, giving thanks to God, and saying:

I was a widow, and behold now I am not so:

I was barren, and behold I have now conceived.

And so they worshipped the Lord, and went into their own house.

And when this was heard of, there was great joy among all their neighbours and acquaintances, so that the whole land of Israel congratulated them.

Footnotes:

1. Gen. xviii. 3.
2. Rev. xix. 10.
3. Judg. xiii. 16.
4. Faustus the Manichaean said that Joachim was of the tribe of Levi (August. xxiii. 4, Contra Faustum). As belonging to the tribe of Judah, he had not the right of sacrifice.
5. Comp. Judg. xiii. 20.
6. Comp. Acts ix. 11.
7. This is the Beautiful gate of Acts iii. 2, to which, according to Josephus, there was an ascent by many steps from the valley of Kedron.

Chapter 4

After these things, her nine months being fulfilled, Anna brought forth a daughter, and called her Mary.

And having weaned her in her third year, Joachim, and Anna his wife, went together to the temple of the Lord to offer sacrifices to God, and placed the infant, Mary by name, in the community of virgins, in which the virgins remained day and night praising God.

And when she was put down before the doors of the temple, she went up the fifteen steps [1] so swiftly, that she did not look back at all; nor did she, as children are wont to do, seek for her parents.

Whereupon her parents, each of them anxiously seeking for the child, were both alike astonished, until they found her in the temple, and the priests of the temple themselves wondered.

Footnote:

1. Corresponding with the fifteen Songs of Degrees, Ps. cxx.-cxxxiv. See Smith's Dict.--art. Songs of Degrees. Another reading is: And there were about the temple, according to the fifteen Psalms of Degrees, fifteen steps of ascent: the temple was on a mountain, and there had been there built the altar of burnt-offering, which could not be reached but by steps.

Chapter 5

Then Anna, filled with the Holy Spirit, said before them all:

The Lord Almighty, the God of Hosts, being mindful of His word, hath visited His people with a good and holy visitation, to bring down the hearts of the Gentiles who were rising against us, and turn them to Himself.

He hath opened His ears to our prayers:

He hath kept away from us the exulting of all our enemies.

The barren hath become a mother, and hath brought forth exultation and gladness to Israel.

Behold the gifts which I have brought to offer to my Lord, and mine enemies have not been able to hinder me.

For God hath turned their hearts to me, and Himself hath given me everlasting joy.

Chapter 6

And Mary was held in admiration by all the people of Israel; and when she was three years old, she walked with a step so mature, she spoke so perfectly, and spent her time so assiduously in the praises of God, that all were astonished at her, and wondered; and she was not reckoned a young infant, but as it were a grown-up person of thirty years old. She was so constant in prayer, and her appearance was so beautiful and glorious, that scarcely any one could look into her face.

And she occupied herself constantly with her wool-work, so that she in her tender years could do all that old women were not able to do.

And this was the order that she had set for herself: [1]From the morning to the third hour she remained in prayer; from the third to the ninth she was occupied with her weaving; and from the ninth she again applied herself to prayer.

She did not retire from praying until there appeared to her the angel of the Lord, from whose hand she used to receive food; and thus she became more and more perfect in the work of God.

Then, when the older virgins rested from the praises of God, she did not rest at all; so that in the praises and vigils of God none were found before her, no one more learned in the wisdom of the law of God, more lowly in humility, more elegant in singing, more perfect in all virtue.

She was indeed stedfast, immoveable, unchangeable, and daily advancing to perfection.

No one saw her angry, nor heard her speaking evil.

All her speech was so full of grace, that her God was acknowledged to be in her tongue.

She was always engaged in prayer and in searching the law, and she was anxious lest by any word of hers she should sin with regard to her companions.

Then she was afraid lest in her laughter, or the sound of her beautiful voice, she should commit any fault, or lest, being elated, she should display any wrong-doing or haughtiness to one of her equals. [2]She blessed God without intermission; and lest perchance, even in her salutation, she might cease from praising God; if any one saluted her, she used to answer by way of salutation:

Thanks be to God.

And from her the custom first began of men saying, Thanks be to God, when they saluted each other. She refreshed herself only with the food which she daily received from the hand of the angel; but the food which she obtained from the priests she divided among the poor.

The angels of God were often seen speaking with her, and they most diligently obeyed her.

If any one who was unwell touched her, the same hour he went home cured.

Footnotes:

1. For the hours of prayer, see Apost. Const., ch. xl.; Jerome's letters to Laeta, Demetrias, etc.
2. One of themss. has: She was anxious about her companions, lest any of them should sin even in one word, lest any of them should raise her voice in laughing, lest any of them should be in the wrong, or proud to her father or her mother.

Chapter 7

Then Abiathar the priest offered gifts without end to the high priests, in order that he might obtain her as wife to his son.

But Mary forbade them, saying:

It cannot be that I should know a man, or that a man should know me.

For all the priests and all her relations kept saying to her:

God is worshipped in children and adored in posterity, as has always happened among the sons of Israel.

But Mary answered and said unto them:

God is worshipped in chastity, as is proved first of all. [1]For before Abel there was none righteous among men, and he by his offerings pleased God, and was without mercy slain by him who displeased Him.

Two crowns, therefore, he received--of oblation and of virginity, because in his flesh there was no pollution.

Elias also, when he was in the flesh, was taken up in the flesh, because he kept his flesh unspotted.

Now I, from my infancy in the temple of God, have learned that virginity can be sufficiently dear to God.

And so, because I can offer what is dear to God, I have resolved in my heart that I should not know a man at all.

Footnote:

1. Or, by the first of all.

Chapter 8

Now it came to pass, when she was fourteen [1] years old, and on this account there was occasion for the Pharisees' saying that it was now a custom that no woman of that age should abide in the temple of God, they fell upon the plan of sending a herald through all the tribes of Israel, that on the third day all should come together into the temple of the Lord.

The Forgotten Bible

And when all the people had come together, Abiathar the high priest rose, and mounted on a higher step, that he might be seen and heard by all the people; and when great silence had been obtained, he said:

Hear me, O sons of Israel, and receive my words into your ears.

Ever since this temple was built by Solomon, there have been in it virgins, the daughters of kings and the daughters of prophets, and of high priests and priests; and they were great, and worthy of admiration.

But when they came to the proper age they were given in marriage, and followed the course of their mothers before them, and were pleasing to God.

But a new order of life has been found out by Mary alone, who promises that she will remain a virgin to God. Wherefore it seems to me, that through our inquiry and the answer of God we should try to ascertain to whose keeping she ought to be entrusted.

Then these words found favour with all the synagogue.

And the lot was cast by the priests upon the twelve tribes, and the lot fell upon the tribe of Judah.

And the priest said:

To-morrow let every one who has no wife come, and bring his rod in his hand.

Whence it happened that Joseph [2] brought his rod along with the young men.

And the rods having been handed over to the high priest, he offered a sacrifice to the Lord God, and inquired of the Lord.

And the Lord said to him:

Put all their rods into the holy of holies of God, and let them remain there, and order them to come to thee on the morrow to get back their rods; and the man from the point of whose rod a dove shall come forth, and fly towards heaven, and in whose hand the rod, when given back, shall exhibit this sign, to him let Mary be delivered to be kept.

On the following day, then, all having assembled early, and an incense-offering having been made, the high priest went into the holy of holies, and brought forth the rods.

And when he had distributed the rods, [3] and the dove came forth out of none of them, the high priest put on the twelve bells [4] and the sacerdotal robe; and entering into the holy of holies, he there made a burnt-offering, and poured forth a prayer.

And the angel of the Lord appeared to him, saying:

There is here the shortest rod, of which thou hast made no account:

thou didst bring it in with the rest, but didst not take it out with them.

When thou hast taken it out, and hast given it him whose it is, in it will appear the sign of which I spoke to thee.

Now that was Joseph's rod; and because he was an old man, he had been cast off, as it were, that he might not receive her, but neither did he himself wish to ask back his rod. [5]And when he was humbly standing last of all, the high priest cried out to him with a loud voice, saying:

Come, Joseph, and receive thy rod; for we are waiting for thee.

And Joseph came up trembling, because the high priest had called him with a very loud voice.

But as soon as he stretched forth his hand, and laid hold of his rod, immediately from the top of it came forth a dove whiter than snow, beautiful exceedingly, which, after long flying about the roofs of the temple, at length flew towards the heavens.

Then all the people congratulated the old man, saying:

Thou hast been made blessed in thine old age, O father Joseph, seeing that God hath shown thee to be fit to receive Mary.

And the priests having said to him, Take her, because of all the tribe of Judah thou alone hast been chosen by God; Joseph began bashfully to address them, saying:

I am an old man, and have children; why do you hand over to me this infant, who is younger than my grandsons?

Then Abiathar the high priest said to him:

Remember, Joseph, how Dathan and Abiron and Core perished, because they despised the will of God.

So will it happen to thee, if thou despise this which is commanded thee by God.

Joseph answered him:

I indeed do not despise the will of God; but I shall be her guardian until I can ascertain concerning the will of God, as to which of my sons can have her as his wife.

Let some virgins of her companions, with whom she may meanwhile spend her time, be given for a consolation to her.

Abiathar the high priest answered and said:

Five virgins indeed shall be given her for consolation, until the appointed day come in which thou mayst receive her; for to no other can she be joined in marriage.

The Forgotten Bible

Then Joseph received Mary, with the other five virgins who were to be with her in Joseph's house.

These virgins were Rebecca, Sephora, Susanna, Abigea, and Cael; to whom the high priest gave the silk, and the blue, [6] and the fine linen, and the scarlet, and the purple, and the fine flax.

For they cast lots among themselves what each virgin should do, and the purple for the veil of the temple of the Lord fell to the lot of Mary.

And when she had got it, those virgins said to her:

Since thou art the last, and humble, and younger than all, thou hast deserved to receive and obtain the purple.

And thus saying, as it were in words of annoyance, they began to call her queen of virgins.

While, however, they were so doing, the angel of the Lord appeared in the midst of them, saying:

These words shall not have been uttered by way of annoyance, but prophesied as a prophecy most true. They trembled, therefore, at the sight of the angel, and at his words, and asked her to pardon them, and pray for them.

Footnotes:

1. Or, twelve.
2. One of themss. adds: Seeing that he had not a wife, and not wishing to slight the order of the high priest.
3. One of themss. inserts: To the number of three thousand.
4. See Protev. James 8.
5. Another and more probable reading is: And this was Joseph's rod; and he was of an abject appearance, seeing that he was old, and he would not ask back his rod, lest perchance he might be forced to receive her.
6. Or, hyacinth.

Chapter 9

And on the second day, while Mary was at the fountain to fill her pitcher, the angel of the Lord appeared to her, saying:

Blessed art thou, Mary; for in thy womb thou hast prepared an habitation for the Lord.

For, lo, the light from heaven shall come and dwell in thee, and by means of thee will shine over the whole world.

Again, on the third day, while she was working at the purple with her fingers, there entered a young man of ineffable beauty.

And when Mary saw him, she exceedingly feared and trembled.

And he said to her: Hail, Mary, full of grace; the Lord is with thee:

blessed art thou among women, and blessed is the fruit of thy womb. [1]And when she heard these words, she trembled, and was exceedingly afraid.

Then the angel of the Lord added:

Fear not, Mary; for thou hast found favour with God:

Behold, thou shalt conceive in thy womb, and shalt bring forth a King, who fills not only the earth, but the heaven, and who reigns from generation to generation.

Footnote:

1. Luke i. 28.

Chapter 10

While these things were doing, Joseph was occupied with his work, house-building, in the districts by the sea-shore; for he was a carpenter.

And after nine months he came back to his house, and found Mary pregnant.

Wherefore, being in the utmost distress, he trembled and cried out, saying:

O Lord God, receive my spirit; for it is better for me to die than to live any longer.

And the virgins who were with Mary said to him:

Joseph, what art thou saying?

We know that no man has touched her; we can testify that she is still a virgin, and untouched.

We have watched over her; always has she continued with us in prayer; daily do the angels of God speak with her; daily does she receive food from the hand of the Lord.

We know not how it is possible that there can be any sin in her.

But if thou wishest us to tell thee what we suspect, nobody but the angel of the Lord [1] has made her pregnant.

Then said Joseph:

Why do you mislead me, to believe that an angel of the Lord has made her pregnant?

But it is possible that some one has pretended to be an angel of the Lord, and has beguiled her. And thus speaking, he wept, and said:

With what face shall I look at the temple of the Lord, or with what face shall I see the priests of God?

What am I to do?

And thus saying, he thought that he would flee, and send her away.

Footnote:

1. Another reading is: The Holy Spirit.

Chapter 11

And when he was thinking of rising up and hiding himself, and dwelling in secret, behold, on that very night, the angel of the Lord appeared to him in sleep, saying:

Joseph, thou son of David, fear not; receive Mary as thy wife:

for that which is in her womb is of the Holy Spirit.

And she shall bring forth a son, and His name shall be called Jesus, for He will save His people from their sins.

And Joseph, rising from his sleep, gave thanks to God, and spoke to Mary and the virgins who were with her, and told them his vision.

And he was comforted about Mary, saying:

I have sinned, in that I suspected thee at all.

Chapter 12

After these things there arose a great report that Mary was with child.

And Joseph was seized by the officers of the temple, and brought along with Mary to the high priest.

And he with the priests began to reproach him, and to say:

Why hast thou beguiled so great and so glorious a virgin, who was fed like a dove in the temple by the angels of God, who never wished either to see or to have a man, who had the most excellent knowledge of the law of God?

If thou hadst not done violence to her, she would still have remained in her virginity.

And Joseph vowed, and swore that he had never touched her at all.

And Abiathar the high priest answered him:

As the Lord liveth, I will give thee to drink of the water of drinking of the Lord, and immediately thy sin will appear.

Then was assembled a multitude of people which could not be numbered, and Mary was brought to the temple.

And the priests, and her relatives, and her parents wept, and said to Mary:

Confess to the priests thy sin, thou that wast like a dove in the temple of God, and didst receive food from the hands of an angel.

And again Joseph was summoned to the altar, and the water of drinking of the Lord was given him to drink.

And when any one that had lied drank this water, and walked seven times round the altar, God used to show some sign in his face.

When, therefore, Joseph had drunk in safety, and had walked round the altar seven times, no sign of sin appeared in him.

Then all the priests, and the officers, and the people justified him, saying: Blessed art thou, seeing that no charge has been found good against thee.

And they summoned Mary, and said:

And what excuse canst thou have? or what greater sign can appear in thee than the conception of thy womb, which betrays thee?

This only we require of thee, that since Joseph is pure regarding thee, thou confess who it is that has beguiled thee.

For it is better that thy confession should betray thee, than that the wrath of God should set a mark on thy face, and expose thee in the midst of the people.

Then Mary said, stedfastly and without trembling:

O Lord God, King over all, who knowest all secrets, if there be any pollution in me, or any sin, or any evil desires, or unchastity, expose me in the sight of all the people, and make me an example of punishment to all.

Thus saying, she went up to the altar of the Lord boldly, and drank the water of drinking, and walked round the altar seven times, and no spot was found in her.

And when all the people were in the utmost astonishment, seeing that she was with child, and that no sign had appeared in her face, they began to be disturbed among themselves by conflicting statements:

some said that she was holy and unspotted, others that she was wicked and defiled.

Then Mary, seeing that she was still suspected by the people, and that on that account she did not seem to them to be wholly cleared, said in the hearing of all, with a loud voice, As the Lord Adonai liveth, the Lord of Hosts before whom I stand, I have not known man; but I am known by Him to whom from my earliest years I have devoted myself.

And this vow I made to my God from my infancy, that I should remain unspotted in Him who created me, and I trust that I shall so live to Him alone, and serve Him alone; and in Him, as long as I shall live, will I remain unpolluted.

Then they all began to kiss her feet and to embrace her knees, asking her to pardon them for their wicked suspicions.

And she was led down to her house with exultation and joy by the people, and the priests, and all the virgins.

And they cried out, and said:

Blessed be the name of the Lord for ever, because He hath manifested thy holiness to all His people Israel.

Chapter 13

And it came to pass some little time after, that an enrolment was made according to the edict of Caesar Augustus, that all the world was to be enrolled, each man in his native place.

This enrolment was made by Cyrinus, the governor of Syria. [1]It was necessary, therefore, that Joseph should enrol with the blessed Mary in Bethlehem, because to it they belonged, being of the tribe of Judah, and of the house and family of David.

When, therefore, Joseph and the blessed Mary were going along the road which leads to Bethlehem, Mary said to Joseph:

I see two peoples before me, the one weeping, and the other rejoicing. And Joseph answered: Sit still on thy beast, and do not speak superfluous words.

Then there appeared before them a beautiful boy, clothed in white raiment, who said to Joseph:

Why didst thou say that the words which Mary spoke about the two peoples were superfluous?

For she saw the people of the Jews weeping, because they have departed from their God; and the people of the Gentiles rejoicing, because they have now been added and made near to the Lord, according to that which He promised to our fathers Abraham, Isaac, and Jacob:

for the time is at hand when in the seed of Abraham all nations shall be blessed. [2]

And when he had thus said, the angel ordered the beast to stand, for the time when she should bring forth was at hand; and he commanded the blessed Mary to come down off the animal, and go into a recess under a cavern, in which there never was light, but always darkness, because the light of day could not reach it.

And when the blessed Mary had gone into it, it began to shine with as much brightness as if it were the sixth hour of the day.

The light from God so shone in the cave, that neither by day nor night was light wanting as long as the blessed Mary was there.

And there she brought forth a son, and the angels surrounded Him when He was being born.

And as soon as He was born, He stood upon His feet, and the angels adored Him, saying:

Glory to God in the highest, and on earth peace to men of good pleasure. [3] Now, when the birth of the Lord was at hand, Joseph had gone away to seek midwives.

And when he had found them, he returned to the cave, and found with Mary the infant which she had brought forth.

And Joseph said to the blessed Mary:

I have brought thee two midwives--Zelomi [4] and Salome; and they are standing outside before the entrance to the cave, not daring to come in hither, because of the exceeding brightness.

And when the blessed Mary heard this, she smiled; and Joseph said to her:

Do not smile; but prudently allow them to visit thee, in case thou shouldst require them for thy cure.

Then she ordered them to enter.

And when Zelomi had come in, Salome having stayed without, Zelomi said to Mary:

Allow me to touch thee.

And when she had permitted her to make an examination, the midwife cried out with a loud voice, and said:

Lord, Lord Almighty, mercy on us!

It has never been heard or thought of, that any one should have her breasts full of milk, and that the birth of a son should show his mother to be a virgin.

But there has been no spilling of blood in his birth, no pain in bringing him forth.

A virgin has conceived, a virgin has brought forth, and a virgin she remains.

And hearing these words, Salome said:

Allow me to handle thee, and prove whether Zelomi have spoken the truth.

And the blessed Mary allowed her to handle her.

And when she had withdrawn her hand from handling her, it dried up, and through excess of pain she began to weep bitterly, and to be in great distress, crying out, and saying:

O Lord God, Thou knowest that I have always feared Thee, and that without recompense I have cared for all the poor; I have taken nothing from the widow and the orphan, and the needy have I not sent empty away.

And, behold, I am made wretched because of mine unbelief, since without a cause I wished to try Thy virgin.

And while she was thus speaking, there stood by her a young man in shining garments, saying:

Go to the child, and adore Him, and touch Him with thy hand, and He will heal thee, because He is the Saviour of the world, and of all that hope in Him.

And she went to the child with haste, and adored Him, and touched the fringe of the cloths in which He was wrapped, and instantly her hand was cured.

And going forth, she began to cry aloud, and to tell the wonderful things which she had seen, and which she had suffered, and how she had been cured; so that many through her statements believed.

And some shepherds also affirmed that they had seen angels singing a hymn at midnight, praising and blessing the God of heaven, and saying: There has been born the Saviour of all, who is Christ the Lord, in whom salvation shall be brought back to Israel. [5]

Moreover, a great star, larger than any that had been seen since the beginning of the world, shone over the cave from the evening till the morning.

And the prophets who were in Jerusalem said that this star pointed out the birth of Christ, who should restore the promise not only to Israel, but to all nations.

Footnotes:

1. Luke ii. 1-6.
2. Gen. xii. 3.
3. See Alford's Greek Testament on Luke ii. 14. [So Rev. Version, following the weight of manuscript authority.--R.]
4. Or Zelemi.
5. Luke ii. 8-12.

Chapter 14

And on the third day after the birth of our Lord Jesus Christ, the most blessed Mary went forth out of the cave, and entering a stable, placed the child in the stall, and the ox and the ass adored Him.

Then was fulfilled that which was said by Isaiah the prophet, saying:

The ox knoweth his owner, and the ass his master's crib. [1] The very animals, therefore, the ox and the ass, having Him in their midst, incessantly adored Him.

Then was fulfilled that which was said by Abacuc the prophet, saying: [2] Between two animals thou art made manifest.

In the same place Joseph remained with Mary three days.

Footnotes:

1. Isa. i. 3.
2. Hab. iii. 2, according to the LXX. reading, snym tyys two living creatures, for snym tyyv years make alive.

Chapter 15

And on the sixth day they entered Bethlehem, where they spent the seventh day.

And on the eighth day they circumcised the child, and called His name Jesus; for so He was called by the angel before He was conceived in the womb. [1] Now, after the days of the purification of Mary were fulfilled according to the law of Moses, then Joseph took the infant to the temple of the Lord.

And when the infant had received parhithomus, [2] --parhithomus, that is, circumcision--they offered for Him a pair of turtle-doves, or two young pigeons. [3]

Now there was in the temple a man of God, perfect and just, whose name was Symeon, a hundred and twelve years old.

He had received the answer from the Lord, that he should not taste of death till he had seen Christ, the Son of God, living in the flesh.

And having seen the child, he cried out with a loud voice, saying:

God hath visited His people, and the Lord hath fulfilled His promise.

And he made haste, and adored Him.

And after this he took Him up into his cloak and kissed His feet, and said:

Lord, now lettest Thou Thy servant depart in peace, according to Thy word:

for mine eyes have seen Thy salvation, which Thou hast prepared before the face of all peoples, to be a light to lighten the Gentiles, and the glory of Thy people Israel. [4]

There was also in the temple of the Lord, Anna, a prophetess, the daughter of Phanuel, of the tribe of Asher, who had lived with her husband seven years from her virginity; and she had now been a widow eighty-four years.

And she never left the temple of the Lord, but spent her time in fasting and prayer.

She also likewise adored the child, saying:

In Him is the redemption of the world. [5]

Footnotes:

1. Luke ii. 21-24.
2. This shows the extent of the writer's, or transcriber's knowledge of Greek.
3. Lev. xii. 8.
4. Luke ii. 22-35.
5. Luke ii. 36-38.

Chapter 16

And when the second year was past, [1] Magi came from the east to Jerusalem, bringing great gifts.

And they made strict inquiry of the Jews, saying:

Where is the king who has been born to you? for we have seen his star in the east, and have come to worship him.

And word of this came to King Herod, and so alarmed him that he called together the scribes and the Pharisees, and the teachers of the people, asking of them where the prophets had foretold that Christ should be born.

And they said:

In Bethlehem of Judah.

For it is written:

And thou Bethelehem, in the land of Judah, art by no means the least among the princes of Judah; for out of thee shall come forth a Leader who shall rule my people Israel. [2]Then King Herod summoned the magi to him, and strictly inquired of them when the star appeared to them. Then, sending them to Bethlehem, he said:

Go and make strict inquiry about the child; and when ye have found him, bring me word again, that I may come and worship him also.

And while the magi were going on their way, there appeared to them the star, which was, as it were, a guide to them, going before them until they came to where the child was.

And when the magi saw the star, they rejoiced with great joy; and going into the house, they saw the child Jesus sitting in His mother's lap.

Then they opened their treasures, and presented great gifts to the blessed Mary and Joseph.

And to the child Himself they offered each of them a piece of gold. [3]And likewise one gave gold, another frankincense, and the third myrrh. [4]And when they were going to return to King Herod, they were warned by an angel in their sleep not to go back to Herod; and they returned to their own country by another road. [5]

Footnotes:

1. One ms. has: When two days were past. Another: On the thirteenth day.
2. Mic. v. 2.
3. The siclus aureus, or gold shekel, was worth -L-1, 16s. 6d.
4. One ms. has: Gaspar gave Myrrh, Melchior frankincense, Balthusar gold.
5. Matt. ii. 1-12.

Chapter 17

And when Herod [1] saw that he had been made sport of by the magi, his heart swelled with rage, and he sent through all the roads, wishing to seize them and put them to death.

But when he could not find them at all, he sent anew to Bethlehem and all its borders, and slew all the male children whom he found of two years old and under, according to the time that he had ascertained from the magi. [2]

Now the day before this was done Joseph was warned in his sleep by the angel of the Lord, who said to him:

Take Mary and the child, and go into Egypt by the way of the desert.

And Joseph went according to the saying of the angel. [3]

Footnotes:

1. One ms. has: And when Herod, coming back from Rome the year after, saw.
2. Matt. ii. 16.
3. Matt. ii. 14.

Chapter 18

And having come to a certain cave, and wishing to rest in it, the blessed [1] Mary dismounted from her beast, and sat down with the child Jesus in her bosom.

And there were with Joseph three boys, and with Mary a girl, going on the journey along with them.

And, lo, suddenly there came forth from the cave many dragons; and when the children saw them, they cried out in great terror.

Then Jesus went down from the bosom of His mother, and stood on His feet before the dragons; and they adored Jesus, and thereafter retired.

Then was fulfilled that which was said by David the prophet, saying:

Praise the Lord from the earth, ye dragons; ye dragons, and all ye deeps. [2] And the young child Jesus, walking before them, commanded them to hurt no man.

But Mary and Joseph were very much afraid lest the child should be hurt by the dragons.

And Jesus said to them:

Do not be afraid, and do not consider me to be a little child; for I am and always have been perfect; and all the beasts of the forest must needs be tame before me.

Footnotes:

1. One of themss. has: Then Joseph put the blessed virgin and the boy upon a beast, and himself mounted another, and took the road through the hill country and the desert, that he might get safe to Egypt; for they did not want to go by the shore, for fear of being waylaid.
2. Ps. cxlviii. 7.

Chapter 19

Lions and panthers adored Him likewise, and accompanied them in the desert.

Wherever Joseph and the blessed Mary went, they went before them showing them the way, and bowing their heads; and showing their submission by wagging their tails, they adored Him with great reverence.

Now at first, when Mary saw the lions and the panthers, and various kinds of wild beasts, coming about them, she was very much afraid.

But the infant Jesus looked into her face with a joyful countenance, and said:

Be not afraid, mother; for they come not to do thee harm, but they make haste to serve both thee and me.

With these words He drove all fear from her heart.

And the lions kept walking with them, and with the oxen, and the asses, and the beasts of burden which carried their baggage, and did not hurt a single one of them, though they kept beside them; but they were tame among the sheep and the rams which they had brought with them from Judaea, and which they had with them.

They walked among wolves, and feared nothing; and no one of them was hurt by another.

Then was fulfilled that which was spoken by the prophet:

Wolves shall feed with lambs; the lion and the ox shall eat straw together. [1] There were together two oxen drawing a waggon with provision for the journey, and the lions directed them in their path.

Footnote:
1. Isa. lxv. 25.

Chapter 20

And it came to pass on the third day of their journey, while they were walking, that the blessed Mary was fatigued by the excessive heat of the sun in the desert; and seeing a palm tree, she said to Joseph:

Let me rest a little under the shade of this tree.

Joseph therefore made haste, and led her to the palm, and made her come down from her beast. And as the blessed Mary was sitting there, she looked up to the foliage of the palm, and saw it full of fruit, and said to Joseph:

I wish it were possible to get some of the fruit of this palm.

And Joseph said to her:

I wonder that thou sayest this, when thou seest how high the palm tree is; and that thou thinkest of eating of its fruit.

I am thinking more of the want of water, because the skins are now empty, and we have none wherewith to refresh ourselves and our cattle.

Then the child Jesus, with a joyful countenance, reposing in the bosom of His mother, said to the palm:

O tree, bend thy branches, and refresh my mother with thy fruit.

And immediately at these words the palm bent its top down to the very feet of the blessed Mary; and they gathered from it fruit, with which they were all refreshed.

And after they had gathered all its fruit, it remained bent down, waiting the order to rise from Him who had commanded it to stoop.

Then Jesus said to it: Raise thyself, O palm tree, and be strong, and be the companion of my trees, which are in the paradise of my Father; and open from thy roots a vein of water which has been hid in the earth, and let the waters flow, so that we may be satisfied from thee.

And it rose up immediately, and at its root there began to come forth a spring of water exceedingly clear and cool and sparkling.

And when they saw the spring of water, they rejoiced with great joy, and were satisfied, themselves and all their cattle and their beasts.

Wherefore they gave thanks to God.

Chapter 21

And on the day after, when they were setting out thence, and in the hour in which they began their journey, Jesus turned to the palm, and said:

This privilege I give thee, O palm tree, that one of thy branches be carried away by my angels, and planted in the paradise of my Father.

And this blessing I will confer upon thee, that it shall be said of all who conquer in any contest, You have attained the palm of victory.

And while He was thus speaking, behold, an angel of the Lord appeared, and stood upon the palm tree; and taking off one of its branches, flew to heaven with the branch in his hand.

And when they saw this, they fell on their faces, and became as it were dead.

And Jesus said to them:

Why are your hearts possessed with fear?

Do you not know that this palm, which I have caused to be transferred to paradise, shall be prepared for all the saints in the place of delights, as it has been prepared for us in this place of the wilderness?

And they were filled with joy; and being strengthened, they all rose up.

Chapter 22

After this, while they were going on their journey, Joseph said to Jesus:

Lord, it is a boiling heat; if it please Thee, let us go by the sea-shore, that we may be able to rest in the cities on the coast. Jesus said to him:

Fear not, Joseph; I will shorten the way for you, so that what you would have taken thirty days to go over, you shall accomplish in this one day.

And while they were thus speaking, behold, they looked forward, and began to see the mountains and cities of Egypt.

And rejoicing and exulting, they came into the regions of Hermopolis, and entered into a certain city of Egypt which is called Sotinen; [1] and because they knew no one there from whom they could ask hospitality, they went into a temple which was called the Capitol of Egypt.

And in this temple there had been set up three hundred and fifty-five idols, [2] to each of which on its own day divine honours and sacred rites were paid.

For the Egyptians belonging to the same city entered the Capitol, in which the priests told them how many sacrifices were offered each day, according to the honour in which the god was held.

Footnotes:

1. Or, Sotrina.
2. No nation was so given to idolatry, and worshipped such a countless number of monsters, as the Egyptians.--Jerome on Isaiah.

Chapter 23

And it came to pass, when the most blessed Mary went into the temple with the little child, that all the idols prostrated themselves on the ground, so that all of them were lying on their faces shattered and broken to pieces; [1] and thus they plainly showed that they were nothing.

Then was fulfilled that which was said by the prophet Isaiah:

Behold, the Lord will come upon a swift cloud, and will enter Egypt, and all the handiwork of the Egyptians shall be moved at His presence. [2]

Footnotes:

1. Cf. 1 Sam. v. 3.
2. Isa. xix. 1.

Chapter 24

Then Affrodosius, that governor of the city, when news of this was brought to him, went to the temple with all his army.

And the priests of the temple, when they saw Affrodosius with all his army coming into the temple, thought that he was making haste only to see vengeance taken on those on whose account the gods had fallen down.

But when he came into the temple, and saw all the gods lying prostrate on their faces, he went up to the blessed Mary, who was carrying the Lord in her bosom, and adored Him, and said to all his army and all his friends: Unless this were the God of our gods, our gods would not have fallen on their faces before Him; nor would they be lying prostrate in His presence:

wherefore they silently confess that He is their Lord. Unless we, therefore, take care to do what we have seen our gods doing, we may run the risk of His anger, and all come to destruction, even as it happened to Pharaoh king of the Egyptians, who, not believing in powers so mighty, was drowned in the sea, with all his army. [1] Then all the people of that same city believed in the Lord God through Jesus Christ.

Footnote:

1. Ex. xv. 4.

Chapter 25

After no long time the angel said to Joseph:

Return to the land of Judah, for they are dead who sought the child's life. [1]

Footnote:

1. Matt. ii. 26. One of the mss. here has: And Joseph and Mary went to live in the house of a certain widow, and spent a year there; and for the events of the year it gives a number of the miracles recorded in the early chapters of the Latin Gospel of Thomas.

Chapter 26

And it came to pass, after Jesus had returned out of Egypt, when He was in Galilee, and entering on the fourth year of His age, that on a Sabbath-day He was playing with some children at the bed of the Jordan.

And as He sat there, Jesus made to Himself seven pools of clay, and to each of them He made passages, through which at His command He brought water from the torrent into the pool, and took it back again.

Then one of those children, a son of the devil, moved with envy, shut the passages which supplied the pools with water, and overthrew what Jesus had built up.

Then said Jesus to him:

Woe unto thee, thou son of death, thou son of Satan! Dost thou destroy the works which I have wrought?

And immediately he who had done this died.

Then with great uproar the parents of the dead boy cried out against Mary and Joseph, saying to them:

Your son has cursed our son, and he is dead.

And when Joseph and Mary heard this, they came forthwith to Jesus, on account of the outcry of the parents of the boy, and the gathering together of the Jews.

But Joseph said privately to Mary:

I dare not speak to Him; but do thou admonish Him, and say:

Why hast Thou raised against us the hatred of the people; and why must the troublesome hatred of men be borne by us?

And His mother having come to Him, asked Him, saying:

My Lord, what was it that he did to bring about his death?

And He said:

He deserved death, because he scattered the works that I had made.

Then His mother asked Him, saying:

Do not so, my Lord, because all men rise up against us.

But He, not wishing to grieve His mother, with His right foot kicked the hinder parts of the dead boy, and said to him:

Rise, thou son of iniquity for thou art not worthy to enter into the rest of my Father, because thou didst destroy the works which I had made.

Then he who had been dead rose up, and went away.

And Jesus, by the word of His power, brought water into the pools by the aqueduct.

Chapter 27

And it came to pass, after these things, that in the sight of all Jesus took clay from the pools which He had made, and of it made twelve sparrows.

And it was the Sabbath when Jesus did this, and there were very many children with Him.

When, therefore, one of the Jews had seen Him doing this, he said to Joseph:

Joseph, dost thou not see the child Jesus working on the Sabbath at what it is not lawful for him to do? for he has made twelve sparrows of clay.

And when Joseph heard this, he reproved him, saying:

Wherefore doest thou on the Sabbath such things as are not lawful for us to do?

And when Jesus heard Joseph, He struck His hands together, and said to His sparrows:

Fly!

And at the voice of His command they began to fly.

And in the sight and hearing of all that stood by, He said to the birds:

Go and fly through the earth, and through all the world, and live.

And when those that were there saw such miracles, they were filled with great astonishment.

And some praised and admired Him, but others reviled Him.

And certain of them went away to the chief priests and the heads of the Pharisees, and reported to them that Jesus the son of Joseph had done great signs and miracles in the sight of all the people of Israel.

And this was reported in the twelve tribes of Israel.

Chapter 28

And again the son of Annas, a priest of the temple, who had come with Joseph, holding his rod in his hand in the sight of all, with great fury broke down the dams which Jesus had made with His own hands, and let out the water which He had collected in them from the torrent. Moreover, he shut the aqueduct by which the water came in, and then broke it down.

And when Jesus saw this, He said to that boy who had destroyed His dams:

O most wicked seed of iniquity!

O son of death! O workshop of Satan! verily the fruit of thy seed shall be without strength, and thy roots without moisture, and thy branches withered, bearing no fruit.

And immediately, in the sight of all, the boy withered away, and died.

Chapter 29

Then Joseph trembled, and took hold of Jesus, and went with Him to his own house, and His mother with Him.

And, behold, suddenly from the opposite direction a boy, also a worker of iniquity, ran up and came against the shoulder of Jesus, wishing to make sport of Him, or to hurt Him, if he could.

And Jesus said to him:

Thou shalt not go back safe and sound from the way that thou goest.

And immediately he fell down, and died.

And the parents of the dead boy, who had seen what happened, cried out, saying:

Where does this child come from?

It is manifest that every word that he says is true; and it is often accomplished before he speaks.

And the parents of the dead boy came to Joseph, and said to him:

Take away that Jesus from this place, for he cannot live with us in this town; or at least teach him to bless, and not to curse.

And Joseph came up to Jesus, and admonished Him, saying:

Why doest thou such things?

For already many are in grief and against thee, and hate us on thy account, and we endure the reproaches of men because of thee.

And Jesus answered and said unto Joseph:

No one is a wise son but he whom his father hath taught, according to the knowledge of this time; and a father's curse can hurt none but evil-doers.

Then they came together against Jesus, and accused him to Joseph.

When Joseph saw this, he was in great terror, fearing the violence and uproar of the people of Israel.

And the same hour Jesus seized the dead boy by the ear, and lifted him up from the earth in the sight of all:

and they saw Jesus speaking to him like a father to his son.

And his spirit came back to him, and he revived.

And all of them wondered.

Chapter 30

Now a certain Jewish schoolmaster named Zachyas [1] heard Jesus thus speaking; and seeing that He could not be overcome, from knowing the power that was in Him, [2] he became angry, and began rudely and foolishly, and without fear, to speak against Joseph.

And he said: Dost thou not wish to entrust me with thy son, that he may be instructed in human learning and in reverence?

But I see that Mary and thyself have more regard for your son than for what the elders of the people of Israel say against him.

You should have given more honour to us, the elders of the whole church of Israel, both that he might be on terms of mutual affection with the children, and that among us he might be instructed in Jewish learning.

Joseph, on the other hand, said to him:

And is there any one who can keep this child, and teach him?

But if thou canst keep him and teach him, we by no means hinder him from being taught by thee those things which are learned by all.

And Jesus, having heard what Zachyas had said, answered and said unto him:

The precepts of the law which thou hast just spoken of, and all the things that thou hast named, must be kept by those who are instructed in human learning; but I am a stranger to your law-courts, because I have no father after the flesh.

Thou who readest the law, and art learned in it, abidest in the law; but I was before the law.

But since thou thinkest that no one is equal to thee in learning, thou shalt be taught by me, that no other can teach anything but those things which thou hast named.

But he alone can who is worthy. [3] For when I shall be exalted on earth, I will cause to cease all mention of your genealogy.

For thou knowest not when thou wast born:

I alone know when you were born, and how long your life on earth will be.

Then all who heard these words were struck with astonishment, and cried out: Oh! oh! oh! this marvellously great and wonderful mystery.

Never have we heard the like!

Never has it been heard from any one else, nor has it been said or at any time heard by the prophets, or the Pharisees, or the scribes.

We know whence he is sprung, and he is scarcely five years old; and whence does he speak these words?

The Pharisees answered:

We have never heard such words spoken by any other child so young.

And Jesus answered and said unto them:

At this do ye wonder, that such things are said by a child?

Why, then, do ye not believe me in those things which I have said to you?

And you all wonder because I said to you that I know when you were born.

I will tell you greater things, that you may wonder more.

I have seen Abraham, whom you call your father, and have spoken with him; and he has seen me. [4]And when they heard this they held their tongues, nor did any of them dare to speak.

And Jesus said to them:

I have been among you with children, and you have not known me; I have spoken to you as to wise men, and you have not understood my words; because you are younger than I am, [5] and of little faith.

Footnotes:

1. Other forms of the name are: Zachias, Zachameus, Zacheus, Zachaeus.
2. Or, seeing that there was in Him an insuperable knowledge of virtue.
3. Tischendorf thinks that the text is corrupt. But the meaning seems to be: You are not a whit better than your neighbours; for all of you teach what you have named, and you can teach nothing else. But he alone (ipse, i.e., Christ) can teach more who is worthy.
4. Comp. John viii. 56-58.
5. Or, literally, inferior to me.

Chapter 31

A second time the master Zachyas, doctor of the law, said to Joseph and Mary:

Give me the boy, and I shall hand him over to master Levi, who shall teach him his letters and instruct him.

Then Joseph and Mary, soothing Jesus, took Him to the schools, that He might be taught His letters by old Levi.

And as soon as He went in He held His tongue. And the master Levi said one letter to Jesus, and, beginning from the first letter Aleph, said to Him:

Answer.

But Jesus was silent, and answered nothing.

Wherefore the preceptor Levi was angry, and seized his storax-tree rod, and struck Him on the head.

And Jesus said to the teacher Levi:

Why dost thou strike me?

Thou shalt know in truth, that He who is struck can teach him who strikes Him more than He can be taught by him.

For I can teach you those very things that you are saying.

But all these are blind who speak and hear, like sounding brass or tinkling cymbal, in which there is no perception of those things which are meant by their sound. [1]And Jesus in addition said to Zachyas:

Every letter from Aleph even to Thet [2] is known by its arrangement.

Say thou first, therefore, what Thet is, and I will tell thee what Aleph is.

And again Jesus said to them:

Those who do not know Aleph, how can they say Thet, the hypocrites?

Tell me what the first one, Aleph, is; and I shall then believe you when you have said Beth.

And Jesus began to ask the names of the letters one by one, and said:

Let the master of the law tell us what the first letter is, or why it has many triangles, gradate, subacute, mediate, obduced, produced, erect, prostrate, curvistrate. [3]And when Levi heard this, he was thunderstruck at such an arrangement of the names of the letters.

Then he began in the hearing of all to cry out, and say: Ought such a one to live on the earth? Yea, he ought to be hung on the great cross.

For he can put out fire, and make sport of other modes of punishment.

I think that he lived before the flood, and was born before the deluge.

For what womb bore him? or what mother brought him forth? or what breasts gave him suck?

I flee before him; I am not able to withstand the words from his mouth, but my heart is astounded to hear such words.

I do not think that any man can understand what he says, except God were with him.

Now I, unfortunate wretch, have given myself up to be a laughing-stock to him.

For when I thought I had a scholar, I, not knowing him, have found my master.

What shall I say? I cannot withstand the words of this child:

I shall now flee from this town, because I cannot understand them.

An old man like me has been beaten by a boy, because I can find neither beginning nor end of what he says.

For it is no easy matter to find a beginning of himself. [4]I tell you of a certainty, I am not lying, that to my eyes the proceedings of this boy, the commencement of his conversation, and the upshot of his intention, seem to have nothing in common with mortal man.

Here then I do not know whether he be a wizard or a god; or at least an angel of God speaks in him.

Whence he is, or where he comes from, or who he will turn out to be, I know not.

Then Jesus, smiling at him with a joyful countenance, said in a commanding voice to all the sons of Israel standing by and hearing:

Let the unfruitful bring forth fruit, and the blind see, and the lame walk right, and the poor enjoy the good things of this life, and the dead live, that each may return to his original state, and abide in Him who is the root of life and of perpetual sweetness.

And when the child Jesus had said this, forthwith all who had fallen under malignant diseases were restored.

And they did not dare to say anything more to Him, or to hear anything from Him.

Footnotes:

1. 1 Cor. xiii. 1, xiv. 7.

2. Tau, and not Teth, is the last letter of the Hebrew alphabet.

3. The original--triangulos gradatos, subacutos, mediatos, obductos, productos, erectos, stratos, curvistratos--is hopelessly corrupt. Compare the passages in the following Apocrypha. [The Gospel of Thomas, first Greek form, chaps. 6, 7, and parallel passages.--R.] It obviously, however, refers to the Pentalpha, Pentacle, or Solomon's Seal, celebrated in the remains of the magical books that have come down to us under the names of Hermas and the Pythagoreans. The Pentalpha was formed by joining by straight lines the alternate angles of a regular pentagon, and thus contained numerous triangles. The Pythagoreans called it the Hygiea or symbol of health, and it was frequently engraved on amulets and coins. It is still, if the books are to be trusted, a symbol of power in the higher grades of freemasonry.

4. i.e., It is not wonderful that we do not understand what he says, for we do not know what he is.

Chapter 32

After these things, Joseph and Mary departed thence with Jesus into the city of Nazareth; and He remained there with His parents.

And on the first of the week, when Jesus was playing with the children on the roof of a certain house, it happened that one of the children pushed another down from the roof to the ground, and he was killed.

And the parents of the dead boy, who had not seen this, cried out against Joseph and Mary, saying:

Your son has thrown our son down to the ground, and he is dead.

But Jesus was silent, and answered them nothing.

And Joseph and Mary came in haste to Jesus; and His mother asked Him, saying:

My lord, tell me if thou didst throw him down.

And immediately Jesus went down from the roof to the ground, and called the boy by his name, Zeno.

And he answered Him:

My lord.

And Jesus said to him:

Was it I that threw thee down from the roof to the ground?

And he said:

No, my lord.

And the parents of the boy who had been dead wondered, and honoured Jesus for the miracle that had been wrought.

And Joseph and Mary departed thence with Jesus to Jericho.

Chapter 33

Now Jesus was six years old, and His mother sent Him with a pitcher to the fountain to draw water with the children.

And it came to pass, after He had drawn the water, that one of the children came against Him, and struck the pitcher, and broke it.

But Jesus stretched out the cloak which He had on, and took up in His cloak as much water as there had been in the pitcher, and carried it to His mother.

And when she saw it she wondered, and reflected within herself, and laid up all these things in her heart. [1]

Footnote:

1. Luke ii. 19.

Chapter 34

Again, on a certain day, He went forth into the field, and took a little wheat from His mother's barn, and sowed it Himself.

And it sprang up, and grew, and multiplied exceedingly.

And at last it came to pass that He Himself reaped it, and gathered as the produce of it three kors, [1] and gave it to His numerous acquaintances. [2]

Footnotes:

1. The kor or chomer was, according to Jahn, equal to 32 pecks 1 pint.
2. Multiplicibus suis.

Chapter 35

There is a road going out of Jericho and leading to the river Jordan, to the place where the children of Israel crossed:

and there the ark of the covenant is said to have rested.

And Jesus was eight years old, and He went out of Jericho, and went towards the Jordan.

And there was beside the road, near the bank of the Jordan, a cave where a lioness was nursing her cubs; and no one was safe to walk that way.

Jesus then, coming from Jericho, and knowing that in that cave the lioness had brought forth her young, went into it in the sight of all.

And when the lions saw Jesus, they ran to meet Him, and adored Him.

And Jesus was sitting in the cavern, and the lion's cubs ran hither and thither round His feet, fawning upon Him, and sporting.

And the older lions, with their heads bowed down, stood at a distance, and adored Him, and fawned upon Him with their tails.

Then the people who were standing afar off, not seeing Jesus, said:

Unless he or his parents had committed grievous sins, he would not of his own accord have offered himself up to the lions.

And when the people were thus reflecting within themselves, and were lying under great sorrow, behold, on a sudden, in the sight of the people, Jesus came out of the cave, and the lions went before Him, and the lion's cubs played with each other before His feet.

And the parents of Jesus stood afar off, with their heads bowed down, and watched; likewise also the people stood at a distance, on account of the lions; for they did not dare to come close to them.

Then Jesus began to say to the people:

How much better are the beasts than you, seeing that they recognise their Lord, and glorify Him; while you men, who have been made after the image and likeness of God, do not know Him!

Beasts know me, and are tame; men see me, and do not acknowledge me.

Chapter 36

After these things Jesus crossed the Jordan, in the sight of them all, with the lions; and the water of the Jordan was divided on the right hand and on the left. [1]Then He said to the lions, in the hearing of all:

Go in peace, and hurt no one; but neither let man injure you, until you return to the place whence you have come forth. And they, bidding Him farewell, not only with their gestures but with their voices, went to their own place.

But Jesus returned to His mother.

Footnote:
1. Josh. iii. 16; 2 Kings ii. 8.

Chapter 37

Now Joseph [1] was a carpenter, and used to make nothing else of wood but ox-yokes, and ploughs, and implements of husbandry, and wooden beds.

And it came to pass that a certain young man ordered him to make for him a couch six cubits long.

And Joseph commanded his servant [2] to cut the wood with an iron saw, according to the measure which he had sent.

But he did not keep to the prescribed measure, but made one piece of wood shorter than the other.

And Joseph was in perplexity, and began to consider what he was to do about this.

And when Jesus saw him in this state of cogitation, seeing that it was a matter of impossibility to him, He addresses him with words of comfort, saying:

Come, let us take hold of the ends of the pieces of wood, and let us put them together, end to end, and let us fit them exactly to each other, and draw to us, for we shall be able to make them equal. Then Joseph did what he was bid, for he knew that He could do whatever He wished.

And Joseph took hold of the ends of the pieces of wood, and brought them together against the wall next himself, and Jesus took hold of the other ends of the pieces of wood, and drew the shorter piece to Him, and made it of the same length as the longer one.

And He said to Joseph:

Go and work, and do what thou hast promised to do. And Joseph did what he had promised. [3]

Footnotes:
1. One of the mss. tells the story, not of Joseph, but of a certain builder, a worker in wood.
2. Lit., boy.
3. One of themss. here inserts: And when Jesus was with other children He repeatedly went up and sat down upon a balcony, and many of them began to do likewise, and they fell down and broke their legs and arms. And the Lord Jesus healed them all.

Chapter 38

And it came to pass a second time, that Joseph and Mary were asked by the people that Jesus should be taught His letters in school.

They did not refuse to do so; and according to the commandment of the elders, they took Him to a master to be instructed in human learning.

Then the master began to teach Him in an imperious tone, saying:

Say Alpha. [1] And Jesus said to him:

Do thou tell me first what Betha is, and I will tell thee what Alpha is.

And upon this the master got angry and struck Jesus; and no sooner had he struck Him, than he fell down dead.

And Jesus went home again to His mother.

And Joseph, being afraid, called Mary to him, and said to her:

Know of a surety that my soul is sorrowful even unto death on account of this child.

For it is very likely that at some time or other some one will strike him in malice, and he will die.

But Mary answered and said:

O man of God! do not believe that this is possible.

You may believe to a certainty that He who has sent him to be born among men will Himself guard him from all mischief, and will in His own name preserve him from evil.

Footnote:
1. Note that the letters are Greek here.

Chapter 39

Again the Jews asked Mary and Joseph a third time to coax Him to go to another master to learn.

And Joseph and Mary, fearing the people, and the overbearing of the princes, and the threats of the priests, led Him again to school, knowing that He could learn nothing from man, because He had perfect knowledge from God only.

And when Jesus had entered the school, led by the Holy Spirit, He took the book out of the hand of the master who was teaching the law, and in the sight and hearing of all the people began to read, not indeed what was written in their book; but He spoke in the Spirit of the living God, as if a stream of water were gushing forth from a living fountain, and the fountain remained always full.

And with such power He taught the people the great things of the living God, that the master himself fell to the ground and adored Him.

And the heart of the people who sat and heard Him saying such things was turned into astonishment.

And when Joseph heard of this, he came running to Jesus, fearing that the master himself was dead.

And when the master saw him, he said to him:

Thou hast given me not a scholar, but a master; and who can withstand his words?

Then was fulfilled that which was spoken by the Psalmist:

The river of God is full of water:

Thou hast prepared them corn, for so is the provision for it. [1]

Footnote:

1. Ps. lxv. 9.

Chapter 40

After these things Joseph departed thence with Mary and Jesus to go into Capernaum by the sea-shore, on account of the malice of his adversaries.

And when Jesus was living in Capernaum, there was in the city a man named Joseph, exceedingly rich.

But he had wasted away under his infirmity, and died, and was lying dead in his couch.

And when Jesus heard them in the city mourning, and weeping, and lamenting over the dead man, He said to Joseph:

Why dost thou not afford the benefit of thy favour to this man, seeing that he is called by thy name?

And Joseph answered him:

How have I any power or ability to afford him a benefit?

And Jesus said to him:

Take the handkerchief which is upon thy head, and go and put it on the face of the dead man, and say to him:

Christ heal thee; and immediately the dead man will be healed, and will rise from his couch.

And when Joseph heard this, he went away at the command of Jesus, and ran, and entered the house of the dead man, and put the handkerchief which he was wearing on his head upon the face of him who was lying in the couch, and said:

Jesus heal thee.

And forthwith the dead man rose from his bed, and asked who Jesus was. [1]

Footnote:

1. In place of this chapter, one of the mss. has a number of miracles copied from the canonical Gospels--the walking on the sea, the feeding of the five thousand, the healing of a blind man, the raising of Lazarus, and the raising of a certain young man.

Chapter 41

And they went away from Capernaum into the city which is called Bethlehem; and Joseph lived with Mary in his own house, and Jesus with them.

And on a certain day Joseph called to him his first-born son James, [1688] and sent him into the vegetable garden to gather vegetables for the purpose of making broth.

And Jesus followed His brother James into the garden; but Joseph and Mary did not know this. And while James was collecting the vegetables, a viper suddenly came out of a hole and struck his hand, [1689] and he began to cry out from excessive pain.

And, becoming exhausted, he said, with a bitter cry: Alas! alas! an accursed viper has struck my hand.

And Jesus, who was standing opposite to him, at the bitter cry ran up to James, and took hold of his hand; and all that He did was to blow on the hand of James, and cool it:

and immediately James was healed, and the serpent died. And Joseph and Mary did not know what had been done; but at the cry of James, and the command of Jesus, they ran to the garden, and found the serpent already dead, and James quite cured.

Footnotes:
1. According to the tradition preserved by Hegesippus and Tertullian, James and Judas were husbandmen.   See Apost. Const., ch. lxvii.
2. Comp. Acts xxviii.

Chapter 42

And Joseph having come to a feast with his sons, James, Joseph, and Judah, and Simeon and his two daughters, Jesus met them, with Mary His mother, along with her sister Mary of Cleophas, whom the Lord God had given to her father Cleophas and her mother Anna, because they had offered Mary the mother of Jesus to the Lord.

And she was called by the same name, Mary, for the consolation of her parents. [1]And when they had come together, Jesus sanctified and blessed them, and He was the first to begin to eat and drink; for none of them dared to eat or drink, or to sit at table, or to break bread, until He had sanctified them, and first done so.

And if He happened to be absent, they used to wait until He should do this.

And when He did not wish to come for refreshment, neither Joseph nor Mary, nor the sons of Joseph, His brothers, came.

And, indeed, these brothers, keeping His life as a lamp before their eyes, observed Him, and feared Him.

And when Jesus slept, whether by day or by night, the brightness of God shone upon Him.

To whom be all praise and glory for ever and ever.

Amen, amen.

Footnote:
1. One of themss. has: And when Joseph, worn out with old age, died and was buried with his parents, the blessed Mary lived with her nephews, or with the children of her sisters; for Anna and Emerina were sisters. Of Emerina was born Elizabeth, the mother of John the Baptist. And as Anna, the mother of the blessed Mary, was very beautiful, when Joachim was dead she was married to Cleophas, by whom she had a second daughter. She called her Mary, and gave her to Alphaeus to wife; and of her was born James the son of Alphaeus, and Philip his brother. And her second husband having died, Anna was married to a third husband named Salome, by whom she had a third daughter. She called her Mary likewise, and gave her to Zebedee to wife; and of her were born James the son of Zebedee, and John the Evangelist. Another passage to the same effect is prefixed to the Gospel. It reads Emeria for Emerina, and Joseph for Philip. It ends with a quotation from Jerome's sermon upon Easter:--We read in the Gospels that there were four Mary's--first, the mother of the Lord the Saviour; second, His maternal aunt, who was called Mary of Cleophas; third, Mary the mother of James and Joseph, fourth, Mary Magdalene--though some maintain that the mother of James and Joseph was His aunt. The same ms. thus concludes: The holy Apostle and Evangelist John with his own hand wrote this little book in Hebrew, and the learned doctor Jerome rendered it from Hebrew into Latin.

The Gospel of the Nativity of Mary

Chapter 1

The blessed and glorious ever-virgin Mary, sprung from the royal stock and family of David, born in the city of Nazareth, was brought up at Jerusalem in the temple of the Lord.

Her father was named Joachim, and her mother Anna.

Her father's house was from Galilee and the city of Nazareth, but her mother's family from Bethlehem.

Their life was guileless and right before the Lord, and irreproachable and pious before men.

For they divided all their substance into three parts. One part they spent upon the temple and the temple servants; another they distributed to strangers and the poor; the third they reserved, for themselves and the necessities of their family.

Thus, dear to God, kind to men, for about twenty years they lived in their own house, a chaste married life, without having any children.

Nevertheless they vowed that, should the Lord happen to give them offspring, they would deliver it to the service of the Lord; on which account also they used to visit the temple of the Lord at each of the feasts during the year.

Chapter 2

And it came to pass that the festival of the dedication [1] was at hand; wherefore also Joachim went up to Jerusalem with some men of his own tribe.

Now at that time Issachar [2] was high priest there. And when he saw Joachim with his offering among his other fellow-citizens, he despised him, and spurned his gifts, asking why he, who had no offspring, presumed to stand among those who had; saying that his gifts could not by any means be acceptable to God, since He had deemed him unworthy of off-spring:

for the Scripture said, Cursed is every one who has not begot a male or a female in Israel. [3] He said, therefore, that he ought first to be freed from this curse by the begetting of children; and then, and then only, that he should come into the presence of the Lord with his offerings.

And Joachim, covered with shame from this reproach that was thrown in his teeth, retired to the shepherds, who were in their pastures with their flocks; nor would he return home, lest perchance he might be branded with the same reproach by those of his own tribe, who were there at the time, and had heard this from the priest.

Footnotes:

1. 1 Macc. iv. 52-59; 2 Macc. x. 1-8; John x. 22; Josephus, Antiq. xii. 7.

2. The spelling in the text is that in the Hebrew, the Samaritan Codex, the Targums, and the Textus Receptus. There is no Issachar in the list of high priests.

3. This statement does not occur in Scripture in so many words; but sterility was looked upon as a punishment from God.

Chapter 3

Now, when he had been there for some time, on a certain day when he was alone, an angel of the Lord stood by him in a great light.

And when he was disturbed at his appearance, the angel who had appeared to him restrained his fear, saying:

Fear not, Joachim, nor be disturbed by my appearance; for I am the angel of the Lord, sent by Him to thee to tell thee that thy prayers have been heard, and that thy charitable deeds have gone up into His presence. [1]For He hath seen thy shame, and hath heard the reproach of unfruitfulness which has been unjustly brought against thee.

For God is the avenger of sin, not of nature: and, therefore, when He shuts up the womb of any one, He does so that He may miraculously open it again; so that that which is born may be acknowledged to be not of lust, but of the gift of God.

For was it not the case that the first mother of your nation--Sarah--was barren up to her eightieth year? ²And, nevertheless, in extreme old age she brought forth Isaac, to whom the promise was renewed of the blessing of all nations.

Rachel also, so favoured of the Lord, and so beloved by holy Jacob, was long barren; and yet she brought forth Joseph, who was not only the lord of Egypt, but the deliverer of many nations who were ready to perish of hunger.

Who among the judges was either stronger than Samson, or more holy than Samuel?

And yet the mothers of both were barren.

If, therefore, the reasonableness of my words does not persuade thee, believe in fact that conceptions very late in life, and births in the case of women that have been barren, are usually attended with something wonderful.

Accordingly thy wife Anna will bring forth a daughter to thee, and thou shalt call her name Mary:

she shall be, as you have vowed, consecrated to the Lord from her infancy, and she shall be filled with the Holy Spirit, even from her mother's womb.

She shall neither eat nor drink any unclean thing, nor shall she spend her life among the crowds of the people without, but in the temple of the Lord, that it may not be possible either to say, or so much as to suspect, any evil concerning her.

Therefore, when she has grown up, just as she herself shall be miraculously born of a barren woman, so in an incomparable manner she, a virgin, shall bring forth the Son of the Most High, who shall be called Jesus, and who, according to the etymology of His name, shall be the Saviour of all nations.

And this shall be the sign to thee of those things which I announce:

When thou shalt come to the Golden gate in Jerusalem, thou shalt there meet Anna thy wife, who, lately anxious from the delay of thy return, will then rejoice at the sight of thee.

Having thus spoken, the angel departed from him.

Footnotes:
1. Comp. Acts x. 4.
2. Gen. xvii. 17. Sarah was ninety years old.

Chapter 4

Thereafter he appeared to Anna his wife, saying:

Fear not, Anna, nor think that it is a phantom which thou seest.

For I am that angel who has presented your prayers and alms before God; and now have I been sent to you to announce to you that thou shalt bring forth a daughter, who shall be called Mary, and who shall be blessed above all women. She, full of the favour of the Lord even from her birth, shall remain three years in her father's house until she be weaned.

Thereafter, being delivered to the service of the Lord, she shall not depart from the temple until she reach the years of discretion.

There, in fine, serving God day and night in fastings and prayers, she shall abstain from every unclean thing; she shall never know man, but alone, without example, immaculate, uncorrupted, without intercourse with man, she, a virgin, shall bring forth a son; she, His hand-maiden, shall bring forth the Lord--both in grace, and in name, and in work, the Saviour of the world.

Wherefore arise, and go up to Jerusalem; and when thou shalt come to the gate which, because it is plated with gold, is called Golden, there, for a sign, thou shalt meet thy husband, for whose safety thou hast been anxious.

And when these things shall have so happened, know that what I announce shall without doubt be fulfilled.

Chapter 5

Therefore, as the angel had commanded, both of them setting out from the place where they were, went up to Jerusalem; and when they had come to the place pointed out by the angel's prophecy, there they met each other.

Then, rejoicing at seeing each other, and secure in the certainty of the promised offspring, they gave the thanks due to the Lord, who exalteth the humble.

And so, having worshipped the Lord, they returned home, and awaited in certainty and in gladness the divine promise.

Anna therefore conceived, and brought forth a daughter; and according to the command of the angel, her parents called her name Mary.

Chapter 6

And when the circle of three years had rolled round, and the time of her weaning was fulfilled, they brought the virgin to the temple of the Lord with offerings.

Now there were round the temple, according to the fifteen Psalms of Degrees, [1] fifteen steps going up; for, on account of the temple having been built on a mountain, the altar of burnt-offering, which stood outside, could not be reached except by steps.

On one of these, then, her parents placed the little girl, the blessed virgin Mary.

And when they were putting off the clothes which they had worn on the journey, and were putting on, as was usual, others that were neater and cleaner, the virgin of the Lord went up all the steps, one after the other, without the help of any one leading her or lifting her, in such a manner that, in this respect at least, you would think that she had already attained full age.

For already the Lord in the infancy of His virgin wrought a great thing, and by the indication of this miracle foreshowed how great she was to be.

Therefore, a sacrifice having been offered according to the custom of the law, and their vow being perfected, they left the virgin within the enclosures of the temple, there to be educated with the other virgins, and themselves returned home.

Footnote:

1. Ps. cxx.-cxxxiv. The fifteen steps led from the court of the women to that of the men.

Chapter 7

But the virgin of the Lord advanced in age and in virtues; and though, in the words of the Psalmist, her father and mother had forsaken her, the Lord took her up. [1] For daily was she visited by angels, daily did she enjoy a divine vision, which preserved her from all evil, and made her to abound in all good.

And so she reached her fourteenth year; and not only were the wicked unable to charge her with anything worthy of reproach, but all the good, who knew her life and conversation, judged her to be worthy of admiration.

Then the high priest publicly announced that the virgins who were publicly settled in the temple, and had reached this time of life, should return home and get married, according to the custom of the nation and the ripeness of their years.

The others readily obeyed this command; but Mary alone, the virgin of the Lord, answered that she could not do this, saying both that her parents had devoted her to the service of the Lord, and that, moreover, she herself had made to the Lord a vow of virginity, which she would never violate by any intercourse with man.

And the high priest, being placed in great perplexity of mind, seeing that neither did he think that the vow should be broken contrary to the Scripture, which says, Vow and pay, [2] nor did he dare to introduce a custom unknown to the nation, gave order that at the festival, which was at hand, all the chief persons from Jerusalem and the neighbourhood should be present, in order that from their advice he might know what was to be done in so doubtful a case.

And when this took place, they resolved unanimously that the Lord should be consulted upon this matter.

And when they all bowed themselves in prayer, the high priest went to consult God in the usual way.

Nor had they long to wait:

in the hearing of all a voice issued from the oracle and from the mercy-seat, that, according to the prophecy of Isaiah, a man should be sought out to whom the virgin ought to be entrusted and espoused.

For it is clear that Isaiah says:

A rod shall come forth from the root of Jesse, and a flower shall ascend from his root; and the Spirit of the Lord shall rest upon him, the spirit of wisdom and understanding, the spirit of counsel and strength, the spirit of wisdom and piety; and he shall be filled with the spirit of the fear of the Lord.[2] According to this prophecy, therefore, he predicted that all of the house and family of David that were unmarried and fit for marriage should bring there rods to the altar; and that he whose rod after it was brought should produce a flower, and upon the end of whose rod the Spirit of the Lord should settle in the form of a dove, was the man to whom the virgin ought to be entrusted and espoused.

Footnotes:

1. Ps. xxvii. 10.
2. Ps. lxxvi. 11.

3. Isa. xi. 1, 2.

Chapter 8

Now there was among the rest Joseph, of the house and family of David, a man of great age: and when all brought there rods, according to the order, he alone withheld his.

Wherefore, when nothing in conformity with the divine voice appeared, the high priest thought it necessary to consult God a second time; and He answered, that of those who had been designated, he alone to whom the virgin ought to be espoused had not brought his rod.

Joseph, therefore, was found out.

For when he had brought his rod, and the dove came from heaven; and settled upon the top of it, it clearly appeared to all that he was the man to whom the virgin should be espoused.

Therefore, the usual ceremonies of betrothal having been gone through, he went back to the city of Bethlehem to put his house in order, and to procure things necessary for the marriage.

But Mary, the virgin of the Lord, with seven other virgins of her own age, and who had been weaned at the same time, whom she had received from the priest, returned to the house of her parents in Galilee.

Chapter 9

And in those days, that is, at the time of her first coming into Galilee, the angel Gabriel was sent to her by God, to announce to her the conception of the Lord, and to explain to her the manner and order of the conception.

Accordingly, going in, he filled the chamber where she was with a great light; and most courteously saluting her, he said:

Hail, Mary!

O virgin highly favoured by the Lord, virgin full of grace, the Lord is with thee; blessed art thou above all women, blessed above all men that have been hitherto born. [1] And the virgin, who was already well acquainted with angelic faces, and was not unused to the light from heaven, was neither terrified by the vision of the angel, nor astonished at the greatness of the light, but only perplexed by his words; and she began to consider of what nature a salutation so unusual could be, or what it could portend, or what end it could have.

And the angel, divinely inspired, taking up this thought, says:

Fear not, Mary, as if anything contrary to thy chastity were hid under this salutation.

For in choosing chastity, thou hast found favour with the Lord; and therefore thou, a virgin, shalt conceive without sin, and shalt bring forth a son.

He shall be great, because He shall rule from sea to sea, and from the river even to the ends of the earth; [2] and He shall be called the Son of the Most High, because He who is born on earth in humiliation, reigns in heaven in exaltation; and the Lord God will give Him the throne of His father David, and He shall reign in the house of Jacob for ever, and of His kingdom there shall be no end; [3] forasmuch as He is King of kings and Lord of lords, [4] and His throne is from everlasting to everlasting.

The virgin did not doubt these words of the angel; but wishing to know the manner of it, she answered:

How can that come to pass?

For while, according to my vow, I never know man, how can I bring forth without the addition of man's seed?

To this the angel says:

Think not, Mary, that thou shalt conceive in the manner of mankind:

for without any intercourse with man, thou, a virgin, wilt conceive; thou, a virgin, wilt bring forth; thou, a virgin, wilt nurse:

for the Holy Spirit shall come upon thee, and the power of the Most High shall overshadow thee, [5] without any of the heats of lust; and therefore that which shall be born of thee shall alone be holy, because it alone, being conceived and born without sin, shall be called the Son of God.

Then Mary stretched forth her hands, and raised her eyes to heaven, and said:

Behold the hand-maiden of the Lord, for I am not worthy of the name of lady; let it be to me according to thy word.

It will be long, and perhaps to some even tedious, if we insert in this little work every thing which we read of as having preceded or followed the Lord's nativity:

wherefore, omitting those things which have been more fully written in the Gospel, let us come to those which are held to be less worthy of being narrated.

Footnotes:
1. Luke i. 26-38.
2. Ps. lxxii. 8.
3. Luke i. 32, 33.
4. Rev. xix. 16.
5. Luke i. 35.

Chapter 10

Joseph therefore came from Judaea into Galilee, intending to marry the virgin who had been betrothed to him; for already three months had elapsed, and it was the beginning of the fourth since she had been betrothed to him.

In the meantime, it was evident from her shape that she was pregnant, nor could she conceal this from Joseph.

For in consequence of his being betrothed to her, coming to her more freely and speaking to her more familiarly, he found out that she was with child.

He began then to be in great doubt and perplexity, because he did not know what was best for him to do.

For, being a just man, he was not willing to expose her; nor, being a pious man, to injure her fair fame by a suspicion of fornication.

He came to the conclusion, therefore, privately to dissolve their contract, and to send her away secretly.

And while he thought on these things, behold, an angel of the Lord appeared to him in his sleep, saying:

Joseph, thou son of David, fear not; that is, do not have any suspicion of fornication in the virgin, or think any evil of her; and fear not to take her as thy wife:

for that which is begotten in her, and which now vexes thy soul, is the work not of man, but of the Holy Spirit.

For she alone of all virgins shall bring forth the Son of God, and thou shalt call His name Jesus, that is, Saviour; for He shall save His people from their sins. Therefore Joseph, according to the command of the angel, took the virgin as his wife; nevertheless he knew her not, but took care of her, and kept her in chastity. [1]And now the ninth month from her conception was at hand, when Joseph, taking with him his wife along with what things he needed, went to Bethlehem, the city from which he came.

And it came to pass, while they were there, that her days were fulfilled that she should bring forth; and she brought forth her first-born son, as the holy evangelists have shown, our Lord Jesus Christ, who with the Father and the Son [2] and the Holy Ghost lives and reigns God from everlasting to everlasting.

Footnotes:
1. Matt. i. 18-24.
2. Thus in the original.

The History of Joseph the Carpenter

In the name of God, of one essence and three persons.
The History of the death of our father, the holy old man, Joseph the carpenter.
May his blessings and prayers preserve us all, O brethren!
Amen.
His whole life was one hundred and eleven years, and his departure from this world happened on the twenty-sixth of the month Abib, which answers to the month Ab.
May his prayer preserve us!
Amen.
And, indeed, it was our Lord Jesus Christ Himself who related this history to His holy disciples on the Mount of Olives, and all Joseph's labour, and the end of his days.
And the holy apostles have preserved this conversation, and have left it written down in the library at Jerusalem.
May their prayers preserve us!
Amen. [1]

1.

It happened one day, when the Saviour, our Master, God, and Saviour Jesus Christ, was sitting along with His disciples, and they were all assembled on the Mount of Olives, that He said to them:
O my brethren and friends, sons of the Father who has chosen you from all men, you know that I have often told you that I must be crucified, and must die for the salvation of Adam and his posterity, and that I shall rise from the dead.
Now I shall commit to you the doctrine of the holy gospel formerly announced to you, that you may declare it throughout the whole world.
And I shall endow you with power from on high, and fill you with the Holy Spirit. [2] And you shall declare to all nations repentance and remission of sins. [3] For a single cup of water, [4] if a man shall find it in the world to come, is greater and better than all the wealth of this whole world.
And as much ground as one foot can occupy in the house of my Father, is greater and more excellent than all the riches of the earth.
Yea, a single hour in the joyful dwelling of the pious is more blessed and more precious than a thousand years among sinners: [5] inasmuch as their weeping and lamentation shall not come to an end, and their tears shall not cease, nor shall they find for themselves consolation and repose at any time for ever.
And now, O my honoured members, go declare to all nations, tell them, and say to them:
Verily the Saviour diligently inquires into the inheritance which is due, and is the administrator of justice.
And the angels will cast down their enemies, and will fight for them in the day of conflict.
And He will examine every single foolish and idle word which men speak, and they shall give an account of it. [6] For as no one shall escape death, so also the works of every man shall be laid open on the day of judgment, whether they have been good or evil. [7] Tell them also this word which I have said to you to-day:
Let not the strong man glory in his strength, nor the rich man in his riches; but let him who wishes to glory, glory in the Lord. [8]

2.

There was a man whose name was Joseph, sprung from a family of Bethlehem, a town of Judah, and the city of King David.
This same man, being well furnished with wisdom and learning, was made a priest in the temple of the Lord.
He was, besides, skilful in his trade, which was that of a carpenter; and after the manner of all men, he married a wife.
Moreover, he begot for himself sons and daughters, four sons, namely, and two daughters.

The Forgotten Bible

Now these are their names--Judas, Justus, James, and Simon.

The names of the two daughters were Assia and Lydia.

At length the wife of righteous Joseph, a woman intent on the divine glory in all her works, departed this life.

But Joseph, that righteous man, my father after the flesh, and the spouse of my mother Mary, went away with his sons to his trade, practising the art of a carpenter.

3.

Now when righteous Joseph became a widower, my mother Mary, blessed, holy, and pure, was already twelve years old.

For her parents offered her in the temple when she was three years of age, and she remained in the temple of the Lord nine years.

Then when the priests saw that the virgin, holy and God-fearing, was growing up, they spoke to each other, saying:

Let us search out a man, righteous and pious, to whom Mary may be entrusted until the time of her marriage; lest, if she remain in the temple, it happen to her as is wont to happen to women, and lest on that account we sin, and God be angry with us.

4.

Therefore they immediately sent out, and assembled twelve old men of the tribe of Judah.

And they wrote down the names of the twelve tribes of Israel.

And the lot fell upon the pious old man, righteous Joseph.

Then the priests answered, and said to my blessed mother:

Go with Joseph, and be with him till the time of your marriage.

Righteous Joseph therefore received my mother, and led her away to his own house.

And Mary found James the Less in his father's house, broken-hearted and sad on account of the loss of his mother, and she brought him up.

Hence Mary was called the mother of James. [9] Thereafter Joseph left her at home, and went away to the shop where he wrought at his trade of a carpenter.

And after the holy virgin had spent two years in his house her age was exactly fourteen years, including the time at which he received her.

5.

And I chose her of my own will, with the concurrence of my Father, and the counsel of the Holy Spirit.

And I was made flesh of her, by a mystery which transcends the grasp of created reason.

And three months after her conception the righteous man Joseph returned from the place where he worked at his trade; and when he found my virgin mother pregnant, he was greatly perplexed, and thought of sending her away secretly. [10]But from fear, and sorrow, and the anguish of his heart, he could endure neither to eat nor drink that day.

6.

But at mid-day there appeared to him in a dream the prince of the angels, the holy Gabriel, furnished with a command from my Father; and he said to him:

Joseph, son of David, fear not to take Mary as thy wife:

for she has conceived of the Holy Spirit; and she will bring forth a son, whose name shall be called Jesus.

He it is who shall rule all nations with a rod of iron. [11]Having thus spoken, the angel departed from him.

And Joseph rose from his sleep, and did as the angel of the Lord had said to him; and Mary abode with him. [12]

7.

Some time after that, there came forth an order from Augustus Caesar the king, that all the habitable world should be enrolled, each man in his own city.

The old man therefore, righteous Joseph, rose up and took the virgin Mary and came to Bethlehem, because the time of her bringing forth was at hand.

Joseph then inscribed his name in the list; for Joseph the son of David, whose spouse Mary was, was of the tribe of Judah.

And indeed Mary, my mother, brought me forth in Bethlehem, in a cave near the tomb of Rachel the wife of the patriarch Jacob, the mother of Joseph and Benjamin.

8.

But Satan went and told this to Herod the Great, the father of Archelaus.

And it was this same Herod [13] who ordered my friend and relative John to be beheaded.

Accordingly he searched for me diligently, thinking that my kingdom was to be of this world. [14] But Joseph, that pious old man, was warned of this by a dream. Therefore he rose and took Mary my mother, and I lay in her bosom. Salome [15] also was their fellow-traveller.

Having therefore set out from home, he retired into Egypt, and remained there the space of one whole year, until the hatred of Herod passed away.

9.

Now Herod died by the worst form of death, atoning for the shedding of the blood of the children whom he wickedly cut off, though there was no sin in them.

And that impious tyrant Herod being dead, they returned into the land of Israel, and lived in a city of Galilee which is called Nazareth.

And Joseph, going back to his trade of a carpenter, earned his living by the work of his hands; for, as the law of Moses had commanded, he never sought to live for nothing by another's labour.[16]

10.

At length, by increasing years, the old man arrived at a very advanced age.

He did not, however, labour under any bodily weakness, nor had his sight failed, nor had any tooth perished from his mouth. In mind also, for the whole time of his life, he never wandered; but like a boy he always in his business displayed youthful vigour, and his limbs remained unimpaired, and free from all pain.

His life, then, in all, amounted to one hundred and eleven years, his old age being prolonged to the utmost limit.

11.

Now Justus and Simeon, the elder sons of Joseph, were married, and had families of their own.

Both the daughters were likewise married, and lived in their own houses.

So there remained in Joseph's house, Judas and James the Less, and my virgin mother.

I moreover dwelt along with them, not otherwise than if I had been one of his sons.

But I passed all my life without fault.

Mary I called my mother, and Joseph father, and I obeyed them in all that they said; nor did I ever contend against them, but complied with their commands, as other men whom earth produces are wont to do; nor did I at any time arouse their anger, or give any word or answer in opposition to them.

On the contrary, I cherished them with great love, like the pupil of my eye.

12.

It came to pass, after these things, that the death of that old man, the pious Joseph, and his departure from this world, were approaching, as happens to other men who owe their origin to this earth.

And as his body was verging on dissolution, an angel of the Lord informed him that his death was now close at hand.

Therefore fear and great perplexity came upon him.

So he rose up and went to Jerusalem; and going into the temple of the Lord, he poured out his prayers there before the sanctuary, and said:

13.

O God! author of all consolation, God of all compassion, and Lord of the whole human race; God of my soul, body, and spirit; with supplications I reverence thee, O Lord and my God.

If now my days are ended, and the time draws near when I must leave this world, send me, I beseech Thee, the great Michael, the prince of Thy holy angels:

let him remain with me, that my wretched soul may depart from this afflicted body without trouble, without terror and impatience.

For great fear and intense sadness take hold of all bodies on the day of their death, whether it be man or woman, beast wild or tame, or whatever creeps on the ground or flies in the air.

At the last all creatures under heaven in whom is the breath of life are struck with horror, and their souls depart from their bodies with strong fear and great depression.

Now therefore, O Lord and my God, let Thy holy angel be present with his help to my soul and body, until they shall be dissevered from each other.

And let not the face of the angel, appointed my guardian from the day of my birth, [17] be turned away from me; but may he be the companion of my journey even until he bring me to Thee: let his countenance be pleasant and gladsome to me, and let him accompany me in peace.

And let not demons of frightful aspect come near me in the way in which I am to go, until I come to Thee in bliss.

And let not the doorkeepers hinder my soul from entering paradise.

And do not uncover my sins, and expose me to condemnation before Thy terrible tribunal.

Let not the lions rush in upon me; nor let the waves of the sea of fire overwhelm my soul--for this must every soul pass through [18] --before I have seen the glory of Thy Godhead.

O God, most righteous Judge, who in justice and equity wilt judge mankind, and wilt render unto each one according to his works, O Lord and my God, I beseech Thee, be present to me in Thy compassion, and enlighten my path that I may come to Thee; for Thou art a fountain overflowing with all good things, and with glory for evermore.

Amen.

14.

It came to pass thereafter, when he returned to his own house in the city of Nazareth, that he was seized by disease, and had to keep his bed.

And it was at this time that he died, according to the destiny of all mankind.

For this disease was very heavy upon him, and he had never been ill, as he now was, from the day of his birth.

And thus assuredly it pleased Christ [19] to order the destiny of righteous Joseph.

He lived forty years unmarried; thereafter his wife remained under his care forty-nine years, and then died.

And a year after her death, my mother, the blessed Mary, was entrusted to him by the priests, that he should keep her until the time of her marriage. She spent two years in his house; and in the third year of her stay with Joseph, in the fifteenth year of her age, she brought me forth on earth by a mystery which no creature can penetrate or understand, except myself, and my Father and the Holy Spirit, constituting one essence with myself. [20]

15.

The whole age of my father, therefore, that righteous old man, was one hundred and eleven years, my Father in heaven having so decreed. And the day on which his soul left his body was the twenty-sixth of the month Abib.

For now the fine gold began to lose its splendour, and the silver to be worn down by use--I mean his understanding and his wisdom.

He also loathed food and drink, and lost all his skill in his trade of carpentry, nor did he any more pay attention to it.

It came to pass, then, in the early dawn of the twenty-sixth day of Abib, that Joseph, that righteous old man, lying in his bed, was giving up his unquiet soul.

Wherefore he opened his mouth with many sighs, and struck his hands one against the other, and with a loud voice cried out, and spoke after the following manner:--

16.

Woe to the day on which I was born into the world!
Woe to the womb which bare me!
Woe to the bowels which admitted me!
Woe to the breasts which suckled me!
Woe to the feet upon which I sat and rested!
Woe to the hands which carried me and reared me until I grew up![21]For I was conceived in iniquity, and in sins did my mother desire me. [22]Woe to my tongue and my lips, which have brought forth and spoken vanity, detraction, falsehood, ignorance, derision, idle tales, craft, and hypocrisy!
Woe to mine eyes, which have looked upon scandalous things!
Woe to mine ears, which have delighted in the words of slanderers!
Woe to my hands, which have seized what did not of right belong to them!
Woe to my belly and my bowels, which have lusted after food unlawful to be eaten!
Woe to my throat, which like a fire has consumed all that it found!
Woe to my feet, which have too often walked in ways displeasing to God!
Woe to my body; and woe to my miserable soul, which has already turned aside from God its Maker! What shall I do when I arrive at that place where I must stand before the most righteous Judge, and when He shall call me to account for the works which I have heaped up in my youth?
Woe to every man dying in his sins!

Assuredly that same dreadful hour, which came upon my father Jacob, [23] when his soul was flying forth from his body, is now, behold, near at hand for me.

Oh! how wretched I am this day, and worthy of lamentation!

But God alone is the disposer of my soul and body; He also will deal with them after His own good pleasure.

17.

These are the words spoken by Joseph, that righteous old man.

And I, going in beside him, found his soul exceedingly troubled, for he was placed in great perplexity.

And I said to him:

Hail! my father Joseph, thou righteous man; how is it with thee?

And he answered me: All hail! my well-beloved son.

Indeed, the agony and fear of death have already environed me; but as soon as I heard Thy voice, my soul was at rest.

O Jesus of Nazareth!

Jesus, my Saviour!

Jesus, the deliverer of my soul!

Jesus, my protector!

Jesus!

O sweetest name in my mouth, and in the mouth of all those that love it!

O eye which seest, and ear which hearest, hear me!

I am Thy servant; this day I most humbly reverence Thee, and before Thy face I pour out my tears. Thou art altogether my God; Thou art my Lord, as the angel has told me times without number, and especially on that day when my soul was driven about with perverse thoughts about the pure and blessed Mary, who was carrying Thee in her womb, and whom I was thinking of secretly sending away.

And while I was thus meditating, behold, there appeared to me in my rest angels of the Lord, saying to me in a wonderful mystery:

O Joseph, thou son of David, fear not to take Mary as thy wife; and do not grieve thy soul, nor speak unbecoming words of her conception, because she is with child of the Holy Spirit, and shall bring forth a son, whose name shall be called Jesus, for He shall save His people from their sins.

Do not for this cause wish me evil, O Lord! for I was ignorant of the mystery of Thy birth.

I call to mind also, my Lord, that day when the boy died of the bite of the serpent. And his relations wished to deliver Thee to Herod, saying that Thou hadst killed him; but Thou didst raise him from the dead, and restore him to them.

Then I went up to Thee, and took hold of Thy hand, saying:

My son, take care of thyself.

But Thou didst say to me in reply:

Art thou not my father after the flesh?

I shall teach thee who I am. [24]Now therefore, O Lord and my God, do not be angry with me, or condemn me on account of that hour.

I am Thy servant, and the son of Thine handmaiden; [25] but Thou art my Lord, my God and Saviour, most surely the Son of God.

18.

When my father Joseph had thus spoken, he was unable to weep more.

And I saw that death now had dominion over him.

And my mother, virgin undefiled, rose and came to me, saying:

O my beloved son, this pious old man Joseph is now dying.

And I answered:

Oh my dearest mother, assuredly upon all creatures produced in this world the same necessity of death lies; for death holds sway over the whole human race.

Even thou, O my virgin mother, must look for the same end of life as other mortals.

And yet thy death, as also the death of this pious man, is not death, but life enduring to eternity.

Nay more, even I must die, as concerns the body which I have received from thee.

But rise, O my venerable mother, and go in to Joseph, that blessed old man, in order that thou mayst see what will happen as his soul ascends from his body.

19.

My undefiled mother Mary, therefore, went and entered the place where Joseph was.

And I was sitting at his feet looking at him, for the signs of death already appeared in his countenance.

And that blessed old man raised his head, and kept his eyes fixed on my face; but he had no power of speaking to me, on account of the agonies of death, which held him in their grasp.

But he kept fetching many sighs.

And I held his hands for a whole hour; and he turned his face to me, and made signs for me not to leave him.

Thereafter I put my hand upon his breast, and perceived his soul now near his throat, preparing to depart from its receptacle.

20.

And when my virgin mother saw me touching his body, she also touched his feet.

And finding them already dead and destitute of heat, she said to me:

O my beloved son, assuredly his feet are already beginning to stiffen, and they are as cold as snow.

Accordingly she summoned his sons and daughters, and said to them:

Come, as many as there are of you, and go to your father; for assuredly he is now at the very point of death.

And Assia, his daughter, answered and said: Woe's me, O my brothers, this is certainly the same disease that my beloved mother died of.

And she lamented and shed tears; and all Joseph's other children mourned along with her.

I also, and my mother Mary, wept along with them. [26]

21.

And turning my eyes towards the region of the south, I saw Death already approaching, and all Gehenna with him, closely attended by his army and his satellites; and their clothes, their faces, and their mouths poured forth flames.

And when my father Joseph saw them coming straight to him, his eyes dissolved in tears, and at the same time he groaned after a strange manner.

Accordingly, when I saw the vehemence of his sighs, I drove back Death and all the host of servants which accompanied him.

And I called upon my good Father, saying:--

22.

O Father of all mercy, eye which seest, and ear which hearest, hearken to my prayers and supplications in behalf of the old man Joseph; and send Michael, the prince of Thine angels, and Gabriel, the herald of light, and all the light of Thine angels, and let their whole array walk with the soul of my father Joseph, until they shall have conducted it to Thee.

This is the hour in which my father has need of compassion.

And I say unto you, that all the saints, yea, as many men as are born in the world, whether they be just or whether they be perverse, must of necessity taste of death.

23.

Therefore Michael and Gabriel came to the soul of my father Joseph, and took it, and wrapped it in a shining wrapper.

Thus he committed his spirit into the hands of my good Father, and He bestowed upon him peace.

But as yet none of his children knew that he had fallen asleep.

And the angels preserved his soul from the demons of darkness which were in the way, and praised God even until they conducted it into the dwelling-place of the pious.

24.

Now his body was lying prostrate and bloodless; wherefore I reached forth my hand, and put right his eyes and shut his mouth, and said to the virgin Mary:

O my mother, where is the skill which he showed in all the time that he lived in this world?

Lo! it has perished, as if it had never existed.

And when his children heard me speaking with my mother, the pure virgin, they knew that he had already breathed his last, and they shed tears, and lamented.

But I said to them:

Assuredly the death of your father is not death, but life everlasting: for he has been freed from the troubles of this life, and has passed to perpetual and everlasting rest.

When they heard these words, they rent their clothes, and wept.

25.

And, indeed, the inhabitants of Nazareth and of Galilee, having heard of their lamentation, flocked to them, and wept from the third hour even to the ninth.

And at the ninth hour they all went together to Joseph's bed.

And they lifted his body, after they had anointed it with costly unguents.

But I entreated my Father in the prayer of the celestials--that same prayer which with my own hand I made before I was carried in the womb of the virgin Mary, my mother.

And as soon as I had finished it, and pronounced the amen, a great multitude of angels came up; and I ordered two of them to stretch out their shining garments, and to wrap in them the body of Joseph, the blessed old man.

26.

And I spoke to Joseph, and said:

The smell or corruption of death shall not have dominion over thee, nor shall a worm ever come forth from thy body.

Not a single limb of it shall be broken, nor shall any hair on thy head be changed.

Nothing of thy body shall perish, O my father Joseph, but it will remain entire and uncorrupted even until the banquet of the thousand years. [27]And whosoever shall make an offering on the day of thy remembrance, him will I bless and recompense in the congregation of the virgins; and whosoever shall give food to the wretched, the poor, the widows, and orphans from the work of his hands, on the day on which thy memory shall be celebrated, and in thy name, shall not be in want of good things all the days of his life. And whosoever shall have given a cup of water, or of wine, to drink to the widow or orphan in thy name, I will give him to thee, that thou mayst go in with him to the banquet of the thousand years.

And every man who shall present an offering on the day of thy commemoration will I bless and recompense in the church of the virgins:

for one I will render unto him thirty, sixty, and a hundred.

And whosoever shall write the history of thy life, of thy labour, and thy departure from this world, and this narrative that has issued from my mouth, him shall I commit to thy keeping as long as he shall have to do with this life. And when his soul departs from the body, and when he must leave this world, I will burn the book of his sins, nor will I torment him with any punishment in the day of judgment; but he shall cross the sea of flames, and shall go through it without trouble or pain. [28]And upon every poor man who can give none of those things which I have mentioned this is incumbent:

viz., if a son is born to him, he shall call his name Joseph.

So there shall not take place in that house either poverty or any sudden death for ever.

27.

Thereafter the chief men of the city came together to the place where the body of the blessed old man Joseph had been laid, bringing with them burial-clothes; and they wished to wrap it up in them after the manner in which the Jews are wont to arrange their dead bodies. And they perceived that he kept his shroud fast; for it adhered to the body in such a way, that when they wished to take it off, it was found to be like iron--impossible to be moved or loosened.

Nor could they find any ends in that piece of linen, which struck them with the greatest astonishment.

At length they carried him out to a place where there was a cave, and opened the gate, that they might bury his body beside the bodies of his fathers.

Then there came into my mind the day on which he walked with me into Egypt, and that extreme trouble which he endured on my account.

Accordingly, I bewailed his death for a long time; and lying upon his body, I said:--

28.

O Death! who makest all knowledge to vanish away, and raisest so many tears and lamentations, surely it is God my Father Himself who hath granted thee this power.

For men die for the transgression of Adam and his wife Eve, and Death spares not so much as one. Nevertheless, nothing happens to any one, or is brought upon him, without the command of my Father.

There have certainly been men who have prolonged their life even to nine hundred years; but they died. Yea, though some of them have lived longer, they have, notwithstanding, succumbed to

The Forgotten Bible

the same fate; nor has any one of them ever said:

I have not tasted death.

For the Lord never sends the same punishment more than once, since it hath pleased my Father to bring it upon men.

And at the very moment when it, going forth, beholds the command descending to it from heaven, it says:

I will go forth against that man, and will greatly move him.

Then, without delay, it makes an onset on the soul, and obtains the mastery of it, doing with it whatever it will.

For, because Adam did not the will of my Father, but transgressed His commandment, the wrath of my Father was kindled against him, and He doomed him to death; and thus it was that death came into the world. But if Adam had observed my Father's precepts, death would never have fallen to his lot.

Think you that I can ask my good Father to send me a chariot of fire, [29] which may take up the body of my father Joseph, and convey it to the place of rest, in order that it may dwell with the spirits?

But on account of the transgression of Adam, that trouble and violence of death has descended upon all the human race. And it is for this cause that I must die according to the flesh, for my work which I have created, that they may obtain grace.

29.

Having thus spoken, I embraced the body of my father Joseph, and wept over it; and they opened the door of the tomb, and placed his body in it, near the body of his father Jacob.

And at the time when he fell asleep he had fulfilled a hundred and eleven years.

Never did a tooth in his mouth hurt him, nor was his eyesight rendered less sharp, nor his body bent, nor his strength impaired; but he worked at his trade of a carpenter to the very last day of his life; and that was the six-and-twentieth of the month Abib.

30.

And we apostles, when we heard these things from our Saviour, rose up joyfully, and prostrated ourselves in honour of Him, and said:

O our Saviour, show us Thy grace.

Now indeed we have heard the word of life:

nevertheless we wonder, O our Saviour, at the fate of Enoch and Elias, inasmuch as they had not to undergo death.

For truly they dwell in the habitation of the righteous even to the present day, nor have their bodies seen corruption.

Yet that old man Joseph the carpenter was, nevertheless, Thy father after the flesh.

And Thou hast ordered us to go into all the world and preach the holy Gospel; and Thou hast said:

Relate to them the death of my father Joseph, and celebrate to him with annual solemnity a festival and sacred day.

And whosoever shall take anything away from this narrative, or add anything to it, commits sin. [30] We wonder especially that Joseph, even from that day on which Thou wast born in Bethlehem, called Thee his son after the flesh.

Wherefore, then, didst Thou not make him immortal as well as them, and Thou sayest that he was righteous and chosen?

31.

And our Saviour answered and said:

Indeed, the prophecy of my Father upon Adam, for his disobedience, has now been fulfilled.

And all things are arranged according to the will and pleasure of my Father.

For if a man rejects the commandment of God, and follows the works of the devil by committing sin, his life is prolonged; for he is preserved in order that he may perhaps repent, and reflect that he must be delivered into the hands of death.

But if any one has been zealous of good works, his life also is prolonged, that, as the fame of his old age increases, upright men may imitate him.

But when you see a man whose mind is prone to anger, assuredly his days are shortened; for it is these that are taken away in the flower of their age.

Every prophecy, therefore, which my Father has pronounced concerning the sons of men, must be fulfilled in every particular.

But with reference to Enoch and Elias, and how they remain alive to this day, keeping the same bodies with which they were born; and as to what concerns my father Joseph, who has not been allowed as well as they to remain in the body:

indeed, though a man live in the world many myriads of years, nevertheless at some time or other he is compelled to exchange life for death.

And I say to you, O my brethren, that they also, Enoch and Elias,[31] must towards the end of time return into the world and die--in the day, namely, of commotion, of terror, of perplexity, and affliction.

For Antichrist will slay four bodies, and will pour out their blood like water, because of the reproach to which they shall expose him, and the ignominy with which they, in their lifetime, shall brand him when they reveal his impiety.

32.

And we said:

O our Lord, our God and Saviour, who are those four whom Thou hast said Antichrist will cut off from the reproach they bring upon him?

The Lord answered:

They are Enoch, Elias, Schila, and Tabitha. [32]When we heard this from our Saviour, we rejoiced and exulted; and we offered all glory and thanksgiving to the Lord God, and our Saviour Jesus Christ.

He it is to whom is due glory, honour, dignity, dominion, power, and praise, as well as to the good Father with Him, and to the Holy Spirit that giveth life, henceforth and in all time for evermore.

Amen.

Footnotes:

1. The Coptic has: The 26th day of Epep. This is the departure from the body of our father Joseph the carpenter, the father of Christ after the flesh, who was 111 years old. Our Saviour narrated all his life to His apostles on Mount Olivet; and His apostles wrote it, and put it in the library which is in Jerusalem. Also that the day on which the holy old man laid down his body was the 26th of the month Epep. In the peace of God, amen. His day is the 19th of March in the Roman calendar.

2. Luke xxiv. 49.
3. Luke xxiv. 37.
4. Comp. Matt. x. 42.
5. Comp. Ps. lxxxiv. 10.
6. Matt. xii. 36.
7. 2 Cor. v. 10.
8. Jer. ix. 23, 24; 1 Cor. i. 31; 2 Cor. x. 17.
9. Luke xxiv. 10.
10. Matt. i. 19.
11. Ps. ii. 9; Rev. xi. 5, xix. 15.
12. Matt. i. 20-24.
13. It was Herod Antipas who ordered John to be beheaded.
14. John xviii. 36.
15. The Salome here mentioned was, according to two of the mss. of Pseudo-Matthew, the third husband of Anna, Mary's mother, and the father of Mary the wife of Zebedee. But compare Matt. xxvii. 56 with Mark xv. 40.
16. Gen. iii. 19.
17. One the subject of guardian angels, see Shepherd of Hermas, iii. 4; Justin, Apol., ii. 5, Tryph., 5; Athenagoras, Legat., 10, 20; Clem. Alex., Strom., vi. 17.
18. This clause looks like an interpolation. But the doctrine of purgatory was held from an early date. Clem. Alex., Paedag., iii. 9; Strom., vii. 6; Origen against Celsus, v. 14, 15.
19. Note the change from the first person.
20. Here the Coptic has: This is the end of the life of my beloved father Joseph. When forty years old he married a wife, with whom he lived nine (? forty-nine) years. After her death he remained a widower one (or two) year: and my mother lived two years in his house before she was married to him, since he had been ordered by the priests to take charge of her until the time of her marriage. And my mother Mary brought me forth in the third year that she was in Joseph's house, in the fifteenth year of her age. My mother bore me in a cave (this seems a mistranslation for mystery), which it is unlawful either to name or seek, and there is not in the whole creation a man who knows it, except me and my Father and the Holy Spirit. It is to be noted that the last clause is omitted in the Coptic. The phrase one essence was first used in regard to the doctrine of the Trinity

The Forgotten Bible
by Augustine.

21. Comp. Job. iii.
22. Comp. Ps. li. 5.
23. Matt. i. 16.
24. The Sahidic has: Joseph entreats Jesus to pardon him likewise, because when, once upon a time, He had recalled to life a boy bitten by a cerastes, he (Joseph) had pulled His right ear, advising Him to refrain from works that brought hatred upon Him. See Second Gospel of Thomas, chap. 5.
25. Ps. cxvi. 16.
26. The argument of the Sahidic is: He sends for Joseph's sons and daughters, of whom the oldest was Lysia the purple-seller. They all wept over their dying father.
27. Barnabas, 15; Hermas, i. 3; Irenaeus, Contra Haer., v. 33; Justin, Tryph., 81; Tertullian, Adv. Marc., iii. 24. Caius and Dionysius imputed grossness and sensuality to Cerinthus, because he spoke of the wedding feast of the thousand years.
28. All the fathers placed the purgatorial fires, as the Greek Church does now, at the day of judgment. Augustine was the first who brought forward the supposition that the purification took place in Hades before the day of judgment. Haag, Histoire des Dogmes, ii. 323.
29. 2 Kings ii. 11.
30. Rev. xxii. 18, 19.
31. Comp. Rev. xi. 3-12.
32. Acts ix. 36. Schila is probably meant for the widow of Nain's son.

The Gospel of Thomas

First Greek Form

Thomas the Israelite Philosopher's Account of the Infancy of the Lord.

1.
   I Thomas, an Israelite, write you this account, that all the brethren from among the heathen may know the miracles of our Lord Jesus Christ in His infancy, which He did after His birth in our country. The beginning of it is as follows:--

2.
   This child Jesus, when five years old, was playing in the ford of a mountain stream; and He collected the flowing waters into pools, and made them clear immediately, and by a word alone He made them obey Him.
   And having made some soft clay, He fashioned out of it twelve sparrows.
   And it was the Sabbath when He did these things.
   And there were also many other children playing with Him.
   And a certain Jew, seeing what Jesus was doing, playing on the Sabbath, went off immediately, and said to his father Joseph:
   Behold, thy son is at the stream, and has taken clay, and made of it twelve birds, and has profaned the Sabbath.
   And Joseph, coming to the place and seeing, cried out to Him, saying:
   Wherefore doest thou on the Sabbath what it is not lawful to do?
   And Jesus clapped His hands, and cried out to the sparrows, and said to them:
   Off you go!
   And the sparrows flew, and went off crying.
   And the Jews seeing this were amazed, and went away and reported to their chief men what they had seen Jesus doing. [1]

3.
   And the son of Annas the scribe was standing there with Joseph; and he took a willow branch, and let out the waters which Jesus had collected.
   And Jesus, seeing what was done, was angry, and said to him:
   O wicked, impious, and foolish! what harm did the pools and the waters do to thee? Behold, even now thou shalt be dried up like a tree, and thou shalt not bring forth either leaves, or root, [2] or fruit.
   And straightway that boy was quite dried up.
   And Jesus departed, and went to Joseph's house.
   But the parents of the boy that had been dried up took him up, bewailing his youth, and brought him to Joseph, and reproached him because, said they, thou hast such a child doing such things. [3]

4.
   After that He was again passing through the village; and a boy ran up against Him, and struck His shoulder.
   And Jesus was angry, and said to him:
   Thou shalt not go back the way thou camest.
   And immediately he fell down dead.
   And some who saw what had taken place, said: Whence was this child begotten, that every word of his is certainly accomplished?
   And the parents of the dead boy went away to Joseph, and blamed him, saying:
   Since thou hast such a child, it is impossible for thee to live with us in the village; or else

teach him to bless, and not to curse: [4]for he is killing our children.

5.

And Joseph called the child apart, and admonished Him, saying:
Why doest thou such things, and these people suffer, and hate us, and persecute us?
And Jesus said:
I know that these words of thine are not thine own; [5] nevertheless for thy sake I will be silent; but they shall bear their punishment.
And straightway those that accused Him were struck blind.
And those who saw it were much afraid and in great perplexity, and said about Him:
Every word which he spoke, whether good or bad, was an act, and became a wonder.
And when they saw that Jesus had done such a thing, Joseph rose and took hold of His ear, and pulled it hard.
And the child was very angry, and said to him:
It is enough for thee to seek, and not to find; and most certainly thou hast not done wisely.
Knowest thou not that I am thine?
Do not trouble me. [6]

6.

And a certain teacher, Zacchaeus by name, was standing in a certain place, and heard Jesus thus speaking to his father; and he wondered exceedingly, that, being a child, he should speak in such a way.
And a few days thereafter he came to Joseph, and said to him:
Thou hast a sensible child, and he has some mind.
Give him to me, then, that he may learn letters; and I shall teach him along with the letters all knowledge, both how to address all the elders, and to honour them as forefathers and fathers, and how to love those of his own age.
And He said to him all the letters from the Alpha even to the Omega, clearly and with great exactness.
And He looked upon the teacher Zacchaeus, and said to him:
Thou who art ignorant of the nature of the Alpha, how canst thou teach others the Beta?
Thou hypocrite! first, if thou knowest, teach the A, and then we shall believe thee about the B.
Then He began to question the teacher about the first letter, and he was not able to answer Him.
And in the hearing of many, the child says to Zacchaeus:
Hear, O teacher, the order of the first letter, and notice here how it has lines, and a middle stroke crossing those which thou seest common; (lines) brought together; the highest part supporting them, and again bringing them under one head; with three points of intersection; of the same kind; principal and subordinate; of equal length.
Thou hast the lines of the A. [7]

7.

And when the teacher Zacchaeus heard the child speaking such and so great allegories of the first letter, he was at a great loss about such a narrative, and about His teaching.
And He said to those that were present:
Alas!
I, wretch that I am, am at a loss, bringing shame upon myself by having dragged this child hither.
Take him away, then, I beseech thee, brother Joseph.
I cannot endure the sternness of his look; I cannot make out his meaning at all.
That child does not belong to this earth; he can tame even fire.
Assuredly he was born before the creation of the world.
What sort of a belly bore him, what sort of a womb nourished him, I do not know.
Alas! my friend, he has carried me away; I cannot get at his meaning:
thrice wretched that I am, I have deceived myself.
I made a struggle to have a scholar, and I was found to have a teacher.
My mind is filled with shame, my friends, because I, an old man, have been conquered by a child.
There is nothing for me but despondency and death on account of this boy, for I am not able at this hour to look him in the face; and when everybody says that I have been beaten by a little child, what can I say?
And how can I give an account of the lines of the first letter that he spoke about?

I know not, O my friends; for I can make neither beginning nor end of him. Therefore, I beseech thee, brother Joseph, take him home.

What great thing he is, either god or angel, or what I am to say, I know not. [8]

8.

And when the Jews were encouraging Zacchaeus, the child laughed aloud, and said:

Now let thy learning bring forth fruit, and let the blind in heart see.

I am here from above, that I may curse them, and call them to the things that are above, as He that sent me on your account has commanded me.

And when the child ceased speaking, immediately all were made whole who had fallen under His curse.

And no one after that dared to make Him angry, lest He should curse him, and he should be maimed.

9.

And some days after, Jesus was playing in an upper room of a certain house, and one of the children that were playing with Him fell down from the house, and was killed.

And, when the other children saw this, they ran away, and Jesus alone stood still.

And the parents of the dead child coming, reproached [9] ...and they threatened Him. And Jesus leaped down from the roof, and stood beside the body of the child, and cried with a loud voice, and said:

Zeno--for that was his name--stand up, and tell me; did I throw thee down?

And he stood up immediately, and said:

Certainly not, my lord; thou didst not throw me down, but hast raised me up.

And those that saw this were struck with astonishment.

And the child's parents glorified God on account of the miracle that had happened, and adored Jesus. [10]

10.

A few days after, a young man was splitting wood in the corner,[11] and the axe came down and cut the sole of his foot in two, and he died from loss of blood.

And there was a great commotion, and people ran together, and the child Jesus ran there too.

And He pressed through the crowd, and laid hold of the young man's wounded foot, and he was cured immediately.

And He said to the young man:

Rise up now, split the wood, and remember me.

And the crowd seeing what had happened, adored the child, saying:

Truly the Spirit of God dwells in this child.

11.

And when He was six years old, His mother gave Him a pitcher, and sent Him to draw water, and bring it into the house.

But He struck against some one in the crowd, and the pitcher was broken.

And Jesus unfolded the cloak which He had on, and filled it with water, and carried it to His mother.

And His mother, seeing the miracle that had happened, kissed Him, and kept within herself the mysteries which she had seen Him doing. [12]

12.

And again in seed-time the child went out with His father to sow corn in their land.

And while His father was sowing, the child Jesus also sowed one grain of corn.

And when He had reaped it, and threshed it, He made a hundred kors; [13] and calling all the poor of the village to the threshing-floor, He gave them the corn, and Joseph took away what was left of the corn.

And He was eight years old when He did this miracle. [14]

13.

And His father was a carpenter, and at that time made ploughs and yokes.

And a certain rich man ordered him to make him a couch.

And one of what is called the cross pieces being too short, they did not know what to do.

The child Jesus said to His father Joseph:

Put down the two pieces of wood, and make them even in the middle.

The Forgotten Bible

And Joseph did as the child said to him.

And Jesus stood at the other end, and took hold of the shorter piece of wood, and stretched it, and made it equal to the other.

And His father Joseph saw it, and wondered, and embraced the child, and blessed Him, saying:

Blessed am I, because God has given me this child. [15]

14.

And Joseph, seeing that the child was vigorous in mind and body, again resolved that He should not remain ignorant of the letters, and took Him away, and handed Him over to another teacher.

And the teacher said to Joseph:

I shall first teach him the Greek letters, and then the Hebrew.

For the teacher was aware of the trial that had been made of the child, and was afraid of Him.

Nevertheless he wrote out the alphabet, and gave Him all his attention for a long time, and He made him no answer.

And Jesus said to him:

If thou art really a teacher, and art well acquainted with the letters, tell me the power of the Alpha, and I will tell thee the power of the Beta.

And the teacher was enraged at this, and struck Him on the head.

And the child, being in pain, cursed him; and immediately he swooned away, and fell to the ground on his face.

And the child returned to Joseph's house; and Joseph was grieved, and gave orders to His mother, saying:

Do not let him go outside of the door, because those that make him angry die. [16]

15.

And after some time, another master again, a genuine friend of Joseph, said to him:

Bring the child to my school; perhaps I shall be able to flatter him into learning his letters.

And Joseph said:

If thou hast the courage, brother, take him with thee.

And he took Him with him in fear and great agony; but the child went along pleasantly. And going boldly into the school, He found a book lying on the reading-desk; and taking it, He read not the letters that were in it, but opening His mouth, He spoke by the Holy Spirit, and taught the law to those that were standing round.

And a great crowd having come together, stood by and heard Him, and wondered at the ripeness of His teaching, and the readiness of His words, and that He, child as He was, spoke in such a way.

And Joseph hearing of it, was afraid, and ran to the school, in doubt lest his master too should be without experience. [17] And the master said to Joseph:

Know, brother, that I have taken the child as a scholar, and he is full of much grace and wisdom; but I beseech thee, brother, take him home.

And when the child heard this, He laughed at him directly, and said:

Since thou hast spoken aright, and witnessed aright, for thy sake he also that was struck down shall be cured.

And immediately the other master was cured.

And Joseph took the child, and went away home. [18]

16.

And Joseph sent his son James to tie up wood and bring it home, and the child Jesus also followed him.

And when James was gathering the fagots, a viper bit James' hand.

And when he was racked with pain, and at the point of death, Jesus came near and blew upon the bite; and the pain ceased directly, and the beast burst, and instantly James remained safe and sound. [19]

17.

And after this the infant of one of Joseph's neighbours fell sick and died, and its mother wept sore.

And Jesus heard that there was great lamentation and commotion, and ran in haste, and found the child dead, and touched his breast, and said:

I say to thee, child, be not dead, but live, and be with thy mother.

And directly it looked up and laughed.
And He said to the woman:
Take it, and give it milk, and remember me.
And seeing this, the crowd that was standing by wondered, and said:
Truly this child was either God or an angel of God, for every word of his is a certain fact.
And Jesus went out thence, playing with the other children. [20]

18.
And some time after there occurred a great commotion while a house was building, and Jesus stood up and went away to the place.
And seeing a man lying dead, He took him by the hand, and said:
Man, I say to thee, arise, and go on with thy work.
And directly he rose up, and adored Him.
And seeing this, the crowd wondered, and said:
This child is from heaven, for he has saved many souls from death, and he continues to save during all his life.

19.
And when He was twelve years old His parents went as usual to Jerusalem to the feast of the passover with their fellow-travellers. And after the passover they were coming home again.
And while they were coming home, the child Jesus went back to Jerusalem.
And His parents thought that He was in the company.
And having gone one day's journey, they sought for Him among their relations; and not finding Him, they were in great grief, and turned back to the city seeking for Him.
And after the third day they found Him in the temple, sitting in the midst of the teachers, both hearing the law and asking them questions.
And they were all attending to Him, and wondering that He, being a child, was shutting the mouths of the elders and teachers of the people, explaining the main points of the law and the parables of the prophets.
And His mother Mary coming up, said to Him:
Why hast thou done this to us, child?
Behold, we have been seeking for thee in great trouble.
And Jesus said to them:
Why do you seek me?
Do you not know that I must be about my Father's business?[21] And the scribes and the Pharisees said:
Art thou the mother of this child? And she said:
I am.
And they said to her:
Blessed art thou among women, for God hath blessed the fruit of thy womb; for such glory, and such virtue and wisdom, we have neither seen nor heard ever.
And Jesus rose up, and followed His mother, and was subject to His parents.
And His mother observed all these things that had happened.
And Jesus advanced in wisdom, and stature, and grace. [22]To whom be glory for ever and ever. Amen.

Footnotes:

1. Pseudo-Matt. 26, etc.
2. Another reading is, branches.
3. One ms. has: And Jesus, at the entreaty of all of them, healed him.
4. Or, either teach him to bless, and not to curse, or depart with him from this place; for, etc.
5. Or, are not mine, but thine.
6. Pseudo-Matt. 29. [The numerous references to the latter part of Pseudo-Matthaei, see pp. 378-383, shows the close relationship. But it is generally agreed that this narrative is the older, and one of the sources of Pseudo-Matthaei.--R.]
7. Pseud.-Matt. 30, 31. Various explanations have been given of this difficult passage by annotators, who refer it to the A of the Hebrew, or of the Greek, or of the Armenian alphabet. It seems, however, to answer very closely to the old Phenician A, which was written *** or ***. The Paris ms. has: And he sat down to teach Jesus the letters, and began the first letter Aleph; and Jesus says the second, Beth, Gimel, and told him all the letters to the end. And shutting the book, He taught the master the prophets.
8. Instead of this chapter, the Paris ms. has: And he was ashamed and perplexed, because he

knew not whence he knew the letters. And he arose, and went home, in great astonishment at this strange thing. It then goes on with a fragment of the history of the dyer's shop, as given in the Arabic Gospel of the Infancy, ch. 37.

9. One of themss. of the Latin Gospel inserts here--Jesus, saying: Indeed, you made him fall down. And Jesus said: I never made him fall.

10. Pseudo-Matt. 32.

11. A better reading would be en te geitonia, in the neighbourhood, for en te gonia, in the corner.

12. Pseudo-Matt. 33.

13. The kor or chomer was, according to Jahn, 32 pecks 1 pint.

14. Pseudo-Matt. 34.

15. Pseudo-Matt. 37.

16. Pseudo-Matt. 38.

17. Tischendorf suggests anaperos, maimed, for apeiros.

18. Pseudo-Matt. 39.

19. Pseudo-Matt. 41.

20. Pseudo-Matt. 40.

21. [This may be rendered, as in R.V., Luke ii. 49, " in my Father's house." The words are the same as in that passage.--R.]

22. Luke ii. 41-52.

Second Greek Form

The Writing of the Holy Apostle Thomas Concerning the Childhood of the Lord.

1.
  I Thomas the Israelite have deemed it necessary to make known to all the brethren of the heathen the great things which our Lord Jesus Christ did in His childhood, when He dwelt in the body in the city of Nazareth, going in the fifth year of His age.

2.
  On one of the days, there being a rainstorm, He went out of the house where His mother was, and played on the ground where the waters were flowing.
  And He made pools, and brought in the waters, and the pools were filled with water.
  Then He says:
  It is my will that you become clear and excellent waters.
  And they became so directly.
  And a certain boy, the son of Annas the scribe, came past, and with a willow branch which he was carrying threw down the pools, and the water flowed out.
  And Jesus turning, said to him:
  O impious and wicked, how have the pools wronged thee, that thou hast emptied them?
  Thou shalt not go on thy way, and thou shalt be dried up like the branch which thou art carrying.
  And as he went along, in a short time he fell down and died.
  And when the children that were playing with him saw this, they wondered, and went away and told the father of the dead boy.
  And he ran and found his child dead, and he went away and reproached Joseph.

3.
  And Jesus made of that clay twelve sparrows, and it was the Sabbath.
  And a child ran and told Joseph, saying:
  Behold, thy child is playing about the stream, and of the clay he has made sparrows, which is not lawful.
  And when he heard this, he went, and said to the child:
  Why dost thou do this, profaning the Sabbath?
  But Jesus gave him no answer, but looked upon the sparrows, and said:
  Go away, fly, and live, and remember me.
  And at this word they flew, and went up into the air.
  And when Joseph saw it, he wondered.

4.
  And some days after, when Jesus was going through the midst of the city, a boy threw a stone at Him, and struck Him on the shoulder.
  And Jesus said to him:
  Thou shalt not go on thy way.
  And directly falling down, he also died.
  And they that happened to be there were struck with astonishment, saying:
  Whence is this child, that every word he says is certainly accomplished?
  And they also went and reproached Joseph, saying:
  It is impossible for thee to live with us in this city:
  but if thou wishest to do so, teach thy child to bless, and not to curse:
  for he is killing our children, and everything that he says is certainly accomplished.

5.
  And Joseph was sitting in his seat, and the child stood before him; and he took hold of Him by the ear, and pinched it hard.
  And Jesus looked at him steadily, and said:
  It is enough for thee.

6.
  And on the day after he took Him by the hand, and led Him to a certain teacher, Zacchaeus by name, and says to him:

O master, take this child, and teach him his letters.

And he says:

Hand him over to me, brother, and I shall teach him the Scripture; and I shall persuade him to bless all, and not to curse.

And Jesus hearing, laughed, and said to them:

You say what you know; but I know more than you, for I am before the ages.

And I know when your fathers' fathers were born; and I know how many are the years of your life.

And hearing this, they were struck with astonishment.

And again Jesus said to them:

You wonder because I said to you that I knew how many are the years of your life.

Assuredly I know when the world was created.

Behold, you do not believe me now.

When you see my cross, then will ye believe that I speak the truth.

And they were struck with astonishment when they heard these things.

7.

And Zacchaeus, having written the alphabet in Hebrew, says to Him: Alpha.

And the child says:

Alpha.

And again the teacher:

Alpha; and the child likewise.

Then again the teacher says the Alpha for the third time.

Then Jesus, looking in the master's face, says:

How canst thou, not knowing the Alpha, teach another the Beta?

And the child, beginning from the Alpha, said by Himself the twenty-two letters.

Then also He says again:

Hear, O teacher, the order of the first letter, and know how many entrances and lines it has, and strokes common, crossing and coming together.[1] And when Zacchaeus heard such an account of the one letter, he was so struck with astonishment, that he could make no answer.

And he turned and said to Joseph:

This child assuredly, brother, does not belong to the earth.

Take him, then, away from me.

8.

And after these things, on one of the days Jesus was playing with other children on the roof of a house.

And one boy was pushed by another, and hurled down upon the ground, and he died.

And seeing this, the boys that were playing with him ran away; and Jesus only was left standing upon the roof from which the boy had been hurled down. And when the news was brought to the parents of the dead boy, they ran weeping; and finding their boy lying dead upon the ground, and Jesus standing above, they supposed that their boy had been thrown down by Him; and fixing their eyes upon Him, they reviled Him.

And seeing this, Jesus directly came down from the roof, and stood at the head of the dead body, and says to him:

Zeno, did I throw thee down?

Stand up, and tell us.

For this was the name of the boy.

And at the word the boy stood up and adored Jesus, and said:

My lord, thou didst not throw me down, but thou hast brought me to life when I was dead.

9.

And a few days after, one of the neighbours, when splitting wood, cut away the lower part of his foot with the axe, and was on the point of death from loss of blood.

And a great number of people ran together, and Jesus came with them to the place.

And He took hold of the young man's wounded foot, and cured him directly, and says to him: Rise up, split thy wood.

And he rose up and adored Him, giving thanks, and splitting the wood.

Likewise also all that were there wondered, and gave thanks to Him.

10.
And when He was six years old, Mary His mother sent Him to bring water from the fountain.

And as He went along, the pitcher was broken.

And going to the fountain He unfolded His overcoat, and drew water from the fountain, and filled it, and took the water to His mother.

And seeing this, she was struck with astonishment, and embraced Him, and kissed Him.

11.
And when Jesus had come to the eighth year of His age, Joseph was ordered by a certain rich man to make him a couch.

For he was a carpenter.

And he went out into the field to get wood; and Jesus went with him.

And having cut two pieces of wood, and smoothed them with the axe, he put the one beside the other; and in measuring he found it too short.

And when he saw this he was grieved, and sought to find another piece.

And seeing this, Jesus says to him:

Put these two pieces together, so as to make both ends even.

And Joseph, in doubt as to what the child should mean, did as he was told.

And He says to him again:

Take a firm hold of the short piece.

And Joseph, in astonishment, took hold of it.

Then Jesus also, taking hold of the other end, drew it towards Himself, and make it equal to the other piece of wood.

And He says to Joseph:

Grieve no more, but do thy work without hindrance.

And seeing this, he wondered greatly, and says to himself:

Blessed am I, because God has given me such a boy.

And when they came back to the city, Joseph gave an account of the matter to Mary.

And when she heard and saw the strange miracles of her son, she rejoiced and glorified Him, with the Father and the Holy Spirit, now and ever, and for evermore.

Amen.

Footnote:

1. [Compare the account in the version of the first Greek form, chap. 6, and the footnote.--R.]

The Forgotten Bible
Latin Form

Here Beginneth the Treatise of the Boyhood of Jesus According to Thomas.

Chapter I - How Mary and Joseph Fled with Him into Egypt

When a commotion took place in consequence of the search made by Herod for our Lord Jesus Christ to kill Him, then an angel said to Joseph: Take Mary and her boy, and flee into Egypt from the face of those who seek to kill Him.

And Jesus was two years old when He went into Egypt.

And as He was walking through a field of corn, He stretched forth His hand, and took of the ears, and put them over the fire, and rubbed them, and began to eat.

And when they had come into Egypt, they received hospitality in the house of a certain widow, and they remained in the same place one year.

And Jesus was in His third year.

And seeing boys playing, He began to play with them.

And He took a dried fish, and put it into a basin, and ordered it to move about.

And it began to move about.

And He said again to the fish:

Throw out thy salt which thou hast, and walk into the water.

And it so came to pass.

And the neighbours, seeing what had been done, told it to the widow woman in whose house Mary His mother lived.

And as soon as she heard it, she thrust them out of her house with great haste.

Chapter II - How a Schoolmaster Thrust Him Out of the City

And as Jesus was walking with Mary His mother through the middle of the city market-place, He looked and saw a schoolmaster teaching his scholars.

And behold twelve sparrows that were quarrelling fell over the wall into the bosom of that schoolmaster, who was teaching the boys.

And seeing this, Jesus was very much amused, and stood still. And when that teacher saw Him making merry, he said to his scholars with great fury:

Go and bring him to me.

And when they had carried Him to the master, he seized Him by the ear, and said:

What didst thou see, to amuse thee so much?

And He said to him:

Master, see my hand full of wheat.

I showed it to them, and scattered the wheat among them, and they carry it out of the middle of the street where they are in danger; and on this account they fought among themselves to divide the wheat.

And Jesus did not pass from the place until it was accomplished.

And this being done, the master began to thrust Him out of the city, along with His mother.

Chapter III - How Jesus Went Out of Egypt

And, lo, the angel of the Lord met Mary, and said to her:

Take up the boy, and return into the land of the Jews, for they who sought His life are dead.

And Mary rose up with Jesus; and they proceeded into the city of Nazareth, which is among the possessions of her father.

And when Joseph went out of Egypt after the death of Herod, he kept Him in the desert until there should be quietness in Jerusalem on the part of those who were seeking the boy's life.

And he gave thanks to God because He had given him understanding, and because he had found favour in the presence of the Lord God.

Amen.

Chapter IV - What the Lord Jesus Did in the City of Nazareth

It is glorious that Thomas the Israelite and apostle of the Lord gives an account also of the works of Jesus after He came out of Egypt into Nazareth.

Understand all of you, my dearest brethren, what the Lord Jesus did when He was in the city of Nazareth; the first chapter of which is as follows:--

And when Jesus was five years old, there fell a great rain upon the earth, and the boy Jesus walked up and down through it.

And there was a terrible rain, and He collected it into a fish-pond, and ordered it by His word to become clear.

And immediately it became so.

Again He took of the clay which was of that fish-pond, and made of it to the number of twelve sparrows.

And it was the Sabbath when Jesus did this among the boys of the Jews.

And the boys of the Jews went away, and said to Joseph His father:

Behold, thy son was playing along with us, and he took clay and made sparrows, which it was not lawful to do on the Sabbath; and he has broken it.

And Joseph went away to the boy Jesus, and said to Him:

Why hast thou done this, which it was not lawful to do on the Sabbath?

And Jesus opened His hands, and ordered the sparrows, saying:

Go up into the air, and fly; nobody shall kill you.

And they flew, and began to cry out, and praise God Almighty. And the Jews seeing what had happened, wondered, and went away and told the miracles which Jesus had done.

But a Pharisee who was with Jesus took an olive branch, and began to let the water out of the fountain which Jesus had made.

And when Jesus saw this, He said to him in a rage:

Thou impious and ignorant Sodomite, what harm have my works the fountains of water done thee?

Behold, thou shalt become like a dry tree, having neither roots, nor leaves, nor fruit.

And immediately he dried up, and fell to the ground, and died.

And his parents took him away dead, and reproached Joseph, saying:

See what thy son has done; teach him to pray, and not to blaspheme.

Chapter V - *How the Citizens Were Enraged Against Joseph on Account of the Doings of Jesus*

And a few days after, as Jesus was walking through the town with Joseph, one of the children ran up and struck Jesus on the arm.

And Jesus said to him:

So shalt thou not finish thy journey.

And immediately he fell to the ground, and died.

And those who saw these wonderful things cried out, saying:

Whence is that boy?

And they said to Joseph:

It is not right for such a boy to be among us.

And Joseph went and brought Him.

And they said to him:

Go away from this place; but if thou must live with us, teach him to pray, and not to blaspheme:

but our children have been killed.

Joseph called Jesus, and reproved Him, saying:

Why dost thou blaspheme?

For these people who live here hate us.

And Jesus said:

I know that these words are not mine, but thine; but I will hold my tongue for thy sake: and let them see to it in their wisdom.

And immediately those who were speaking against Jesus became blind.

And they walked up and down, and said:

All the words which proceed from his mouth are accomplished. And Joseph seeing what Jesus had done, in a fury seized Him by the ear; and Jesus said to Joseph in anger:

It is enough for thee to see me, not to touch me.

For thou knowest not who I am; but if thou didst know, thou wouldst not make me angry.

And although just now I am with thee, I was made before thee.

Chapter VI - *How Jesus Was Treated by the Schoolmaster*

Therefore a certain man named Zacheus [1] listened to all that Jesus was saying to Joseph, and in great astonishment said to himself:

Such a boy speaking in this way I have never seen.

And he went up to Joseph, and said:

That is an intelligent boy of thine; hand him over to me to learn his letters; and when he has thoroughly learned his letters, I shall teach him honourably, so that he may be no fool.

The Forgotten Bible

But Joseph answered and said to him:

No one can teach him but God alone. You do not believe that that little boy will be of little consequence? And when Jesus heard Joseph speaking in this way, He said to Zacheus: Indeed, master, whatever proceeds from my mouth is true.

And before all I was Lord, but you are foreigners.

To me has been given the glory of the ages, to you has been given nothing; because I am before the ages.

And I know how many years of life thou wilt have, and that thou wilt be carried into exile:

and my Father hath appointed this, that thou mayest understand that whatever proceeds from my mouth is true. And the Jews who were standing by, and hearing the words which Jesus spoke, were astonished, and said:

We have seen such wonderful things, and heard such words from that boy, as we have never heard, nor are likely to hear from any other human being,--either from the high priests, or the masters, or the Pharisees.

Jesus answered and said to them:

Why do you wonder?

Do you consider it incredible that I have spoken the truth?

I know when both you and your fathers were born, and to tell you more, when the world was made:

I know also who sent me to you. [2]And when the Jews heard the words which the child had spoken, they wondered, because that they were not able to answer.

And, communing with Himself, the child exulted and said:

I have told you a proverb; and I know that you are weak and ignorant.

And that schoolmaster said to Joseph:

Bring him to me, and I shall teach him letters.

And Joseph took hold of the boy Jesus, and led Him to the house of a certain schoolmaster, where other boys were being taught.

Now the master in soothing words began to teach Him His letters, and wrote for Him the first line, which is from A to T, [3] and began to stroke Him and teach Him.

And that teacher struck the child on the head:

and when He had received the blow, the child said to him:

I should teach thee, and not thou me; I know the letters which thou wishest to teach me, and I know that you are to me like vessels from which there come forth only sounds, and no wisdom.

And, beginning the line, He said the letters from A to T in full, and very fast.

And He looked at the master, and said to him:

Thou indeed canst not tell us what A and B are; how dost thou wish to teach others?

O hypocrite, if thou knowest and will tell me about the A, then will I tell thee about the B.

And when that teacher began to tell [4] about the first letter, he was unable to give any answer.

And Jesus said to Zacheus:

Listen to me, master; understand the first letter.

See how it has two lines; advancing in the middle, standing still, giving, scattering, varying, threatening; triple intermingled with double; at the same time homogeneous, having all common. [5]

And Zacheus, seeing that He so divided the first letter, was stupefied about the first letter, and about such a human being and such learning; and he cried out, and said:

Woe's me, for I am quite stupefied; I have brought disgrace upon myself through that child.

And he said to Joseph:

I earnestly entreat thee, brother, take him away from me, because I cannot look upon his face, nor hear his mighty words. Because that child can tame fire and bridle the sea:

for he was born before the ages.

What womb brought him forth, or what mother [6] nursed him, I know not.

Oh, my friends, I am driven out of my senses; I have become a wretched laughing-stock.

And I said that I had got a scholar; but he has been found to be my master.

And my disgrace I cannot get over, because I am an old man; and what to say to him I cannot find.

All I have to do is to fall into some grievous illness, and depart from this world; or to leave this town, because all have seen my disgrace.

An infant has deceived me.

What answer can I give to others, or what words can I say, because he has got the better of me in the first letter?

I am struck dumb, O my friends and acquaintances; neither beginning nor end can I find of an answer to him.

And now I beseech thee, brother Joseph, take him away from me, and lead him home, because he is a master, or the Lord, or an angel.

What to say I do not know.

And Jesus turned to the Jews who were with Zacheus, and said to them:

Let all not seeing see, and not understanding understand; let the deaf hear, and let those who are dead through me rise again; and those who are exalted, let me call to still higher things, as He who sent me to you hath commanded me.

And when Jesus ceased speaking, all who had been affected with any infirmity through His words were made whole.

And they did not dare to speak to Him.

Footnotes:

1. [In this book, the name Zacheus is given in different form, following the Latin.--R.]
2. A slight alteration is here made upon the punctuation of the original.
3. This refers to the Hebrew alphabet.
4. Better, perhaps: And when He began to tell that teacher.
5. This passage is hopelessly corrupt. The writer of this Gospel knew very little Greek, and probably the text from which he was translating was also here in a bad state. [Compare the accounts in the versions from the Greek forms.--R.]
6. The Greek original has metra, which he seems to have confounded with meter.

Chapter VII - How Jesus Raised a Boy to Life

One day, when Jesus was climbing on a certain house, along with the children, He began to play with them.

And one of the boys fell down through a back-door, and died immediately.

And when the children saw this, they all ran away; but Jesus remained in the house. [1]And when the parents of the boy who had died had come, they spoke against Jesus:

Surely it was thou who made him fall down; and they reviled Him.

And Jesus, coming down from the house, stood over the dead child, and with a loud voice called out the name of the child:

Sinoo, Sinoo, rise and say whether it was I that made thee fall down.

And suddenly he rose up, and said:

No, my lord.

And his parents, seeing such a great miracle done by Jesus, glorified God, and adored Jesus.

Footnote:

1. Or, on the house.

Chapter VIII - How Jesus Healed a Boy's Foot

And a few days thereafter, a boy in that town was splitting wood, and struck his foot.

And a great crowd went to him, and Jesus too went with them.

And He touched the foot which had been hurt, and immediately it was made whole.

And Jesus said to him:

Rise, and split the wood, and remember me.

And when the crowd saw the miracles that were done by Him, they adored Jesus, and said:

Indeed we most surely believe that Thou art God.

Chapter IX - How Jesus Carried Water in a Cloak

And when Jesus was six years old, His mother sent Him to draw water. And when Jesus had come to the fountain, or to the well, there were great crowds there, and they broke His pitcher.

And He took the cloak which He had on, and filled it with water, and carried it to His mother Mary.

And His mother, seeing the miracles which Jesus had done, kissed Him, and said:

O Lord, hear me, and save my son.

Chapter X - How Jesus Sowed Wheat

In the time of sowing, Joseph went out to sow wheat, and Jesus followed him.

And when Joseph began to sow, Jesus stretched out His hand, and took as much wheat as He could hold in His fist, and scattered it. Joseph therefore came at reaping-time to reap his harvest.

Jesus came also, and collected the ears which He had scattered, and they made a hundred pecks [1] of the best grain; and he called the poor, and the widows, and the orphans, and distributed to them the wheat which He had made.

Joseph also took a little of the same wheat, for the blessing of Jesus to his house.

Footnote:
1. The modius or modium was almost exactly two gallons.

Chapter XI - How Jesus Made a Short Piece of Wood of the Same Length as a Longer One

And Jesus reached the age of eight years.

Joseph was a master builder, [1] and used to make ploughs and ox-yokes.

And one day a rich man said to Joseph:

Master, make me a couch, both useful and beautiful. And Joseph was in distress, because the wood which he had brought [2] for the work was too short.

And Jesus said to him:

Do not be annoyed.

Take hold of this piece of wood by one end, and I by the other; I and let us draw it out.

And they did so; and immediately he found it useful for that which he wished.

And He said to Joseph: Behold, do the work which thou wishest.

And Joseph, seeing what He had done, embraced Him, and said:

Blessed am I, because God hath given me such a son.

Footnotes:
1. But probably architector here is equal to tekton, a carpenter.
2. Perhaps sectum, cut, is the true reading, and not actum.

Chapter XII - How Jesus Was Handed Over to Learn His Letters

And Joseph, seeing that He had such favour, and that He was increasing in stature, thought it right to take Him to learn His letters.

And he handed Him over to another teacher to be taught.

And that teacher said to Joseph:

What letters dost thou wish me to teach that boy?

Joseph answered and said:

First teach him the Gentile letters, and then the Hebrew.

For the teacher knew that He was very intelligent, and willingly took Him in hand.

And writing for Him the first line, which is A and B, he taught Him for some hours. [1]But Jesus was silent, and made him no answer.

Jesus said to the master:

If thou art indeed a master, and if thou indeed knowest the letters, tell me the power [2] of the A, and I shall tell thee the power of the B.

Then His master was filled with fury, and struck Him on the head.

And Jesus was angry, and cursed him; and he suddenly fell down, and died.

And Jesus returned home.

And Joseph gave orders to Mary His mother, not to let Him go out of the court of his house.

Footnotes:
1. This is his translation of epi pollen oran.
2. Here again he makes a mistranslation--dunamis, fortitudo.

Chapter XIII - How He Was Handed Over to Another Master

Many days after came another teacher, a friend of Joseph, and said to him:

Hand him over to me, and I with much sweetness will teach him his letters.

And Joseph said to him:

If thou art able, take him and teach him.

May it be attended with joy.

When the teacher had taken Him, he went along in fear and in great firmness, and held Him with exultation.

And when He had come to the teacher's house, He found a book lying there, and took it and opened it, and did not read what was written in the book; but opened His mouth, and spoke from the Holy Spirit, and taught the law.

And, indeed, all who were standing there listened to Him attentively; and the master sat down beside Him, and listened to Him with pleasure, and entreated Him to teach them more. And a great crowd being gathered together, they heard all the holy teaching which He taught, and the choice words which came forth from the mouth of Him who, child as He was, spake such things.

And Joseph, hearing of this, was afraid, and running [1] ...the master, where Jesus was, said to Joseph:

Know, brother, that I have received thy child to teach him or train him; but he is filled with much gravity and wisdom.

Lo, now, take him home with joy, my brother; because the gravity which he has, has been given him by the Lord.

And Jesus, hearing the master thus speaking, became cheerful, and said:

Lo, now, master, thou hast truly said.

For thy sake, he who is dead shall rise again.

And Joseph took Him home.

Footnote:

1. Some words have been omitted here in the ms., but the sense is obvious enough.

Chapter XIV - How Jesus Delivered James from the Bite of a Serpent

And Joseph sent James to gather straw, and Jesus followed him.

And while James was gathering the straw, a viper bit him; and he fell to the ground, as if dead from the poison.

And Jesus seeing this, blew upon his wound; and immediately James was made whole, and the viper died.

Chapter XV - How Jesus Raised a Boy to Life

A few days after, a child, His neighbour, died, and his mother mourned for him sore.

Jesus, hearing this, went and stood over the boy, and knocked upon his breast, and said:

I say to thee, child, do not die, but live.

And immediately the child rose up.

And Jesus said to the boy's mother:

Take thy son, and give him the breast, and remember me. And the crowd, seeing this miracle, said:

In truth, this child is from heaven; for already has he freed many souls from death, and he has made whole all that hope in him.

The scribes and Pharisees said to Mary:

Art thou the mother of this child?

And Mary said:

Indeed I am.

And they said to her:

Blessed art thou among women, [1] since God hath blessed the fruit of thy womb, seeing that He hath given thee such a glorious child, and such a gift of wisdom, as we have never seen nor heard of.

Jesus rose up and followed His mother.

And Mary kept in her heart all the great miracles that Jesus had done among the people, in healing many that were diseased.

And Jesus grew in stature and wisdom; and all who saw Him glorified God the Father Almighty, who is blessed for ever and ever. Amen.

And all these things I Thomas the Israelite have written what I have seen, and have recounted them to the Gentiles and to our brethren, and many other things done by Jesus, who was born in the land of Judah. Behold, the house of Israel has seen all, from the first even to the last; how great signs and wonders Jesus did among them, which were exceedingly good, and invisible to their father, [2] as holy Scripture relates, and the prophets have borne witness to His works in all the peoples of Israel.

And He it is who is to judge the world according to the will of immortality, since He is the Son of God throughout all the world.

To Him is due all glory and honour for ever, who lives and reigns God through all ages of ages.

Amen.

Footnotes:

1. Luke i. 28.
2. This, I think, means: and which their father Israel, i.e. their fathers generally, had not seen.

The Arabic Gospel of the Infancy of the Saviour

In the name of the Father, and the Son, and the Holy Spirit, one God.
With the help and favour of the Most High we begin to write a book of the miracles of our Lord and Master and Saviour Jesus Christ, which is called the Gospel of the Infancy:
in the peace of the Lord.
Amen.

1.
We find [1] what follows in the book of Joseph the high priest, who lived in the time of Christ. Some say that he is Caiaphas. [2]
He has said that Jesus spoke, and, indeed, when He was lying in His cradle said to Mary His mother:
I am Jesus, the Son of God, the Logos, whom thou hast brought forth, as the Angel Gabriel announced to thee; and my Father has sent me for the salvation of the world.

2.
In the three hundred and ninth year of the era of Alexander, Augustus put forth an edict, that every man should be enrolled in his native place.
Joseph therefore arose, and taking Mary his spouse, went away to [3] Jerusalem, and came to Bethlehem, to be enrolled along with his family in his native city.
And having come to a cave, Mary told Joseph that the time of the birth was at hand, and that she could not go into the city; but, said she, let us go into this cave.
This took place at sunset.
And Joseph went out in haste to go for a woman to be near her.
When, therefore, he was busy about that, he saw an Hebrew old woman belonging to Jerusalem, and said:
Come hither, my good woman, and go into this cave, in which there is a woman near her time.

3.
Wherefore, after sunset, the old woman, and Joseph with her, came to the cave, and they both went in.
And, behold, it was filled with lights more beautiful than the gleaming of lamps and candles, [4] and more splendid than the light of the sun.
The child, enwrapped in swaddling clothes, was sucking the breast of the Lady Mary His mother, being placed in a stall.
And when both were wondering at this light, the old woman asks the Lady Mary:
Art thou the mother of this Child? And when the Lady Mary gave her assent, she says:
Thou art not at all like the daughters of Eve.
The Lady Mary said:
As my son has no equal among children, so his mother has no equal among women.
The old woman replied:
My mistress, I came to get payment; I have been for a long time affected with palsy.
Our mistress the Lady Mary said to her: Place thy hands upon the child.
And the old woman did so, and was immediately cured.
Then she went forth, saying:
Henceforth I will be the attendant and servant of this child all the days of my life.

4.

Then came shepherds; and when they had lighted a fire, and were rejoicing greatly, there appeared to them the hosts of heaven praising and celebrating God Most High.

And while the shepherds were doing the same, the cave was at that time made like a temple of the upper world, since both heavenly and earthly voices glorified and magnified God on account of the birth of the Lord Christ.

And when that old Hebrew woman saw the manifestation of those miracles, she thanked God, saying:

I give Thee thanks, O God, the God of Israel, because mine eyes have seen the birth of the Saviour of the world.

5.

And the time of circumcision, that is, the eighth day, being at hand, the child was to be circumcised according to the law.

Wherefore they circumcised Him in the cave.

And the old Hebrew woman took the piece of skin; but some say that she took the navel-string, and laid it past in a jar of old oil of nard.

And she had a son, a dealer in unguents, and she gave it to him, saying:

See that thou do not sell this jar of unguent of nard, even although three hundred denarii [5] should be offered thee for it.

And this is that jar which Mary the sinner bought and poured upon the head and feet of our Lord Jesus Christ, which thereafter she wiped with the hair of her head. [6] Ten days after, they took Him to Jerusalem; and on the fortieth day [7] after His birth they carried Him into the temple, and set Him before the Lord, and offered sacrifices for Him, according to the commandment of the law of Moses, which is:

Every male that openeth the womb shall be called the holy of God. [8]

6.

Then old Simeon saw Him shining like a pillar of light, when the Lady Mary, His virgin mother, rejoicing over Him, was carrying Him in her arms.

And angels, praising Him, stood round Him in a circle, like life guards standing by a king.

Simeon therefore went up in haste to the Lady Mary, and, with hands stretched out before her, said to the Lord Christ:

Now, O my Lord, let Thy servant depart in peace, according to Thy word; for mine eyes have seen Thy compassion, which Thou hast prepared for the salvation of all peoples, a light to all nations, and glory to Thy people Israel.

Hanna also, a prophetess, was present, and came up, giving thanks to God, and calling the Lady Mary blessed. [9]

7.

And it came to pass, when the Lord Jesus was born at Bethlehem of Judaea, in the time of King Herod, behold, magi came from the east to Jerusalem, as Zeraduscht [10] had predicted; and there were with them gifts, gold, and frankincense, and myrrh.

And they adored Him, and presented to Him their gifts.

Then the Lady Mary took one of the swaddling-bands, and, on account of the smallness of her means, gave it to them; and they received it from her with the greatest marks of honour.

And in the same hour there appeared to them an angel in the form of that star which had before guided them on their journey; and they went away, following the guidance of its light, until they arrived in their own country. [11]

8.

And their kings and chief men came together to them, asking what they had seen or done, how they had gone and come back, what they had brought with them.

And they showed them that swathing-cloth which the Lady Mary had given them.

Wherefore they celebrated a feast, and, according to their custom, lighted a fire and worshipped it, and threw that swathing-cloth into it; and the fire laid hold of it, and enveloped it.

And when the fire had gone out, they took out the swathing-cloth exactly as it had been before, just as if the fire had not touched it.

Wherefore they began to kiss it, and to put it on their heads and their eyes, saying:

This verily is the truth without doubt.

Assuredly it is a great thing that the fire was not able to burn or destroy it.

Then they took it, and with the greatest honour laid it up among their treasures.

The Forgotten Bible

9.

And when Herod saw that the magi had left him, and not come back to him, he summoned the priests and the wise men, and said to them:

Show me where Christ is to be born.

And when they answered, In Bethlehem of Judaea, he began to think of putting the Lord Jesus Christ to death. Then appeared an angel of the Lord to Joseph in his sleep, and said: Rise, take the boy and His mother, and go away into Egypt. [12]He rose, therefore, towards cockcrow, and set out.

10.

While he is reflecting how he is to set about his journey, morning came upon him after he had gone a very little way.

And now he was approaching a great city, in which there was an idol, to which the other idols and gods of the Egyptians offered gifts and vows.

And there stood before this idol a priest ministering to him, who, as often as Satan spoke from that idol, reported it to the inhabitants of Egypt and its territories.

This priest had a son, three years old, beset by several demons; and he made many speeches and utterances; and when the demons seized him, he tore his clothes, and remained naked, and threw stones at the people.

And there was a hospital in that city dedicated to that idol.

And when Joseph and the Lady Mary had come to the city, and had turned aside into that hospital, the citizens were very much afraid; and all the chief men and the priests of the idols came together to that idol, and said to it:

What agitation and commotion is this that has arisen in our land?

The idol answered them:

A God has come here in secret, who is God indeed; nor is any god besides Him worthy of divine worship, because He is truly the Son of God.

And when this land became aware of His presence, it trembled at His arrival, and was moved and shaken; and we are exceedingly afraid from the greatness of His power.

And in the same hour that idol fell down, and at its fall all, inhabitants of Egypt and others, ran together.

11.

And the son of the priest, his usual disease having come upon him, entered the hospital, and there came upon Joseph and the Lady Mary, from whom all others had fled.

The Lady Mary had washed the cloths of the Lord Christ, and had spread them over some wood.

That demoniac boy, therefore, came and took one of the cloths, and put it on his head.

Then the demons, fleeing in the shape of ravens and serpents, began to go forth out of his mouth.

The boy, being immediately healed at the command of the Lord Christ, began to praise God, and then to give thanks to the Lord who had healed him.

And when his father saw him restored to health, My son, said he, what has happened to thee? and by what means hast thou been healed?

The son answered:

When the demons had thrown me on the ground, I went into the hospital, and there I found an august woman with a boy, whose newly-washed cloths she had thrown upon some wood:

one of these I took up and put upon my head, and the demons left me and fled.

At this the father rejoiced greatly, and said:

My son, it is possible that this boy is the Son of the living God who created the heavens and the earth:

for when he came over to us, the idol was broken, and all the gods fell, and perished by the power of his magnificence.

12.

Here was fulfilled the prophecy which says, Out of Egypt have I called my son. [13]Joseph indeed, and Mary, when they heard that that idol had fallen down and perished, trembled, and were afraid. Then they said:

When we were in the land of Israel, Herod thought to put Jesus to death, and on that account slew all the children of Bethlehem and its confines; and there is no doubt that the Egyptians, as soon as they have heard that this idol has been broken, will burn us with fire. [14]

13.
Going out thence, they came to a place where there were robbers who had plundered several men of their baggage and clothes, and had bound them.

Then the robbers heard a great noise, like the noise of a magnificent king going out of his city with his army, and his chariots and his drums; and at this the robbers were terrified, and left all their plunder.

And their captives rose up, loosed each other's bonds, recovered their baggage, and went away.

And when they saw Joseph and Mary coming up to the place, they said to them:

Where is that king, at the hearing of the magnificent sound of whose approach the robbers have left us, so that we have escaped safe?

Joseph answered them:

He will come behind us.

14.
Thereafter they came into another city, where there was a demoniac woman whom Satan, accursed and rebellious, had beset, when on one occasion she had gone out by night for water.

She could neither bear clothes, nor live in a house; and as often as they tied her up with chains and thongs, she broke them, and fled naked into waste places; and, standing in cross-roads and cemeteries, she kept throwing stones at people, and brought very heavy calamities upon her friends.

And when the Lady Mary saw her, she pitied her; and upon this Satan immediately left her, and fled away in the form of a young man, saying:

Woe to me from thee, Mary, and from thy son.

So that woman was cured of her torment, and being restored to her senses, she blushed on account of her nakedness; and shunning the sight of men, went home to her friends.

And after she put on her clothes, she gave an account of the matter to her father and her friends; and as they were the chief men of the city, they received the Lady Mary and Joseph with the greatest honour and hospitality.

15.
On the day after, being supplied by them with provision for their journey, they went away, and on the evening of that day arrived at another town, in which they were celebrating a marriage; but, by the arts of accursed Satan and the work of enchanters, the bride had become dumb, and could not speak a word.

And after the Lady Mary entered the town, carrying her son the Lord Christ, that dumb bride saw her, and stretched out her hands towards the Lord Christ, and drew Him to her, and took Him into her arms, and held Him close and kissed Him, and leaned over Him, moving His body back and forwards.

Immediately the knot of her tongue was loosened, and her ears were opened; and she gave thanks and praise to God, because He had restored her to health.

And that night the inhabitants of that town exulted with joy, and thought that God and His angels had come down to them.

16.
There they remained three days, being held in great honour, and living splendidly.

Thereafter, being supplied by them with provision for their journey, they went away and came to another city, in which, because it was very populous, they thought of passing the night.

And there was in that city an excellent woman:

and once, when she had gone to the river to bathe, lo, accursed Satan, in the form of a serpent, had leapt upon her, and twisted himself round her belly; and as often as night came on, he tyrannically tormented her.

This woman, seeing the mistress the Lady Mary, and the child, the Lord Christ, in her bosom, was struck with a longing for Him, and said to the mistress the Lady Mary:

O mistress, give me this child, that I may carry him, and kiss him.

She therefore gave Him to the woman; and when He was brought to her, Satan let her go, and fled and left her, nor did the woman ever see him after that day.

Wherefore all who were present praised God Most High, and that woman bestowed on them liberal gifts

17.

On the day after, the same woman took scented water to wash the Lord Jesus; and after she had washed Him, she took the water with which she had done it, and poured part of it upon a girl who was living there, whose body was white with leprosy, and washed her with it.

And as soon as this was done, the girl was cleansed from her leprosy.

And the townspeople said:

There is no doubt that Joseph and Mary and that boy are gods, not men.

And when they were getting ready to go away from them, the girl who had laboured under the leprosy came up to them, and asked them to let her go with them.

18.

When they had given her permission, she went with them.

And afterwards they came to a city, in which was the castle of a most illustrious prince, who kept a house for the entertainment of strangers.

They turned into this place; and the girl went away to the prince's wife; and she found her weeping and sorrowful, and she asked why she was weeping.

Do not be surprised, said she, at my tears; for I am overwhelmed by a great affliction, which as yet I have not endured to tell to any one.

Perhaps, said the girl, if you reveal it and disclose it to me, I may have a remedy for it.

Hide this secret, then, replied the princess, and tell it to no one.

I was married to this prince, who is a king and ruler over many cities, and I lived long with him, but by me he had no son.

And when at length I produced him a son, he was leprous; and as soon as he saw him, he turned away with loathing, and said to me:

Either kill him, or give him to the nurse to be brought up in some place from which we shall never hear of him more.

After this I can have nothing to do with thee, and I will never see thee more.

On this account I know not what to do, and I am overwhelmed with grief.

Alas! my son.

Alas! my husband.

Did I not say so? said the girl.

I have found a cure for thy disease, and I shall tell it thee.

For I too was a leper; but I was cleansed by God, who is Jesus, the son of the Lady Mary.

And the woman asking her where this God was whom she had spoken of, Here, with thee, said the girl; He is living in the same house.

But how is this possible? said she. Where is he?

There, said the girl, are Joseph and Mary; and the child who is with them is called Jesus; and He it is who cured me of my disease and my torment.

But by what means, said she, wast thou cured of thy leprosy?

Wilt thou not tell me that?

Why not? said the girl. I got from His mother the water in which He had been washed, and poured it over myself; and so I was cleansed from my leprosy.

Then the princess rose up, and invited them to avail themselves of her hospitality.

And she prepared a splendid banquet for Joseph in a great assembly of the men of the place.

And on the following day she took scented water with which to wash the Lord Jesus, and thereafter poured the same water over her son, whom she had taken with her; and immediately her son was cleansed from his leprosy.

Therefore, singing thanks and praises to God, she said:

Blessed is the mother who bore thee, O Jesus; dost thou so cleanse those who share the same nature with thee with the water in which thy body has been washed?

Besides, she bestowed great gifts upon the mistress the Lady Mary, and sent her away with great honour.

19.

Coming thereafter to another city, they wished to spend the night in it.

They turned aside, therefore, to the house of a man newly married, but who, under the influence of witchcraft, was not able to enjoy his wife; and when they had spent that night with him, his bond was loosed.

And at daybreak, when they were girding themselves for their journey, the bridegroom would not let them go, and prepared for them a great banquet.

20.

They set out, therefore, on the following day; and as they came near another city, they saw three women weeping as they came out of a cemetery.

And when the Lady Mary beheld them, she said to the girl who accompanied her:

Ask them what is the matter with them, or what calamity has befallen them.

And to the girl's questions they made no reply, but asked in their turn:

Whence are you, and whither are you going? for the day is already past, and night is coming on apace.

We are travellers, said the girl, and are seeking a house of entertainment in which we may pass the night.

They said:

Go with us, and spend the night with us.

They followed them, therefore, and were brought into a new house with splendid decorations and furniture.

Now it was winter; and the girl, going into the chamber of these women, found them again weeping and lamenting.

There stood beside them a mule, covered with housings of cloth of gold, and sesame was put before him; and the women were kissing him, and giving him food.

And the girl said:

What is all the ado, my ladies, about this mule?

They answered her with tears, and said:

This mule, which thou seest, was our brother, born of the same mother with ourselves.

And when our father died, and left us great wealth, and this only brother, we did our best to get him married, and were preparing his nuptials for him, after the manner of men.

But some women, moved by mutual jealousy, bewitched him unknown to us; and one night, a little before daybreak, when the door of our house was shut, we saw that this our brother had been turned into a mule, as thou now beholdest him.

And we are sorrowful, as thou seest, having no father to comfort us:

there is no wise man, or magician, or enchanter in the world that we have omitted to send for; but nothing has done us any good.

And as often as our hearts are overwhelmed with grief, we rise and go away with our mother here, and weep at our father's grave, and come back again.

21.

And when the girl heard these things, Be of good courage, said she, and weep not:

for the cure of your calamity is near; yea, it is beside you, and in the middle of your own house.

For I also was a leper; but when I saw that woman, and along with her that young child, whose name is Jesus, I sprinkled my body with the water with which His mother had washed Him, and I was cured.

And I know that He can cure your affliction also.

But rise, go to Mary my mistress; bring her into your house, and tell her your secret; and entreat and supplicate her to have pity upon you.

After the woman had heard the girl's words, they went in haste to the Lady Mary, and brought her into their chamber, and sat down before her weeping, and saying:

O our mistress, Lady Mary, have pity on thy hand-maidens; for no one older than ourselves, and no head of the family, is left--neither father nor brother--to live with us; but this mule which thou seest was our brother, and women have made him such as thou seest by witchcraft.

We beseech thee, therefore, to have pity upon us.

Then, grieving at their lot, the Lady Mary took up the Lord Jesus, and put Him on the mule's back; and she wept as well as the women, and said to Jesus Christ:

Alas! my son, heal this mule by Thy mighty power, and make him a man endowed with reason as he was before.

And when these words were uttered by the Lady Mary, his form was changed, and the mule became a young man, free from every defect. Then he and his mother and his sisters adored the Lady Mary, and lifted the boy above their heads, and began to kiss Him, saying:

Blessed is she that bore Thee, O Jesus, O Saviour of the world; blessed are the eyes which enjoy the felicity of seeing Thee.

22.

Moreover, both the sisters said to their mother:

Our brother indeed, by the aid of the Lord Jesus Christ, and by the salutary intervention of this girl, who pointed out to us Mary and her son, has been raised to human form.

Now, indeed, since our brother is unmarried, it would do very well for us to give him as his wife this girl, their servant.

And having asked the Lady Mary, and obtained her consent, they made a splendid wedding for the girl; and their sorrow being changed into joy, and the beating of their breasts into dancing, they began to be glad, to rejoice, to exult, and sing--adorned, on account of their great joy, in most splendid and gorgeous attire.

Then they began to recite songs and praises, and to say:

O Jesus, son of David, who turnest sorrow into gladness, and lamentations into joy! And Joseph and Mary remained there ten days.

Thereafter they set out, treated with great honours by these people, who bade them farewell, and from bidding them farewell returned weeping, especially the girl.

23.

And turning away from this place, they came to a desert; and hearing that it was infested by robbers, Joseph and the Lady Mary resolved to cross this region by night.

But as they go along, behold, they see two robbers lying in the way, and along with them a great number of robbers, who were their associates, sleeping.

Now those two robbers, into whose hands they had fallen, were Titus and Dumachus. Titus therefore said to Dumachus:

I beseech thee to let these persons go freely, and so that our comrades may not see them.

And as Dumachus refused, Titus said to him again:

Take to thyself forty drachmas from me, and hold this as a pledge.

At the same time he held out to him the belt which he had about his waist, to keep him from opening his mouth or speaking.

And the Lady Mary, seeing that the robber had done them a kindness, said to him:

The Lord God will sustain thee by His right hand, and will grant thee remission of thy sins.

And the Lord Jesus answered, and said to His mother:

Thirty years hence, O my mother, the Jews will crucify me at Jerusalem, and these two robbers will be raised upon the cross along with me, Titus on my right hand and Dumachus on my left; and after that day Titus shall go before me into Paradise.

And she said:

God keep this from thee, my son.

And they went thence towards a city of idols, which, as they came near it, was changed into sand-hills.

24.

Hence they turned aside to that sycamore which is now called Matarea, [15] and the Lord Jesus brought forth in Matarea a fountain in which the Lady Mary washed His shirt.

And from the sweat of the Lord Jesus which she sprinkled there, balsam was produced in that region.

25.

Thence they came down to Memphis, and saw Pharaoh, and remained three years in Egypt; and the Lord Jesus did in Egypt very many miracles which are recorded neither in the Gospel of the Infancy nor in the perfect Gospel.

26.

And at the end of the three years He came back out of Egypt, and returned.

And when they had arrived at Judaea, Joseph was afraid to enter it; but hearing that Herod was dead, and that Archelaus his son had succeeded him, he was afraid indeed, but he went into Judaea.

And an angel of the Lord appeared to him, and said:

O Joseph, go into the city of Nazareth, and there abide.

Wonderful indeed, that the Lord of the world should be thus borne and carried about through the world!

27.

Thereafter, going into the city of Bethlehem, they saw there many and grievous diseases infesting the eyes of the children, who were dying in consequence.

And a woman was there with a sick son, whom, now very near death, she brought to the Lady Mary, who saw him as she was washing Jesus Christ.

Then said the woman to her:

O my Lady Mary, look upon this son of mine, who is labouring under a grievous disease. And the Lady Mary listened to her, and said:

Take a little of that water in which I have washed my son, and sprinkle him with it.

She therefore took a little of the water, as the Lady Mary had told her, and sprinkled it over her son.

And when this was done his illness abated; and after sleeping a little, he rose up from sleep safe and sound.

His mother rejoicing at this, again took him to the Lady Mary. And she said to her:

Give thanks to God, because He hath healed this thy son.

28.

There was in the same place another woman, a neighbour of her whose son had lately been restored to health.

And as her son was labouring under the same disease, and his eyes were now almost blinded, she wept night and day.

And the mother of the child that had been cured said to her:

Why dost thou not take thy son to the Lady Mary, as I did with mine when he was nearly dead?

And he got well with that water with which the body of her son Jesus had been washed.

And when the woman heard this from her, she too went and got some of the same water, and washed her son with it, and his body and his eyes were instantly made well.

Her also, when she had brought her son to her, and disclosed to her all that had happened, the Lady Mary ordered to give thanks to God for her son's restoration to health, and to tell nobody of this matter.

29.

There were in the same city two women, wives of one man, each having a son ill with fever.

The one was called Mary, and her son's name was Cleopas.

She rose and took up her son, and went to the Lady Mary, the mother of Jesus, and offering her a beautiful mantle, said: O my Lady Mary, accept this mantle, and for it give me one small bandage.

Mary did so, and the mother of Cleopas went away, and made a shirt of it, and put it on her son.

So he was cured of his disease; but the son of her rival died.

Hence there sprung up hatred between them; and as they did the house-work week about, and as it was the turn of Mary the mother of Cleopas, she heated the oven to bake bread; and going away to bring the lump that she had kneaded, she left her son Cleopas beside the oven.

Her rival seeing him alone--and the oven was very hot with the fire blazing under it--seized him and threw him into the oven, and took herself off.

Mary coming back, and seeing her son Cleopas lying in the oven laughing, and the oven quite cold, as if no fire had ever come near it, knew that her rival had thrown him into the fire.

She drew him out, therefore, and took him to the Lady Mary, and told her of what had happened to him.

And she said:

Keep silence, and tell nobody of the affair; for I am afraid for you if you divulge it. After this her rival went to the well to draw water; and seeing Cleopas playing beside the well, and nobody near, she seized him and threw him into the well, and went home herself.

And some men who had gone to the well for water saw the boy sitting on the surface of the water; and so they went down and drew him out.

And they were seized with a great admiration of that boy, and praised God.

Then came his mother, and took him up, and went weeping to the Lady Mary, and said:

O my lady, see what my rival has done to my son, and how she has thrown him into the well; she will be sure to destroy him some day or other.

The Lady Mary said to her:

God will avenge thee upon her.

Thereafter, when her rival went to the well to draw water, her feet got entangled in the rope,

The Forgotten Bible

and she fell into the well.

Some men came to draw her out, but they found her skull fractured and her bones broken.

Thus she died a miserable death, and in her came to pass that saying:

They have digged a well deep, but have fallen into the pit which they had prepared. [16]

30.

Another woman there had twin sons who had fallen into disease, and one of them died, and the other was at his last breath.

And his mother, weeping, lifted him up, and took him to the Lady Mary, and said:

O my lady, aid me and succour me.

For I had two sons, and I have just buried the one, and the other is at the point of death. See how I am going to entreat and pray to God.

And she began to say:

O Lord, Thou art compassionate, and merciful, and full of affection. Thou gavest me two sons, of whom Thou hast taken away the one:

this one at least leave to me.

Wherefore the Lady Mary, seeing the fervour of her weeping, had compassion on her, and said:

Put thy son in my son's bed, and cover him with his clothes.

And when she had put him in the bed in which Christ was lying, he had already closed his eyes in death; but as soon as the smell of the clothes of the Lord Jesus Christ reached the boy, he opened his eyes, and, calling upon his mother with a loud voice, he asked for bread, and took it and sucked it.

Then his mother said:

O Lady Mary, now I know that the power of God dwelleth in thee, so that thy son heals those that partake of the same nature with himself, as soon as they have touched his clothes.

This boy that was healed is he who in the Gospel is called Bartholomew.

31.

Moreover, there was there a leprous woman, and she went to the Lady Mary, the mother of Jesus, and said:

My lady, help me.

And the Lady Mary answered:

What help dost thou seek?

Is it gold or silver? or is it that thy body be made clean from the leprosy?

And that woman asked:

Who can grant me this?

And the Lady Mary said to her:

Wait a little, until I shall have washed my son Jesus, and put him to bed. The woman waited, as Mary had told her; and when she had put Jesus to bed, she held out to the woman the water in which she had washed His body, and said:

Take a little of this water, and pour it over thy body.

And as soon as she had done so, she was cleansed, and gave praise and thanks to God.

32.

Therefore, after staying with her three days, she went away; and coming to a city, saw there one of the chief men, who had married the daughter of another of the chief men.

But when he saw the woman, he beheld between her eyes the mark of leprosy in the shape of a star; and so the marriage was dissolved, and became null and void.

And when that woman saw them in this condition, weeping and overwhelmed with sorrow, she asked the cause of their grief.

But they said:

Inquire not into our condition, for to no one living can we tell our grief, and to none but ourselves can we disclose it.

She urged them, however, and entreated them to entrust it to her, saying that she would perhaps be able to tell them of a remedy.

And when they showed her the girl, and the sign of leprosy which appeared between her eyes, as soon as she saw it, the woman said:

I also, whom you see here, laboured under the same disease, when, upon some business which happened to come in my way, I went to Bethlehem.

There going into a cave, I saw a woman named Mary, whose son was he who was named Jesus; and when she saw that I was a leper, she took pity on me, and handed me the water with which she had washed her son's body.

With it I sprinkled my body, and came out clean.

Then the woman said to her:

Wilt thou not, O lady, rise and go with us, and show us the Lady Mary?

And she assented; and they rose and went to the Lady Mary, carrying with them splendid gifts.

And when they had gone in, and presented to her the gifts, they showed her the leprous girl whom they had brought.

The Lady Mary therefore said:

May the compassion of the Lord Jesus Christ descend upon you; and handling to them also a little of the water in which she had washed the body of Jesus Christ, she ordered the wretched woman to be bathed in it.

And when this had been done, she was immediately cured; and they, and all standing by, praised God.

Joyfully therefore they returned to their own city, praising the Lord for what He had done.

And when the chief heard that his wife had been cured, he took her home, and made a second marriage, and gave thanks to God for the recovery of his wife's health.

33.

There was there also a young woman afflicted by Satan; for that accursed wretch repeatedly appeared to her in the form of a huge dragon, and prepared to swallow her.

He also sucked out all her blood, so that she was left like a corpse.

As often as he came near her, she, with her hands clasped over her head, cried out, and said:

Woe, woe's me, for nobody is near to free me from that accursed dragon.

And her father and mother, and all who were about her or saw her, bewailed her lot; and men stood round her in a crowd, and all wept and lamented, especially when she wept, and said:

Oh, my brethren and friends, is there no one to free me from that murderer?

And the daughter of the chief who had been healed of her leprosy, hearing the girl's voice, went up to the roof of her castle, and saw her with her hands clasped over her head weeping, and all the crowds standing round her weeping as well.

She therefore asked the demoniac's husband whether his wife's mother were alive.

And when he answered that both her parents were living, she said:

Send for her mother to come to me.

And when she saw that he had sent for her, and she had come, she said:

Is that distracted girl thy daughter?

Yes, O lady, said that sorrowful and weeping woman, she is my daughter.

The chief's daughter answered: Keep my secret, for I confess to thee that I was formerly a leper; but now the Lady Mary, the mother of Jesus Christ, has healed me.

But if thou wishest thy daughter to be healed, take her to Bethlehem, and seek Mary the mother of Jesus, and believe that thy daughter will be healed; I indeed believe that thou wilt come back with joy, with thy daughter healed.

As soon as the woman heard the words of the chief's daughter, she led away her daughter in haste; and going to the place indicated, she went to the Lady Mary, and revealed to her the state of her daughter.

And the Lady Mary hearing her words, gave her a little of the water in which she had washed the body of her son Jesus, and ordered her to pour it on the body of her daughter.

She gave her also from the clothes of the Lord Jesus a swathing-cloth, saying:

Take this cloth, and show it to thine enemy as often as thou shalt see him.

And she saluted them, and sent them away.

34.

When, therefore, they had gone away from her, and returned to their own district, and the time was at hand at which Satan was wont to attack her, at this very time that accursed one appeared to her in the shape of a huge dragon, and the girl was afraid at the sight of him. And her mother said to her:

Fear not, my daughter; allow him to come near thee, and then show him the cloth which the Lady Mary hath given us, and let us see what will happen.

Satan, therefore, having come near in the likeness of a terrible dragon, the body of the girl shuddered for fear of him; but as soon as she took out the cloth, and placed it on her head, and covered her eyes with it, flames and live coals began to dart forth from it, and to be cast upon the dragon.

O the great miracle which was done as soon as the dragon saw the cloth of the Lord Jesus, from which the fire darted, and was cast upon his head and eyes!

He cried out with a loud voice:

What have I to do with thee, O Jesus, son of Mary?

Whither shall I fly from thee?

And with great fear he turned his back and departed from the girl, and never afterwards appeared to her.

And the girl now had rest from him, and gave praise and thanks to God, and along with her all who were present at that miracle.

35.

Another woman was living in the same place, whose son was tormented by Satan.

He, Judas by name, as often as Satan seized him, used to bite all who came near him; and if he found no one near him, he used to bite his own hands and other limbs.

The mother of this wretched creature, then, hearing the fame of the Lady Mary and her son Jesus, rose up and brought her son Judas with her to the Lady Mary.

In the meantime, James and Joses had taken the child the Lord Jesus with them to play with the other children; and they had gone out of the house and sat down, and the Lord Jesus with them.

And the demoniac Judas came up, and sat down at Jesus' right hand:

then, being attacked by Satan in the same manner as usual, he wished to bite the Lord Jesus, but was not able; nevertheless he struck Jesus on the right side, whereupon He began to weep.

And immediately Satan went forth out of that boy, fleeing like a mad dog.

And this boy who struck Jesus, and out of whom Satan went forth in the shape of a dog, was Judas Iscariot, who betrayed Him to the Jews; and that same side on which Judas struck Him, the Jews transfixed with a lance. [17]

36.

Now, when the Lord Jesus had completed seven years from His birth, on a certain day He was occupied with boys of His own age.

For they were playing among clay, from which they were making images of asses, oxen, birds, and other animals; and each one boasting of his skill, was praising his own work.

Then the Lord Jesus said to the boys:

The images that I have made I will order to walk.

The boys asked Him whether then he were the son of the Creator; and the Lord Jesus bade them walk.

And they immediately began to leap; and then, when He had given them leave, they again stood still.

And He had made figures of birds and sparrows, which flew when He told them to fly, and stood still when He told them to stand, and ate and drank when He handed them food and drink.

After the boys had gone away and told this to their parents, their fathers said to them:

My sons, take care not to keep company with him again, for he is a wizard:

flee from him, therefore, and avoid him, and do not play with him again after this.

37.

On a certain day the Lord Jesus, running about and playing with the boys, passed the shop of a dyer, whose name was Salem; and he had in his shop many pieces of cloth which he was to dye.

The Lord Jesus then, going into his shop, took up all the pieces of cloth, and threw them into a tub full of indigo.

And when Salem came and saw his cloths destroyed, he began to cry out with a loud voice, and to reproach Jesus, saying:

Why hast thou done this to me, O son of Mary?

Thou hast disgraced me before all my townsmen:

for, seeing that every one wished the colour that suited himself, thou indeed hast come and destroyed them all.

The Lord Jesus answered:

I shall change for thee the colour of any piece of cloth which thou shalt wish to be changed.

And immediately He began to take the pieces of cloth out of the tub, each of them of that colour which the dyer wished, until He had taken them all out.

When the Jews saw this miracle and prodigy, they praised God.

38.
And Joseph used to go about through the whole city, and take the Lord Jesus with him, when people sent for him in the way of his trade to make for them doors, and milk-pails, and beds, and chests; and the Lord Jesus was with him wherever he went.

As often, therefore, as Joseph had to make anything a cubit or a span longer or shorter, wider or narrower, the Lord Jesus stretched His hand towards it; and as soon as He did so, it became such as Joseph wished.

Nor was it necessary for him to make anything with his own hand, for Joseph was not very skilful in carpentry.

39.
Now, on a certain day, the king of Jerusalem sent for him, and said:
I wish thee, Joseph, to make for me a throne to fit that place in which I usually sit.
Joseph obeyed, and began the work immediately, and remained in the palace two years, until he finished the work of that throne.
And when he had it carried to its place, he perceived that each side wanted two spans of the prescribed measure.
And the king, seeing this, was angry with Joseph; and Joseph, being in great fear of the king, spent the night without supper, nor did he taste anything at all.
Then, being asked by the Lord Jesus why he was afraid, Joseph said:
Because I have spoiled all the work that I have been two years at.
And the Lord Jesus said to him:
Fear not, and do not lose heart; but do thou take hold of one side of the throne; I shall take the other; and we shall put that to rights.
And Joseph, having done as the Lord Jesus had said and each having drawn by his own side, the throne was put to rights, and brought to the exact measure of the place.
And those that stood by and saw this miracle were struck with astonishment, and praised God.
And the woods used in that throne were of those which are celebrated in the time of Solomon the son of David; that is, woods of many and various kinds.

40.
On another day the Lord Jesus went out into the road, and saw the boys that had come together to play, and followed them; but the boys hid themselves from Him.
The Lord Jesus, therefore, having come to the door of a certain house, and seen some women standing there, asked them where the boys had gone; and when they answered that there was no one there, He said again:
Who are these whom you see in the furnace? [18]They replied that they were kids of three years old.
And the Lord Jesus cried out, and said:
Come out hither, O kids, to your Shepherd.
Then the boys, in the form of kids, came out, and began to dance round Him; and the women, seeing this, were very much astonished, and were seized with trembling, and speedily supplicated and adored the Lord Jesus, saying:
O our Lord Jesus, son of Mary, Thou art of a truth that good Shepherd of Israel; have mercy on Thy handmaidens who stand before Thee, and who have never doubted:
for Thou hast come, O our Lord, to heal, and not to destroy.
And when the Lord Jesus answered that the sons of Israel were like the Ethiopians among the nations, the women said:
Thou, O Lord, knowest all things, nor is anything hid from Thee; now, indeed, we beseech Thee, and ask Thee of Thy affection to restore these boys Thy servants to their former condition.
The Lord Jesus therefore said:
Come, boys, let us go and play.
And immediately, while these women were standing by, the kids were changed into boys.

41.
Now in the month Adar, Jesus, after the manner of a king, assembled the boys together.
They spread their clothes on the ground, and He sat down upon them.
Then they put on His head a crown made of flowers, and, like chamber-servants, stood in His presence, on the right and on the left, as if He were a king.
And whoever passed by that way was forcibly dragged by the boys, saying:
Come hither, and adore the king; then go thy way.

42.

In the meantime, while these things were going on, some men came up carrying a boy.

For this boy had gone into the mountain with those of his own age to seek wood, and there he found a partridge's nest; and when he stretched out his hand to take the eggs from it, a venomous serpent bit him from the middle of the nest, so that he called out for help.

His comrades accordingly went to him with haste, and found him lying on the ground like one dead.

Then his relations came and took him up to carry him back to the city.

And after they had come to that place where the Lord Jesus was sitting like a king, and the rest of the boys standing round Him like His servants, the boys went hastily forward to meet him who had been bitten by the serpent, and said to his relations:

Come and salute the king.

But when they were unwilling to go, on account of the sorrow in which they were, the boys dragged them by force against their will.

And when they had come up to the Lord Jesus, He asked them why they were carrying the boy.

And when they answered that a serpent had bitten him, the Lord Jesus said to the boys:

Let us go and kill that serpent.

And the parents of the boy asked leave to go away, because their son was in the agony of death; but the boys answered them, saying:

Did you not hear the king saying: Let us go kill the serpent? and will you not obey him?

And so, against their will the couch was carried back.

And when they came to the nest, the Lord Jesus said to the boys:

Is this the serpent's place?

They said that it was; and the serpent, at the call of the Lord, came forth without delay, and submitted itself to Him.

And He said to it:

Go away, and suck out all the poison which thou hast infused into this boy.

And so the serpent crawled to the boy, and sucked out all its poison.

Then the Lord Jesus cursed it, and immediately on this being done it burst asunder; and the Lord Jesus stroked the boy with his hand, and he was healed.

And he began to weep; but Jesus said:

Do not weep, for by and by thou shalt be my disciple.

And this is Simon the Cananite, [19] of whom mention is made in the Gospel. [20]

43.

On another day, Joseph sent his son James to gather wood, and the Lord Jesus went with him as his companion.

And when they had come to the place where the wood was, and James had begun to gather it, behold, a venomous viper bit his hand, so that he began to cry out and weep. The Lord Jesus then, seeing him in this condition, went up to him, and blew upon the place where the viper had bitten him; and this being done, he was healed immediately.

44.

One day, when the Lord Jesus was again with the boys playing on the roof of a house, one of the boys fell down from above, and immediately expired.

And the rest of the boys fled in all directions, and the Lord Jesus was left alone on the roof.

And the relations of the boy came up and said to the Lord Jesus:

It was thou who didst throw our son headlong from the roof.

And when He denied it, they cried out, saying:

Our son is dead, and here is he who has killed him.

And the Lord Jesus said to them:

Do not bring an evil report against me; but if you do not believe me, come and let us ask the boy himself, that he may bring the truth to light.

Then the Lord Jesus went down, and standing over the dead body, said, with a loud voice:

Zeno, Zeno, who threw thee down from the roof?

Then the dead boy answered and said:

My lord, it was not thou who didst throw me down, but such a one cast me down from it.

And when the Lord commanded those who were standing by to attend to His words, all who were present praised God for this miracle.

45.

Once upon a time the Lady Mary had ordered the Lord Jesus to go and bring her water from the well.

And when He had gone to get the water, the pitcher already full was knocked against something, and broken.

And the Lord Jesus stretched out His handkerchief, and collected the water, and carried it to His mother; and she was astonished at it.

And she hid and preserved in her heart all that she saw.

46.

Again, on another day, the Lord Jesus was with the boys at a stream of water, and they had again made little fish-ponds.

And the Lord Jesus had made twelve sparrows, and had arranged them round His fish-pond, three on each side.

And it was the Sabbath-day.

Wherefore a Jew, the son of Hanan, coming up, and seeing them thus engaged, said in anger and great indignation:

Do you make figures of clay on the Sabbath-day?

And he ran quickly, and destroyed their fish-ponds.

But when the Lord Jesus clapped His hands over the sparrows which He had made, they flew away chirping.

Then the son of Hanan came up to the fish-pond of Jesus also, and kicked it with his shoes, and the water of it vanished away.

And the Lord Jesus said to him:

As that water has vanished away, so thy life shall likewise vanish away.

And immediately that boy dried up.

47.

At another time, when the Lord Jesus was returning home with Joseph in the evening, He met a boy, who ran up against Him with so much force that He fell.

And the Lord Jesus said to him:

As thou hast thrown me down, so thou shalt fall and not rise again.

And the same hour the boy fell down, and expired.

48.

There was, moreover, at Jerusalem, a certain man named Zacchaeus, who taught boys.

He said to Joseph:

Why, O Joseph, dost thou not bring Jesus to the to learn his letters?

Joseph agreed to do so, and reported the matter to the Lady Mary.

They therefore took Him to the master; and he, as soon as he saw Him, wrote out the alphabet for Him, and told Him to say Aleph.

And when He had said Aleph, the master ordered Him to pronounce Beth.

And the Lord Jesus said to him:

Tell me first the meaning of the letter Aleph, and then I shall pronounce Beth.

And when the master threatened to flog Him, the Lord Jesus explained to him the meanings of the letters Aleph and Beth; also which figures of the letter were straight, which crooked, which drawn round into a spiral, which marked with points, which without them, why one letter went before another; and many other things He began to recount and to elucidate which the master himself had never either heard or read in any book.

The Lord Jesus, moreover, said to the master: Listen, and I shall say them to thee.

And He began clearly and distinctly to repeat Aleph, Beth, Gimel, Daleth, on to Tau.

And the master was astonished, and said:

I think that this boy was born before Noah.

And turning to Joseph, he said:

Thou hast brought to me to be taught a boy more learned than all the masters.

To the Lady Mary also he said:

This son of thine has no need of instruction.

49.

Thereafter they took Him to another and a more learned master, who, when he saw Him, said: Say Aleph.

And when He had said Aleph, the master ordered him to pronounce Beth.

The Forgotten Bible

And the Lord Jesus answered him, and said:

First tell me the meaning of the letter Aleph, and then I shall pronounce Beth.

And when the master hereupon raised his hand and flogged Him, immediately his hand dried up, and he died.

Then said Joseph, to the Lady Mary:

From this time we shall not let him go out of the house, since every one who opposes him is struck dead.

50.

And when He was twelve years old, they took Him to Jerusalem to the feast.

And when the feast was finished, they indeed returned; but the Lord Jesus remained in the temple among the teachers and elders and learned men of the sons of Israel, to whom He put various questions upon the sciences, and gave answers in His turn. [21]For He said to them:

Whose son is the Messias?

They answered Him:

The son of David.

Wherefore then, said He, does he in the Spirit call him his lord, when he says, The Lord said to my lord, Sit at my right hand, that I may put thine enemies under thy footsteps? [22]Again the chief of the teachers said to Him:

Hast thou read the books?

Both the books, said the Lord Jesus, and the things contained in the books.

And He explained the books, and the law, and the precepts, and the statutes, and the mysteries, which are contained in the books of the prophets--things which the understanding of no creature attains to. That teacher therefore said:

I hitherto have neither attained to nor heard of such knowledge:

Who, pray, do you think that boy will be?

51.

And a philosopher who was there present, a skilful astronomer, asked the Lord Jesus whether He had studied astronomy.

And the Lord Jesus answered him, and explained the number of the spheres, and of the heavenly bodies, their natures and operations; their opposition; their aspect, triangular, square, and sextile; their course, direct and retrograde; the twenty-fourths, [23] and sixtieths of twenty-fourths; and other things beyond the reach of reason.

52.

There was also among those philosophers one very skilled in treating of natural science, and he asked the Lord Jesus whether He had studied medicine.

And He, in reply, explained to him physics and metaphysics, hyperphysics and hypophysics, the powers likewise and humours of the body, and the effects of the same; also the number of members and bones, of veins, arteries, and nerves; also the effect of heat and dryness, of cold and moisture, and what these give rise to; what was the operation of the soul upon the body, and its perceptions and powers; what was the operation of the faculty of speech, of anger, of desire; lastly, their conjunction and disjunction, and other things beyond the reach of any created intellect.

Then that philosopher rose up, and adored the Lord Jesus, and said:

O Lord, from this time I will be thy disciple and slave.

53.

While they were speaking to each other of these and other things, the Lady Mary came, after having gone about seeking Him for three days along with Joseph.

She therefore, seeing Him sitting among the teachers asking them questions, and answering in His turn, said to Him:

My son, why hast thou treated us thus?

Behold, thy father and I have sought thee with great trouble.

But He said:

Why do you seek me?

Do you not know that I ought to occupy myself in my Father's house?

But they did not understand the words that He spoke to them. Then those teachers asked Mary whether He were her son; and when she signified that He was, they said:

Blessed art thou, O Mary, who hast brought forth such a son.

And returning with them to Nazareth, He obeyed them in all things.

And His mother kept all these words of His in her heart.

And the Lord Jesus advanced in stature, and in wisdom, and in favour with God and man. [24]

54.

And from this day He began to hide His miracles and mysteries and secrets, and to give attention to the law, until He completed His thirtieth year, when His Father publicly declared Him at the Jordan by this voice sent down from heaven:

This is my beloved Son, in whom I am well pleased; the Holy Spirit being present in the form of a white dove. [25]

55.

This is He whom we adore with supplications, who hath given us being and life, and who hath brought us from our mothers' wombs; who for our sakes assumed a human body, and redeemed us, that He might embrace us in eternal compassion, and show to us His mercy according to His liberality, and beneficence, and generosity, and benevolence.

To Him is glory, and beneficence, and power, and dominion from this time forth for evermore.

Amen.

Here endeth the whole Gospel of the Infancy, with the aid of God Most High, according to what we have found in the original.

Footnotes:

1. Or, have found.
2. He is called Joseph Caiaphas in Josephus, Antiq., xviii. 2. 2.
3. The Latin translation in Tischendorf has Hierosolyma, which, as the form in the rest of the translation is feminine, means "from Jerusalem."

But as the Arabic can mean only "to Jerusalem," the acc. plural of the neut. form may be here intended.

4. Or, with the lights of lamps and candles, more beautiful than lightning, and more splendid than sunlight.
5. John xii. 5. The denarius was worth about 7-3/4 d.
6. Luke vii. 37, 38.
7. Lev. xii. 4.
8. Ex. xiii. 2; Luke ii. 23.
9. Luke ii. 25-38.
10. For this prediction of Zoroaster, see Smith's Dict. of the Bible, art. Magi.
11. Matt. ii. 1-12.
12. Matt. ii. 13, 14.
13. Hos. xi. 1; Matt. ii. 15.
14. Burning to death was the punishment of those convicted of sacrilege and the practice of magic. It was inflicted also on slaves for grave offences against their masters.
15. Matarea, or Matariyeh, the site of Heliopolis or On, is a little way to the N.E. of Cairo. Ismail Pasha is said to have presented, on his visit to the Paris Exhibition of 1867, the tree and the ground surrounding it to the Empress of the French. For some interesting particulars about the tree, see a paragraph, by B.H.C. (i.e., Mr. B. Harris Cowper, who has translated the Apocryphal Gospels), in the Leisure Hour for 2d November, 1867.
16. Ps. vii. 15, lvii. 6.
17. John xix. 34.
18. Perhaps the correct reading is fornice, archway, and not fornace.
19. [So the Latin; but the Greek word in the Gospels is equivalent to "zealot." See Rev. Vers. in the lists of the Apostles.--R.]
20. Matt. x. 4, etc.
21. Luke ii. 42-47. [A comparison of the two narratives is very suggestive. The Evangelist Luke does not present any such monster of precocity, nor does he adventure into discussions "upon the sciences."--R.]
22. Ps. cx. 1; Matt. xxii. 42-45. [The Latin reads: vestigiis pedum tuorum, "the footsteps of thy feet." The original term, "footstool," has evidently been misunderstood by some transcriber.--R.]
23. The scripulum was the twenty-fourth part of the as. It is likely here put for the motion of a planet during one hour. Pliny, N. H., ii. 10, uses the word to signify an undefined number of degrees, or parts of a degree.
24. Luke ii. 46-52.
25. Matt. iii. 13-17; Luke iii. 21-23.

The Gospel of Nicodemus

Part I - The Acts of Pilate

First Greek Form

Memorials of Our Lord Jesus Christ, Done in the Time of Pontius Pilate

Prologue.--I Ananias, of the propraetor's body-guard, being learned in the law, knowing our Lord Jesus Christ from the Holy Scriptures, coming to Him by faith, and counted worthy of the holy baptism, searching also the memorials written at that time of what was done in the case of our Lord Jesus Christ, which the Jews had laid up in the time of Pontius Pilate, found these memorials written in Hebrew, and by the favour of God have translated them into Greek for the information of all who call upon the name of our Master Jesus Christ, in the seventeenth year of the reign of our Lord Flavius Theodosius, and the sixth of Flavius Valentinianus, in the ninth indiction. [1]

All ye, therefore, who read and transfer into other books, remember me, and pray for me, that God may be merciful to me, and pardon my sins which I have sinned against Him.

Peace be to those who read, and to those who hear and to their households.

Amen.

In the fifteenth year [2] of the government of Tiberius Caesar, emperor of the Romans, and Herod being king of Galilee, in the nineteenth year of his rule, on the eighth day before the Kalends of April, which is the twenty-fifth of March, in the consulship of Rufus and Rubellio, in the fourth year of the two hundred and second Olympiad, Joseph Caiaphas being high priest of the Jews.

The account that Nicodemus wrote in Hebrew, after the cross and passion of our Lord Jesus Christ, the Saviour God, and left to those that came after him, is as follows:--

Footnotes:

1. [The works which precede sought to supplement the evangelical narrative in regard to the early life of our Lord, and Mary His mother; those which follow are also supplementary, but refer to the closing events.--R.]

2. The 15th year of Tiberius, reckoning from the death of Augustus, was a.d. 29, a.u.c. 782, the first year of the 202d Olympiad, in the consulship of C. Fugus Geminus and L. Rubellius Geminus, and the 34th year of Herod Antipas. Other readings are: In the eighteenth year--In the nineteenth year. [Compare the Acts of Pilate in both forms. The variations here correspond with the various theories of the length of our Lord's ministry. The text seems to confuse the statement of Luke (iii. 1) respecting the beginning of the public ministry with the time of our Lord's death.--R.]

Chapter 1

Having called a council, the high priests and scribes Annas and Caiaphas and Semes and Dathaes, and Gamaliel, Judas, Levi and Nephthalim, Alexander and Jairus, [1] and the rest of the Jews, came to Pilate accusing Jesus about many things, saying:

We know this man to be the son of Joseph the carpenter, born of Mary; and he says that he is the Son of God, and a king; moreover, he profanes the Sabbath, and wishes to do away with the law of our fathers.

Pilate says:

And what are the things which he does, to show that he wishes to do away with it? [2]The Jews say:

We have a law not to cure any one on the Sabbath; but this man[3] has on the Sabbath cured the lame and the crooked, the withered and the blind and the paralytic, the dumb and the demoniac, by evil practices.

Pilate says to them:

What evil practices?

They say to him:
He is a magician, and by Beelzebul prince of the demons he casts out the demons, and all are subject to him. Pilate says to them:
This is not casting out the demons by an unclean spirit, but by the god AEsculapius.
The Jews say to Pilate:
we entreat your highness that he stand at thy tribunal, and be heard. [4]And Pilate having called them, says: Tell me how I, being a procurator, can try a king?
They say to him: We do not say that he is a king, but he himself says that he is.
And Pilate having called the runner, says to him:
Let Jesus be brought in with respect.
And the runner going out, and recognising Him, adored Him, and took his cloak into his hand, and spread it on the ground, and says to him:
My lord, walk on this, and come in, for the procurator calls thee.
And the Jews seeing what the runner had done, cried out against Pilate, saying:
Why hast thou ordered him to come in by a runner, and not by a crier? for assuredly the runner, when he saw him, adored him, and spread his doublet on the ground, and made him walk like a king.
And Pilate having called the runner, says to him:
Why hast thou done this, and spread out thy cloak upon the earth, and made Jesus walk upon it?
The runner says to him:
My lord procurator, when thou didst send me to Jerusalem to Alexander, [5] I saw him sitting upon an ass, and the sons of the Hebrews held branches in their hands, and shouted; and other spread their clothes under him saying, Save now, thou who art in the highest:
blessed is he that cometh in the name of the Lord. [6]
The Jews cry out, and say to the runner:
The sons of the Hebrews shouted in Hebrew; whence then hast thou the Greek?
The runner says to them:
I asked one of the Jews, and said, What is it they are shouting in Hebrew?
And he interpreted it for me.
Pilate says to them:
And what did they shout in Hebrew?
The Jews say to him:
Hosanna membrome Baruchamma Adonai. [7]Pilate says to them:
And this hosanna, etc., how is it interpreted?
The Jews say to him:
Save now in the highest; blessed is he that cometh in the name of the Lord.
Pilate says to them:
If you bear witness to the words spoken by the children, in what has the runner done wrong?
And they were silent.
And the procurator says to the runner:
Go out, and bring him in what way thou wilt.
And the runner going out, did in the same manner as before, and says to Jesus:
My lord, come in; the procurator calleth thee.
And Jesus going in, and the standard-bearers holding their standards, the tops of the standards were bent down, and adored Jesus.
And the Jews seeing the bearing of the standards, how they were bent down and adored Jesus, cried [8] out vehemently against the standard-bearers.
And Pilate says to the Jews:
Do you not wonder how the tops of the standards were bent down, and adored Jesus?
The Jews say to Pilate:
We saw how the standard-bearers bent them down, and adored him.
And the procurator having called the standard-bearers, says to them:
Why have you done this?
They say to Pilate:
We are Greeks and temple-slaves, and how could we adore him? and assuredly, as we were holding them up, the tops bent down of their own accord, and adored him.
Pilate says to the rulers of the synagogue and the elders of the people:
Do you choose for yourselves men strong and powerful, and let them hold up the standards, and let us see whether they will bend down with them.
And the elders of the Jews picked out twelve men powerful and strong, and made them hold up the standards six by six; and they were placed in front of the procurator's tribunal.

And Pilate says to the runner:

Take him outside of the praetorium, and bring him in again in whatever way may please thee.

And Jesus and the runner went out of the praetorium.

And Pilate, summoning those who had formerly held up the standards, says to them:

I have sworn by the health of Caesar, that if the standards do not bend down when Jesus comes in, I will cut off your heads.

And the procurator ordered Jesus to come in the second time.

And the runner did in the same manner as before, and made many entreaties to Jesus to walk on his cloak.

And He walked on it, and went in.

And as He went in, the standards were again bent down, and adored Jesus.

Footnotes:

1. There is in themss. great variation as to these names.

2. Lit., and wishes to do away with it.

3. Compare with this, Lactantius, iv. 17. The Jews brought charges against Jesus, that He did away with the law of God given by Moses; that is, that He did not rest on the Sabbath, etc.

4. Another reading is: We entreat your highness to go into the praetorium, and question him. For Jesus was standing outside with the crowd.

5. Probably the Alexander mentioned in Acts iv. 6.

6. Matt. xxi. 8, 9.

7. Ps. cxviii. 25: Hosyah na bimromim baruch hobba (b'shem) Adonai.

8. Another reading is: Annas and Caiaphas and Joseph, the three false witnesses, began to cry out, etc.

Chapter 2

And Pilate seeing this, was afraid, and sought to go away from the tribunal; but when he was still thinking of going away, his wife sent to him, saying:

Have nothing to do with this just man, for many things have I suffered on his account this night. [1]And Pilate, summoning the Jews, says to them:

You know that my wife is a worshipper of God, and prefers to adhere to the Jewish religion along with you.

They say to him:

Yes; we know.

Pilate says to them: Behold, my wife [2] has sent to me, saying, Have nothing to do with this just man, for many things have I suffered on account of him this night.

And the Jews answering, say unto Pilate:

Did we not tell thee that he was a sorcerer? [3] behold, he has sent a dream to thy wife.

And Pilate, having summoned Jesus, says to Him:

What do these witness against thee?

Sayest thou nothing?

And Jesus said:

Unless they had the power, they would say nothing; for every one has the power of his own mouth to speak both good and evil.

They shall see to it. [4]

And the elders of the Jews answered, and said to Jesus:

What shall we see? first, that thou wast born of fornication; secondly, that thy birth in Bethlehem was the cause of the murder of the infants; thirdly, that thy father Joseph and thy mother Mary fled into Egypt because they had no confidence in the people.

Some of the bystanders, pious men of the Jews, say:

we deny that he was born of fornication; for we know that Joseph espoused Mary, and he was not born of fornication.

Pilate says to the Jews who said that he was of fornication:

This story of yours is not true, because they were betrothed, as also these fellow-countrymen of yours say.

Annas and Caiaphas say to Pilate:

All the multitude of us cry out that he was born of fornication, and are not believed; these are proselytes, and his disciples.

And Pilate, calling Annas and Caiaphas, says to them: What are proselytes?

They say to him:

They are by birth children of the Greeks, and have now become Jews.

And those that said that He was not born of fornication, viz.--Lazarus, Asterius, Antonius,

James, Amnes, Zeras, Samuel, Isaac, Phinees, Crispus, Agrippas, and Judas [5] --say:

We are not proselytes, but are children of the Jews, and speak of the truth; for we were present at the betrothal of Joseph and Mary.

And Pilate, calling these twelve men who said that He was not born of fornication, says to them:

I adjure you by the health of Caesar, to tell me whether it be true that you say, that he was not born of fornication.

They say to Pilate:

We have a law against taking oaths, because it is a sin; but they will swear by the health of Caesar, [6] that it is not as we have said, and we are liable to death. Pilate says to Annas and Caiaphas:

Have you nothing to answer to this?

Annas and Caiaphas say to Pilate:

These twelve are believed when they say that he was not born of fornication; all the multitude of us cry out that he was born of fornication, and that he is a sorcerer, and he says that he is the Son of God and a king, and we are not believed.

And Pilate orders all the multitude to go out, except the twelve men who said that He was not born of fornication, and he ordered Jesus to be separated from them.

And Pilate says to them:

For what reason do they wish to put him to death?

They say to him:

They are angry because he cures on the Sabbath.

Pilate says:

For a good work do they wish to put him to death?

They say to him:

Yes.

Footnotes:

1. Matt. xxvii. 19.

2. One ms. adds: Procla,--the traditional name of Pilate's wife.

3. Three mss. add: And by Beelzebul, prince of the demons, he casts out the demons, and they are all subject to him.

4. i.e., let them see to it.

5. There is considerable variation in the mss. as to these names.

6. Or, let them swear.

Chapter 3

And Pilate, filled with rage, went outside of the praetorium, and said to them:

I take the sun to witness [1] that I find no fault in this man.

The Jews answered and said to the procurator:

Unless this man were an evil-doer, we should not have delivered him to thee.

And Pilate said, Do you take him, and judge him according to your law.

The Jews said to Pilate:

It is not lawful for us to put any one to death. Pilate said:

Has God said that you are not to put to death, but that I am?

And Pilate went again into the praetorium, and spoke to Jesus privately, and said to Him:

Art thou the king of the Jews?

Jesus answered Pilate:

Dost thou say this of thyself, or have others said it to thee of me?

Pilate answered Jesus:

Am I also a Jew? [2]Thy nation and the chief priests have given thee up to me.

What hast thou done?

Jesus answered:

My kingdom is not of this world; for if my kingdom were of this world, my servants would fight in order that I should not be given up to the Jews:

but now my kingdom is not from thence.

Pilate said to Him:

Art thou then a king?

Jesus answered him:

Thou sayest that I am a king.

Because for this have I been born, and have I come, in order that every one who is of the truth might hear my voice.

The Forgotten Bible

Pilate says to him:
What is truth?
Jesus says to him: Truth is from heaven.
Pilate says:
Is truth not upon earth?
Jesus says to Pilate:
Thou seest how those who speak the truth are judged by those that have the power upon earth.

Footnotes:

1. See Apost. Const., ii. 56. At last he who is going to pronounce sentence of death upon the culprit raises his hands aloft, and takes the sun to witness that he is innocent of his blood.
2. The full force of the expression is: You do not mean to say that I too am a Jew?

Chapter 4

And leaving Jesus within the praetorium, Pilate went out to the Jews, and said to them:
I find no fault in him.
The Jews say to him:
He said, I can destroy this temple, and in three days build it.
Pilate says:
What temple?
The Jews say:
The one that Solomon [1] built in forty-six years, and this man speaks of pulling it down and building it in three days.
Pilate says to them:
I am innocent of the blood of this just man.
See you to it.
The Jews say:
His blood be upon us, and upon our children.
And Pilate having summoned the elders and priests and Levites, said to them privately:
Do not act thus, because no charge that you bring against him is worthy of death; for your charge is about curing and Sabbath profanation.
The elders and the priests and the Levites say: If any one speak evil against Caesar, is he worthy of death or not? Pilate says:
He is worthy of death.
The Jews say to Pilate:
If any one speak evil against Caesar, he is worthy of death; but this man has spoken evil against God.
And the procurator ordered the Jews to go outside of the praetorium; and summoning Jesus, he says to Him:
What shall I do to thee?
Jesus says to Pilate:
As it has been given to thee.
Pilate says:
How given?
Jesus says:
Moses and the prophets have proclaimed beforehand of my death and resurrection.
And the Jews noticing this, and hearing it, say to Pilate:
What more wilt thou hear of this blasphemy?
Pilate says to the Jews:
If these words be blasphemous, do you take him for the blasphemy, and lead him away to your synagogue, and judge him according to your law.
The Jews say to Pilate:
Our law bears that a man who wrongs his fellow-men is worthy to receive forty save one; but he that blasphemeth God is to be stoned with stones.[2]
Pilate says to them:
Do you take him, and punish him in whatever way you please.
The Jews say to Pilate:
We wish that he be crucified. Pilate says:
He is not deserving of crucifixion.
And the procurator, looking round upon the crowds of the Jews standing by, sees many of the Jews weeping, and says:
All the multitude do not wish him to die.

The elders of the Jews say:
For this reason all the multitude of us have come, that he should die.
Pilate says to the Jews:
Why should he die?
The Jews say:
Because he called himself Son of God, and King.

Footnotes:

1. Comp. John ii. 20.
2. Deut. xxv. 3; Lev. xxiv. 16.

Chapter 5

And one Nicodemus, a Jew, stood before the procurator, and said:
I beseech your honour, let me say a few words.
Pilate says:
Say on. Nicodemus says:
I said to the elders and the priests and Levites, and to all the multitude of the Jews in the synagogue, What do you seek to do with this man?
This man does many miracles and strange things, which no one has done or will do.
Let him go, and do not wish any evil against him.
If the miracles which he does are of God, they will stand; but if man, they will come to nothing. [1]For assuredly Moses, being sent by God into Egypt, did many miracles, which the Lord commanded him to do before Pharaoh king of Egypt.
And there were there Jannes and Jambres, servants of Pharaoh, and they also did not a few of the miracles which Moses did; and the Egyptians took them to be gods--this Jannes and this Jambres. [2]But, since the miracles which they did were not of God, both they and those who believed in them were destroyed.
And now release this man, for he is not deserving of death.
The Jews say to Nicodemus:
Thou hast become his disciple, and therefore thou defendest him.
Nicodemus says to them:
Perhaps, too, the procurator has become his disciple, because he defends him.
Has the emperor not appointed him to this place of dignity?
And the Jews were vehemently enraged, and gnashed their teeth against Nicodemus. Pilate says to them:
Why do you gnash your teeth against him when you hear the truth?
The Jews say to Nicodemus:
Mayst thou receive his truth and his portion.
Nicodemus says:
Amen, amen; may I receive it, as you have said.

Footnotes:

1. Acts v. 38.
2. 2 Tim. iii. 8, 9.

Chapter 6

One of the Jews, stepping up, asked leave of the procurator to say a word.
The procurator says:
If thou wishest to say any thing, say on. And the Jew said:
Thirty-eight years I lay in my bed in great agony. And when Jesus came, many demoniacs, and many lying ill of various diseases, were cured by him.
And some young men, taking pity on me, carried me, bed and all, and took me to him.
And when Jesus saw me, he had compassion on me, and said to me:
Take up thy couch and walk.
And I took up my couch, and walked.
The Jews say to Pilate:
Ask him on what day it was that he was cured.
He that had been cured says:
On a Sabbath. [1]The Jews say:
Is not this the very thing that we said, that on a Sabbath he cures and casts out demons?
And another Jew stepped up and said:

The Forgotten Bible

I was born blind; I heard sounds, but saw not a face.
And as Jesus passed by, I cried out with a loud voice, Pity me, O son of David.
And he pitied me, and put his hands upon my eyes, and I instantly received my sight. ²And another Jew stepped up and said:
I was crooked, and he straightened me with a word.
And another said:
I was a leper, and he cured me with a word. ³

Footnotes:
1. John v. 5-9.
2. Mark x. 46, etc.
3. Matt. viii. 1-4, etc.

Chapter 7

And a woman ¹ cried out from a distance, and said:
I had an issue of blood, and I touched the hem of his garment, and the issue of blood which I had had for twelve years was stopped. ²The Jews say: we have a law, that a woman's evidence is not to be received.³

Footnotes:
1. Some mss. add the name Bernice, or Veronica.
2. Matt. ix. 20-26.
3. Jos. Ant., iv. 8, S: 15.

Chapter 8

And others, a multitude both of men and women, cried out, saying:
This man is a prophet, and the demons are subject to him.
Pilate says to them who said that the demons were subject to Him:
Why, then, were not your teachers also subject to him?
They say to Pilate:
We do not know.
And others said:
He raised Lazarus from the tomb after he had been dead four days. ¹And the procurator trembled, and said to all the multitude of the Jews:
Why do you wish to pour out innocent blood?

Footnote:
1. John xi. 1-16.

Chapter 9

And having summoned Nicodemus and the twelve men that said He was not born of fornication, he says to them:
What shall I do, because there is an insurrection among the people?
They say to him:
We know not; let them see to it.
Again Pilate, having summoned all the multitude of the Jews, says:
You know that it is customary, at the feast of unleavened bread, to release one prisoner to you.
I have one condemned prisoner in the prison, a murderer named Barabbas, and this man standing in your presence, Jesus, in whom I find no fault.
Which of them do you wish me to release to you?
And they cry out:
Barabbas. Pilate says:
What, then, shall we do to Jesus who is called Christ? The Jews say:
Let him be crucified.
And others said:
Thou art no friend of Caesar's if thou release this man, because he called himself Son of God and king.
You wish, then, this man to be king, and not Caesar? ¹
And Pilate, in a rage, says to the Jews:
Always has your nation been rebellious, and you always speak against your benefactors.

The Jews say:
What benefactors?
He says to them:
Your God led you out of the land of Egypt from bitter slavery, and brought you safe through the sea as through dry land, and in the desert fed you with manna, and gave you quails, and quenched your thirst with water from a rock, and gave you a law; and in all these things you provoked your God to anger, and sought a molten calf.

And you exasperated your God, and He sought to slay you.

And Moses prayed for you, and you were not put to death.

And now you charge me with hating the emperor. [2]

And rising up from the tribunal, he sought to go out.

And the Jews cry out, and say:
We know that Caesar is king, and not Jesus.
For assuredly the magi brought gifts to him as to a king.

And when Herod heard from the magi that a king had been born, he sought to slay him; and his father Joseph, knowing this, took him and his mother, and they fled into Egypt.

And Herod hearing of it, destroyed the children of the Hebrews that had been born in Bethlehem. [3]

And when Pilate heard these words, he was afraid; and ordering the crowd to keep silence, because they were crying out, he said to them: So this is he whom Herod sought?

The Jews say:
Yes, it is he.

And, taking water, Pilate washed his hands in the face of the sun, saying: I am innocent of the blood of this just man; see you to it.

Again the Jews cry out:
His blood be upon us, and upon our children.

Then Pilate ordered the curtain of the tribunal where he was sitting to be drawn, [4] and says to Jesus:
Thy nation has charged thee with being a king.

On this account I sentence thee, first to be scourged, according to the enactment of venerable kings, and then to be fastened on the cross in the garden where thou wast seized.

And let Dysmas and Gestas, the two malefactors, be crucified with thee.

Footnotes:

1. Matt. xxvii. 15-26, etc.
2. Lit., king. Other readings are: with wishing another king; with seeking Jesus for king.
3. One ms. adds: from two years old and under.
4. This was customary before pronouncing sentence. See Apost. Const., ii. 56.

Chapter 10

And Jesus went forth out of the praetorium, and the two malefactors with Him.

And when they came to the place, they stripped Him of his clothes, and girded Him with a towel, and put a crown of thorns on Him round His head.

And they crucified Him; and at the same time also they hung up the two malefactors along with Him.

And Jesus said:
Father, forgive them, for they know not what they do.

And the soldiers parted His clothes among them; and the people stood looking at Him.

And the chief priests, and the rulers with them, mocked Him, saying:
He saved others; let him save himself.

If he be the Son of God, let him come down from the cross.

And the soldiers made sport of Him, coming near and offering Him vinegar mixed with gall, and said:
Thou art the king of the Jews; save thyself. [1]

And Pilate, after the sentence, ordered the charge made against Him to be inscribed as a superscription in Greek, and Latin, and Hebrew, according to what the Jews had said:
He is king of the Jews.

And one of the malefactors hanging up spoke to Him, saying:
If thou be the Christ, save thyself and us.

And Dysmas answering, reproved him, saying:
Dost thou not fear God, because thou art in the same condemnation?

And we indeed justly, for we receive the fit punishment of our deeds; but this man has done no evil.

And he said to Jesus: Remember me, Lord, in Thy kingdom.

And Jesus said to him:

Amen, amen; I say to thee, To-day shalt thou be [2] with me in Paradise.

Footnotes:

1. Some of themss. add: And the soldier Longinus, taking a spear, pierced His side, and there came forth blood and water.

2. Lit., art.

Chapter 11

And it was about the sixth hour, and there was darkness over the earth until the ninth hour, the sun being darkened; and the curtain of the temple was split in the middle.

And crying out with a loud voice, Jesus said:

Father, Baddach ephkid ruel, which is, interpreted:

Into Thy hands I commit my spirit. [1] And having said this, He gave up the ghost.

And the centurion, seeing what had happened, glorified God, and said:

This was a just man.

And all the crowds that were present at this spectacle, when they saw what had happened, beat their breasts and went away.

And the centurion reported what had happened to the procurator.

And when the procurator and his wife heard it, they were exceedingly grieved, and neither ate nor drank that day.

And Pilate sent for the Jews, and said to them:

Have you seen what has happened?

And they say:

There has been an eclipse of the sun in the usual way. [2]

And His acquaintances were standing at a distance, and the women who came with Him from Galilee, seeing these things.

And a man named Joseph, a councillor from the city of Arimathaea, who also waited for the kingdom of God, went to Pilate, and begged the body of Jesus.

And he took it down, and wrapped it in clean linen, and placed it in a tomb hewn out of the rock, in which no one had ever lain.

Footnotes:

1. Luke xxiii. 46. Ps. xxxi. 5 is, b'yadcha aphkid ruchi.

2. One ms. adds: Pilate said to them: You scoundrels! is this the way you tell the truth about everything? I know that that never happens but at new moon. Now you ate your passover yesterday, the fourteenth of the month, and you say that it was an eclipse of the sun.

Chapter 12

And the Jews, hearing that Joseph had begged the body of Jesus, sought him and the twelve who said that Jesus was not born of fornication, and Nicodemus, and many others who had stepped up before Pilate and declared His good works.

And of all these that were hid, Nicodemus alone was seen by them, because he was a ruler of the Jews.

And Nicodemus says to them:

How have you come into the synagogue?

The Jews say to him:

How hast thou come into the synagogue? for thou art a confederate of his, and his portion is with thee in the world to come. Nicodemus says:

Amen, amen.

And likewise Joseph also stepped out and said to them:

Why are you angry against me because I begged the body of Jesus?

Behold, I have put him in my new tomb, wrapping him in clean linen; and I have rolled a stone to the door of the tomb.

And you have acted not well against the just man, because you have not repented of crucifying him, but also have pierced him with a spear.

And the Jews seized Joseph, and ordered him to be secured until the first day of the week, and said to him:

Know that the time does not allow us to do anything against thee, because the Sabbath is dawning; and know that thou shalt not be deemed worthy of burial, but we shall give thy flesh to the birds of the air.

Joseph says to them:

These are the words of the arrogant Goliath, who reproached the living God and holy David. [1]For God has said by the prophet, Vengeance is mine, and I will repay, saith the Lord. [2]And now he that is uncircumcised in flesh, but circumcised in heart, has taken water, and washed his hands in the face of the sun, saying, I am innocent of the blood of this just man; see ye to it.

And you answered and said to Pilate, His blood be upon us, and upon our children.

And now I am afraid lest the wrath of God come upon you, and upon your children, as you have said.

And the Jews, hearing these words, were embittered in their souls, and seized Joseph, and locked him into a room where there was no window; and guards were stationed at the door, and they sealed the door where Joseph was locked in.

And on the Sabbath, the rulers of the synagogue, [3] and the priests and the Levites, made a decree that all should be found in the synagogue on the first day of the week.

And rising up early, all the multitude in the synagogue consulted by what death they should slay him.

And when the Sanhedrin was sitting, they ordered him to be brought with much indignity.

And having opened the door, they found him not.

And all the people were surprised, and struck with dismay, because they found the seals unbroken, and because Caiaphas had the key.

And they no longer dared to lay hands upon those who had spoken before Pilate in Jesus' behalf.

Footnotes:

1. 1 Sam. xvii. 44.
2. Deut. xxxii. 35; Rom. xii. 19; Heb. x. 30.
3. [This is an evident blunder, one of many pointing to a late origin.--R.]

Chapter 13

And while they were still sitting in the synagogue, and wondering about Joseph, there come some of the guard whom the Jews had begged of Pilate to guard the tomb of Jesus, that His disciples might not come and steal Him.

And they reported to the rulers of the synagogue, and the priests and the Levites, what had happened:

how there had been a great earthquake; and we saw an angel coming down from heaven, and he rolled away the stone from the mouth of the tomb, and sat upon it; and he shone like snow, and like lightning.

And we were very much afraid, and lay like dead men; and we heard the voice of the angel saying to the women who remained beside the tomb, Be not afraid, for I know that you seek Jesus who was crucified.

He is not here:

He is risen, as He said.

Come, see the place where the Lord lay:

and go quickly, and tell His disciples that He is risen from the dead, and is in Galilee. [1]

The Jews say:

To what women did he speak?

The men of the guard say: We do not know who they were.

The Jews say:

At what time was this? The men of the guard say:

At midnight.

The Jews say:

And wherefore did you not lay hold of them?

The men of the guard say:

We were like dead men from fear, not expecting to see the light of day, and how could we lay hold of them?

The Jews say:

As the Lord liveth, we do not believe you.

The men of the guard say to the Jews:

You have seen so great miracles in the case of this man, and have not believed; and how can you believe us?

And assuredly you have done well to swear that the Lord liveth, for indeed He does live.

The Forgotten Bible

Again the men of the guard say:

We have heard that you have locked up the man that begged the body of Jesus, and put a seal on the door; and that you have opened it, and not found him.

Do you then give us the man whom you were guarding, and we shall give you Jesus.

The Jews say:

Joseph has gone away to his own city.

The men of the guard say to the Jews:

And Jesus has risen, as we heard from the angel, and is in Galilee.

And when the Jews heard these words, they were very much afraid, and said:

We must take care lest this story be heard, and all incline to Jesus.

And the Jews called a council, and paid down a considerable sum of money, and gave it to the soldiers, saying:

Say, while we slept, his disciples came by night and stole him; and if this come to the ears of the procurator, we shall persuade him, and keep you out of trouble. And they took it, and said as they had been instructed. [2]

Footnotes:

1. Matt. xxviii. 5-7.

2. Three of the Latin versions say: And they took the money, but could not hide the truth. For they wanted to say, His disciples stole him while we slept, and could not utter it; but said, Truly the Lord Jesus Christ has risen from the dead; and we saw an angel of God coming down from heaven, and he rolled back the stone, and sat on it. And this saying has been spread abroad among the Jews even to this day.

Chapter 14

And Phinees a priest, and Adas a teacher, and Haggai a Levite, came down from Galilee to Jerusalem, and said to the rulers of the synagogue, and the priests and the Levites:

We saw Jesus and his disciples sitting on the mountain called Mamilch; [1] and he said to his disciples, Go into all the world, and preach to every creature:

he that believeth and is baptized shall be saved, and he that believeth not shall be condemned.

And these signs shall attend those who have believed:

in my name they shall cast out demons, speak new tongues, take up serpents; and if they drink any deadly thing, it shall by no means hurt them; they shall lay hands on the sick, and they shall be well.

And while Jesus was speaking to his disciples, we saw him taken up to heaven. [2]

The elders and the priests and Levites say:

Give glory to the God of Israel, and confess to Him whether you have heard and seen those things of which you have given us an account.

And those who had given the account said:

As the Lord liveth, the God of our fathers Abraham, Isaac, and Jacob, we heard these things, and saw him taken up into heaven.

The elders and the priests and the Levites say to them:

Have you come to give us this announcement, or to offer prayer to God?

And they say:

To offer prayer to God.

The elders and the chief priests and the Levites say to them:

If you have come to offer prayer to God, why then have you told these idle tales in the presence of all the people? [3]Says Phinees the priest, and Adas the teacher, and Haggai the Levite to the rulers of the synagogues, and the priests and the Levites:

If what we have said and seen be sinful, behold, we are before you; do to us as seems good in your eyes.

And they took the law, and made them swear upon it, not to give any more an account of these matters to any one.

And they gave them to eat and drink, and sent them out of the city, having given them also money, and three men with them; and they sent them away to Galilee.

And these men having gone into Galilee, the chief priests, and the rulers of the synagogue, and the elders, came together into the synagogue, and locked the door, and lamented with a great lamentation, saying:

Is this a miracle that has happened in Israel?

And Annas and Caiaphas said:

Why are you so much moved?

Why do you weep?

Do you not know that his disciples have given a sum of gold to the guards of the tomb, and have instructed them to say that an angel came down and rolled away the stone from the door of the tomb?

And the priests and the elders said:

Be it that his disciples have stolen his body; how is it that the life has come into his body, and that he is going about in Galilee?

And they being unable to give an answer to these things, said, after great hesitation:

It is not lawful for us to believe the uncircumcised.

Footnotes:

1. Other readings are: Malek, Mophek, Mambre, Mabrech. Comp. 2 Kings xxiii. 13.
2. Mark xvi. 15-18.
3. Lit., why then this trifling which ye have trifled, etc.

Chapter 15

And Nicodemus stood up, and stood before the Sanhedrin, saying:

You say well; [1] you are not ignorant, you people of the Lord, of these men that come down from Galilee, that they fear God, and are men of substance, haters of covetousness, men of peace; and they have declared with an oath, We saw Jesus upon the mountain Mamilch with his disciples, and he taught what we heard from him, and we saw him taken up into heaven.

And no one asked them in what form he went up.

For assuredly, as the book of the Holy Scriptures taught us, Helias also was taken up into heaven, and Elissaeus cried out with a loud voice, and Helias threw his sheepskin upon Elissaeus, and Elissaeus threw his sheepskin upon the Jordan, and crossed, and came into Jericho.

And the children of the prophets met him, and said, O Elissaeus, where is thy master Helias?

And he said, He has been taken up into heaven.

And they said to Elissaeus, Has not a spirit seized him, and thrown him upon one of the mountains?

But let us take our servants [2] with us, and seek him.

And they persuaded Elissaeus, and he went away with them.

And they sought him three days, and did not find him; and they knew he had been taken up.

[3] And now listen to me, and let us send into every district of Israel, and see lest perchance Christ has been taken up by a spirit, and thrown upon one of the mountains?

And this proposal pleased all.

And they sent into every district of Israel, and sought Jesus, and did not find Him; but they found Joseph in Arimathaea, and no one dared to lay hands on him.

And they reported to the elders, and the priests, and the Levites:

We have gone round to every district of Israel, and have not found Jesus; but Joseph we have found in Arimathaea.

And hearing about Joseph, they were glad, and gave glory to the God of Israel.

And the rulers of the synagogue, and the priests and the Levites, having held a council as to the manner in which they should meet with Joseph, took a piece of paper, and wrote to Joseph as follows:--

Peace to thee!

We know that we have sinned against God, and against thee; and we have prayed to the God of Israel, that thou shouldst deign to come to thy fathers, and to thy children, because we have all been grieved.

For having opened the door, we did not find thee.

And we know that we have counselled evil counsel against thee; but the Lord has defended thee, and the Lord Himself has scattered to the winds our counsel against thee, O honourable father Joseph.

And they chose from all Israel seven men, friends of Joseph, whom also Joseph himself was acquainted with; and the rulers of the synagogue, and the priests and the Levites, say to them:

Take notice:

if, after receiving our letter, he read it, know that he will come with you to us; but if he do not read it, know that he is ill-disposed towards us. And having saluted him in peace, return to us.

And having blessed the men, they dismissed them.

And the men came to Joseph, and did reverence to him, and said to him:

Peace to thee!

And he said:

Peace to you, and to all the people of Israel!

And they gave him the roll of the letter.

And Joseph having received it, read the letter and rolled it up, and blessed God, and said:

Blessed be the Lord God, who has delivered Israel, that they should not shed innocent blood; and blessed be the Lord, who sent out His angel, and covered me under his wings. And he set a table for them; and they ate and drank, and slept there. And they rose up early, and prayed.

And Joseph saddled his ass, and set out with the men; and they came to the holy city Jerusalem.

And all the people met Joseph, and cried out:

Peace to thee in thy coming in!

And he said to all the people:

Peace to you! and he kissed them. And the people prayed with Joseph, and they were astonished at the sight of him.

And Nicodemus received him into his house, and made a great feast, and called Annas and Caiaphas, and the elders, and the priests, and the Levites to his house.

And they rejoiced, eating and drinking with Joseph; and after singing hymns, each proceeded to his own house.

But Joseph remained in the house of Nicodemus.

And on the following day, which was the preparation, the rulers of the synagogue and the priests and the Levites went early to the house of Nicodemus; and Nicodemus met them, and said:

Peace to you!

And they said:

Peace to thee, and to Joseph, and to all thy house, and to all the house of Joseph!

And he brought them into his house.

And all the Sanhedrin sat down, and Joseph sat down between Annas and Caiaphas: and no one dared to say a word to him.

And Joseph said:

Why have you called me?

And they signalled to Nicodemus to speak to Joseph.

And Nicodemus, opening his mouth, said to Joseph:

Father, thou knowest that the honourable teachers, and the priests and the Levites, see to learn a word from thee.

And Joseph said:

Ask.

And Annas and Caiaphas having taken the law, made Joseph swear, saying:

Give glory to the God of Israel, and give Him confession; for Achar being made to swear by the prophet Jesus, [4] did not forswear himself, but declared unto him all, and did not hide a word from him.

Do thou also accordingly not hide from us to the extent of a word.

And Joseph said:

I shall not hide from you one word.

And they said to him:

With grief were we grieved because thou didst beg the body of Jesus, and wrap it in clean linen, and lay it in a tomb.

And on account of this we secured thee in a room where there was no windows:

and we put locks and seals upon the doors and guards kept watching where thou wast locked in.

And on the first day of the week we opened, and found thee not, and were grieved exceedingly; and astonishment fell upon all the people of the Lord until yesterday.

And now relate to us what has happened to thee.

And Joseph said:

On the preparation, about the tenth hour, you locked me up, and I remained all the Sabbath.

And at midnight, as I was standing and praying, the room where you locked me in was hung up by the four corners, and I saw a light like lightning into my eyes. [5]

And I was afraid, and fell to the ground.

And some one took me by the hand, and removed me from the place where I had fallen; and moisture of water was poured from my head even to my feet, and a smell of perfumes came about my nostrils.

And he wiped my face, and kissed me, and said to me, Fear not, Joseph; open thine eyes, and see who it is that speaks to thee.

And looking up, I saw Jesus.

And I trembled and thought it was a phantom; and I said the commandments, and he said them with me. [6]Even so you are not ignorant that a phantom, if it meet anybody, and hear the commandments, takes to flight.

And seeing that he said them with me, I said to him, Rabbi Helias.

And he said to me, I am not Helias.

And I said to him, Who art thou, my lord?

And he said to me, I am Jesus, whose body thou didst beg from Pilate; and thou didst clothe me with clean linen, and didst put a napkin on my face, and didst lay me in thy new tomb, and didst roll a great stone to the door of the tomb.

And I said to him that was speaking to me, Show me the place where I laid thee.

And he carried me away, and showed me the place where I laid him; and the linen cloth was lying in it, and the napkin for his face.

And I knew that it was Jesus.

And he took me by the hand, and placed me, though the doors were locked, in the middle of my house, and led me away to my bed, and said to me, Peace to thee!

And he kissed me, and said to me, For forty days go not forth out of thy house; for, behold, I go to my brethren into Galilee.

Footnotes:

1. Perhaps better as a question.
2. Lit., boys.
3. 2 Kings ii. 12-18.
4. i.e., Joshua. Josh. vii. 19, 20.
5. Comp. Acts x. 11.
6. Or, and he spoke to me.

Chapter 16

And the rulers of the synagogue, and the priests and the Levites, when they heard these words from Joseph, became as dead, and fell to the ground, and fasted until the ninth hour.

And Nicodemus, along with Joseph, exhorted Annas and Caiaphas, the priests and the Levites, saying:

Rise up and stand upon your feet, and taste bread, and strengthen your souls, because to-morrow is the Sabbath of the Lord. And they rose up, and prayed to God, and ate and drank, and departed every man to his own house.

And on the Sabbath our teachers and the priests and Levites sat questioning each other, and saying:

What is this wrath that has come upon us? for we know his father and mother.

Levi, a teacher, says:

I know that his parents fear God, and do not withdraw themselves from the prayers, and give the tithes thrice a year. [1]And when Jesus was born, his parents brought him to this place, and gave sacrifices and burnt-offerings to God.

And when the great teacher Symeon took him into his arms, he said, Now Thou sendest away Thy servant, Lord, according to Thy word, in peace; for mine eyes have seen Thy salvation, which Thou hast prepared before the face of all the peoples:

a light for the revelation of the Gentiles, and the glory of Thy people Israel.

And Symeon blessed them, and said to Mary his mother, I give thee good news about this child.

And Mary said, It is well, my lord. And Symeon said to her, It is well; behold, he lies for the fall and rising again of many in Israel, and for a sign spoken against; and of thee thyself a sword shall go through the soul, in order that the reasoning of many hearts may be revealed. [2]

They say to the teacher Levi:

How knowest thou these things?

Levi says to them:

Do you not know that from him I learned the law?

The Sanhedrin say to him:

We wish to see thy father.

And they sent for his father.

And they asked him; and he said to them:

Why have you not believed my son?

The blessed and just Symeon himself taught him the law.

The Sanhedrin says to Rabbi Levi:

Is the word that you have said true?

And he said:

It is true.

And the rulers of the synagogue, and the priests and the Levites, said to themselves:

Come, let us send into Galilee to the three men that came and told about his teaching and his taking up, and let them tell us how they saw him taken up.

And this saying pleased all.

And they sent away the three men who had already gone away into Galilee with them; and they say to them:

Say to Rabbi Adas, and Rabbi Phinees, and Rabbi Haggai:

Peace to you, and all who are with you!

A great inquiry having taken place in the Sanhedrin, we have been sent to you to call you to this holy place, Jerusalem.

And the men set out into Galilee, and found them sitting and considering the law; and they saluted them in peace.

And the men who were in Galilee said to those who had come to them:

Peace upon all Israel!

And they said:

Peace to you!

And they again said to them: Why have you come?

And those who had been sent said:

The Sanhedrin call you to the holy city Jerusalem.

And when the men heard that they were sought by the Sanhedrin, they prayed to God, and reclined with the men, and ate and drank, and rose up, and set out in peace to Jerusalem.

And on the following day the Sanhedrin sat in the synagogue, and asked them, saying:

Did you really see Jesus sitting on the mountain Mamilch teaching his eleven disciples, and did you see him taken up?

And the men answered them, and said:

As we saw him taken up, so also we said.

Annas says:

Take them away from one another, and let us see whether their account agrees.

And they took them away from one another.

And first they call Adas, and say to him:

How didst thou see Jesus taken up?

Adas says:

While he was yet sitting on the mountain Mamilch, and teaching his disciples, we saw a cloud overshadowing both him and his disciples.

And the cloud took him up into heaven, and his disciples lay upon their face upon the earth.

And they call Phinees the priest, and ask him also, saying:

How didst thou see Jesus taken up?

And he spoke in like manner.

And they again asked Haggai, and he spoke in like manner.

And the Sanhedrin said:

The law of Moses holds:

At the mouth of two or three every word shall be established. ^{3}Buthem, a teacher, says:

It is written in the law, And Enoch walked with God, and is not, because God took him.

^{4}Jairus, a teacher, said: And the death of holy Moses we have heard of, and have not seen it; for it is written in the law of the Lord, And Moses died from the mouth of the Lord, and no man knoweth of his sepulchre unto this day. ^{5} And Rabbi Levi said:

Why did Rabbi Symeon say, when he saw Jesus, "Behold, he lies for the fall and rising again of many in Israel, and for a sign spoken against?" ^{6}And Rabbi Isaac said:

It is written in the law, Behold, I send my messenger before thy face, who shall go before thee to keep thee in every good way, because my name has been called upon him. ^{7}

Then Annas and Caiaphas said:

Rightly have you said what is written in the law of Moses, that no one saw the death of Enoch, and no one has named the death of Moses; but Jesus was tried before Pilate, and we saw him receiving blows and spittings on his face, and the soldiers put about him a crown of thorns, and he was scourged, and received sentence from Pilate, and was crucified upon the Cranium, and two robbers with him; and they gave him to drink vinegar with gall, and Longinus the soldier pierced his side with a spear; and Joseph our honourable father begged his body, and, as he says, he is risen; and as the three teachers say, We saw him taken up into heaven; and Rabbi Levi has given evidence of what was said by Rabbi Symeon, and that he said, Behold, he lies for the fall and rising again of many in Israel, and for a sign spoken against.

And all the teachers said to all the people of the Lord:

If this was from the Lord, and is wonderful in your eyes, ^{8} knowing you shall know, O house of Jacob, that it is written, Cursed is every one that hangeth upon a tree. ^{9}And another Scripture teaches:

The gods which have not made the heaven and the earth shall be destroyed. [10]And the priests and the Levites said to each other:

If his memorial be until the year that is called Jobel, [11] know that it shall it endure for ever, and he hath raised for himself a new people.

Then the rulers of the synagogue, and the priests and the Levites, announced to all Israel, saying:

Cursed is that man who shall worship the work of man's hand, and cursed is the man who shall worship the creatures more than the Creator.

And all the people said, Amen, amen. [12]

And all the people praised [13] the Lord, and said:

Blessed is the Lord, who hath given rest to His people Israel, according to all that He hath spoken; there hath not fallen one word of every good word of His that He spoke to Moses His servant.

May the Lord our God be with us, as He was with our fathers:

let Him not destroy us.

And let Him not destroy us, that we may incline our hearts to Him, that we may walk in all His ways, that we may keep His commandments and His judgments which He commanded to our fathers. [14]And the Lord shall be for a king over all the earth in that day; and there shall be one Lord, and His name one. [15]The Lord is our king:

He shall save us. [16]

There is none like Thee, O Lord. [17]Great art Thou, O Lord, and great is Thy name.

By Thy power heal us, O Lord, and we shall be healed:

save us, O Lord, and we shall be saved; [18] because we are Thy lot and heritage.

And the Lord will not leave His people, for His great name's sake; for the Lord has begun to make us into His people. [19]

And all, having sung praises, went away each man to his own house, glorifying God; for His is the glory for ever and ever.

Amen.

Footnotes:

1. This would seem to confirm the opinion that there were three tithes paid in the year. Comp. Smith's Dict., sub voce.

2. Luke ii. 25-35.
3. Deut. xvii. 6.
4. Gen. v. 24; Heb. xi. 5.
5. Deut. xxxiv. 5, 6.
6. Luke ii. 34.
7. Ex. xxiii. 20, 21; Mal. iii. 1; Matt. xi. 10.
8. Ps. cxviii. 23.
9. Deut. xxi. 23; Gal. iii. 13.
10. Jer. x. 11.
11. i.e., the year of jubilee. The original, heos tou sommou, is not Greek. It is not easy to see what the passage means. It may refer to Isa. lxi. 1-3.
12. Deut. xxvii. 15; Rom. i. 25.
13. Or, sang hymns to.
14. 1 Kings viii. 56-58.
15. Zech. xiv. 9.
16. Isa. xxxiii. 22.
17. Ps. lxxxvi. 8.
18. Comp. Jer. xvii. 14.
19. Comp. 1 Sam. xii. 22.

The Forgotten Bible
Second Greek Form

A narrative about the suffering of our Lord Jesus Christ, and His holy resurrection

Written by a Jew, AEneas by name, and translated out of the Hebrew tongue into the Romaic language by Nicodemus, a Roman toparch.

After the dissolution of the kingdom of the Hebrews, four hundred years having run their course, and the Hebrews also coming at last under the kingdom of the Romans, and the king of the Romans appointing them a king; when Tiberius Caesar at last swayed the Roman sceptre, in the eighteenth year of his reign, [1] he appointed as king of Judaea, Herod, the son of the Herod who had formerly slaughtered the infants in Bethlehem, and he made Pilate procurator in Jerusalem; when Annas and Caiaphas held the high-priesthood of Jerusalem, Nicodemus, a Roman toparch, having summoned a Jew, AEneas by name, asked him to write an account of the things done in Jerusalem about Christ in the times of Annas and Caiaphas.

The Jew accordingly did this, and delivered it to Nicodemus; and he, again, translated it from the Hebrew writing into the Romaic language.

And the account is as follows:--

Footnote:
1. [Compare the first Greek form, prologue and footnote.--R.]

Chapter 1

Our Lord Jesus Christ having wrought in Judaea many and great and extraordinary miracles, and on account of this being hated by the Hebrews, while Pilate was procurator in Jerusalem, and Annas and Caiaphas high priests, there came of the Jews to the chief priests, Judas, Levi, Nephthalim, Alexander, Syrus, and many others, speaking against Christ.

And these chief priests sent them away to say these things to Pilate also.

And they went away, and said to him:

A man walks about in this city whose father is called Joseph, and his mother Mary; and he calls himself king and Son of God; and being a Jew, he overturns the Scriptures, and does away with the Sabbath.

Pilate then asked, in order to learn from them in what manner he did away with the Sabbath.

And they answered, saying:

He cures the sick on the Sabbath.

Pilate says:

If he makes the sick whole, he does no evil. They say to him:

If he effected the cures properly, small would be the evil; but by using magic he does these things, and by having the demons on his side.

Pilate says:

To cure a person that is ill is not a diabolic work, but a grace from God.

The Hebrews said:

We beseech your highness to summon him, in order that thou mayst make accurate inquiry into what we say.

Pilate therefore, throwing off his cloak, gave it to one of his officers, [1] saying:

Go away, and show this to Jesus, and say to him, Pilate the procurator calls thee to come before him.

The officer accordingly went away, and finding Jesus, summoned Him, having unfolded on the ground also Pilate's mantle, and urged Him to walk upon it.

And the Hebrews, seeing this, and being greatly enraged, came to Pilate, murmuring against him, how he had deemed Jesus worthy of so great honour.

And he, having inquired of the officer who had been sent how he had done so, the officer answered:

When thou didst send me to the Jew Alexander, I came upon Jesus entering the gate of the city, sitting upon an ass.

And I saw that the Hebrews spread their garments in the way, and the ass walked upon the garments; and others cut branches, and they went forth to meet him, and cried out, Hosanna in the highest! Thus, therefore, it was necessary for me also to do.

The Jews, hearing these words, said to him:

How didst thou, being a Roman, know what was said by the Hebrews?

The officer answered:

I asked one of the Hebrews, and he told me these things.
Pilate said: What means Hosanna?
The Jews said:
Save us, O Lord.
Pilate answered:
Since you confess that your children said so, how now do you bring charges, and say against Jesus what you do say?
The Jews were silent, and had nothing to answer. [2]
Now, as Jesus was coming to Pilate, the soldiers of Pilate adored Him. And others also were standing before Pilate holding standards.
And as Jesus was coming, the standards also bowed down, and adored Him.
As Pilate, therefore, was wondering at what had happened, the Jews said to him:
My lord, it was not the standards that adored Jesus, but the soldiers who were holding them carelessly.
Pilate says to the ruler of the synagogue:
Choose twelve powerful men, and give them the standards, so that they may hold them firmly.
And this having taken place, Pilate ordered the officer to take Jesus outside, and bring Him in again.
And as He was coming in, the standards again bowed down, and adored Him.
Pilate therefore wondered greatly.
But the Jews said:
He is a magician, and through that he does these things.

Footnotes:

1. One ms. inserts: by name Rachaab, the messenger.
2. Instead of these four sections, ms. C has a minute account of the suicide of Judas, of which the following specimen may be given:--And he went home to make a halter to hang himself, and he found his wife roasting a cock on the coals. And he says to her: Rise, wife, and get a rope ready for me; for I mean to hang myself, as I deserve. And his wife said to him: Why do you speak like that? And Judas says: Know in truth that I unjustly betrayed my master, etc., and that he is going to rise on the third day; and woe to us! And his wife says: Do not speak or think in that way. It is just as likely as that this cock roasting on the coals will crow, that Jesus will rise, as you say. No sooner said than the cock flapped his wings, and crew thrice. This decided Judas, and he immediately made the halter, and hanged himself. [Themss. of the "Second Greek Form" are designated by Tischendorf (Evang. Apocry., pp. lxxii., lxxiii.) as follows: A, a Venice ms., comparatively recent; B., a Paris ms. of the fifteenth century; C. a Venice ms. of the same century.--R.]

Chapter 2

Pilate says to Jesus:
Hearest thou what these testify against thee, and answerest thou not? [1] And Jesus answered and said:
Every man has power to speak either good or bad, as he wishes; these also, therefore, having power, say what they wish. [2]
The Jews said to Him:
What have we to say about thee?
First, that thou wast begotten from sin; second, that on account of thee, when thou wast born, the infants [3] were murdered; third, that thy father and thy mother fled into Egypt, because they had no confidence in the people.
To these the Jews who were there present, God-fearing men, answered and said:
We say that his birth is not from sin; for we know that Joseph received into keeping his mother Mary, according to the practice of betrothal.
Pilate said:
Consequently you lie who say that his birth is from sin.
They say again to Pilate:
All the people testify that he is a magician.
The God-fearing Jews answered and said:
We also were at the betrothal of his mother, and we are Jews, and know all his daily life; but that he is a magician, that we do not know.
And the Jews that thus said were these:
Lazarus, Astharius, Antonius, James, Zaras, Samuel, Isaac, Phinees, Crispus, Dagrippus, Amese, and Judas.
Pilate therefore says to them:

The Forgotten Bible

By the life of Caesar, I wish you to swear whether the birth of this man is without sin.

They answered: Our law lays down that we are to swear not at all, because an oath is great sin.

Notwithstanding, by the life of Caesar we swear that his birth is without sin; and if we lie, order us all to be beheaded.

And when they had thus spoken, the Jews that were bringing the charge answered Pilate, and said:

And dost thou believe these twelve single Jews more than all the multitude and us, who know for certain that he is a magician and blasphemer, and that he names himself Son of God?

Then Pilate ordered them all to go forth out of the praetorium except the said twelve alone.

And when this had been done, Pilate says to them privately:

As to this man, it appears that from envy and madness the Jews wish to murder him:

for of one thing--that he does away with the Sabbath--they accuse him; but he then does a good work, because he cures the sick.

For this, sentence of death is not upon the man.

The twelve also say to him:

Assuredly, my lord, it is so.

Footnotes:

1. Matt. xxvii. 13, 14.
2. Comp. John xix. 11.
3. ms. A, 14,000 infants; B, 44,000 infants.

Chapter 3

Pilate therefore went outside in rage and anger, and says to Annas and Caiaphas, and to the crowd who brought Jesus:

I take the sun to witness that I find no fault in this man.

The crowd answered:

If he were not a sorcerer, and a magician, and a blasphemer, we should not have brought him to your highness.

Pilate said:

Try him yourselves; and since you have a law, do as your law says.

The Jews said:

Our law permits to put no man to death. [1]Pilate says:

If you are unwilling to put him to death, how much more am I!

Then Pilate returned to the palace, and says to Jesus:

Tell me, art thou the king of the Jews?

Jesus answered:

Dost thou say this, or have the other Jews said this to thee, that thou mightst question me? Pilate said:

Thou dost not think that I am a Hebrew?

I am not a Hebrew.

Thy people and the chief priests have delivered thee into my hands; and tell me if thou art king of the Jews?

Jesus answered:

My kingdom is not of this world; for if my kingdom were in this world, my soldiers would not be unconcerned at my being seized;

wherefore my kingdom is not in this world.

Pilate says:

But art thou a king? Jesus said:

Thou hast said;

for this was I born, to bear witness to the truth; and if any one be a man of the truth, he believes my word, and does it.

Pilate says:

What is the truth? [2]Jesus answered:

The truth is from the heavens.

Pilate says:

On earth, then, is there no truth?

Christ says:

I am the truth; and how is the truth judged on earth by those that have earthly power!

Footnotes:
1. John xix. 6, 7.
2. John xviii. 33-38.

Chapter 4

Pilate therefore, leaving Christ alone, went outside, and says to the Jews:
I find no fault in this man.
The Jews answered:
Let us tell your highness what he said.
He said, I am able to destroy the temple of God, and in three days to build it.
Pilate says:
And what temple did he say that he was to destroy?
The Hebrews say:
The temple of Solomon, which Solomon built in forty-six years.[1]
Pilate says privately to the chief priests and the scribes and the Pharisees:
I entreat you, do nothing evil against this man; for if you do evil against him, you will do unjustly:
for it is not just that such a man should die, who has done great good to many men.
They said to Pilate:
If, my lord, he who has dishonoured Caesar is worthy of death, how much more this man who dishonours God!
Then Pilate dismissed them, and they all went outside.
Thereupon he says to Jesus:
What dost thou wish that I shall do to thee?
Jesus says to Pilate:
Do to me as is determined.
Pilate says:
How is it determined?
Jesus answered:
Moses and the prophets wrote about me being crucified, and rising again.
The Hebrews, hearing this, said to Pilate:
Why do you seek to hear a greater insult out of him against God?
Pilate says:
These words are not an insult against God, since they are written in the books of the prophets.
The Hebrews said:
Our Scripture says, If a man offend against a man, that is to say, if he insult him, he is worthy to receive forty strokes with a rod; but if any one insult God, to be stoned.[2]
Then came a messenger from Procle, the wife of Pilate, to him; and the message said:
Take care that thou do not agree that any evil should happen to Jesus the good man; because during this night I have seen fearful dreams on account of him.[3] And Pilate spoke to the Hebrews, saying:
If you hold as insult against God the words which you declare Jesus to have spoken, take and judge him yourselves according to your law.[4] The Jews said to Pilate:
We wish that you should crucify him.
Pilate says:
This is not good.
And Pilate, turning towards the people, saw many weeping, and said:
To me it seems that it is not the wish of all the people that this man should die.
The priests and the scribes say:
We on this account have brought all the people, that thou mightst have full conviction that all wish his death.
Pilate says:
For what evil hath he done?
The Hebrews said:
He says that he is a king, and the Son of God.

Footnotes:
1. Comp. John ii. 20.
2. Deut. xxv. 3; Lev. xxiv. 16.
3. Matt. xxvii. 19.
4. John xviii. 31.

The Forgotten Bible

Chapter 5

A God-fearing Jew, therefore, Nicodemus by name, stood up in the midst, and said to Pilate: I entreat your highness to permit me to say a few words.

Say on, said Pilate.

Nicodemus says:

I, being present in the synagogue, said to the priests, and the Levites, and the scribes, and the people, What have you to say against this man?

This man does many miracles, such as man has never yet done nor will do.

Let him go, therefore; and if indeed what he does be from God, it will stand; but if from man, it will be destroyed. [1] Just as happened also when God sent Moses into Egypt, and Pharoah king of Egypt told him to do a miracle, and he did it.

Then Pharoah had also two magicians, Jannes and Jambres; and they also did miracles by the use of magic art, but not such as Moses did. [2] And the Egyptians held these magicians to be gods; but because they were not from God, what they did was destroyed.

This Jesus, then, raised up Lazarus, and he is alive.

On this account I entreat thee, my lord, by no means to allow this man to be put to death.

The Hebrews were enraged against Nicodemus, and said:

Mayst thou receive the truth of Jesus, and have a portion with him.

Nicodemus says:

Amen, amen; be it to me as you say.

Footnotes:
1. Comp. Acts v. 38.
2. Ex. vii. 10-14.

Chapter 6

And when Nicodemus had thus spoken, another Hebrew rose up, and said to Pilate:

I beg of thee, my lord Pilate, hear me also.

Pilate answered:

Say what thou wishest.

The Hebrew says:

I lay sick in bed thirty-eight years; and when he saw me he was grieved, and said to me, Rise, take up thy couch, and go into thine house.

And while he was saying the word to me, I rose and walked about.

The Hebrews say:

Ask him on what day of the week this happened.

He says:

On Sabbath. [1] The Jews said:

And consequently we say truly, that he does not keep the Sabbath.

Another, again, standing in the midst, said:

I was born blind; and as Jesus was going along the road, I cried to him, saying, Have mercy upon me, Lord, thou son of David.

And he took clay, and anointed mine eyes; and straightway I received my sight. [2] Another said:

I was crooked; and seeing him, I cried, Have mercy upon me, O Lord.

And he took me by the hand, and I was immediately raised. [3] Another said:

I was a leper, and he healed me merely by a word. [4]

Footnotes:
1. John v. 5-9.
2. John ix. 6, 7.
3. Comp. Acts iii. 7.
4. Luke xvii. 11-19.

Chapter 7

There was found there also a woman named Veronica, and she said: Twelve years I was in an issue of blood, and I only touched the edge of his garment, and directly I was cured. [1] The Jews say: Our law does not admit the testimony of a woman. [2]

Footnotes:
1. Matt. ix. 20-22.
2. See note 9, p. 419.

Chapter 8

Other men cried:
This man is a prophet, and the demons are afraid of him.
Pilate says:
And how were the demons not at all thus afraid of your parents also?
They say:
We do not know.
Others, again, said: Lazarus, after having been four days in the tomb, he raised by a single word. [1] Pilate therefore, hearing of the raising of Lazarus, was afraid, and said to the people:
Why do you wish to shed the blood of a just man?

Footnote:
1. John xi. 43.

Chapter 9

Then he summoned Nicodemus and the twelve God-fearing Jews, and said to them:
What do you say that I should do? because the people are in commotion.
They say:
We do not know:
do as thou wilt; but what the people do, they do unjustly, in order to kill him.
Pilate again went outside, and said to the people:
You know that in the feasts of unleavened bread it is customary that I free on your account one of the criminals kept in custody.
I have, then, one malefactor in the prison, a robber named Barabbas.
I have also Jesus, who has never done any evil.
Which of the two, then, do you wish that I release to you?
The people answered:
Release to us Barabbas.
Pilate says:
What then shall I do with Jesus?
They say:
Let him be crucified. [1] Again, others of them cried out:
If thou release Jesus, thou art no friend of Caesar, [2] because he calls himself Son of God, and king.
And if thou free him, he becomes a king, and will take Caesar's kingdom.
Pilate therefore was enraged, and said:
Always has your nation been devilish [3] and unbelieving; and ever have you been adversaries to your benefactors.
The Hebrews say:
And who were our benefactors? Pilate says:
God, who freed you out of the hand of Pharaoh, and brought you through the Red Sea as upon dry land, and fed you with quails, and gave you water to drink out of the dry rock, and who gave you a law which, denying God you broke; and if Moses had not stood and entreated God, you would have perished by a bitter death.
All these, then, you have forgotten.
Thus also, even now, you say that I do not at all love Caesar, but hate him, and wish to plot against his kingdom.
And having thus spoken, Pilate rose up from the throne with anger, wishing to flee from them.
The Jews therefore cried out, saying:
We wish Caesar to be king over us, not Jesus, because Jesus received gifts [4] from the Magi.
And Herod also heard this--that there was going to be a king--and wished to put him to death, and for this purpose sent and put to death all the infants that were in Bethlehem.
And on this account also his father Joseph and his mother fled from fear of him into Egypt. [5]
So then Pilate, hearing this, silenced all the people, and said:
This, then, is the Jesus whom Herod then sought that he might put him to death?
They say to him:
Yes.

Pilate therefore, having ascertained that he was of the jurisdiction of Herod, as being derived of the race of the Jews, sent Jesus to him.

And Herod, seeing Him, rejoiced greatly, because he had been long desiring to see Him, hearing of the miracles which He did.

He put on Him, therefore, white garments.

Then he began to question Him.

But Jesus did not give him an answer.

And Herod, wishing to see also some miracle or other done by Jesus, and not seeing it, and also because He did not answer him a single word, sent Him back again to Pilate. [6]Pilate, seeing this, ordered his officers to bring water.

Washing, then, his hands with the water, he said to the people:

I am innocent of the blood of this good man.

See you to it, that he is unjustly put to death, since neither I have found a fault in him, nor Herod; for because of this he has sent him back again to me.

The Jews said:

His blood be upon us, and upon our children. [7]

Then Pilate sat down upon his throne to pass sentence.

He gave order, therefore, and Jesus came before him.

And they brought a crown of thorns, and put it on His head, and a reed into His right hand. [8]
Then he passed sentence, and said to Him:

Thy nation says, and testifies against thee, that thou wishest to be a king.

Therefore I decree that they shall beat thee first with a rod forty strokes, as the laws of the kings decree, and that they shall mock thee; and finally, that they shall crucify thee.

Footnotes:

1. Matt. xxvii. 15-18, 21-23.
2. John xix. 12.
3. Or, slanderous.
4. The word here, charisma, is used in the New Testament only of gifts and graces bestowed by God, and specially of the miraculous gifts imparted to the early Christians by the Holy Ghost. The word in Matt. ii. 11 is dora.
5. Matt. ii. 14-16. [The writer seems to identify Herod the Great and Herod Antipas.--R.]
6. Luke xxiii. 6-11. [The only passage directly interpolated into Luke's narrative is "as being derived of the race of the Jews." A curious blunder of the compiler!--R.]
7. Matt. xxvii. 25.
8. John xix. 2, 3; Matt. xxvii. 29.

Chapter 10

The sentence to this effect, then, having been passed by Pilate, the Jews began to strike Jesus, some with rods, others with their hands, others with their feet; some also spat in His face.

Immediately, therefore, they got ready the cross, and gave it to Him, and flew to take the road.

And thus going along, bearing also the cross, He came as far as the gate of the city of Jerusalem.

But as He, from the many blows and the weight of the cross, was unable to walk, the Jews, out of the eager desire they had to crucify Him as quickly as possible, took the cross from Him, and gave it to a man that met them, Simon by name, who had also two sons, Alexander and Rufus.

And he was from the city of Cyrene. [1]They gave the cross, then, to him, not because they pitied Jesus, and wished to lighten Him of the weight, but because they eagerly desired, as has been said, to put Him to death more speedily.

Of His disciples, therefore, John followed Him there.

Then he came fleeing to the mother of God, [2] and said to her:

Where hast thou been, that thou hast not come to see what has happened?

She answered: What is it that has happened?

John says:

Know that the Jews have laid hold of my Master, and are taking Him away to crucify Him.

Hearing this, His mother cried out with a loud voice, saying:

My son, my son, what evil then hast thou done, that [3] they are taking thee away to crucify thee?

And she rose up as if blinded, [4] and goes along the road weeping.

And women followed her--Martha, and Mary Magdalene, and Salome, and other virgins.

And John also was with her.

When, therefore, they came to the multitude of the crowd, the mother of God says to John:

Where is my son?

John says:

Seest thou Him bearing the crown of thorns, and having His hands bound?

And the mother of God, hearing this, and seeing Him, fainted, and fell backwards to the ground, and lay a considerable time.

And the women, as many as followed her, stood round her, and wept.

And as soon as she revived and rose up, she cried out with a loud voice:

My Lord, my son, where has the beauty of thy form sunk? how shall I endure to see thee suffering such things?

And thus saying, she tore her face with her nails, and beat her breast.

Where are they gone, said she, the good deeds which thou didst in Judaea?

What evil hast thou done to the Jews?

The Jews, then, seeing her thus lamenting and crying, came and drove her from the road; but she would not flee, but remained, saying: Kill me first, ye lawless Jews.

Then they got safe to the place called Cranium, which was paved with stone; ⁵ and there the Jews set up the cross.

Then they stripped Jesus, and the soldiers took His garments, and divided them among themselves; and they put on Him a tattered robe of scarlet, and raised Him, and drew Him up on the cross at the sixth hour of the day.

After this they brought also two robbers, the one on His right, the other on His left.

Then the mother of God, standing and looking, cried out with a loud voice, saying:

My son! my son!

And Jesus, turning to her, and seeing John near her, and weeping with the rest of the women, said:

Behold thy son!

Then He says also to John:

Behold thy mother! ⁶And she wept much, saying:

For this I weep, my son, because thou sufferest unjustly, because the lawless Jews have delivered thee to a bitter death.

Without thee, my son, what will become of me?

How shall I live without thee?

What sort of life shall I spend?

Where are thy disciples, who boasted that they would die with thee?

Where those healed by thee?

How has no one been found to help thee?

And looking to the cross, she said:

Bend down, O cross, that I may embrace and kiss my son, whom I suckled at these breasts after a strange manner, as not having known man.

Bend down, O cross; I wish to throw my arms round my son.

Bend down, O cross, that I may bid farewell to my son like a mother.

The Jews, hearing these words, came forward, and drove to a distance both her and the women and John.

Then Jesus cried out with a loud voice, saying:

Father, let not this sin stand against them; for they know not what they do. ⁷Then He says: I thirst.

And immediately there ran one of the soldiers, and took a sponge, and filled it with gall and vinegar mixed, and put it on a reed, and gave Jesus to drink.

And having tasted it, He would not drink it. ⁸And the Jews standing and looking on laughed at Him, and said:

If thou truly sayst that thou art the Son of God, come down from the cross, and immediately, that we may believe in thee.

Others said mocking:

Others he saved, others he cured, and he healed the sick, the paralytic, the lepers, the demoniacs, the blind, the lame, the dead; and himself he cannot cure. ⁹

In the same manner also, the robber crucified on His left hand said to Him:

If thou art the Son of God, come down and save both thyself and us.

His name was Gistas.

And he that was crucified on the right, Dysmas by name, reproved that robber, saying:

O wretched and miserable man, dost thou not fear God?

We suffer the due punishment of what we have done; but this man has done no evil at all.

And turning to Jesus, he says to Him:

Lord, when Thou shalt reign do not forget me.

And He said to him:
To-day, I tell thee truth, I shall have thee in paradise with me.[10]

Footnotes:

1. Mark xv. 21.
2. Theotokos-- a word used several times by Athanasius (died 373), e.g., in Orat. iii. Contra Arianos, c. 14 and 29. The refusal of Nestorius to give this epithet to Mary was the commencement, in 428, of the long struggle between the rival sees of Constantinople and Alexandria. See Haag, Histoire des Dogmes Chretiens, i. 190. The paragraphs about the Theotokos in this chapter are interpolations.
3. Lit., and.
4. Lit., darkened.
5. A mistaken reference to John xix. 13.
6. John xix. 26, 27.
7. Luke xxiii. 34; cf. Acts vii. 60.
8. John xix. 28; Matt. xxvii. 48.
9. Comp. Matt. xxvii. 40-42.
10. Luke xxiii. 39-43. ms. C here inserts the early history of the robber Dysmas. [See note 3, p. 426.--R.]

Chapter 11

Then Jesus, crying out with a loud voice, Father, into Thy hands I shall commit my spirit, breathed His last. [1]And immediately one could see the rocks rent:

for there was an earthquake over all the earth; and from the earthquake being violent and great, the rocks also were rent.

And the tombs of the dead were opened, and the curtain of the temple was rent, and there was darkness from the sixth hour till the ninth.

And from all these things that had happened the Jews were afraid, and said:

Certainly this was a just man.

And Longinus, the centurion who stood by, said:

Truly this was a son of God.

Others coming and seeing Him, beat their breasts from fear, and again turned back. [2]

And the centurion having perceived all these so great miracles, went away and reported them to Pilate.

And when he heard, he wondered and was astonished, and from his fear and grief would neither eat nor drink that day.

And he sent notice, and all the Sanhedrin came to him as soon as the darkness was past; and he said to the people:

You know how the sun has been darkened; you know how the curtain has been rent. Certainly I did well in being by no means willing to put to death the good man.

And the malefactors said to Pilate:

This darkness is an eclipse of the sun, such as has happened also at other times.

Then they say to him:

We hold the feast of unleavened bread to-morrow; and we entreat thee, since the crucified are still breathing, that their bones be broken, and that they be brought down.

Pilate said:

It shall be so.

He therefore sent soldiers, and they found the two robbers yet breathing, and they broke their legs; but finding Jesus dead, they did not touch Him at all, except that a soldier speared Him in the right side, and immediately there came forth blood and water. [3]

And as the day of the preparation [4] was drawing towards evening, Joseph, a man well-born and rich, a God-fearing Jew, finding Nicodemus, whose sentiments his foregoing speech had shown, says to him:

I know that thou didst love Jesus when living, and didst gladly hear his words, and I saw thee fighting with the Jews on his account.

If, then, it seem good to thee, let us go to Pilate, and beg the body of Jesus for burial, because it is a great sin for him to lie unburied.

I am afraid, said Nicodemus, lest Pilate should be enraged, and some evil should befall me.

But if thou wilt go alone, and beg the dead, and take him, then will I also go with thee, and help thee to do everything necessary for the burial.

Nicodemus having thus spoken, Joseph directed his eyes to heaven, and prayed that he might not fail in his request; and he went away to Pilate, and having saluted him, sat down. Then he says to him:

I entreat thee, my lord, not to be angry with me, if I shall ask anything contrary to what seems good to your highness. And he said:

And what is it that thou askest?

Joseph says:

Jesus, the good man whom through hatred the Jews have taken away to crucify, him I entreat that thou give me for burial.

Pilate says:

And what has happened, that we should deliver to be honoured again the dead body of him against whom evidence of sorcery was brought by his nation, and who was in suspicion of taking the kingdom of Caesar, and so was given up by us to death?

And Joseph, weeping and in great grief, fell at the feet of Pilate, saying:

My lord, let no hatred fall upon a dead man; for all the evil that a man has done should perish with him in his death.

And I know your highness, how eager thou wast that Jesus should not be crucified, and how much thou saidst to the Jews on his behalf, now in entreaty and again in anger, and at last how thou didst wash thy hands, and declare that thou wouldst by no means take part with those who wished him to be put to death; for all which reasons I entreat thee not to refuse my request.

Pilate, therefore, seeing Joseph thus lying, and supplicating, and weeping, raised him up, and said:

Go, I grant thee this dead man; take him, and do whatever thou wilt.

And then Joseph, having thanked Pilate, and kissed his hands and his garments, went forth, rejoicing indeed in heart as having obtained his desire, but carrying tears in his eyes.

Thus also, though grieved, he was glad.

Accordingly he goes away to Nicodemus, and discloses to him all that had happened.

Then, having bought myrrh and aloes a hundred pounds, and a new tomb, [5] they, along with the mother of God and Mary Magdalene and Salome, along with John, and the rest of the women, did what was customary for the body with white linen, and placed it in the tomb. [6]

And the mother of God said, weeping:

How am I not to lament thee, my son?

How should I not tear my face with my nails?

This is that, my son, which Symeon the elder foretold to me when I brought thee, an infant of forty days old, into the temple.

This is the sword which now goes through my soul. [7]Who shall put a stop to my tears, my sweetest son?

No one at all except thyself alone, if, as thou saidst, thou shalt rise again in three days.

Mary Magdalene said, weeping:

Hear, O peoples, tribes, and tongues, and learn to what death the lawless Jews have delivered him who did them ten thousand good deeds.

Hear, and be astonished.

Who will let these things be heard by all the world?

I shall go alone to Rome, to the Caesar.

I shall show him what evil Pilate hath done in obeying the lawless Jews.

Likewise also, Joseph lamented, saying:

Ah, me! sweetest Jesus, most excellent of men, if indeed it be proper to call thee man, who hast wrought such miracles as no man has ever done.

How shall I enshroud thee?

How shall I entomb thee?

There should now have been here those whom thou fedst with a few loaves; for thus should I not have seemed to fail in what is due.

Then Joseph, along with Nicodemus, went home; and likewise also the mother of God, with the women, John [8] also being present with them.

Footnotes:

1. Luke xxiii. 46.
2. Comp. Luke xxiii. 44-49.
3. John xix. 31-34.
4. [Or simply, "the Preparation;" comp. Matt. xxvii. 62, and elsewhere, in the Rev. Vers.--R.]
5. Comp. Matt. xxvii. 60.
6. John xix. 38-42.
7. Luke ii. 35.
8. It is to be observed that John's Gospel is much more frequently quoted in this book than

any of the others.

Chapter 12

When the Jews were made acquainted with these things done by Joseph and Nicodemus, they were greatly stirred up against them.

And the chief priests Annas and Caiaphas sent for Joseph, and said:

Why hast thou done this service to Jesus?

Joseph says:

I know that Jesus was a man just, and true, and good in all respects; and I know also that you, through hatred, managed to murder him:

and therefore I buried him. Then the high priests were enraged, and laid hold of Joseph, and threw him into prison, and said to him:

If we had not to-morrow the feast of unleavened bread, tomorrow also should we have put thee, like him, to death; but being kept in the meantime, early in the morning of the Lord's day [1] thou shalt be given up to death.

Thus they spoke, and affixed their seal to the prison, having secured it by fastenings of all sorts.

Thus, therefore, when the Preparation was ended, early on the Sabbath the Jews went away to Pilate, and said to him:

My lord, that deceiver said, that after three days he should rise again.

Lest, therefore, his disciples should steal him by night, and lead the people astray by such deceit, order his tomb to be guarded.

Pilate therefore, upon this, gave them five hundred soldiers, who also sat round the sepulchre so as to guard it, after having put seals upon the stone of the tomb. [2]

The Lord's day, then, having dawned, the chief priests, along with the Jews, called a council, and sent to take Joseph out of the prison, in order to put him to death.

But having opened it, they found him not. And they were astonished at this--how, with the doors shut, and the bolts safe, and the seals unbroken, Joseph had disappeared.

Footnotes:

1. Observe the anachronism.
2. Matt. xxvii. 62-66.

Chapter 13

And upon this there came up one of the soldiers guarding the tomb, and he said in the synagogue:

Learn that Jesus has risen.

The Jews say: How?

And he said:

First there was an earthquake; then an angel of the Lord, clothed with lightning, came from heaven, and rolled the stone from the tomb, and sat upon it.

And from fear of him, all of us soldiers became as dead, and were able neither to flee nor speak.

And we heard the angels saying to the women who came there to see the tomb:

Be not you afraid, for I know that you seek Jesus.

He is not here, but is risen, as He told you before.

Bend down and see the tomb where His body lay; but go and tell His disciples that He is risen from the dead, and let them go into Galilee, for there shall they find Him. For this reason I tell you this first. [1]

The Jews say to the soldiers:

What sort of women were they who came to the tomb? and why did you not lay hold of them?

The soldiers say: From the fear and the mere sight of the angel, we were able neither to speak nor move.

The Jews said:

As the God of Israel liveth, we do not believe a word you say.

The soldiers say:

Jesus did so great wonders, and you believed not, and are you going to believe us?

You say truly that God liveth; and certainly he whom you crucified truly liveth.

But we have heard that you had Joseph shut up in the prison, and that you afterwards opened the doors, and did not find him.

Do you then present Joseph, and so we also shall present Jesus.

The Jews say:

Joseph, that fled from the prison, you will find in Arimathaea, his own country.

And the soldiers say:

Go you too into Galilee, and you will find Jesus, as the angel said to the women.

At these words the Jews were afraid, and said to the soldiers:

See that you tell this story to nobody, or all will believe in Jesus.

And for this reason they gave them also much money.

And the soldiers said:

We are afraid lest by any chance Pilate hear that we have taken money, and he will kill us.

And the Jews said:

Take it; and we pledge ourselves that we shall speak to Pilate in your defence.

Only say that you were asleep, and in your slumber the disciples of Jesus came and stole him from the tomb.

The soldiers therefore took the money, and said as they were bid.

And up to this day this same lying tale is told among the Jews. [2]

Footnotes:
1. Matt. xxviii. 1-8.
2. Matt. xxviii. 11-15.

Chapter 14

And a few days after there came from Galilee to Jerusalem three men. One of them was a priest, by name Phinees; the second a Levite, by name Aggai; and the third a soldier, by name Adas.

These came to the chief priests, and said to them and to the people:

Jesus, whom you crucified, we have seen in Galilee with his eleven disciples upon the Mount of Olives, teaching them, and saying, Go into all the world, and proclaim the good news; and whosoever will believe and be baptized shall be saved; but whosoever will not believe shall be condemned.

And having thus spoken, he went up into heaven. [1] And both we and many others of the five hundred [2] besides were looking on.

And when the chief priests and the Jews heard these things, they said to these three:

Give glory to the God of Israel, and repent of these lies that you have told.

They answered:

As the God of our fathers Abraham, Isaac, and Jacob liveth, we do not lie, but tell you the truth.

Then the high priest spoke, and they brought the old covenant of the Hebrews out of the temple, and he made them swear, and giving them also money, he sent them into another place, in order that they might not proclaim in Jerusalem the resurrection of Christ.

And when these stories had been heard by all the people, the crowd came together into the temple, and there was a great commotion.

For many said:

Jesus has risen from the dead, as we hear, and why did you crucify him?

And Annas and Caiaphas said:

Do not believe, ye Jews, what the soldiers say; and do not believe that they saw an angel coming down from heaven.

For we have given money to the soldiers, in order that they should not tell such tales to any one; and thus also have the disciples of Jesus given them money, in order that they should say that Jesus has risen from the dead.

Footnotes:
1. Mark xvi. 16.
2. 1 Cor. xv. 6.

Chapter 15

Nicodemus says:

O children of the inhabitants of Jerusalem, the prophet Helias went up into the height of heaven with a fiery chariot, and it is nothing incredible if Jesus too has risen; for the prophet Helias was a prototype of Jesus, in order that you, hearing that Jesus has risen, might not disbelieve.

I therefore say and advise, that it is befitting that we send soldiers into Galilee, to that place where these men testify that they saw him with his disciples, in order that they may go round about and find him, and that thus we may ask pardon of him for the evil which we have done to him.

The Forgotten Bible

This proposal pleased them; and they chose soldiers, and sent them away into Galilee.

And Jesus indeed they did not find; but they found Joseph in Arimathaea.

When, therefore, the soldiers had returned, the chief priests, having ascertained that Joseph was found, brought the people together, and said:

What shall we do to get Joseph to come to us?

After deliberating, therefore, they wrote to him a letter to the following effect:--O father Joseph, peace be to thee and all thy house, and thy friends!

We know that we have offended against God, and against thee His servant.

On account of this, we entreat thee to come here to us thy children.

For we have wondered much how thou didst escape from the prison, and we say in truth that we had an evil design against thee. But God, seeing that our designs against thee were unjust, has delivered thee out of our hands.

But come to us, for thou art the honour of our people.

This letter the Jews sent to Arimathaea, with seven soldiers, friends of Joseph.

And they went away and found him; and having respectfully saluted him, as they had been ordered, they gave him the letter.

And after receiving it and reading it, he glorified God, and embraced the soldiers; and having set a table, ate and drank with them during all the day and the night.

And on the following day he set out with them to Jerusalem; and the people came forth to meet him, and embraced him.

And Nicodemus received him into his own house.

And the day after, Annas and Caiaphas, the chief priests, having summoned him to the temple, said to him:

Give glory to the God of Israel, and tell us the truth.

For we know that thou didst bury Jesus; and on this account we laid hold of thee, and locked thee up in the prison.

Thereafter, when we sought to bring thee out to be put to death, we did not find thee, and we were greatly astonished and afraid.

Moreover, we prayed to God that we might find thee, and ask thee.

Tell us therefore the truth.

Joseph said to them:

In the evening of the Preparation, when you secured me in prison, I fell a-praying throughout the whole night, and throughout the whole day of the Sabbath.

And at midnight I see the prison-house that four angels lifted it up, [1] holding it by the four corners.

And Jesus came in like lightning, and I fell to the ground from fear.

Taking hold of me, therefore, by the hand, he raised me, saying, Fear not, Joseph.

Thereafter, embracing me, he kissed me, and said, Turn thyself, and see who I am.

Turning myself, therefore, and looking, I said, My lord, I know not who thou art.

He says, I am Jesus, whom thou didst bury the day before yesterday.

I say to him, Show me the tomb, and then I shall believe.

He took me, therefore, by the hand, and led me away to the tomb, which had been opened.

And seeing the linen and the napkin, and recognising him, I said, Blessed is he that cometh in the name of the Lord; [2] and I adored him. Then taking me by the hand, and accompanied by the angels, he brought me to my house in Arimathaea, and said to me, Sit here for forty days; for I go to my disciples, in order that I may enable them fully to proclaim my resurrection.

Footnotes:

1. esikosan, which should be esekosan, is a modern Greek word, the aorist of sekono.
2. Ps. cxviii. 26; Matt. xxi. 9.

Chapter 16

When Joseph had thus spoken, the chief priests cried out to the people:

We know that Jesus had a father and mother; how can we believe that he is the Christ?

One of the Levites answered and said:

I know the family of Jesus, noble-minded men, [1] great servants of God, and receiving tithes from the people of the Jews.

And I know also Symeon the elder, that he received him when he was an infant, and said to him:

Now thou sendest away Thy servant, O Lord.

The Jews said:

Let us now find the three men that saw him on the Mount of Olives, that we may question them, and learn the truth more accurately.

They found them, and brought them before all, and made them swear to tell the truth.

And they said:

As the God of Israel liveth, we saw Jesus alive on the Mount of Olives, and going up into heaven.

Then Annas and Caiaphas took the three apart, one by one, and questioned them singly in private.

They agreed with one another, therefore, and gave, even the three, one account.

The chief priests answered, saying:

Our Scripture says that every word shall be established by two or three witnesses. [2]Joseph, then, has confessed that he, along with Nicodemus, attended to his body, and buried him, and how it is the truth that he has risen. [3]

Footnotes:

1. Or, literally, men of good family.
2. Deut. xix. 15; Matt. xviii. 16.
3. This last clause would be better as a question: And how is it the truth that he has risen?

The Forgotten Bible
Part II - The Descent of Christ into Hell

Greek Form

Chapter 1 (17)
Joseph says:
And why do you wonder that Jesus has risen?
But it is wonderful that He has not risen alone, but that He has also raised many others of the dead who have appeared in Jerusalem to many. [1]And if you do not know the others, Symeon at least, who received Jesus, and his two sons whom He has raised up--them at least you know.
For we buried them not long ago; but now their tombs are seen open and empty, and they are alive, and dwelling in Arimathaea.
They therefore sent men, and they found their tombs open and empty.
Joseph says:
Let us go to Arimathaea and find them.
Then rose up the chief priests Annas and Caiaphas, and Joseph, and Nicodemus, and Gamaliel, and others with them, and went away to Arimathaea, and found those whom Joseph spoke of.
They made prayer, therefore, and saluted each other.
Then they came with them to Jerusalem, and brought them into the synagogue, and secured the doors, and placed in the midst the old covenant of the Jews; and the chief priests said to them:
We wish you to swear by the God of Israel and Adonai, and so that you tell the truth, how you have risen, and who has raised you from the dead.
The men who had risen having heard this, made upon their faces the sign of the cross, and said to the chief priests:
Give us paper and ink and pen.
These therefore they brought.
And sitting down, they wrote thus:--

Footnote:
1. Matt. xxvii. 53.

Chapter 2 (18)
O Lord Jesus Christ, the resurrection and the life of the world, grant us grace that we may give an account of Thy resurrection, and Thy miracles which Thou didst in Hades.
We then were in Hades, with all who had fallen asleep since the beginning of the world.
And at the hour of midnight there rose a light as if of the sun, and shone into these dark regions; and we were all lighted up, and saw each other. And straightway our father Abraham was united with the patriarchs and the prophets, and at the same time they were filled with joy, and said to each other:
This light is from a great source of light.
The prophet Hesaias, who was there present, said:
This light is from the Father, and from the Son, and from the Holy Spirit; about whom I prophesied when yet alive, saying, The land of Zabulon, and the land of Nephthalim, the people that sat in darkness, have seen a great light. [1]
Then there came into the midst another, an ascetic from the desert; and the patriarchs said to him:
Who art thou?
And he said:
I am John, the last of the prophets, who made the paths of the Son of God straight, [2] and proclaimed to the people repentance for the remission of sins. [3]And the Son of God came to me; and I, seeing Him a long way off, said to the people:
Behold the Lamb of God, who taketh away the sin of the world.[4]And with my hand I baptized Him in the river Jordan, and I saw like a dove also the Holy Spirit coming upon Him; [5] and I heard also the voice of God, even the Father, [6] thus saying:
This is my beloved Son, in whom I am well pleased. [17]And on this account He sent me also to you, to proclaim how the only begotten Son of God is coming here, that whosoever shall believe in Him shall be saved, and whosoever shall not believe in Him shall be condemned. [8]On this account I say to you all, in order that when you see Him you all may adore Him, that now only is for you the time of repentance for having adored idols in the vain upper world, and for the sins you have

committed, and that this is impossible at any other time.

Footnotes:
1. Isa. ix. 1, 2.
2. Matt. iii. 3.
3. Mark i. 4.
4. John i. 29.
5. Or: and I saw, as it were, a dove and the Holy Spirit, etc.
6. Or, of the God and Father.
7. Luke iii. 22.
8. [Mark xvi. 16.]; John iii. 18.

Chapter 3 (19)

While John, therefore, was thus teaching those in Hades, the first created and forefather Adam heard, and said to his son Seth:

My son, I wish thee to tell the forefathers of the race of men and the prophets where I sent thee, when it fell to my lot to die.

And Seth said: Prophets and patriarchs, hear.

When my father Adam, the first created, was about to fall once upon a time into death, he sent me to make entreaty to God very close by the gate of paradise, that He would guide me by an angel to the tree of compassion and that I might take oil and anoint my father, and that he might rise up from his sickness:

which thing, therefore, I also did.

And after the prayer an angel of the Lord came, and said to me:

What, Seth, dost thou ask?

Dost thou ask oil which raiseth up the sick, or the tree from which this oil flows, on account of the sickness of thy father?

This is not to be found now.

Go, therefore, and tell thy father, that after the accomplishing of five thousand five hundred years [1] from the creation of the world, then shalt come into the earth the only begotten Son of God, being made man; and He shall anoint him with this oil, and shall raise him up; and shall wash clean, with water and with the Holy Spirit, both him and those out of him, and then shall he be healed of every disease; but now this is impossible. [2]

When the patriarchs and the prophets heard these words, they rejoiced greatly.

Footnotes:
1. 5300 b.c. was the date commonly assigned to the creation. See Clem., Strom., i.; Theoph. Ant., ad Autol., iii.; comp. Just., Apol., xxxix.
2. For this legend, see the Revelation of Moses.

Chapter 4 (20)

And when all were in such joy, came Satan the heir of darkness, and said to Hades:

O all-devouring and insatiable, hear my words.

There is of the race of the Jews one named Jesus, calling himself the Son of God; and being a man, by our working with them the Jews have crucified him:

and now when he is dead, be ready that we may secure him here. For I know that he is a man, and I heard him also saying, My soul is exceeding sorrowful, even unto death. [1]He has also done me many evils when living with mortals in the upper world.

For wherever he found my servants, he persecuted them; and whatever men I made crooked, blind, lame, lepers, or any such thing, by a single word he healed them; and many whom I had got ready to be buried, even these through a single word he brought to life again.

Hades says:

And is this man so powerful as to do such things by a single word? or if he be so, canst thou withstand him?

It seems to me that, if he be so, no one will be able to withstand him.

And if thou sayest that thou didst hear him dreading death, he said this mocking thee, and laughing, wishing to seize thee with the strong hand; and woe, woe to thee, to all eternity!

Satan says:

O all-devouring and insatiable Hades, art thou so afraid at hearing of our common enemy?

I was not afraid of him, but worked in the Jews, and they crucified him, and gave him also to drink gall with vinegar. [2]Make ready, then, in order that you may lay fast hold of him when he comes.

Hades answered:

Heir of darkness, son of destruction, devil, thou hast just now told me that many whom thou hadst made ready to be buried, be brought to life again by a single word.

And if he has delivered others from the tomb, how and with what power shall he be laid hold of by us? For I not long ago swallowed down one dead, Lazarus by name; and not long after, one of the living by a single word dragged him up by force out of my bowels:

and I think that it was he of whom thou speakest. If, therefore, we receive him here, I am afraid lest perchance we be in danger even about the rest.

For, lo, all those that I have swallowed from eternity I perceive to be in commotion, and I am pained in my belly.

And the snatching away of Lazarus beforehand seems to me to be no good sign:

for not like a dead body, but like an eagle, he flew out of me; for so suddenly did the earth throw him out.

Wherefore also I adjure even thee, for thy benefit and for mine, not to bring him here; for I think that he is coming here to raise all the dead.

And this I tell thee:

by the darkness in which we live, if thou bring him here, not one of the dead will be left behind in it to me.

Footnotes:

1. Mark xv. 34.
2. Matt. xxvii. 34.

Chapter 5 (21)

While Satan and Hades were thus speaking to each other, there was a great voice like thunder, saying:

Lift up your gates, O ye rulers; and be ye lifted up, ye everlasting gates; and the King of glory shall come in. [1] When Hades heard, he said to Satan:

Go forth, if thou art able, and withstand him.

Satan therefore went forth to the outside. Then Hades says to his demons:

Secure well and strongly the gates of brass and the bars of iron, and attend to my bolts, and stand in order, [2] and see to everything; for if he come in here, woe will seize us.

The forefathers having heard this, began all to revile him, saying:

O all-devouring and insatiable! open, that the King of glory may come in.

David the prophet says:

Dost thou not know, O blind, that I when living in the world prophesied this saying:

Lift up your gates, O ye rulers?

Hesaias said:

I, foreseeing this by the Holy Spirit, wrote: The dead shall rise up, and those in their tombs shall be raised, and those in the earth shall rejoice. [3] And where, O death, is thy sting? where, O Hades, is thy victory? [4]

There came, then, again a voice saying:

Lift up the gates.

Hades, hearing the voice the second time, answered as if forsooth he did not know, and says:

Who is this King of glory?

The angels of the Lord say:

The Lord strong and mighty, the Lord mighty in battle. [5] And immediately with these words the brazen gates were shattered, and the iron bars broken, and all the dead who had been bound came out of the prisons, and we with them.

And the King of glory came in in the form of a man, and all the dark places of Hades were lighted up.

Footnotes:

1. Ps. xxiv. 7.
2. Lit., erect.
3. Isa. xxvi. 19, according to the LXX.
4. Hos. xiii. 14.
5. Ps. xxiv. 8.

Chapter 6 (22)

Immediately Hades cried out:
We have been conquered:
woe to us!
But who art thou, that hast such power and might? and what art thou, who comest here without sin who art seen to be small and yet of great power, lowly and exalted, the slave and the master, the soldier and the king, who hast power over the dead and the living?

Thou wast nailed on the cross, and placed in the tomb; and now thou art free, and hast destroyed all our power.

Art thou then the Jesus about whom the chief satrap Satan told us, that through cross and death thou art to inherit the whole world?

Then the King of glory seized the chief satrap Satan by the head, and delivered him to His angels, and said:
With iron chains bind his hands and his feet, and his neck, and his mouth.
Then He delivered him to Hades, and said:
Take him, and keep him secure till my second appearing.

Chapter 7 (23)

And Hades receiving Satan, said to him:
Beelzebul, heir of fire and punishment, enemy of the saints, through what necessity didst thou bring about that the King of glory should be crucified, so that he should come here and deprive us of our power?

Turn and see that not one of the dead has been left in me, but all that thou hast gained through the tree of knowledge, all hast thou lost through the tree of the cross:

and all thy joy has been turned into grief; and wishing to put to death the King of glory, thou hast put thyself to death.

For, since I have received thee to keep thee safe, by experience shalt thou learn how many evils I shall do unto thee.

O arch-devil, the beginning of death, root of sin, end of all evil, what evil didst thou find in Jesus, that thou shouldst compass his destruction? how hast thou dared to do such evil? how hast thou busied thyself to bring down such a man into this darkness, through whom thou hast been deprived of all who have died from eternity?

Chapter 8 (24)

While Hades was thus discoursing to Satan, the King of glory stretched out His right hand, and took hold of our forefather Adam, and raised him.

Then turning also to the rest, He said:
Come all with me, as many as have died through the tree which he touched:
for, behold, I again raise you all up through the tree of the cross.

Thereupon He brought them all out, and our forefather Adam seemed to be filled with joy, and said:
I thank Thy majesty, O Lord, that Thou hast brought me up out of the lowest Hades.
[1]Likewise also all the prophets and the saints said:
We thank Thee, O Christ, Saviour of the world, that Thou hast brought our life up out of destruction. [2]

And after they had thus spoken, the Saviour blessed Adam with the sign of the cross on his forehead, and did this also to the patriarchs, and prophets, and martyrs, and forefathers; and He took them, and sprang up out of Hades.

And while He was going, the holy fathers accompanying Him sang praises, saying:
Blessed is He that cometh in the name of the Lord: [3]Alleluia; to Him be the glory of all the saints.

Footnotes:

1. Ps. lxxxvi. 13.
2. Comp. Ps. ciii. 4.
3. Ps. cxviii. 26.

The Forgotten Bible

Chapter 9 (25)

And setting out to paradise, He took hold of our forefather Adam by the hand, and delivered him, and all the just, to the archangel Michael. And as they were going into the door of paradise, there met them two old men, to whom the holy fathers said:

Who are you, who have not seen death, and have not come down into Hades, but who dwell in paradise in your bodies and your souls?

One of them answered, and said:

I am Enoch, who was well-pleasing to God, and who was translated hither by Him; and this is Helias the Thesbite; and we are also to live until the end of the world; and then we are to be sent by God to withstand Antichrist, and to be slain by him, and after three days to rise again, and to be snatched up in clouds to meet the Lord. [1]

Footnote:

1. 1 Thess. iv. 17; Rev. xi. 3-12.

Chapter 10 (26)

While they were thus speaking, there came another lowly man, carrying also upon his shoulders a cross, to whom the holy fathers said:

Who art thou, who hast the look of a robber; and what is the cross which thou bearest upon thy shoulders?

He answered:

I, as you say, was a robber and a thief in the world, and for these things the Jews laid hold of me, and delivered me to the death of the cross, along with our Lord Jesus Christ.

While, then, He was hanging upon the cross, I, seeing the miracles that were done, believed in Him, and entreated Him, and said, Lord, when Thou shalt be King, do not forget me.

And immediately He said to me, Amen, amen:

to-day, I say unto thee, shalt thou be with me in paradise.

Therefore I came to paradise carrying my cross; and finding the archangel Michael, I said to him, Our Lord Jesus, who has been crucified, has sent me here; bring me, therefore, to the gate of Eden.

And the flaming sword, seeing the sign of the cross, opened to me, and I went in.

Then the archangel says to me, Wait a little, for there cometh also the forefather of the race of men, Adam, with the just, that they too may come in.

And now, seeing you, I came to meet you.

The saints hearing these things, all cried out with a loud voice: Great is our Lord, and great is His strength. [1]

Footnote:

1. Ps. cxlvii. 5.

Chapter 11 (27)

All these things we saw and heard; we, the two brothers, who also have been sent by Michael the archangel, and have been ordered to proclaim the resurrection of the Lord, but first to go away to the Jordan and to be baptized.

Thither also we have gone, and have been baptized with the rest of the dead who have risen.

Thereafter also we came to Jerusalem, and celebrated the passover of the resurrection.

But now we are going away, being unable to stay here.

And the love of God, even the Father, and the grace of our Lord Jesus Christ, and the communion of the Holy Spirit, be with you all. [1]

Having written these things, and secured the rolls, they gave the half to the chief priests, and the half to Joseph and Nicodemus.

And they immediately disappeared:

to the glory of our Lord Jesus Christ.

Amen.

Footnote:

1. 2 Cor. xiii. 15.

Part I - The Acts of Pilate

Latin Form

I Aeneas was at first a protector of the Hebrews, and follower of the law; then the grace of the Saviour and His great gift took possession of me.

I recognised Christ Jesus in holy Scripture; I came to Him, and embraced His faith, so that I might become worthy of His holy baptism. First of all I searched for the memoirs written in those times about our Lord Jesus Christ, which the Jews published in the age of Pontius Pilate, and we found them in Hebrew writings, drawn up in the age of the Lord Jesus Christ; and I translated them into the language of the Gentiles, in the reign of the eminent Theodosius, who was fulfilling his seventeenth consulship, and of Valentinian, consul for the fifth time in the ninth indiction.

Whosoever of you read this book, and transfer it to other copies, remember me, and pray for me, Aeneas, least of the servants of God, that He be merciful to me, and pardon my sins which I have committed against Him.

Peace be to all who shall read these, and to all their house, for ever!
Amen.

Now it came to pass, in the nineteenth year of the reign of Tiberius Caesar, emperor of the Romans, and of Herod, son of Herod king of Galilee, in the nineteenth year of his rule, on the eighth day before the kalends of April, which is the twenty-fifth day of the month of March, in the consulship of Rufinus and Rubellio, in the fourth year of the 202d Olympiad, under the rule of Joseph and Caiaphas, priests of the Jews:

the things done by the chief priests and the rest of the Jews, which Nicodemus recorded after the cross and passion of the Lord, Nicodemus himself committed to Hebrew letters.

Chapter 1

Annas and Caiaphas, Summas and Datam, Gamaliel, Judas, Levi, Neptalim, Alexander and Jairus, and the rest of the Jews, came to Pilate, accusing the Lord Jesus Christ of many things, and saying:

We know him to be the son of Joseph the carpenter, born of Mary; and he says that he is the Son of God, and a king.

Not only so, but he also breaks the Sabbath, and wishes to do away with the law of our fathers.

Pilate says:

What is it that he does, and wishes to destroy the law?

The Jews say:

We have a law, not to heal any one on the Sabbath; but he, by evil arts, heals on the Sabbath the lame and the hunchbacked, the blind, the palsied, the lepers, and the demoniacs.

Pilate says to them:

By what evil arts?

They say to him:

He is a sorcerer; and by Beelzebub, prince of the demons, he casts out demons, and they are all subject to him.

Pilate says to them:

It is not in an unclean spirit to cast out demons, but in the god of Scolapius.

The Jews say:

We pray thy majesty to set him before thy tribunal to be heard.

Pilate, calling the Jews to him, says to them:

How can I, seeing that I am a governor, [1] hear a king?

They say to him:

We do not say that he is a king, but he himself says he is.

And Pilate, calling a runner, says to him:

Let Jesus be brought in with kindness. And the runner, going out and recognising Him, adored Him, and spread on the ground the cloak which he carried in his hand, saying:

My lord, walk upon this, and come in, because the governor calls thee.

But the Jews, seeing what the runner did, cried out against Pilate, saying: Why didst not thou make him come in by the voice of a crier, but by a runner? for the runner, too, seeing him, has adored him, and has spread out before him on the ground the cloak which he held in his hand, and has said to him:

My lord, the governor calls thee.

The Forgotten Bible

And Pilate, calling the runner, says to him:

Wherefore hast thou done this, and honoured Jesus, who is called Christ?

The runner says to him:

When thou didst send me into Jerusalem to Alexander, I saw him sitting upon an ass, and the children of the Hebrews breaking branches from the trees, strewing them in the way; and others held branches in their hands; and others spread their garments in the way, shouting and saying, Save, therefore, Thou who art in the highest; blessed is He that cometh in the name of the Lord!

The Jews cried out, saying against the runner:

The children of the Hebrews indeed cried out in Hebrew.

How canst thou, a Gentile, know this?

The runner says to them:

I asked one of the Jews, and said, What is it that they cry out in Hebrew? and he explained to me.

Pilate says to them:

And how did they cry out in Hebrew?

The Jews said: Osanna in the highest!

Pilate says to them:

What is the meaning of Osanna in the highest?

They say to him:

Save us, Thou who art in the highest.

Pilate says to them:

If you yourselves bear witness to the terms and words in which the children cried out, in what has the runner sinned?

And they were silent.

The governor says to the runner:

Go out, and lead him in, in whatever way thou wilt.

And the runner, going forth, did after the same form as before, and says to Jesus:

My lord, go in, because the governor calls thee.

As Jesus, then, was going in, and the standard-bearers bearing the standards, the heads of the standards were bowed of themselves, and adored Jesus.

And the Jews, seeing the standards, how they bowed themselves and adored Jesus, cried out the more against the standard-bearers.

And Pilate says to the Jews:

Do you not wonder at the way in which the standards have bowed themselves and adored Jesus? The Jews say to Pilate:

we saw how the men carrying the standards bowed themselves and adored Jesus.

And the governor, calling the standard-bearers, says to them:

Why have you so done?

They say to Pilate:

We are Gentile men, and slaves of the temples:

how had we [2] to adore him? for when we were holding the figures, [3] they themselves bowed and adored him.

Pilate says to the chiefs of the synagogue and the elders of the people:

Choose ye men powerful and strong, and let them hold the standards, and let us see whether they will bow of themselves.

And the elders of the Jews, taking twelve men very strong and powerful, made them hold the standards, six and six; and they stood before the governor's tribunal.

Pilate says to the runner:

Take out Jesus outside of the praetorium, and bring him in again, in whatever way thou wilt.

And Jesus and the runner went outside of the praetorium.

And Pilate, calling those who had formerly held the standards, said to them:

By the health of Caesar, if the standards do not bow themselves when Jesus comes in, I will cut off your heads.

And the governor ordered Jesus to come in a second time.

And the runner did after the same form as before, and besought Jesus much that He would go up and walk upon his cloak.

And He walked upon it, and went in.

And as Jesus was going in, immediately the standards bowed themselves, and adored Jesus.

Footnotes:
1. The word in the original is the general term praeses, which the Vulgate uses for procurator.
2. i.e., was it possible for us.
3. Vultus. He seems to have read prosopa, and not protomai, as in the Greek.

Chapter 2

And Pilate seeing, fear seized him, and immediately he wished to rise from the tribunal.
And while he was thinking of this, viz., to rise and go away, his wife sent to him, saying:
Have nothing to do with that just man, [1] for I have suffered much on account of him this night.
And Pilate, calling the Jews, said to them:
Ye know that my wife is a worshipper of God, and in Judaism thinks rather with you. The Jews say to him:
So it is, and we know.
Pilate says to them:
Lo, my wife has sent to me, saying:
Have nothing to do with that just man, [2] for I have suffered much on account of him this night.
And the Jews answering, said to Pilate:
Did we not say to thee that he is a magician?
Lo, he has sent a vision of dreams to thy wife.
Pilate called Jesus, and said to him:
What is it that these witness against thee, and sayest thou nothing to them?
And Jesus answered:
If they had not the power, they would not speak.
Every one has power over his own mouth to say good and evil; let them see [3] to it.
And the elders of the Jews answering, say to Jesus:
What shall we see?
First, that thou wast born of fornication; second, that at thy birth in Bethlehem there took place a massacre of infants; third, that thy father Joseph and thy mother Mary fled into Egypt, because they had no confidence in the people.
Some of the bystanders, kind men of the Jews, say:
We say that he was not born of fornication; but we know that Mary was espoused to Joseph, and that he was not born of fornication.
Pilate says to the Jews who said that he was of fornication:
This speech of yours is not true, seeing that the betrothal took place, as these of your nation say. Annas and Caiaphas say to Pilate:
We with all the multitude say that he was born of fornication, and that he is a magician; but these are proselytes, and his disciples.
And Pilate, calling Annas and Caiaphas, says to them:
What are proselytes?
They say to him:
They have been born sons of the Gentiles, and then have become Jews.
Then answered those who testified that Jesus was not born of fornication, Lazarus and Asterius, Antonius and James, Annes and Azaras, Samuel and Isaac, Finees and Crispus, Agrippa and Judas:
We were not born proselytes, but are sons of the Jews, and we speak the truth; for we were present at the betrothal of Mary.
And Pilate, calling to him those twelve men who proved that Jesus had not been born of fornication, said to them:
I adjure you by the health of Caesar, tell me if it be true that Jesus was not born of fornication.
They say to Pilate:
We have a law not to swear, because it is a sin; but let them swear by the health of Caesar that it is not as we say, and we are worthy of death.
Then said Pilate to Annas and Caiaphas:
Answer you nothing to those things which these testify? Annas and Caiaphas say to Pilate:
Those twelve are believed that he is not born of fornication; we--all the people--cry out that he was born of fornication, and is a magician, and says that he himself is the Son of God and a king, and we are not believed.
And Pilate ordered all the multitude to go outside, except the twelve men who said that He was not born of fornication, and ordered to separate Jesus from them.
And Pilate says to them:

The Forgotten Bible

For what reason do the Jews wish to put Jesus to death?
And they say to him:
They are angry because he heals on the Sabbath.
Pilate said:
For a good work do they wish to put him to death?
They say to him:
Yes, my lord.

Footnotes:

1. Lit., nothing to thee and that just man.
2. Lit., nothing to thee and that just man.
3. Lit., they will see.

Chapter 3

Pilate, filled with fury, went forth outside of the praetorium, and says to them:
I take the sun to witness that I find in this man not even one fault.
The Jews answered and said to the governor:
If he were not an evil-doer, we should never have delivered him to thee. Pilate says to them:
Take him, and judge him according to your law. The Jews answered:
It is not permitted to us to put any one to death. Pilate says to them:
Has God said to you not to put any one to death? has He therefore said to me that I am to kill?
Pilate, having again gone into the praetorium, called Jesus to him privately, and said to Him:
Art thou the king of the Jews?
Jesus answered Pilate:
Speakest thou this of thyself, or have others said it to thee of me?
Pilate answered:
Am I a Jew?
Thy nation and the chief priests have delivered thee to me.
What hast thou done?
Jesus answering, said:
My kingdom is not of this world.
If my kingdom were of this world, my servants would assuredly strive that I should not be delivered to the Jews; but now my kingdom is not from hence.
Pilate said to Him:
Art thou then a king?
Jesus said to him:
Thou sayest that I am a king.
For I for this was born, and for this have I come, that I should bear witness to the truth; and every one who is of the truth hears my voice.
Pilate says to him:
What is truth?
Jesus says:
Truth is from heaven.
Pilate says:
Is not there truth upon earth?
Jesus says to Pilate:
Notice how the truth-speaking are judged by those who have power upon earth.

Chapter 4

Pilate therefore, leaving Jesus within the praetorium, went out to the Jews, and says to them:
I find not even one fault in him.
The Jews say to him:
He said, I can destroy that temple, and in three days raise it again.
Pilate said to them:
What temple?
The Jews say to him:
The temple which Solomon built in forty and six years; and he says that he can destroy and build it in three days.
Pilate says to them:
I am innocent of the blood of this man; see ye to it.
The Jews say to him:
His blood be upon us, and upon our children.

And Pilate, calling the elders and priests and Levites, says to them privately:
Do not do so; for in nothing, though you accuse him, do I find him deserving of death, not even about the healing and the breaking of the Sabbath.
The priests and Levites and elders say:
Tell us, if any one blaspheme Caesar, is he deserving of death or not? Pilate says to them:
He deserves to die.
The Jews answered him:
How much more is he who has blasphemed God deserving to die!
And the governor ordered the Jews to go outside of the praetorium; and calling Jesus, said to Him:
What am I to do to thee?
Jesus says to Pilate:
As it has been given thee.
Pilate says:
How has it been given?
Jesus says:
Moses and the prophets made proclamation of my death and resurrection.
And the Jews, hearing this, say to Pilate: Why do you desire any more to hear blasphemy?
And Pilate said:
If this speech is blasphemous, do you take him, and lead him to your synagogue, and judge him according to your law.
The Jews say to Pilate:
Our law holds, If a man have sinned against a man, he is worthy to receive forty less one; but he who has blasphemed against God, to be stoned.
Pilate says to them:
Then judge him according to your law.
The Jews say to Pilate:
We wish that he be crucified.
Pilate says to them:
He does not deserve to be crucified.
And the governor, looking upon the people of the Jews standing round, saw very many of the Jews weeping, and said:
All the multitude does not wish him to die.
The elders say to Pilate:
And for this reason have we come--the whole multitude--that he should die.
Pilate said to the Jews:
What has he done that he should die?
They say:
Because he said that he was the Son of God, and a king.

Chapter 5

But one Nicodemus, a Jew, stood before the governor, and said:
I entreat, mercifully allow me to say a few words.
Pilate says to him: Say on.
Nicodemus says:
I said to the elders and the priests and the Levites, and to all the multitude of the Jews, in the synagogue, What have you to do with this man?
This man does many wonders and signs, which no one of men has done or can do.
Let him go, and do not devise any evil against him:
if the signs which he does are of God, they will stand; but if of men, they will come to nothing.
For Moses also, being sent by God into Egypt, did many signs, which God told him to do before Pharaoh king of Egypt.
And the sorcerers Jamnes and Mambres were there healing, and they did, they also, the signs which Moses did, but not all; and the Egyptians deemed them as gods, Jamnes and Mambres.
And since the signs which they did were not of God, they perished, both they and those who believed in them.
And now let this man go, for he is not deserving of death.
The Jews say to Nicodemus:
Thou hast become his disciple, and takest his part. [1]Nicodemus says to them:
Has the governor also become his disciple, and does he take his part?
Has not Caesar set him over that dignity?

And the Jews were raging and gnashing with their teeth against Nicodemus.
Pilate says to them:
Why do you gnash with your teeth against him, when you are hearing the truth?
The Jews say to Nicodemus:
Mayst thou receive his truth, and a portion with him! Nicodemus says:
Amen, amen, amen; may I receive it, as you have said!

Footnote:

1. Lit., makest a word for him.

Chapter 6

And of the Jews a certain other one, starting up, asks the governor that he might say a word.
The governor says:
What thou wishest to say, say.
And he said:
For thirty-eight years I lay in infirmity in my bed in very grievous pain.
And at the coming of Jesus, many demoniacs, and persons held down by divers infirmities, were healed by him.
And some young men had pity on me; and carrying me in my bed, laid me before him.
And Jesus, seeing, had pity on me, and said the word to me, Take up thy bed, and walk.
And immediately I was made whole; I took up my bed, and walked.
The Jews say to Pilate:
Ask him what was the day on which he was healed.
He said:
The Sabbath.
The Jews say:
Have we not so informed thee, that on the Sabbath he heals, and drives out demons?
And a certain other Jew starting up, said:
I was born blind; I heard a voice, and saw no man.
And as Jesus was passing by, I cried out with a loud voice, Have pity upon me, thou son of David.
And he had pity upon me, and laid his hands upon my eyes, and I saw immediately.
And another Jew starting up, said:
I was hunchbacked, and he straightened me with a word.
And another said:
I was leprous, and he healed me with a word.

Chapter 7

And also a certain woman, Veronica by name, from afar off cried out to the governor:
I was flowing with blood for twelve years; and I touched the fringe of his garment, and immediately the flowing of my blood stopped.
The Jews say:
We have a law, that a woman does not come to bear witness.

Chapter 8

And certain others, a multitude of men and women, cried out, saying: That man is a prophet, and the demons are subject to him.
Pilate says to those who said the demons are subject to him:
And your masters, why are they not subject to him?
They say to Pilate:
We do not know.
And others said to Pilate:
He raised up dead Lazarus from the tomb after four days.
The governor, hearing this, said trembling to all the multitude of the Jews:
Why do you wish to shed innocent blood?

Chapter 9

And Pilate, calling Nicodemus and the twelve men who said that He was not born of fornication, says to them:
What am I to do, seeing that there is a sedition among the people?
They say to him:

We do not know; let them see to it.

Again Pilate, calling all the multitude of the Jews, said:

You know that you have a custom during the day of unleavened bread, that I should release to you one that is bound.

I have a notable one bound in the prison, a murderer who is called Barabbas, and Jesus who is called Christ, in whom I find no cause of death.

Whom do you wish that I should release unto you?

And they all cried out, saying:

Release unto us Barabbas.

Pilate says to them: What, then, am I to do with Jesus who is called Christ?

They all say: Let him be crucified.

Again the Jews said:

Thou art no friend of Caesar's if thou release this man, for he called himself the Son of God, and a king; unless, perhaps, thou wishest this man to be king, and not Caesar.

Then, filled with fury, Pilate said to them:

Always has your nation been seditious, and always have you been opposed to those who were for you.

The Jews answered:

Who are for us?

Pilate says to them:

Your God,--who rescued you from the hard slavery of the Egyptians, and led you forth out of Egypt through the sea as if through dry land, and fed you in the desert with manna and quail, and brought water to you out of the rock, and gave you to drink, and gave you a law; and in all these things you provoked your God, and sought for yourselves a god, a molten calf.

And you exasperated your God, and He wished to slay you; and Moses made supplication for you, that ye should not die.

And now you say that I hate the king.

And rising up from the tribunal, he wished to go outside.

And the Jews cried out, and said to him:

We know that Caesar is king, and not Jesus.

For the Magi also presented gifts to him as to a king; and Herod, hearing from the Magi that a king was born, wished to slay him. But when this was known, his father Joseph took him and his mother, and fled into Egypt; and Herod hearing, destroyed the infants of the Jews which were born in Bethlehem.

Pilate, hearing those words, was afraid.

And silence being made among the people, who were crying out, Pilate said:

This, then, is he whom Herod sought?

They say to him:

It is he.

And taking water, Pilate washed his hands in presence of the people, saying:

I am innocent of the blood of this just man; see ye to it.

Again the Jews cried out, saying:

His blood be upon us, and upon our children.

Then Pilate ordered the veil to be loosened, [1] and said to Jesus: Thine own nation have brought charges against thee as a king; and therefore I have sentenced thee first to be scourged on account of the statutes of the emperors, and then to be crucified on a cross.

Footnote:

1. See note 5, p. 420.

Chapter 10

And when Jesus was scourged, he delivered Him to the Jews to be crucified, and two robbers with Him; one by name Dismas, and the other by name Gestas.

And when they came to the place, they stripped Him of His garments, and girt Him about with a linen cloth, and put a crown of thorns upon His head.

Likewise also they hanged the two robbers with Him, Dismas on the right and Gestas on the left.

And Jesus said: Father, forgive them, for they know not what they do.

And the soldiers parted His garments among them.

And the people stood waiting; and their chief priests and judges mocked Him, saying among themselves:

He saved others, now let him save himself; if he is the Son of God, let him come down from

The Forgotten Bible

the cross.

And the soldiers mocked Him, falling prostrate [1] before Him, and offering vinegar with gall, and saying:

If thou art the King of the Jews, set thyself free.

And Pilate, after sentence, ordered a title to be written in Hebrew, Greek, and Latin letters, according to what the Jews said:

This is the King of the Jews.

And one of the robbers who were hanged, by name Gestas, said to Him: If thou art the Christ, free thyself and us.

And Dismas answering, rebuked him, saying:

Dost not even thou fear God, who art in this condemnation? for we justly and deservedly have received those things which we endure; but He has done no evil.

And he kept saying to Jesus:

Remember me, Lord, in Thy kingdom.

And Jesus said to him: Verily I say unto thee, that to-day shalt thou be with me in paradise.

Footnote:

1. Procidentes; but this, according to the Greek, should be procedentes, coming before Him.

Chapter 11

And it was about the sixth hour, and there was darkness over the whole earth; and the sun was obscured, and the veil of the temple was rent in the midst.

And crying out with a loud voice, He said:

Father, into Thy hands I commend my spirit.

And thus saying, He gave up the ghost. And the centurion, seeing what was done, glorified God, saying:

This was a just man.

And all the people who were present at that spectacle, seeing what was done, beating their breasts, returned.

And the centurion reported to the governor what was done.

And the governor and his wife hearing, were very sorrowful, and neither ate nor drank that day.

And Pilate, calling together the Jews, said to them: Have you seen what has been done?

And they said to the governor: There has been an eclipse of the sun, as is usual.

And his acquaintances also stood afar off, and the women who had followed Him from Galilee, seeing these things.

And lo, a certain man, by name Joseph, holding office, a man good and just, who did not consent to their counsels nor their deeds, from Arimathaea, [1] a city of the Jews, waiting, he also, for the kingdom of God, went to Pilate and begged the body of Jesus.

And taking Him down from the cross, he wrapped Him in clean linen, and laid Him in his own new tomb, in which no one had been laid.

Footnote:

1. [The Latin has Arimathia; and in the next clause there are variations in the mss.--R.]

Chapter 12

And the Jews, hearing that Joseph had begged the body of Jesus, sought for him; and those twelve men who had said that He was not born of fornication, and Nicodemus, and many others, who had stood before Pilate and declared His good works.

And all of them being hid, Nicodemus alone appeared to them, because he was a chief man of the Jews; and he says to them:

How have ye come into the synagogue?

The Jews say to him:

And thou, how hast thou come into the synagogue, seeing that thou consentest with him? May his portion be with thee in the world to come!

Nicodemus said:

Amen, amen, amen.

Likewise also Joseph, coming forth, said to them:

Why are you enraged against me because I begged the body of Jesus?

Lo, I have laid him in my own new tomb, wrapping him in clean linen; and I have rolled a stone to the door of the cave.

And ye have not acted well against a just man, since you have not borne in mind how you crucified him, and pierced him with a lance.

The Jews therefore, laying hold of Joseph, ordered him to be imprisoned because of the Sabbath-day; and they say to him:

Know that the hour compels us not to do anything against thee, because the Sabbath is dawning.

But understand that thou art worthy not even of burial, but we will give thy flesh to the birds of the air and the beasts of the earth.

Joseph says to them:

That is the speech of proud Goliath, who reviled the living God against holy David.

And God hath said, Vengeance is mine; I will repay, saith the Lord.

And Pilate, intercepted [1] in his heart, took water, and washed his hands before the sun, saying, I am innocent of the blood of this just man; see ye to it.

And you answered and said to Pilate, His blood be upon us, and upon our children.

And now I fear that some time or other the wrath of God will come upon you and your children, as you have said. And the Jews, hearing this, were embittered in heart; and taking Joseph, shut him up in a house where there was no window, and set guards at the gates, and sealed the gate where Joseph had been shut up.

And on the Sabbath morning they took counsel with the priests and the Levites, that they should all be assembled after the Sabbath-day.

And awaking at dawn, all the multitude in the synagogue took counsel by what death they should slay him.

And when the assembly was sitting, they ordered him to be brought with much indignity; and opening the gate, they found him not.

All the people therefore were in terror, and wondered with exceeding astonishment, because they found the seals sealed, and because Caiaphas had the keys.

And no longer did they dare to lay hand upon those who spoke before Pilate in Jesus' defence.

Footnote:

1. Another reading is compunctus, pricked. The reading in the text, obstructus, is a curious mistranslation of the word in the Greek, peritetmemenos, cut away all round, i.e., circumcised; or, by an obvious transition, hemmed in--the meaning adopted in the version before us.

Chapter 13

And while they were sitting in the synagogue, and recriminating about Joseph, there came certain of the guards whom they had asked from Pilate to guard the sepulchre of Jesus, lest His disciples coming should steal Him.

And they reported, saying to the rulers of the synagogue, and the priests and the Levites, what had happened:

how there had happened a great earthquake, and we saw how an angel of the Lord came down from heaven, and rolled away the stone from the door of the tomb, and sat upon it; and his countenance was like lightning, and his raiment like snow.

And for fear, we became as dead.

And we heard the voice of the angel speaking to the women who had come to the sepulchre, and saying, Be not ye afraid; for I know that ye seek Jesus who was crucified:

He is not here; He has risen, as He said:

come and see the place where the Lord was laid.

And go immediately and tell His disciples that He has risen from the dead, and will go before you into Galilee, as He said to you.

The Jews say:

To what women was he speaking?

The soldiers say:

We do not know who the women were.

The Jews say:

At what hour was it?

The guards say:

At midnight.

The Jews say:

And why did you not detain them?

The guards say:

We became as dead from fear of the angel, not hoping now to see the light of day; and how could we detain them?

The Jews says:

As the Lord God liveth, we do not believe you.

And the guards said to the Jews:

You have seen so great signs in that man, and have not believed; and how can you believe us, that the Lord lives? For well have ye sworn that the Lord Jesus Christ lives.

Again the guards say to the Jews:

we have heard that you have shut up Joseph, who begged the body of Jesus, in the prison, and have sealed it with your rings; and on opening, that you have not found him.

Give us Joseph, then, and we shall give you Jesus Christ.

The Jews said: Joseph has gone to Arimathea, his own city.

The guards say to the Jews:

And Jesus, as we have heard from the angel, is in Galilee.

And the Jews, hearing these sayings, feared exceedingly, saying:

Lest at some time or other this saying be heard, and all believe in Jesus. And the Jews, taking counsel among themselves, brought forth a sufficient number of silver pieces, and gave to the soldiers, saying: Say that, while we slept, his disciples came and stole him.

And if this be heard by the governor, we shall persuade [1] him, and make you secure.

And the soldiers, taking the money, said as they were advised by the Jews; and their saying was spread abroad among all.

Footnote:

1. Confirmabimus.

Chapter 14

And Finees a certain priest, and Addas a teacher, and Egias a Levite, coming down from Galilee to Jerusalem, reported to the rulers of the synagogue, and the priests and the Levites, how they had seen Jesus sitting, and his disciples with him, on the Mount of Olivet, which is called Mambre or Malech.

And he said to his disciples:

Go into all the world, and declare to every creature the Gospel of the kingdom of God.

He who believeth and is baptized shall be saved; but he who believeth not shall be condemned.

And these signs shall follow them who believe:

In my name shall they cast out demons; they shall speak in new tongues; they shall take up serpents; and if they have drunk any deadly thing, it shall not hurt them; they shall lay hands upon the sick, and they shall be well.

And as Jesus was thus speaking to his disciples, we saw him taken up into heaven. [1]

The priests and the Levites and the elders say to them:

Give glory to the God of Israel, and give confession to Him, whether you have both heard and seen those things which you have related.

Those who had made the report say:

As the Lord God of our fathers liveth, the God of Abraham, and the God of Isaac, and the God of Jacob, we have heard and seen.

The Jews say to them:

Have you come for this--to tell us? or have you come to give prayer to God?

They said:

We have come to give prayer to God.

The elders and chief priests and Levites say to them: And if you have come to give prayer to God, why have you murmured before all the people about that foolish tale?

Finees the priest, and Addas the teacher, and Egias the Levite, say to the rulers of the synagogue, and the priests and the Levites:

If those words which we have spoken, which we have seen and heard, be sin, behold, we are in your presence; do unto us according to that which is good in your eyes.

And they, taking the law, adjured them to report the words to no one thereafter.

And they gave them to eat and drink, and put them outside of the city, giving them silver and pieces, and three men with them, who should conduct them as far as Galilee.

Then the Jews took counsel among themselves when those men had gone up into Galilee; and the rulers of the synagogue shut themselves in, and were cut up [2] with great fury, saying:

What sign is this which hath come to pass in Israel?

And Annas and Caiaphas say:

Why are your souls sorrowful?

Are we to believe the soldiers, that an angel of the Lord came down from heaven, and rolled away the stone from the door of the tomb?

No; but that his disciples have given much gold to those who were guarding the sepulchre, and have taken Jesus away, and have taught them thus to say:

Say ye that an angel of the Lord came down from heaven, and rolled away the stone from the door of the tomb.

Do you not know that it is unlawful for Jews to believe foreigners in a single word, knowing that these same who received sufficient gold from us have said as we taught them?

Footnotes:

1. [Comp. Mark xvi. 15-19; from the disputed ending of that Gospel.--R.]
2. Concidebantur, a mistranslation from considering ekoptonto as passive, they were cut, instead of middle, they beat their breasts.

Chapter 15

And Nicodemus rising up, stood in the midst of the counsel, and said: You have said rightly.

And are not the men who have come down from Galilee God-fearing, men of peace, hating a lie?

And they recounted with an oath, how "we saw Jesus sitting on Mount Mambre with his disciples, and he taught them in our hearing," and that they saw him taken up into heaven.

And no one asked them this:

How he was taken up into heaven.

And, as the writing of the holy book teaches us, holy Elias too was taken up into heaven, and Elisaeus cried out with a loud voice, and Elias threw his sheepskin over Elisaeus; and again Elisaeus threw that sheepskin over the Jordan, and went over and came to Jericho.

And the sons of the prophets met him, and said to Elisaeus, Where is thy master Elias?

And he said, He has been taken up into heaven.

And they said to Elisaeus, Has a spirit snatched him away, and thrown him upon one of the mountains?

But rather let us take our boys [1] with us and seek him.

And they persuaded Elisaeus, and he went with them.

And they sought him for three days and three nights, and found him not, because he was taken up.

And now, men, hear me, and let us send into all Israel, and see lest Jesus can have been taken up somewhere or other, and thrown upon one of the mountains.

And that saying pleased all.

And they sent to all the mountains of Israel to seek Jesus, and they found Him not; but they found Joseph of Arimathaea, and no one dared to lay hold of him.

And they reported to the elders and priests and Levites:

We have gone round all the mountains of Israel, and not found Jesus; but we have found Joseph in Arimathaea.

And hearing of Joseph, they rejoiced, and gave glory to the God of Israel.

And the rulers of the synagogue, and the priests and the Levites, taking counsel in what manner they should send to Joseph, took paper, and wrote to Joseph:--

Peace to thee and all that is thine!

We know that we have sinned against God, and against thee; and thou hast prayed to the God of Israel, and He has delivered thee out of our hands.

And now deign to come to thy fathers and thy children, because we have been vehemently grieved.

We have all sought for thee--we who opened the door, and found thee not.

We know that we counselled evil counsel against thee; but the Lord hath supplanted our counsel against thee.

Thou art worthy to be honoured, father Joseph, by all the people.

And they chose out of all Israel seven men friendly to Joseph, whom also Joseph knew to be friendly; and the rulers of the synagogue and the priests and the Levites say to them:

See, if he take the letter and read it, for certain he will come with you to us; but if he do not read it, you may know that he is ill-disposed toward us, and, saluting him in peace, return to us.

And blessing them, they sent them away. And they came to Arimathaea to Joseph, and adored him on their face upon the ground, and said:

Peace to thee and all thine!

And Joseph said:

Peace to you, and to all the people of Israel!

And they gave him the roll of the letter.

And Joseph took and read it, and rolled up the letter, and blessed God, and said:

Blessed be the Lord God, who hath delivered Israel from shedding innocent blood; and blessed be God, who sent His angel, and covered me under his wings.

And he kissed them, and set a table for them; and they ate and drank, and slept there.

And they rose in the morning; and Joseph saddled his ass, and travelled with them, and they came into the holy city Jerusalem.

And there met them all the people, crying out, and saying:

Peace be in thy coming in, father Joseph!

To whom he answered and said:

The peace of the Lord be upon all the people!

And they all kissed him.

And they prayed with Joseph, and were terrified at the sight of him.

And Nicodemus took him into his house, and made a great feast, and called Annas and Caiaphas, and the elders and chief priests and Levites, to his house. And making merry, and eating and drinking with Joseph, they blessed God, and went every one to his own house.

And Joseph remained in the house of Nicodemus.

And on the next day, which is the preparation, the priests and the rulers of the synagogue and the Levites rose early, and came to the house of Nicodemus.

And Nicodemus met them, and said to them:

Peace to you!

And they said to him:

Peace to thee and Joseph, and to thy house and Joseph's house!

And Nicodemus brought them into his house. And the council sat; and Joseph sat between Annas and Caiaphas, and no one dared to say a word.

And Joseph said to them:

Why have you called me?

And they made signs with their eyes to Nicodemus, that he should speak with Joseph.

And Nicodemus, opening his mouth, said:

Father Joseph, thou knowest that the reverend teachers, priests, and Levites seek to hear a word from thee.

And Joseph said:

Ask.

And Annas and Caiaphas, taking up the law, adjured Joseph, saying:

Give glory to the God of Israel, and give confession to Him, that thou wilt not hide any word [2] from us.

And they said to him:

With grief were we grieved that thou didst beg the body of Jesus, and wrap it in clean linen, and lay it in a tomb.

Therefore we shut thee up in a house where there was no window, and put a lock and a seal on the gate; and on the first day of the week we opened the gates, and found thee not.

We were therefore exceedingly grieved, and astonishment came over all the people of God. And therefore hast thou been sent for; and now tell us what has happened.

Then said Joseph:

On the day of the Preparation, about the tenth hour, you shut me in, and I remained there the whole Sabbath in full.

And when midnight came, as I was standing and praying, the house where you shut me in was hung up by the four corners, and there was a flashing of light in mine eyes.

And I fell to the ground trembling.

Then some one lifted me up from the place where I had fallen, and poured over me an abundance of water from the head even to the feet, and put round my nostrils the odour of a wonderful ointment, and rubbed my face with the water itself, as if washing me, and kissed me, and said to me, Joseph, fear not; but open thine eyes, and see who it is that speaks to thee. And looking, I saw Jesus; and being terrified, I thought it was a phantom.

And with prayer and the commandments I spoke to him, and he spoke with me.

And I said to him:

Art thou Rabbi Elias?

And he said to me:

I am not Elias.

And I said:

Who art thou, my lord?

And he said to me:

I am Jesus, whose body thou didst beg from Pilate, and wrap in clean linen; and thou didst lay a napkin on my face, and didst lay me in thy new tomb, and roll a stone to the door of the tomb.

Then I said to him that was speaking to me:

Show me, Lord, where I laid thee.

And he led me, and showed me the place where I laid him, and the linen which I had put on him, and the napkin which I had wrapped upon his face; and I knew that it was Jesus.

And he took hold of me with his hand, and put me in the midst of my house though the gates were shut, and put me in my bed, and said to me:

Peace to thee!

And he kissed me, and said to me:

For forty days go not out of thy house; for, lo, I go to my brethren into Galilee.

Footnotes:
1. i.e., servants.
2. The Greek rhemameans thing as well as word.

Chapter 16

And the rulers of the synagogue, and the priests and the Levites, hearing these words from Joseph, became as it were dead, and fell to the ground, and fasted until the ninth hour.

And Joseph and Nicodemus entreated them, saying:

Arise and stand upon your feet, and taste bread, and comfort your souls, seeing that tomorrow is the Sabbath of the Lord.

And they arose, and entreated the Lord, and ate and drank, and went every man to his own house.

And on the Sabbath the teachers and doctors sat questioning each other, and saying:

What is this wrath that has come upon us? because we know his father and mother.

Levi the teacher said:

I know that his parents fear God, and never depart from prayer, and give tithes thrice a-year. And when Jesus was born, his parents brought him up to this place, and gave to God sacrifices and burnt-offerings.

And assuredly the great teacher Simeon took him into his arms, saying:

Now Thou sendest away Thy servant, O Lord, according to Thy word, in peace; for mine eyes have seen Thy salvation, which Thou hast prepared before the face of all peoples, a light for the revealing of the nations, and the glory of Thy people Israel.

And he blessed Mary his mother, and said, I make an announcement to thee concerning this child.

And Mary said, Well, my lord. [1]And Simeon said, Well.

And he said again, Lo, he has been set for the fall and rising again of many in Israel, and for a sign which shall be spoken against; and a sword shall pierce thine own soul, that the thoughts of many hearts may be revealed.

And the Jews said to Levi:

And how knowest thou these things?

Levi says:

Do you not know that from him I learned the law?

They of the council say:

We wish to see thy father.

And they searched out his father, and got information; for he said:

Why did you not believe my son?

The blessed and just Simeon taught him the law.

The council says to Rabbi Levi:

The saying which thou hast spoken is true.

The chief priests and rulers of the synagogue, and Levites, said to each other: Come, let us send into Galilee to the three men who came hither and gave an account of his teaching and his being taken up, and let them tell us how they saw him taken up into heaven.

And that saying pleased all.

Then they sent three men into Galilee; and Go, said they, say to Rabbi Addas and Rabbi Finees and Rabbi Egias, Peace to you and yours! Many investigations have been made in the council concerning Jesus; therefore have we been instructed to call you to the holy place, to Jerusalem.

The men went to Galilee, and found them sitting, and meditating on the law.

And they saluted them in peace.

And they said:

Why have you come?

The messengers said:

The council summon you to the holy city Jerusalem.

And the men, hearing that they were sought for by the council, prayed to God, and reclined with the men, and ate and drank with them.

And rising in the morning, they went to Jerusalem in peace.

And on the morrow the council sat; and they questioned them, saying: Did you plainly see Jesus sitting on Mount Mambre teaching his disciples, and taken up into heaven?

First Addas the teacher says:

I really saw him sitting on Mount Mambre teaching his disciples; and a shining cloud overshadowed him and his disciples, and he went up into heaven; and his disciples prayed upon their faces on the ground.

And calling Finees the priest, they questioned him also, saying:

How didst thou see Jesus taken up?

And he said the same as the other.

And again they called the third, Rabbi Egias, and questioned him, and he said the same as the first and second.

And those who were in the council said:

The law of Moses holds that by the mouth of two or three every word should stand. Abudem, a teacher, one of the doctors, says:

It is written in the law, Enoch walked with God, and was translated; for God took him.

Jairus, a teacher, said:

And we have heard of the death of holy Moses, and have not seen it; for it is written in the law of the Lord, And Moses died according to the word [2] of the Lord, and no man knoweth of his burying even to the present day.

Rabbi Levi said:

What is it that Rabbi Simeon said:

Lo, he lies for the fall and rising again of many in Israel, and for a sign which shall be spoken against?

Rabbi Isaac said:

It is written in the law, Lo, I send mine angel, who shall go before thy face to keep thee in every good way, because I have brought his [3] new name.

Then Annas and Caiaphas said:

Rightly have ye said that these things are written in the law of Moses, that no one saw the death of Enoch, and no one has named the burying of holy Moses.

And Jesus gave account to [4] Pilate, and we saw him scourged, and receiving spitting on his face; and the soldiers put a crown of thorns on him, and he received sentence from Pilate; and then he was crucified, and they gave him gall and vinegar to drink, and two robbers were crucified with him, and the soldier Longinus pierced his side with a lance; and our honourable father Joseph begged his body, and he has risen again, and, as they say, the three teachers have seen him taken up into heaven. And Rabbi Levi has borne witness to what was said by Simeon the elder--that he has been set for the fall and rising again of many in Israel, and for a sign which shall be spoken against.

Then Didas, a teacher, said to all the assembly:

If all the things which these have borne witness to have come to pass in Jesus, they are from God, and let it not be wonderful in our eyes. [5]The chiefs of the synagogue, and the priests and the Levites, said to each other how our law holds, saying:

His name shall be blessed for ever:

His place endureth before the sun, and His seat before the moon:

and all the tribes of earth shall be blessed in Him, and all nations shall serve Him; and kings shall come from far, adoring and magnifying Him. [6]

Footnotes:

1. Perhaps this would be better as a question: Is it good?
2. Lit., mouth.
3. Or, its. The text of the clause is corrupt.
4. i.e., was tried before.
5. Comp. Ps. cxviii. 23.
6. Ps. lxxii. 11, 17.

Part II - Christ's Descent into Hell

Latin First Version

Chapter 1 (17)

And Joseph rose up and said to Annas and Caiaphas:

Truly and well do you wonder, since you have heard that Jesus has been seen alive from the dead, ascending up into heaven.

But it is more to be wondered at that he is not the only one who has risen from the dead: but he has raised up alive out of their tombs many others of the dead, and they have been seen by many in Jerusalem.

And hear me now, that we all know the blessed Simeon, the great priest, who took up with his hands Jesus, when an infant, in the temple.

And Simeon himself had two sons, full brothers; and we all were at their falling asleep, and at their burial.

Go, therefore, and see their tombs:

for they are open, because they have risen; and, behold, they are in the city of Arimathaea, living together in prayers.

And, indeed, they are heard crying out, but speaking with nobody, and they are silent as the dead. But come, let us go to them; let us conduct them to us with all honour and respect.

And if we adjure them, perhaps they will speak to us of the mystery of their resurrection.

At hearing this they all rejoiced.

And Annas and Caiaphas, Nicodemus, and Joseph, and Gamaliel, went, and did not find them in their sepulchres; but, walking into the city of Arimathea, they found them there, on their bended knees, and spending their time in prayer.

And kissing them, they conducted them to Jerusalem, into the synagogue, with all veneration and fear of God.

And shutting the doors, and lifting up the law of the Lord, they put it in their hands, adjuring them by the God Adonai, and the God of Israel, who by the law and the prophets spoke to our fathers, saying:

Do you believe that it was Jesus who raised you from the dead?

Tell us how you have risen from the dead.

Karinus and Leucius, hearing this adjuration, trembled in their body, and groaned, being disturbed in heart.

And together they looked towards heaven, and with their fingers made the sign of the cross on their tongues, and immediately they spoke together, saying:

Give each of us sheets of paper, and let us write what we have seen and heard. And they gave it to them.

And they sat down, and each of them wrote, saying:--

Chapter 2 (18)

O Lord Jesus Christ, the resurrection and the life of the dead, permit us to speak mysteries through the death of Thy cross, because we have been adjured by Thee.

For Thou didst order Thy servants to relate to no one the secrets of Thy divine majesty which Thou didst in Hades. And when we were, along with all our fathers, lying in the deep, in the blackness of darkness, suddenly there appeared a golden heat [1] of the sun, and a purple royal light shining upon us.

And immediately the father of all the human race, with all the patriarchs and prophets, exulted, saying:

That light is the source of eternal light, which hath promised to transmit to us co-eternal light.

And Esaias cried out, and said:

This is the light of the Father, the Son of God, as I predicted when I was alive upon earth:

The land of Zabulon and the land of Nephthalim across Jordan, Galilee of the nations, the people who sat in darkness, have seen a great light; and light was shining among those who are in the region of the shadow of death.

And now it has come and shone upon us sitting in death.

And when we were all exulting in the light which shone over us, there came up to us our father Simeon; and he said, exulting:

Glorify the Lord Jesus Christ, the Son of God; because I took Him up when born, an infant, in my hands in the temple; and instigated by the Holy Spirit, I said to Him, confessing:

Now mine eyes have seen Thy salvation, which Thou hast prepared in the sight of all peoples, a light for the revealing of the nations, and the glory of Thy people Israel.

When they heard this, all the multitude of the saints exulted more.

And after this there comes up, as it were, a dweller in the desert; and he is asked by all: Who art thou?

To whom he says in answer:

I am John, the voice and prophet of the Most High, going before the face of His coming to prepare His ways, to give the knowledge of salvation to His people for the remission of their sins.

And seeing Him coming to me, instigated by the Holy Spirit, I said:

Behold the Lamb of God! behold Him who taketh away the sins of the world!

And I baptized Him in the river of Jordan, and I saw the Holy Spirit descending upon Him in the form of a dove; and I heard a voice from the heavens saying, This is my beloved Son, in whom I am well pleased.

And now I have gone before His face, and have descended to announce to you that the rising Son of God is close at hand to visit us, coming from on high to us sitting in darkness and the shadow of death.

Footnote:

1. Calor; another ms. has color, hue.

Chapter 3 (19)

And when the first created, father Adam, had heard this, that Jesus was baptized in Jordan, he cried out to his son Seth:

Tell thy sons, the patriarchs and the prophets, all that thou heardest from Michael the archangel when I sent thee to the gates of paradise to implore God that he might send thee His angel to give thee oil from the tree of mercy, with which to anoint my body when I was sick.

Then Seth, coming near to the holy patriarchs and prophets, said:

When I, Seth, was praying to the Lord at the gates of paradise, behold Michael, the angel of the Lord, appeared to me, saying, I have been sent to thee by the Lord.

I am set over the human race. [1]And to thee, Seth, I say, do not labour with tears in prayers and supplications on account of the oil of the tree of mercy to anoint thy father Adam for the pain of his body, because in no wise shalt thou receive of it, except in the last days and times, except when five thousand and five hundred years have been fulfilled:

then will come upon the earth the most beloved Son of God, to raise up again the body of Adam, and the bodies of the dead; and He, when He comes, will be baptized in Jordan.

And when he shall have come out of the water of Jordan, then with the oil of His mercy shall He anoint all that believe on Him; and that oil of mercy shall be for the generation of those who shall be born out of water and the Holy Spirit into life eternal.

Then, descending upon earth, Christ Jesus, the most beloved Son of God, will lead our father Adam into paradise to the tree of mercy.

And when they heard all these things from Seth, all the patriarchs and prophets exulted with great exultation.

Footnote:

1. Lit., body.

Chapter 4 (20)

And when all the saints were exulting, lo, Satan, the prince and leader of death, said to Hades:

Make thyself ready to receive Jesus, who boasts himself to be the Son of God, and is a man fearing death, and saying, My soul is sorrowful, even unto death.

And he has withstood me much, doing me evil; and many whom I made blind, lame, deaf, leprous, and demoniac, he has healed with a word; and those whom I have brought to thee dead, he has dragged away from thee.

Hades, answering, said to Prince Satan:

Who is he that is so powerful, when he is a man in fear of death?

For all the powerful of the earth are kept in subjection by my power, whom thou hast brought into subjection by thy power.

If then, thou art powerful, what is that man Jesus like, who, though fearing death, withstands thy power?

If he is so powerful in humanity, verily I say unto thee, he is all-powerful in divinity, and his power can no one resist.

And when he says that he fears death, he wishes to lay hold on thee, and woe will be to thee to the ages of eternity.

And Satan, prince of Tartarus, answered and said:

Why hast thou doubted, and feared to receive this Jesus, thy adversary and mine?

For I have tempted him, and I have roused up my ancient people the Jews with hatred and anger against him; I have sharpened a lance to strike him; I have mixed gall and vinegar to give him to drink; and I have prepared wood to crucify him, and nails to pierce him, and his death is near at hand, that I may bring him to thee, subject to thee and me.

Tartarus answered and said:

Thou hast told me that it is he himself who has dragged away the dead from me.

Now there are many who are here kept by me, who, while they lived on earth, took the dead from me, not by their own powers, but by godly prayers, and their almighty God dragged them away from me.

Who is that Jesus, who by his word has withdrawn the dead from me without prayers?

Perhaps he is the same who, by, the word of his command, brought alive Lazarus, after he had been four days in stench and corruption, whom I kept dead.

Satan prince of death answered and said:

That Jesus is the same.

And when Hades heard this he said to him:

I adjure thee by thy powers and mine, do not bring him to me.

For I at that time, when I heard the command of his word, trembled with terror and dismay, and all my officers at the same time were confounded along with me.

Nor could we keep that Lazarus; but, shaking himself like an eagle, he sprang out, and went forth from us with all activity and speed, and the same ground which held the dead body of Lazarus immediately gave him forth alive.

So now, I know that that man who could do these things is God, strong in authority, powerful in humanity, and He is the Saviour of the human race.

But if thou bring Him to me, all who are here shut up in the cruelty of the prison, and bound by their sins in chains that cannot be loosened, He will let loose, and will bring to the life of His divinity for ever.

Chapter 5 (21)

And as Prince Satan and Hades were thus speaking to each other in turn, suddenly there was a voice as of thunders, and a shouting of spirits: Lift up your gates, ye princes; and be ye lifted up, ye everlasting gates; and the King of glory shall come in. [1]Hades hearing this, said to Prince Satan:

Retire from me, and go outside of my realms:

if thou art a powerful warrior, fight against the King of glory.

But what hast thou to do with Him?

And Hades thrust Satan outside of his realms.

And Hades said to his impious officers:

Shut the cruel gates of brass, and put up the bars of iron, and resist bravely, that we, holding captivity, may not take Him captive. [2]

And all the multitude of the saints, hearing this, said to Hades, with the voice of reproach:

Open thy gates, that the King of glory may come in.

And David cried out, saying:

Did I not, when I was alive upon earth, prophesy to you:

Let them confess to the Lord His tender mercies and His wonderful works to the children of men:

for He has shattered the brazen gates, and burst the iron bars; He has taken them up out of the way of their iniquity? [3]And after this, in like manner, Esaias said:

Did not I, when I was alive upon earth, prophesy to you:

The dead shall rise up, and those who are in their tombs shall rise again, and those who are upon earth shall exult; because the dew, which is from the Lord, is their health? [4]And again I said, Where, O Death, is thy sting? where, O Hades, is thy victory? [5]

And when all the saints heard this from Esaias, they said to Hades: Open thy gates.

Since thou art now conquered, thou wilt be weak and powerless.

And there was a great voice, as of thunders, saying:

Lift up your gates, ye princes; and be ye lifted up, ye infernal gates; and the King of glory shall come in.

Hades, seeing that they had twice shouted out this, says, as if not knowing:

Who is the king of glory? David says, in answer to Hades:

I recognise those words of the shout, since I prophesied the same by His Spirit.

And now, what I have said above I say to thee, The Lord strong and mighty, the Lord mighty in battle; He is the King of glory. [6]And the Lord Himself hath looked down from heaven upon earth, to hear the groans of the prisoners, and to release the sons of the slain. [7]And now, most filthy and most foul Hades, open thy gates, that the King of glory may come in.

While David was thus speaking, there came to Hades, in the form of a man, the Lord of majesty, and lighted up the eternal darkness, and burst asunder the indissoluble chains; and the aid of unconquered power visited us, sitting in the profound darkness of transgressions, and in the shadow of death of sins. [8]

Footnotes:

1. Ps. xxiv. 7.
2. Ps. lxviii. 18. Captivemus in the text is probably a misprint for captivemur, may not be taken captive.
3. Ps. cvii. 15-17, according to the LXX. and the Vulgate.
4. Isa. xxvi. 19, according to the LXX.
5. Hos. xiii. 14; 1 Cor. xv. 55.
6. Ps. xxiv. 7, 8.
7. Ps. cii. 19, 20.
8. Comp. Isa. ix. 2; Luke i. 79.

Chapter 6 (22)

When this was seen by Hades and Death, and their impious officers, along with their cruel servants, they trembled at perceiving in their own dominions the clearness of so great a light, when they saw Christ suddenly in their abodes; and they cried out, saying:

We have been overcome by thee.

Who art thou, that to the Lord directest our confusion? [1]Who art thou, that, undestroyed by corruption, the uncorrupted proof of thy majesty, with fury condemnest our power?

Who art thou, so great and little, lowly and exalted, soldier and commander, wonderful warrior in the form of a slave, and the king of glory dead and alive, whom slain the cross has carried?

Thou, who didst lie dead in the sepulchre, hast come down to us alive; and in thy death every creature trembled, and the stars in a body were moved; and now thou hast been made free among the dead, and disturbest our legions.

Who art thou, that settest free those who art held captive, bound by original sin, and recallest them to their former liberty?

Who art thou, who sheddest a divine, and splendid, and illuminating light upon those who have been blinded by the darkness of their sins?

In like manner, also, all the legions of the demons, terror-stricken with like fear from their fearful overthrow, cried out, saying:

Whence art thou, O Jesus, a man so powerful and splendid in majesty, so excellent, without spot, and free from guilt?

For that world of earth which has been subject to us always until now, which used to pay tribute for our uses, has never sent us such a dead man, has never destined such gifts for the powers below.

Who therefore art thou, that hast so intrepidly entered our bounds, and who hast not only no fear of our punishments, but, moreover, attemptest to take all away from our chains?

Perhaps thou art that Jesus of whom our prince Satan said, that by thy death of the cross thou wast destined to receive the dominion of the whole world.

Then the King of glory, trampling on death by His majesty, and seizing Prince Satan, delivered him to the power of Hades, and drew Adam to His brightness.

Footnote:

1. Some mss. have: Who art thou, O man, that to God directest thy prayer to our confusion? The correct reading may be: Who art thou, that bringest confusion upon our master?

Chapter 7 (23)

Then Hades, receiving Prince Satan, said to him, with vehement revilings:

O prince of perdition, and leader of extermination, Beelzebub, derision of angels, to be spit upon by the just, why didst thou wish to do this?

Didst thou wish to crucify the King of glory, in whose death thou didst promise us so great spoils?

Like a fool, thou didst not know what thou wast doing.

For, behold, that Jesus by the splendour of His divinity is putting to flight all the darkness of death, and He has broken into the strong lowest depths of our dungeons, and has brought out the captives, and released those who were bound. And all who used to groan under our torments insult us, and by their prayers our dominions are taken by storm, and our realms conquered, and no race of men has now any respect for us.

Moreover, also, we are grievously threatened by the dead, who have never been haughty to us, and who have not at any time been joyful as captives.

O Prince Satan, father of all impious wretches and renegades, why didst thou wish to do this?

Of those who from the beginning, even until now, have despaired of salvation and life, no bellowing after the usual fashion is now heard here; and no groaning of theirs resounds, nor in any of their faces is a trace of tears found.

O Prince Satan, possessor of the keys of the lower regions, all thy riches which thou hadst acquired by the tree of transgression and the loss of paradise, thou hast now lost by the tree of the cross, and all thy joy has perished.

When thou didst hang up that Christ Jesus the King of glory, thou wast acting against thyself and against me.

Henceforth thou shalt know what eternal torments and infinite punishments thou art to endure in my everlasting keeping.

O Prince Satan, author of death, and source of all pride, thou oughtest first to have inquired into the bad cause of that Jesus. Him in whom thou perceivedst no fault, why, without reason, didst thou dare unjustly to crucify? and why hast thou brought to our regions one innocent and just, and lost the guilty, the impious, and the unjust of the whole world?

And when Hades had thus spoken to Prince Satan, then the King of glory said to Hades:

Satan the prince will be in thy power for ever, in place of Adam and his sons, my just ones.

Chapter 8 (24)

And the Lord stretched out His hand, and said:

Come to me, all my saints, who have my image and likeness.

Do you, who have been condemned through the tree and the devil and death, now see the devil and death condemned through the tree.

Immediately all the saints were brought together under the hand of the Lord.

And the Lord, holding Adam by the right hand, said to him:

Peace be to thee, with all thy children, my righteous ones!

And Adam fell down at the knees of the Lord, and with tearful entreaty praying, said with a loud voice:

I will extol Thee, O Lord; for Thou hast lifted me up, and hast not made my foes to rejoice over me.

O Lord God, I cried unto Thee, and Thou hast healed me.

O Lord, Thou hast brought out my soul from the powers below; Thou hast saved me from them that go down into the pit.

Sing praises to the Lord, all His saints, and confess to the memory of His holiness; since there is anger in His indignation, and life in His goodwill. [1]In like manner also all the saints of God, falling on their knees at the feet of the Lord, said with one voice:

Thou hast come, O Redeemer of the world:

as Thou hast foretold by the law and Thy prophets, so hast Thou fulfilled by Thy deeds.

Thou hast redeemed the living by Thy cross; and by the death of the cross Thou hast come down to us, to rescue us from the powers below, and from death, by Thy majesty.

O Lord, as Thou hast set the title of Thy glory in heaven, and hast erected as the title of redemption Thy cross upon earth, so, O Lord, set in Hades the sign of the victory of Thy cross, that death may no more have dominion.

And the Lord, stretching forth His hand, made the sign of the cross upon Adam and upon all His saints; and holding Adam by the right hand, went up from the powers below:

and all the saints followed Him.

Then holy David cried out aloud, saying:

Sing unto the Lord a new song, for He hath done wonderful things; His right hand and His holy arm have brought salvation to Himself.

The Lord hath made known His salvation; His righteousness hath He revealed in the sight of the heathen. [2]

And all the multitude of the saints answered, saying:

This is glory to all His saints.

Amen, alleluia.

The Forgotten Bible

And after this the prophet Habacuc cried out, saying:

Thou wentest forth for the salvation of Thy people, to deliver Thine elect. [3] And all the saints answered, saying:

Blessed is He who cometh in the name of the Lord; God is the Lord, and He hath shone upon us. [4] Amen, alleluia.

In like manner after this the prophet Michaeas as also cried out, saying:

Who is a God like unto thee, O Lord, taking away iniquities and passing by sins?

And now Thou dost withhold Thine anger for a testimony against us, because Thou delightest in mercy.

And Thou turnest again, and hast compassion upon us, and pardonest all our iniquities; and all our sins hast Thou sunk in the multitude of death, [5] as Thou hast sworn unto our fathers in the days of old. [6] And all the saints answered, saying:

This is our God to eternity, and for ever and ever; and He will direct us for evermore. [7] Amen, alleluia.

So also all the prophets, quoting the sacred writings concerning His praises, [8] and all the saints crying, Amen, alleluia, followed the Lord.

Footnotes:

1. Ps. xxx. 1-6 (Vulg.).
2. Ps. xcviii. 1, 2.
3. Hab. iii. 13.
4. Ps. cxviii. 26, 27.
5. So the text, multitudine mortis; but the mss. must have had altitudine maris, in the depth of the sea, with the LXX. and the Hebrew.
6. Mic. vii. 18-20.
7. Ps. xlviii. 14.
8. Or, bringing sacred words from their praises.

Chapter 9 (25)

And the Lord, holding the hand of Adam, delivered him to Michael the archangel:

and all the saints followed Michael the archangel, and he led them all into the glorious grace of paradise.

And there met them two men, ancient of days.

The saints asked them:

Who are you, that have not yet been dead, along with us in the regions below, and have been placed in paradise in the body?

One of them answered, and said: I am Enoch, who by the word of the Lord have been translated hither; and he who is with me is Elias the Thesbite, who was taken up by a fiery chariot.

Here also even until now we have not tasted death, but have been reserved to the coming of Antichrist, by divine signs and wonders to do battle with him, and, being killed by him in Jerusalem, after three days and half a day to be taken up alive again in the clouds. [1]

Footnote:

1. Rev. xi. 3-12; 1 Thess. iv. 17.

Chapter 10 (26)

And while the saints Enoch and Elias were thus speaking, behold, there came up another man, most wretched, carrying on his shoulders the sign of the cross.

And seeing him, all the saints said to him:

Who art thou? because thy appearance is that of a robber.

And what is the sign which thou carriest on thy shoulders?

In answer to them, he said: Truly have you said that I was a robber, doing all sorts of evil upon the earth.

And the Jews crucified me along with Jesus; and I saw the miracles in created things which were done through the cross of Jesus crucified, and I believed Him to be the Creator of all created things, and the King omnipotent; and I entreated Him, saying, Be mindful of me, Lord, when Thou shalt have come into Thy kingdom.

Immediately He accepted my entreaty, and said to me, Amen; I say to thee, To-day shalt thou be with me in paradise. [1] And He gave me this sign of the cross, saying, Walk into paradise carrying this; and if the guardian angel of paradise will not let thee go in, show him the sign of the cross, and thou shalt say to him, Jesus Christ, the Son of God, who has now been crucified, has sent me.

Having done so, I said all this to the guardian angel of paradise.

And when he heard this, he immediately opened, and led me in, and placed me at the right of paradise, saying, Lo, hold a little, and there will come in the father of the whole human race, Adam, with all his children, holy and just, after the triumph and glory of the ascension of Christ the crucified Lord.

Hearing all these words of the robber, all the holy patriarchs and prophets with one voice said:

Blessed art Thou, O Lord Almighty, Father of everlasting benefits, and Father of mercies, who hast given such grace to Thy sinners, and hast brought them back into the grace of paradise, and into Thy rich pastures; for this is spiritual life most sure.

Amen, amen.

Footnote:
1. Luke xxiii. 42, 43.

Chapter 11 (27)

These are the divine and sacred mysteries which we saw and heard, I Karinus, and Leucius.

More we are not allowed to tell of the other mysteries of God, as Michael the archangel adjured us, and said:

You shall go into Jerusalem with your brethren, and continue in prayers, and you shall cry out, and glorify the resurrection of the Lord Jesus Christ, who has raised you up again from the dead with Himself.

And with none of men shall you speak; and you shall sit as if dumb, until the hour shall come when the Lord Himself shall permit you to relate the mysteries of His divinity.

And Michael the archangel ordered us to walk across Jordan into a place rich and fertile, where there are many who rose again along with us for an evidence of the resurrection of Christ the Lord; because only three days were allowed to us who have risen from the dead to celebrate in Jerusalem the passover of the Lord, with our living relations, for an evidence of the resurrection of Christ the Lord:

and we have been baptized in the holy river of Jordan, receiving each of us white robes.

And after three days, when we had celebrated the passover of the Lord, all who rose again along with us were snatched up into the clouds, and taken across the Jordan, and were no longer seen by any one.

But we were told to remain in the city of Arimathaea in prayers.

These are the things which the Lord commanded us to relate to you. Give Him praise and confession, and be penitent, that He may have mercy upon you.

Peace be to you from the same Lord Jesus Christ, and the Saviour of all of us!

Amen.

And after they had finished all, writing on separate sheets of paper, they arose.

And Karinus gave what he wrote into the hands of Annas and Caiaphas and Gamaliel; in like manner also Leucius gave what he wrote into the hands of Nicodemus and Joseph.

And being suddenly transfigured, they became exceedingly white, and were seen no more. And their writings were found exactly the same, not one letter more or less.

All the synagogue of the Jews, hearing all these wonderful sayings of Karinus and Leucius, said to each other:

Truly all these things have been done by the Lord, and blessed be the Lord for ever and ever. Amen.

And they all went out with great anxiety, beating their breasts with fear and trembling; and they went away, each to his own house.

All these things which were said by the Jews in their synagogue Joseph and Nicodemus immediately reported to the proconsul.

And Pilate himself wrote all which had been done and said concerning Jesus by the Jews, and he placed all the words in the public records of his praetorium.

Chapter 12 (28)

After this, Pilate going into the temple of the Jews, assembled all the chief priests, and learned men, and scribes, and teachers of the law, and went in with them into the sanctuary of the temple, and ordered that all the gates should be shut, and said to them:

We have heard that you have a certain great collection of books in this temple: therefore I ask you that it be presented before us.

And when four officers brought in that collection of books, adorned with gold and precious gems, Pilate said to all:

I adjure you by the God of your fathers, who ordered you to build this temple in the place of his sanctuary, not to conceal the truth from me.

You all know what is written in that collection of books; but now say whether you have found in the writings that Jesus, whom you have crucified, to be the Son of God that was to come for the salvation of the human race, and in how many revolutions of the seasons he ought to come.

Declare to me whether you crucified him in ignorance of this, or knowing it.

Being thus adjured, Annas and Caiaphas ordered all the others who were with them to go out of the sanctuary; and themselves shut all the gates of the temple and the sanctuary, and said to Pilate:

We have been adjured by thee, O good judge, by the building of this temple, to give thee the truth, and a clear account of this matter.

After we had crucified Jesus, not knowing Him to be the Son of God, thinking that He did miracles by means of some charm, we made a great synagogue in this temple.

And conferring with each other of the signs of the miracles which Jesus had done, we found many witnesses of our nation who said that they had seen Jesus alive after suffering death, and that He had penetrated into the height of heaven.

And we have seen two witnesses, whom Jesus raised up again from the dead, who told us many wonderful things that Jesus did among the dead, which we have in our hands, written out.

And our custom is, every year before our synagogue, to open that holy collection of books, and seek out the testimony of God. And we have found in the first book of the LXX., where the archangel Michael spoke to the third son of Adam, the first man, of five thousand and five hundred years, in which the Christ, the most beloved Son of God, was to come from the heavens; and upon this we have considered that perhaps He was the God of Israel who said to Moses, [1] Make to thee the ark of the covenant, two cubits and a half in length, one cubit and a half in breadth, one cubit and a half in height.

In these five and a half cubits we have understood and recognised, from the structure of the ark of the old covenant, that in five and a half thousands of years, Jesus Christ was to come in the ark of the body; and we have found Him to be the God of Israel, the Son of God.

Because after His passion, we, the chief priests, wondering at the signs which happened on account of Him, opened this collection of books, searching out all the generations, even to the generation of Joseph, and reckoning that Mary the mother of Christ was of the seed of David; and we have found that from the time that God made the heaven and the earth and the first man, to the deluge, are two thousand two hundred and twelve [2] years; and from the deluge to the building of the tower, five hundred and thirty-one [3] years; and from the building of the tower to Abraham, six hundred and six [4] years; and from Abraham to the arrival of the children of Israel from Egypt, four hundred and seventy years; from the coming of the children of Israel out of Egypt to the building of the temple, five hundred and eleven years; and from the building of the temple to the destruction of the same temple, four hundred and sixty-four years.

Thus far have we found in the book of Esdras.

After searching, we find that from the burning of the temple to the advent of Christ, and His birth, there are six hundred and thirty-six [5] years, which together were five thousand five hundred years, as we have found written in the book that Michael the archangel foretold to Seth the third son of Adam, that in five and a half thousands of years Christ the Son of God would come. [6]Even until now we have told no one, that there might be no dissension in our synagogues.

And now thou hast adjured us, O good judge, by this holy book of the testimonies of God, and we make it manifest to thee.

And now we adjure thee, by thy life and safety, to make manifest these words to no one in Jerusalem.

Footnotes:
1. Ex. xxv. 10.
2. Should be 2262--bsob in place of bsib.
3. This includes the second Cainan.
4. Should be 676.
5. Should be 586--dlxxxvi. instead of dcxxxvi.
6. Lit., has come.

Chapter 13 (29)

Pilate, hearing these words of Annas and Caiaphas, laid them all up in the acts of our Lord and Saviour, in the public records of his praetorium, and wrote a letter to Claudius, king of the city of Rome, [1] saying:--

Pontius Pilate to Claudius his king, greeting.

It has lately happened, as I myself have also proved, that the Jews, through envy, have punished themselves and their posterity by a cruel condemnation.

In short, when their fathers had a promise that their God would send them from heaven his holy one, who should deservedly be called their king, and promised that he would send him by a virgin upon the earth:

when, therefore, while I was procurator, he had come into Judaea, and when they saw him enlightening the blind, cleansing the lepers, curing the paralytics, making demons flee from men, even raising the dead, commanding the winds, walking dryshod upon the waves of the sea, and doing many other signs of miracles; and when all the people of the Jews said that he was the Son of God, the chief priests felt envy against him, and seized him, and delivered him to me; and, telling me one lie after another, they said that he was a sorcerer, and was acting contrary to their law.

And I believed that it was so, and delivered him to be scourged, according to their will.

And they crucified him, and set guards over him when buried.

And he rose again on the third day, while my soldiers were keeping guard.

But so flagrant was the iniquity of the Jews, that they gave money to my soldiers, saying, Say that his disciples have stolen his body.

But after receiving the money they could not keep secret what had been done; for they bore witness both that he had risen again, that they had seen him, [2] and that they had received money from the Jews.

This accordingly I have done, lest any one should give a different and a false account of it, and lest thou shouldst think that the lies of the Jews are to be believed.

Footnotes:

1. [Compare the other Latin form of this letter, as translated on p. 459; also the version of the Greek form of a similar letter, included in the Acts of Peter and Paul.--R.]

2. Or, that they had seen that he rose from the dead.

The Forgotten Bible
Latin Second Version

Chapter 1 (17)

Then Rabbi Addas, and Rabbi Finees, and Rabbi Egias, the three men who had come from Galilee, testifying that they had seen Jesus taken up into heaven, rose up in the midst of the multitude of the chiefs of the Jews, and said before the priests and the Levites, who had been called together to the council of the Lord:

When we were coming from Galilee, we met at the Jordan a very great multitude of men, fathers [1] who had been some time dead.

And present among them we saw Karinus and Leucius.

And they came up to us, and we kissed each other, because they were dear friends of ours; and we asked them, Tell us, friends and brothers, what is this breath of life and flesh? and who are those with whom you are going? and how do you, who have been some time dead, remain in the body?

And they said in answer:

We have risen again along with Christ from the lower world, and He has raised us up again from the dead.

And from this you may know that the gates of death and darkness have been destroyed, and the souls of the saints have been brought out thence, and have ascended into heaven along with Christ the Lord.

And indeed to us it has been commanded by the Lord Himself, that for an appointed time we should walk over the banks of Jordan and the mountains; not, however, appearing to every one, nor speaking to every one, except to those to whom He has permitted us.

And just now we could neither have spoken nor appeared to you, unless it had been allowed to us by the Holy Spirit.

And when they heard this, all the multitude who were present in the council were struck with fear and trembling, and wondered whether these things had really happened which these Galilaeans testified.

Then Caiaphas and Annas said to the council:

What these have testified, first and last, must shortly be altogether made clear:

If it shall be found to be true that Karinus and Leucius remain alive in the body, and if we shall be able to behold them with our own eyes, then what they testify is altogether true; and if we find them, they will inform us of everything; but if not, you may know that it is all lies.

Then the council having suddenly risen, it pleased them to choose men fit for the duty, fearing God, and who knew when they died, and where they were buried, to inquire diligently, and to see whether it was as they had heard.

The men therefore proceeded to the same place, fifteen in number, who through all were present at their falling asleep, and had stood at their feet when they were buried, and had beheld their tombs.

And they came and found their tombs open, and very many others besides, and found a sign neither of their bones nor of their dust. And they returned in all haste, and reported what they had seen.

Then all their synagogue was in great grief and perplexity, and they said to each other: What shall we do?

Annas and Caiaphas said:

Let us turn to where we have heard that they are, and let us send to them men of rank, asking and entreating them:

perhaps they will deign to come to us.

Then they sent to them Nicodemus and Joseph, and the three men, the Galilaean rabbis who had seen them, asking that they should deign to come to them.

And they went, and walked round all the region of Jordan and of the mountains, and they were coming back without finding them.

And, behold, suddenly there appeared coming down from Mount Amalech a very great number, as it were, twelve thousand men, who had risen with the Lord.

And though they recognised very many there, they were not able to say anything to them for fear and the angelic vision; and they stood at a distance gazing and hearing them, how they walked along singing praises, and saying:

The Lord has risen again from the dead, as He had said; let us all exult and be glad, since He reigns for ever.

Then those who had been sent were astonished, and fell to the ground for fear, and received the answer from them, that they should see Karinus and Leucius in their own houses.

And they rose up and went to their houses, and found them spending their time in prayer.

And going in to them, they fell on their faces to the ground, saluting them; and being raised up, they said:

O friends of God, all the multitude of the Jews have directed us to you, hearing that you have risen from the dead, asking and beseeching you to come to them, that we all may know the great things of God which have happened around us in our times.

And they immediately, at a sign from God, rose up, and came with them, and entered their synagogue.

Then the multitude of the Jews, with the priests, put the books of the law in their hands, and adjured them by the God Heloi, and the God Adonai, and by the law and the prophets, saying:

Tell us how you have risen from the dead, and what are those wonderful things which have happened in our times, such as we have never heard to have happened at any other time; because already for fear all our bones have been benumbed, and have dried up, and the earth moves itself under our feet:

for we have joined all our hearts to shed righteous and holy blood.

Then Karinus and Leucius signed to them with their hands to give them a sheet of paper and ink.

And this they did, because the Holy Spirit did not allow them to speak to them.

And they gave each of them paper, and put them apart, the one from the other in separate cells.

And they, making with their fingers the sign of the cross of Christ, began to write on the separate sheets; and after they had finished, as if out of one mouth from the separate cells, they cried out, Amen.

And rising up, Karinus gave his paper to Annas, and Leucius to Caiaphas; and saluting each other, they went out, and returned to their sepulchres.

Then Annas and Caiaphas, opening the sheet of paper, began each to read it in secret.

But all the people took it ill, and so all cried out: Read these writings to us openly; and after they have been read through we shall keep them, lest perchance this truth of God be turned through wilful blindness, by unclean and deceitful men, into falsehood.

At this Annas and Caiaphas fell a-trembling, and delivered the sheet of paper to Rabbi Addas, and Rabbi Finees, and Rabbi Egias, who had come from Galilee, and announced that Jesus had been taken up into heaven. All the multitude of the Jews trusted to them to read this writing. And they read the paper containing these words:--

Footnote:
1. Abbatorum.

Chapter 2 (18)
I Karinus.

O Lord Jesus Christ, Son of the living God, permit me to speak of Thy wonders which Thou hast done in the lower world.

When, therefore, we were kept in darkness and the shadow of death in the lower world, suddenly there shone upon us a great light, and Hades and the gates of death trembled.

And then was heard the voice of the Son of the Father most high, as if the voice of a great thunder; and loudly proclaiming, He thus charged them:

Lift up your gates, ye princes; lift up the everlasting gates; the King of glory, Christ the Lord, will come up to enter in.

Then Satan, the leader of death, came up, fleeing in terror, saying to his officers and the powers below:

My officers, and all the powers below, run together, shut your gates, put up the iron bars, and fight bravely, and resist, lest they lay hold of us, and keep us captive in chains.

Then all his impious officers were perplexed, and began to shut the gates of death with all diligence, and by little and little to fasten the locks and the iron bars, and to hold all their weapons [1] grasped in their hands, and to utter howlings in a direful and most hideous voice.

Footnote:
1. Ornamenta; another ms. has armamenta.

The Forgotten Bible

Chapter 3 (19)

Then Satan said to Hades:

Make thyself ready to receive him whom I shall bring down to thee.

Thereupon Hades thus replied to Satan:

That voice was from nothing else than the cry of the Son of the Father most high, because the earth and all the places of the world below so trembled under it:

wherefore I think that myself and all my dungeons are now lying open.

But I adjure thee, Satan, head of all evils, [1] by thy power and my own, bring him not to me, lest, while we wish to take him, we be taken captive by him.

For if, at his voice only, all my power has been thus destroyed, what do you think he will do when he shall come in person?

To him Satan, the leader of death, thus replied:

What art thou crying out about?

Do not be afraid, my old most wicked friend, because I have stirred up the people of the Jews against him; I have told them to strike him with blows on the face, and I have brought upon him betrayal by one of his disciples; and he is a man in great fear of death, because from fear he said, My soul is sorrowful, even unto death; and I have brought him to this, that he has just been lifted up and hanged on the cross.

Then Hades said to him:

If he be the same who, by the mere word of his command, made Lazarus fly away like an eagle from my bosom, when he had already been dead four days, he is not a man in humanity, but God in majesty.

I entreat thee not to bring him to me.

And Satan says to him:

Make thyself ready nevertheless; be not afraid; because he is already hanging on the cross, I can do nothing else.

Then Hades thus replied to Satan:

If, then, thou canst do nothing else, behold, thy destruction is at hand.

I, in short, shall remain cast down and dishonoured; thou, however, wilt be tortured under my power.

Footnote:

1. Or, of all the wicked.

Chapter 4 (20)

And the saints of God heard the wrangling of Satan and Hades.

They, however, though as yet not at all recognising each other, were, notwithstanding, in the possession of their faculties.

But our holy father Adam thus replied to Satan at once:

O captain of death, why dost thou fear and tremble?

Behold, the Lord is coming, who will now destroy all thy inventions; and thou shalt be taken by Him, and bound throughout eternity.

Then all the saints, hearing the voice of our father Adam, how boldly he replied to Satan in all points, were strengthened in joy; and all running together to father Adam, were crowded in one place.

Then our father Adam, gazing on all that multitude, wondered greatly whether all of them had been begotten from him into the world.

And embracing those who were standing everywhere around him, and shedding most bitter tears, he addressed his son Seth, saying:

Relate, my son Seth, to the holy patriarchs and prophets what the guardian of paradise said to thee, when I sent thee to bring to me of that oil of compassion, in order to anoint my body when I was ill.

Then he answered:

I, when thou sentest me before the gates of paradise, prayed and entreated the Lord with tears, and called upon the guardian of paradise to give me of it therefrom.

Then Michael the archangel came out, and said to me, Seth, why then dost thou weep? Know, being informed beforehand, that thy father Adam will not receive of this oil of compassion now, but after many generations of time.

For the most beloved Son of God will come down from heaven into the world, and will be baptized by John in the river Jordan; and then shall thy father Adam receive of this oil [1] of compassion, and all that believe in him.

And of those who have believed in him, their kingdom will endure for ever.

Footnote:
1. The text has deo, God, obviously a misprint for oleo, oil.

Chapter 5 (21)

Then all the saints, hearing this again, exulted in joy.

And one of those standing round, Isaias by name, cried out aloud, and thundered: Father Adam, and all standing round, hear my declaration.

When I was on earth, and by the teaching of the Holy Spirit, in prophecy I sang of this light:

The people who sat in darkness have seen a great light; to them dwelling in the region of the shadow of death light has arisen. At these words father Adam, and all of them, turned and asked him:

Who art thou? because what thou sayest is true.

And he subjoined, and said:

My name is Isaias.

Then appeared another near him, as if a hermit.

And they asked him, saying:

Who art thou, who bearest such an appearance in thy body?[1] And he firmly answered:

I am John the Baptist, voice and prophet of the Most High.

I went before the face of the same Lord, that I might make the waste and rough places into plain ways.

I with my finger pointed out and made manifest the Lamb of the Lord, and Son of God, to the inhabitants of Jerusalem.

I baptized Him in the river Jordan.

I heard the voice of the Father from heaven thundering over Him, and proclaiming, This is my beloved Son, in whom I am well pleased.

I received from Him the answer that He would descend to the lower world

Then father Adam, hearing this, cried with a loud voice, exclaiming: Alleluia! which is, interpreted, The Lord is certainly coming.

Footnote:
1. Or, who wearest such (things) on thy body.

Chapter 6 (22)

After that, another standing there, pre-eminent as it were, with a certain mark of an emperor, David by name, thus cried out, and said: When I was upon earth, I made revelations to the people of the mercy of God and His visitation, prophesying future joys, saying through all ages, Let them make confession to the Lord of His tender mercy and His wonderful works to the sons of men, because He has shattered the gates of brass, and broken the bars of iron.

Then the holy patriarchs and prophets began mutually to recognise each other, and each to quote his prophecies.

Then holy Jeremias, examining his prophecies, said to the patriarchs and prophets:

When I was upon earth, I prophesied of the Son of God, that He was seen upon earth, and dwelt with men.

Then all the saints, exulting in the light of the Lord, and in the sight of father Adam, and in the answering of all the patriarchs and prophets, cried out, saying:

Alleluia! blessed is He who cometh in the name of the Lord; so that at their crying out Satan trembled, and sought a way of escape.

And he could not, because Hades and his satellites kept him bound in the lower regions, and guarded at all points.

And they said to him:

Why dost thou tremble?

We by no means allow thee to go forth hence.

But receive this, as thou art worthy, from Him whom thou didst daily assail; but if not, know that thou, bound by Him, shall be in my keeping.

Chapter 7 (23)

And again there came the voice of the Son of the Father most high, as it were the voice of a great thunder, saying:

Lift up your gates, ye princes; and be ye lifted up, ye everlasting gates, and the King of glory will come in.

Then Satan and Hades cried out, saying:

Who is the king of glory?
And it was answered to them in the voice of the Lord:
The Lord strong and mighty, the Lord mighty in battle.

After this voice there came a man, whose appearance was that of a robber, carrying a cross on his shoulder, crying from the outside of the door, and saying:

Open to me, that I may come in.

And Satan, opening to him a little, brought him inside into his dwelling, [1] and again shut the door after him.

And all the saints saw him most clearly, and said to him forthwith:

Thy appearance is that of a robber.

Tell us what it is that thou carriest on thy back.

And he answered, and said with humility:

Truly I was a robber altogether; and the Jews hung me up on a cross, along with my Lord Jesus Christ, the Son of the Father most high.

I, in fine, have come heralding [2] Him; He indeed is coming immediately behind me.

Then holy David, inflamed with anger against Satan, cried out aloud: Open thy gates, most vile wretch, that the King of glory may come in. In like manner also all the saints of God rose up against Satan, and would have seized him, and divided him among them.

And again a cry was heard within:

Lift up your gates, ye princes; and be ye lifted up, ye everlasting gates; and the King of glory shall come in.

Hades and Satan, at that clear voice, again asked, saying:

Who is this king of glory?

And it was said to them by that wonderful voice:

The Lord of powers, He is the King of glory.

Footnotes:
1. Hospitio.
2. Praeconcitus, corrected to praeconatus or ans.

Chapter 8 (24)

And, behold, suddenly Hades trembled, and the gates of death and the bolts were shattered, and the iron bars were broken and fell to the ground, and everything was laid open.

And Satan remained in the midst, and stood confounded and downcast, bound with fetters on his feet. And, behold, the Lord Jesus Christ, coming in the brightness of light from on high, compassionate, great, and lowly, carrying a chain in His hand, bound Satan by the neck; and again tying his hands behind him, dashed him on his back into Tartarus, and placed His holy foot on his throat, saying:

Through all ages thou hast done many evils; thou hast not in any wise rested.

To-day I deliver thee to everlasting fire. And Hades being suddenly summoned, He commanded him, and said:

Take this most wicked and impious one, and have him in thy keeping even to that day in which I shall command thee.

And he, as soon as he received him, was plunged under the feet of the Lord along with him into the depth of the abyss.

Chapter 9 (25)

Then the Lord Jesus, the Saviour of all, affectionate and most mild, saluting Adam kindly, said to him:

Peace be to thee, Adam, with thy children, through immeasurable ages of ages!
Amen.

Then father Adam, falling forward at the feet of the Lord, and being raised erect, kissed His hands, and shed many tears, saying, testifying to all:

Behold the hands which fashioned me!

And he said to the Lord:

Thou hast come, O King of glory, delivering men, and bringing them into Thy everlasting kingdom.

Then also our mother Eve in like manner fell forward at the feet of our Lord, and was raised erect, and kissed His hands, and poured forth tears in abundance, and said, testifying to all:

Behold the hands which made me!

Then all the saints, adoring Him, cried out, saying:

Blessed is He who cometh in the name of the Lord!

The Lord God hath shone upon us--amen--through all ages.

Alleluia for ever and ever!

Praise, honour, power, glory! because Thou hast come from on high to visit us. Singing Alleluia continually, and rejoicing together concerning His glory, they ran together under the hands of the Lord.

Then the Saviour, inquiring thoroughly about all, seized Hades,[1] immediately threw some down into Tartarus, and led some with Him to the upper world.

Footnote:

1. Momordidit infernum, which is obviously corrupt. The translator may have read dedeche haden, bit Hades, for dedeiche haden, brought Hades to light.

Chapter 10 (26)

Then all the saints of God asked the Lord to leave as a sign of victory the sign of His holy cross in the lower world, that its most impious officers might not retain as an offender any one whom the Lord had absolved.

And so it was done.

And the Lord set His cross in the midst of Hades, which is the sign of victory, and which will remain even to eternity.

Then we all went forth thence along with the Lord, leaving Satan and Hades in Tartarus.

And to us and many others it was commanded that we should rise in the body, giving in the world a testimony of the resurrection of our Lord Jesus Christ, and of those things which had been done in the lower world.

These are the things, dearest brethren, which we have seen, and which, adjured by you, we testify, He bearing witness who died for us, and rose again; because, as it was written, so has it been done in all points.

Chapter 11 (27)

And when the paper was finished and read through, all that heard it fell on their faces, weeping bitterly, and cruelly beating their breasts, crying out, and saying through all:

Woe to us!

Why has this happened to us wretched?

Pilate flees; Annas and Caiaphas flee; the priests and Levites flee; moreover also the people of the Jews, weeping and saying, Woe to us wretched! we have shed sacred blood upon the earth.

For three days, therefore, and three nights, they did not taste bread and water at all; nor did any of them return to the synagogue.

But on the third day again the council was assembled, and the other paper of Leucius was read through; and it was found neither more nor less, to a single letter, than that which the writing of Karinus contained.

Then the synagogue was perplexed; and they all lamented forty days and forty nights, looking for destruction from God, and the vengeance of God. But He, pitier affectionate and most high, did not immediately destroy them, bountifully giving them a place of repentance.

But they were not found worthy to be turned to the Lord.

These are the testimonies of Karinus and Leucius, dearest brethren, concerning Christ the Son of God, and His holy deeds in the lower world; to whom let us all give praise and glory through immeasurable age of ages.

Amen.

The Letter of Pontius Pilate,
Which He Wrote to the Roman Emperor, Concerning Our Lord Jesus Christ.

Pontius Pilate to Tiberius Caesar the emperor, greeting.[1]

Upon Jesus Christ, whose case I had clearly set forth to thee in my last, at length by the will of the people a bitter punishment has been inflicted, myself being in a sort unwilling and rather afraid.

A man, by Hercules, so pious and strict, no age has ever had nor will have. But wonderful were the efforts of the people themselves, and the unanimity of all the scribes and chief men and elders, to crucify this ambassador of truth, notwithstanding that their own prophets, and after our manner the sibyls, warned them against it:

and supernatural signs appeared while he was hanging, and, in the opinion of philosophers, threatened destruction to the whole world.

His disciples are flourishing, in their work and the regulation of their lives not belying their master; yea, in his name most beneficent.

Had I not been afraid of the rising of a sedition among the people, who were just on the point of breaking out, perhaps this man would still have been alive to us; although, urged more by fidelity to thy dignity than induced by my own wishes, I did not according to my strength resist that innocent blood free from the whole charge brought against it, but unjustly, through the malignity of men, should be sold and suffer, yet, as the Scriptures signify, to their own destruction.

Farewell.

28th March.

Footnote:
1. [Compare the translation of the letter of Pilate to Claudius, found in the Acts of Peter and Paul; also a similar letter incorporated in The Gospel of Nicodemus, second part, Latin, first version, chap. 13 (29), p. 454.--R.]

The Report of Pilate the Procurator Concerning Our Lord Jesus Christ
Sent to the August [1] Caesar in Rome.

First Greek Form

In those days, our Lord Jesus Christ having been crucified under Pontius Pilate, procurator of Palestine and Phoenicia, these records were made in Jerusalem as to what was done by the Jews against the Lord.

Pilate therefore, along with his private report, sent them to the Caesar in Rome, writing thus:--

To the most mighty, venerable, most divine, and most terrible, the august [2] Caesar, Pilate the governor of the East sends greeting. I have, O most mighty, a narrative to give thee, on account of which I am seized with fear and trembling.

For in this government of mine, of which one of the cities is called Jerusalem, all the people of the Jews have delivered to me a man named Jesus, bringing many charges against him, which they were not able to convict him of by the consistency of their evidence.

And one of the heresies they had against him was, that Jesus said that their Sabbath should not be a day of leisure, and should not be observed.

For he performed many cures on that day:

he made the blind receive their sight, the lame walk; he raised up the dead, he cleansed the lepers; he healed paralytics that were not at all able to make any movement of their body, or to keep their nerves steady, but who had only speech and the modulation of their voice, and he gave them the power of walking and running, removing their illness by a single word.

Another thing again, more powerful still, which is strange even with our gods: he raised up one that had been dead four days, summoning him by a single word, when the dead man had his blood corrupted, and when his body was destroyed by the worms produced in it, and when it had the stink of a dog.

And seeing him lying in the tomb, he ordered him to run.

Nor had he anything of a dead body about him at all; but as a bridegroom from the bridal chamber, so he came forth from the tomb filled with very great fragrance.

And strangers that were manifestly demoniac, and that had their dwelling in deserts, and ate their own flesh, living like beasts and creeping things, even these he made to be dwellers in cities, and by his word restored them to soundness of mind, and rendered them wise and able and reputable, eating with all the enemies of the unclean spirits that dwelt in them for their destruction, which he cast down into the depths of the sea. And again there was another having a withered hand; and not the hand only, but rather the half of the body of the man, was petrified, so that he had not the form of a man, or the power of moving his body. And him by a word he healed, and made sound.

And a woman that had an issue of blood for many years, and whose joints [3] and veins were drained by the flowing of the blood, so that she did not present the appearance of a human being, but was like a corpse, and was speechless every day, so that all the physicians of the district could not cure her.

For there was not any hope of life left to her.

And when Jesus passed by, she mysteriously received strength through his overshadowing her; and she took hold of his fringe behind, and immediately in the same hour power filled up what in her was empty, so that, no longer suffering any pain, she began to run swiftly to her own city Kepharnaum, so as to accomplish the journey in six days.

And these are the things which I lately had in my mind to report, which Jesus accomplished on the Sabbath.

And other signs greater than these he did, so that I have perceived that the wonderful works done by him are greater than can be done by the gods whom we worship.

And him Herod and Archelaus and Philip, Annas and Caiaphas, with all the people, delivered to me, making a great uproar against me that I should try him.

I therefore ordered him to be crucified, having first scourged him, and having found against him no cause of evil accusations or deeds.

And at the time he was crucified there was darkness over all the world, the sun being darkened at mid-day, and the stars appearing, but in them there appeared no lustre; and the moon, as if turned into blood, failed in her light.

And the world was swallowed up by the lower regions, so that the very sanctuary of the temple, as they call it, could not be seen by the Jews in their fall; and they saw below them a chasm of the earth, with the roar of the thunders that fell upon it. [4] And in that terror dead men were seen that had risen, as the Jews themselves testified; and they said that it was Abraham, and Isaac, and Jacob, and the twelve patriarchs, and Moses and Job, that had died, as they say, three thousand five hundred years before.

And there were very many whom I also saw appearing in the body; and they were making a lamentation about the Jews, on account of the wickedness that had come to pass through them, and the destruction of the Jews and of their law.

And the fear of the earthquake remained from the sixth hour of the preparation until the ninth hour.

And on the evening of the first day of the week there was a sound out of the heaven, so that the heaven became enlightened sevenfold more than all the days.

And at the third hour of the night also the sun was seen brighter than it had ever shone before, lighting up all the heaven.

And as lightnings come suddenly in winter, so majestic men appeared [5] in glorious robes, an innumerable multitude, whose voice was heard as that of a very great thunder, crying out:

Jesus that was crucified is risen:

come up out of Hades, ye that have been enslaved in the underground regions of Hades.

And the chasm of the earth was as if it had no bottom; but it was as if the very foundations of the earth appeared along with those that cried out in the heavens, and walked about in the body in the midst of the dead that had risen.

And he that raised up all the dead, and bound Hades, said:

Say to my disciples, He goes before you into Galilee; there shall you see him.

And all that night the light did not cease shining.

And many of the Jews died, swallowed up in the chasm of the earth, so that on the following day most of those who had been against Jesus could not be found.

Others saw the appearing of those that had risen, whom no one of us had ever seen. [6] And only one [7] synagogue of the Jews was left in this Jerusalem, since all disappeared in that fall.

With that terror, being in perplexity, and seized with a most frightful trembling, I have written what I saw at that time, and have reported to thy majesty.

Having set in order also what was done by the Jews against Jesus, I have sent it, my lord, to thy divinity.

Footnotes:
1. Or, Augustus.
2. Or, Augustus.
3. Codex A has a better reading--arteries. [Thems. here referred to is in Paris, of the fourteenth century (a.d. 1315).--R.]
4. The text here is very corrupt.
5. Or, so men appeared on high.
6. This sentence also is very corrupt.
7. Another and more probably reading is, not one. [So B, a Parisms. of the fourteenth century.--R.]

The Report of Pontius Pilate, Procurator of Judaea,
Sent to Rome to Tiberius Caesar.

Second Greek Form

To the most mighty, venerable, awful, most divine, the august,--Pilatus Pontius, the governor of the East:

I have to report to thy reverence, through this writing of mine, being seized with great trembling and fear, O most mighty emperor, the conjuncture of the present times, as the end of these things has shown.

For while I, my lord, according to the commandment of thy clemency, was discharging the duties of my government, which is one of the cities of the East, Jerusalem by name, in which is built the temple of the Jewish nation, all the multitude of the Jews came together, and delivered to me a certain man named Jesus, bringing against him many and groundless charges; and they were not able to convict him in anything.

And one heresy of theirs against him was, that he said that the Sabbath was not their right rest.

And that man wrought many cures, in addition to good works.

He made the blind see; he cleansed lepers; he raised the dead; he healed paralytics who could not move at all, except that they only had their voice, and the joining of their bones; and he gave them the power of walking about and running, commanding them by a single word.

And another mightier work he did, which was strange even with our gods:

he raised up a dead man, Lazarus, who had been dead four days, by a single word ordering the dead man to be raised, although his body was already corrupted by the worms that grow in wounds; and that ill-smelling body lying in the tomb he ordered to run; and as a bridegroom from the bridal chamber, so he came forth out of the tomb, filled with exceeding fragrance.

And some that were cruelly vexed by demons, and had their dwellings in deserts, and ate the flesh of their own limbs, and lived along with reptiles and wild beasts, he made to be dwellers in cities in their own houses, and by a word he rendered them sound-minded; and he made those that were troubled by unclean spirits to be intelligent and reputable; and sending away the demons in them into a herd of swine, he suffocated them in the sea.

Another man, again, who had a withered hand, and lived in sorrow, and had not even the half of his body sound, he rendered sound by a single word.

And a woman that had a flow of blood for many years, so that, in consequence of the flowing of her blood, all the joinings of her bones appeared, and were transparent like glass; and assuredly all the physicians had left her without hope, and had not cleansed her, for there was not in her a single hope of health:

once, then, as Jesus was passing by, she took hold of the fringe of his clothes behind, and that same hour the power of her body was completely restored, and she became whole, as if nothing were the matter with her, and she began to run swiftly to her own city Paneas.[1]

And these things indeed were so.

And the Jews gave information that Jesus did these things on the Sabbath.

And I also ascertained that the miracles done by him were greater than any which the gods whom we worship could do.

Him then Herod and Archelaus and Philip, and Annas and Caiaphas, with all the people, delivered to me to try him.

And as many were exciting an insurrection against me, I ordered him to be crucified.

And when he had been crucified, there was darkness over the whole earth, the sun having been completely hidden, and the heaven appearing dark though it was day, so that the stars appeared, but had at the same time their brightness darkened, as I suppose your reverence is not ignorant of, because in all the world they lighted lamps from the sixth hour until evening.

And the moon, being like blood, did not shine the whole night, and yet she happened to be at the full.

And the stars also, and Orion, made a lament about the Jews, on account of the wickedness that had been done by them. [2]

And on the first of the week, about the third hour of the night, the sun was seen such as it had never at any time shone, and all the heaven was lighted up.

And as lightnings come on in winter, so majestic men of indescribable splendour of dress and of glory appeared in the air, and an innumerable multitude of angels crying out, and saying:

Glory in the highest to God, and on earth peace, among men goodwill:
come up out of Hades, ye who have been kept in slavery in the underground regions of Hades.

And at their voice all the mountains and hills were shaken, and the rocks were burst asunder; and great chasms were made in the earth, so that also what was in the abyss appeared.

And there were seen in that terror dead men raised up, [3] as the Jews that saw them said:

We have seen Abraham, and Isaac, and Jacob, and the twelve patriarchs, that died two thousand five hundred years ago; and we have seen Noah manifestly in the body.

And all the multitude walked about, and sang praises to God with aloud voice, saying:

The Lord our God that has risen from the dead has brought to life all the dead, and has plundered Hades, and put him to death.

All that night therefore, my lord, O king, the light ceased not.

And many of the Jews died, and were engulphed and swallowed up in the chasms in that night, so that not even their bodies appeared.

Those, I say, of the Jews suffered that had spoken against Jesus.

And one synagogue was left in Jerusalem, since all those synagogues that had been against Jesus were engulphed.

From that fear, then, being in perplexity, and seized with much trembling, at that same hour I ordered what had been done by them all to be written; and I have reported it to thy mightiness.

Footnotes:

1. This is a conjecture of Thilo's. Themss. have Spania.
2. Instead of this last sentence, one of the mss. has: And the whole world was shaken by unspeakable miracles, and all the creation was like to be swallowed up by the lower regions; so that also the sanctuary of their temple was rent from top to bottom. And again there was thunder, and a mighty noise from heaven, so that all our land shook and trembled. Another: And there began to be earthquakes in the hour in which the nails were fixed in Jesus' hands and feet, until evening.
3. One ms. adds: To the number of five hundred.

The Giving Up of Pontius Pilate

And the writings having come to the city of the Romans, and having been read to the Caesar, with not a few standing by, all were astounded, because through the wickedness of Pilate the darkness and the earthquake had come over the whole world.

And the Caesar, filled with rage, sent soldiers, and ordered them to bring Pilate a prisoner.

And when he was brought to the city of the Romans, the Caesar, hearing that Pilate had arrived, sat in the temple of the gods, in the presence of all the senate, and with all the army, and all the multitude of his power; and he ordered Pilate to stand forward. [1] And the Caesar says to him:

Why hast thou, O most impious, dared to do such things, having seen so great miracles in that man?

By daring to do an evil deed, thou hast destroyed the whole world.

And Pilate said:

O almighty [2] king, I am innocent of these things; but the multitude of the Jews are violent and guilty.

And the Caesar said:
And who are they?
Pilate says:
Herod, Archelaus, Philip, Annas and Caiaphas, and all the multitude of the Jews.
The Caesar says:
For what reason didst thou follow out their counsel?
And Pilate says:
Their nation is rebellious and insubmissive, not submitting themselves to thy power.
And the Caesar said:
When they delivered him to thee, thou oughtest to have made him secure, and to have sent

him to me, and not to have obeyed them in crucifying such a man, righteous as he was, and one that did such good miracles, as thou hast said in thy report.

For from such miracles Jesus was manifestly the Christ, the King of the Jews.

And as the Caesar was thus speaking, when he named the name of Christ, all the multitude of the gods fell down in a body, and became as dust, where the Caesar was sitting with the senate.

And the people standing beside the Caesar all began to tremble, on account of the speaking of the word, and the fall of their gods; and being seized with terror, they all went away, each to his own house, wondering at what had happened.

And the Caesar ordered Pilate to be kept in security, in order that he might know the truth about Jesus.

And on the following day, the Caesar, sitting in the Capitol with all the senate, tried again to question Pilate.

And the Caesar says:

Tell the truth, O most impious, because through thy impious action which thou hast perpetrated against Jesus, even here the doing of thy wicked deeds has been shown by the gods having been cast down.

Say, then, who is he that has been crucified; because even his name has destroyed all the gods?

Pilate said:

And indeed the records of him are true; for assuredly I myself was persuaded from his works that he was greater than all the gods whom we worship.

And the Caesar said:

For what reason, then, didst thou bring against him such audacity and such doings, if thou wert not ignorant of him, and altogether devising mischief against my kingdom?

Pilate said:

On account of the wickedness and rebellion of the lawless and ungodly Jews, I did this.

And the Caesar, being filled with rage, held a council with all his senate and his power, and ordered a decree to be written against the Jews as follows:--To Licianus, the governor of the chief places of the East, greeting.

The reckless deed which has been done at the present time by the inhabitants of Jerusalem, and the cities of the Jews round about, and their wicked action, has come to my knowledge, that they have forced Pilate to crucify a certain god named Jesus, and on account of this great fault of theirs the world has been darkened and dragged to destruction.

Do thou then speedily, with a multitude of soldiers, go to them there, and make them prisoners, in accordance with this decree.

Be obedient, and take action against them, and scatter them, and make them slaves among all the nations; and having driven them out of the whole of Judaea, make them the smallest of nations, so that it may not any longer be seen at all, because they are full of wickedness. [3]

And this decree having come into the region of the East, Licianus, obeying from fear of the decree, seized all the nation of the Jews; and those that were left in Judaea he scattered among the nations, and sold for slaves: [4]so that it was known to the Caesar that these things had been done by Licianus against the Jews in the region of the East; and it pleased him.

And again the Caesar set himself to question Pilate; and he orders a captain named Albius to cut off Pilate's head, saying:

Just as he laid hands upon the just man named Christ, in like manner also shall he fall, and not find safety.

And Pilate, going away to the place, prayed in silence, saying:

Lord, do not destroy me along with the wicked Hebrews, because I would not have laid hands upon Thee, except for the nation of the lawless Jews, because they were exciting rebellion against me.

But Thou knowest that I did it in ignorance.

Do not then destroy me for this my sin; but remember not evil against me, O Lord, and against Thy servant Procla, who is standing with me in this hour of my death, whom Thou didst appoint to prophesy that Thou shouldest be nailed to the cross.

Do not condemn her also in my sin; but pardon us, and make us to be numbered in the portion of Thy righteous.

And, behold, when Pilate had finished his prayer, there came a voice out of the heaven, saying:

All the generations and families of the nations shall count thee blessed, because under thee have been fulfilled all those things said about me by the prophets; and thou thyself shall be seen as my witness at my second appearing, when I shall judge the twelve tribes of Israel, and those that have not owned my name.

And the prefect struck off the head of Pilate; and, behold, an angel of the Lord received it.

And his wife Procla, seeing the angel coming and receiving his head, being filled with joy herself also, immediately gave up the ghost, and was buried along with her husband. [5]

Footnotes:

1. Or, in the entrance.
2. autokrator.
3. The text is very corrupt.
4. Lit., he made to be slaves in the dispersion of the Gentiles.
5. One of themss. adds: By the will and good pleasure of our Lord Jesus Christ, to whom be the glory of the Father, and the Son, and the Holy Ghost, now and ever, and to ages of ages. Amen.

The Death of Pilate, Who Condemned Jesus

And when Tiberius Caesar, the emperor of the Romans, was labouring under a grievous disease, and understanding that there was at Jerusalem a certain physician, Jesus by name, who by a single word cured all infirmities, he, not knowing that the Jews and Pilate had put Him to death, ordered a certain friend of his named Volusianus:

Go as quickly as possible across the seas; and thou shalt tell Pilate, my servant and friend, to send me this physician, that he may restore me to my former health.

And this Volusianus, having heard the emperor's command, immediately departed, and came to Pilate, as he had been commanded. And he related to the same Pilate what had been entrusted to him by Tiberius Caesar, saying:

Tiberius Caesar, the emperor of the Romans, thy master, having heard that in this city there is a physician who by his word alone heals infirmities, begs thee earnestly to send him to him for the curing of his infirmity.

Pilate, hearing this, was very much afraid, knowing that through envy he had caused Him to be put to death.

Pilate answered the same messenger thus, saying:

This man was a malefactor, and a man who drew to himself all the people; so a council of the wise men of the city was held, and I caused him to be crucified.

And this messenger returning to his inn, met a certain woman named Veronica, who had been a friend of Jesus; and he said:

O woman, a certain physician who was in this city, who cured the sick by a word alone, why have the Jews put him to death?

And she began to weep, saying:

Ah me! my lord, my God and my Lord, whom Pilate for envy delivered, condemned, and ordered to be crucified.

Then he, being exceedingly grieved, said:

I am vehemently grieved that I am unable to accomplish that for which my lord had sent me.

And Veronica said to him:

When my Lord was going about preaching, and I, much against my will, was deprived of His presence, I wished His picture to be painted for me, in order that, while I was deprived of His presence, the figure of His picture might at least afford me consolation.

And when I was carrying the canvas to the painter to be painted, my Lord met me, and asked whither I was going.

And when I had disclosed to Him the cause of my journey, He asked of me the cloth, and gave it back to me impressed with the image of His venerable face.

Therefore, if thy lord will devoutly gaze upon His face, [1] he shall obtain forthwith the benefit of health.

And he said to her:

Is a picture of such a sort procurable by gold or silver?

She said to him:

No; but by the pious influence of devotion.

I shall therefore set out with thee, and shall carry the picture to be seen by Caesar, and shall come back again.

Volusianus therefore came with Veronica to Rome, and said to Tiberius the emperor:

Jesus, whom thou hast been longing for, Pilate and the Jews have delivered to an unjust death, and have through envy affixed to the gibbet of the cross.

There has therefore come with me a certain matron, bringing a picture of Jesus himself; and if thou wilt devoutly look upon it, thou shalt immediately obtain the benefit of thy health. Caesar therefore ordered the way to be strewn with silk cloths, and the picture to be presented to him; and as soon as he had looked upon it, he regained his former health.

Pontius Pilate, therefore, by the command of Caesar, is taken and brought through to Rome.

Caesar, hearing that Pilate had arrived at Rome, was filled with exceeding fury against him, and caused him to be brought to him.

But Pilate brought down with him the seamless tunic of Jesus; and he wore it on him in presence of the emperor.

And as soon as the emperor saw him, he laid aside all his anger, and forthwith rose up to meet him.

Nor was he able to speak harshly to him in anything; and he who seemed so terrible and fierce in his absence, now in his presence is somehow found to be mild.

And when he had sent him away, immediately he blazed out against him terribly, crying out that he was a wretch, inasmuch as he had not at all shown him the fury of his heart.

And immediately he made him be called back, swearing and declaring that he was the son of death, and that it was infamous that he should live upon the earth.

And as soon as he saw him, he forthwith saluted him, and threw away all the ferocity of his mind.

All wondered; and he himself wondered that he should thus blaze out against Pilate when he was absent, and that while he was present he could say nothing to him roughly.

Then, by a divine impulse, or perhaps by the advice of some Christian, [2] he caused him to be stripped of that tunic, and immediately resumed against him his former ferocity of mind.

And when at this the emperor wondered very much, it was told him that that tunic had belonged to the Lord Jesus.

Then the emperor ordered him to be kept in prison, until he should deliberate in a council of the wise men what ought to be done with him.

And a few days after, sentence was therefore passed upon Pilate, that he should be condemned to the most disgraceful death.

Pilate, hearing this, killed himself with his own knife, and by such a death ended his life.

When Caesar knew of the death of Pilate, he said:

Truly he has died by a most disgraceful death, whom his own hand has not spared.

He is therefore bound to a great mass, and sunk into the river Tiber.

But malignant and filthy spirits in his malignant and filthy body, all rejoicing together, kept moving themselves in the waters, and in a terrible manner brought lightnings and tempests, thunders and hail-storms, in the air, so that all men were kept in horrible fear. Wherefore the Romans, drawing him out of the river Tiber, in derision carried him down to Vienna, and sunk him in the river Rhone.

For Vienna is called, as it were, Via Gehennae, the way of Gehenna, because it was then a place of cursing.

But there evil spirits were present, working the same things in the same place.

Those men therefore, not enduring such a visitation of demons, removed from themselves that vessel of malediction, and sent him to be buried in the territory of Losania. [3] And they, seeing that they were troubled by the aforesaid visitations, removed him from themselves, and sunk him in a certain pit surrounded by mountains, where to this day, according to the account of some, certain diabolical machinations are said to bubble up.

Footnotes:

1. Or, upon the sight of this.

2. This is the first appearance of the word Christian in these writings.

3. Losonium was the Roman name of Lausanne. For a discussion of this legend concerning Mont Pilate, near Lucerne, see Smith's Dictionary of the Bible, under Pilate.

The Narrative of Joseph

Narrative of Joseph of Arimathaea, That Begged the Lord's Body; In Which Also He Brings In the Cases of the Two Robbers.

Chapter 1

I am Joseph of Arimathaea, who begged from Pilate the body of the Lord Jesus for burial, and who for this cause was kept close in prison by the murderous and God-fighting [1] Jews, who also, keeping to the law, have by Moses himself become partakers in tribulation and having provoked their Lawgiver to anger, and not knowing that He was God, crucified Him and made Him manifest to those that knew God.

In those days in which they condemned the Son of God to be crucified, seven days before Christ suffered, two condemned robbers were sent from Jericho to the procurator Pilate; and their case was as follows:--

The first, his name Gestas, put travellers to death, murdering them with the sword, and others he exposed naked.

And he hung up women by the heels, head down, and cut off their breasts, and drank the blood of infants limbs, never having known God, not obeying the laws, being violent from the beginning, and doing such deeds.

And the case of the other was as follows:

He was called Demas, and was by birth a Galilaean, and kept an inn.

He made attacks upon the rich, but was good to the poor--a thief like Tobit, for he buried the bodies of the poor. [2] And he set his hand to robbing the multitude of the Jews, and stole the law [3] itself in Jerusalem, and stripped naked the daughter of Caiaphas, who was priestess of the sanctuary, and took away from its place the mysterious deposit itself placed there by Solomon.

Such were his doings.

And Jesus also was taken on the third day before the passover, in the evening.

And to Caiaphas and the multitude of the Jews it was not a passover, but it was a great mourning to them, on account of the plundering of the sanctuary by the robber.

And they summoned Judas Iscariot, and spoke to him, for he was son of the brother [4] of Caiaphas the priest.

He was not a disciple before the face of Jesus; but all the multitude of the Jews craftily supported him, that he might follow Jesus, not that he might be obedient to the miracles done by Him, nor that he might confess Him, but that he might betray Him to them, wishing to catch up some lying word of Him, giving him gifts for such brave, honest conduct to the amount of a half shekel of gold each day.

And he did this for two years with Jesus, as says one of His disciples called John.

And on the third day, before Jesus was laid hold of, Judas says to the Jews:

Come, let us hold a council; for perhaps it was not the robber that stole the law, but Jesus himself, and I accuse him.

And when these words had been spoken, Nicodemus, who kept the keys of the sanctuary, came in to us, and said to all:

Do not do such a deed.

For Nicodemus was true, more than all the multitude of the Jews.

And the daughter of Caiaphas, Sarah by name, cried out, and said:

He himself said before all against this holy place, I am able to destroy this temple, and in three days to raise it.

The Jews say to her:

Thou hast credit with all of us.

For they regarded her as a prophetess.

And assuredly, after the council had been held, Jesus was laid hold of.

Footnotes:

1. ms. C. has God-killing. [C is the designation given by Tischendorf to the ms. from which Birch made his edition of the text. It is in Paris; date a.d. 1315. Themss. which Tischendorf himself collated are designated A (in the Ambrosian library at Milan, of about the twelfth century), B (Paris, fifteenth century), D (Harleian codex, of the same century). Only a small part of the last ms. was used by Tischendorf; see his prolegomena. p. lxxxi.--R.]
2. Tobit i. 17, 18.
3. Perhaps the true reading is naon, and not nomon: plundered the temple.
4. ms. B has: And they say that he was of the family of the sister, etc.

Chapter 2

And on the following day, the fourth day of the week, they brought Him at the ninth hour into the hall of Caiaphas.

And Annas and Caiaphas say to Him:

Tell us, why hast thou stolen our law, and renounced [1] the ordinances of Moses and the prophets?

And Jesus answered nothing.

And again a second time, the multitude also being present, they say to Him:

The sanctuary which Solomon built in forty and six years, why dost thou wish to destroy in one moment?

And to these things Jesus answered nothing.

For the sanctuary of the synagogue had been plundered by the robber.

And the evening of the fourth day being ended, all the multitude sought to burn the daughter of Caiaphas, on account of the loss of the law; for they did not know how they were to keep the passover.

And she said to them:

Wait, my children, and let us destroy this Jesus, and the law will be found, and the holy feast will be fully accomplished.

And secretly Annas and Caiaphas gave considerable money to Judas Iscariot, saying:

Say as thou saidst to us before, I know that the law has been stolen by Jesus, that the accusation may be turned against him, and not against this maiden, who is free from blame.

And Judas having received this command, said to them:

Let not all the multitude know that I have been instructed by you to do this against Jesus; but release Jesus, and I persuade the multitude that it is so.

And craftily they released Jesus.

And Judas, going into the sanctuary at the dawn of the fifth day, says to all the people:

What will you give me, and I will give up to you the overthrower[2] of the law, and the plunderer of the prophets? The Jews say to him:

If thou wilt give him up to us, we will give thee thirty pieces of gold.

And the people did not know that Judas was speaking about Jesus, for many of them confessed that he was the Son of God.

And Judas received the thirty pieces of gold.

And going out at the fourth hour, and at the fifth, he finds Jesus walking in the street.

And as evening was coming on, Judas says to the Jews:

Give me the aid of soldiers with swords and staves, and I will give him up to you.

They therefore gave him officers for the purpose of seizing Him.

And as they were going along, Judas says to them:

Lay hold of the man whom I shall kiss, for he has stolen the law and the prophets.

Going up to Jesus, therefore, he kissed Him, saying:

Hail, Rabbi! it being the evening of the fifth day.

And having laid hold of Him, they gave Him up to Caiaphas and the chief priests, Judas saying: This is he who stole the law and the prophets.

And the Jews gave Jesus an unjust trial, saying:

Why hast thou done these things?

And he answered nothing.

And Nicodemus and I Joseph, seeing the seat of the plagues,[3] stood off from them, not wishing to perish along with the counsel of the ungodly.

Footnotes:

1. Tischendorf suggests aekrupsas, hidden, for apekeruxas.
2. Or, taker away.
3. Following the reading of the LXX. in Ps. i. 1.

Chapter 3

Having therefore done many and dreadful things against Jesus that night, they gave Him up to Pilate the procurator at the dawn of the preparation, that he might crucify Him; and for this purpose they all came together.

After a trial, therefore, Pilate the procurator ordered Him to be nailed to the cross, along with the two robbers.

And they were nailed up along with Jesus, Gestas on the left, and Demas on the right.

And he that was on the left began to cry out, saying to Jesus:

See how many evil deeds I have done in the earth; and if I had known that thou wast the king, I should have cut off thee also.

And why dost thou call thyself Son of God, and canst not help thyself in necessity? how canst thou afford it to another one praying for help?

If thou art the Christ, come down from the cross, that I may believe in thee.

But now I see thee perishing along with me, not like a man, but like a wild beast.

And many other things he began to say against Jesus, blaspheming and gnashing his teeth upon Him.

For the robber was taken alive in the snare of the devil. [1]

But the robber on the right hand, whose name was Demas, seeing the Godlike grace of Jesus, thus cried out:

I know Thee, Jesus Christ, that Thou art the Son of God.

I see Thee, Christ, adored by myriads of myriads of angels.

Pardon me my sins which I have done.

Do not in my trial make the stars come against me, or the moon, when Thou shalt judge all the world; because in the night I have accomplished my wicked purposes.

Do not urge the sun, which is now darkened on account of Thee, to tell the evils of my heart, for no gift can I give Thee for the remission of my sins.

Already death is coming upon me because of my sins; but Thine is the propitiation.

Deliver me, O Lord of all, from Thy fearful judgment.

Do not give the enemy power to swallow me up, and to become heir of my soul, as of that of him who is hanging on the left; for I see how the devil joyfully takes his soul, and his body disappears.

Do not even order me to go away into the portion of the Jews; for I see Moses and the patriarchs in great weeping, and the devil rejoicing over them.

Before, then, O Lord, my spirit departs, order my sins to be washed away, and remember me the sinner in Thy kingdom, when upon the great most lofty throne [2] thou shalt judge the twelve tribes of Israel. [3] For Thou hast prepared great punishment for Thy world on account of Thyself.

And the robber having thus spoken, Jesus says to him:

Amen, amen; I say to thee, Demas, that to-day thou shalt be with me in paradise. [4] And the sons of the kingdom, the children of Abraham, and Isaac, and Jacob, and Moses, shall be cast out into outer darkness; there shall be weeping and gnashing of teeth. [5] And thou alone shalt dwell in paradise until my second appearing, when I am to judge those who do not confess my name.

And He said to the robber:

Go away, and tell the cherubim and the powers, that turn the flaming sword, that guard paradise from the time that Adam, the first created, was in paradise, and sinned, and kept not my commandments, and I cast him out thence.

And none of the first shall see paradise until I am to come the second time to judge living and dead.

And He wrote thus:

Jesus Christ the Son of God, who have come down from the heights of the heavens, who have come forth out of the bosom of the invisible Father without being separated from Him, [6] and who have come down into the world to be made flesh, and to be nailed to a cross, in order that I might save Adam, whom I fashioned,--to my archangelic powers, the gatekeepers of paradise, to the officers of my Father:

I will and order that he who has been crucified along with me should go in, should receive remission of sins through me; and that he, having put on an incorruptible body, should go in to paradise, and dwell where no one has ever been able to dwell.

And, behold, after He had said this, Jesus gave up the ghost, on the day of the preparation, at the ninth hour.

And there was darkness over all the earth; and from a great earthquake that happened, the sanctuary fell down, and the wing of the temple.

The Forgotten Bible

Footnotes:
1. 2 Tim. ii. 26.
2. Or, upon the great throne of the Most High.
3. Matt. xix. 28.
4. Luke xxiii. 43.
5. Matt. viii. 11, 12.
6. Lit., inseparably.

Chapter 4

And I Joseph begged the body of Jesus, and put it in a new tomb, where no one had been put.

And of the robber on the right the body was not found; but of him on the left, as the form of a dragon, so was his body.

And after I had begged the body of Jesus to bury, the Jews, carried away by hatred and rage, shut me up in prison, where evil-doers were kept under restraint.

And this happened to me on the evening of the Sabbath, whereby our nation transgressed the law.

And, behold, that same nation of ours endured fearful tribulations on the Sabbath.

And now, on the evening of the first of the week, at the fifth hour of the night, Jesus comes to me in the prison, along with the robber who had been crucified with Him on the right, whom He sent into paradise. And there was a great light in the building.

And the house was hung up by the four corners, and the place was opened, and I came out.

Then I first recognised Jesus, and again the robber, bringing a letter to Jesus.

And as we were going into Galilee, there shone a great light, which the creation did not produce.

And there was also with the robber a great fragrance out of paradise.

And Jesus, having sat down in a certain place, thus read:

We, the cherubim and the six-winged, who have been ordered by Thy Godhead to watch the garden of paradise, make the following statement through the robber who was crucified along with Thee, by Thy arrangement:

When we saw the print of the nails of the robber crucified along with Thee, and the shining light of the letter of Thy Godhead, [1] the fire indeed was extinguished, not being able to bear the splendour of the print; [2] and we crouched down, being in great fear.

For we heard that the Maker of heaven and earth, and of the whole creation, had come down from on high to dwell in the lower parts of the earth, on account of Adam, the first created.

And when we beheld the undefiled cross shining like lightning from the robber, gleaming with sevenfold the light of the sun, trembling fell upon us.

We felt a violent shaking of the world below; [3] and with a loud voice, the ministers of Hades said, along with us:

Holy, holy, holy is He who in the beginning was in the highest.

And the powers sent up a cry:

O Lord, Thou hast been made manifest in heaven and in earth, bringing joy to the world; and, a greater gift than this, Thou hast freed Thine own image from death by the invisible purpose of the ages.

Footnotes:
1. Or, the shining light of the letter, the fire of the Godhead, we indeed were extinguished.
2. i.e., of the nails.
3. The text is here corrupt; but this seems to be the meaning.

Chapter 5

After I had beheld these things, as I was going into Galilee with Jesus and the robber, Jesus was transfigured, and was not as formerly, before He was crucified, but was altogether light; and angels always ministered to Him, and Jesus spoke with them.

And I remained with Him three days.

And no one of His disciples was with Him, except the robber alone.

And in the middle of the feast of unleavened bread, His disciple John comes, and we no longer beheld the robber as to what took place.

And John asked Jesus:

Who is this, that Thou hast not made me to be seen by him?

But Jesus answered him nothing.

And falling down before Him, he said:

Lord, I know that Thou hast loved me from the beginning, and why dost Thou not reveal to me that man?

Jesus says to him:

Why dost thou seek what is hidden?

Art thou still without understanding?

Dost thou not perceive the fragrance of paradise filling the place?

Dost thou not know who it is?

The robber on the cross has become heir of paradise.

Amen, amen; I say to thee, that it shall belong to him alone until that the great day shall come.

And John said:

Make me worthy to behold him.

And while John was yet speaking, the robber suddenly appeared; and John, struck with astonishment, fell to the earth.

And the robber was not in his first form, as before John came; but he was like a king in great power, having on him the cross.

And the voice of a great multitude was sent forth:

Thou hast come to the place prepared for thee in paradise.

We have been commanded by Him that has sent thee, to serve thee until the great day.

And after this voice, both the robber and I Joseph vanished, and I was found in my own house; and I no longer saw Jesus.

And I, having seen these things, have written them down, in order that all may believe in the crucified Jesus Christ our Lord, and may no longer obey the law of Moses, but may believe in the signs and wonders that have happened through Him, and in order that we who have believed may inherit eternal life, and be found in the kingdom of the heavens. For to Him are due glory, strength, praise, and majesty for ever and ever.

Amen.

The Forgotten Bible

The Avenging of the Saviour

This version of the legend of Veronica is written in very barbarous Latin, probably of the seventh or eighth century.

An Anglo-Saxon version, which Tischendorf concludes to be derived from the Latin, was edited and translated for the Cambridge Antiquarian Society, by C. W. Goodwin, in 1851.

The Anglo-Saxon text is from a ms. in the Cambridge Library, one of a number presented to the Cathedral of Exeter by Bishop Leofric in the beginning of the eleventh century.

The reader will observe that there are in this document two distinct legends, somewhat clumsily joined together--that of Nathan's embassy, and that of Veronica.

Here Beginneth the Avenging of the Saviour

In the days of the Emperor Tiberius Caesar, when Herod was tetrarch, Christ was delivered under Pontius Pilate by the Jews, and revealed by Tiberius.

In those days Titus [1] was a prince under Tiberius in the region of Equitania, in a city of Libia which is called Burgidalla.

And Titus had a sore in his right nostril, on account of a cancer, and he had his face torn even to the eye.

There went forth a certain man from Judaea, by name Nathan the son of Nahum; for he was an Ishmaelite who went from land to land, and from sea to sea, and in all the ends of the earth. Now Nathan was sent from Judaea to the Emperor Tiberius, to carry their treaty to the city of Rome.

And Tiberius was ill, and full of ulcers and fevers, and had nine kinds of leprosy.

And Nathan wished to go to the city of Rome.

But the north wind blew and hindered his sailing, and carried him down to the harbour of a city of Libia.

Now Titus, seeing the ship coming, knew that it was from Judaea; and they all wondered, and said that they had never seen any vessel so coming from that quarter.

And Titus ordered the captain to come to him, and asked him who he was.

And he said:

I am Nathan the son of Nahum, of the race of the Ishmaelites, and I am a subject of Pontius Pilate in Judaea.

And I have been sent to go to Tiberius the Roman emperor, to carry a treaty from Judaea.

And a strong wind came down upon the sea, and has brought me to a country that I do not know.

And Titus says:

If thou couldst at any time find anything either of cosmetics or herbs which could cure the wound that I have in my face, as thou seest, so that I should become whole, and regain my former health, I should bestow upon thee many good things.

And Nathan said to him:

I do not know, nor have I ever known, of such things as thou speakest to me about.

But for all that, if thou hadst been some time ago in Jerusalem, there thou wouldst have found a choice prophet, whose name was Emanuel, for He will save His people from their sins.

And He, as His first miracle in Cana of Galilee, made wine from water; and by His word He cleansed lepers, He enlightened the eyes of one born blind, He healed paralytics, He made demons flee, He raised up three dead; a woman caught in adultery, and condemned by the Jews to be stoned, He set free; and another woman, named Veronica, who suffered twelve years from an issue of blood, and came up to Him behind, and touched the fringe of His garment, He healed; and with five loaves and two fishes He satisfied five thousand men, to say nothing of little ones and women, and there remained of the fragments twelve baskets.

All these things, and many others, were accomplished before His passion.

After His resurrection we saw Him in the flesh as He had been before.

And Titus said to Him:

How did he rise again from the dead, seeing that he was dead?

And Nathan answered and said:

He was manifestly dead, and hung up on the cross, and again taken down from the cross, and for three days He lay in the tomb:

thereafter He rose again from the dead, and went down to Hades, and freed the patriarchs and the prophets, and the whole human race; thereafter He appeared to His disciples, and ate with them; thereafter they saw Him going up into heaven.

And so it is the truth, all this that I tell you.

For I saw it with my own eyes, and all the house of Israel.

And Titus said in his own words:

Woe to thee, O Emperor Tiberius, full of ulcers, and enveloped in leprosy, because such a scandal has been committed in thy kingdom; because thou hast made such laws [2] in Judaea, in the land of the birth of our Lord Jesus Christ, and they have seized the King, and put to death the Ruler of the peoples; and they have not made Him come to us to cure thee of thy leprosy, and cleanse me from mine infirmity:

on which account, if they had been before my face, with my own hands I should have slain the carcases of those Jews, and hung them up on the cruel tree, because they have destroyed my Lord, and mine eyes have not been worthy to see His face.

And when he had thus spoken, immediately the wound fell from the face of Titus, and his flesh and his face were restored to health.

And all the sick who were in the same place were made whole in that hour.

And Titus cried out, and all the rest with him, in a loud voice, saying:

My King and my God, because I have never seen Thee, and Thou hast made me whole, bid me go with the ship over the waters to the land of Thy birth, to take vengeance on Thine enemies; and help me, O Lord, that I may be able to destroy them, and avenge Thy death:

do Thou, Lord, deliver them into my hand.

And having thus spoken, he ordered that he should be baptized.

And he called Nathan to him, and said to him:

How hast thou seen those baptized who believe in Christ?

Come to me, and baptize me in the name of the Father, and of the Son, and of the Holy Ghost. Amen. [3] For I also firmly believe in the Lord Jesus Christ with all my heart, and with all my soul; because nowhere in the whole world is there another who has created me, and made me whole from my wounds.

And having thus spoken, he sent messengers to Vespasian to come with all haste with his bravest men, so prepared as if for war.

Then Vespasian brought with him five thousand armed men, and they went to meet Titus.

And when they had come to the city of Libia, he said to Titus:

Why is it that thou hast made me come hither?

And he said: Know that Jesus has come into this world, and has been born in Judaea, in a place which is called Bethlehem, and has been given up by the Jews, and scourged, and crucified on Mount Calvary,[4] and has risen again from the dead on the third day.

And His disciples have seen Him in the same flesh in which he was born, and He has shown Himself to His disciples, and they have believed in Him.

And we indeed wish to become His disciples.

Now, let us go and destroy His enemies from the earth, that they may now know that there is none like the Lord our God on the face of the earth.

With this design, then, they went forth from the city of Libia which is called Burgidalla, [5] and went on board a ship, and proceeded to Jerusalem, and surrounded the kingdom of the Jews, and began to send them to destruction.

And when the kings of the Jews heard of their doings, and the wasting of their land, fear came upon them, and they were in great perplexity.

Then Archelaus [6] was perplexed in his words, and said to his son:

My son, take my kingdom and judge it; and take counsel with the other kings who are in the land of Judah, that you may be able to escape from our enemies.

And having thus said, he unsheathed his sword and leant upon it; and turned his sword, which was very sharp, and thrust it into his breast, and died.

And his son allied himself with the other kings who were under him, and they took counsel among themselves, and went into Jerusalem with their chief men who were in their counsel, and stood in the same place seven years. And Titus and Vespasian took counsel to surround their city.

And they did so.

And the seven years being fulfilled, there was a very sore famine, and for want of bread they began to eat earth.

Then all the soldiers who were of the four kings took counsel among themselves, and said:

Now we are sure to die:

The Forgotten Bible

what will God do to us? or of what good is our life to us, because the Romans have come to take our place and nation?

It is better for us to kill each other, than that the Romans should say that they have slain us, and gained the victory over us. And they drew their swords and smote themselves, and died, to the number of twelve thousand men of them.

Then there was a great stench in that city from the corpses of those dead men.

And their kings feared with a very great fear even unto death; and they could not bear the stench of them, nor bury them, nor throw them forth out of the city.

And they said to each other:

What shall we do?

We indeed gave up Christ to death, and now we given up to death ourselves.

Let us bow our heads, and give up the keys of the city to the Romans, because God has already given us up to death.

And immediately they went up upon the walls of the city, and all cried out with a loud voice, saying: Titus and Vespasian, take the keys of the city, which have been given to you by Messiah, who is called Christ.

Then they gave themselves up into the hands of Titus and Vespasian, and said:

Judge us, seeing that we ought to die, because we judged Christ; and he was given up without cause.

Titus and Vespasian seized them, and some they stoned, and some they hanged on a tree, feet up and head down, and struck them through with lances; and others they gave up to be sold, and others they divided among themselves, and made four parts of them, just as they had done of the garments of the Lord.

And they said:

They sold Christ for thirty pieces of silver, and we shall sell thirty of them for one denarius.

And so they did.

And having done so, they seized all the lands of Judaea and Jerusalem.

Then they made a search about the face or portrait [7] of Jesus, how they might find it. [8]And they found a woman named Veronica who had it.

Then they seized Pilate, and sent him to prison, to be guarded by four quaternions of soldiers at the door of the prison.

Then they forthwith sent their messengers to Tiberius, the emperor of the city of Rome, that he should send Velosianus to them.

And he said to him: Take all that is necessary for thee in the sea, and go down into Judaea, and seek out one of the disciples of him who is called Christ and Lord, that he may come to me, and in the name of his God cure me of the leprosy and the infirmities by which I am daily exceedingly burdened, and of my wounds, because I am ill at ease.

And send upon the kings of the Jews, who are subject to my authority, thy forces and terrible engines, because they have put to death Jesus Christ our Lord, and condemn them to death.

And if thou shalt there find a man as may be able to free me from this infirmity of mine, I will believe in Christ the Son of God, and will baptize myself in his name.

And Velosianus said:

My lord emperor, if I find such a man as may be able to help and free us, what reward shall I promise him?

Tiberius said to him: The half of my kingdom, without fail, to be in his hand.

Then Velosianus immediately went forth, and went on board the ship, and hoisted the sail in the vessel, and went on sailing through the sea. And he sailed a year and seven days, after which he arrived at Jerusalem.

And immediately he ordered some of the Jews to come to his power, and began carefully to ask what had been the acts of Christ. Then Joseph, of the city of Arimathaea, and Nicodemus, came at the same time.

And Nicodemus said:

I saw Him, and I know indeed that He is the Saviour of the world.

And Joseph said to him:

And I took Him down from the cross, and laid Him in a new tomb, which had been cut out of the rock.

And the Jews kept me shut up on the day of the preparation, at evening; and while I was standing in prayer on the Sabbath-day, the house was hung up by the four corners, and I saw the Lord Jesus Christ like a gleam of light, and for fear I fell to the ground.

And He said to me, Look upon me, for I am Jesus, whose body thou buriedst in thy tomb.

And I said to Him, Show me the sepulchre where I laid Thee.

And Jesus, holding my hand in His right hand, led me to the place where I buried Him. [9]

And there came also the woman named Veronica, and said to him:

And I touched in the crowd the fringe of His garment, because for twelve years I had suffered from an issue of blood; and He immediately healed me.

Then Velosianus said to Pilate:

Thou, Pilate, impious and cruel, why hast thou slain the Son of God?

And Pilate answered:

His own nation, and the chief priests Annas and Caiaphas, gave him to me. Velosianus said:

Impious and cruel, thou art worthy of death and cruel punishment.

And he sent him back to prison.

And Velosianus at last sought for the face or the countenance of the Lord.

And all who were in that same place said:

It is the woman called Veronica who has the portrait of the Lord in her house.

And immediately he ordered her to be brought before his power.

And he said to her:

Hast thou the portrait of the Lord in thy house?

But she said, No.

Then Velosianus ordered her to be put to the torture, until she should give up the portrait of the Lord.

And she was forced to say:

I have it in clean linen, my lord, and I daily adore it.

Velosianus said:

Show it to me.

Then she showed the portrait of the Lord.

When Velosianus saw it, he prostrated himself on the ground; and with a ready heart and true faith he took hold of it, and wrapped it in cloth of gold, and placed it in a casket, and sealed it with his ring.

And he swore with an oath, and said:

As the Lord God liveth, and by the health of Caesar, no man shall any more see it upon the face of the earth, until I see the face of my lord Tiberius.

And when he had thus spoken, the princes, who were the chief men of Judaea, seized Pilate to take him to a seaport.

And he took the portrait of the Lord, with all His disciples, and all in his pay, and they went on board the ship the same day.

Then the woman Veronica, for the love of Christ, left all that she possessed, and followed Velosianus.

And Velosianus said to her: What dost thou wish, woman, or what dost thou seek?

And she answered: I am seeking the portrait of our Lord Jesus Christ, who enlightened me, not for my own merits, but through His own holy affection. [10] Give back to me the portrait of my Lord Jesus Christ; for because of this I die with a righteous longing.

But if thou do not give it back to me, I will not leave it until I see where thou wilt put it, because I, most miserable woman that I am, will serve Him all the days of my life; because I believe that He, my Redeemer, liveth for everlasting.

Then Velosianus ordered the woman Veronica to be taken down with him into the ship.

And the sails being hoisted, they began to go in the vessel in the name of the Lord, and they sailed through the sea.

But Titus, along with Vespasian, went up into Judaea, avenging all nations upon their land.

[11] At the end of a year Velosianus came to the city of Rome, brought his vessel into the river which is called Tiberis, or Tiber, and entered the city which is called Rome.

And he sent his messenger to his lord Tiberius the emperor in the Lateran about his prosperous arrival.

Then Tiberius the emperor, when he heard the message of Velosianus, rejoiced greatly, and ordered him to come before his face.

And when he had come, he called him, saying:

Velosianus, how hast thou come, and what hast thou seen in the region of Judaea of Christ the Lord and his disciples?

Tell me, I beseech thee, that he is going to cure me of mine infirmity, that I may be at once cleansed from that leprosy which I have over my body, and I give up my whole kingdom into thy power and his.

And Velosianus said:

My lord emperor, I found thy servants Titus and Vespasian in Judaea fearing the Lord, and they were cleansed from all their ulcers and sufferings.

And I found that all the kings and rulers of Judaea have been hanged by Titus; Annas and

Caiaphas have been stoned, Archelaus has killed himself with his own lance; and I have sent Pilate to Damascus in bonds, and kept him in prison under safe keeping.

But I have also found out about Jesus, whom the Jews most wickedly attacked with swords, and staves, and weapons; and they crucified him who ought to have freed and enlightened us, and to have come to us, and they hanged him on a tree.

And Joseph came from Arimathaea, and Nicodemus with him, bringing a mixture of myrrh and aloes, about a hundred pounds, to anoint the body of Jesus; and they took him down from the cross, and laid him in a new tomb.

And on the third day he most assuredly rose again from the dead, and showed himself to his disciples in the same flesh in which he had been born. At length, after forty days, they saw him going up into heaven.

Many, indeed, and other miracles did Jesus before his passion and after. First, of water he made wine; he raised the dead, he cleansed lepers, he enlightened the blind, he cured paralytics, he put demons to flight; he made the deaf hear, the dumb speak; Lazarus, when four days dead, he raised from the tomb; the woman Veronica, who suffered from an issue of blood twelve years, and touched the fringe of his garment, he made whole.

Then it pleased the Lord in the heavens, that the Son of God, who, sent into this world as the first-created, had died upon earth, should send his angel; and he commanded Titus and Vespasian, whom I knew in that place where thy throne is.

And it pleased God Almighty that they went into Judaea and Jerusalem, and seized thy subjects, and put them under that sentence, as it were, in the same manner as they did when thy subjects seized Jesus and bound him.

And Vespasian afterwards said:

What shall we do about those who shall remain?

Titus answered:

They hanged our Lord on a green tree, and struck him with a lance; now let us hang them on a dry tree, and pierce their bodies through and through with the lance.

And they did so.

And Vespasian said:

What about those who are left?

Titus answered:

They seized the tunic of our Lord Jesus Christ, and of it made four parts; now let us seize them, and divide them into four parts,--to thee one, to me one, to thy men another, and to my servants the fourth part.

And they did so.

And Vespasian said:

But what shall we do about those who are left?

Titus answered him:

The Jews sold our Lord for thirty pieces of silver:

now let us sell thirty of them for one piece of silver.

And they did so.

And they seized Pilate, and gave him up to me, and I put him in prison, to be guarded by four quaternions of soldiers in Damascus.

Then they made a search with great diligence to seek the portrait of the Lord; and they found a woman named Veronica who had the portrait of the Lord.

Then the Emperor Tiberius said to Velosianus: How hast thou it?

And he answered:

I have it in clean cloth of gold, rolled up in a shawl.

And the Emperor Tiberius said:

Bring it to me, and spread it before my face, that I, falling to the ground and bending my knees, may adore it on the ground.

Then Velosianus spread out his shawl with the cloth of gold on which the portrait of the Lord had been imprinted; and the Emperor Tiberius saw it.

And he immediately adored the image of the Lord with a pure heart, and his flesh was cleansed as the flesh of a little child.

And all the blind, the lepers, the lame, the dumb, the deaf, and those possessed by various diseases, who were there present, were healed, and cured, and cleansed.

And the Emperor Tiberius bowed his head and bent his knees, considering that saying: Blessed is the womb which bore Thee, and the breasts which Thou hast sucked; and he groaned to the Lord, saying with tears:

God of heaven and earth, do not permit me to sin, but confirm my soul and my body, and place me in Thy kingdom, because in Thy name do I trust always: free me from all evils, as Thou didst free the three children from the furnace of blazing fire.

Then said the Emperor Tiberius to Velosianus:

Velosianus, hast thou seen any of those men who saw Christ?

Velosianus answered:

I have. He said:

Didst thou ask how they baptize those who believed in Christ?

Velosianus said:

Here, my Lord, we have one of the disciples of Christ himself.

Then he ordered Nathan to be summoned to come to him.

Nathan therefore came and baptized him in the name of the Father, and of the Son, and of the Holy Ghost.

Amen.

Immediately the Emperor Tiberius, made whole from all his diseases, ascended upon his throne, and said:

Blessed art Thou, O Lord God Almighty, and worthy to be praised, who hast freed me from the snare of death, and cleansed me from all mine iniquities; because I have greatly sinned before Thee, O Lord my God, and I am not worthy to see Thy face.

And then the Emperor Tiberius was instructed in all the articles of the faith, fully, and with strong faith.

May that same God Almighty, who is King of kings and Lord of lords, Himself shield us in His faith, and defend us, and deliver us from all danger and evil, and deign to bring us to life everlasting, when this life, which is temporary, shall fail; who is blessed for ever and ever.

Amen.

Footnotes:

1. The Saxon version has Tirus.
2. Reges, kings, instead of leges, as suggested by Mr. Cowper, is a much better reading.
3. Sax.: Then Nathan came, and baptized him in the name of the Father, and the Son, and the Holy Ghost, and took away from him his name of Tirus, and called him in his baptism Titus, which is in our language Pius.
4. Note this popular but erroneous appellation of Mount.
5. Sax. omits which is called Burgidalla.
6. Sax.: And Herod the king was so terrified, that he said to Archelaus his son.
7. Lit., countenance.
8. Sax.: And they inquired diligently whether perchance there were there any one who had miraculous relics of the Saviour, of His clothing, or other precious things; and they sought so diligently, that they found a woman, etc.
9. In the Saxon, Joseph's speech is: I know that they took Him down from the cross, and laid Him in the tomb which I had cut out of the rock. And I was one of those who guarded His tomb: and I bent my head and thought I should see Him, but I beheld nothing of Him, but saw two angels, one at the head and the other at the foot, and they asked me whom I was seeking. I answered and said to them, I seek Jesus who was crucified. Again they said to me, Go into Galilee; there shall you see Him, as He said to you before.
10. A few lines of the text are here very corrupt, and are omitted by Tischendorf. The meaning of them is: And woe's me, because, contrary to the law, thou hast treated me most unjustly. Ah! woe's me, because thou hast taken my Lord from me; just as the Jews did contrary to the law in crucifying in this world the Lord Jesus Christ, whom the eyes of your Caesar have not seen. But woe's me! have I done contrary to the law? Have I deserved to suffer this punishment?
11. Or, taking vengeance upon all the nations of their land.

Acts of the Holy Apostles Peter and Paul

It came to pass, after Paul went out of the island Gaudomeleta, [1] that he came to Italy; and it was heard of by the Jews who were in Rome, the elder of the cities, that Paul demanded to come to Caesar. Having fallen, therefore, into great grief and much despondency, they said among themselves:

It does not please him that he alone has afflicted all our brethren and parents in Judaea and Samaria, and in all Palestine; and he has not been pleased with these, but, behold, he comes here also, having through imposition asked Caesar to destroy us.

Having therefore made an assembly against Paul, and having considered many proposals, [2] it seemed good to them to go to Nero the emperor, to ask him not to allow Paul to come to Rome.

Having therefore got in readiness not a few presents, and having carried them with them, with supplication they came before him, saying:

We beseech thee, O good emperor, send orders into all the governments of your worship, to the effect that Paul is not to come near these parts; because this Paul, having afflicted all the nation of our fathers, has been seeking to come hither to destroy us also.

And the affliction, O most worshipful emperor, which we have from Peter is enough for us.

And the Emperor Nero, having heard these things, answered them:

It is [3] according to your wish.

And we write to all our governments that he shall not on any account come to anchor in the parts of Italy. And they also informed Simon the magian, having sent for him, that, as has been said, he should not come into the parts of Italy.

And while they were thus doing, some of those that had repented out of the nations, and that had been baptized at the preaching of Peter, sent elders to Paul with a letter to the following effect:

Paul, dear servant of our Lord Jesus Christ, and brother of Peter, the first of the apostles, we have heard from the rabbis of the Jews that are in this Rome, the greatest of the cities, that they have asked Caesar to send into all his governments, in order that, wherever thou mayst be found, thou mayst be put to death.

But we have believed, and do believe, that as God does not separate the two great lights which He has made, so He is not to part you from each other, that is, neither Peter from Paul, nor Paul from Peter; but we positively believe in our Lord Jesus Christ, into whom we have been baptized, that we have become worthy also of your teaching.

And Paul, having received the two men sent with the letter on the twentieth of the month of May, became eager to go, and gave thanks to the Lord and Master Jesus Christ.

And having sailed from Gaudomeleta, he did not now come through Africa to the parts of Italy, but ran to Sicily, until he came to the city of Syracuse with the two men who had been sent from Rome to him.

And having sailed thence, he came to Rhegium of Calabria, and from Rhegium he crossed to Mesina, and there ordained a bishop, Bacchylus by name.

And when he came out of Mesina he sailed to Didymus, and remained there one night.

And having sailed thence, he came to Pontiole [4] on the second day.

And Dioscorus the shipmaster, who brought him to Syracuse, sympathizing with Paul because he had delivered his son from death, having left his own ship in Syracuse, accompanied him to Pontiole.

And some of Peter's disciples having been found there, and having received Paul, exhorted him to stay with them.

And he stayed a week, in hiding, because of the command of Caesar.

And all the toparchs were watching to seize and kill him.

But Dioscorus the shipmaster, being himself also bald, wearing his shipmaster's dress, and speaking boldly, on the first day went out into the city of Pontiole.

Thinking therefore that he was Paul, they seized him, and beheaded him, and sent his head to Caesar.

Caesar therefore, having summoned the first men of the Jews, announced to them, saying:

Rejoice with great joy, for Paul your enemy is dead. And he showed them the head.

Having therefore made great rejoicing on that day, which was the fourteenth of the month of June, each of the Jews fully believed it.

And Paul, being in Pontiole, and having heard that Dioscorus had been beheaded, being grieved with great grief, gazing into the height of the heaven, said:

O Lord Almighty in heaven, who hast appeared to me in every place whither I have gone on account of Thine only-begotten Word, our Lord Jesus Christ, punish this city, and bring out all who have believed in God and followed His word.

He said to them therefore: Follow me:

And going forth from Pontiole with those who had believed in the word of God, they came to a place called Baias;[5] and looking up with their eyes, they all see that city called Pontiole sunk into the sea-shore about one fathom; and there it is until this day, for a remembrance, under the sea.

And having gone forth from Baias, they went to Gaitas, and there he taught the word of God.

And he stayed there three days in the house of Erasmus, whom Peter sent from Rome to teach the Gospel of God.

And having come forth from Gaitas, he came to the castle called Taracinas, and stayed there seven days in the house of Caesarius the deacon, whom Peter had ordained by the laying on of hands.

And sailing thence, he came by the river to a place called Tribus Tabernes.

And those who had been saved out of the city of Pontiole that had been swallowed up, reported to Caesar in Rome that Pontiole had been swallowed up, with all its multitude.

And the emperor, being in great grief on account of the city, having summoned the chief of the Jews, said to them:

Behold, on account of what I heard from you, I have caused Paul to be beheaded, and on account of this the city has been swallowed up.

And the chief of the Jews said to Caesar:

Most worshipful emperor, did we not say to thee that he troubled all the country of the East, and perverted our fathers?

It is better therefore, most worshipful emperor, that one city be destroyed, and not the seat of thine empire; for this had Rome to suffer.

And the emperor, having heard their words, was appeased.

And Paul stayed in Tribus Tabernes four days.

And departing thence, he came to Appii Forum, which is called Vicusarape; and having slept there that night, he saw one sitting on a golden chair, and a multitude of blacks standing beside him, saying:

I have to-day made a son murder his father.

Another said:

And I have made a house fall, and kill parents with children.

And they reported to him many evil deeds--some of one kind, some of another.

And another coming, reported to him:

I have managed that the bishop Juvenalius, whom Peter ordained, should sleep with the abbess Juliana.

And having heard all these things when sleeping in that Appii Forum, near Vicusarape, straightway and immediately he sent to Rome one of those who had followed him from Pontiole to the bishop Juvenalius, telling him this same thing which had just been done.

And on the following day, Juvenalius, running, threw himself at the feet of Peter, weeping and lamenting, and saying what had just befallen; and he recounted to him the matter, and said: I believe that this is the light which thou wast awaiting.

And Peter said to him:

How is it possible that it is he when he is dead?

And Juvenalius the bishop took to Peter him that had been sent by Paul, and he reported to him that he was alive, and on his way, and that he was at Appii Forum.

And Peter thanked and glorified the God and Father of our Lord Jesus Christ.

Then having summoned his disciples that believed, he sent them to Paul as far as Tribus Tabernes.

And the distance from Rome to Tribus Tabernes is thirty-eight miles.[6] And Paul seeing them, having given thanks to our Lord Jesus Christ, took courage; and departing thence, they slept in the city called Aricia.

And a report went about in the city of Rome that Paul the brother of Peter was coming.

And those that believed in God rejoiced with great joy.

And there was great consternation among the Jews; and having gone to Simon the magian,

The Forgotten Bible

they entreated him, saying:

Report to the emperor that Paul is not dead, but that he is alive, and has come.

And Simon said to the Jews:

What head is it, then, which came to Caesar from Pontiole?

Was it not bald also?

And Paul having come to Rome, great fear fell upon the Jews.

They came together therefore to him, and exhorted him, saying:

Vindicate the faith in which thou wast born; for it is not right that thou, being a Hebrew, and of the Hebrews, shouldst call thyself teacher of Gentiles, and vindicator of the uncircumcised; and, being thyself circumcised, that thou shouldst bring to nought the faith of the circumcision. [7]And when thou seest Peter, contend against his teaching, because he has destroyed all the bulwarks of our law; for he has prevented the keeping of Sabbaths and new moons, and the holidays appointed by the law.

And Paul, answering, said to them:

That I am a true Jew, by this you can prove; because also you have been able to keep the Sabbath, and to observe the true circumcision; for assuredly on the day of the Sabbath God rested from all His works.

We have fathers, and patriarchs, and the law.

What, then, does Peter preach in the kingdom of the Gentiles?

But if he shall wish to bring in any new teaching, without any tumult, and envy, and trouble, send him word, that we may see, and in your presence I shall convict him.

But if his teaching be true, supported by the book and testimony of the Hebrews, it becomes all of us to submit to him.

Paul saying these and such like things, the Jews went and said to Peter:

Paul of the Hebrews has come, and entreats thee to come to him, since those who have brought him say that he cannot meet whomsoever he may wish until he appear before Caesar.

And Peter having heard, rejoiced with great joy; and rising up, immediately went to him.

And seeing each other, they wept for joy; and long embracing each other, they bedewed each other with tears.

And when Paul had related to Peter the substance [8] of all his doings, and how, through the disasters of the ship, he had come, Peter also told him what he had suffered from Simon the magian, and all his plots.

And having told these things, he went away towards evening.

And in the morning of the following day, at dawn, behold, Peter coming, finds a multitude of the Jews before Paul's door.

And there was a great uproar between the Christian Jews and the Gentiles.

For, on the one hand, the Jews said:

We are a chosen race, a royal priesthood, the friends of Abraham, and Isaac, and Jacob, and all the prophets, with whom God spake, to whom He showed His own mysteries and His great wonders.

But you of the Gentiles are no great thing in your lineage; if otherwise, you have become polluted and abominable by idols and graven images.

While the Jews were saying such things, and such-like, those of the Gentiles answered, saying:

We, when we heard the truth, straightway followed it, having abandoned our errors.

But you, both knowing the mighty deeds of your fathers, and seeing the signs of the prophets, and having received the law, and gone through the sea with dry feet, and seen your enemies sunk in its depths, and the pillar of fire by night and of cloud by day shining upon you, and manna having been given to you out of heaven, and water flowing to you out of a rock,--after all these things you fashioned to yourselves the idol of a calf, and worshipped the graven image.

But we, having seen none of the signs, believe to be a Saviour the God whom you have forsaken in unbelief.

While they were contending in these and such-like words, the Apostle Paul said that they ought not to make such attacks upon each other, but that they should rather give heed to this, that God had fulfilled His promises which He swore to Abraham our father, that in his seed he should inherit all the nations. [9]For there is no respect of persons with God. [10]As many as have sinned in law shall be judged according to law, and as many as have sinned without law shall perish without law. [11]But we, brethren, ought to thank God that, according to His mercy, He has chosen us to be a holy people to Himself:

so that in this we ought to boast, whether Jews or Greeks; for you are all one in the belief of His name.

And Paul having thus spoken, both the Jews and they of the Gentiles were appeased.

But the rulers of the Jews assailed Peter.

And Peter, when they accused him of having renounced their synagogues, said: Hear, brethren, the holy Spirit about the patriarch David, promising, Of the fruit of thy womb shall He set upon thy throne. [12]Him therefore to whom the Father said, Thou art my Son, this day have I begotten Thee, the chief priests through envy crucified; but that He might accomplish the salvation of the world, it was allowed that He should suffer all these things. [13]Just as, therefore, from the side of Adam Eve was created, so also from the side of Christ was created the Church, which has no spot nor blemish.

In Him, [14] therefore, God has opened an entrance to all the sons of Abraham, and Isaac, and Jacob, in order that they may be in the faith of profession towards Him, [15] and have life and salvation in His name.

Turn, therefore, and enter into the joy of your father Abraham, because God hath fulfilled what He promised to him.

Whence also the prophet says, The Lord hath sworn, and will not repent:

Thou art a priest for ever, after the order of Melchizedec. [16]For a priest He became upon the cross, when He offered the whole burnt-offering of His own body and blood as a sacrifice for all the world.

And Peter saying this and such-like, the most part of the people believed.

And it happened also that Nero's wife Libia, and the yoke-fellow of Agrippa the prefect, Agrippina by name, thus believed, so that also they went away from beside their own husbands.

And on account of the teaching of Paul, many, despising military life, clung to God; so that even from the emperor's bed-chamber some came to him, and having become Christians, were no longer willing to return to the army or the palace.

When, consequently, the people were making a seditious murmuring, Simon, moved with zeal, rouses himself, and began to say many evil things about Peter, saying that he was a wizard and a cheat.

And they believed him, wondering at his miracles; for he made a brazen serpent move itself, and stone statues to laugh and move themselves, and himself to run and suddenly to be raised into the air.

But as a set-off to these, Peter healed the sick by a word, by praying made the blind to see, put demons to flight by a command; sometimes he even raised the dead.

And he said to the people that they should not only flee from Simon's deceit, but also that they should expose him, that they might not seem to be slaves to the devil.

And thus it happened that all pious men abhorred Simon the magian, and proclaimed him impious.

But those who adhered to Simon strongly affirmed Peter to be a magian, bearing false witness as many of them as were with Simon the magian; so that the matter came even to the ears of Nero the Caesar, and he gave order to bring Simon the magian before him.

And he, coming in, stood before him, and began suddenly to assume different forms, so that on a sudden he became a child, and after a little an old man, and at other times a young man; for he changed himself both in face and stature into different forms, and was in a frenzy, having the devil as his servant.

And Nero beholding this, supposed him to be truly the son of God; but the Apostle Peter showed him to be both a liar and a wizard, base and impious and apostate, and in all things opposed to the truth of God, and that nothing yet remained except that his wickedness, being made apparent by the command of God, might be made manifest to them all.

Then Simon, having gone in to Nero, said:

Hear, O good emperor:

I am the son of God come down from heaven.

Until now I have endured Peter only calling himself an apostle; but now he has doubled the evil:

for Paul also himself teaches the same things, and having his mind turned against me, is said to preach along with him; in reference to whom, if thou shalt not contrive their destruction, it is very plain that thy kingdom cannot stand.

Then Nero, filled with concern, ordered to bring them speedily before him.

And on the following day Simon the magian, and Peter and Paul the apostles of Christ, having come in to Nero, Simon said:

These are the disciples of the Nazarene, and it is not at all well that they should be of the people of the Jews, Nero said:

What is a Nazarene?

Simon said:

There is a city of Judah which has always been opposed to us, called Nazareth, and to it the

The Forgotten Bible

teacher of these men belonged.

Nero said:

God commands us to love every man; why, then, dost thou persecute them?

Simon said:

This is a race of men who have turned aside all Judaea from believing in me.

Nero said to Peter:

Why are you thus unbelieving, according to your race? [17]Then Peter said to Simon:

Thou hast been able to impose upon all, but upon me never; and those who have been deceived, God has through me recalled from their error.

And since thou hast learned by experience that thou canst not get the better of me, I wonder with what face thou boastest thyself before the emperor, and supposest that through thy magic art thou shalt overcome the disciples of Christ.

Nero said:

Who is Christ?

Peter said:

He is what this Simon the magian affirms himself to be; but this is a most wicked man, and his works are of the devil.

But if thou wishest to know, O good emperor, the things that have been done in Judaea about Christ, take the writings of Pontius Pilate sent to Claudius, and thus thou wilt know all.

And Nero ordered them to be brought, and to be read in their presence; and they were to the following effect: [18] --

Pontius Pilate to Claudius, greeting.

There has lately happened an event which I myself was concerned in.

For the Jews through envy have inflicted on themselves, and those coming after them, dreadful judgments.

Their fathers had promises that their God would send them his holy one from heaven, who according to reason should be called their king, and he had promised to send him to the earth by means of a virgin.

He, then, when I was procurator, came into Judaea.

And they saw [19] him enlightening the blind, cleansing lepers, healing paralytics, expelling demons from men, raising the dead, subduing the winds, walking upon the waves of the sea, and doing many other wonders, and all the people of the Jews calling him Son of God.

Then the chief priests, moved with envy against him, seized him, and delivered him to me; and telling one lie after another, they said that he was a wizard, and did contrary to their law.

And I, having believed that these things were so, gave him up, after scourging him, to their will; [20] and they crucified him, and after he was buried set guards over him. But he, while my soldiers were guarding him, rose on the third day. And to such a degree was the wickedness of the Jews inflamed against him, that they gave money to the soldiers, saying, Say his disciples have stolen his body.

But they, having taken the money, were not able to keep silence as to what had happened; for they have testified that they have seen him (after he was) risen, and that they have received money from the Jews.

These things, therefore, have I reported, that no one should falsely speak otherwise, and that thou shouldest not suppose that the falsehoods of the Jews are to be believed.

And the letter having been read, Nero said:

Tell me, Peter, were all these things thus done by him?

Peter said:

They were, with your permission, O good emperor.

For this Simon is full of lies and deceit, even if it should seem that he is what he is not--a god.

And in Christ there is all excellent victory through God and through man, [21] which that incomprehensible glory assumed which through man deigned to come to the assistance of men.

But in this Simon there are two essences, of man and of devil, who through man endeavours to ensnare men.

Simon said:

I wonder, O good emperor, that you reckon this man of any consequence--a man uneducated, a fisherman of the poorest, and endowed with power neither in word nor by rank.

But, that I may not long endure him as an enemy, I shall forthwith order my angels to come and avenge me upon him.

Peter said:

I am not afraid of thy angels; but they shall be much more afraid of me in the power and trust of my Lord Jesus Christ, whom thou falsely declarest thyself to be.

Nero said:

Art thou not afraid, Peter, of Simon, who confirms his godhead by deeds?

Peter said:

Godhead is in Him who searcheth the hidden things of the heart.[22]Now then, tell me what I am thinking about, or what I am doing.

I disclose to thy servants who are here what my thought is, before he tells lies about it, in order that he may not dare to lie as to what I am thinking about.

Nero said: Come hither, and tell me what thou art thinking about.

Peter said: Order a barley loaf to be brought, and to be given to me secretly.

And when he ordered it to be brought, and secretly given to Peter, Peter said:

Now tell us, Simon, what has been thought about, or what said, or what done.

Nero said:

Do you mean me to believe that Simon does not know these things, who both raised a dead man, and presented himself on the third day after he had been beheaded, and who has done whatever he said he would do?

Peter said:

But he did not do it before me.

Nero said: But he did all these before me.

For assuredly he ordered angels to come to him, and they came.

Peter said:

If he has done what is very great, why does he not do what is very small?

Let him tell what I had in my mind, and what I have done.

Nero said:

Between you, I do not know myself.

Simon said:

Let Peter say what I am thinking of, or what I am doing.

Peter said:

What Simon has in his mind I shall show that I know, by my doing what he is thinking about.

Simon said:

Know this, O emperor, that no one knows the thoughts of men, but God alone.

Is not, therefore, Peter lying?

Peter said:

Do thou, then, who sayest that thou art the Son of God, tell what I have in my mind; disclose, if thou canst, what I have just done in secret.

For Peter, having blessed the barley loaf which he had received, and hawing broken it with his right hand and his left, had heaped it up in his sleeves.

Then Simon, enraged that he was not able to tell the secret of the apostle, cried out, saying:

Let great dogs come forth, and eat him up before Caesar. And suddenly there appeared great dogs, and rushed at Peter.

But Peter, stretching forth his hands [23] to pray, showed to the dogs the loaf which he had blessed; which the dogs seeing, no longer appeared.

Then Peter said to Nero:

Behold, I have shown thee that I knew what Simon was thinking of, not by words, but by deeds; for he, having promised that he would bring angels against me, has brought dogs, in order that he might show that he had not god-like but dog-like angels.

Then Nero said to Simon:

What is it, Simon?

I think we have got the worst of it.

Simon said:

This man, both in Judaea and in all Palestine and Caesarea, has done the same to me; [24] and from very often striving with me, he has learned that this is adverse to them. This, then, he has learned how to escape from me; for the thoughts of men no one knows but God alone.

And Peter said to Simon:

Certainly thou feignest thyself to be a god; why, then, dost thou not reveal the thoughts of every man?

Then Nero, turning to Paul, said:

Why dost thou say nothing, Paul? Paul answered and said:

Know this, O emperor, that if thou permittest this magician to do such things, it will bring an access of the greatest mischief to thy country, and will bring down thine empire from its position.

Nero said to Simon:

What sayest thou?

Simon said:

If I do not manifestly hold myself out to be a god, no one will bestow upon me due reverence.

The Forgotten Bible

Nero said:

And now, why dost thou delay, and not show thyself to be a god, in order that these men may be punished? Simon said:

Give orders to build for me a lofty tower of wood, and I, going up upon it, will call my angels, and order them to take me, in the sight of all, to my father in heaven; and these men, not being able to do this, are put to shame as [25] uneducated men.

And Nero said to Peter:

Hast thou heard, Peter, what has been said by Simon?

From this will appear how much power either he or thy god has.

Peter said: O most mighty emperor, if thou wert willing, thou mightst perceive that he is full of demons.

Nero said:

Why do you make to me roundabouts of circumlocutions?

To-morrow will prove you.

Simon said:

Dost thou believe, O good emperor, that I who was dead, and rose again, am a magician?

For it had been brought about by his own cleverness that the unbelieving Simon had said to Nero:

Order me to be beheaded in a dark place, and there to be left slain; and if I do not rise on the third day, know that I am a magician; but if I rise again, know that I am the Son of God.

And Nero having ordered this, in the dark, by his magic art he managed that a ram should be beheaded.

And for so long did the ram appear to be Simon until he was beheaded.

And when he had been beheaded in the dark, he that had beheaded him, taking the head, found it to be that of a ram; but he would not say anything to the emperor, lest he should scourge him, having ordered this to be done in secret.

Thereafter, accordingly. Simon said that he had risen on the third day, because he took away the head of the ram and the limbs--but the blood had been there congealed--and on the third day he showed himself to Nero, and said:

Cause to be wiped away my blood that has been poured out; for, behold, having been beheaded, as I promised, I have risen again on the third day.

And when Nero said, To-morrow will prove you, turning to Paul, he says:

Thou Paul, why dost thou say nothing?

Either who taught thee, or whom thou hast for a master, or how thou hast taught in the cities, or what things have happened through thy teaching?

For I think that thou hast not any wisdom, and art not able to accomplish any work of power. Paul answered:

Dost thou suppose that I ought to speak against a desperate man, a magician, who has given his soul up to death, whose destruction and perdition will come speedily?

For he ought to speak who pretends to be what he is not, and deceives men by magic art.

If thou consentest to hear his words, and to shield him, thou shalt destroy thy soul and thy kingdom, for he is a most base man.

And as the Egyptians Jannes and Jambres led Pharaoh and his army astray until they were swallowed up in the sea, so also he, through the instruction of his father the devil, persuades men to do many evils to themselves, and thus deceives many of the innocent, to the peril of thy kingdom. But as for the word of the devil, which I see has been poured out through this man, with groanings of my heart I am dealing with the Holy Spirit, that it may be clearly shown what it is; for as far as he seems to raise himself towards heaven, so far will he be sunk down into the depth of Hades, where there is weeping and gnashing of teeth.

But about the teaching of my Master, of which thou didst ask me, none attain it except the pure, who allow faith to come into their heart.[26]For as many things as belong to peace and love, these have I taught.

Round about from Jerusalem, and as far as Illyricum, [27] I have fulfilled the word of peace.

For I have taught that in honour they should prefer one another;[28] I have taught those that are eminent and rich not to be lifted up, and hope in uncertainty of riches, but to place their hope in God; [29] I have taught those in a middle station to be content with food and covering; [30] I have taught the poor to rejoice in their own poverty; I have taught fathers to teach their children instruction in the fear of the Lord, children to obey their parents in wholesome admonition; [31] I have taught wives to love their own husbands, and to fear them as masters, and husbands to observe fidelity to their wives; I have taught masters to treat their slaves with clemency, and slaves to serve their own masters faithfully; [32] I have taught the churches of the believers to reverence one almighty, invisible, and incomprehensible God.

And this teaching has been given me, not from men, nor through men, but through Jesus Christ, [33] who spoke to me out of heaven, who also has sent me to preach, saying to me, Go forth, for I will be with thee; and all things, as many as thou shalt say or do, I shall make just.

Nero said:

What sayest thou, Peter?

He answered and said:

All that Paul has said is true. [34]For when he was a persecutor of the faith of Christ, a voice called him out of heaven, and taught him the truth; for he was not an adversary of our faith from hatred, but from ignorance.

For there were before us false Christs, like Simon, false apostles, and false prophets, who, contrary to the sacred writings, set themselves to make void the truth; and against these it was necessary to have in readiness this man, who from his youth up set himself to no other thing than to search out the mysteries of the divine law, by which [35] he might become a vindicator of truth and a persecutor of falsehood.

Since, then, his persecution was not on account of hatred, but on account of the vindication of the law, the very truth out of heaven held intercourse with him, saying, I am the truth which you persecutest; cease persecuting me.

When, therefore, he knew that this was so, leaving off that which he was vindicating, he began to vindicate this way of Christ which he was persecuting.

Simon said:

O good emperor, take notice that these two have conspired against me; for I am the truth, and they purpose evil against me. Peter said:

There is no truth in thee; but all thou sayest is false.

Nero said:

Paul, what sayest thou?

Paul said:

Those things which thou hast heard from Peter, believe to have been spoken by me also; for we purpose the same thing, for we have the same Lord Jesus the Christ. Simon said:

Dost thou expect me, O good emperor, to hold an argument with these men, who have come to an agreement against me?

And having turned to the apostles of Christ, he said:

Listen, Peter and Paul:

if I can do nothing for you here, we are going to the place where I must judge you.

Paul said:

O good emperor, see what threats he holds out against us.

Peter said:

Why was it necessary to keep from laughing outright at a foolish man, made the sport of demons, so as to suppose that he cannot be made manifest?

Simon said:

I spare you until I shall receive my power.

Paul said: See if you will go out hence safe.

Peter said:

If thou do not see, Simon, the power of our Lord Jesus Christ, thou wilt not believe thyself not to be Christ.

Simon said:

Most sacred emperor, do not believe them, for they are circumcised knaves.

Paul said:

Before we knew the truth, we had the circumcision of the flesh; but when the truth appeared, in the circumcision of the heart we both are circumcised, and circumcise.

Peter said:

If circumcision be a disgrace, why hast thou been circumcised, Simon?

Nero said:

Has, then, Simon also been circumcised?

Peter said:

For not otherwise could he have deceived souls, unless he feigned himself to be a Jew, and made a show of teaching the law of God.

Nero said: Simon, thou, as I see, being carried away with envy, persecutest these men.

For, as it seems, there is great hatred between thee and their Christ; and I am afraid that thou wilt be worsted by them, and involved in great evils.

Simon said:

Thou art led astray, O emperor.

Nero said:

How am I led astray?
What I see in thee, I say.
I see that thou art manifestly an enemy of Peter and Paul and their master.
Simon said:
Christ was not Paul's master.
Paul said:
Yes; through revelation He taught me also.
But tell me what I asked thee--Why wast thou circumcised?
Simon said:
Why have you asked me this?
Paul said:
We have a reason for asking you this.
Nero said:
Why art thou afraid to answer them?
Simon said:
Listen, O emperor.
At that time circumcision was enjoined by God when I received it.
For this reason was I circumcised.
Paul said:
Hearest thou, O good emperor, what has been said by Simon? If, therefore, circumcision be a good thing, why hast thou, Simon, given up those who have been circumcised, and forced them, after being condemned, to be put to death?
Nero said:
Neither about you do I perceive anything good.
Peter and Paul said:
Whether this thought about us be good or evil has no reference to the matter; but to us it was necessary that what our Master promised should come to pass.
Nero said:
If I should not be willing?
Peter said:
Not as thou willest, but as He promised to us.
Simon said:
O good emperor, these men have reckoned upon thy clemency, and have bound thee.
Nero said:
But neither hast thou yet made me sure about thyself.
Simon said:
Since so many excellent deeds and signs have been shown to thee by me, I wonder how thou shouldst be in doubt.
Nero said:
I neither doubt nor favour any of you; but answer me rather what I ask.
Simon said:
Henceforward I answer thee nothing.
Nero said:
Seeing that thou liest, therefore thou sayest this.
But if even I can do nothing to thee, God, who can, will do it.
Simon said:
I no longer answer thee.
Nero said:
Nor do I consider thee to be anything:
for, as I perceive, thou art a liar in everything.
But why do I say so much?
The three of you show that your reasoning is uncertain; and thus in all things you have made me doubt, so that I find that I can give credit to none of you. [36]
Peter said:
We preach one God and Father of our Lord Jesus Christ, that has made the heaven and the earth and the sea, and all that therein is, who is the true King; and of His kingdom there shall be no end. [37]Nero said:
What king is lord?
Paul said:
The Saviour of all the nations.
Simon said:
I am he whom you speak of.

Peter and Paul said:
May it never be well with thee, Simon, magician, and full of bitterness.
Simon said:
Listen, O Caesar Nero, that thou mayst know that these men are liars, and that I have been sent from the heavens:
to-morrow I go up into the heavens, that I may make those who believe in me blessed, and show my wrath upon those who have denied me.
Peter and Paul said: Us long ago God called to His own glory; but thou, called by the devil, hastenest to punishment.
Simon said:
Caesar Nero, listen to me. Separate these madmen from thee, in order that when I go into heaven to my father, I may be very merciful to thee.
Nero said:
And whence shall we prove this, that thou goest away into heaven?
Simon said: Order a lofty tower to be made of wood, and of great beams, that I may go up upon it, and that my angels may find me in the air; for they cannot come to me upon earth among the sinners.
Nero said:
I will see whether thou wilt fulfil what thou sayest.
Then Nero ordered a lofty tower to be made in the Campus Martius, and all the people and the dignities to be present at the spectacle.
And on the following day, all the multitude having come together, Nero ordered Peter and Paul to be present, to whom also he said:
Now the truth has to be made manifest.
Peter and Paul said:
We do not expose him, but our Lord Jesus Christ, the Son of God, whom he has falsely declared himself to be.
And Paul, having turned to Peter, said:
It is my part to bend the knee, and to pray to God; and thine to produce the effect, if thou shouldst see him attempting anything, because thou wast first taken in hand [38] by the Lord.
And Paul, bending his knees, prayed.
And Peter, looking stedfastly upon Simon, said:
Accomplish what thou hast begun; for both thy exposure and our call is at hand:
for I see my Christ calling both me and Paul.
Nero said:
And where will you go to against my will?
Peter said:
Whithersoever our Lord has called us. Nero said:
And who is your lord?
Peter said:
Jesus the Christ, whom I see calling us to Himself.
Nero said:
Do you also then intend to go away to heaven?
Peter said:
If it shall seem good to Him that calls us.
Simon said:
In order that thou mayst know, O emperor, that these are deceivers, as soon as ever I ascend into heaven, I will send my angels to thee, and will make thee come to me.
Nero said:
Do at once what thou sayest.
Then Simon went up upon the tower in the face of all, and, crowned with laurels, he stretched forth his hands, and began to fly.
And when Nero saw him flying, he said to Peter:
This Simon is true; but thou and Paul are deceivers.
To whom Peter said:
Immediately shalt thou know that we are true disciples of Christ; but that he is not Christ, but a magician, and a malefactor.
Nero said:
Do you still persist?
Behold, you see him going up into heaven.
Then Peter, looking stedfastly upon Paul, said:
Paul, look up and see.

The Forgotten Bible

And Paul, having looked up, full of tears, and seeing Simon flying, said:

Peter, why art thou idle? finish what thou hast begun; for already our Lord Jesus Christ is calling us.

And Nero hearing them, smiled a little, and said:

These men see themselves worsted already, and are gone mad.

Peter said:

Now thou shalt know that we are not mad.

Paul said to Peter:

Do at once what thou doest.

And Peter, looking stedfastly against Simon, said:

I adjure you, ye angels of Satan, who are carrying him into the air, to deceive the hearts of the unbelievers, by the God that created all things, and by Jesus Christ, whom on the third day He raised from the dead, no longer from this hour to keep him up, but to let him go.

And immediately, being let go, he fell into a place called Sacra Via, that is, Holy Way, and was divided into four parts, having perished by an evil fate.

Then Nero ordered Peter and Paul to be put in irons, and the body of Simon to be carefully kept three days, thinking that he would rise on the third day.

To whom Peter said:

He will no longer rise, since he is truly dead, being condemned to everlasting punishment.

And Nero said to him:

Who commanded thee to do such a dreadful deed?

Peter said:

His reflections and blasphemy against my Lord Jesus Christ have brought him into this gulf of destruction.

Nero said:

I will destroy you by an evil taking off.

Peter said:

This is not in thy power, even if it should seem good to thee to destroy us; but it is necessary that what our Master promised to us should be fulfilled.

Then Nero, having summoned Agrippa the propraetor, said to him:

It is necessary that men introducing mischievous religious observances should die. Wherefore I order them to take iron clubs, [39] and to be killed in the sea-fight.

Agrippa the propraetor said:

Most sacred emperor, what thou hast ordered is not fitting for these men, since Paul seems innocent beside Peter.

Nero said:

By what fate, then, shall they die?

Agrippa answered and said:

As seems to me, it is just that Paul's head should be cut off, and that Peter should be raised on a cross as the cause of the murder.

Nero said:

Thou hast most excellently judged.

Then both Peter and Paul were led away from the presence of Nero.

And Paul was beheaded on the Ostesian road. [40]

And Peter, having come to the cross, said:

Since my Lord Jesus Christ, who came down from the heaven upon the earth, was raised upon the cross upright, [41] and He has deigned to call to heaven me, who am of the earth, my cross ought to be fixed head down most, so as to direct my feet towards heaven; for I am not worthy to be crucified like my Lord. Then, having reversed the cross, they nailed his feet up.

And the multitude was assembled reviling Caesar, and wishing to kill him.

But Peter restrained them, saying: [42] A few days ago, being exhorted by the brethren, I was going away; and my Lord Jesus Christ met me, and having adored Him, I said, Lord, whither art Thou going? And He said to me, I am going to Rome to be crucified.

And I said to Him, Lord, wast Thou not crucified once for all?

And the Lord answering, said, I saw thee fleeing from death, and I wish to be crucified instead of thee.

And I said, Lord, I go; I fulfil Thy command.

And He said to me, Fear not, for I am with thee. [43] On this account, then, children, do not hinder my going; for already my feet are going on the road to heaven.

Do not grieve, therefore, but rather rejoice with me, for to-day I receive the fruit of my labours. And thus speaking, he said:

I thank Thee, good Shepherd, that the sheep which Thou hast entrusted to me, sympathize with me; I ask, then, that with me they may have a part in Thy kingdom. [44]And having thus spoken, he gave up the ghost.

And immediately there appeared men glorious and strange in appearance; and they said:

We are here, on account of the holy and chief apostles, from Jerusalem.

And they, along with Marcellus, an illustrious man, who, having left Simon, had believed in Peter, took up his body secretly, and put it under the terebinth near the place for the exhibition of sea-fights in the place called the Vatican. [45]

And the men who had said that they came from Jerusalem said to the people:

Rejoice, and be exceeding glad, because you have been deemed worthy to have great champions.

And know that Nero himself, after these not many days, will be utterly destroyed, and his kingdom shall be given to another.

And after these things the people revolted against him; and when he knew of it, he fled into desert places, and through hunger and cold he gave up the ghost, and his body became food for the wild beasts.

And some devout men of the regions of the East wished to carry off the relics of the saints, and immediately there was a great earthquake in the city; [46] and those that dwelt in the city having become aware of it, ran and seized the men, but they fled.

But the Romans having taken them, put them in a place three miles from the city, and there they were guarded a year and seven months, until they had built the place in which they intended to put them.

And after these things, all having assembled with glory and singing of praise, they put them in the place built for them.

And the consummation of the holy glorious Apostles Peter and Paul was on the 29th of the month of June--in Christ Jesus our Lord, to whom be glory and strength.

Footnotes:

1. Lambecius proposes to read Gaudos and Melita. In the Latin version of the famous Greek scholar Lascaris, 1490, it is a Melita et Gaudisio insulis. [Comp. Acts xxvii. 16, xxviii. 1. The two names are apparently combined here.--R.]

2. traktaisantes: from the Byzantine verb traktaizein = tractare. The various readings in the mss. are: Being very disorderly; having been much disturbed.

3. Various reading: Let it be...and we will write, etc.

4. Puteoli.

5. The geographical names are given in the peculiar forms of the text. Occasionally the usual forms, such as Baiae, occur.

6. The distance was thirty-three miles. In the Antonine Itinerary, "To Aricia is sixteen miles, to Tres Tabernae seventeen miles, to Appii Forum ten miles."

7. Or, do away with belief in circumcision.

8. Lit., web or tissue.

9. Gen. xii. 3, xvii. 5.

10. Rom. ii. 11; Eph. vi. 9; Col. iii. 25; Jas. ii. 1.

11. Rom. ii. 12.

12. Ps. cxxxii. 11.

13. Or, He allowed Himself to suffer all these things.

14. Or, by Him.

15. i.e., That all may profess their faith in Him. For similar expressions, see 2 Cor. ix. 13, Heb. x. 23.

16. Ps. cx. 4; Heb. vii. 21.

17. i.e., How do you happen, as a race, to be so unbelieving? The Latin translation has: against your race--kata tou genous for kata to genos.

18. For another translation of this letter, see Latin Gospel of Nicodemus, chap. xiii. (xxix.) [This occurs on p. 454; there is another form on p. 459.--R.]

19. Or, I saw.

20. Or, to their council.

21. i.e., human nature.

22. Jer. xvii. 10; Rev. ii. 23.

23. Lam. iii. 41; Mark xi. 25; 1 Tim. ii. 8.

24. See the Clementines, Homilies II., III., VI., XVI., XX.

25. Or, are proved to be.

26. Or, the pure in heart admitting the faith.

27. Rom. xv. 19.

The Forgotten Bible

28. Rom. xii. 10.
29. 1 Tim. vi. 17.
30. Or, those who have a moderate quantity of food and covering to be content (1 Tim. vi. 8).
31. Or, in the admonition of the Saviour (Eph. vi. 4.).
32. Col. iii. 18-22.
33. Gal. i. 1.
34. Four of themss. and the Latin version here add: For assuredly I have for a long time past received letters from our bishops throughout all the world about the things done and said by him.
35. i.e., mysteries.
36. Or, to nothing.
37. Luke i. 33.
38. Or, chosen.
39. The text has kinaras, artichokes, for which I have read korunas, clubs. Sea-fights were a favourite spectacle of the Roman emperors (Suet., Nero, xii.; Claud., xxi.; Dom., iv.). The combatants were captives, or persons condemned to death (Dion Cass., lx. 33).
40. For the episode of Perpetua, contained in three of the Greek mss., but not in the Latin versions, see the end of this book.
41. i.e., head uppermost.
42. One of the mss. here inserts: Do not be hard upon him, for he is the servant of this father Satan; but I must fulfil the command of my Lord.
43. Some of themss. insert: Until I bring thee into my Father's house.
44. Several of themss. here add: I commend unto Thee the sheep whom Thou didst entrust unto me, that they may not feel that they are without me, having for a shepherd Thee, through whom I have been able to feed this flock.
45. In three of the Greek mss., but not in the Latin versions, the story of Perpetua is here continued.
46. Severalmss. here add: And the people of the Romans ran, and took them into the place called the Catacombs on the Appian Way, at the third milestone; and there the bodies of the saints were guarded a year and six months, until places were built for them in which they might be put. And the body of St. Peter was put into the Vatican, near the place for the sea-fights, and that of St. Paul into the Vostesian (or Ostesian) Way, two mile from the city; and in these places, through their prayers, many good deeds are wrought to the faithful in the name of our Lord Jesus Christ.

The Story of Perpetua

And as Paul was being led away to be beheaded at a place about three miles from the city, he was in irons.

And there were three soldiers guarding him who were of a great family.

And when they had gone out of the gate about the length of a bow-shot, there met them a God-fearing woman; and she, seeing Paul dragged along in irons, had compassion on him, and wept bitterly.

And the name of the woman was called Perpetua; and she was one-eyed.

And Paul, seeing her weeping, says to her:

Give me thy handkerchief, and when I turn back I shall give it to thee.

And she, having taken the handkerchief, gave it to him willingly.

And the soldiers laughed, and said to the woman:

Why dost thou wish, woman, to lose thy handkerchief?

Knowest thou not that he is going away to be beheaded?

And Perpetua said to them:

I adjure you by the health of Caesar to bind his eyes with this handkerchief when you cut off his head.

Which also was done.

And they beheaded him at the place called Aquae Salviae, near the pine tree. And as God had willed, before the soldiers came back, the handkerchief, having on it drops of blood, was restored to the woman.

And as she was carrying it, straightway and immediately her eye was opened.

And the three soldiers who had cut off the head of Saint Paul, when after three hours they came on the same day with the Bulla bringing it to Nero, having met Perpetua, they said to her:

What is it, woman? Behold, by thy confidence thou hast lost thy handkerchief.

But she said to them:

I have both got my handkerchief, and my eye has recovered its sight.

And as the Lord, the God of Paul, liveth, I also have entreated him that I may be deemed worthy to become the slave of his Lord.

Then the soldiers who had the Bulla, recognising the handkerchief, and seeing that her eye had been opened, cried out with a loud voice, as if from one mouth, and said:

We too are the slaves of Paul's master.

Perpetua therefore having gone away, reported in the palace of the Emperor Nero that the soldiers who had beheaded Paul said:

We shall no longer go into the city, for we believe in Christ whom Paul preached, and we are Christians.

Then Nero, filled with rage, ordered Perpetua, who had informed him of the soldiers, to be kept fast in irons; and as to the soldiers, he ordered one to be beheaded outside of the gate about one mile from the city, another to be cut in two, and the third to be stoned.

And Perpetua was in the prison; and in this prison there was kept Potentiana, a noble maiden, because she had said:

I forsake my parents and all the substance of my father, and I wish to become a Christian.

She therefore joined herself to Perpetua, and ascertained from her everything about Paul, and was in much anxiety about the faith in Christ.

And the wife of Nero was Potentiana's sister; and she secretly informed her about Christ, that those who believe in Him see everlasting joy, and that everything here is temporary, but there eternal:

so that also she fled out of the palace, and some of the senators' wives with her.

Then Nero, having inflicted many tortures upon Perpetua, at last tied a great stone to her neck, and ordered her to be thrown over a precipice.

And her remains lie at the Momentan [1] gate.

And Potentiana also underwent many torments; and at last, having made a furnace one day, they burned her.

Footnote:

1. This is a slip for Nomentan.

Acts of Paul and Thecla

As Paul was going up to Iconium after the flight from Antioch, his fellow-travellers were Demas and Ermogenes, full of hypocrisy; and they were importunate with Paul, [1] as if they loved him.

But Paul, looking only to the goodness of Christ, did them no harm, but loved them exceedingly, so that he made the oracles of the Lord sweet to them in the teaching both of the birth and the resurrection of the Beloved; and he gave them an account, word for word, of the great things of Christ, how He [2] had been revealed to him.

And a certain man, by name Onesiphorus, hearing that Paul had come to Iconium, went out to meet him with his children Silas and Zeno, and his wife Lectra, in order that he might entertain him:

for Titus had informed him what Paul was like in appearance:

for he had not seen him in the flesh, but only in the spirit.

And he went along the road to Lystra, and stood waiting for him, and kept looking at the passers by according to the description of Titus.

And he saw Paul coming, a man small in size, bald-headed, bandy-legged, well-built, [3] with eyebrows meeting, rather long-nosed, full of grace.

For sometimes he seemed like a man, and sometimes he had the countenance of an angel. And Paul, seeing Onesiphorus, smiled; and Onesiphorus said:

Hail, O servant of the blessed God!

And he said:

Grace be with thee and thy house.

And Demas and Ermogenes were jealous, and showed greater hypocrisy; so that Demas said:

Are not we of the blessed God, that thou hast not thus saluted us?

And Onesiphorus said:

I do not see in you the fruit of righteousness; but if such you be, come you also into my house and rest yourselves.

And Paul having gone into the house of Onesiphorus, there was great joy, and bending of knees, and breaking of bread, and the word of God about self-control and the resurrection; Paul saying:

Blessed are the pure in heart, for they shall see God: [4]blessed are they that have kept the flesh chaste, for they shall become a temple of God: [5]blessed are they that control themselves, for God shall speak with them:

blessed are they that have kept aloof from this world, for they shall be called upright: [6]blessed are they that have wives as not having them, for they shall receive God for their portion: [7]blessed are they that have the fear of God, for they shall become angels of God: [8]blessed are they that have kept the baptism, for they shall rest beside the Father and the Son:

blessed are the merciful, for they shall obtain mercy, [9] and shall not see the bitter day of judgment:

blessed are the bodies of the virgins, for they shall be well pleasing to God, and shall not lose the reward of their chastity; for the word of the Father shall become to them a work of salvation against the day of His Son, and they shall have rest for ever and ever. [10]

And while Paul was thus speaking in the midst of the church in the house of Onesiphorus, a certain virgin Thecla, the daughter of Theocleia, betrothed to a man named Thamyris, sitting at the window close by, listened night and day to the discourse of virginity and prayer, and did not look away from the window, but paid earnest heed to the faith, rejoicing exceedingly.

And when she still saw many women going in beside Paul, she also had an eager desire to be deemed worthy to stand in the presence of Paul, and to hear the word of Christ; for never had she seen his figure, but heard his word only.

And as she did not stand away from the window, her mother sends to Thamyris; and he comes gladly, as if already receiving her in marriage.

And Theocleia said:

I have a strange story to tell thee, Thamyris; for assuredly for three days and three nights

Thecla does not rise from the window, neither to eat nor to drink; but looking earnestly as if upon some pleasant sight, she is so devoted to a foreigner teaching deceitful and artful discourses, that I wonder how a virgin of such modesty is so painfully put about.

Thamyris, this man will overturn the city of the Iconians, and thy Thecla too besides; for all the women and the young men go in beside him, being taught to fear God and to live in chastity.

Moreover also my daughter, tied to the window like a spider, lays hold of what is said by Paul with a strange eagerness and awful emotion; for the virgin looks eagerly at what is said by him, and has been captivated.

But do thou go near and speak to her, for she has been betrothed to thee.

And Thamyris going near, and kissing her, but at the same time also being afraid of her overpowering emotion, said:

Thecla, my betrothed, why dost thou sit thus? and what sort of feeling holds thee overpowered?

Turn round to thy Thamyris, and be ashamed.

Moreover also her mother said the same things:

Why dost thou sit thus looking down, my child, and answering nothing, but like a mad woman?

And they wept fearfully, Thamyris indeed for the loss of a wife, and Theocleia of a child, and the maidservants of a mistress:

there was accordingly much confusion in the house of mourning.[11] And while these things were thus going on, Thecla did not turn round, but kept attending earnestly to the word of Paul.

And Thamyris starting up, went forth into the street, and kept watching those going in to him and coming out.

And he saw two men bitterly contending with each other; and he said:

Men, tell me who this is among you, leading astray the souls of young men, and deceiving virgins, so that they do not marry, but remain as they are.

I promise, therefore, to give you money enough if you tell me about him; for I am the first man [12] of the city.

And Demas and Ermogenes said to him:

Who this is, indeed, we do not know; but he deprives young men of wives, and maidens of husbands, saying, There is for you a resurrection in no other way, unless you remain chaste, and pollute not the flesh, but keep it chaste.

And Thamyris said to them:

Come into my house, and rest yourselves.

And they went to a sumptuous dinner, and much wine, and great wealth, and a splendid table; and Thamyris made them drink, from his love to Thecla, and his wish to get her as his wife. And Thamyris said during the dinner:

Ye men, what is his teaching, tell me, that I also may know; for I am no little distressed about Thecla, because she thus loves the stranger, and I am prevented from marrying.

Demas and Ermogenes said:

Bring him before the governor Castelios on the charge of persuading the multitudes to embrace the new teaching of the Christians, and he will speedily destroy him, and thou shalt have Thecla as thy wife.

And we shall teach thee that the resurrection of which this man speaks has taken place, because it has already taken place in the children which we have; [13] and we rose again when we came to the knowledge of the true God.

And Thamyris, hearing these things, being filled with anger and rage, rising up early, went to the house of Onesiphorus with archons and public officers, and a great crowd with batons, saying:

Thou hast corrupted the city of the Iconians, and her that was betrothed to me, so that she will not have me:

let us go to the governor Castelios. And all the multitude said:

Away with the magician; for he has corrupted all our wives, and the multitudes have been persuaded to change their opinions.

And Thamyris, standing before the tribunal, said with a great shout:

O proconsul, this man, who he is we know not, who makes virgins averse to marriage; let him say before thee on what [14] account he teaches these things.

And Demas and Ermogenes said to Thamyris:

Say that he is a Christian, and thus thou wilt do away with him.

But the proconsul stayed his intention, and called Paul, saying:

Who art thou, and what dost thou teach? for they bring no small charges against thee.

And Paul lifted up his voice, saying:

Since I am this day examined as to what I teach, listen, O proconsul:

A living God, a God of retributions, a jealous God, a God in need of nothing, consulting for the salvation of men, has sent me that I may reclaim them from corruption and uncleanness, and from all pleasure, and from death, that they may not sin.

Wherefore God sent His own Son, whom I preach, and in whom I teach men to rest their hope, who alone has had compassion upon a world led astray, that they may be no longer under judgment, O proconsul, but may have faith, and the fear of God, and the knowledge of holiness, and the love of truth.

If, therefore, I teach what has been revealed to me by God, wherein do I do wrong?

And the proconsul having heard, ordered Paul to be bound, and sent to prison, until, said he, I, being at leisure, shall hear him more attentively.

And Thecla by night having taken off her bracelets, gave them to the gatekeeper; and the door having been opened to her, she went into the prison; and having given the jailor a silver mirror, she went in beside Paul, and, sitting at his feet, she heard the great things of God.

And Paul was afraid of nothing, but ordered his life in the confidence of God.

And her faith also was increased, and she kissed his bonds.

And when Thecla was sought for by her friends, and Thamyris, as if she had been lost, was running up and down the streets, one of the gatekeeper's fellow-slaves informed him that she had gone out by night.

And having gone out, they examined the gatekeeper; and he said to them:

She has gone to the foreigner into the prison.

And having gone, they found her, as it were, enchained by affection.

And having gone forth thence, they drew the multitudes together, and informed the governor of the circumstance.

And he ordered Paul to be brought to the tribunal; but Thecla was wallowing on the ground [15] in the place where he sat and taught her in the prison; and he ordered her too to be brought to the tribunal.

And she came, exulting with joy.

And the crowd, when Paul had been brought, vehemently cried out:

He is a magician! away with him!

But the proconsul gladly heard Paul upon the holy works of Christ.

And having called a council, he summoned Thecla, and said to her:

Why dost thou not obey Thamyris, according to the law of the Iconians?

But she stood looking earnestly at Paul.

And when she gave no answer, her mother cried out, saying:

Burn the wicked wretch; burn in the midst of the theatre her that will not marry, in order that all the women that have been taught by this man may be afraid.

And the governor was greatly moved; and having scourged Paul, he cast him out of the city, and condemned Thecla to be burned.

And immediately the governor went away to the theatre, and all the crowd went forth to the spectacle of Thecla.

But as a lamb in the wilderness looks round for the shepherd, so she kept searching for Paul.

And having looked upon the crowd, she saw the Lord sitting in the likeness of Paul, and said:

As I am unable to endure my lot, Paul has come to see me.

And she gazed upon him with great earnestness, and he went up into heaven.

But the maid-servants [16] and virgins brought the faggots, in order that Thecla might be burned.

And when she came in naked, the governor wept, and wondered at the power [17] that was in her.

And the public executioners arranged the faggots for her to go up on the pile.

And she, having made the sign of the cross, went up on the faggots; and they lighted them.

And though a great fire was blazing, it did not touch her; for God, having compassion upon her, made an underground rumbling, and a cloud overshadowed them from above, full of water and hail; and all that was in the cavity of it was poured out, so that many were in danger of death.

And the fire was put out, and Thecla saved.

And Paul was fasting with Onesiphorus and his wife, and his children, in a new tomb, as they were going from Iconium to Daphne.

And when many days were past, the fasting children said to Paul:

We are hungry, and we cannot buy loaves; for Onesiphorus had left the things of the world, and followed Paul, with all his house.

And Paul, having taken off his cloak, said:

Go, my child, buy more loaves, and bring them. And when the child was buying, he saw Thecla their neighbour, and was astonished, and said:

Thecla, whither art thou going?

And she said: I have been saved from the fire, and am following Paul.

And the boy said:

Come, I shall take thee to him; for he is distressed about thee, and is praying six days.

And she stood beside the tomb where Paul was with bended knees, and praying, and saying:

O Saviour Christ, let not the fire touch Thecla, but stand by her, for she is Thine.

And she, standing behind him, cried out:

O Father, who hast made the heaven and the earth, the Father of Thy holy Son, I bless Thee that Thou hast saved me that I may see Paul.

And Paul, rising up, saw her, and said: O God, that knowest the heart, the Father of our Lord Jesus Christ, I bless Thee that Thou, having heard me, hast done quickly what I wished.

And they had five loaves, and herbs, and water; and they rejoiced in the holy works of Christ.

And Thecla said to Paul:

I shall cut my hair, and follow thee whithersoever thou mayst go.

And he said:

It is a shameless age, and thou art beautiful.

I am afraid lest another temptation come upon thee worse than the first, and that thou withstand it not, but be cowardly.

And Thecla said:

Only give me the seal [18] in Christ, and temptation shall not touch me.

And Paul said: Thecla, wait with patience, and thou shalt receive the water.

And Paul sent away Onesiphorus and all his house to Iconium; and thus, having taken Thecla, he went into Antioch.

And as they were going in, a certain Syriarch, Alexander by name, seeing Thecla, became enamoured of her, and tried to gain over Paul by gifts and presents.

But Paul said:

I know not the woman whom thou speakest of, nor is she mine. But he, being of great power, himself embraced her in the street.

But she would not endure it, but looked about for Paul.

And she cried out bitterly, saying:

Do not force the stranger; do not force the servant of God.

I am one of the chief persons of the Iconians; and because I would not have Thamyris, I have been cast out of the city.

And taking hold of Alexander, she tore his cloak, and pulled off his crown, and made him a laughing-stock.

And he, at the same time loving her, and at the same time ashamed of what had happened, led her before the governor; and when she had confessed that she had done these things, he condemned her to the wild beasts.

And the women were struck with astonishment, and cried out beside the tribunal:

Evil judgment! impious judgment!

And she asked the governor, that, said she, I may remain pure until I shall fight with the wild beasts.

And a certain Tryphaena, [19] whose daughter was dead, took her into keeping, and had her for a consolation.

And when the beasts were exhibited, they bound her to a fierce lioness; and Tryphaena accompanied her.

But the lioness, with Thecla sitting upon her, licked her feet; and all the multitude was astonished.

And the charge on her inscription was:

Sacrilegious.

And the women cried out from above:

An impious sentence has been passed in this city!

And after the exhibition, Tryphaena again receives her.

For her daughter Falconilla had died, and said to her in a dream:

Mother, thou shalt have this stranger Thecla in my place, in order that she may pray concerning me, and that I may be transferred to the place of the just.

And when, after the exhibition, Tryphaena received her, at the same time indeed she grieved that she had to fight with the wild beasts on the day following; and at the same time, loving her as much as her daughter Falconilla, she said:

My second child Thecla, come and pray for my child, that she may live for ever; for this I saw in my sleep. And she, nothing hesitating, lifted up her voice, and said:

God most high, [20] grant to this woman according to her wish, that her daughter Falconilla may live for ever.

And when Thecla had thus spoken, Tryphaena lamented, considering so much beauty thrown to the wild beasts.

And when it was dawn, Alexander came to take her, for it was he that gave the hunt, [21] saying: The governor is sitting, and the crowd is in uproar against us.

Allow me to take away her that is to fight with the wild beasts.

And Tryphaena cried aloud, so that he even fled, saying:

A second mourning for my Falconilla has come upon my house and there is no one to help; neither child, for she is dead, nor kinsman, for I am a widow.

God of Thecla, help her!

And immediately the governor sends an order that Thecla should be brought.

And Tryphaena, taking her by the hand, said:

My daughter Falconilla, indeed, I took away to the tomb; and thee, Thecla, I am taking to the wild-beast fight.

And Thecla wept bitterly, saying:

O Lord, the God in whom I believe, to whom I have fled for refuge, who deliveredst me from the fire, do Thou grant a recompense to Tryphaena, who has had compassion on Thy servant, and because she has kept me pure.

Then a tumult arose, and a cry of the people, and the women sitting together, the one saying:

Away with the sacrilegious person! the others saying:

Let the city be raised [22] against this wickedness.

Take off all of us, O proconsul!

Cruel sight! evil sentence!

And Thecla, having been taken out of the hand of Tryphaena, was stripped, and received a girdle, [23] and was thrown into the arena, and lions and bears and a fierce lioness were let loose upon her; and the lioness having run up to her feet, lay down; and the multitude of the women cried aloud.

And a bear ran upon her; but the lioness, meeting the bear, tore her to pieces.

And again a lion that had been trained against men, which belonged to Alexander, ran upon her; and she, the lioness, encountering the lion, was killed along with him. And the women made great lamentation, since also the lioness, her protector, was dead.

Then they send in many wild beasts, she standing and stretching forth her hands, and praying.

And when she had finished her prayer, she turned and saw a ditch full of water, and said:

Now it is time to wash myself.

And she threw herself in, saying:

In the name of Jesus Christ I am baptized on my last day.

And the women seeing, and the multitude, wept, saying:

Do not throw thyself into the water; so that also the governor shed tears, because the seals were going to devour such beauty.

She then threw herself in in the name of Jesus Christ; but the seals having seen the glare of the fire of lightning, floated about dead.

And there was round her, as she was naked, a cloud of fire; so that neither could the wild beasts touch her, nor could she be seen naked.

And the women, when other wild beasts were being thrown in, wailed. And some threw sweet-smelling herbs, others nard, others cassia, others amomum, so that there was abundance of perfumes.

And all the wild beasts that had been thrown in, as if they had been withheld by sleep, did not touch her; so that Alexander said to the governor:

I have bulls exceedingly terrible; let us bind to them her that is to fight with the beasts.

And the governor, looking gloomy, turned, and said: Do what thou wilt.

And they bound her by the feet between them, and put red-hot irons under the privy parts of the bulls, so that they, being rendered more furious, might kill her.

They rushed about, therefore; but the burning flame consumed the ropes, and she was as if she had not been bound.

But Tryphaena fainted standing beside the arena, so that the crowd said:

Queen Tryphaena is dead.

And the governor put a stop to the games, and the city was in dismay.

And Alexander entreated the governor, saying:

Have mercy both on me and the city, and release this woman.

For if Caesar hear of these things, he will speedily destroy the city also along with us, because his kinswoman Queen Tryphaena has died beside the Abaci. [24]

And the governor summoned Thecla out of the midst of the wild beasts, and said to her:

Who art thou? and what is there about thee, that not one of the wild beasts touches thee?
And she said:
I indeed am a servant of the living God; and as to what there is about me, I have believed in the Son of God, in whom He is well pleased; wherefore not one of the beasts has touched me.

For He alone is the end [25] of salvation, and the basis of immortal life; for He is a refuge to the tempest-tossed, a solace to the afflicted, a shelter to the despairing; and, once for all, whoever shall not believe on Him, shall not live for ever.

And the governor having heard this, ordered her garments to be brought, and to be put on.
And Thecla said:
He that clothed me naked among the wild beasts, will in the day of judgment clothe thee with salvation. And taking the garments, she put them on.
The governor therefore immediately issued an edict, saying:
I release to you the God-fearing Thecla, the servant of God.
And the women shouted aloud, and with one mouth returned thanks to God, saying:
There is one God, the God of Thecla; so that the foundations of the theatre were shaken by their voice.
And Tryphaena having received the good news, went to meet the holy Thecla, and said:
Now I believe that the dead are raised:
now I believe that my child lives.
Come within, and I shall assign to thee all that is mine.
She therefore went in along with her, and rested eight days, having instructed her in the word of God, so that most even of the maid-servants believed.
And there was great joy in the house.
And Thecla kept seeking Paul; and it was told her that he was in Myra of Lycia.
And taking young men and maidens, she girded herself; and having sewed the tunic so as to make a man's cloak, she came to Myra, and found Paul speaking the word of God.
And Paul was astonished at seeing her, and the crowd with her, thinking that some new trial was coming upon her.
And when she saw him, she said:
I have received the baptism, Paul; for He that wrought along with thee for the Gospel has wrought in me also for baptism.
And Paul, taking her, led her to the house of Hermaeus, and hears everything from her, so that those that heard greatly wondered, and were comforted, and prayed over Tryphaena. And she rose up, and said:
I am going to Iconium.
And Paul said:
Go, and teach the word of God.
And Tryphaena sent her much clothing and gold, so that she left to Paul many things for the service of the poor.
And she went to Iconium.
And she goes into the house of Onesiphorus, and fell upon the pavement where Paul used to sit and teach her, and wept, saying:
God of myself and of this house, where Thou didst make the light to shine upon me, O Christ Jesus, the Son of the living God, my help in the fire, my help among the wild beasts, Thou art glorified for ever.
Amen.
And she found Thamyris dead, but her mother alive. And having sent for her mother, she said:
Theocleia, my mother, canst thou believe that the Lord liveth in the heavens?
For whether thou desirest wealth, God gives it to thee through me; or thy child, I am standing beside thee.
And having thus testified, she departed to Seleucia, and dwelt in a cave seventy-two years, living upon herbs and water.
And she enlightened many by the word of God.
And certain men of the city, being Greeks by religion, and physicians by profession, sent to her insolent young men to destroy [26] her. For they said:
She is a virgin, and serves Artemis, and from this she has virtue in healing.
And by the providence of God she entered into the rock alive, and went under ground.
And she departed to Rome to see Paul, and found that he had fallen asleep. [27] And after staying there no long time, she rested in a glorious sleep; and she is buried about two or three stadia from the tomb of her master Paul.
She was cast, then, into the fire when seventeen years old, and among the wild beasts when eighteen.

The Forgotten Bible

And she was an ascetic in the cave, as has been said, seventy-two years, so that all the years of her life were ninety.

And having accomplished many cures, she rests in the place of the saints, having fallen asleep on the twenty-fourth of the month of September in Christ Jesus our Lord, to whom be glory and strength for ever and ever.

Amen.

***

Instead of the last two sections, the ms. which Dr. Grabe used has the following:--
And a cloud of light guided her.

And having come into Seleucia, she went forth outside of the city one stadium.

And she was afraid of them also, for they worshipped idols.

And it guided her to the mountain called Calamon or Rhodeon; and having there found a cave, she went into it.

And she was there many years, and underwent many and grievous trials by the devil, and bore them nobly, being assisted by Christ. And some of the well-born women, having learned about the virgin Thecla, went to her, and learned the oracles of God.

And many of them bade adieu to the world, and lived an ascetic life with her.

And a good report was spread everywhere concerning her, and cures were done by her.

All the city, therefore, and country round, having known this, brought their sick to the mountain; and before they came near the door they were speedily released from whatever disease they were afflicted by; and the unclean spirits went out shrieking, and all received their own in health, glorifying God, who had given such grace to the virgin Thecla.

The physicians, therefore, of the city of the Seleucians were thought nothing of, having lost their trade, and no one any longer had regard to them; and being filled with envy and hatred, they plotted against the servant of Christ, what they should do to her.

The devil then suggests to them a wicked device; and one day, being assembled, and having taken counsel, they consult with each other, saying:

This virgin is a priestess of the great goddess Artemis; and if she ask anything of her, she hears her as being a virgin, and all the gods love her.

Come, then, let us take men of disorderly lives, and make them drunk with much wine, and let us give them much gold, and say to them, If you can corrupt and defile her, we shall give you even more money. The physicians therefore said to themselves, that if they should be able to defile her, neither the gods nor Artemis would listen to her in the case of the sick.

They therefore did so.

And the wicked men, having gone to the mountain, and rushed upon the cave like lions, knocked at the door.

And the holy martyr Thecla opened, emboldened by the God in whom she believed; for she knew of their plot beforehand. And she says to them:

What do you want, my children?

And they said: Is there one here called Thecla?

And she said:

What do you want with her?

They say to her:

We want to sleep with her.

The blessed Thecla says to them:

I am a humble old woman, but the servant of my Lord Jesus Christ; and even though you want to do something to me out of place, you cannot.

They say to her:

It is impossible for us not to do to thee what we want.

And having said this, they laid fast hold of her, and wished to insult her.

And she says to them with mildness: Wait, my children, that you may see the glory of the Lord.

And being laid hold of by them, she looked up into heaven, and said:

God, terrible and incomparable, and glorious to Thine adversaries, who didst deliver me out of the fire, who didst not give me up to Thamyris, who didst not give me up to Alexander, who didst deliver me from the wild beasts, who didst save me in the abyss, who hast everywhere worked with me, and glorified Thy name in me, now also deliver me from these lawless men, and let me not insult my virginity, which through Thy name I have preserved till now, because I love Thee, and desire Thee, and adore Thee, the Father, and the Son, and the Holy Ghost for ever. Amen.

And there came a voice out of the heaven, saying:

Fear not, Thecla, my true servant, for I am with thee.

Look and see where an opening has been made before thee, for there shall be for thee an everlasting house, and there thou shalt obtain shelter.

And the blessed Thecla regarding it, saw the rock opened as far as to allow a man to enter, and did according to what had been said to her: and nobly fleeing from the lawless ones entered into the rock; and the rock was straightway shut together, so that not even a joining appeared.

And they, beholding the extraordinary wonder, became as it were distracted; and they were not able to detain the servant of God, but only caught hold of her veil, and were able to tear off a certain part; and that by the permission of God for the faith of those seeing the venerable place, and for a blessing in the generations afterwards to those that believe in our Lord Jesus Christ out of a pure heart.

Thus, then, suffered the first martyr of God, and apostle, and virgin, Thecla, who came from Iconium at eighteen years old; and with the journeying, and the going round, and the retirement in the mountain, she lived other seventy-two years.

And when the Lord took her, she was ninety years old.

And thus is her consummation.

And her holy commemoration is on the twenty-fourth of the month of September, to the glory of the Father, and the Son, and the Holy Spirit, now and ever, and to ages of ages.

Amen.

Footnotes:

1. Or, persisted in staying with Paul.
2. Or, how they.
3. Or, healthy.
4. Matt. v. 8.
5. Comp. 1 Cor. vi. 18, 19.
6. Comp. Rom. xii. 2.
7. Comp. 1 Cor. vii. 29.
8. Comp. Luke xx. 36.
9. Matt. v. 7.
10. Some mss. add the following beatitudes: Blessed are they that tremble at the words of God, for they shall be comforted: blessed are they that have received the wisdom of Jesus Christ, for they shall be called the sons of the Most High: blessed are they that through love of Christ have come out from conformity with the world, for they shall judge the angels, and shall be blessed at the right hand of the Father.
11. Or, a great outpouring of lamentation in the house.
12. Or, a chief man.
13. i.e., we rise again in our children.
14. Or, whose.
15. i.e., in sign of grief.
16. One ms. has, boys.
17. Or, virtue.
18. 2 Cor. i. 22; Eph. i. 13, iv. 30.
19. Some mss. add: A widow, very rich.
20. One ms. has: God of our fathers, Son of the Most High. Another: O Lord God, who has made the heaven and the earth, Son of the Most High, Lord Jesus Christ.
21. i.e., the exhibition of wild beasts.
22. Or, be taken off, i.e., put to death.
23. Or, drawers.
24. A part of the ancient theatres on or near the stage.
25. Or, way.
26. Or, corrupt.
27. i.e., that he was dead.

The Acts of Barnabus

The Journeyings and Martyrdom of St. Barnabas the Apostle.

Since from the descent of the presence of our Saviour Jesus Christ, the unwearied and benevolent and mighty Shepherd and Teacher and Physician, I beheld and saw the ineffable and holy and unspotted mystery of the Christians, who hold the hope in holiness, and who have been sealed; and since I have zealously served Him, I have deemed it necessary to give account of the mysteries which I have heard and seen.

I John, accompanying the holy apostles Barnabas and Paul, being formerly a servant of Cyrillus the high priest of Jupiter, but now having received the gift of the Holy Spirit through Paul and Barnabas and Silas, who were worthy of the calling, and who baptized me in Iconium.

After I was baptized, then, I saw a certain man standing clothed in white raiment; and he said to me:

Be of good courage, John, for assuredly thy name shall be changed to Mark, and thy glory shall be proclaimed in all the world.

And the darkness in thee has passed away from thee, and there has been given to thee understanding to know the mysteries of God.

And when I saw the vision, becoming greatly terrified, I went to the feet of Barnabas, and related to him the mysteries which I had seen and heard from that man.

And the Apostle Paul was not by when I disclosed the mysteries.

And Barnabas said to me:

Tell no one the miracle which thou hast seen.

For by me also this night the Lord stood, saying, Be of good courage:

for as thou hast given thy life for my name to death and banishment from thy nation, thus also shalt thou be made perfect. Moreover, as for the servant who is with you, take him also with thyself; for he has certain mysteries.

Now then, my child, keep to thyself the things which thou hast seen and heard; for a time will come for thee to reveal them. [1]

And I, having been instructed in these things by him, remained in Iconium [2] many days; for there was there a holy man and a pious, who also entertained us, whose house also Paul had sanctified.

Thence, therefore, we came to Seleucia, and after staying three days sailed away to Cyprus; and I was ministering to them until we had gone round all Cyprus.

And setting sail from Cyprus, we landed in Perga of Pamphylia.

And there I then stayed about two months, wishing to sail to the regions of the West; and the Holy Spirit did not allow me. Turning, therefore, I again sought the apostles; and having learned that they were in Antioch, I went to them.

And I found Paul in bed in Antioch from the toil of the journey, who also seeing me, was exceedingly grieved on account of my delaying in Pamphylia.

And Barnabas coming, encouraged him, and tasted bread, and he took a little of it.

And they preached the word of the Lord, and enlightened many of the Jews and Greeks.

And I only attended to them, and was afraid of Paul to come near him, both because he held me as having spent much time in Pamphylia, and because he was quite enraged against me.

And I gave repentance on my knees upon the earth to Paul, and he would not endure it.

And when I remained for three Sabbaths in entreaty and prayer on my knees, I was unable to prevail upon him about myself; for his great grievance against me was on account of my keeping several parchments in Pamphylia.

And when it came to pass that they finished teaching in Antioch, on the first of the week they took counsel together to set out for the places of the East, and after that to go into Cyprus, and oversee all the churches in which they had spoken the word of God.

And Barnabas entreated Paul to go first to Cyprus, and oversee his own in his village; and Lucius [3] entreated him to take the oversight of his city Cyrene.

And a vision was seen by Paul in sleep, that he should hasten to Jerusalem, because the brethren expected him there.

But Barnabas urged that they should go to Cyprus, and pass the winter, and then that they should go to Jerusalem at the feast.

Great contention, therefore, arose between them. [4]And Barnabas urged me also to accompany them, on account of my being their servant from the beginning, and on account of my having served them in all Cyprus until they came to Perga of Pamphylia; and I there had remained many days. But Paul cried out against Barnabas, saying:

It is impossible for him to go with us.

And those who were with us there urged me also to accompany them, because there was a vow upon me to follow them to the end.

So that Paul said to Barnabas:

If thou wilt take John who also is surnamed Mark with thee, go another road; for he shall not come with us.

And Barnabas coming to himself, said:

The grace of God does not desert [5] him who has once served the Gospel and journeyed with us.

If, therefore, this be agreeable to thee, Father Paul, I take him and go.

And he said:

Go thou in the grace of Christ, and we in the power of the Spirit.

Therefore, bending their knees, they prayed to God.

And Paul, groaning aloud, wept, and in like manner also Barnabas, saying to one another: It would have been good for us, as at first, so also at last, to work in common among men; but since it has thus seemed good to thee, Father Paul, pray for me that my labour may be made perfect to commendation: for thou knowest how I have served thee also to the grace of Christ that has been given to thee.

For I go to Cyprus, and hasten to be made perfect; [6] for I know that I shall no more see thy face, O Father Paul.

And falling on the ground at his feet, he wept long.

And Paul said to him:

The Lord stood by me also this night, saying, Do not force Barnabas not to go to Cyprus, for there it has been prepared for him to enlighten many; and do thou also, in the grace that has been given to thee, go to Jerusalem to worship in the holy place, and there it shall be shown thee where thy martyrdom has been prepared.

And we saluted one another, and Barnabas took me to himself.

And having come down to Laodiceia, [7] we sought to cross to Cyprus; and having found a ship going to Cyprus, we embarked.

And when we had set sail, the wind was found to be contrary.

And we came to Corasium; [8] and having gone down to the shore where there was a fountain, we rested there, showing ourselves to no one, that no one might know that Barnabas had separated from Paul.

And having set sail from Corasium, we came to the regions of Isauria, and thence came to a certain island called Pityusa; [9] and a storm having come on, we remained there three days; and a certain pious man entertained us, by name Euphemus, whom also Barnabas instructed in many things in the faith, with all his house.

And thence we sailed past the Aconesiae, [10] and came to the city of Anemurium; and having gone into it, we found two Greeks.

And coming to us, they asked whence and who we were.

And Barnabas said to them:

If you wish to know whence and who we are, throw away the clothing which you have, and I shall put on you clothing which never becomes soiled; for neither is there in it anything filthy, but it is altogether splendid.

And being astonished at the saying, they asked us:

What is that garment which you are going to give us?

And Barnabas said to them:

If you shall confess your sins, and submit yourselves to our Lord Jesus Christ, you shall receive that garment which is incorruptible for ever.

And being pricked at heart by the Holy Spirit, they fell at his feet, entreating and saying:

We beseech thee, father, give us that garment; for we believe in the living and true God whom thou proclaimest.

And leading them down to [11] the fountain, he baptized them into the name of Father, and Son, and Holy Ghost.

And they knew that they were clothed with power, and a holy robe.

And having taken from me one robe, he put it on the one; and his own robe he put on the other.

And they brought money to him, and straightway Barnabas distributed it to the poor.

And from them also the sailors were able to gain many things. [12]

And they having come down to the shore, he spoke to them the word of God; and he having blessed them, we saluted them, and went on board the ship.

And the one of them who was named Stephanus wished to accompany us, and Barnabas did not permit him.

And we, having gone across, sailed down to Cyprus by night; and having come to the place called Crommyacita, [13] we found Timon and Ariston the temple servants, at whose house also we were entertained.

And Timon was afflicted by much fever.

And having laid our hands upon him, we straightway removed his fever, having called upon the name of the Lord Jesus.

And Barnabas had received documents from Matthew, a book of the word [14] of God, and a narrative of miracles and doctrines.

This Barnabas laid upon the sick in each place that we came to, and it immediately made a cure of their sufferings.

And when we had come to Lapithus, [15] and an idol festival [16] being celebrated in the theatre, they did not allow us to go into the city, but we rested a little at the gate.

And Timon, after he rose up from his disease, came with us.

And having gone forth from Lapithus, we travelled through the mountains, and came to the city of Lampadistus, of which also Timon was a native; in addition to whom, having found also that Heracleius was there, we were entertained by him.

He was of the city of Tamasus, [17] and had come to visit his relations; and Barnabas, looking stedfastly at him, recognised him, having met with him formerly at Citium with Paul; to whom also the Holy Spirit was given at baptism, and he changed his name to Heracleides. And having ordained him bishop over Cyprus, and having confirmed the church in Tamasus, we left him in the house of his brethren that dwelt there.

And having crossed the mountain called Chionodes, [18] we came to Old Paphos, and there found Rhodon, a temple servant, who also, having himself believed, accompanied us.

And we met a certain Jew, by name Barjesus, coming from Paphos, who also recognised Barnabas, as having been formerly with Paul.

He did not wish us to go into Paphos; but having turned away, we came to Curium. [19]

And we found that a certain abominable race was being performed [20] in the road near the city, where a multitude of women and men naked were performing the race.

And there was great deception and error in that place.

And Barnabas turning, rebuked it; and the western part fell, so that many were wounded, and many of them also died and the rest fled to the temple of Apollo, which was close at hand in the city, which was called sacred. [21]And when we came near the temple, a great multitude of Jews who were there, having been put up to it by Barjesus, stood outside of the city, and did not allow us to go into the city; but we spent the evening under a tree near the city, and rested there.

And on the following day, we came to a certain village where Aristoclianus dwelt.

He being a leper, had been cleansed in Antioch, whom also Paul and Barnabas sealed to be a bishop, and sent to his village in Cyprus, because there were many Greeks there.

And we were entertained in the cave by him in the mountain, and there we remained one day.

And thence we came to Amathus and there was a great multitude of Greeks in the temple in the mountain, low women and men pouring libations.

There also Barjesus, getting the start of us, gained over the nation of the Jews, and did not allow us to enter into the city; but a certain widow woman, eighty years old, being outside of the city, and she also not worshipping the idols, coming forward to us, took us into her house one hour.

And when we came out we shook the dust off our feet over against that temple where the libation of the abominable took place.

And having gone out thence, we came through desert places, and Timon also accompanied us.

And having come to Citium, and there being a great uproar there also in their hippodrome, having learned this, we came forth out of the city, having all shaken the dust off our feet; for no one received us, except that we rested one hour in the gate near the aqueduct.

And having set sail in a ship from Citium, we came to Salamis, and landed in the so-called islands, where there was a place full of idols; and there there took place high festivals [22] and libations.

And having found Heracleides there again, we instructed him to proclaim the Gospel of God, and to set up churches, and ministers in them.

And having gone into Salamis, we came to the synagogue near the place called Biblia; and when we had gone into it, Barnabas, having unrolled the Gospel which he had received from Matthew his fellow-labourer, began to teach the Jews.

And Barjesus, having arrived after two days, after not a few Jews had been instructed, was enraged, and brought together all the multitude of the Jews; and they having laid hold of Barnabas, wished to hand him over to Hypatius, the governor of Salamis.

And having bound him to take him away to the governor, and a pious Jebusite, [23] a kinsman of Nero, having come to Cyprus, the Jews, learning this, took Barnabas by night, and bound him with a rope by the neck; and having dragged him to the hippodrome from the synagogue, and having gone out of the city, standing round him, they burned him with fire, so that even his bones became dust.

And straightway that night, having taken his dust, they cast it into a cloth; and having secured it with lead, they intended to throw it into the sea.

But I, finding an opportunity in the night, and being able along with Timon and Rhodon to carry it. we came to a certain place, and having found a cave, put it down there, where the nation of the Jebusites formerly dwelt.

And having found a secret place in it, we put it away, with the documents which he had received from Matthew.

And it was the fourth hour of the night of the second of the week.[24]

And when we were hid in the place, the Jews made no little search after us; and having almost found us, they pursued us as far as the village of the Ledrians; and we, having found there also a cave near the village, took refuge in it, and thus escaped them.

And we were hid in the cave three days; and the Jews having gone away, we came forth and left the place by night.

And taking with us Ariston and Rhodon, we came to the village of Limnes. [25]

And having come to the shore, we found an Egyptian ship; and having embarked in it, we landed at Alexandria.

And there I remained, teaching the brethren that came the word of the Lord, enlightening them, and preaching what I had been taught by the apostles of Christ, who also baptized me into the name of Father, and Son, and Holy Ghost; who also changed my name to Mark in the water of baptism, by which also I hope to bring many to the glory of God through His grace; because to Him is due honour and everlasting glory.

Amen.

The journeyings and martyrdom of the holy apostle Barnabas have been fulfilled through God.

Footnotes:

1. Or, will come to reveal thee.
2. One ms. has Jerusalem, and adds, and we came to Antioch, which suits the geography better.
3. Acts xiii. 1; Rom. xvi. 21.
4. Acts xv. 39.
5. Or, turn away.
6. i.e., to finish my course.
7. This is the Syrian Laodiceia, opposite Cyprus.
8. Perhaps Corycus.
9. Or, Pityussa, close to the Zephyrian promontory.
10. Perhaps Aphrodisias.
11. Or, into.
12. To make much profit.
13. Crommyon Pr.
14. Lit., the voice.
15. Lapethus.
16. Lit., an idol-frenzy,--a term often applied to the worship of Bacchus.
17. Tamassus.
18. i.e., snowy, an epithet of Olympus, the mountain they crossed.
19. Perhaps Curtium, which was nearer Palaeo Paphos than Curias Pr. was.
20. i.e., as a religious service.
21. Another reading is: In the city called Curium.
22. Lit., assemblies of the whole nation.
23. Another reading is: Eusebius the Jebusite. There is a legend that the Jebusites colonized

The Forgotten Bible
Cyprus after they were driven out of Palestine by King David.

24. The Vaticanms. adds: on the 17th of the month Pauen according to the Egyptians, and according to the Romans the 11th of the month of June.

25. This place does not appear on the ancient maps, but there is a modern C. Limniti.

The Acts of Philip

Of the Journeyings of Philip the Apostle.
From the Fifteenth Acts Until the End, and Among Them the Martyrdom. [1]
About the time when the Emperor Trajan received the government of the Romans, after Simon the son of Clopas, who was bishop of Jerusalem, had suffered martyrdom in the eighth year of his reign, being the second bishop of the church there after James who bore the name of brother of the Lord, [2] Philip the apostle, going through the cities and regions of Lydia and Asia, preached to all the Gospel of Christ.

And having come to the city of Ophioryma, which is called Hierapolis of Asia, he was entertained by a certain believer, Stachys by name.

And there was with him also Bartholomew, one of the seventy disciples of the Lord, and his sister Mariamme, and his disciples that followed him.

All the men of the city therefore, having left their work, ran to the house of Stachys, hearing about the works which Philip did.

And many men and women having assembled in the house of Stachys, Philip along with Bartholomew taught them the things of Jesus.

And Philip's sister Mariamme, sitting in the entry of the house of Stachys, addressed herself to those coming, persuading them to listen to the apostles, saying to them:

Our brethren, and sons of my Father in heaven, ye are the excellent riches, and the substance of the city above, the delight of the habitation which God has prepared for those that love Him.

Trample under foot the snares of the enemy, the writhing serpent.

For his path is crooked, since he is the son of the wicked one, and the poison of wickedness is in him; and his father is the devil, the author of death, and his mother corruption; rage in his eyes and destruction in his mouth, and his path is Hades.

Wherefore flee from him that has no substance, the shapeless one that has no shape in all the creation, whether in the heaven or in the earth, whether in the flying creatures or the beasts.

For everything is taken away from his shape; for among the beasts of the earth and the fowls of the heaven is the knowledge of him, that the serpent trails his belly and his breast; and Tartarus is his dwelling-place, and he goes in the darkness, since he has confidence in nothing. [3]Flee therefore from him, that his poison may not be poured out into your mouth.

But be rather believing, holy, of good works, having no deceit.

Take away from yourselves the wicked disposition, that is, the evil desires through which the serpent, the wicked dragon, the prince of evil, has produced the pasture of destruction and death for the soul, since all the desire of the wicked has proceeded from him.

And this is the root of iniquity, the maintenance of evils, the death of souls:

for the desire of the enemy is armed against the believers, and comes forth from the darkness, and walks in the darkness, taking in hand to war with those who are in the light.

For this is the beginning of concupiscence. [4]Wherefore you who wish to come to us, and the rather that God has come through us to you as a father to his own children, wishing to have mercy upon you, and to deliver you from the wicked snare of the enemy, flee from the evil lusts of the enemy, and cast them completely out of your mind, hating openly the father of evils, and loving Jesus, who is light, and life, and truth, and the Saviour of all who desire Him.

Having run, therefore, to Him, take hold of Him in love, that He may bring you up out of the pit of the wicked, and having cleansed you, set you blameless, living in truth, in the presence of His Father.

And all these things Philip said to the multitudes that had come together to worship as in old times the serpents and the viper, of which also they set up images and worshipped them.

Wherefore also they called Hierapolis Ophioryma. [5]And these things having been said by Philip, Bartholomew and Mariamme and his disciples, and Stachys being along with him, all the people gave ear, and a great multitude of them fleeing from the enemy were turned to Jesus, and were added to Philip and those about him.

And the faithful were the more confirmed in the love of Christ.

And Nicanora, the wife of the proconsul, lying in bed under various diseases, especially of the eyes, having heard about the Apostle Philip and his teaching, believed in the Lord.

For she had even before this heard about Him; and having called upon His name, she was released from the troubles that afflicted her.

And rising up, she went forth out of her house through the side door, carried by her own slaves in a silver litter, and went into the house of Stachys, where the apostles were.

And when she came before the gate of the house, Mariamme, the sister of Philip the apostle, seeing her, spoke to her in the Hebrew tongue before Philip and Bartholomew, and all the multitude of those who had believed, saying:

Alemakan, ikasame, marmare, nachaman, [6] mastranan, achaman; which is, Daughter of the father, thou art my mistress, thou hast been given as a pledge to the serpent; but Jesus our Redeemer has come to deliver thee through us, to break thy bands, and cut them, and to remove them from thee from their root, because thou art my sister, one mother brought us forth twins.

Thou hast forsaken thy father, thou hast forsaken the path leading thee to the dwelling-place of thy mother, being in error; thou hast left the temple of that deception, and of the temporary glory, and hast come to us, fleeing from the enemy, because he is the dwelling-place of death. Behold, now thy Redeemer has come to redeem thee; Christ the Sun of righteousness has risen upon thee, to enlighten thee. [7]

And when Nicanora, standing before the door, heard these things, she took courage before all, crying out, and saying:

I am a Hebrew, and a daughter of the Hebrews; speak with me in the language of my fathers. For, having heard the preaching of my fathers, I was straightway cured of the disease and the troubles that encompassed me.

I therefore adore the goodness of God who has caused you to be spoiled even to this city, on account of His true stone [8] held in honour, in order that through you we may receive the knowledge of Him, and may live with you, having believed in Him.

Nicanora having thus spoken, the Apostle Philip, along with Bartholomew and Mariamme and those with them, prayed for her to God, saying:

Thou who bringest the dead to life, Christ Jesus the Lord, who hast freed us through baptism from the slavery of death, [9] completely deliver also this woman from the error, the enemy; make her alive in Thy life, and perfect her in Thy perfection, in order that she may be found in the country of her fathers in freedom, having a portion in Thy goodness, O Lord Jesus.

And all having sent up the amen along with the Apostle Philip, behold, there came the tyrant, the husband of Nicanora, raging like an unbroken horse; and having laid hold of his wife's garments, he cried out, saying:

O Nicanora, did not I leave thee in bed? how hadst thou so much strength as to come to these magicians?

And how hast thou been cured of the inflammation of thine eyes?

Now, therefore, unless thou tell me who thy physician is, and what is his name, I shall punish thee with various punishments, and shall not have compassion upon thee.

And she answering, says to him:

O tyrant, cast out from thee this tyranny of thine, forsake this wickedness of thine; abandon this life lasting only for a season; run away from the brutality of thy worthless disposition; flee from the wicked dragon and his lusts; throw from thee the works and the dart of the man-slaying serpent; renounce the abominable and wicked sacrifices of the idols, which are the husbandry of the enemy, the hedge of darkness; make for thyself a life chaste and pure, that being in holiness thou mayst be able to know my Physician, and to get His name.

If therefore thou wishest me to be beside thee, prepare thyself to live in chastity and self-restraint, and in fear of the true God, and I shall live with thee all my life; only cleanse thyself from the idols, and from all their filth.

And when the gloomy tyrant her husband heard these words of hers, he seized her by the hair of her head, and dragged her along, kicking her, and saying:

It will be a fine thing for thee to be cut off by the sword, or to see thee from beside me committing fornication with these foreign magicians; for I see that thou hast fallen into the madness of these deceivers.

Thee first of them, therefore, I shall cut off by an evil death; and then, not sparing them, I shall cut their sinews, and put them to a most cruel death.

And having turned, he said to those about him:

Bring out for me those impostors of magicians.

And the public executioners having run into the house of Stachys, and laid hold of the Apostle Philip, and Bartholomew and Mariamme, dragged them along, leading them to where the proconsul was.

And the most faithful Stachys followed, and all the faithful.

And the proconsul seeing them, gnashed his teeth, saying:

Torture these deceivers that have deceived many women, and young men and girls, saying that they are worshippers of God, while they are an abomination.

And he ordered thongs of raw hide to be brought, and Philip and Bartholomew and Mariamme to be beaten; and after they had been scourged with the thongs, he ordered their feet to be tied, and them to be dragged through the streets of the city as far as the gate of their temple.

And a great crowd was assembled, so that scarcely any one stayed at home; and they all wondered at their patience, as they were being violently and inhumanly dragged along.

And the proconsul, having tortured the Apostle Philip and the saints who were with him, ordered them to be brought, and secured in the temple of the idol of the viper by its priests, until he should decide by what death he should destroy each of them.

And many of the crowd believed in the grace of Christ, and were added to the Apostle Philip, and those with him, having renounced the idol of the viper, and were confirmed in the faith, being magnified by the endurance of the saints; and all together with their voice glorified God, saying the amen.

And when they were shut up in the temple of the viper--both Philip the Apostle, and Bartholomew and Mariamme--the priests of the viper assembled in the same place, and a great crowd, about seven thousand men; and having run to the proconsul, they cried out, saying:

Avenge us of the foreigners, and magicians, and corrupters and seducers of men.

For ever since they came to us, our city has been filled with every evil deed; and they have also killed the serpents, the sons of our goddess; and they have also shut the temple, and the altar has been desolated; and we have not found the wine which had been brought in order that the viper, having drunk of it, might go to sleep.

But if thou wishest to know that they are really magicians, look and see how they wish to bewitch us, saying, Live in chastity and piety, after believing in God; and how also they have come into the city; and how also the dragons have not struck them blind, or even killed them; and how also they have not drunk their blood; but even they who keep our city from every foreigner have been cast down by these men.

And the proconsul, having heard these things, was the more inflamed with rage, and filled with wrath and threatening; and he was exceedingly enraged, and said to the priests:

Why need you speak, when they have bewitched my own wife?

And from that time she has spoken to me with strange words; and praying all the night through, she speaks in a strange tongue with a light shining round her; and groaning aloud, she says, Jesus the true light has come to me.

And I, having gone forth from my chamber, wished to look down through the window and see Jesus, the light which she spoke of; and like lightning it came upon me, so that I was within a little of being blinded; and from that time forth I am afraid of my wife, on account of her luminous Jesus.

Tell me, ye priests, what I am to do.

And they said to him:

O proconsul, assuredly we are no longer priests; for ever since thou didst shut them up, in consequence of them praying, not only has the temple been shaken from the foundations, but it is also assuredly falling down.

Then the proconsul ordered to bring Philip and those with him forth out of the temple, and to bring them up to the tribunal, saying to the public executioner:

Strip Philip and Bartholomew and Mariamme, and search thoroughly to try to find their enchantments.

Having therefore first stripped Philip, then Bartholomew, they came also to Mariamme; and dragging her along, they said:

Let us strip her naked, that all may see her, how she follows men; for she especially deceives all the women.

And the tyrant says to the priests:

Proclaim throughout the whole city round about that all should come, men and women, that they may see her indecency, that she travels about with these magicians, and no doubt commits adultery with them.

And he ordered Philip to be hanged, and his ankles to be pierced, and to bring also iron hooks, and his heels also to be driven through, and to be hanged head downwards, opposite the temple on a certain tree; and stretch out Bartholomew opposite Philip, having nailed his hands on the wall of the gate of the temple.

And both of them smiled, seeing each other, both Philip and Bartholomew; for they were as if they were not tortured:

for their punishments were prizes and crowns.

And when also they had stripped Mariamme, behold, straightway the semblance of her body

The Forgotten Bible

was changed in the presence of all, and straightway there was about her a cloud of fire before all; and they could not longer look at all on the place in which the holy Mariamme was, but they all fled from her.

And Philip spoke with Bartholomew in the Hebrew tongue saying:

Where is our brother John? for, behold, I am being released from the body; and who is he that has prayed for us?

Because they have also laid hands on our sister Mariamme, contrary to what is meet; and, behold, they have set fire to the house of Stachys, saying, Let us burn it, since he entertained them.

Dost thou wish then, Bartholomew, fire to come from heaven, and that we should burn them up?

And as Philip was thus speaking, behold, also John entered into the city like one of their fellow-citizens; and moving about in the street, he asked:

Who are these men, and why are they punished?

And they say to him:

It cannot be that thou art of our city, and askest about these men, who have wronged many: for they have shut up our gods, and by their magic have cut off both the serpents and the dragons; and they have also raised many of the dead, who have struck us with amazement, detailing many punishments against us, and they wish also, these strangers who are hanging, to pray for fire out of heaven, and to burn up us and our city.

Then says John:

Let us go, and do you show me them.

They led John, therefore, as their fellow-citizen, to where Philip was; and there was there a great crowd, and the proconsul, and the priests.

And Philip, seeing John, said to Bartholomew in Hebrew:

Brother, John has come, who was in Barek, where the living water is. [10]And John saw Philip hanging head downwards both by the ankles and the heels; [11] and he also saw Bartholomew stretched out on the wall of the temple; and he said to them:

The mystery of him that was hanged between the heaven and the earth shall be with you.

And he said also to the men of that city:

Ye men who dwell in Ophioryma Hierapolis, great is the ignorance which is among you, for you have erred in the path of error.

The dragon breathing has breathed upon you, and blinded you in three ways; that is, he has made you blind in body, and blind in soul, and blind in spirit:

and you have been struck by the destroyer.

Look upon the whole creation, whether in the earth, or in the heaven, or in the waters, that the serpent has no resemblance to anything above;[12] but he is of the stock of corruption, and has been brought to nothing by God; and on this account he is twisted and crooked, and there is no life in him; and anger, and rage, and darkness, and fire, and smoke are in all his members.

And now, therefore, why do you punish these men because they have told you that the serpent is your enemy?

And when they heard these words from John, they raised their hands against him, saying:

We thought thee to be a fellow-citizen, but now thou hast shown thyself that thou art their companion.

Like them, so also thou shalt be put to death; for the priests have intended to squeeze out your blood, and having mixed it with wine, to bring it to the viper to drink it.

When, therefore, the priests attempted to lay hold of John, their hands were paralyzed.

And John said to Philip: Let us not at all render evil for evil.

And Philip said to John: Behold now, where is my Lord Jesus, who told me not to avenge myself? But for my part, I shall not endure it longer; but I will accomplish upon them my threat, and will destroy them all [13].

And John and Bartholomew and Mariamme restrained him, saying:

Our Master was beaten, was scourged, was extended on the cross, was made to drink gall and vinegar, and said, Father, forgive them, for they know not what they do. [14]And this He taught, saying:

Learn of me, for I am meek and lowly in heart. [15]Let us also therefore be patient.

Philip says:

Go away, and do not mollify me; for I will not bear that they have hanged me head down, and pierced my ankles and my heels with irons.

And thou, John, beloved of God, how much hast thou reasoned with them, and thou hast not been listened to!

Wherefore go away from me, and I will curse them, and they shall be destroyed utterly to a man.

And he began to curse them, invoking, and crying out in Hebrew:

Abalo, aremun, iduthael, tharseleon, nachoth, aidunaph, teletoloi:[16]that is, O Father of Christ, the only and Almighty God; O God, whom all ages dread, powerful and impartial Judge, whose name is in Thy dynasty Sabaoth, [17] blessed art Thou for everlasting:

before Thee tremble dominions and powers of the celestials, and the fire-breathing threats of the cherubic living ones; the King, holy in majesty, whose name came upon the wild beasts of the desert, and they were tamed, and praised Thee with a rational voice; who lookest upon us, and readily grantest our requests; who knewest us before we were fashioned; the Overseer of all:

now, I pray, let the great Hades open its mouth; let the great abyss swallow up these the ungodly, who have not been willing to receive the word of truth in this city.

So let it be, Sabaoth.

And, behold, suddenly the abyss was opened, and the whole of the place in which the proconsul was sitting was swallowed up, and the whole of the temple, and the viper which they worshipped, and great crowds, and the priests of the viper, about seven thousand men, besides women and children, except where the apostles were:

they remained unshaken.

And the proconsul was swallowed up into the abyss; and their voices came up from beneath, saying, with weeping:

Have mercy upon us, O God of Thy glorious apostles, because we now see the judgments of those who have not confessed the crucified One:

behold, the cross illumines us.

O Jesus Christ, manifest Thyself to us, because we are all coming down alive into Hades, and are being scourged because we have unjustly crucified Thine apostles.

And a voice was heard of one, saying:

I shall be merciful to you in the cross of light.

And there remained both Stachys and all his house, and the wife of the proconsul, and fifty other women who had believed with her upon the Lord, and a multitude besides, both of men and women, and a hundred virgins who had not been swallowed up because of their chastity, having been sealed with the seal of Christ.

Then the Lord, having appeared unto Philip, said:

O Philip, didst thou not hear:

Thou shalt not render evil for evil? and why hast thou inflicted such destruction?

O Philip, whosoever putteth his hand to the plough, and looketh backwards, [18] is his furrow well set? or who gives up his own lamp to another, and himself sits in darkness? or who forsakes his own dwelling-place, and dwells on a dunghill himself? And who, giving away his own garment in winter, goes naked? or what enemy rejoices in the joy of the man that hates him? and what soldier goes to war without a full suit of armour? and what slave who has fulfilled his master's order will not be commended? and who in the race-course, having nobly run, does not receive the prize? and who that has washed his garments willingly defiles them?

Behold, my bride chamber is ready; but blessed is he who has been found in it wearing the shining garment: [19]he it is who receives the crown upon his head.

Behold, the supper is ready; and blessed is he who is invited, and is ready to go to Him that has invited him.

The harvest of the field is much, [20] and blessed is the good labourer.

Behold the lilies and all the flowers, and it is the good husbandman who is the first to get a share of them.

And how hast thou become, O Philip, unmerciful, having cursed thine enemies in wrath?

Philip says:

Why art Thou angry with me, Lord, because I have cursed mine enemies? for why dost Thou not tread them under foot, because they are yet alive in the abyss?

And knowest Thou, Lord, that because of Thee I came into this city, and in Thy name I have persecuted all the error of the idols, and all the demons?

The dragons have withered away, and the serpents.

And since these men have not received Thy light, therefore have I cursed them, and they have gone down to Hades alive.

And the Saviour says to Philip:

But since thou hast disobeyed me, and hast requited evil for evil, and hast not kept my commandment, on this account thou shalt finish thy course gloriously indeed, and shalt be led by the hand by my holy angels, and shalt come with them even to the paradise of delight; and they indeed shall come beside me into paradise, but thee will I order to be shut outside of paradise for forty days, in terror under the flaming and turning sword, and thou shalt groan because thou hast done evil to those who have done evil to thee.

And after forty days I shall send my archangel Michael; and he, having taken hold of the sword guarding paradise, shall bring thee into it, and thou shalt see all the righteous who have walked in their innocence, and then thou shalt worship the glory of my Father in the heavens.

Nevertheless the sign of thy departure shall be glorified in my cross.

And Bartholomew having gone away into Lycaonia, shall there also be himself crucified; and Mariamme shall lay her body in the river Jordan.

But I, O Philip, will not endure thee, because thou hast swallowed up the men into the abyss; but, behold, my Spirit is in them, and I shall bring them up from the dead; and thus they, seeing thee, shall believe in the glory of Him that sent thee.

And the Saviour having turned, stretched up His hand, and marked a cross in the air coming down from above even to the abyss, and it was full of light, and had its form after the likeness of a ladder.

And all the multitude that had gone down from the city into the abyss came up on the ladder of the luminous cross; but there remained below the proconsul, and the viper which they worshipped.

And when the multitude had come up, having looked upon Philip hanging head downwards, they lamented with a great lamentation at the lawless action which they had done.

And they also saw Bartholomew, and Mariamme having her former appearance.

And, behold, the Lord went up into the heavens in the sight of Philip, and Bartholomew and Mariamme, and Stachys, and all the unbelieving people, and silently they glorified God in fear and trembling.

And all the multitudes cried out, saying:

He alone is God, whom these men proclaim in truth; He alone is God, who sent these men for our salvation.

Let us therefore truly repent for our great error, because we are by no means worthy of everlasting life.

Now we believe, because we have seen great wonders, because the Saviour has brought us up from the abyss.

And they all fell upon their face, and adored Philip, and entreated him, ready to flee:

Do not do another miracle, and again send us away into the abyss.

And they prayed that they might become worthy of the appearing of Christ.

And Philip, yet hanging, addressed them, and said:

Hear and learn how great are the powers of my God, remembering what you have seen below, and how your city has been overturned, with the exception of the house which received me; and now the sweetness of my God has brought you up out of the abyss, and I am obliged to walk round paradise for forty days on your account, because I was enraged against you into requiting you.

And this commandment alone I have not kept, in that I did not give you good in return for evil.

But I say unto you, From this time forth, in the goodness of God, reject the evil, that you may become worthy of the thanksgiving [21] of the Lord.

And some of the faithful ran up to take down Philip, and take off him the iron grapnels, and the hooks out of his ankles.

But Philip said: Do not, my children, do not come near me on account of this, for thus shall be my end.

Listen to me, ye who have been enlightened in the Lord, that I came to this city, not to make any merchandise, or do any other thing; but I have been destined to go out of my body in this city in the case in which you see me.

Grieve not, then, that I am hanging thus; for I bear the stamp [22] of the first man, who was brought to the earth head downwards, and again, through the wood of the cross brought to life out of the death of the transgression.

And now I accomplish that which hath been enjoined upon me; for the Lord said to me, Unless you shall make that of you which is down to be up, and that which is on the left to be on the right, you shall not enter into my kingdom.

Be ye not therefore likened to the unchanged type, for all the world has been changed, and every soul dwelling in a body is in forgetfulness of heavenly things; but let not us possessing the glory of the heavenly seek that which is without, which is the body and the house of slavery.

Be not unbelieving, but believing, and forgive each other's faults.

Behold, I hang six days, and I have blame from the true Judge, because I altogether requited you evil, and put a stumbling-block in the way of my rectitude.

And now I am going up on high; be not sorrowful, but rather rejoice, because I am leaving this dwelling-place, my body, having escaped from the corruption of the dragon, who punishes every soul that is in sins.

And Philip, having looked round upon the multitudes, said:

O ye who have come up out of the dead from Hades, and the swallowing up of the abyss,--and the luminous cross led you up on high, through the goodness of the Father, and the Son, and the Holy Ghost,--He being God became man, having been made flesh out of the Virgin Mary, immortal, abiding in flesh; and having died, He raised the dead, having had pity on mankind, having taken away the sting of sin.

He was great, and became small for our sake, until He should enlarge the small, and bring them into His greatness.

And He it is who has sweetness; and they spat upon Him, giving Him gall to drink, in order that He might make those who were bitter against Him to taste of His sweetness.

Cleave then to Him, and do not forsake Him, for He is our life to everlasting.

And when Philip had finished this announcement, he says to them, Loose Bartholomew; and having gone up, they loosed him.

And after loosing him, Philip says to him:

Bartholomew, my brother in the Lord, thou knowest that the Lord has sent thee with me to this city, and thou hast shared with me in all the dangers with our sister Mariamme; but I know that the going forth from thy body has been appointed in Lycaonia, and it has been decreed to Mariamme to go forth from the body in the river Jordan.

Now therefore I command you, that when I have gone forth from my body, you shall build a church in this place; and let the leopard and the kid of the goats [23] come into the church, for a sign to those that believe; and let Nicanora provide for them until they shall go forth from the body; and when they shall have gone forth, bury them by the gate of the church.

And lay your peace upon the house of Stachys, as Christ laid His peace on this city.

And let all the virgins who believe stand in that house each day, watching over the sick, walking two and two; but let them have no communication with young men, that Satan may not tempt them: [24]for he is a creeping serpent, and he caused Adam by means of Eve to slip into death.

Let it not be so again in this time as in the case of Eve.

But do thou, O Bartholomew, look to them well: [25]and thou shalt give these injunctions to Stachys, and appoint him bishop.

Do not entrust the place of the bishopric to a young man, that the Gospel of Christ may not be brought to shame; and let every one that teacheth have his works equal to his words.

But I am going to the Lord, and take my body and prepare it for burial with Syriac sheets of paper; and do not put round me flaxen cloth, because the body of my Lord was wrapped in linen.

And having prepared my body for burial in the sheets of paper, bind it tight with papyrus reeds, and bury it in the church; and pray for me [26] forty days, in order that the Lord may forgive me the transgression wherein I transgressed, in requiting those who did evil to me.

See, O Bartholomew, where my blood shall drop upon the earth, a plant shall spring up from my blood, and shall become a vine, and shall produce fruit of a bunch of grapes; and having taken the cluster, press it into the cup; and having partaken of it on the third day, send up on high the Amen, in order that the offering may be complete.

And Philip, having said these things, prayed thus:

O Lord Jesus Christ, Father of the ages, King of the light, who hast made us wise in Thy wisdom, and hast given us Thine understanding, and hast bestowed upon us the counsel of Thy goodness, who hast never at any time left us, Thou art He who taketh away the disease of those who flee to Thee for refuge; Thou art the Son of the living God, who hast given us Thy presence of wisdom, who hast given us signs and wonders, and hast turned those who have gone astray; who crownest those who overcome the adversary, Thou excellent Judge. [27]Come now, Jesus, and give me the everlasting crown of victory against every adverse dominion and power, and do not let their dark air hide me when I shall cross the waters of fire and all the abyss.

O my Lord Jesus Christ, let not the enemy have ground to accuse me at Thy tribunal:

but put on me Thy glorious robe, Thy seal of light that ever shines, until I shall pass by all the powers of the world, and the wicked dragon that lieth in wait for us.

Now therefore, my Lord Jesus Christ, make me to meet Thee in the air, having forgiven me the recompense which I recompensed to my enemies; and transform the form of my body into angelic glory, and give me rest in Thy blessedness; and let me receive the promise from Thee which Thou hast promised to Thy saints to everlasting.

And having thus spoken, Philip gave up the ghost, while all the multitudes were looking upon him, and weeping, and saying:

The life of this spirit has been accomplished in peace.

And they said the Amen.

And Bartholomew and Mariamme took down his body, and did as Philip had commanded them, and buried it in that place.

And there was straightway a voice out of the heavens:

Philip the apostle has been crowned with an incorruptible crown by Jesus Christ, the Judge of the contest.

And all shouted out the Amen.

And after the three days the plant of the vine sprouted up where the blood of the holy Philip had dropped.

And they did all that had been commanded them by him, offering an offering for forty days, praying without ceasing.

And they built the church in that place, having appointed Stachys bishop in the church.

And Nicanora and all the faithful assembled, and did not cease, all of them, glorifying God on account of the wonders that had happened among them.

And all the city believed in the name of Jesus.

And Bartholomew commanded Stachys to baptize those who believed into the name of the Father, and the Son, and the Holy Ghost.

And after the forty days, the Saviour, having appeared in the form of Philip, said to Bartholomew and Mariamme:

My beloved brethren, do you wish to rest in the rest of God?

Paradise has been opened to me, and I have entered into the glory of Jesus.

Go away to the place appointed for you; for the plant that has been set apart and planted in this city shall bear excellent fruit.

Having therefore saluted the brethren, and prayed for each of them, they departed from the city of Ophioryma, the Hierapolis of Asia; and Bartholomew departed into Lycaonia, and Mariamme proceeded to the Jordan; and Stachys and those with him remained, maintaining the church in Christ Jesus our Lord, to whom be glory and strength for ever and ever.

Amen.

Footnotes:

1. [This enlarged title is from the Venetian ms.; see p. 355.--R.]
2. Comp. Euseb., H. E., iii. 32.
3. Or, in no one.
4. Or, covetousness.
5. i.e., Serpent's town.
6. Or, iachaman.
7. Comp. Mal. iv. 2.
8. Isa. xxviii. 16; 1 Pet. ii. 4, etc.
9. Comp. Rom. vi. 3, 4.
10. Another and more probable reading is: He who is the son of Barek, which means living water.
11. Or, hams.
12. One of themss. has: has no resemblance to a man in anything.
13. A Bodleianms. adds: for because I am wrathful, Jesus named me Son of thunder. [This is the ms. from which Grabe derived his text of the Acts of Paul and Thecla; comp. pp. 355 and 491.--R.]
14. Luke xxiii. 34.
15. Matt. xi. 29.
16. The Bodleianms. has the Hebrew thus: Saballon, prumeni, duthael, tharseli, annachathaei; adonab batelo teloe.
17. The Bodleianms. has Ailoel.
18. Comp. Luke ix. 62.
19. Comp. Matt. xxii. 11.
20. Comp. Matt. ix. 37.
21. Or, the Eucharist.
22. Or, type.
23. Alluding to Isa. xi. 6.
24. Comp. 1 Cor. vii. 5.
25. Lit., be a good trier.
26. On the subject of the immemorial practice of prayers for the dead, see Apostolical Constitutions, vi. 30, viii. 47. Comp. 2 Macc. xii. 44 and 2 Tim. i. 18.
27. Lit., president of the games.

Acts of Saint Philip the Apostle When He Went to Upper Hellas

And it came to pass in those days, when Philip entered into the city of Athens called Hellas, there assembled to him three hundred philosophers, saying:

Let us go and see what his wisdom is; for they say about the wise men of Asia, that their wisdom is great.

For they thought that Philip was a philosopher, since he was travelling in the dress of a recluse; and they did not know that he was an apostle of Christ.

For the dress which Jesus gave to His disciples was a mantle only, and a linen cloth. [1]Thus, then, Philip was going about. On this account, therefore, when the philosophers of Hellas saw him, they were afraid.

They assembled therefore into one place, and said to each other:

Come, let us look into our books, lest somehow this stranger overcome us, and put us to shame.

And having done so, they came together to the same place, and say to Philip:

We have doctrines of our fathers in which we are pleased, seeking after knowledge; but if thou hast anything new, O stranger, show it to us without envy boldly:

for we have need of nothing else, but only to hear something new.[2]

And Philip answering, said to them:

O philosophers of Hellas, if you wish to hear some new thing, and are desirous of something new, you ought to throw away from you the disposition of the old man; as my Lord said, It is impossible to put new wine into old bottles, since the bottle is burst, and the wine spilled, and the bottle destroyed.[3]

But they put new wine into fresh bottles, so that both may be preserved.

And these things the Lord said in parables, teaching us in His holy wisdom, that many will love the new wine, not having a bottle fresh and new.

And I love you, O men of Hellas, and I congratulate you for having said, We love something new.

For instruction really new and fresh my Lord has brought into the world, in order that He might sweep away all worldly instruction.

The philosophers say:

Who is it that thou callest thy Lord?

Philip says:

My Lord is Jesus in heaven.

And they said to him:

Show him to our comprehension without envy, that we also may believe in him.

And Philip said:

He with whom I am about to make you acquainted as Lord, is above every name; there is no other. [4]And this only I say: As you have said, Do not refuse us through envy, let it not be that I should refuse you; but rather in great exultation and in great joy I have to reveal to you that name, for I have no other work in this world than this proclamation.[5]For when my Lord came into this world, He chose us, being twelve in number, having filled us with the Holy Spirit; from His light He made us know who He was, and commanded us to preach all salvation through Him, because there is no other name named out of heaven than this. [6]On this account I have come to you, to make you fully assured, not in word only, but also in the showing forth of wonderful works in the name of our Lord Jesus Christ.

And when the philosophers heard this, they say to Philip:

This name that has been heard of by us from thee we have never found in the books of our fathers; now, therefore, how can we know about thy words?

And moreover, in addition, they say to him:

Allow us three days, that we may consult with each other about this name; for we lay no little stress upon this--to apostatize from our fathers' religion.

Philip therefore says to them:

Consult as you wish; for there is no deceit in the matter.

And the three hundred philosophers having assembled, spoke with each other, saying:

You know that this man has brought a strange philosophy, and the words spoken by him bring us to distraction.

What, then, shall we do about him, or about the name of him who is called Jesus, the king of the ages, whom he speaks of?

And moreover they say to each other:

Assuredly we cannot reason with him, but the high priest of the Jews can.

If therefore it seem good, let us send to him, in order that he may stand up to this stranger, and that we may learn accurately the name that is preached.

They wrote therefore to Jerusalem after this manner:--The philosophers of Hellas to Ananias, the great high priest of the Jews in Jerusalem. There being between thee and us at all times great [7] ...as thou knowest that we Athenians are searchers after truth.

A certain foreigner has come to Hellas, Philip by name; and, in a word, he has disturbed us exceedingly, both by words and by extraordinary miracles, and he introduces a glorious name, Jesus, professing himself to be his disciple.

And he does also wonders of which we write to you, in that he has cast out demons that have been long in men, and makes the deaf hear, the blind see; and what is more wonderful--which also we should have first mentioned--he has raised up men after they were dead, that have fairly completed the number of their days. [8] And the fame of him has gone abroad into all Hellas and Macedonia; and there are many coming to him from the cities round about, bringing those who are ill with various diseases, and he heals them all through the name of Jesus.

On this account, therefore, come to us without any reluctance, that thou thyself mayst announce to us what Jesus, this name which he teaches, means.

For on this account also we have sent this letter to thee, O high priest.

And when he had read, he was filled with great wrath, and rent his clothes, and said:

Has that deceiver gone even to Athens, among the philosophers, to lead them astray?

And the Mansemat--that is, Satan--entered into Ananias unawares, and filled him with anger and rage; and he said:

If I allow that Philip himself, and those with him, to live, the law will be entirely destroyed, and their teaching will likely fill the whole earth.

And the high priest went into his own house, and the teachers of the law, and the Pharisees; and they consulted with each other, saying:

What shall we do about these things? [9] And they say to the high priest Ananias:

Stand up and arm thyself, and five hundred able men out of the people, and go away to Athens, and by all means kill Philip, and thus thou shalt overturn his teaching.

And having put on the high priest's robe, he came to Hellas in great pomp, with the five hundred men.

And Philip was in the house of a certain chief man of the city, with the brethren who had believed.

And the high priest and those with him, and the three hundred philosophers, went up to the gateway of the house where Philip was; and it was told Philip that they were outside.

And he rose up and went out.

And when the high priest saw him, he says to him:

O Philip, sorcerer and magician, for I know thee, that in Jerusalem thy master the deceiver called thee Son of Thunder. [10] Was not the whole of Judaea sufficient for you, but you have come here also to deceive men who are searchers after wisdom?

And Philip said:

Would that, O Ananias, thy covering of unbelief were taken away from thy heart, that thou mightst know my words, and from them learn whether I am a deceiver, or thou!

Ananias having heard this, said to Philip:

I shall give answer to all.

And Philip said:

Speak.

The high priest says:

O men of Hellas, this Philip believes in a man called Jesus, who was born among us, who also taught this heresy, and destroyed the law and the temple, and brought to nought the purification through Moses, and the new moons, because he says, These have not been commanded by God.

And when we saw that he thus destroyed the law, we stood up against him, and crucified him, that his teaching might not be fulfilled.

For many changes were brought in by him; and he gave an evil testimony, for he ate all things in common, and mixed with blood, after the manner of the Gentiles. [11]And having given him up, we put him to death, and buried him in a tomb; and these disciples of his having stolen him, have proclaimed everywhere that he has risen from the dead, and have led astray a great multitude by professing that he is at the right hand of God in heaven. [12]But now these men, themselves having the circumcision as we also have, have not followed it, since they began to do many deeds of power in Jerusalem through the name of Jesus; and having been cast out of Jerusalem, they go about the world, and deceive all men by the magic of that Jesus, as also now this Philip has come to you to deceive you by the same means.

But I shall carry him away with myself to Jerusalem, because Archelaus the king is also searching for him to kill him.

And when the multitude standing round heard this, those indeed who had been confirmed in the faith were not shaken nor made to waver; for they knew that Philip would conquer in the glory of Jesus.

Philip therefore stated his case in the power of Christ with great boldness, exulting and saying:

I, O men of Athens, and those of you who are philosophers, have come to you, not to teach you with words, but by the showing forth of miracles; and in part you have quickly seen [13] the things that have come to pass through me, in that name by which the high priest himself is cast off. [14]For, behold, I shall cry to my God, and teach you, and you will prove the words of both.

The high priest having heard this, ran to Philip, wishing to scourge him, and that same hour his whole hand was dried up, and his eyes were blinded; and in like manner also the five hundred who were with him were also themselves blinded.

And they reviled and cursed the high priest, saying:

Coming out of Jerusalem we said to thee, Refrain; for, being men, we cannot fight against God. [15]But we entreat thee, O Philip, apostle of the God Jesus, give us the light that is through him, that we also may truly be his slaves.

And Philip, having seen what had come to pass, said:

O weak nature! which has thrown itself upon us, but straightway has been brought down low into itself; O bitter sea! which rouses its waves against us, and thinks to cast us out, but which by itself lulls its waves to rest. Now therefore, O our good steward Jesus, the holy light, Thou hast not overlooked us who are all together crying up to Thee in all good works, but hast come to finish them through us.

Now therefore come, Lord Jesus; reprove the folly of these men.

The high priest says to Philip:

Dost thou then think to turn us away from the traditions of our fathers, and the God of the desert, and Moses; and dost thou imagine that thou wilt make us followers of Jesus the Nazarene?

Then Philip says to him:

Behold, I shall pray to my God to come and manifest Himself before thee and the five hundred, and before all here; for perhaps thou wilt change thy mind, and believe. But if even to the end thou remain in unbelief, there is coming upon thee an extraordinary thing, which shall be spoken of to generations of generations--that also thou shalt go down alive, down into Hades, before the face of all seeing thee, because thou yet abidest in unbelief, because also thou seekest to turn away this multitude from the true life.

And Philip prayed, saying:

O holy Father of the holy Son Jesus Christ, who hast granted to me to believe in Him, send Thy beloved Son Jesus Christ to reprove the unbelieving high priest, that Thy name may be glorified in Christ the Beloved.

And while Philip was yet crying out this, suddenly the heavens were opened, and Jesus appeared coming down in most excellent glory, and in lightning; and His face was shining sevenfold more than the sun, and His garments were whiter than snow, so that also all the idols of Athens fell suddenly to the ground.

And the people fled in anguish; and the demons dwelling among them cried out:

Behold, we also flee because of Him who has appeared to the city, Jesus the Son of God.

Then Philip says to the high priest:

Hearest thou the demons crying out because of Him who has been seen, and believest thou not in Him who is present that He is Lord of all?

The high priest says:

I have no other God than the one in the desert.

And as Jesus was going up into heaven there happened a very great earthquake, so that the place on which they stood was cleft; and the crowds ran and fell at the feet of the apostle, crying out:

Have mercy upon us, O man of God!

The Forgotten Bible

In like manner also the five hundred men cried out themselves also again:

Have mercy upon us, O Philip, that we may know thee, and through thee Jesus the light of life:

for we said to this unbelieving high priest, Being sinful men, we cannot fight against God.

Then Philip says:

There is no hatred in us, but the grace of Christ will make you receive your sight; but I will make the high priest receive his sight before you, that at this you may the more believe. And a voice out of heaven was brought to Philip:

O Philip, son once of thunder, but now of meekness, whatever thou mayst ask of my Father, He shall do for thee.

And all the crowd was terror-struck at the voice, for the sound of it was greater than that of thunder.

Then Philip says to the high priest:

In the name of the power of the voice of my Lord, receive thy sight, Ananias.

And immediately he received his sight, and looked round, and said:

What is there in the magic of Jesus, that this Philip within a short time has made me blind, and again within a short time has made me receive my sight?

Dost thou then, said Philip, believe in Jesus?

The high priest says:

You do not think, do you, that you can bewitch me, and persuade me?

And the five hundred who were with him, having heard that their high priest, having received his sight, was yet unbelieving, said to the bystanders to pray Philip that he should make them receive their sight, that, said they, we may cut off this unbelieving high priest.

And Philip said:

Do not avenge yourselves upon the wicked.

And he says to the high priest:

There will be a certain great sign upon thee.

He says to Philip:

I know that thou art a sorcerer and a disciple of Jesus:

thou dost not bewitch me.

And the apostle said to Jesus:

Sabarthan, sabathabt, bramanuch, come quickly.

And immediately the earth was cleft in the place where Ananias was, and swallowed him up as far as the knees.

And Ananias cried out:

O great is the power of the true witchcraft, because it has cleft the earth, when Philip threatened it in Hebrew, and adjured it; and it holds me even to the knees, and by the heels some hooks as it were drag me downwards, that I may believe in Philip; but he cannot persuade me, for from Jerusalem I know his magic tricks.

And Philip, enraged, said:

O earth, lay fast hold of him, even to the navel.

And immediately it dragged him down.

And he said:

The one of my feet underneath is turned into ice, and the other is frightfully hot; but by thy magic, Philip, I will not be overcome.

Except, therefore, that I am sore tortured underneath, I do not believe at all.

And the crowds wished to stone him.

And Philip says:

Not so; for this has in the meantime happened, that he has been swallowed up as far as the navel, that the salvation of your souls may be effected, because he would almost have drawn you by his wicked words into unbelief.

But if even he repented, I should bring him up out of the earth to the salvation of his soul; but assuredly he is not worthy of salvation.

If, then, he remain in unbelief, you shall see him sunk down into the abyss, unless the Lord intends to raise those who are in Hades, that they may confess that Jesus is Lord.

For in that day every tongue shall confess that Jesus is Lord, [16] and that there is one glory of the Father, and the Son, with the Holy Spirit for evermore.

And Philip, having said this, extended his right hand, stretching it through the air over the five hundred men in the name of Jesus.

And their eyes were opened, and they all praised God with one mouth, saying:

We bless Thee, O Christ Jesus, the God of Philip, that thou hast driven the blindness away from us, and hast given us Thy light, the Gospel.

And Philip rejoiced exceedingly at their words, because they were thus confirmed in the faith.

And after this, Philip, having turned to the high priest, said:

Confess thou also in a pure heart that Jesus is Lord, that thou mayst be saved, like those with thee. But the high priest laughed at Philip, and remained in unbelief.

Philip then, seeing that he remained in unbelief, having looked at him, says to the earth:

Open thy mouth, and swallow him up as far as his neck in the presence of those who have believed in Christ Jesus.

And in the same hour the earth, having opened its mouth, received him as far as the neck.

And the multitude communed with each other on account of the wonders that had happened.

A certain chief man of the city came crying out, and saying:

O blessed apostle, a certain demon has assailed my son, and cried out, saying to me, Since thou hast allowed a foreigner to come into your city, thou who hast been the first to do away with [17] our worship and our sacrifices, what shall I do for thee, except to kill this thine only begotten son?

And after he said this, he strangled my son.

Now therefore, I beseech thee, O apostle of Christ, do not allow my joy to be turned into sorrow, because I also have believed thy words.

And the apostle, having heard this, said:

I wonder at the activity of the demons, that it is active in every place, and dares to assail those to whose help I have not been able to come, [18] as now they have tried you, wishing to cause you to offend.

And he says to the man: Bring me thy son, and I will give him to thee alive, through my Christ.

And rejoicing, he ran to bring his son.

And when he came near his house, he cried out, saying:

My son, I have come to thee to carry thee to the apostle, so that he may present thee to me living.

And he ordered his slaves to carry the bed; and his son was twenty-three years old.

And when Philip saw him, he was moved; and he turned to the high priest, and said:

This has happened as a chance for thee:

if, therefore, I shall raise him up, wilt thou henceforth believe?

And he says:

I know your magic arts, that thou wilt raise him up; but I will not believe thee.

And Philip, enraged, said:

A curse upon thee! then go down altogether into the abyss before the face of all these.

And at the same hour he went down into Hades alive, except that the high priest's robe flew off from him; and because of this, from that day, no one knew what became of the priest's robe.

And the apostle turned round and prayed for the boy; and having driven the demon away from him, he raised him up, and set him beside his father alive.

And the multitude having beheld this, cried out:

The God of Philip is the only God, who has punished the unbelief of the high priest, and driven away the demon from the young man, and raised him up from the dead.

And the five hundred having seen the high priest swallowed up into the abyss, and the other miracles, besought Philip, and he gave them the seal in Christ.

And Philip abode in Athens two years; and having founded a church, appointed a bishop and a presbyter, and so went away to Parthia, preaching Christ.

To whom be glory for ever. Amen.

Footnotes:

1. Comp. Matt. x. 10; Mark vi. 9.
2. Acts xvii. 21.
3. Comp. Matt. ix. 17, etc.
4. Eph. i. 21.
5. Or, preaching.
6. Acts iv. 12.
7. There seems to be some omission in the mss. here.
8. Lit., of life.
9. Or, these men.
10. It was James and John who were called sons of thunder (Mark iii. 17).
11. This last sentence is very corrupt in the original. A few changes give it the meaning above.
12. Rom. viii. 34, etc.
13. Better tach an theasesthe--you will perhaps see.

14. Or, which the high priest casts off for himself.
15. Comp. Acts v. 39 and xxiii. 9 in Textus Receptus.
16. Phil. ii. 11.
17. Or, thou being a chief man who has done away with.
18. There is some doubt about the reading here.

Addition to Acts of Philip
(From a Paris ms.) [1]

And he taught them thus:
My brethren, sons of my Father--for you are of my family as to Christ, substance of my city, the Jerusalem above, the delight of my dwelling-place--why have you been taken captive by your enemy the serpent, twisted, crooked, and perverse, to whom God has given neither hands nor feet?

And crooked is his going, since he is the son of the wicked one; for his father is death, and his mother corruption, and ruin is in his body.

Do not go then into his destruction; for you are in bondage by the unbelief and deception of his son, who is without order, and has no substance; [2] formless, and has no form in the whole creation, either in the heaven or in the earth, or among the fishes that are in the waters.

But if you see him, flee from him, since he has no resemblance to men:
his dwelling is the abyss, and he walks in darkness.
Flee, then, from him, that his venom may not be poured out upon you:
if his venom be poured out upon your body, you walk in his wickedness.
But remain rather in the true worship, being faithful, reverent, and good, without guile.
Flee from Satan the dragon, and remove from you his wicked seed, namely desire, by which he begets disease in the soul, which is the venom of the serpent.

For desire is of the serpent from the beginning, and she it is who arms herself against the faithful; for she came forth out of the darkness, and returns to the darkness.

You ought therefore, after coming to us, or rather through us to God, to throw out the venom of the devil from your bodies.

And as the apostle was saying this, behold, Nicanora came forth from her house, and went with her slaves into the house of Stachys.

And when she came near the door of the house, behold, Mariamme spoke to her in the Syriac language:
Helikomaei, kosma, etaa, mariacha.
And she explained her words, saying:
O daughter of the Spirit, thou art my lady, who hast been given in pledge to the serpent; but I have come to deliver thee:
I shall break thy bonds, and cut them from their root. Behold, the Deliverer that frees thee has come:
behold, the Sun of righteousness has risen to enlighten thee.

And when she was thus speaking, the gloomy tyrant came running and panting.
And Nicanora, who was before the door, heard this, and took courage before them all, crying out and saying:
I am a Hebrew, a daughter of the Hebrews; speak with me in the language of my fathers, because I have heard your preaching, and have been cured of this my disease.

I reverence and glorify the goodness of God, in that He hath made you to be utterly spoiled in this earth.

And when she said this, the tyrant came, and took hold of her garments, and said:
O Nicanora, did I not leave thee lying on the bed from thy disease?
Whence, then, hast thou found this power and strength, so as to be able to come to these magicians?
Unless, then, thou tell who is the healer, I shall punish thee most severely.
And Nicanora answered, and said:
O rearer of tyrants, cast away from thyself this tyranny, and forget thy wicked works, and abandon this temporary life, and put away vainglory, because it passes like a shadow:
seek rather what is everlasting, and take away from thyself the beastly and impious work of base desire, and reject vain intercourse, which is the husbandry of death, the dark prison; and overturn the middle wall of corruption, and prepare for thyself a life chaste and spotless, that we may altogether live in sanctity.

If, then, thou wishest me to remain with thee, I will live with thee in continence.

And when the tyrant heard these words, he seized her by the hair of the head, and dragged her along, kicking her, and saying:

It would be better for thee to be put to death by my sword, than to be seen with these foreign magicians and deceivers.

I will punish thee, therefore, and put to death those who have deceived thee.

And he turned in a rage to the executioners who followed him, and said:

Bring me these impostors.

And the executioners ran to the house of Stachys, and laid hold of Philip, and Bartholomew, and Mariamme, with the leopard and the kid of the goats, and dragged them along, and brought them.

When the tyrant saw them, he gnashed his teeth against them, and said: Drag along these magicians and deceivers that have deceived many souls of women by saying, We are worshippers of God.

And he caused thongs to be brought, and bound their feet.

And he ordered them to be dragged along from the gate as far as the temple.

And great multitudes came together to that place.

And they wondered exceedingly at the leopard and the kid; for they were speaking like men, and some of the multitude believed the words of the apostles.

And the priests said to the tyrant:

These men are magicians.

And when he heard that, he burned with rage, and was filled with anger; and he ordered Philip, and Bartholomew, and Mariamne to be stripped, saying: Search them.

Perhaps you will find their sorcery.

And the executioners stripped them, and laid hold of Mariamne, and dragged her along, saying:

Uncover her, that they may learn that it is a woman who follows them.

And he ordered to bring clubs and strong cords; and after piercing Philip's ankles they brought hooks, and put the cords through his ankles, and hung him head downwards on a tree that was before the door of the temple; and they fixed pegs into the temple wall, and left him.

And after binding Bartholomew hand and foot, they extended him naked on the wall; and when they had stripped Mariamne, the appearance of her body was changed, and became a glass chest filled with light, and they could not come near her.

And Philip spoke with Bartholomew in Hebrew:

Where is John to-day, in the day of our need? for behold, we are being delivered from our bodies.

And they have laid hands on Mariamne beyond what is seemly, and they have scourged the leopard and the kid of the goats, and have set fire to the house of Stachys, because he took us in.

Let us therefore speak, that fire may come down from heaven and burn them up.

And as Philip was thus speaking, behold, John came into the city, and walked about the street, and asked those in the city:

What is the commotion, and who are these men, and why are they punished?

And they say to him:

Art thou not of this city?

And dost thou not know about these men, how they disturbed our houses, and the whole city? Moreover, they have even persuaded our wives to go away from us on the pretence of religion, proclaiming a foreign name, viz. Christ's; and they have also shut our temples by the sorcery they have, and they have put to death the serpents that are in the city by foreign names that we have never known.

And they have fixed their abode in the house of Stachys the blind man, whom they made to recover his sight through the spittle of a woman who accompanies them; and it is perhaps she who has all the sorcery:

and there accompany them a leopard and a kid, speaking like men.

But if ever you have seen such doings, you will not be put about by them.

And John answered, and said to them:

Show me them.

And they brought him to the temple where Philip was hanging. And when Philip saw John, he said to Bartholomew:

O my brother, behold the son of Barega--that is the living water--has come.

And John saw Philip hanging head down, tied by his ankles; and saw Bartholomew also bound to the temple wall.

And he said to the men of the city:

O children of the serpent, how great is your folly! for the way of deceit has deceived you, the

wicked dragon breathing has breathed upon you:
why do you punish these men for saying the serpent is your enemy?

And when they heard these words from John, they laid their hands upon him, saying:

We called thee our fellow-citizen, but now thy speech has made thee manifest that thou also art in communion with them.

Thou also, therefore, shalt be put to the same death as they, for the priests have decided thus:

Let us drain out their blood as they hang head downward, and mix it with wine, and offer it to the viper.

And when they were thus speaking, behold, Mariamne rose up from the place in which she was, and came back to her former appearance.

And the priests reached forth their hands towards John, wishing to lay hold of him, and they could not.

Then Philip with Bartholomew said to John:

Where is Jesus, who enjoins upon us not to take into our own hands vengeance on those that torture us? for after this I will not endure them.

And Philip spoke in Hebrew, and said:

My Father Uthael, i.e., O Christ, Father of majesty, whose name all the ages [3] fear, who art powerful, and the power of the universe, whose name goes forth in lordship, [4] Eloa:

Blessed art Thou to the ages; Thou whom dominions and powers fear, trembling before Thy face; King of honour! Father of majesty! whose name has gone forth to the wild beasts of the desert, and they have become quiet because of Thee, and through Thee the serpents have departed from us:

Hear us before we ask.

Thou who seest us before we call, who knowest our thoughts, the All-surveyor [5] of all, who sends forth from Himself unnumbered compassions; let the abyss open its mouth, and swallow up these godless persons who will not accept the word of Thy truth.

And in that very hour the abyss opened its mouth, and all that place was violently shaken, from the proconsul to all the multitude along with the priests; and they were all sunk down.

And the places where the apostles and all who were with them were remained unshaken, and the house of Stachys, and Nicanora the tyrant's wife, and the twenty-four wives who fled from their husbands, and the forty virgins who had not known men.

These alone did not go down into the abyss, because they had become servants, and had received the word of God, and His seal; but all the rest of the city were swallowed down into the abyss.

And the Saviour having appeared at that hour, said to Philip:

Who is it that has put his hand to the plough, and has turned back from making the furrow straight? or who gives his light to others, and himself remains sitting in darkness? or who dwells in the dirt, and leaves his dwelling-place to strangers? or who lays down his garment, and goes out in the days of winter naked? or what slave that has done his master's service, shall not be called by him to supper? or who runs with zeal in the racecourse, and does not get the prize?

Philip, behold my bridal chamber is ready, and blessed is he who has his own shining garment; for he it is who gets the crown of joy upon his head.

Behold, the supper is ready, and blessed is he who is called by the bridegroom. Great is the harvest of the field; blessed is the able workman.

And when Philip heard these words from the Saviour, he answered and said to him:

Thou didst give us leave, O Jesus of Nazareth, and dost Thou not enjoin us to smite those who do not wish Thee to reign over them?

But this we know, that Thy name has not been proclaimed in all the world, and Thou hast sent us to this city.

And I did not intend to come into this city, and Thou didst send me, after giving me Thy true commandment, that I should drive away all deceit, and bring to nothing every idol and demon, and all the power of the unclean one.

And when I came here, the demons fled from our faces through Thy name, and the dragons and the serpents withered away, but these men did not take to themselves Thy true light; and for this reason I resolved to bring them low, according to their folly.

And the Saviour said:

O Philip, since thou hast forsaken this commandment of mine, not to render evil for evil, [6] for this reason thou shalt be debarred in the next world for forty years from being in the place of my promise:

besides, this is the end of thy departure from the body in this place; and Bartholomew has his lot in Lycaonia, and shall be crucified there; and Mariamne shall lay down her body in the river Jordan.

And the Saviour turned and stretched out His hand, and made the sign of the cross in the air; and it was full of light, and had its form after the likeness of a ladder.

And all the multitude of the men of the city who had gone down into the abyss came up upon the ladder of the cross of light and none of them remained in the abyss, but only the tyrant and the priests, and the viper which they worshipped.

And when the multitudes came up from the abyss, they looked and saw Philip hanging head down, and Bartholomew upon the wall of the temple, and they also found Mariamne in her first shape.

And the Saviour went up into heaven in the sight of Philip and Bartholomew and Mariamne, and the leopard and the kid of the goats, and Nicanora and Stachys; and they all with a loud voice glorified God with fear and trembling, crying out:

There is one God who has sent us His salvation, whose name these men proclaim: we repent therefore of the error in which we were before yesterday, not being worthy of eternal life; and we believe, having seen the wonderful things that have come to pass through us.

And some of them threw themselves on their faces, and worshipped the apostles; and others made ready to flee, saying:

There may be another earthquake like the one that has just happened.

And stretching out his hands, the Apostle Philip, hanging head down, said:

Men of the city, hear these words which I am going to say to you, hanging head down.

Ye have learned how great are the powers of God, and the wonders which you saw when your city was destroyed by the earthquake which came upon it.

And this was manifest to you, that the house of Stachys was not destroyed and that he did not go down into the abyss, because he believed on the true God, and received us His servants.

And I, having fulfilled all the will of my God, am His debtor for what I requited to him that did evil to me.

And some of those who had been baptized ran to loose Philip hanging head down.

And he answered and said to them:

My brethren,... [7] those who are virgins in the members of their flesh and commit fornication in their hearts, and the fornication of their eyes, shall abound like the deluge.

And they grow immoderate from listening to persuasive pleasures, forgetting the God of the knowledge of the Gospel; and their hearts are full of arrogance, eating and drinking in their worship, forgetting the holy commandment, and despising it.

That generation is turned aside; but blessed is he that retires into his retreat, for he shall obtain rest in his departure.

Knowest thou not, Bartholomew, that the word of our Lord is true life and knowledge? for the Lord said to us in His teaching, Every one who shall look upon a woman, and lust after her in his heart, has completed adultery. [8]

And on this account our brother Peter fled from every place in which a woman was, and yet there was scandal on account of his own daughter; and he prayed to the Lord, and she had paralysis of her side, that she might not be deceived.

Thou seest, brother, that the sight of the eyes brings gainsaying, and the beginning of sin, as it is written, [9] She looked, and saw the tree, that it was pleasing to her eyes, and good for food, and she was deceived.

Let the hearing, then, of the virgins be holy; and in their going out let them walk two and two, for many are the wiles of the enemy.

Let their walk and conversation be well ordered, that they may be saved; but if not, let their fruit be common.

My brother Bartholomew, give these promises to Stachys, and appoint him ruler and bishop in the Church, that he may be like thee, teaching well.

Do not entrust the office to a man too young:

appoint not such a one to the chair of the teachers, lest thou profane the witness of Christ.

For he that teaches should have his works corresponding to his words, that the word may be ready on every occasion in its own glory. But I am being released from my body, hanging head down.

Take, then, my body, and prepare it for burial in Syrian paper, and do not put about it linen cloth, since they put it upon the body of our Lord, and wrap it close in paper and papyrus, and put it in the vestibule of the holy church.

And pray over me for forty days, that God may forgive the transgression which I did, in that I requited evil to him that did evil to me, and there may not be for me in the world to come the forty years.

And after thus speaking, Philip prayed, saying:

My Lord Jesus Christ, Father of the ages, King of all light, who makest us wise in Thy wisdom, who hast given us the exalted knowledge, who hast graciously conferred upon us the counsel of Thy goodness, who hast never departed from us; Thou who takest away disease from those who take refuge in Thee; Thou who hast given us the Word, to turn unto Thee those who have been led astray; Thou who hast given us signs and wonders on behalf of those of little faith; Thou who presentest the crown to those who have conquered; Thou who art the judge of the games, who hast given us the crown of joy, who speakest with us, that we may be able to withstand those that hurt us; Thou art He who sows and reaps, and completes, and increases, and vivifies all Thine own servants:

reproaches and threats are to us help and power through those who turn to Thee through us, who are Thy servants.

Come, Lord, and give me the crown of victory in the presence of men.

Let not their dark air envelope me, nor their smoke burn the shape of my soul, that I may cross the waters of the abyss, and not sink in them.

My Lord Jesus Christ, let not the enemy find anything that he can bring against me in the presence of Thee, the true Judge, but clothe me in Thy shining robe, and...(The rest is wanting.)

Footnotes:

1. [The Greek text of this addition is given by Tischendorf in the supplement appended to his volume containing Apocalypses Apocryphae, pp. 141-150. The ms. from which it is taken is of the eleventh century. Tischendorf regards this form as of Gnostic origin.--R.]

2. upostasin.

3. Or, aeons.

4. dunasteia.

5. panepiskopos.

6. Matt. v. 39; 1 Pet. iii. 9.

7. Here a good deal of the text is wanting. The Bodleianms. fills up the blank to some extent:--Walking two and two, but let them not talk with the young men, lest Satan tempt them. For he is a creeping serpent, and made Adam be destroyed even to death. And thus shall it be again at this time, for the time and the season shall be wicked. Many women and men shall leave the work of marriage, and the women shall assume the name of virginity, but knowing nothing at all about it, and that it has a great and glorious seal. And there shall be many men in those days in word only, and not in its power; for they shall observe virginity in the members of the flesh, and commit fornication in their hearts, etc. [Thems. is that referred to on p. 500. Tischendorf gives large extracts from it; the Greek text of this paragraph may be found on pp. 154, 155, supplement to Apocalypses Apocryphae.--R.]

8. Matt. v. 28.

9. Gen. iii. 6.

Acts and Martyrdom of the Holy Apostle Andrew

What we have all, both presbyters and deacons of the churches of Achaia, beheld with our eyes, we have written to all the churches established in the name of Christ Jesus, both in the east and west, north and south.

Peace to you, and to all who believe in one God, perfect Trinity, true Father unbegotten, true Son only-begotten, true Holy Spirit proceeding from the Father, and abiding in the Son, in order that there may be shown one Holy Spirit subsisting in the Father and Son in precious Godhead.

This faith we have learned from the blessed Andrew, the apostle of our Lord Jesus Christ, whose passion also we, having seen it set forth before our eyes, have not hesitated to give an account of, according to the degree of ability we have.

Accordingly the proconsul AEgeates, [1] having come into the city of Patras, began to compel those believing in Christ to worship the idols; to whom the blessed Andrew, running up, said:

It behoved thee, being a judge of men, to acknowledge thy Judge who is in the heaven, and having acknowledged Him, to worship Him; and worshipping Him who is the true God, to turn away thy thoughts from those which are not true gods.

To whom AEgeates said:

Art thou Andrew, who destroyest the temples of the gods, and persuadest men about the religion which, having lately made its appearance, the emperors of the Romans have given orders to suppress?

The blessed Andrew said:

The emperors of the Romans have never recognised the truth.

And this the Son of God, who came on account of the salvation of men, manifestly teaches-- that these idols are not only not gods, but also most shameful demons, [2] and hostile to the human race, teaching men to offend God, so that, by being offended, He turns away and will not hearken; that therefore, by His turning away and not hearkening, they may be held captive by the devil; and that they might work them to such a degree, that when they go out of the body they may be found deserted and naked, carrying nothing with them but sins.

AEgeates said:

These are superfluous and vain words:

as for your Jesus, for proclaiming these things to the Jews they nailed him to the tree of the cross.

The blessed Andrew answering, said:

Oh, if thou wouldst recognise the mystery of the cross, with what reasonable love the Author [3] of the life of the human race for our restoration endured this tree of the cross, not unwillingly, but willingly!

AEgeates said:

Seeing that, betrayed by his own disciple, and seized by the Jews, he was brought before the procurator, and according to their request was nailed up by the procurator's soldiers, in what way dost thou say that he willingly endured the tree of the cross?

The holy Andrew said:

For this reason I say willingly, since I was with Him when he was betrayed by His disciple.

For before He was betrayed, He spoke to us to the effect that He should be betrayed and crucified for the salvation of men, and foretold that He should rise again on the third day.

To whom my brother Peter said, [4] Far be it from thee, Lord; let this by no means be.

And so, being angry, He said to Peter, Get thee behind me, Satan; for thou art not disposed to the things of God.

And in order that He might most fully explain that He willingly underwent the passion, He said to us, [5] I have power to lay down my life, and I have power to take it again.

And, last of all, while He was supping with us, He said, [6] One of you will betray me.

At these words, therefore, all becoming exceedingly grieved, in order that the surmise might be free from doubt, He made it clear, saying, To whomsoever I shall give the piece of bread out of my hand, he it is who betrays me.

When, therefore, He gave it to one of our fellow-disciples, and gave an account of things to come as if they were already present, He showed that He was to be willingly betrayed. For neither did He run away, and leave His betrayer at fault; but remaining in the place in which He knew that he was, He awaited him.

AEgeates said:

I wonder that thou, being a sensible man, shouldst wish to uphold him on any terms whatever; for, whether willingly or unwillingly, all the same, thou admittest that he was fastened to the cross.

The blessed Andrew said:

This is what I said, if now thou apprehendest, that great is the mystery of the cross, which, if thou wishest, as is likely, to hear, attend to me. [7]

AEgeates said:

A mystery it cannot be called, but a punishment.

The blessed Andrew said:

This punishment is the mystery of man's restoration.

If thou wilt listen with any attention, thou wilt prove it.

AEgeates said:

I indeed will hear patiently; but thou, unless thou submissively obey me, shalt receive [8] the mystery of the cross in thyself.

The blessed Andrew answered:

If I had been afraid of the tree of the cross, I should not have proclaimed the glory of the cross.

AEgeates said:

Thy speech is foolish, because thou proclaimest that the cross is not a punishment, and through thy foolhardiness thou art not afraid of the punishment of death.

The holy Andrew said:

It is not through foolhardiness, but through faith, that I am not afraid of the punishment of death; for the death of sins [9] is hard.

And on this account I wish thee to hear the mystery of the cross, in order that thou perhaps, acknowledging it, mayst believe, and believing, mayst come somehow or other to the renewing of thy soul.

AEgeates said:

That which is shown to have perished is for renewing. Do you mean that my soul has perished, that thou makest me come to the renewing of it through the faith, I know not what, of which thou hast spoken?

The blessed Andrew answered:

This it is which I desired time to learn, which also I shall teach and make manifest, that though the souls of men are destroyed, they shall be renewed through the mystery of the cross.

For the first man through the tree of transgression brought in death; and it was necessary for the human race, that through the suffering of the tree, death, which had come into the world, should be driven out.

And since the first man, who brought death into the world through the transgression of the tree, had been produced from the spotless earth, it was necessary that the Son of God should be begotten a perfect man from the spotless virgin, that He should restore eternal life, which men had lost through Adam, and should cut off [10] the tree of carnal appetite through the tree of the cross.

Hanging upon the cross, He stretched out His blameless hands for the hands which had been incontinently stretched out; for the most sweet food of the forbidden tree He received gall for food; and taking our mortality upon Himself, He made a gift of His immortality to us.

AEgeates said:

With these words thou shalt be able to lead away those who shall believe in thee; but unless thou hast come to grant me this, that thou offer sacrifices to the almighty gods, I shall order thee, after having been scourged, to be fastened to that very cross which thou commendest.

The blessed Andrew said:

To God Almighty, who alone is true, I bring sacrifice day by day; not the smoke of incense, nor the flesh of bellowing bulls, nor the blood of goats, but sacrificing a spotless lamb day by day on the altar of the cross; and though all the people of the faithful partake of His body and drink His blood, the Lamb that has been sacrificed remains after this entire and alive.

Truly, therefore, is He sacrificed, and truly is His body eaten by the people, and His blood is likewise drunk; nevertheless, as I have said, He remains entire, and spotless, and alive.

AEgeates said:

How can this be?

The blessed Andrew said:

If thou wouldest know, take the form of a disciple, that thou mayst learn what thou art inquiring after.

AEgeates said:

I will exact of thee through tortures the gift of this knowledge.

The blessed Andrew declared:

I wonder that thou, being an intelligent man, shouldest fall into [11] the folly of thinking that thou mayst be able to persuade me, through thy tortures, to disclose to thee the sacred things of God.

Thou hast heard the mystery of the cross, thou hast heard the mystery of the sacrifice.

If thou believest in Christ the Son of God, who was crucified, I shall altogether disclose to thee in what manner the Lamb that has been slain may live, after having been sacrificed and eaten, remaining in His kingdom entire and spotless.

AEgeates said:

And by what means does the lamb remain in his kingdom after he has been slain and eaten by all the people, as thou hast said?

The blessed Andrew said:

If thou believest with all thy heart, thou shalt be able to learn:

but if thou believest not, thou shalt not by any means attain to the idea of such truth.

Then AEgeates, enraged, ordered him to be shut up in prison, where, when he was shut up, a multitude of the people came together to him from almost all the province, so that they wished to kill AEgeates, and by breaking down the doors of the prison to set free the blessed Andrew the apostle.

Them the blessed Andrew admonished in these words, saying:

Do not stir up the peace of our Lord Jesus Christ into seditious and devilish uproar.

For my Lord, when He was betrayed, endured it with all patience; He did not strive, He did not cry out, nor in the streets did any one hear Him crying out. [12]Therefore do ye also keep silence, quietness, and peace; and hinder not my martyrdom, but rather get yourselves also ready beforehand as athletes to the Lord, in order that you may overcome threatenings by a soul that has no fear of man, and that you may get the better of injuries through the endurance of the body.

For this temporary fall is not to be feared; but that should be feared which has no end.

The fear of men, then, is like smoke which, while it is raised and gathered together, disappears.

And those torments ought to be feared which never have an end.

For these torments, which happen to be somewhat light, any one can bear; but if they are heavy, they soon destroy life.

But those torments are everlasting, where there are daily weepings, and mournings, and lamentations, and never-ending torture, to which the proconsul AEgeates is not afraid to go.

Be ye therefore rather prepared for this, that through temporary afflictions ye may attain to everlasting rest, and may flourish for ever, and reign with Christ. [13]

The holy Apostle Andrew having admonished the people with these and such like words through the whole night, when the light of day dawned, AEgeates having sent for him, ordered the blessed Andrew to be brought to him; and having sat down upon the tribunal, he said:

I have thought that thou, by thy reflection during the night, hast turned away thy thoughts from folly, and given up thy commendation of Christ that thou mightst be able to be with us, and not throw away the pleasures of life; for it is folly to come for any purpose to the suffering of the cross, and to give oneself up to most shameful punishments and burnings.

The holy Andrew answered:

I shall be able to have joy with thee, if thou wilt believe in Christ, and throw away the worship of idols; for Christ has sent me to this province, in which I have acquired for Christ a people not the smallest.

AEgeates said:

For this reason I compel thee to make a libation, that these people who have been deceived by thee may forsake the vanity of thy teaching, and may themselves offer grateful libations to the gods; for not even one city has remained in Achaia in which their temples [14] have not been forsaken and deserted.

And now, through thee, let them be again restored to the worship of the images, in order that the gods also, who have been enraged against thee, being pleased by this, may bring it about that thou mayst return to their friendship and ours.

But if not, thou awaitest varied tortures, on account of the vengeance of the gods; and after these, fastened to the tree of the cross which thou commendest, thou shalt die.

The holy Andrew said:

Listen, O son of death and chaff made ready for eternal burnings,[15] to me, the servant of God and apostle of Jesus Christ.

Until now I have conversed with thee kindly about the perfection of the faith, in order that thou, receiving the exposition of the truth, being made perfect as its vindicator, mightst despise vain idols, and worship God, who is in the heavens; but since thou remainest in the same shamelessness at last, and thinkest me to be afraid because of thy threats, bring against me whatever may seem to thee greater in the way of tortures.

For the more shall I be well pleasing to my King, the more I shall endure in tortures for the confession of His name.

Then the proconsul AEgeates, being enraged, ordered the apostle of Christ to be afflicted by tortures.

Being stretched out, therefore, by seven times three [16] soldiers, and beaten with violence, he was lifted up and brought before the impious AEgeates.

And he spoke to him thus:

Listen to me, Andrew, and withdraw thy thoughts from the outpouring of thy blood; but if thou wilt not hearken to me, I shall cause thee to perish on the tree of the cross.

The holy Andrew said:

I am a slave of the cross of Christ, and I ought rather to pray to attain to the trophy of the cross than to be afraid; but for thee is laid up eternal torment, which, however, thou mayst escape after thou hast tested my endurance, if thou wilt believe in my Christ.

For I am afflicted about thy destruction, and I am not disturbed about my own suffering.

For my suffering takes up a space of one day, or two at most; but thy torment for endless ages shall never come to a close.

Wherefore henceforward cease from adding to thy miseries, and lighting up everlasting fire for thyself.

AEgeates then being enraged, ordered the blessed Andrew to be fastened to the cross. [17] And he having left them all, goes up to the cross, and says to it with a clear voice:

Rejoice, O cross, which has been consecrated by the body of Christ, and adorned by His limbs as if with pearls.

Assuredly before my Lord went up on thee, thou hadst much earthly fear; but now invested with heavenly longing, thou art fitted up [18] according to my prayer.

For I know, from those who believe, how many graces thou hast in Him, how many gifts prepared beforehand. Free from care, then, and with joy, I come to thee, that thou also exulting mayst receive me, the disciple of Him that was hanged upon thee; because thou hast been always faithful to me, and I have desired to embrace thee.

O good cross, which hast received comeliness and beauty from the limbs of the Lord; O much longed for, and earnestly desired, and fervently sought after, and already prepared beforehand for my soul longing for thee, take me away from men, and restore me to my Master, in order that through thee He may accept me who through thee has redeemed me.

And having thus spoken, the blessed Andrew, standing on the ground, and looking earnestly upon the cross, stripped himself and gave his clothes to the executioners, having urged the brethren that the executioners should come and do what had been commanded them; for they were standing at some distance.

And they having come up, lifted him on the cross; and having stretched his body across with ropes, they only bound his feet, but did not sever his joints, [19] having received this order from the proconsul:

for he wished him to be in distress while hanging, and in the night-time, as he was suspended, to be eaten up alive by dogs. [20]

And a great multitude of the brethren stood by, nearly twenty thousand; and having beheld the executioners standing off, and that they had done to the blessed one nothing of what those who were hanged up suffer, they thought that they would again hear something from him; for assuredly, as he was hanging, he moved his head smiling.

And Stratocles inquired of him:

Why art thou smiling, Andrew, servant of God?

Thy laughter makes us mourn and weep, because we are deprived of thee.

And the blessed Andrew answered him:

Shall I not laugh at all, my son Stratocles, at the empty stratagem of AEgeates, through which he thinks to take vengeance upon us?

We have nothing to do with him and his plans.

He cannot hear; for if he could, he would be aware, having learned it by experience, that a man of Jesus is unpunished. [21]

And having thus spoken, he discoursed to them all in common, for the people ran together enraged at the unjust judgment of AEgeates:

Ye men standing by me, and women, and children, and elders, bond and free, and as many as will hear; I beseech you, forsake all this life, ye who have for my sake assembled here; and hasten to take upon you my life, which leads to heavenly things, and once for all despise all temporary things, confirming the purposes of those who believe in Christ.

And he exhorted them all, teaching that the sufferings of this transitory life are not worthy to be compared with the future recompense of the eternal life.

And the multitude hearing what was said by him, did not stand off from the place, and the blessed Andrew continued the rather to say to them more than he had spoken.

And so much was said by him, that a space of three days and nights was taken up, and no one was tired and went away from him.

And when also on the fourth day they beheld his nobleness, and the unweariedness of his intellect, and the multitude of his words, and the serviceableness of his exhortations, and the stedfastness of his soul, and the sobriety of his spirit, and the fixedness of his mind, and the perfection of his reason, they were enraged against AEgeates; and all with one accord hastened to the tribunal, and cried out against AEgeates, who was sitting, saying:

What is thy judgment, O proconsul?

Thou hast judged wickedly; thy awards are impious.

In what has the man done wrong; what evil has he done?

The city has been put in an uproar; thou grievest us all; do not betray Caesar's city.

Grant willingly to the Achaians a just man; grant willingly to us a God-fearing man; do not put to death a godly man.

Four days he has been hanging, and is alive; having eaten nothing, he has filled us all.

Take down the man from the cross, and we shall all seek after wisdom; release the man, and to all Achaia will mercy be shown.

It is not necessary that he should suffer this, because, though hanging, he does not cease proclaiming the truth.

And when the proconsul refused to listen to them, at first indeed signing with his hand to the crowd to take themselves off, they began to be emboldened against him, being in number about twenty thousand. And the proconsul having beheld that they had somehow become maddened, afraid that something frightful would befall him, rose up from the tribunal and went away with them, having promised to set free the blessed Andrew.

And some went on before to tell the apostle the cause for which they came to the place.

While all the crowd, therefore, was exulting that the blessed Andrew was going to be set free, the proconsul having come up, and all the brethren rejoicing along with Maximilla, [22] the blessed Andrew, having heard this, said to the brethren standing by:

What is it necessary for me to say to him, when I am departing to the Lord, that will I also say.

For what reason hast thou again come to us, AEgeates?

On what account dost thou, being a stranger to us, [23] come to us?

What wilt thou again dare to do, what to contrive?

Tell us.

Hast thou come to release us, as having changed thy mind?

I would not agree with thee that thou hadst really changed thy mind.

Nor would I believe thee, saying that thou art my friend.

Dost thou, O proconsul, release him that has been bound?

By no means.

For I have One with whom I shall be for ever; I have One with whom I shall live to countless ages.

To Him I go; to Him I hasten, who also having made thee known to me, has said to me, Let not that fearful man terrify thee; do not think that he will lay hold of thee, who art mine:

for he is thine enemy.

Therefore, having known thee through him who has turned towards me, I am delivered from thee.

But if thou wishest to believe in Christ, there will be opened up for time, as I promised thee, a way of access; but if thou hast come only to release me, I shall not be able after this to be brought down from this cross alive in the body.

For I and my kinsmen depart to our own, allowing thee to be what thou art, and what thou dost not know about thyself.

For already I see my King, already I worship Him, already I stand before Him, where the fellowship [24] of the angels is, where He reigns the only emperor, where there is light without night, where the flowers never fade, where trouble is never known, nor the name of grief heard, where there are cheerfulness and exultation that have no end.

O blessed cross! without the longing for thee, no one enters into that place.

But I am distressed, AEgeates, about thine own miseries, because eternal perdition is ready to receive thee.

Run then, for thine own sake, O pitiable one, while yet thou canst, lest perchance thou shouldst wish then when thou canst not.

When, therefore, he attempted to come near the tree of the cross, so as to release the blessed Andrew, with all the city applauding him, the holy Andrew said with a loud voice:

Do not suffer Andrew, bound upon Thy tree, to be released, O Lord; do not give me who am in Thy mystery to the shameless devil.

O Jesus Christ, let not Thine adversary release me, who have been hanged by Thy favour; O Father, let this insignificant man no longer humble him who has known Thy greatness. The executioners, therefore, putting out their hands, were not able at all to touch him.

Others, then, and others endeavoured to release him, and no one at all was able to come near him; for their arms were benumbed.

Then the blessed Andrew, having adjured the people, said:

I entreat you earnestly, brethren, that I may first make one prayer to my Lord. So then set about releasing me.

All the people therefore kept quiet because of the adjuration.

Then the blessed Andrew, with a loud cry, said:

Do not permit, O Lord, Thy servant at this time to be removed from Thee; for it is time that my body be committed to the earth, and Thou shalt order me to come to Thee.

Thou who givest eternal life, my Teacher whom I have loved, whom on this cross I confess, whom I know, whom I possess, receive me, O Lord; and as I have confessed Thee and obeyed Thee, so now in this word hearken to me; and, before my body come down from the cross, receive me to Thyself, that through my departure there may be access to Thee of many of my kindred, finding rest for themselves in Thy majesty.

When, therefore, he had said this, he became in the sight of all glad and exulting; for an exceeding splendour like lightning coming forth out of heaven shone down upon him, and so encircled him, that in consequence of such brightness mortal eyes could not look upon him at all.

And the dazzling light remained about the space of half an hour. And when he had thus spoken and glorified the Lord still more, the light withdrew itself, and he gave up the ghost, and along with the brightness itself he departed to the Lord in giving Him thanks.

And after the decease of the most blessed Andrew the apostle, Maximilla being the most powerful of the notable women, [25] and continuing among those who had come, as soon as she learned that the apostle had departed to the Lord, came up and turned her attention to the cross, along with Stratocles, taking no heed at all of those standing by, and with reverence took down the body of the most blessed apostle from the cross.

And when it was evening, bestowing upon him the necessary care, she prepared the body for burial with costly spices, and laid it in her own tomb.

For she had been parted from AEgeates on account of his brutal disposition and lawless conduct, having chosen for herself a holy and quiet life; and having been united to the love of Christ, she spent her life blessedly along with the brethren.

AEgeates had been very importunate with her, and promised that he would make her mistress of his wealth; but not having been able to persuade her, he was greatly enraged, and was determined to make a public charge against all the people, and to send to Caesar an accusation against both Maximilla and all the people.

And while he was arranging these things in the presence of his officers, at the dead of night he rose up, and unseen by all his people, having been tormented by the devil, he fell down from a great height, and rolling into the midst of the market-place of the city, breathed his last.

And this was reported to his brother Stratocles; and he sent his servants, having told them that they should bury him among those who had died a violent death.

But he sought nothing of his substance, saying:

Let not my Lord Jesus Christ, in whom I have believed, suffer me to touch anything whatever of the goods of my brother, that the condemnation of him who dared to cut off the apostle of the Lord may not disgrace me.

These things were done in the province of Achaia, in the city of Patras on the day before the kalends of December, [26] where his good deeds are kept in mind even to this day, to the glory and praise of our Lord Jesus Christ, to whom be glory for ever and ever.

Amen. [27]

Footnotes:

1. Another reading is AEgeas. [This is the reading of the Bodleian ms., already frequently referred to (see p. 355). In most cases its text is followed in the Latin version collated by Tischendorf.--R.]
2. Deut. xxxii. 17; 1 Cor. x. 20, 21.
3. Or, Prince.
4. Matt. xvi. 22.
5. John x. 18.
6. Matt. xxvi. 21.
7. Another reading is: This is what I spoke of, as you know-- that great is the mystery of the cross; and if so be that you are willing to listen, I will reveal it.
8. Perhaps we should read anadeixei, shalt exhibit, for anadexei.
9. Two mss., of sinners.
10. Or, shut out.
11. Lit., be rolled towards.
12. Matt. xii. 19.
13. Comp. 2 Cor. iv. 17.
14. Or, their sacred rites.
15. Comp. Matt. iii. 12.
16. Another reading is, seven quaternions.
17. One of themss. [the Bodleian] has here: Giving orders to the centurions that he should be bound hand and foot as if he were stretched on the rack, and not pierced with nails, that he might not die soon, but be tormented with long-continuing torture.
18. Another reading is: I am attached to thee.
19. The original is obscure. The meaning seems to be that he was tied only, not nailed. The nailing, however, seems to have been an essential part of the punishment of crucifixion.
20. It was common to let loose wild beasts on the crucified (Sueton., Nero, 49).
21. Instead of this paragraph, on ms. [the Bodleian] has: And there ran up a great multitude, about twenty thousand in number, among whom was the brother of AEgeas, Stratocles by name; and he cried out with the people, It is an unjust judgment. And the holy Andrew, hitting upon the thoughts of the believers, exhorted them to endure the temporary trial, saying that the suffering counted for nothing when compared with the eternal recompense.
22. One ms. calls her the proconsul's wife. [So Pseudo-Abdias; but the Greek mss., collated by Tischendorf, do not give this reading.--R.]
23. i.e., having nothing to do with us.
24. homonoiai.
25. Lit., females.
26. i.e., 30th November, St. Andrew's day.
27. One ms. thus ends: These things were done in the province of Achaia, in the city of Patras, on the day before the kalends of December; where also his glorious good deeds are shown even to this day; and so great fear came upon all, that no one remained who did not believe in God our Saviour, who wishes all to be saved, and to come to the knowledge of the truth. To Him be glory to ages of ages. Amen. [This is the ending of the Latin version (in Tischendorf); the Bodleian ms. has a similar conclusion, but the text is differently arranged.--R.]

Acts of Andrew and Matthias [1]
In the City of the Man-eaters

About that time all the apostles had come together to the same place, and shared among themselves the countries, casting lots, in order that each might go away into the part that had fallen to him.

By lot, then, it fell to Matthias to set out to the country of the man-eaters.

And the men of that city used neither to eat bread nor drink wine; but they ate the flesh of men, and drank their blood.

Every man, therefore, who came into their city they laid hold of, and digging they thrust out his eyes, and gave him a drug to drink, prepared by sorcery and magic; and from drinking the drug his heart was altered and his mind deranged.

Matthias then having come into the gate of their city, the men of that city laid hold of him, and thrust out his eyes; and after putting them out they made him drink the drug of their magical deception, and led him away to the prison, and put beside him grass to eat, and he ate it not.

For when he had partaken of their drug, his heart was not altered, nor his mind deranged; but he kept praying to God, weeping, and saying:

Lord Jesus Christ, for whose sake we have forsaken all things and have followed Thee, knowing that Thou art the helper of all who hope in Thee, attend then and behold what they have done to Matthias Thy servant, how they have made me nigh to the brutes; for Thou art He who knowest all things.

If, therefore, Thou hast ordained that the wicked men in this city should eat me up, I will not by any means flee from Thy dispensation.

Afford to me then, O Lord, the light of mine eyes, that at least I may behold what the wicked men in this city have in hand for me; do not forsake me, O my Lord Jesus Christ, and do not give me up to this bitter death.

While Matthias was thus praying in the prison, a light shone, and there came forth out of the light a voice saying:

Beloved Matthias, receive thy sight.

And immediately he received his sight.

And again there came forth a voice saying:

Be of good courage, our Matthias, and be not dismayed; for I shall not by any means forsake thee, for I shall deliver thee from all danger; and not only thee, but also all thy brethren who are with thee:

for I am with thee everywhere and at all times.

But remain here twenty-seven days for the edification [2] of many souls; and after that I shall send forth Andrew to thee, and he shall lead thee forth out of this prison; and not thee only, but also all who hear.

Having said this, the Saviour said again to Matthias, Peace be to thee, our Matthias, and went into heaven.

Then Matthias having beheld Him, said to the Lord:

Let thy grace abide with me, O my Lord Jesus.

Then Matthias therefore [3] sat down in the prison, and sang.

And it came to pass that, when the executioners came into the prison to bring forth the men to eat them, Matthias also shut his eyes, that they might not behold that he saw.

And the executioners having come to him, read the ticket in his hand, and said among themselves:

Yet three days, and we shall bring out this one also from the prison, and slay him.

Because in the case of every man whom they laid hold of, they noted that day on which they laid hold of him, and tied a ticket to his right hand, that they might know the completion of the thirty days.

And it came to pass when the twenty-seven days were fulfilled since Matthias was seized, the Lord appeared in the country where Andrew was teaching, and said to him:

Rise up, and set out with thy disciples to the country of the man-eaters, and bring forth

Matthias out of that place; for yet three days, and the men of the city will bring him forth and slay him for their food.

And Andrew answered and said:

My Lord, I shall not be able to accomplish the journey thither before the limited period of the three days; but send Thine angel quickly, that he may bring him out thence:

for thou knowest, Lord, that I also am flesh, and shall not be able to go there quickly.

And He says to Andrew: Obey Him who made thee, and Him who is able to say in a word, and that city shall be removed thence, and all that dwell in it.

For I command the horns of the winds, [4] and they drive it thence.

But rise up early, and go down to the sea with thy disciples, and thou shalt find a boat upon the shore, and thou shalt go aboard with thy disciples.

And having said this, the Saviour again said:

Peace to thee, Andrew, along with those with thee!

And He went into the heavens.

And Andrew having risen up early, proceeded to the sea along with his disciples; and having come down to the shore, he saw a little boat, and in the boat three men sitting.

For the Lord by His own power had prepared a boat, and He it was in human shape a pilot in the boat; and He brought two angels whom He made to appear like men, and they were in the boat sitting. [5]Andrew, therefore, having beheld the boat, and the three who were in it, rejoiced with exceeding great joy; and having gone to them, he said:

Where are you going, brethren, with this little boat?

And the Lord answered and said to him:

We are going to the country of the man-eaters.

And Andrew having beheld Jesus, did not recognise Him; for Jesus was hiding His Godhead, and He appeared to Andrew like a pilot.

And Jesus having heard Andrew saying, I too am going to the country of the man-eaters, says to him:

Every man avoids that city, and how are you going there?

And Andrew answered and said: We have some small business to do there, and we must get through with it; but if thou canst, do us this kindness to convey us to the country of the man-eaters, to which also you intend to go.

Jesus answered and said to them:

Come on board.

And Andrew said:

I wish to make some explanation to thee, young man, before we come on board thy boat.

And Jesus said:

Say what thou wilt.

And Andrew said to Him:

We have no passage-money to give thee; we have not even bread for our nourishment.

And Jesus answered and said to him:

How, then, are you going away without giving us the passage-money, and without having bread for your nourishment?

And Andrew said to Jesus, Listen, brother; do not think that it is through masterfulness that we do not give thee our passage-money, but we are disciples of our Lord Jesus Christ, the good God.

For He chose for Himself us twelve, and gave us such a commandment, saying, When you go to preach, do not carry money in the journey, nor bread, nor bag, nor shoes, nor staff, nor two coats. [6]If, therefore, thou wilt do us the kindness, brother, tell us at once; if not, let us know, and we shall go and seek another boat for ourselves.

And Jesus answered and said to Andrew:

If this is the commandment which you received, and you keep it, come on board my boat with all joy.

For I really wish you, the disciples of Him who is called Jesus, to come on board my boat, rather than those who give me of their silver and gold; for I am altogether worthy that the apostle of the Lord should come on board my boat.

And Andrew answered and said:

Permit me, brother, may the Lord grant thee glory and honour.

And Andrew went on board the boat with his disciples.

And having gone on board, he sat down by the boat's sail.

And Jesus answered and said to one of the angels:

Rise and go down to the hold of the boat, and bring up three loaves, that the men may eat, lest perchance they be hungry, from having come to us off a long journey. And he rose and went down to the hold of the boat, and brought up three loaves, as the Lord commanded him; and he gave them the loaves.

Then Jesus said to Andrew:

Rise up, brother, with thy friends; partake of food, that you may be strong to bear the tossing of the sea.

And Andrew answered and said to his disciples:

My children, we have found great kindness from this man.

Stand up, then, and partake of the nourishment of bread, that you may be strong to bear the tossing of the sea.

And his disciples were not able to answer him a word, for they were in distress because of the sea.

Then Jesus forced Andrew to partake himself also of the nourishment of bread along with his disciples.

And Andrew answered and said to Jesus, not knowing that it was Jesus:

Brother, may the Lord give thee heavenly bread out of His kingdom.

Allow me then brother; for thou seest the children, that they are distressed because of the sea.

And Jesus answered and said to Andrew:

Assuredly the brethren are without experience of the sea; but inquire of them whether they want to go to land, and thyself to remain, until thou shalt finish thy business, and again come back to them. Then Andrew said to his disciples:

My children, do you wish to go to the land, and me to remain here until I shall finish my business for which I have been sent?

And they answered and said to Andrew:

If we go away from thee, may we become strangers to the good things which the Lord hath provided for us.

Now, therefore, we are with thee, wherever thou mayst go.

Jesus answered and said to Andrew:

If thou art truly a disciple of Him who is called Jesus, tell thy disciples the miracles which thy Teacher did, that their soul may rejoice, and that they may forget the fear of the sea; for, behold, we are going to take the boat off from the land. And immediately Jesus said to one of the angels:

Let go the boat; and he let go the boat from the land.

And Jesus came and sat down beside the rudder, and steered the boat.

Then Andrew exhorted and comforted his disciples, saying:

My children, who have given up your life to the Lord, fear not; for the Lord will not at all forsake you for ever.

For at that time when I was alone with our Lord, we went on board the boat with Him, and He lay down to sleep in the boat, trying us; for He was not [7] fast asleep.

And a great wind having arisen, and the sea being stormy, so that the waves were uplifted, and came under the sail of the boat, and when we were in great fear, the Lord stood up and rebuked the winds, and there was a calm in the sea; for all things feared Him, as being made by Him.[8] Now, therefore, my children, fear not.

For the Lord Jesus will not at all forsake us.

And having said this, the holy Andrew prayed in his heart that his disciples might be led to sleep.

And as Andrew was praying, his disciples fell asleep.

And Andrew, turning round to the Lord, not knowing that it was the Lord, said to Him:

Tell me, O man, and show me the skill of thy steering; for I have never seen any man so steering in the sea as I now see thee.

For sixteen years have I sailed the sea, and behold this is the seventeenth, and I have not seen such skill; for truly the boat is just as if on land.

Show me then, young man, thy skill.

Then Jesus answered and said to Andrew:

We also have often sailed the sea, and been in danger; but since thou art a disciple of Him called Jesus, the sea has recognised thee that thou art righteous, and has become calm, and has not lifted its waves against the boat.

Then Andrew cried out with a loud voice, saying:

I thank Thee, my Lord Jesus Christ, that I have met a man who glorifies Thy name.

And Jesus answered and said:

O Andrew, tell me, thou disciple of Him called Jesus, wherefore the unbelieving Jews did not believe in Him, saying that He was not God, but man.

Show me, O disciple of Him called Jesus; for I have heard that He showed His Godhead to His disciples. And Andrew answered and said:

Truly, brother, He showed us that He was God.
Do not think, then, that He is man.
For He made the heaven, and the earth, and the sea, and all that is in them.
And Jesus answered and said:
How then did the Jews not believe Him?
Perhaps He did not do miracles before them?
Andrew said:
Hast thou not heard of the miracles which He did before them?

He made the blind see, the lame walk, the deaf hear; He cleansed lepers, He changed water into wine; and having taken five loaves and two fishes, He made a crowd recline on the grass, and having blessed, He gave them to eat; and those that ate were five thousand men, [9] and they were filled:

and they took up what was over to them twelve baskets of fragments.[10] And after all these things they did not believe Him.

And Jesus answered and said to Andrew:
Perhaps He did these miracles before the people, and not before the chief priests, and because of this they did not believe Him.

And Andrew answered and said:
Nay, brother, He did them also before the chief priests, not only openly, but also in secret, and they did not believe Him.

Jesus answered and said:
What are the miracles which He did in secret?
Disclose them to me.

And Andrew answered and said: O man, who hast the spirit of inquisitiveness, why dost thou put me to the test?

And Jesus answered and said:
I do not put thee to the test by saying this, O disciple of Him called Jesus; but my soul rejoices and exults, and not only mine, but also every soul that hears the wonders of Jesus.

And Andrew answered and said:
O child, the Lord shall fill thy soul with all joy and all good, as thou hast persuaded me now to relate to thee the miracles which our Lord did in secret.

It came to pass as we, the twelve disciples, were going with our Lord into a temple of the Gentiles, that He might make known to us the ignorance of the devil, that the chief priests, having beheld us following Jesus, said to us, O wretches, why do you walk with him who says, I am the Son of God?

Do you mean to say that God has a son? Which of you has ever at any time seen God associating with a woman? Is not this the son of Joseph the carpenter, and his mother is Mary, and his brothers James and Simon?[11] And when we heard these words, our hearts were turned into weakness.

And Jesus, having known that our hearts were giving way, took us into a desert place, and did great miracles before us, and displayed to us all His Godhead.

And we spoke to the chief priests, saying, Come ye also, and see; for, behold, He has persuaded us.

And the chief priests having come, went with us; and when we had gone into the temple of the Gentiles, Jesus showed us the heaven, [12] that we might know whether the things were true or not.

And there went in along with us thirty men of the people, and four chief priests.

And Jesus, having looked on the right hand and on the left of the temple, saw two sculptured sphinxes, one on the right and one on the left.

And Jesus having turned to us, said, Behold the sign of the cross; for these are like the cherubim and the seraphim which are in heaven.

Then Jesus, having looked to the right, where the sphinx was, said to it, I say unto thee, thou image of that which is in heaven, which the hands of craftsmen have sculptured, be separated from thy place, and come down, and answer and convict the chief priests, and show them whether I am God or man.

And immediately at that very time the sphinx removed from its place, and having assumed a human voice, said, O foolish sons of Israel, not only has the blinding of their own hearts not been enough for them, but they also wish others to be blind like themselves, saying that God is man, who in the beginning fashioned man, and put His breath into all, who gave motion to those things which moved not; He it is who called Abraham, who loved his son Isaac, who brought back his beloved Jacob into his land; He is the Judge of living and dead; He it is who prepareth great benefits for those who obey Him, and prepareth punishment for those who believe Him not.

Heed not that I am an idol that can be handled; for I say unto you, that the sacred places of your synagogue are more excellent. [13]For though we are stones, the priests have given us only the name of a god; and those priests who serve the temple purify themselves, being afraid of the demons:

for if they have had intercourse with women, they purify themselves seven days, because of their fear; so that they do not come into the temple because of us, because of the name which they have given us, that we are a god.

But you, if you have committed fornication, take up the law of God, and go into the synagogue of God, and purify, and read, and do not reverence the glorious words of God.

Because of this, I say unto you, that the holy things purify your synagogues, so that they also become churches of His only begotten Son.

The sphinx having said this, ceased speaking.

And we said to the chief priests, Now it is fitting that you should believe, because even the stones have convicted you.

And the Jews answered and said, By magic these stones speak, and do not you think that it is a god?

For if you have tested what has been said by the stone, you have ascertained its deception.

For where did he find Abraham, or how did he see him?

For Abraham died many years before he was born, and how does he know him?

And Jesus, having again turned to the image, said to it, Because these believe not that I have spoken with Abraham, go away into the land of the Canaanites, and go away to the double [14] cave in the field of Mamre, where the body of Abraham is, and cry outside of the tomb, saying, Abraham, Abraham, whose body is in the tomb, and whose soul is in paradise, thus speaks He who fashioned man, who made thee from the beginning his friend, Rise up, thou and thy son Isaac, and the son of thy son Jacob, and come to the temples of the Jebusites, that we may convict the chief priests, in order that they may know that I am acquainted with thee, and thou with me.

And when the sphinx heard these words, immediately she walked about in the presence of us all, and set out for the land of the Canaanites to the field of Mamre, and cried outside of the tomb, as God had commanded her.

And straightway the twelve patriarchs [15] came forth alive out of the tomb, and answered and said to her, To which of us hast thou been sent?

And the sphinx answered and said, I have been sent to the three patriarchs for testimony; but do ye go in, and rest until the time of the resurrection.

And having heard, they went into the tomb and fell asleep.

And the three patriarchs set out along with the sphinx to Jesus, and convicted the chief priests.

And Jesus said to them, Go away to your places; and they went away.

And He said also to the image, Go up to thy place; and straightway she went up and stood in her place.

And He did also many other miracles, and they did not believe Him; which miracles, if I shall recount, thou wilt not be able to bear.

And Jesus answered and said to him:

I can bear it; for I prudently listen to profitable words.

And when the boat was about to come near the land, Jesus bent down His head upon one of His angels, and was quiet.

And Andrew ceased speaking; and he also, reclining his head upon one of his disciples, fell asleep.

And Jesus said to His angels:

Spread your hands under him, and carry Andrew and his disciples, and go put them outside of the city of the man-eaters; and having laid them on the ground, return to me.

And the angels did as Jesus commanded them, and the angels returned to Jesus:

and He went up into the heavens with His angels.

And when it was morning, Andrew, having awakened and looked up, found himself sitting on the ground; and having looked, [16] he saw his disciples sleeping on the ground:

and he wakened them, and said to them:

Rise up, my children, and know the great dispensation that has happened to us, and learn that the Lord was with us in the boat, and we knew Him not; for He transformed Himself as if He were a pilot in the boat, and humbled Himself, and appeared to us as a man, putting us to the test.

And Andrew, recovering himself, said:

Lord, I recognised Thy excellent words, but Thou didst not manifest Thyself to me, and because of this I did not know Thee.

And his disciples answered and said to him:

Father Andrew, do not think that we knew when thou wast speaking with Him in the boat, for we were weighed down by a most heavy sleep; and eagles came down out of the heavens, and lifted up our souls, and took them away into the paradise in heaven, and we saw great wonders.

For we beheld our Lord Jesus sitting on a throne of glory, and all the angels round about Him.

We beheld also Abraham, and Isaac, and Jacob, and all the saints; and David praised Him with a song upon his harp.

And we beheld there you the twelve apostles standing by in the presence of our Lord Jesus Christ, and outside of you twelve angels round about you, and each angel standing behind each of you, and they were like you in appearance.

And we heard the Lord saying to the angels, Listen to the apostles in all things whatsoever they shall ask you.

These are the things which we have seen, father Andrew, until thou didst awake us; and angels, who appeared like eagles, brought our souls into our bodies.

Then Andrew, having heard, rejoiced with great joy that his disciples had been deemed worthy to behold these wonderful things.

And Andrew looked up into heaven, and said:

Appear to me, Lord Jesus Christ; for I know that Thou art not far from Thy servants.

Pardon me, Lord, for what I have done; for I have beheld Thee as a man in the boat, and I have conversed with Thee as with a man.

Now therefore, Lord, manifest Thyself to me in this place.

And when Andrew had said this, Jesus appeared to him in the likeness of a most beautiful little child.

And Jesus answered and said:

Hail, our Andrew!

And Andrew, having beheld Him, worshipped Him, saying:

Pardon me, Lord Jesus Christ, for I saw Thee like a man on the sea, and conversed with Thee.

What is there, then, wherein I have sinned, my Lord Jesus, that Thou didst not manifest Thyself to me on the sea?

And Jesus answered and said to Andrew:

Thou hast not sinned, but I did this to thee because thou saidst, I shall not be able to go to the city of the man-eaters in three days; and I have showed thee that I am able to do all things, and to appear to every one as I wish.

Now therefore rise up, go into the city to Matthias, and bring him forth out of the prison, and all the strangers that are with him.

For, behold, I show thee, Andrew, what thou must suffer before going into this city.

They will heap upon thee tortures and insults, and scatter thy flesh in the ways and the streets, and thy blood shall flow to the ground, but they are not able to put thee to death; but endure, just as thou sawest me beaten, insulted, and crucified:

for there are those who are destined to believe in this city.

And having said this, the Saviour went into the heavens.

And Andrew went into the city along with his disciples, and no one beheld him.

And when he came to the prison, he saw seven warders standing at the gate guarding, and he prayed within himself, and they fell down and expired; and he marked the gate with the sign of the cross, and it opened of its own accord.

And having gone in with his disciples, he found Matthias sitting and singing; and seeing him, he stood up, and they saluted each other with a holy kiss; and he said to Matthias:

Brother, how hast thou been found here?

For yet three days, and they will bring thee out to be food for them.

Where are the great mysteries which thou hast been taught, and the wonderful things which we have believed?

And Matthias said to him:

Didst thou not hear the Lord saying, I shall send you like sheep into the midst of wolves? [17]They straightway brought me into the prison, and I prayed to the Lord; and He said to me, Remain here twenty-seven days, and I shall send thee Andrew, and he will bring thee forth out of the prison.

And now, behold, it has come to pass as the Lord said.

Then Andrew, having looked, saw three men shut up eating grass naked; and he beat his breast, and said:

Consider, O Lord, what the men suffer; how have they made them like the irrational brutes?

And he says to Satan:

Woe to thee, the devil, the enemy of God, and to thine angels, because the strangers here have done nothing to thee; and how hast thou brought upon them the punishment? how long dost thou war against the human race?

Thou didst bring forth Adam out of paradise, and didst cause men to be mixed up with transgression; and the Lord was enraged, and brought on the deluge so as to sweep man away.

And again hast thou made thy appearance in this city too, in order that thou mayst make those who are here eat men, [18] that the end of them also may be in execration and destruction, thinking in thyself that God will sweep away the work of His hands.

Hast thou not heard that God said, I will not bring a deluge upon the earth? [19] but if there is any punishment prepared, it is for the sake of taking vengeance upon thee.

Then he stood up, and Andrew and Matthias prayed; and after the prayer Andrew laid his hands upon the faces of the blind men who were in the prison, and straightway they all received their sight.

And again he laid his hand upon their hearts, and their minds were changed into human reason.

Then Andrew answered them:

Rise up, and go into the lower parts of the city, and you shall find in the way a great fig-tree, and sit under the fig-tree, and eat of its fruit, until I come to you; but if I delay coming there, you will find abundance of food for yourselves:

for the fruit shall not fail from the fig-tree, but according as you eat it shall produce more fruit, and nourish you, as the Lord has said.

And they answered and said to Andrew:

Go along with us, O our master, lest perchance the wicked men of this city again see us, and shut us up, and inflict upon us greater and more dreadful tortures than they have inflicted upon us.

And Andrew answered and said to them:

Go; for in truth I say to you, that as you go, not a dog shall bark with his tongue against you.

And there were in all two hundred and seventy men and forty-nine women [20] whom Andrew released from the prison.

And the men went as the blessed Andrew said to them; and he made Matthias go along with his disciples out of the eastern gate of the city.

And Andrew commanded a cloud, and the cloud took up Matthias and the disciples of Andrew; and the cloud set them down on the mountain where Peter was teaching, [21] and they remained beside him.

And Andrew, having gone forth from the prison, walked about in the city; and having seen a brazen pillar, and a statue standing upon it, he came and sat down behind that pillar until he should see what should happen.

And it happened that the executioners went to the prison to bring out the men for their food, [22] according to the custom; and they found the doors of the prison opened, and the guards that guarded it lying dead upon the ground.

And straightway they went, and reported to the rulers of the city, saying:

We found the prison opened, and having gone inside we found nobody; [23] but we found the guards lying dead upon the ground.

And the rulers having heard this, said among themselves:

What, then, has happened?

You do not mean to say that some persons have gone into the prison of the city, and have killed the warders, and taken away those that were shut up?

And they spoke to the executioners, saying:

Go to the prison, and bring the men that are dead, that we may eat them up to-day.

And let us go to-morrow, and bring together all the old men of the city, that they may cast lots upon themselves, until the seven lots come, and we slay seven each day.

And they shall be to us for food until we may choose young men, and put them in boats as sailors, that they may go away to the countries round about, and attack them, and bring some men here, that they may be for food to us.

And the executioners went to the prison, and brought the seven men that were dead; and there was an oven built in the midst of the city, and there lay in the oven a large trough in which they killed the men, and their blood ran down into the trough, and they drew out of the blood and drank it.

And they brought the men, and. put them into the trough.

And when the executioners were lifting their hands against them, Andrew heard a voice, saying:

Behold, Andrew, what is happening in this city.

And Andrew having beheld, prayed to the Lord, saying: Lord Jesus Christ, who didst order me to come into this city, do not suffer those in this city to do any evil, but let the knives go out of the hands of the wicked ones.

And straightway the knives of the wicked men fell, and their hands were turned into stone.

And the rulers, having seen what had happened, wept, saying:

Woe unto us, for here are the magicians who have gone into the prison, and brought out the men; for, behold, they have bewitched these also.

What, then, shall we do? Let us go now, and gather together the old men of the city, seeing that we are hungry.

And they went and gathered them together, and found two hundred and seventeen; and they brought them to the rulers, and they made them cast lots, and the lot came upon seven old men.

And one of those taken by lot answered and said to the officers:

I pray you, I have for myself one son; take him, and slay him instead of me, and let me go.

And the officers answered and said to him:

We cannot take thy son, unless we bring him first to our superiors.

And the officers went and told the rulers.

And the rulers answered and said to the officers:

If he give us his son instead of himself, let him go.

And the officers went and told the old man.

And the old man answered and said to them:

I have also a daughter along with my son; take them, and kill them, only let me go.

And he gave his children to the officers, that they might kill them.

And the children wept to each other, and prayed the officers, saying:

We pray you do not kill us, as we are of so small a size; but let us complete our size, and so kill us.

For it was a custom in that city, and they did not bury their dead, but ate them up.

And the officers did not hearken to the children, nor take pity upon them, but carried them to the trough weeping and praying.

And it happened, as they were leading them away to kill them, that Andrew, having beheld what happened, shed tears; and weeping, he looked up to heaven and said:

Lord Jesus Christ, as Thou didst hear me in the case of the dead men, and didst not suffer them to be eaten up, so also now hear me, that the executioners may not inflict death upon these children, but that the knives may be loosened out of the hands of the executioners. [24]And straightway the knives were loosened, and fell out of the hands of the executioners.

And when this came to pass, the executioners, having beheld what had happened, were exceedingly afraid.

And Andrew, seeing what had happened, glorified the Lord because He had listened to him in every work.

And the rulers, having beheld what had happened, wept with a great weeping, saying:

Woe unto us! what are we to do?

And, behold, the devil appeared in the likeness of an old man, and began to say in the midst of all:

Woe unto you! because you are now dying, having no food; what can sheep and oxen do for you?

They will not at all be enough for you.

But rise up, and make a search here for one who has come to the city, a stranger named Andrew, and kill him; for if you do not, he will not permit you to carry on this practice longer:

for it was he who let loose the men out of the prison.

Assuredly the man is in this city, and you have not seen [25] him.

Now, therefore, rise and make search for him, in order that henceforward you may be able to collect your food.

And Andrew saw the devil, how he was talking to the multitudes; but the devil did not see the blessed Andrew.

Then Andrew answered the devil, and said:

O Belial most fiendish, who art the foe of every creature; [26] but my Lord Jesus Christ will bring thee down to the abyss.

And the devil, having heard this, said:

I hear thy voice indeed, and I know thy voice, but where thou art standing I know not.

And Andrew answered and said to the devil:

Why, then, hast thou been called Amael? [27] is it not because thou art blind, not seeing all the saints?

And the devil, having heard this, said to the citizens:

Look round now for him speaking to me, for he is the man.

And the citizens, having run in different directions, shut the gates of the city, and searched for the blessed one, and did not see him. [28]Then the Lord showed Himself to Andrew, and said to him; Andrew, rise up and show thyself to them, that they may learn my power, and the powerlessness of the devil working in them.

Then Andrew rose up, and said in presence of all:

Behold, I am Andrew whom you seek.
And the multitudes ran upon him, and laid hold of him, saying:
What thou hast done to us, we also will do to thee.
And they reasoned among themselves, saying:
By what death shall we kill him? And they said to each other:
If we take off his head, his death is not torture; and if we burn him, he will not be for food to us.
Then one of them, the devil having entered into him, answered and said to the multitudes:
As he has done to us, so let us also do to him.
Let us rise up, then, and fasten a rope to his neck, and drag him through all the streets and lanes of the city; and when he is dead, we shall share his body.
And they did as he said to them; and having fastened a rope round his neck, they dragged him through the streets and lanes of the city, and the flesh of the blessed Andrew stuck to the ground, and his blood flowed to the ground like water.
And when it was evening they cast him into the prison, having bound his hands behind him; and he was in sore distress.
And in the morning again they brought him out, and having fastened a rope round his neck, they dragged him about; and again his flesh stuck to the ground, and his blood flowed.
And the blessed one wept and prayed, saying:
Do not forsake me, my Lord Jesus Christ; for I know that Thou art not far from Thy servants.
And as he was praying, the devil walked behind, and said to the multitudes:
Strike him on the mouth, that he may not speak. [29]
And when it was evening they took him again to the prison, having bound his hands behind him, and left him till the morrow again.
And the devil having taken with himself seven demons [30] whom the blessed one had cast out of the countries round about, and having gone into the prison, they stood before him, wishing to kill him.
And the demons answered and said to Andrew:
Now hast thou fallen into our hands; where is thy glory and thy exultation, thou that raisest thyself up against us, and dishonourest us, and tellest our doings to the people in every place and country, and hast made our workshops and our temples to become desolate, in order that sacrifices may not be brought to them?
Because of this, then, we shall also kill thee, like thy teacher called Jesus, and John whom Herod beheaded. [31]
And they stood before Andrew, wishing to kill him; and having beheld the seal upon his forehead which the Lord gave him, they were afraid, and did not come near him, but fled.
And the devil said to them:
Why have you fled from him, my children, and not killed him?
And the demons answered and said to the devil:
We cannot kill him, but kill him if thou art able; for we knew him before he came into the distress of his humiliation.
Then one of the demons answered and said:
We cannot kill him, but come let us mock him in the distress of his humiliation.
And the demons came and stood before him, and scoffed at him.
And the blessed one hearing, wept; and there came to him a voice saying:
Andrew, why weepest thou?
And it was the voice of the devil changed.
And Andrew answered and said:
I am weeping because God commanded me, saying, Be patient toward them.
And the devil said:
If thou canst do anything, do it.
And Andrew answered and said:
Is it for this, then, that you do these things to me?
But forbid it that I should disobey the commandment of my Lord; for if the Lord shall make for me a charge [32] in this city, I shall chastise you as you deserve.
And having heard this, they fled.
And when it was morning they brought him out again, and having fastened a rope about his neck, they dragged him; and again his flesh stuck to the ground, and his blood flowed to the ground like water.
And the blessed one, as he was being dragged along, wept, saying:
Lord Jesus Christ, be not displeased with me; for Thou knowest, Lord, what the fiend has inflicted upon me, along with his demons.

The Forgotten Bible

These tortures are enough, my Lord; for, behold, I am dragged about for three days. But do Thou, Lord, remember that Thou wast three hours upon the cross, and didst cry out to the Father, My Father, why hast Thou forsaken me? ³³Where are Thy words, Lord, which Thou spakest to us, confirming us, when we walked about with Thee, saying to us, Ye shall not lose one hair? ³⁴Consider, then, Lord, what has become of my flesh, and the hairs of my head.

Then Jesus said to Andrew:

O our Andrew, the heaven and the earth shall pass away, but my words shall not pass away. ³⁵Turn thyself then, Andrew, and behold thy flesh that has fallen, and thy hair, what has become of them.

And Andrew turned, and saw great trees springing up, bearing fruit; and he glorified God.

And when it was evening they took him up again, and cast him into the prison, having bound his hands behind him; and he was exceedingly exhausted.

And the men of the city said among themselves:

Perhaps he dies in the night, and we do not find him alive on the following day; for he was languid, and his flesh was spent.

And the Lord appeared in the prison, and having stretched out His hand, said to Andrew:

Give me thy hand, and rise up whole.

And Andrew, having beheld the Lord Jesus, gave Him his hand, and rose up whole. And falling down, he worshipped Him, and said:

I thank Thee, my Lord Jesus Christ, that Thou hast speedily brought help to me.

And Andrew, having looked into the middle of the prison, saw a pillar standing, and upon the pillar there stood an alabaster statue.

And Andrew, having gone up to the statue, unfolded his hands seven times, and said to the pillar, and the statue upon it:

Fear the sign of the cross, which the heaven and the earth dread; and let the statue set upon the pillar bring up much water through its mouth, until all who are in this city be punished.

And say not, I am stone, and am not worthy to praise the Lord, for the Lord fashioned us from the earth; but you are pure, because that out of you He gave the tables of the law. ³⁶When the blessed Andrew had said this, straightway the stone statue cast out of its mouth water in abundance, as if out of a canal.

And the water stood high upon the earth; and it was exceedingly acrid, eating into the flesh of men.

And when it was morning, the men of the city saw it, and began to flee, saying in themselves:

Woe to us! because we are now dying.

And the water killed their cattle and their children; and they began to flee out of the city.

Then Andrew prayed, saying:

Lord Jesus Christ, in whom I have hoped that this miracle should come upon this city, forsake me not, but send Michael Thy archangel in a cloud of fire, and be a wall round the city, that no one may be able to escape out of the fire.

And straightway a cloud of fire came down and encircled the city like a wall; and the water was as high as the neck of those men, and it was eating them up exceedingly.

And they wept, saying:

Woe to us! for all these things have come upon us because of the stranger who is in the prison.

Let us go and release him, lest perchance we die.

And they went out, crying with a loud voice:

God of the stranger, take away from us this water.

And the apostle knew that they were in great affliction, and said to the alabaster statue:

Stop the water, for they have repented.

And I say to thee, that if the citizens of this city shall believe, I will build a church, and place thee in it, because thou hast done me this service.

And the statue ceased flowing, and no longer brought forth water.

And the men of the city, having come out to the doors of the prison, cried out, saying:

Have pity upon us, God of the stranger, and do not according to our unbelief, and according to what we have done to this man, but take away from us this water.

And Andrew came forth out of the prison; and the water ran this way and that from the feet of the blessed Andrew.

Then all the multitude seeing him, all cried out:

Have pity upon us.

And the old man having come who gave up his children that they should slay them instead of him, prayed at the feet of the blessed Andrew, saying:

Have pity upon me.

And the holy Andrew answered and said to the old man:

I wonder how thou sayest, Have pity upon me; for thou hadst no pity upon thy children, but gavest them up to be slain instead of thee.

Therefore I say unto thee, At what hour this water goes away, into the abyss shalt thou go, with the fourteen [37] executioners who slay the men every day.

And he came to the place of the trough, where they used to slay the men.

And the blessed one, having looked up to heaven, prayed before all the multitude; and the earth was opened, and swallowed up the water, along with the old man.

He was carried down into the abyss, with the executioners.

And the men, having seen what had happened, were exceedingly afraid, and began to say:

Woe unto us because this man is from God; and now he will kill us because of the afflictions which we have caused him.

For, behold, what he said to the executioners and the old man has befallen them.

Now, therefore, he will command the fire, and it will burn us.

And Andrew, having heard, said to them:

Fear not, children; for I shall not send these also to Hades; but those have gone, that you may believe in our Lord Jesus Christ.

Then the holy Andrew ordered to be brought up all who had died in the water.

And they were not able to bring them; for there had died a great multitude both of men, and women, and children, and cattle.

Then Andrew prayed, and they all came to life.

And after these things he drew a plan of a church, and he caused the church to be built.

And he baptized them, and gave them the ordinances of our Lord Jesus Christ, saying to them:

Stand by these, in order that you may know the mysteries of our Lord Jesus Christ.

And they all prayed him:

We pray thee, stay with us a few days, that we may be filled with thy fountain, because we are newly planted. [38] And he did not comply with their request, but said to them:

I shall go first to my disciples.

And the children followed after, weeping and praying, with the men; and they cast ashes [39] upon their heads.

And he did not comply with them, but said:

I shall go to my disciples, and after that I shall come again to you.

And he went his way.

And the Lord Jesus Christ came down, being like a comely little child, and met Andrew, and said:

Andrew, why hast thou come out and left them without fruit, and hast not had compassion upon the children that followed after thee, and the men entreating thee, Stay with us a few days?

For the cry of them and the weeping has come up to heaven.

Now therefore return, and go into the city, and remain there seven days, until I shall confirm their souls in the faith; and then thou shalt go away into the country of the barbarians, thou and thy disciples.

And after going into this city, thou shalt proclaim my Gospel, and bring up the men who are in the abyss.

And thou shalt do what I command thee.

Then Andrew turned and went into the city, saying:

I thank Thee, my Lord Jesus Christ, who wishest to save every soul, that Thou hast not allowed me to go forth out of this city in mine anger.

And when he had come into the city, they, seeing him, rejoiced with exceeding great joy.

And he stayed there seven days, teaching and confirming them in the Lord Jesus Christ.

And the seven days having been fulfilled, it came to pass, while the blessed Andrew was going out, all came together to him, from the child even to the elder, and sent him on his way, saying:

There is one God, the God of Andrew, and one Lord Jesus Christ, who alone doeth wonders; to whom [40] be glory and strength for ever.

Amen.

Footnotes:

1. The oldestms. has Matthias; the four or five others have Matthew.
2. Lit., oeconomy.
3. One ms. inserts: having given thanks to God.
4. The winds from the four quarters of the heavens.
5. One ms. has: and the Lord prepared a small boat, and put angels in it for sailors; and Jesus

The Forgotten Bible

was, as it were, the master of the boat.

6. Matt. x. 10; Mark vi. 9.
7. One ms. omits the negative.
8. Comp. Matt. viii. 26.
9. One ms. inserts, besides women and children.
10. Mark vi. 37-44.
11. Mark vi. 3.
12. There seems to be something wrong here. One ms. has, the structure of the temple, and omits the following clause.
13. One ms. has: Do not say that I am a carved stone, and that you alone have a name, and are called high priests.
14. Gen. xxiii. 9, 17, following the version of the LXX. and the older interpreters.
15. Not one of the twelve patriarchs was buried in Machpelah.
16. One ms. inserts: And he saw the gate of that city.
17. Matt. x. 16.
18. Another ms. has: make men eat their like.
19. Gen. ix. 11.
20. Two mss. have: two hundred and forty-nine men.
21. Another reading is, praying.
22. i.e., to be eaten by them.
23. Comp. Acts v. 20-25.
24. One ms. adds: like wax before fire.
25. Or, do not know.
26. One ms. has: Thou art always warring against the race of the Christians.
27. One of the mss. has Samael.
28. One ms. adds: And Andrew answered and said: O Belial! foe of the whole creation, thou hast always been a robber, warring against the race of men: thou in the beginning didst cause Adam to be cast out of paradise; thou didst cause the loaves upon the table to be turned into stones; and again thou hast appeared in this city, to cause the people here to eat up men.
29. Comp. Acts xxiii. 2.
30. Comp. Matt. xii. 45.
31. One ms. adds: And the devil answered and said to the seven wicked demons, My children, kill him that dishonours us.
32. Or, a bishopric.
33. Matt. xxvii. 46.
34. Comp. Matt. x. 30.
35. Matt. v. 18.
36. One ms. has: Yea, for assuredly you have been honoured: for God did not write the law for His people on plates of gold or silver, but on plates of stone. Now therefore, O statue, do this that I require of thee.
37. One ms. has, four.
38. i.e., neophytes.
39. Or, dust.
40. One ms. adds: With the Father, and the Son, and the all-holy and good and life-giving and holy Spirit. Another ms. ends thus: Then the Apostle Andrew wished to go out again to preach. And they assembled from small to great of them, and said: There is one God and Father of all, one Lord, one faith, one baptism, which we have been taught by our father Andrew, the first called in (or by) Christ Jesus or Lord; to whom be glory for ever. Amen.

Acts of Peter and Andrew
From a Bodleian ms. [1]

Acts of the Holy Apostles Peter and Andrew.

It came to pass when Andrew the apostle of Christ went forth from the city of the man-eaters, behold a luminous cloud snatched him up, and carried him away to the mountain where Peter and Matthew and Alexander were sitting.

And when he saw them, they saluted him with great joy. Then Peter says to him:

What has happened to thee, brother Andrew? Hast thou sown the word of truth in the country of the man-eaters or not?

Andrew says to him:

Yes, father Peter, through thy prayers; but the men of that city have done me many mischiefs, for they dragged me through their street three days, so that my blood stained the whole street.

Peter says to him:

Be a man in the Lord, brother Andrew, and come hither, and rest from thy labour.

For if the good husbandman laboriously till the ground, it will also bear fruit, and straightway all his toil will be turned into joy; but if he toil, and his land bring forth no fruit, he has double toil.

And while he was thus speaking, the Lord Jesus Christ appeared to them in the form of a child, and said to them:

Hail, Peter, bishop of the whole of my Church! hail, Andrew!

My co-heirs, be courageous, and struggle for mankind; for verily I say unto you, you shall endure toils in this world for mankind.

But be bold; I will give you rest in one hour of repose in the kingdom of my Father.

Arise, then, and go into the city of the barbarians, and preach in it; and I will be with you in the wonders that shall happen in it by your hands.

And the Lord Jesus, after saluting them, went up into the heavens in glory.

And Peter, and Andrew, and Alexander, and Rufus, and Matthias, went into the city of the barbarians.

And after they had come near the city, Andrew answered and said to Peter:

Father Peter, have we again to undergo toils in this city, as in the country of the man-eaters? Peter says to him:

I do not know.

But, behold, there is an old man before us sowing in his field:

if we go up to him, let us say to him, Give us bread; and if he give us bread, we may know that we are not to suffer in this city; but if he say to us, We have no bread, on the other hand, we shall know that suffering again awaits us.

And when they came up to the old man, Peter says to him:

Hail, farmer!

And the farmer says to them:

Hail you too, merchants!

Peter says to him: Have you bread to give to these children, for we have been in want? The old man says to them:

Wait a little, and look after the oxen, and the plough, and the land, that I may go into the city, and get you loaves.

Peter says to him:

If you provide hospitality for us, we shall took after the cattle and the field.

The old man says:

So be it.

Peter says to him:

Are the oxen your own?

The old man says:

No; I have them on hire.

Peter says to him:

Go into the city.

And the old man went into the city.

And Peter arose, and girded up his cloak and his under-garment, and says to Andrew:

It is not right for us to rest and be idle; above all, when the old man is working for us, having left his own work.

Then Peter took hold of the plough, and sowed the wheat.

And Andrew was behind the oxen, and says to Peter:

Father Peter, why dost thou bring toil upon us, especially when we have work enough already!

Then Andrew took the plough out of Peter's hand, and sowed the wheat, saying:

O seed cast into the ground in the field of the righteous, come up, and come to the light.

Let the young men of the city therefore come forth, whom I found in the pit of destruction until to-day; for, behold, the apostles of Christ are coming into the city, pardoning the sins of those who believe in them, and healing every disease, and every sickness.

Pray ye for me, that He may have mercy upon me, and that I may be delivered from this strait.

And many of the multitude believed in Christ, because of the saying of the woman; [2] and they fell at the feet of the apostles, and adored them.

And they laid their hands upon them.

And they healed those in the city that were sick, and gave sight to the blind and, hearing to the deaf, and drove out the demons.

All the multitude glorified the Father, and the Son, and the Holy Spirit.

And there was a certain rich man in the city, by name Onesiphorus.

He, having seen the miracles done by the apostles, says to them:

If I believe in your God, can I also do a miracle like you?

Andrew says to him:

If thou wilt forsake all that belongs to thee, and thy wife and thy children, as we also have done, then thou also shalt do miracles. When Onesiphorus heard this, he was filled with rage, and took his scarf and threw it over Andrew's neck, and struck him, and said to him:

Thou art a sorcerer.

How dost thou force me to abandon my wife, and my children, and my goods?

Then Peter, having turned and seen him striking Andrew, says to him:

Man, stop now striking Andrew. Onesiphorus says to him:

I see that thou art more sensible than he. Do thou then tell me to leave my wife, and my children, and my goods. What dost thou say?

Peter says to him:

One thing I say unto thee:

it is easier for a camel to go through the eye of a needle, than for a rich man to go into the kingdom of heaven. [3]When Onesiphorus heard this, he was even more filled with rage and anger, and took his scarf off the neck of Andrew, and threw it upon the neck of Peter; and so he dragged him along, saying:

Verily thou art a great sorcerer, more than the other; for a camel cannot go through the eye of a needle.

But if thou wilt show me this miracle, I will believe in thy God; and not only I, but also the whole city.

But if not, thou shalt be grievously punished in the midst of the city.

And when Peter heard this, he was exceedingly grieved, and stood and stretched forth his hands towards heaven, and prayed, saying:

O Lord our God, listen to me at this time; for they will ensnare us from Thine own words:

for no prophet has spoken to set forth this his explanation, and no patriarch that we might learn the interpretation of it; and now we seek for ourselves the explanation with boldness.

Do Thou then, Lord, not overlook us:

for thou art He who is praised by the cherubim.

And after he had said this, the Saviour appeared in the form of a child of twelve years old, wearing a linen garment; and He says to them:

Be courageous, and tremble not, my chosen disciples; for I am with you always.

Let the needle and the camel be brought.

And after saying this, He went up into the heavens.

And there was a certain merchant [4] in the city who had believed in the Lord through the Apostle Philip; and when he heard of this, he ran and searched for a needle with a big eye, to do a favour to the apostles.

When Peter learned this, he said:

My son, do not search for a big needle; for nothing is impossible with God:

rather bring us a small needle.

And after the needle had been brought, and all the multitude of the city were standing by to see, Peter looked up and saw a camel coming.

And he ordered her to be brought.

Then he fixed the needle in the ground, and cried out with a loud voice, saying:

In the name of Jesus Christ, who was crucified under Pontius Pilate, I order thee, O camel, to go through the eye of the needle.

Then the eye of the needle was opened like a gate, and the camel went through it, and all the multitude saw it.

Again Peter says to the camel:

Go again through the needle.

And the camel went a second time.

When Onesiphorus saw this, he said to Peter; Truly thou art a great sorcerer; but I do not believe unless I send and bring a camel and a needle.

And he called one of his servants, and said to him privately:

Go and bring me here a camel and a needle; find also a polluted woman, and force her to come here:

for these men are sorcerers.

And Peter having learned the mystery through the Spirit, says to Onesiphorus:

Send and bring the camel, and the woman, and the needle.

And when they brought them, Peter took the needle, and fixed it in the ground.

And the woman was sitting on the camel.

Then Peter says:

In the name of our Lord Jesus Christ the crucified, I order thee, O camel, to go through this needle.

And immediately the eye of the needle was opened, and became like a gate, and the camel went through it.

Peter again says to the camel:

Go through it again, that all may see the glory of our Lord Jesus Christ, in order that some may believe on Him.

Then the camel again went through the needle.

And Onesiphorus seeing it, cried out, and said: Truly great is the God of Peter and Andrew, and I from this time forth believe in the name of our Lord Jesus Christ.

Now then, hear my words, O Peter.

I have corn lands, vineyards, and fields; I have also twenty-seven pounds of gold, and fifty pounds of silver; and I have very many slaves.

I give my possessions to the poor, that I also may do one miracle like you.

And Peter was grieved lest the powers should not work in him, seeing that he had not received the seal in Christ. And while he was considering this, behold, a voice out of the heaven saying to him:

Do to him what he wishes, because I will accomplish for him what he desires.

Peter says to him:

My son, come hither; do as we do.

And Onesiphorus came up, and stood before the camel and the needle, and said:

In the n... (Here the ms. ends.)

Footnotes:

1. [This is thems. frequently referred to in the previous pages. The Greek text of this fragment is given by Tischendorf in the supplement to Apocalypses Apocr., pp. 161-167.--R.]

2. Something seems to have fallen out here.

3. Matt. xix. 24, etc.

4. pantapoles.

Acts and Martyrdom of St. Matthew the Apostle

About that time Matthew, the holy apostle and evangelist of Christ, was abiding in the mountain resting, and praying in his tunic and apostolic robes without sandals; and, behold, Jesus came to Matthew in the likeness of the infants who sing in paradise, and said to him:

Peace to thee, Matthew!

And Matthew having gazed upon Him, and not known who He was, said:

Grace to thee, and peace, O child highly favoured!

And why hast thou come hither to me, having left those who sing in paradise, and the delights there?

Because here the place is desert; and what sort of a table I shall lay for thee, O child, I know not, because I have no bread nor oil in a jar.

Moreover, even the winds are at rest, so as not to cast down from the trees to the ground anything for food; because, for the accomplishing of my fast of forty days, I, partaking only of the fruits falling by the movement of the winds, am glorifying my Jesus.

Now, therefore, what shall I bring thee, beautiful boy?

There is not even water near, that I may wash thy feet.

And the child said:

Why sayest thou, O Matthew?

Understand and know that good discourse is better than a calf, and words of meekness better than every herb of the field, and a sweet saying as the perfume of love, and cheerfulness of countenance better than feeding, and a pleasant look is as the appearance of sweetness.

Understand, Matthew, and know that I am paradise, that I am the comforter, I am the power of the powers above, I the strength of those that restrain themselves, I the crown of the virgins, I the self-control of the once married, I the boast of the widowed, I the defence of the infants, I the foundation of the Church, I the kingdom of the bishops, I the glory of the presbyters, I the praise of the deacons.

Be a man, and be strong, Matthew, in, these words.

And Matthew said:

The sight of thee hast altogether delighted me, O child; moreover also, thy words are full of life.

For assuredly thy face shines more than the lightning, and thy words are altogether most sweet.

And that indeed I saw thee in paradise when thou didst sing with the other infants who were killed in Bethlehem, I know right well; but how thou hast suddenly come hither, this altogether astonishes me. But I shall ask thee one thing, O child:

that impious Herod, where is he?

The child says to him:

Since thou hast asked, hear his dwelling-place.

He dwells, indeed, in Hades; and there has been prepared for him fire unquenchable, Gehenna without end, bubbling mire, worm that sleeps not, [1] because he cut off three [2] thousand infants, wishing to slay the child Jesus, the ancient of the ages; but of all these ages I am father.

Now therefore, O Matthew, take this rod of mine, and go down from the mountain, and go into Myrna, the city of the man-eaters, and plant it by the gate of the church which thou [3] and Andrew founded; and as soon as thou hast planted it, it shall be a tree, great and lofty and with many branches, and its branches shall extend to thirty cubits, and of each single branch the fruit shall be different both to the sight and the eating, [4] and from the top of the tree shall flow down much honey; and from its root there shall come forth a great fountain, giving drink to this country round about, and in it creatures that swim and creep; and in it the man-eaters shall wash themselves, and eat of the fruit of the trees of the vine and of the honey; and their bodies shall be changed, and their forms shall be altered so as to be like those of other men; and they shall be ashamed of the nakedness of their body, and they shall put on clothing of the rams of the sheep, and they shall no

The Forgotten Bible

longer eat unclean things; and there shall be to them fire in superabundance, preparing the sacrifices for offerings, and they shall bake their bread with fire; and they shall see each other in the likeness of the rest of men, and they shall acknowledge me, and glorify my Father who is in the heavens.

Now therefore make haste, Matthew, and go down hence, because the departure from thy body through fire is at hand, and the crown of thy endurance.

And the child having said this, and given him the rod, was taken up into the heavens.

And Matthew went down from the mountain, hastening to the city.

And as he was about to enter into the city, there met him Fulvana the wife of the king, and his son Fulvanus and his wife Erva, who were possessed by an unclean spirit, and cried out shouting:

Who has brought thee here again, Matthew? or who has given thee the rod for our destruction? for we see also the child Jesus, the Son of God, who is with thee.

Do not go then, O Matthew, to plant the rod for the food, and for the transformation of the man-eaters:

for I have found what I shall do to thee.

For since thou didst drive me out of this city, and prevent me from fulfilling my wishes among the man-eaters, behold, I will raise up against thee the king of this city, and he will burn thee alive.

And Matthew, having laid his hands on each one of the demoniacs, put the demons to flight, and made the people whole; and they followed him.

And thus the affair being made manifest, Plato the bishop, having heard of the presence of the holy Apostle Matthew, met him with all the clergy; and having fallen to the ground, they kissed his feet.

And Matthew raised them, and went with them into the church, and the child Jesus was also with him.

And Matthew, having come to the gate of the church, stood upon a certain lofty and immoveable stone; and when the whole city ran together, especially the brethren who had believed, began to say:

Men and women who appear in our sight, heretofore believing in the universe, [5] but now knowing Him who has upheld and made the universe; until now worshipping the Satyr, and mocked by ten thousand false gods, but now through Jesus Christ acknowledging the one and only God, Lord, Judge; who have laid aside the immeasurable greatness of evil, and put on love, which is of like nature with affectionateness, towards men; once strangers to Christ, but now confessing Him Lord and God; formerly without form, but now transformed through Christ;--behold, the staff which you see in my hand, which Jesus, in whom you have believed and will believe, gave me; perceive now what comes to pass through me, and acknowledge the riches of the greatness which He will this day make for you.

For, behold, I shall plant this rod in this place, and it shall be a sign to your generations, and it shall become a tree, great and lofty and flourishing, and its fruit beautiful to the view and good to the sight; and the fragrance of perfumes shall come forth from it, and there shall be a vine twining round it, full of clusters; and from the top of it honey coming down, and every flying creature shall find covert in its branches; and a fountain of water shall come forth from the root of it, having swimming and creeping things, giving drink to all the country round about.

And having said this, and called upon the name of the Lord Jesus, he fixed his rod in the ground, and straightway it sprung up to one cubit; and the sight was strange and wonderful.

For the rod having straightway shot up, increased in size, and grew into a great tree, as Matthew had said.

And the apostle said:

Go into the fountain and wash your bodies in it, and then thus partake both of the fruits of the tree, and of the vine and the honey, and drink of the fountain, and you shall be transformed in your likeness to that of men; and after that, having gone into the church, you will clearly recognise that you have believed in the living and true God.

And having done all these things, they saw themselves changed into the likeness of Matthew; then, having thus gone into the church, they worshipped and glorified God.

And when they had been changed, they knew that they were naked; and they ran in haste each to his own house to cover their nakedness, because they were ashamed.

And Matthew and Plato remained in the church spending the night, and glorifying God.

And there remained also the king's wife, and his son and his wife, and they prayed the apostle to give them the seal in Christ.

And Matthew gave orders to Plato; and he, having gone forth, baptized them in the water of the fountain of the tree, in the name of the Father, and the Son, and the Holy Ghost.

And so thereafter, having gone into the church, they communicated in the holy mysteries of Christ; [6] and they exulted and passed the night, they also along with the apostle, many others having also come with them; and all in the church sang the whole night, glorifying God.

And when the dawn had fully come, the blessed Matthew, having gone along with the bishop Plato, stood in the place in which the rod had been planted, and he sees the rod grown into a great tree, and near it a vine twined round it, and honey coming down from above even to its root; and that tree was at once beautiful and flourishing, like the plants in paradise, and a river proceeded from its root watering [7] all the land of the city of Myrna. [8]And all ran together, and ate of the fruit of the tree and the vine, just as any one wished.

And when what had come to pass was reported in the palace, the king Fulvanus, having learned what had been done by Matthew about his wife, and his son, and his daughter-in-law, rejoiced for a time at their purification; but seeing that they were inseparable from Matthew, he was seized with rage and anger, and endeavoured to put him to death by fire.

And on that night [9] in which the king intended to lay hands on Matthew, Matthew saw Jesus saying to him:

I am with thee always to save thee, Matthew; be strong, and be a man.

And the blessed Matthew, having awoke, and sealed himself over all the body, rose up at dawn, and proceeded into the church; and having bent his knees, prayed earnestly.

Then the bishop having come, and the clergy, they stood in common in prayer, glorifying God.

And after they had ended the prayer, the bishop Plato said:

Peace to thee, Matthew, apostle of Christ!

And the blessed Matthew said to him:

Peace to you!

And when they had sat down, the apostle said to the bishop Plato, and to all the clergy:

I wish you, children, to know, Jesus having declared it to me, that the king of this city is going to send soldiers against me, the devil having entered into him, and manifestly armed him against us.

But let us give ourselves up to Jesus, and He will deliver us from every trial, and all who have believed in Him.

And the king, plotting against the blessed Matthew how he should lay hands on him, and seeing also that the believers were very many, was very much at fault, and was in great difficulty.

Therefore the wicked and unclean devil who had come forth from the king's wife, and his son, and his daughter-in-law, put to flight by Matthew, having transformed himself into the likeness of a soldier, stood before the king, and said to him:

O king, why art thou thus put to the worse by this stranger and sorcerer?

Knowest thou not that he was a publican, but now he has been called an apostle [10] by Jesus, who was crucified by the Jews?

For, behold, thy wife, and thy son, and thy daughter-in-law, instructed by him, have believed in him, and along with him sing in the church.

And now, behold, Matthew is going forth, and Plato with him, and they are going to the gate called Heavy; but make haste, and thou wilt find them, and thou shalt do to him all that may be pleasing in thine eyes.

The king having heard this, and being the more exasperated by the pretended soldier, sent against the blessed Matthew four soldiers, having threatened them, and said:

Unless you bring Matthew to me, I shall burn you alive with fire; and the punishment which he is to undergo, you shall endure.

And the soldiers, having been thus threatened by the king, go in arms to where the Apostle Matthew and the bishop Plato are.

And when they came near them, they heard their speaking indeed, but saw no one.

And having come, they said to the king:

We pray thee, O king, we went and found no one, but only heard the voices of persons talking.

And the king, being enraged, and having blazed up like fire, gave orders to send other ten soldiers--man-eaters--saying to them:

Go stealthily to the place, and tear them in pieces alive, and eat up Matthew, and Plato, who is with him.

And when they were about to come near the blessed Matthew, the Lord Jesus Christ, having come in the likeness of a most beautiful boy, holding a torch of fire, ran to meet them, burning out their eyes.

And they, having cried out and thrown their arms from them, fled, and came to the king, being speechless.

And the demon who had before appeared to the king in the form of a soldier, being again transformed into the form of a soldier, stood before the king, and said to him:

Thou seest, O king, this stranger has bewitched them all.

Learn, then, how thou shalt take him.

The king says to him:

Tell me first wherein his strength is, that I may know, and then I will draw up against him with a great force.

And the demon, compelled by an angel, says to the king:

Since thou wishest to hear accurately about him, O king, I will tell thee all the truth. Really, unless he shall be willing to be taken by thee of his own accord, thou labourest in vain, and thou wilt not be able to hurt him; but if thou wishest to lay hands on him, thou wilt be struck by him with blindness, and thou wilt be paralyzed.

And if thou send a multitude of soldiers against him, they also will be struck with blindness, and will be paralyzed.

And we shall go, even seven unclean demons, and immediately make away with thee and thy whole camp, and destroy all the city with lightning, except those naming that awful and holy name of Christ; for wherever a footstep of theirs has come, thence, pursued, we flee.

And even if thou shalt apply fire to him, to him the fire will be dew; and if thou shalt shut him up in a furnace, to him the furnace will be a church; and if thou shalt put him in chains in prison, and seal up the floors, the doors will open to him of their own accord, and all who believe in that name will go in, even they, and say, This prison is a church of the living God, and a holy habitation of those that live alone. [11]Behold, O king, I have told thee all the truth.

The king therefore says to the pretended soldier:

Since I do not know Matthew, come with me, and point him out to me from a distance, and take from me gold, as much as thou mayst wish, or go thyself, and with thy sword kill him, and Plato his associate. [12]The demon says to him:

I cannot kill him.

I dare not even look into his face, seeing that he has destroyed all our generation through the name of Christ, proclaimed through him.

The king says to him:

And who art thou?

And he says:

I am the demon who dwelt in thy wife, and in thy son, and in thy daughter-in-law; and my name is Asmodaeus; and this Matthew drove me out of them.

And now, behold, thy wife, and thy son, and thy daughter-in-law sing along with him in the church.

And I know, O king, that thou also after this wilt believe in him.

The king says to him:

Whoever thou art, spirit of many shapes, I adjure thee by the God whom he whom thou callest Matthew proclaims, depart hence without doing hurt to any one.

And straightway the demon, no longer like a soldier, but like smoke, became invisible; and as he fled he cried out:

O secret name, armed against us, I pray thee, Matthew, servant of the holy God, pardon me, and I will no longer remain in this city.

Keep thou thine own; but I go away into the fire everlasting.

Then the king, affected with great fear at the answer of the demon, remained quiet that day.

And the night having come, and he not being able to sleep because he was hungry, [13] leaped up at dawn, and went into the church, with only two soldiers without arms, to take Matthew by craft, that he might kill him.

And having summoned two friends of Matthew, he said to them:

Show to Matthew, says he, that I wish to be his disciple.

And Matthew hearing, and knowing the craft of the tyrant, and having been warned also by the vision of the Lord to him, went forth out of the church, led by the hand by Plato, and stood in the gate of the church.

And they say to the king:

Behold Matthew in the gate!

And he says: Who he is, or where he is, I see not.

And they said to him:

Behold, he is in sight of thee.

And he says:

All the while I see nobody.

For he had been blinded by the power of God.

And he began to cry out:

Woe to me, miserable! what evil has come upon me, for my eyes have been blinded, and all my limbs paralyzed?

The Forgotten Bible

O Asmodaeus Beelzebul Satan! all that thou hast said to me has come upon me.

But I pray thee, Matthew, servant of God, forgive me as the herald of the good God; for assuredly the Jesus proclaimed by thee three days ago through the night appeared to me altogether resplendent as with lightning, like a beautiful young man, and said to me, Since thou art entertaining evil counsels in the wickedness of thine heart in regard to my servant Matthew, know I have disclosed to him that through thee will be the release of his body. And straightway I saw him going up into heaven.

If therefore he is thy God, and if he wishes thy body to be buried in our city for a testimony of the salvation of the generations after this, and for the banishing [14] of the demons, I shall know the truth for myself by this, by thee laying on hands upon me, and I shall receive my sight.

And the apostle having laid his hands upon his eyes, and saying Ephphatha, Jesus, [15] he made him receive his sight instantly.

And straightway the king, laying hold of the apostle, and leading him by the right hand, brought him by craft into the palace; and Plato was on Matthew's left hand, going along with him, and keeping hold of him.[16] Then Matthew says:

O crafty tyrant, how long dost thou not fulfil the works of thy father the devil?

And he was enraged at what had been said; for he perceived that he would inflict upon him a more bitter death.

For he resolved to put him to death by fire.

And he commanded several executioners to come, and to lead him away to the place by the seashore, where the execution of malefactors was wont to take place, saying to the executioners:

I hear, says he, that the God whom he proclaims delivers from fire those who believe in him.

Having laid him, therefore, on the ground on his back, and stretched him out, pierce his hands and feet with iron nails, and cover him over with paper, having smeared it with dolphins' oil, and cover him up with brimstone and asphalt and pitch, and put tow and brushwood above.

Thus apply the fire to him; and if any of the same tribe with him rise up against you, he shall get the same punishment.

And the apostle exhorted the brethren to remain undismayed, and that they should rejoice, and accompany him with great meekness, singing and praising God, because they were deemed worthy to have the relics of the apostle.

Having therefore come to the place, the executioners, like most evil wild beasts, pinned down to the ground Matthew's hands and feet with long nails; and having done everything as they had been bid, applied the fire.

And they indeed laboured [17] closely, kindling it all round; but all the fire was changed into dew, so that the brethren, rejoicing, cried out:

The only God is the Christians', who assists Matthew, in whom also we have believed:

the only God is the Christians', who preserves His own apostle in the fire.

And by the voice the city was shaken.

And some of the executioners, having gone forth, said to the king:

We indeed, O king, by every contrivance of vengeance, have kindled the fire; but the sorcerer by a certain name puts it out, calling upon Christ, and invoking his cross; and the Christians surrounding him play with the fire, and walking in it with naked feet, laugh at us, [18] and we have fled ashamed.

Then he ordered a multitude to carry coals of fire from the furnace of the bath in the palace, and the twelve gods of gold and silver; and place them, says he, in a circle round the sorcerer, lest he may even somehow bewitch the fire from the furnace of the palace.

And there being many executioners and soldiers, some carried the coals; and others, bearing the gods, brought them.

And the king accompanied them, watching lest any of the Christians should steal one of his gods, or bewitch the fire.

And when they came near the place where the apostle was nailed down, his face was looking towards heaven, and all his body was covered over with the paper, and much brushwood over his body to the height of ten cubits.

And having ordered the soldiers to set the gods in a circle round Matthew, five cubits off, securely fastened that they might not fall, again he ordered the coal to be thrown on, and to kindle the fire at all points.

And Matthew, having looked up to heaven, cried out, Adonai eloi sabaoth marmari marmunth; that is, O God the Father, O Lord Jesus Christ, deliver me, and burn down their gods which they worship; and let the fire also pursue the king even to his palace, but not to his destruction:

for perhaps he will repent and be converted.

And when he saw the fire to be monstrous in height, the king, thinking that Matthew was burnt up, laughed aloud, and said:

Has thy magic been of any avail to thee, Matthew?

Can thy Jesus now give thee any help?

And as he said this a dreadful wonder appeared; for all the fire along with the wood went away from Matthew, and was poured round about their gods, so that nothing of the gold or the silver was any more seen; and the king fled, and said:

Woe's me, that my gods are destroyed by the rebuke of Matthew, of which the weight was a thousand talents of gold and a thousand talents of silver.

Better are the gods of stone and of earthenware, in that they are neither melted nor stolen. [19]

And when the fire had thus utterly destroyed their gods, and burnt up many soldiers, there came to pass again another stranger wonder.

For the fire, in the likeness of a great and dreadful dragon, chased the tyrant as far as the palace, and ran hither and thither round the king, not letting him go into the palace.

And the king, chased by the fire, and not allowed to go into his palace, turned back to where Matthew was, and cried out, saying:

I beseech thee, whoever thou art, O man, whether magician or sorcerer or god, or angel of God, whom so great a pyre has not touched, remove from me this dreadful and fiery dragon; forget the evil I have done, as also when thou madest me receive my sight.

And Matthew, having rebuked the fire, and the flames having been extinguished, and the dragon having become invisible, stretching his eyes to heaven, and praying in Hebrew, and commending his spirit to the Lord, said:

Peace to you!

And having glorified the Lord, he went to his rest about the sixth hour.

Then the king, having ordered more soldiers to come, and the bed to be brought from the palace, which had a great show of gold, he ordered the apostle to be laid on it, and carried to the palace.

And the body of the apostle was lying as if in sleep, and his robe and his tunic unstained by the fire; and sometimes they saw him on the bed, and sometimes following, and sometimes going before the bed, and with his right hand put upon Plato's head, and singing along with the multitude, so that both the king and the soldiers, with the crowd, were struck with astonishment.

And many diseased persons and demoniacs, having only touched the bed, were made sound; and as many as were savage in appearance, in that same hour were changed into the likeness of other men.

And as the bed was going into the palace, we [20] all saw Matthew rising up, as it were, from the bed, and going into heaven, led by the hand by a beautiful boy; and twelve men in shining garments came to meet him, having never-fading and golden crowns on their head; and we saw how that child crowned Matthew, so as to be like them, and in a flash of lightning they went away to heaven.

And the king stood at the gate of the palace, and ordered that no one should come in but the soldiers carrying the bed.

And having shut the doors, [21] he ordered an iron coffin to be made, put the body of Matthew into it, and sealed it up with lead; through the eastern gate of the palace at midnight put it into a boat, no one knowing of it, and threw it into the deep part of the sea.

And through the whole night the brethren remained before the gate of the palace, spending the night, and singing; and when the dawn rose there was a voice:

O bishop Plato, carry the Gospel and the Psalter of David; go along with the multitude of the brethren to the east of the palace, and sing the Alleluia, and read the Gospel, and bring as an offering the holy bread; and having pressed three clusters from the vine into a cup, communicate with me, as the Lord Jesus showed us how to offer up when He rose from the dead on the third day.

And the bishop having run into the church, and taken the Gospel and the Psalter of David, and having assembled the presbyters and the multitude of the brethren, came to the east of the palace at the hour of sunrise; and having ordered the one who was singing to go upon a certain lofty stone, he began to praise in singing of a song to God:

Precious in the sight of God is the death of His saints. [22] And again:

I laid me down and slept; I arose:

because the Lord will sustain me. [23] And they listened to the singing of a song of David:

Shall he that is dead not rise again?

Now I shall raise him up for myself, saith the Lord.

And all shouted out the Alleluia.

And the bishop read the Gospel, and all cried out:

Glory to Thee, Thou who hast been glorified in heaven and on earth.

And so then they offered the gift of the holy offering for Matthew; and having partaken for thanksgiving [24] of the undefiled and life-giving mysteries of Christ, they all glorified God.

And it was about the sixth hour, and Plato sees the sea opposite about seven furlongs off; and, behold, Matthew was standing on the sea, and two men, one on each side, in shining garments, and the beautiful boy in front of them.

And all the brethren saw these things, and they heard them saying Amen, Alleluia.

And one could see the sea fixed like a stone of crystal, and the beautiful boy in front of them, when out of the depth of the sea a cross came up, and at the end of the cross the coffin going up in which was the body of Matthew; and in the hour of the piercing on the cross, [25] the boy placed the coffin on the ground, behind the palace towards the east, where the bishop had offered the offering for Matthew.

And the king having seen these things from the upper part of the house, and being terror-struck, went forth from the palace, and ran and worshipped towards the east at the coffin, and fell down before the bishop, and the presbyters, and the deacons, in repentance and confession, saying: [26]"Truly I believe in the true God, Christ Jesus.

I entreat, give me the seal in Christ, and I will give you my palace, in testimony of Matthew, and you shall put the coffin upon my golden bed, in the great dining-room; only, having baptized me in it, communicate to me the Eucharist of Christ.

And the bishop having prayed, and ordered him to take off his clothes, and having examined him for a long time, and he having confessed and wept over what he had done, having sealed him, and anointed him with oil, put him down into the sea, in the name of Father, and Son, and Holy Ghost.

And when he came up from the water he ordered him to put on himself splendid garments, and so then having given praise and thanks, communicating the holy bread and mixed cup, the bishop first gave them to the king, saying:

Let this body of Christ, and this cup, His blood shed for us, be to thee for the remission of sins unto life.

And a voice was heard from on high:

Amen, amen, amen.

And when he had thus communicated in fear and joy, the apostle appeared and said:

King Fulvanus, thy name shall no longer be Fulvanus; but thou shalt be called Matthew.

And thou, the son of the king, shall no longer be called Fulvanus, but Matthew also; and thou Ziphagia, the wife of the king, shall be called Sophia; [27] and Erva, the wife of your son, shall be called Synesis.[28] And these names of yours shall be written in the heavens, and there shall not fail of your loins from generation to generation.

And in that same hour Matthew appointed the king a presbyter, and he was thirty-seven years old; and the king's son he appointed deacon, being seventeen years old; and the king's wife he appointed a presbyteress; and his son's wife he appointed a deaconess, [29] and she also was seventeen years old.

And then he thus blessed them, saying:

The blessing and the grace of our Lord Jesus Christ shall be with you to time everlasting.

Then the king, having awakened out of sleep, and rejoiced with all his house at the vision of the holy Apostle Matthew, praised God.

And the king, having gone into his palace, broke all the idols to pieces, and gave a decree to those in his kingdom, writing thus:

King Matthew, to all those under my kingdom, greeting.

Christ having appeared upon earth, and having saved the human race, the so-called gods have been found to be deceivers, and soul-destroyers, and plotters against the human race.

Whence, divine grace having shone abroad, and come even to us, and we having come to the knowledge of the deception of the idols, that it is vain and false, it has seemed good to our divinity that there should not be many gods, but one, and one only, the God in the heavens.

And you, having received this our decree, keep to the purport of it, and break to pieces and destroy every idol; and if any one shall be detected from this time forth serving idols, or concealing them, let such an one be subjected to punishment by the sword.

Farewell all, because we also are well.

And when this order was given out, all, rejoicing and exulting, broke their idols to pieces, crying out and saying:

There is one only God, He who is in the heavens, who does good to men.

And after all these things had come to pass, Matthew the apostle of Christ appeared to the bishop Plato, and said to him:

Plato, servant of God, and our brother, be it known unto thee, that after three years shall be thy rest in the Lord, and exultation to ages of ages.

And the king himself, whom after my own name I have called Matthew, shall receive the throne of thy bishopric, and after him his son.

And he, having said Peace to thee and all the saints, went to heaven.

And after three years the bishop Plato rested in the Lord.

And King Matthew succeeded him, having given up his kingdom willingly to another, whence there was given him grace against unclean demons, and he cured every affliction.

And he advanced his son to be a presbyter, and made him second to himself.

And Saint Matthew finished his course in the country of the man-eaters, in the city of Myrna, on the sixteenth of the month of November, our Lord Jesus Christ reigning, to whom be glory and strength, now and ever, and to ages of ages.

Amen. [30]

Footnotes:

1. Or, that dies not.
2. The other [Vienna] ms. has, eleven.
3. In some of themss. of the previous book the name of Matthew appears in place of that of Matthias--Matthaios for Mattheias.
4. Comp. Rev. xxii. 2.
5. The other [Vienna] ms. has: heretofore worshipping every evil thing.
6. The other [Paris]ms. has: having communicated in the Eucharist.
7. Or, giving drink to.
8. The other [Paris]ms. has Smyrna. Nicephorus calls it Myrmene.
9. Comp. Acts xviii. 9, xxiii. 11.
10. Or, as an apostle.
11. i.e., monks.
12. Lit., of the same form with him.
13. The other [Vienna] ms. has: for he neither ate nor drank, in his concern about these things.
14. The word thus translated is used by the LXX. in the sense of an asylum, or place of refuge.
15. Comp. Mark vii. 34. The addition of Jesus here shows that the writer did not know the meaning of the Aramaic word.
16. Or, holding him back.
17. I should be disposed to read ekaion, set fire to, for ekamnon, laboured.
18. The other [Vienna] ms. has: at our gods.
19. The other [Vienna] ms. adds: How my forefathers toiled, and with great trouble made the gods; and now, behold, they have been destroyed by one magician.
20. The change of person is noticable.
21. In the otherms. the king prays: And now, since there is still in me a little unbelief, I beseech thee that thou wilt bring the body of Matthew from the sea. For, behold, I will order the body to be thrown into the depths of the sea; and if thou deliver it as thou didst deliver it, in the funeral pile, I will forsake all my gods at once, and believe in thee alone. [The Viennams., here cited, interpolates still more.--R.]
22. Ps. cxvi. 15.
23. Ps. iii. 5 according to the LXX.
24. Or, of the Eucharist.
25. The meaning is not clear. The otherms. has: After one hour he sees in that place an image of a cross coming up from the depth of the sea. [The Viennams. varies more than this extract indicates.--R.]
26. The other [Vienna] ms. is much fuller here: And the cry of the multitude came to the king. And he asked: What is the uproar and shouting among the people? And he learned that Matthew's coffin had come of itself. Then, filled with great joy, the king straightway goes to the coffin, crying out, and saying with a loud voice: The God of Matthew is the only God, and there is none other but Him. And he fell on his face near the coffin, saying: Pardon me, Lord Jesus Christ, for what I have done against this holy man, for I was in ignorance. And the bishop, seeing the repentance and tears of the king, gave him a hand, and raised him from the ground, and said to him: Rise up, and be of good courage; for the Lord God hath accepted thy repentance and conversion through the good offices of His servant and apostle Thomas. And the king rose up from the ground, and fell at the bishop's feet, etc.--as in the text.
27. Wisdom.
28. Understanding.
29. The other [Vienna] ms. has: And likewise his wife and his daughter-in-law deaconesses.
30. The other [Paris]ms. ends differently: And there came a voice, Peace to you, and joy, for there shall not be war nor stroke of sword in this city, because of Matthew, mine elect, whom I have

The Forgotten Bible

loved for ever. Blessed are they who observe his memory, for they shall be glorified to ages of ages. And the day of his commemoration shall be the fourteenth of the month of Gorpiaeus.* Glory, honour, and worship to God, and to the Son, and to the Holy Spirit, now and ever, and to the ages. [The Paris ms. is usually followed by Tischendorf. But in the three concluding paragraphs, as given in the text above, he follows the Vienna ms.--R.] *Gorpiaeus was the eleventh month of the Macedonian year, and fell partly in August and partly in September.

Acts of the Holy Apostle Thomas

At that time we the apostles were all in Jerusalem--Simon called Peter, and Andrew his brother; James the son of Zebedee, and John his brother; Philip and Bartholomew; Thomas, and Matthew the tax-gatherer; James of Alphaeus and Simon the Cananaean; and Judas of James; [1] -- and we portioned out the regions of the world, in order that each one of us might go into the region that fell to him, and to the nation to which the Lord sent him.

By lot, then, India fell to Judas Thomas, [2] also called Didymus.

And he did not wish to go, saying that he was not able to go on account of the weakness of the flesh; and how can I, being an Hebrew man, go among the Indians to proclaim the truth?

And while he was thus reasoning and speaking, the Saviour appeared to him through the night, and said to him:

Fear not, Thomas; go away to India, and proclaim the word; for my grace shall be with thee.

But he did not obey, saying:

Wherever Thou wishest to send me, send me elsewhere; for to the Indians I am not going.

And as he was thus speaking and growing angry, there happened to be there a certain merchant come from India, by name Abbanes, sent from the king Gundaphoros, and having received an order from him to buy a carpenter and bring him to him.

And the Lord, having seen him walking about in the market at noon, said to him:

Dost thou wish to buy a carpenter?

And he said to Him:

Yes.

And the Lord said to him:

I have a slave a carpenter, and I wish to sell him.

And having said this, He showed him Thomas at a distance, and agreed with him for three pounds of uncoined silver; and He wrote a bill of sale, saying:

I Jesus, the son of Joseph the carpenter, declare that I have sold my slave, Judas by name, to thee Abbanes, a merchant of Gundaphoros, the king of the Indians.

And the purchase [3] being completed, the Saviour taking Judas, who also is Thomas, led him to Abbanes the merchant; and Abbanes seeing him, said to him:

Is this thy master? And the apostle answered and said:

Yes, He is my Lord.

And he says: I have bought thee from him.

And the apostle held his peace.

And at dawn of the following day, the apostle having prayed and entreated the Lord, said:

I go wherever Thou wishest, O Lord Jesus; Thy will be done.

And he went to Abbanes the merchant, carrying nothing at all with him, but only his price. For the Lord had given it to him, saying:

Let thy worth also be with thee along with my grace, wherever thou mayst go.

And the apostle came up with Abbanes, who was carrying his effects into the boat.

He began therefore also to carry them along with him.

And when they had gone on board and sat down, Abbanes questioned the apostle, saying:

What kind of work dost thou know?

And he said:

In wood, ploughs, and yokes, and balances, [4] and boats, and boats' oars, and masts, and blocks; in stone, slabs, [5] and temples, and royal palaces.

And Abbanes the merchant said to him:

Of such a workman, to be sure, we have need.

They began, therefore, to sail away.

And they had a fair wind, and they sailed fast until they came to Andrapolis, a royal city.

And having gone out of the boat, they went into the city.

And, behold, the voices of flute-players, and of water-organs, and trumpets, sounding round them; and the apostle inquired, saying:

What festival is this in this city?

And those who were there said to him:

The gods have brought thee also, that thou mayst be feasted in this city.

For the king has an only-begotten daughter, and he is now giving her to a husband in marriage:

this festival, then, which thou seest to-day, is the rejoicing and public assembly for the marriage.

And the king has sent forth heralds to proclaim everywhere that all are to come to the marriage, rich and poor, bond and free, strangers and citizens.

And if any one shall refuse and not come to the marriage, he will be answerable to the king.
[6]And Abbanes having heard, said to the apostle:

Let us also go, then, that we may not offend the king, and especially as we are strangers.

And he said:

Let us go.

And having turned into the inn, and rested a little, they went to the marriage. And the apostle seeing them all reclining, reclined he also in the midst.

And they all looked at him as a stranger, and coming from a foreign land.

And Abbanes the merchant, as being a lord, reclined in another place.

And when they had dined and drunk, the apostle tasted nothing.

Those, then, about him said to him:

Why hast thou come hither, neither eating nor drinking?

And he answered and said to them:

For something greater than food or even drink have I come hither, even that I might accomplish the will of the King.

For the heralds proclaim the wishes of the King, and whoever will not hear the heralds will be liable to the judgment of the King.

When, therefore, they had dined and drunk, and crowns and perfumes had been brought, each took perfume, and one anointed his face, another his cheek, [7] and one one part of his body, and another another.

And the apostle anointed the crown of his head, and put a little of the ointment in his nostrils, and dropped it also into his ears, and applied it also to his teeth, and carefully anointed the parts round about his heart; and having taken the crown that was brought to him wreathed of myrtle and other flowers, he put it on his head, and took a branch of reed in his hand, and held it.

And the flute-girl, holding the flutes in her hand, went round them all; and when she came to the place where the apostle was, she stood over him, playing the flute over his head a long time.

And that flute-girl was Hebrew by race.

And as the apostle looked away to the ground, a certain one of the wine-pourers [8] stretched forth his hand and struck him.

And the apostle, having raised his eyes, and regarded him who had struck him, said:

My God will forgive thee this wrong in the world to come, but in this world He will show His wonders, and I shall soon see that hand that struck me dragged along by a dog.

And having thus spoken, he began to sing and to repeat this song:--

Maiden, daughter of the light, in whom there exists and abides the majestic splendour of kings; and delightsome is the sight of her, resplendent with brilliant beauty.

Her garments are like spring flowers, and the odour of a sweet smell is given forth from them; and on the crown of her head the king is seated, feeding with his own ambrosia those who are seated beside him; and truth rests upon her head, and she shows forth joy with her feet; and becomingly does she open her mouth; thirty-and-two are they who sing her praises, and their tongue is like a curtain of the door which is drawn for them who go in; and her neck is made in the likeness of the stairs which the first Creator created; and her two hands signify and represent the choral dance of the blessed ages, proclaiming it; and her fingers represent the gates of the city.

Her chamber lighted up breathes forth scent from balsam and every perfume, and gives forth a sweet odour of myrrh and savoury herbs; and within are strewn myrtles and sweet-smelling flowers of all kinds; and the bridal chambers are adorned with calamus. [9]And her groomsmen, of whom the number is seven, whom she has chosen for herself, surround her like a wall; and her bridesmaids are seven, who dance before her; and twelve are they in number who minister before her and are at her bidding, having their gaze and their sight upon the bridegroom, that through the sight of him they may be enlightened.

And they shall be with him to everlasting in that everlasting joy, and they shall sit down in that wedding to which the great ones are gathered together, and they shall abide in the festivities of which the eternals are deemed worthy; and they shall be arrayed in royal raiment, and shall put on shining robes; and in joy and exultation both of them shall be, and they shall glorify the Father of the universe, whose majestic light they have received, and they have been enlightened by the sight of Him their Lord, whose ambrosial food they have received, of which there is no failing at all; and they have drunk also of the wine which brings to them no thirst, neither desire of the flesh; and they have with the living spirit glorified and praised the father of truth and the mother of wisdom.

And when he had sung and finished this song, all who were there present looked upon him and kept silence, and they also saw his form changed; and what had been said by him they did not understand, since he was a Hebrew, and what had been said by him had been said in Hebrew.

But the flute-girl alone heard all, for she was Hebrew by race, and standing off from him she played the flute to the others; but at him she mostly turned her eyes and looked, for she altogether loved him as a man of the same nation with herself, and he was also beautiful in appearance above all who were there.

And when the flute-girl had come to the end of all her flute-playing, she sat down opposite him, and looked and gazed upon him.

But he looked at no one at all, neither did he regard any one, but only kept his eyes on the ground, waiting until he should depart thence.

And that wine-pourer that struck him came down to the fountain to draw water; and there happened to be a lion there, and it came forth and killed him, and left him lying in the place, after tearing up his limbs; and dogs immediately seized his limbs, among which also one black dog, laying hold of his right hand in his mouth, brought it to the place of the banquet.

And all seeing were terror-struck, inquiring which of them had been taken off.

And when it was clear that it was the hand of the wine-pourer who had struck the apostle, the flute-girl broke her flutes in pieces, and threw them away, and went and sat down at the feet of the apostle, saying:

This man is either God or God's apostle; for I heard him saying in Hebrew to the wine-pourer, I shall soon see the hand that struck me dragged about by dogs, which also you have now seen; for as he said, so also it has come to pass.

And some believed her, and some not.

And the king, having heard, came up and said to him:

Rise up, and go with me, and pray for my daughter; for she is my only child, and today I give her away.

And the apostle would not go with him; for his Lord had not at all been revealed to him there.

And the king took him away against his will to the bridal-chamber, that he might pray for them.

And the apostle stood, and began to pray and speak thus:

My Lord and my God, who accompanies His servants on their way, guiding and directing those who trust in Him, the refuge and the repose of the afflicted, the hope of the mourners, and the deliverer of the captives, the physician of the souls that are lying under disease, and Saviour of every creature, who gives life to the world, and invigorates our souls!

Thou knowest what will come to pass, who also for our sakes makest these things perfect:

Thou, Lord, who revealest hidden mysteries, and declarest unspeakable words; Thou, Lord, the planter of the good tree, also through the tree makest words to spring up; Thou, Lord, who art in all, and camest through all, and existest in all Thy works, and makest Thyself manifest through the working of them all; Jesus Christ, the Son of compassion, and perfect Saviour; Christ, Son of the living God, the undaunted Power which has overthrown the enemy; and the voice heard by the rulers, [10] which shook all their powers; the ambassador who was sent to them from on high, and who wentest down even to Hades; who also, having opened the doors, didst bring out thence those that had been shut in for many ages by the controller of the world, and didst show them the way up that leads up on high:

I beseech Thee, Lord Jesus Christ, I offer Thee supplication for these young persons, that Thou mayst make what happens and befalls them to be for their good.

And having laid his hands on them, and said, The Lord will be with you, he left them in the place, and went away. [11]

And the king requested the groomsmen to go out of the bridal-chamber; and all having gone forth, and the doors having been shut, the bridegroom raised the curtain of the bridal-chamber, that he might bring the bride to himself.

And he saw the Lord Jesus talking with the bride, and having the appearance of Judas Thomas, who shortly before had blessed them, and gone out from them; and he says to him:

Didst thou not go out before them all?

And how art thou found here?

And the Lord said to him:

I am not Judas, who also is Thomas; I am his brother.

And the Lord sat down on the bed, and ordered them also to sit down on the seats; [12] and He began to say to them:--

Keep in mind, my children, what my brother said to you, and to whom he commended you; and this know, that if you refrain from this filthy intercourse, you become temples holy and pure, being released from afflictions and troubles, known and unknown, and you will not be involved in the cares of life, and of children, whose end is destruction; but if you get many children, for their sakes you become grasping and avaricious, plundering orphans, coveting the property of widows, and by doing this you subject yourselves to most grievous punishments.

For many children become unprofitable, being harassed by demons, some openly and others secretly:

for they become either lunatics, or half-withered, or lame, or deaf, or dumb, or paralytics, or idiots; and even if they be in good health, they will be again good-for-nothing, doing unprofitable and abominable works:

for they will be detected either in adultery, or in murder, or in theft, or in fornication, and by all these you will be afflicted.

But if you will be persuaded, and preserve your souls pure to God, there will be born to you living children, whom these hurtful things do not touch; and you will be without care, spending an untroubled life, free from grief and care, looking forward to receive that marriage incorruptible and true; and you will be in it companions of the bridegroom, going in along with Him into that bridal-chamber full of immortality and light. [13]

And when the young people heard this, they believed the Lord, and gave themselves over into His keeping, and refrained from filthy lust, and remained thus spending the night in the place.

And the Lord went out from before them, having spoken thus to them:

The grace of the Lord shall be with you.

And the dawn having come on, the king arrived, and having supplied the table, brought it in before the bridegroom and the bride; and he found them sitting opposite each other, and he found the face of the bride uncovered, and the bridegroom was quite cheerful. And the mother having come to the bride, said:

Wherefore dost thou sit thus, child, and art not ashamed, but thus as if thou hadst for a long time lived with thine own husband?

And her father said:

Is it because of thy great love to thy husband that thou art uncovered?

And the bride answered and said:

Truly, father, I am in great love, and I pray to my Lord to continue to me the love which I have experienced this night, and I shall beg for myself this husband whom I have experienced today.

For this reason, then, I am no longer covered, since the mirror [14] of shame has been taken away from me, and I am no longer ashamed nor abashed, since the work of shame and bashfulness has been removed far from me; and because I am not under any violent emotion, since violent emotion does not abide in me; and because I am in cheerfulness and joy, since the day of joy has not been disturbed; and because I hold of no account this husband, and these nuptials that have passed away from before mine eyes, since I have been joined in a different marriage; and because I have had no intercourse with a temporary husband, whose end is with lewdness and bitterness of soul, since I have been united to a true Husband.

And when the bride is saying yet more, the bridegroom answers and says:

I thank Thee, Lord, who hast been proclaimed by the stranger and found by us; [15] who hast put corruption far from me, and hast sown life in me; who hast delivered me from this disease, hard to heal, and hard to cure, and abiding for ever, and established in me sound health; who hast shown Thyself to me, and hast revealed to me all that concerns me, in which I am; who hast redeemed me from falling, and hast led me to something better, and who hast released me from things temporary, and hast deemed me worthy of things immortal and ever existing; who hast brought Thyself down even to me and to my littleness, in order that, having placed me beside Thy greatness, Thou mightest unite me to Thyself; who hast not withheld Thine own compassion from me lost, but hast shown me how to search myself, and to know what [16] I was and what [17] and how I am now, in order that I may again become as I was; whom I indeed did not know, but Thou Thyself whom I knew not hast sought me out and taken me to Thyself; whom I have experienced, and am not now able to forget, whose love is fervent in me; and speak indeed as I ought I cannot.

But what I have time to say about Him is short, and altogether little, and not in proportion to His glory; but He does not find fault with me for not being ashamed to say to Him even what I do not know; because it is through the love of Him that I say even this.

And the king, having heard these things from the bridegroom and the bride, rent his garments, and said to those standing near him:

Go out quickly, and go round the whole city, and seize and bring me that man, the sorcerer, who has come for evil into this city:

for I led him with my own hands into my house, and I told him to pray for my most unfortunate daughter; and whoever shall find him and bring him to me, whatever service he shall ask of me, I give him.

They went away, therefore, and went round seeking him, and found him not; for he had sailed.

They went, therefore, also into the inn where he had stayed, and found there the flute-girl weeping and in distress, because he had not taken her with him.

And they having recounted what had happened in the case of the young people, she was altogether glad when she heard it, and dismissed her grief, and said:

Now have I found, even I, repose here.

And she arose and went to them, and was with them a long time, until they had instructed the king also.

And many also of the brethren were gathered together there, until they heard word of the apostle, that he had gone down to the cities of India, and was teaching there.

And they went away, and joined him.

Footnotes:

1. This list is a transcript of Matt. x. 2-4, except in the last name.
2. This double name is in accordance with a tradition preserved by Eusebius (H. E., i. 13), that the true name of Thomas was Judas.
3. Or, bill of sale.
4. Or, scales.
5. i.e., monuments.
6. Comp. Matt. xxii. 3-14.
7. Or, chin.
8. Or, cup-bearers.
9. Ex. xxx. 23; Cant. iv. 14; Ezek. xxvii. 19.
10. Comp. Ps. xxiv. 7, according to the LXX.
11. Three of the fivemss. either omit the prayer altogether, or give it very briefly.
12. Or, couches.
13. The text of this exhortation also varies much in the four mss. which give it.
14. Or, look.
15. Or, in us.
16. Or, who.
17. Or, who.

The Forgotten Bible
When He Came into India, and Built the Palace in the Heavens

And when the apostle came into the cities of India, with Abbanes the merchant, Abbanes went away to salute Gundaphoros the king, and reported to him about the carpenter whom he had brought with him; and the king was glad, and ordered him to come in to himself.

And when he had come in, the king said to him:

What trade knowest thou?

The apostle says to him:

The carpenter's and house builder's.

The king says to him:

What work in wood knowest thou, then, and what in stone? The apostle says:

In wood, ploughs, yokes, balances, pulleys, and boats, and oars, and masts; and in stone, monuments, temples, royal palaces.

And the king said:

Wilt thou build me a palace?

And he answered:

Yes, I shall build it, and finish it; for because of this I came, to build houses, and to do carpenter's work.

And the king having taken him, went forth out of the gates of the city, and began to talk with him on the way about the building of the palace, and about the foundations, how they should be laid, until they came to that place in which he wished the building to be.

And he said:

Here I wish the building to be.

And the apostle says:

Yes; for assuredly this place is convenient for the building.

For the place was well wooded, and there was much water there.

The king therefore says: Begin to build.

And he said:

I cannot begin to build at this time.

And the king says:

When wilt thou be able?

And he says:

I shall begin in Dius and end in Xanthicus. [1]And the king wondering, said:

Every building is built in summer; but canst thou build and make a palace in winter itself?

And the apostle said:

Thus it must be, and otherwise it is impossible.

And the king said:

If, therefore, this be thy opinion, mark out for me how the work is to be, since I shall come here after some time.

And the apostle, having taken a reed, measured the place, and marked it out; and he set the doors towards the rising of the sun, to look to the light, and the windows towards its setting, to the winds; and he made the bakehouse to be towards the south, and the water-tank, for abundance, towards the north.

And the king seeing this, said to the apostle:

Thou art a craftsman indeed, and it is fitting that thou shouldst serve kings.

And having left many things for him, he went away.

And from time to time he also sent the money that was necessary, for the living both of him and the other workmen.

And he taking it, dispenses it all, going about the cities and the places round, distributing and doing kindnesses to the poor and the afflicted, and gave them rest, [2] saying:

The king knows how to obtain royal recompense, and it is necessary for the poor to have repose for the present.

And after this, the king sent a messenger to the apostle, having written to him as follows:

Show me what thou hast done, or what I am to send thee, or what thou needest.

The apostle sends to him, saying: The palace is built, and only the roof remains to be done.

And the king, having heard, sent him again gold and silver uncoined, and wrote to him:

Let the palace, if it be done, be roofed.

And the apostle said to the Lord:

I thank Thee, Lord, as to all things, that Thou didst die for a short time, that I might live in

Thee for ever; and hast sold me, so that Thou mayst deliver many through me.

And he did not cease to teach and refresh the afflicted, saying:

These things the Lord hath dispensed to us, and He gives to each his food; for He is the support of the orphans, and the provider of the widows, and to all that are afflicted He is rest and repose.

And when the king came into the city, he inquired of his friends about the palace which Judas, who also is Thomas, had built; and they said to him:

He has neither built a palace, nor done anything else of what he promised to do; but he goes round the cities and the districts, and if he has anything he gives all to the poor, and teaches one new God, [3] and heals the diseased, and drives out demons, and does many other extraordinary things; and we think that he is a magician.

But his acts of compassion, and the cures done by him as a free gift, and still more, his single-mindedness, and gentleness, and fidelity, show that he is a just man, or an apostle of the new God whom he preaches; for he continually fasts and prays, and eats only bread with salt, and his drink is water, and he carries one coat, whether in warm weather or in cold, and he takes nothing from any one, but gives to others even what he has.

The king having heard this, stroked his face with his hands, shaking his head for a long time.

And he sent for the merchant that had brought him, and for the apostle, and said to him:

Hast thou built me the palace?

And he said:

Yes, I have built it.

And the king said:

When, then, are we to go and see it?

And he answered and said:

Now thou canst not see it; but when thou hast departed this life, thou shalt see it.

And the king, quite enraged, ordered both the merchant, and Judas who also is Thomas, to be put in chains, and to be cast into prison, until he should examine, and learn to whom he had given the king's property.

And thus I shall destroy him along with the merchant.

And the apostle went to prison rejoicing, and said to the merchant:

Fear nothing at all, but only believe in the God proclaimed by me, and thou shalt be freed from this world, and thou shalt obtain life in the world to come.

And the king considered by what death he should kill them; and when it seemed good to him to flay them, and burn them with fire, on that very night Gad the king's brother fell ill, and through the grief and imposition which the king suffered he was grievously depressed; and having sent for the king, he said to him:

My brother the king, I commend to thee my house and my children; for I, on account of the insult that has befallen thee, have been grieved, and am dying; and if thou do not come down with vengeance upon the head of that magician, thou wilt give my soul no rest in Hades.

And the king said to his brother:

During the whole night I have considered this, how I shall put him to death; and this has seemed good to me--to flay him and burn him up with fire, both him and with him the merchant that brought him.

And as they were talking together, the soul of Gad his brother departed.

And the king mourned for Gad exceedingly, for he altogether loved him.

And he ordered him to be prepared for burial in a royal and costly robe.

And as this was being done, angels received the soul of Gad the king's brother, and took it up into heaven, showing him the places and dwellings there, asking him:

In what sort of a place dost thou wish to dwell?

And when they came near the edifice of Thomas the apostle, which he had built for the king, Gad, seeing it, said to the angels, I entreat you, my lords, permit me to dwell in one of the underground chambers of this palace.

And they said to him:

Thou canst not dwell in this building. [4]And he said:

Wherefore?

They say to him:

This palace is the one which that Christian built for thy brother.

And he said:

I entreat you, my lords, permit me to go to my brother, that I may buy this palace from him; for my brother does not know what it is like, and he will sell it to me.

Then the angels let the soul of Gad go.

And as they were putting on him the burial robe, his soul came into him.

And he said to those standing round him:

Call my brother to me, that I may beg of him one request.

Straightway, therefore, they sent the good news to their king, saying:

Thy brother has come alive again.

And the king started up, and along with a great multitude went to his brother, and went in and stood beside his bed as if thunderstruck, not being able to speak to him.

And his brother said:

I know and am persuaded, brother, that if any one asked of thee the half of thy kingdom, thou wouldst give it for my sake; wherefore I entreat thee to grant me one favour, which I beg of thee to do me.

And the king answered and said:

And what is it that thou askest me to do for thee?

And he said:

Assure me by an oath that thou wilt grant it me.

And the king swore to him:

Of what belongs to me, whatever thou shalt ask, I will give thee.

And he says to him:

Sell me that palace which thou hast in the heavens.

And the king said:

Whence does a palace in the heavens belong to me?

And he said:

That which the Christian who is now in the prison, whom the merchant bought from a certain Jesus, and brought to thee, built for thee.

And as he was at a loss, he says to him again:

I speak of that Hebrew slave whom thou didst wish to punish, as having suffered some imposition from him, on account of whom I also was grieved and died, and now have come alive again.

Then the king, having come to know, understood about the eternal benefits that were conferred upon him and destined for him, and said: That palace I cannot sell thee, but I pray thee to go into it, and dwell there, and become worthy to be of its inhabitants; but if thou really wishest to buy such a palace, behold, the man is alive, and will build thee a better than that. [5]And having sent immediately, he brought out of the prison the apostle, and the merchant who had been shut up along with him, saying:

I entreat thee, as a man entreating the servant of God, that thou wilt pray for me, and entreat him whose servant thou art, to pardon me, and overlook what I have done to thee, or even what I meant to do, and that I may be worthy to be an inhabitant of that house for which indeed I have laboured nothing, but which thou labouring alone hast built for me, the grace of thy God working with thee; and that I may become a servant, I also, and slave of this God whom thou proclaimest.

And his brother, falling down before the apostle, said:

I entreat thee, and supplicate before thy God, that I may become worthy of this ministry and service, and may be allotted to become worthy of those things which were shown me by his angels.

And the apostle, seized with joy, said:

I make full confession [6] to Thee, Lord Jesus, that Thou hast revealed Thy truth in these men: for Thou alone art a God of truth, and not another; and Thou art He who knowest all things that are unknown to many:

Thou art He, Lord, who in all things showest compassion and mercy to men; for men, through the error that is in them, have overlooked Thee, but Thou hast not overlooked them.

And now, when I am entreating and supplicating Thee, accept the king and his brother, and unite them into Thy fold, having cleansed them by Thy purification, and anointed them with Thy oil, from the error which encompasseth them; and protect them also from the wolves, bringing them into Thy meadows; and give them to drink of Thy ambrosial fountain, that is never muddy and never faileth:

for they entreat Thee, and supplicate, and wish to become Thy ministers and servants; and on account of this they are well pleased even to be persecuted by Thine enemies, and for Thy sake to be hated by them, and insulted, and to die; as Thou also for our sakes didst suffer all these things, that Thou mightst gain us to Thyself, as being Lord, and truly a good shepherd.

And do Thou grant them that they may have confidence in Thee alone, and aid from Thee, and hope of their salvation, which they obtain from Thee alone, and that they may be confirmed in Thy mysteries; and they shall receive the perfect benefits of Thy graces and gifts, and flourish in Thy service, and bear fruit to perfection in Thy Father.

King Gundaphoros, therefore, and Gad, having been altogether set apart by the apostle, followed him, not at all going back, they also providing for those that begged of them, giving to all, and relieving all.

And they entreated him that they might also then receive the seal of baptism; and they said to him:

As our souls are at ease, and as we are earnest about God, give us the seal; for we have heard thee saying that the God whom thou proclaimest recognises through his seal his own sheep.

And the apostle said to them:

And I am glad, and entreat you to receive this seal, and to communicate with me in this thanksgiving [7] and blessing of God, and to be made perfect in it; [8] for this Jesus Christ whom I proclaim is Lord and God of all, and He is the Father of truth, in whom I have taught you to believe.

And he ordered to bring them oil, in order that through the oil they might receive the seal.

They brought the oil, therefore, and lighted many lamps, for it was night. [9]

And the apostle arose, and sealed them; and the Lord was revealed to them, through a voice saying, Peace to you, brethren!

And they heard His voice only, but His form they saw not; for they had not yet received the ratification [10] of the seal.

And the apostle, having taken oil, and poured it over their head, and salved and anointed them, began to say:

Come, holy name of Christ, which is above every name; come, power of the Most High, and perfect compassion; come, grace most high; come, compassionate mother; come, thou that hast charge [11] of the male child; come, thou who revealest secret mysteries; come, mother of the seven houses, that there may be rest for thee in the eighth house; come, thou presbyter of the five members--intelligence, thought, purpose, reflection, reasoning--communicate with these young persons; come, Holy Spirit, and purify their reins and heart, and seal them in the name of Father, and Son, and Holy Spirit.

And when they had been sealed, there appeared to them a young man holding a burning torch, so that their lamps were even darkened by the approach [12] of its light.

And he went out, and disappeared from their sight.

And the apostle said to the Lord:

Thy light, Lord, is too great for us, and we cannot bear it; for it is too much for our sight.

And when light came, and it was dawn, having broken bread, he made them partakers of the thanksgiving [13] of Christ.

And they rejoiced and exulted; and many others also believed, and were added, and came to the refuge of the Saviour.

And the apostle ceased not proclaiming, and saying to them:

Men and women, boys and girls, young men and maidens, vigorous and aged, both bond and free, withhold yourselves from fornication, and covetousness, and the service of the belly; for under these three heads all wickedness comes.

For fornication maims the mind, and darkens the eyes of the soul, and becomes a hindrance of the due regulation of the body, changing the whole man into feebleness, and throwing the whole body into disease.

And insatiableness puts the soul into fear and shame, existing by what pertains to the body, [14] and forcibly seizing what belongs to another;...and the service of the belly throws the soul into cares and troubles and griefs....Since, therefore, you have been set free from these, you are without care, and without grief, and without fear; and there remains to you that which was said by the Saviour: Take no care for the morrow, for the morrow will take care of itself. [15]Keep in mind also that saying before mentioned:

Look upon the ravens, and behold the fowls of the heaven, that they neither sow nor reap, nor gather into barns, and God takes care of them; how much more you, O ye of little faith! [16]But look for His appearing, and have your hopes in Him, and believe in His name:

for He is the Judge of living and dead, and He requites to each one according to his deeds; and at His coming and appearance at last no one will have as a ground of excuse, when he comes to be judged by Him, that he has not heard. For His heralds are proclaiming in the four quarters of the world. Repent, therefore, and believe the message, [17] and accept the yoke of gentleness and the light burden, [18] that you may live and not die.

These things lay hold of, these things keep; come forth from the darkness, that the light may receive you; come to Him who is truly good, that from Him you may receive grace, and place His sign upon your souls.

When he had thus said, some of the bystanders said to him:

It is time for this debtor to receive his debt.

And he said to them:

The creditor, [19] indeed, always wishes to receive more; but let us give him what is proper.

And having blessed them, he took bread and oil, and herbs and salt, and gave them to eat.

But he continued in his fasting, for the Lord's day was about to dawn.

And on the night following, while he was asleep, the Lord came and stood by his head, saying:

Thomas, rise up early and bless them all; and after the prayer and service go along the eastern road two miles, and there I shall show in thee my glory.

For because thou goest away, many shall flee to me for refuge, and thou shalt reprove the nature and the power of the enemy.

And having risen up from sleep, he said to the brethren who were with him:

Children and brethren, the Lord wishes to do something or other to-day through me; but let us pray and entreat Him that nothing may be a hindrance to us towards Him, but as at all times let it now also be done unto us according to His purpose and will.

And having thus spoken, he laid his hands upon them and blessed them.

And having broken the bread of the Eucharist, he gave it to them, saying: This Eucharist shall be [20] to you for compassion, and mercy, and recompense, and not for judgment.

And they said:

Amen.

Footnotes:

1. Dius was the first, and Xanthicus the sixth, of the twelve lunar months of the Macedonian calendar, which after the time of Alexander was adopted by the Greek cities of Asia generally. Dius fell partly in October and partly in November; Xanthicus answered generally to April.--Smith's Dict. of Antiq., s.v. Mensis. Another reading is: I shall begin in Hyperberetaeus--the twelfth month.

2. Or, remission.

3. One of themss. has: that there is one God, namely Jesus.

4. One ms. has: But if thou buy it, thou shalt live in it. And he said to them: Can I buy it? And they said to him: See that thou obtain one like this which thou seest, or better if thou wilt, that when thou comest hither again, thou mayst not be driven into the darkness.

5. One of themss. here ends the history in these words:--And he sent, and brought out Thomas, and said to him: Pardon us if we have in ignorance been in any way harsh to thee; and make us to be partakers of him whom thou preachest. And the apostle says: I too rejoice with you, that you are made partakers of His kingdom. And he took and enlightened them, having given them the washing of grace in the name of Father, and Son, and Holy Spirit, to whom is due all glory and kingdom without end. And when they had gone up straightway out of the water, the Saviour appeared to them, so that the apostle wondered, and a great light shone brighter than the rays of the sun. And having confirmed their faith, he went out, going on his way in the Lord.

6. i.e., give thanks, as in Matt. xi. 25, Luke x. 21, etc.

7. Or, Eucharist.

8. i.e., by it.

9. One ms. for this whole section has: The two brothers having been set apart by the apostle, said to him, Give us the seal in Christ. And he ordered them to bring him oil. And ends the history thus: And he arose, and sealed them in the name of Father, and Son, and Holy Spirit, and baptized them. And the Lord was revealed to them, through a voice saying to them, peace unto you! And the apostle sealed also all that were with them. And they all believed in our Lord Jesus Christ: and the whole of India became believing. The last sentence in the text seems to be an interpolation. The oil was not for the lamps, but for the ceremony of baptism. The practice of baptizing with oil instead of water--one of the "notable and execrable" heresies of the Manichaeans--is said to have been founded on this passage.

10. Lit., the sealing up.

11. Lit., the administration.

12. Perhaps for prosbole we should read probole, projection or emanation.

13. Or, communicants of the Eucharist.

14. Or, arising from the things of the body.

15. Comp. Matt. vi. 34.

16. Luke xii. 24.

17. Or, announcement.

18. Matt. xi. 30.

19. Lit., master of the debt.

20. i.e., be.

The Forgotten Bible

About the Dragon and the Young Man

And the apostle went forth to go where the Lord had bidden him.

And when he came near the second milestone he turned a little out of the way, and saw the body of a beautiful youth lying; and he said:

Lord, was it for this that Thou broughtest me out to come here, that I might see this trial? Thy will therefore be done, as Thou purposest.

And he began to pray, and to say:

Lord, Judge of the living, and of those that are lying dead, and Lord of all, and Father--Father not only of the souls that are in bodies, but also of those that have gone out of them; for of the souls that are in pollutions Thou art Lord and Judge--come at this time, when I call upon Thee, and show Thy glory upon him that is lying down here.

And he turned and said to those that followed him:

This affair has not happened idly; but the enemy has wrought and effected this, that he might make an assault upon him; and you see that he has availed himself of no other form, and has wrought through no other living being, but through his subject.

And when the apostle had thus spoken, behold, a great dragon came forth from his den, knocking his head, and brandishing his tail down to the ground, and, using a loud voice, said to the apostle:

I shall say before thee for what cause I have put him to death, since thou art here in order to reprove my works.

And the apostle says:

Yes, say on.

And the dragon:

There is a certain woman in this place exceedingly beautiful; and as she was once passing by, I saw her, and fell in love with her, and I followed and watched her; and I found this young man kissing her, and he also had intercourse with her, and did with her other shameful things.

And to me indeed it was pleasant to tell thee this, for I know that thou art the twin-brother of Christ, and always bringest our race to nought.

But, not wishing to harass her, I did not at this time put him to death; but I watched him passing by in the evening, and struck him, and killed him, and especially as he had dared to do this on the Lord's day. [1] And the apostle inquired of him, saying:

Tell me, of what seed and of what race art thou?

And he said to him:

I am the offspring of the race of the serpent, and hurtful of the hurtful; I am son of him who hurt and struck the four brothers that stood; I am son of him who sits on the throne of destruction, and takes his own from what he has lent; [2] I am son of that apostate who encircles the globe; I am kinsman to him who is outside of the ocean, whose tail lies in his mouth; I am he who went into paradise through the hedge, and spoke with Eve what my father bade me speak to her; I am he who inflamed and fired Cain to kill his brother, and through me thorns and prickles sprang up in the ground; I am he who cast down the angels from above, and bound them down by the desires of women, that earth-born [3] children might be produced from them, and that I might work my will in them; [4] I am he who hardened the heart of Pharaoh, that he should murder the children of Israel, and keep them down by the hard yoke of slavery; I am he who caused the multitude to err in the desert when they made the calf; I am he who inflamed Herod and incited Caiaphas to the lying tales of falsehood before Pilate, for this became me; I am he who inflamed Judas, and bought him, that he should betray Christ; I am he who inhabits and holds the abyss of Tartarus, and the Son of God has wronged me against my will, and has gathered his own out of me; I am the kinsman of him who is to come from the east, to whom also power has been given to do whatever he will upon the earth.

And that dragon having thus spoken in the hearing of all the multitude, the apostle raised his voice on high, and said:

Cease henceforth, O thou most unabashed, and be ashamed and altogether put to death; for the end of thy destruction is at hand, and do not dare to say what thou hast done through thy dependants.

And I order thee, in the name of that Jesus who even until now makes a struggle against you for the sake of His own human beings, to suck out the poison which thou hast put into this man, and to draw it forth, and take it out of him.

And the dragon said:

The time of our end is by no means at hand, as thou hast said.

Why dost thou force me to take out what I have put into him, and to die before the time?

Assuredly, when my father shall draw forth and suck out what he has put into the creation, then his end will come. And the apostle said to him:

Show us, therefore, now the nature of thy father.

And the dragon went up, and put his mouth upon the wound of the young man, and sucked the gall out of it.

And in a short time the skin of the young man, which was like purple, grew white, and the dragon swelled.

And when the dragon had drawn up all the gall into himself, the young man sprang up and stood, and ran and fell at the apostle's feet.

And the dragon, being swelled up, shrieked out and died, and his poison and gall were poured forth; and in the place where his poison was poured forth there was made a great chasm, and that dragon was swallowed up.

And the apostle said to the king and his brother:

Take workmen, and fill up the place in which the dragon has been swallowed up, and lay foundations, and build houses-above it, that it may be made a dwelling-place for the strangers.

And the young man said to the apostle, with many tears:

I have sinned against the God proclaimed by thee, and against thee, but I ask pardon of thee; for thou art a man having two forms, and wherever thou wishest there art thou found, and thou art held in by no one, as I see.

For I beheld that man, when I stood beside thee, who also said to thee, I have many wonders to show by means of thee, and I have great works to accomplish by means of thee, for which thou shalt obtain a reward; and thou shalt make many to live, and they shall be in repose and eternal light as the children of God:

do thou therefore bring alive--he says, speaking to thee about me--this young man who has been cast down by the enemy, and in all time be the overseer of him.

Thou hast, then, well come hither, and again thou shalt well go away to him, he being not at all forsaken by thee.

And I am without care and reproach, for the dawn has risen upon me from the care of the night, and I am at rest; and I have also been released from him who exasperated me to do these things:

for I have sinned against Him who taught me the contrary, and I have destroyed him who is the kinsman of the night, who forced me to sin by his own practices; and I have found that kinsman of mine who is like the light.

I have destroyed him who darkens and blinds those who are subject to him, lest they should know what they are doing, and, ashamed of their works, withdraw themselves from them, and their deeds have an end:

and I have found Him whose works are light, and whose deeds are truth, of which whoever does them shall not repent.

I have been set free also from him in whom falsehood abides, whom darkness as a covering goes before, and shame conducting herself impudently in idleness follows after.

And I have found also Him who shows me what is beautiful, that I should lay hold of it, the Son of the truth, who is kinsman of concord, who, driving away the mist, enlightens His own creation, and heals its wounds, and overturns its enemies.

But I entreat thee, O man of God, make me again to behold and see Him, now become hidden from me, that I may also hear His voice, the wonders of which I cannot declare:

for it is not of the nature of this bodily organ.

And the apostle said to him:

If, as thou hast also said, thou hast cast off the knowledge of those things which thou hast received, and if thou knowest who has wrought these things in thee, and if thou shalt become a disciple and hearer of Him of whom, through thy living love, thou now desirest the sight, thou shalt both see Him, and shalt be with Him for ever, and shalt rest in His rest, and shalt be in His joy.

But if thou art rather carelessly disposed towards Him, and again returnest to thy former deeds, and lettest go that beauty and that beaming countenance which has now been displayed to thee, and if the splendour of the light of Him whom thou now desirest be forgotten by thee, thou shalt be deprived not only of this life, but also of that which is to come; and thou shalt go to him whom thou hast said thou hast destroyed, and shalt no longer behold Him whom thou hast said thou hast found.

And when the apostle had thus spoken, he went into the city, holding that young man by the hand, and saying to him:

Those things which thou hast beheld, my child, are a few out of the many which God has:

for it is not about these things that appear that the good news is brought to us, but greater things than these are promised to us; but inasmuch as we are in the body, we cannot tell and speak out what He will do for our souls.

If we say that He affords us light, it is seen by us, and we have it; and if riches, they exist and appear in this world, and we name them, since it has been said, With difficulty will a rich man enter into the kingdom of the heavens. ⁵And if we speak of fine clothing, which they who delight in this life put on, it has been said, They that wear soft things are in kings' palaces; ⁶ and if costly dinners, about these we have received a commandment to keep away from them, not to be burdened by carousing and drunkenness and the cares of life; ⁷ as also in the Gospel it has been said, Take no heed for your life, what ye shall eat, or what ye shall drink; nor for your body, what ye shall put on:

because the life is more than food, and the body than clothing. ⁸And if we speak of this rest lasting only for a season, its judgment has also been ordained.

But we speak about the upper world, about God and angels, about ambrosial food, about garments that last and become not old, about those things which eye hath not seen, nor ear heard, nor hath there come into the heart of sinful men what God has prepared for those that love Him. ⁹Do thou also therefore believe in Him, that thou mayst live; and have confidence in Him, and thou shalt never die.

For He is not persuaded by gifts, that thou shouldst offer them to Him; nor does He want sacrifices, that thou shouldst sacrifice to Him.

But look to Him, and thou shalt not look in vain, for His comeliness and desirable beauty will make thee love Him; and neither will He allow thee to turn thyself away from Him.

And when the apostle was thus speaking to that young man, a great multitude joined them.

And the apostle looked, and saw them lifting themselves up that they might see him; and they went up into elevated places.

And the apostle said to them:

Ye men who have come to the assembly of Christ, and who wish to believe in Jesus, take an example from this, and see that if you do not get high up, you cannot see me, who am small, and cannot get a look of me, who am like yourselves.

If, then, you cannot see me, who am like yourselves, unless you raise yourselves a little from the earth, how can you see Him who lives above, and is now found below, unless you first raise yourselves out of your former behaviour, and unprofitable deeds, and troublesome desires, and the riches that are left behind here, and create things that are of the earth, and that grow old, and the garments that are destroyed, and the beauty that ages and vanishes away, yea, even out of the whole body in which all these have been stored past, and which grows old, and becomes dust, returning into its own nature? for all these things the body itself sets up. ¹⁰But rather believe in our Lord Jesus Christ, whom we proclaim to you, in order that your hope may be upon Him, and that you may have life in Him to ages of ages, that He may be your fellow-traveller in this land, and may release you from error, and may become ¹¹ a haven for you in this troublous sea.

And there shall be for you also a fountain welling out in this thirsty land, and a fold full of food in the place of the hungry, and rest for your souls, and also a physician for your bodies.

Then the multitude of those assembled that heard, wept, and said to the apostle:

O man of God, as for the God whom thou proclaimest, we dare not say that we are his, because our works which we have done are alien from him, not pleasing to him; but if he has compassion upon us, and pities us, and delivers us, overlooking our former doings; and if he set us free from the evil things which we did when we were in error, and shall not take into account nor keep the recollection of our former sins, we shall become his servants, and we shall do his will to the end.

And the apostle answered and said to them:

He does not reckon against you the sins which you did, being in error; but He overlooks your transgressions which you have done in ignorance. ¹²

Footnotes:

1. In this passage we have one of the data for fixing the date of the writing.
2. Or, from those to whom he was lent.
3. And, by implication, gigantic.
4. Or, by them.
5. Matt. xix. 23.
6. Matt. xi. 8.
7. Rom. xiii. 13; Luke xii. 34.
8. Matt. vi. 25.
9. 1 Cor. ii. 9; Isa. lxiv. 4.
10. Or, establishes.
11. Or, and that there may be.
12. Comp. Acts xvii. 30.

The Forgotten Bible
About the Demon that Dwelt in the Woman

And the apostle went into the city, all the multitude accompanying him; and he thought of going to the parents of the young man whom, when killed by the dragon, he had brought to life; for they earnestly entreated him to come to them, and to enter into their house.

And a certain woman, exceedingly beautiful, suddenly uttered a loud cry, saying:

O apostle of the new God, who hast come into India, and servant of that holy and only good God--for through thee he is proclaimed the Saviour of the souls that come unto him, and through thee he heals the bodies of those that are punished by the enemy, and thou hast become the cause of life to all who turn to him--order me to be brought before thee, that I may declare to thee what has happened to me, and that perhaps there may be hope to me from thee and those who stand beside thee may have more and more hope in the God whom thou proclaimest.

For I am not a little tormented by the adversary, who has assailed me for now a period of five years.

As a woman, I formerly sat down in peace, and peace encompassed me on all sides and I had nothing to trouble me, for of nothing else [1] had I a care.

And it happened on one of the days as I was coming forth from the bath, there met me one like a man troubled and disturbed; and his voice and utterance seemed to me to be indistinct and very weak.

And he said, standing over against me, Thou and I shall be in one love, and we shall have intercourse with each other, as a man is coupled with his wife. And I answered him, saying, To my betrothed I consented not, entreating him not to marry me; and to thee, wishing to have intercourse with me as it were in adultery, how shall I give myself up?

And having thus spoken, I went away from him.

And to my maid I said, Hast thou seen the young man and his shamelessness, how shamelessly and boldly he talks to me?

And she said to me, It was an old man I saw talking with thee.

And when I was in my own house, and had supped, my mind suggested to me some suspicion, and especially because he had appeared to me in two forms.

I fell asleep, having this same thing in my thoughts.

And he came that night, and made me share in his filthy commerce.

And I saw him when it was day, and fled from him; but, according to his wont, he came at night and abused me.

And now, as thou seest me, I have been tormented by him five years, and he has not departed from me.

But I know and am persuaded that even demons, and spirits, and avenging deities, are subject to thee, and tremble at thy prayer.

Pray, then, for me, and drive away from me the demon that torments me, that I also may become free, and may be brought to my former nature, and I shall receive the gift [2] that has been granted to my kindred.

And the apostle said:

O irrepressible wickedness!

O the shamelessness of the enemy!

O the sorcerer that is never at rest!

O the ill-favoured one, bring to subjection the well-favoured!

O the many-formed one!

He appears just as he may wish, but his essence cannot be changed.

O offspring of the crafty and insatiable one!

O bitter tree, which also his fruits are like!

O thou who art of the devil, who fights over those who do not belong to him!

O thou who art of the deceit that uses shamelessness!

O thou who art of the wickedness that creeps like a serpent, and art thyself his kindred! And when the apostle had thus spoken the fiend stood before him, no one seeing him but the woman and the apostle, and with a very loud voice he said in the hearing of all:

What have we to do with thee, O apostle of the Most High?

What have we to do with thee, O servant of Jesus Christ?

What have we to do with thee, O thou that sittest in council with the Holy Spirit.

Wherefore dost thou wish to destroy us, when our time has not yet come?

On what account dost thou wish to take away our power? for until the present hour we have had hope and time left us. [3] What have we to do with thee?

Thou hast power over thine own, and we over our own.

Why dost thou wish to use tyranny against us, and especially thou who teachest others not to use tyranny?

Why dost thou want those who do not belong to thee, as if thou wert not satisfied with thine own?

Why dost thou liken thyself to the Son of God, who has done us hurt?

For thou art like him altogether, just as if thou hadst been brought forth by him.

For we thought to bring him also under the yoke, like the rest; but he turned, and held us under his hand.

For we did not know him; but he deceived us by the form which he had put on, and his poverty and his want; for when we saw him such, we thought him to be a man clothed with flesh, not knowing that it was he who makes men live.

And he gave us power over our own, and, in the time in which we live, not to let our own go, but to employ ourselves about them. But thou wishest to get more than is necessary, or than has been given thee, and to overpower us.

And having thus spoken, the demon wept, saying:

I let thee go, my most lovely yoke-fellow, [4] whom I found long ago and was at rest; I leave thee, my beloved and trusty sister, in whom I was well pleased. What I shall do I know not, or whom I shall call upon to hear me and protect me.

I know what I shall do.

I shall go to some place where the fame of this man has not been heard, and perhaps I shall call thee, my beloved, by a new name. [5]And lifting up his voice, he said: Abide in peace, having received an asylum with a greater than I; but I, as I have said, will go away and seek thy like, and if I find her not I shall again return to thee:

for I know that when thou art beside this man, thou hast an asylum in him; but when he has gone away, thou shalt be as thou wast before he made his appearance, and him indeed wilt thou forget, and to me there will again be opportunity and boldness; but now I am afraid of the name of him who has delivered thee.

And having thus said, the demon disappeared.

And just when he had disappeared, fire and smoke were seen there, and all there present were struck with amazement.

And the apostle seeing this, said to them:

Nothing strange or unusual has that demon shown, but his own nature, in which also he shall be burnt up; for the fire shall consume him, and the smoke of him shall be scattered abroad.

And he began to say:

O Jesus Christ, the secret mystery which has been revealed to us, Thou art He who disclosest to us all manner of mysteries, who hast set me apart from all my companions, and who hast told me three words with which I am set on fire, and I cannot tell them to others; O Jesus, man slain, dead, buried; Jesus, God of God, and Saviour who bringest the dead to life, and healest those who are diseased; O Jesus, who appearest to be in want, and savest as if in want of nothing, catching the fishes for the morning and the evening meal, and establishing all in abundance with a little bread; Jesus, who didst rest from the toil of the journey as a man, and walk upon the waves as God; [6] Jesus Most High, voice arising from perfect compassion, Saviour of all, the right hand of the light overthrowing him that is wicked in his own kind, and bringing all his kind into one place; Thou who art only begotten, the first-born of many brethren, [7] God of God Most High, man despised until now; Jesus Christ, who overlookest us not when we call upon Thee; who hast been shown forth to all in Thy human life; who for our sakes hast been judged and kept in prison, and freest all that are in bonds; who hast been called a deceiver, [8] and who deliverest Thine own from deception:

I entreat Thee in behalf of those standing and entreating Thee, and those that believe in Thee; for they pray to obtain Thy gifts, being of good hope in Thine aid, occupying Thy place of refuge in Thy majesty; they give audience, so as to hear from us the words that have been spoken to them.

Let Thy peace come and dwell in them, that they may be purified from their former deeds, and may put off the old man with his deeds, and put on the new now declared to them by me. [9]

And having laid his hands on them, he blessed them, saying:

The grace of our Lord Jesus Christ be upon you for ever! [10]And they said, Amen.

And the woman begged of him, saying:

Apostle of the Most High, give me the seal, that that foe may not come back upon me again.

Then he made her come near him; and putting his hand upon her, he sealed her in the name of Father, and Son, and Holy Ghost.

And many others also were sealed along with her.

And the apostle ordered his servant [11] to set out a table; and they set out a bench [12] which they found there.

And having spread a linen cloth upon it, he put on it the bread of the blessing.

And the apostle standing by it, said:

Jesus Christ, Son of God, who hast deemed us worthy to communicate of the Eucharist of Thy sacred body and honourable blood, behold, we are emboldened by the thanksgiving [13] and invocation of Thy sacred name; come now, and communicate with us.

And he began to say:

Come, perfect compassion; come, communion with mankind; come, Thou that knowest the mysteries of the chosen one; come, Thou that communicatest in all the combats [14] of the noble combatant; come, peace that revealest the great things of all greatness; come, Thou that disclosest secrets, and makest manifest things not to be spoken; the sacred dove which has brought forth twin young; come, thou secret mother; come, Thou who art manifest in Thy deeds, and givest joy and rest to those who are united to Thee; come and communicate with us in this Eucharist, which we make in Thy name, and in the love [15] in which we are united in calling upon Thee. [16] And having thus said, he made the sign of the cross upon the bread, and broke it, and began to distribute it.

And first he gave it to the woman, saying:

This shall be to thee for remission of sins, and the ransom of everlasting transgressions.

And after her, he gave also to all the others who had received the seal.

Footnotes:

1. Or, no one else.
2. Or, grace.
3. Comp. Matt. viii. 29.
4. Or, wife.
5. i.e., get another instead of thee, my beloved.
6. Matt. xiv. 17; John xxi. 11; John iv. 6; Matt. xiv. 25.
7. Rom. viii. 29.
8. Matt. xxvii. 63.
9. Col. iii. 9.
10. Rom. xvi. 20.
11. Or, deacon.
12. sumpsellion, which is not Greek, is obviously the Latin subsellium.
13. Or, Eucharist.
14. Or, prizes.
15. Or, love-feast.
16. Or, in Thy calling.

The Forgotten Bible

About the Young Man Who Killed the Maiden.

And there was a certain young man who had done a nefarious deed; and having come to the apostle, he took the bread of the Eucharist into his mouth, and his two hands immediately withered, so that he could no longer bring them to his mouth.

And those who were present and saw him told the apostle what had happened.

And he, having summoned him, said:

Tell me, my child, and be ashamed of nothing, [1] what thou hast done, and why thou hast come hither; for the Eucharist of the Lord has convicted thee.

For this gracious gift coming to many is especially healing to those who approach it through faith and love; but thee it has withered away, and what has happened has happened not without some working cause.

And the young man who had been convicted by the Eucharist of the Lord came up, and fell at the apostle's feet, and prayed him, saying:

An evil deed has been done by me, yet I thought to do something good.

I was in love with a certain woman living outside of the city in an inn, and she loved me.

And I having heard from thee, and believed that thou proclaimest the living God, came and received the seal from thee along with the others; and thou saidst, Whoever shall indulge in filthy intercourse, and especially in adultery, shall not have life with the God whom I proclaim. [2] Since, then, I altogether loved her, I begged of her, and persuaded her to live with me in chaste and pure intercourse, as thou thyself teachest; but she would not.

When therefore she would not, I took a sword and killed her; for I could not see her living in adultery with another.

The apostle, having heard this, said:

O maddening intercourse, into what shamelessness dost thou lead!

O unrestrained lust, how hast thou brought him into subjection to do this!

O work of the serpent, how dost thou rage in thine own!

And the apostle ordered water to be brought him in a dish.

And when the water had been brought, he said: Come waters from the living waters, existing from the existing, and sent to us; the fountain sent to us from repose, the power of salvation coming from that power that subdues all things, and subjects them to its own will; come and dwell in these waters, that the gracious gift of the Holy Spirit may be fully perfected in them.

And he said to the young man:

Go, wash thy hands in these waters.

And when he had washed, they were restored.

And the apostle said to him:

Dost thou believe in our Lord Jesus Christ, that He can do all things?

And he said:

Even though I am least of all, I believe; but this I did, thinking to do a good thing:

for I implored her, as also I told thee; but she would not be persuaded by me to keep herself chaste.

And the apostle said to him:

Come, let us go to the inn where thou didst this deed, and let us see what has happened.

And the young man went before the apostle on the road; and when they came to the inn, they found her lying.

And the apostle, seeing her, was disheartened, for she was a beautiful maiden; and he ordered her to be brought into the middle of the inn.

And having put her on a couch, they brought it, and set it in the midst of the court-yard of the inn.

And the apostle laid his hand on her, and began to say:

Jesus, who always appearest to us--for this Thou always wishest, that we should seek Thee-- and Thou Thyself hast given us this power of asking and receiving; [3] and not only hast Thou given us this, but hast also taught us how to pray; [4] who art not seen by bodily eyes, but who art not altogether hidden from those of our soul, and who art hidden in Thy form, but manifested to us by Thy works; and by Thy many deeds we have recognised Thee as we go on, and Thou hast given us Thy gifts without measure, saying, Ask, and it shall be given you; seek, and ye shall find; knock, and it shall be opened unto you. [5]We pray, therefore, having suspicion of our sins; [6] and we ask of Thee not riches, nor gold, nor silver, nor possessions, nor any of those things that come from the earth and go into the earth again; but this we beg of Thee, and entreat that in Thy holy name Thou raise this woman lying here by Thy power, to the glory and faith of those standing by.

And when he had thus prayed, he sealed the young man, and said to him: Go, and take her by the hand, and say to her, I through my hands killed thee with the sword; [7] and again I raise thee by my hands, in the faith of our Lord Jesus Christ.

And the young man went and stood by her, saying:

I have believed in Thee, O Christ Jesus.

And looking upon Judas Thomas the apostle, he said to him:

Pray for me, that my Lord, upon whom also I call, may come to my help.

And having laid his hand on her hand, he said:

Come, Lord Jesus Christ, giving this woman life, and me the earnest of Thy faith.

And immediately, as he drew her hand, she sprang up, and sat, looking at the great multitude standing round.

And she also saw the apostle standing opposite to her; and having left the couch, she sprang up, and fell at his feet, and took hold of his garments, saying:

I pray thee, my lord, where is that other who is with thee, who has not left me to remain in that fearful and grievous place, but has given me up to thee, saying, Do thou take her, that she may be made perfect, and thereafter brought into her own place?

And the apostle says to her:

Tell us where thou hast been.

And she answered:

Dost thou, who wast with me, to whom also I was entrusted, wish to hear?

And she began to say:

A certain man received me, hateful in appearance, all black, and his clothing exceedingly filthy; and he led me away to a place where there were many chasms, and a great stench and most hateful odour were given forth thence; and he made me bend down into each chasm, and I saw in the chasm blazing fire; and wheels of fire ran there, and souls were hung upon those wheels, and were dashed against each other.

And there was there crying and great lamentation, and there was none released.

And that man said to me, These souls are of thine own nation, and for a certain number of days [8] they have been given over to punishment and torture; and then others are brought in instead of them; and likewise also these are again succeeded by others.

These are they who have exchanged the intercourse of man and wife.

And again I looked down, and saw infants heaped upon each other, and struggling and lying upon each other; and he answered and said to me, These are their children, and for this have they been placed here for a testimony against them.

And he brought me to another chasm, and I bent down and saw mud, and worms spouting forth, and souls wallowing there; and a great gnashing of teeth was heard thence from them.

And that man said to me, These are the souls of women that left their own husbands, and went and committed adultery with others, and who have been brought to this torment.

He showed me another chasm, into which I bent down and saw souls hung up, some by the tongue, some by the hair, some by the hands, some by the feet, head downwards, and smoked with smoke and sulphur; about whom that man who was with me answered me, These souls which are hung up by the tongue are slanderers, and such as have uttered false and disgraceful words; those that are hung up by the hair [9] are those that are shameless, and that have gone about with uncovered heads in the world; these hung up by the hands are those who have taken what belongs to others, and have stolen, and who have never given anything to the poor, nor assisted the afflicted; but they so acted, wishing to get everything, and giving no heed at all to justice and the laws; and these hung up by the feet are those who lightly and eagerly ran in wicked ways, and disorderly wickedness, not looking after the sick, and not aiding those departing this life, and on account of this each individual soul is requited for what has been done by it.

Again leading me away, he showed me a cavern, exceedingly dark, exhaling a great stench; and many souls were peeping out thence, wishing to get some share of the air, but their keepers would not let them peep out.

And he who was with me said, This is the prison of those souls which thou seest; for when they shall complete their punishments for those things which each one has done, afterwards again others succeed them--and there are some also quite used up--and are given up to other punishments.

Those, then, who guarded the souls that were in the dark cave said to the man that had charge of me, Give her to us, that we may take her in beside the others, until the time comes for her to be given up to punishment.

And he answered them, I will not give her to you, for I am afraid of him who gave her up to me; for I received no orders to leave her here, and I shall take her up with me until I get some injunction about her.

And he took me and brought me to another place, in which were men who were bitterly tortured.

And he that is like thee took me and gave me up to thee, having thus said to thee, Take her, since she is one of the creatures that have been led astray.

And I was taken by thee, and am now before thee.

I beg, therefore, and supplicate thee that I may not go into those places of punishment which I saw.

And the apostle said to the multitudes standing by:

You have heard, brethren, what this woman has recounted; and these are not the only punishments, but there are others worse than these; and if you do not turn to this God whom I proclaim, and refrain from your former works and deeds which you have done without knowledge, in these punishments you shall have your end.

Believe, therefore, in our Lord Jesus Christ, and He will forgive you the sins done by you heretofore, and will purify you from all the bodily desires that abide in the earth, and will heal you from the faults that follow after you, and go along with you, and are found before you.

And let each of you put off the old man, and put on the new, and leave your former course of conduct and behaviour; and let those that steal steal no more, but let them live, labouring and working; [10] and let the adulterers no more commit adultery, lest they give themselves up to everlasting punishment; for adultery is with God an evil altogether grievous above other evils. Put away also from yourselves covetousness, and lying, and drunkenness, and slandering, and requiting evil for evil:

for all these are alien and strange to the God proclaimed by us; but rather live in faith, and meekness, and holiness, and hope, in which God rejoices, that ye may become His servants, having received from Him gracious gifts, which few or none receive.

All the people therefore believed, and presented their souls obedient to the living God and Christ Jesus, enjoying His blessed works, and His holy service.

And they brought much money for the service of the widows; for he had them collected in the cities, and he sent to all of them by his own servants [11] what was necessary, both clothing and food.

But he did not cease proclaiming and saying to them, and showing that this is Jesus the Christ, concerning whom the Scriptures proclaimed that He should come, and be crucified, and be raised from the dead after three days.

And he showed them a second time, beginning from the prophets, and explaining the things concerning Christ, and that it was necessary for Him to come, and for all things to be fulfilled that had been said to us beforehand concerning Him. [12]

And the report of him ran through all the cities and countries; and all who had persons sick or tormented by unclean spirits brought them, and they were healed.

Some also they laid on the road by which he was to pass, and he healed them all by the power of the Lord. [13]Then said all with one accord who had been healed by him, with one voice: Glory to Thee, Jesus, who givest Thy healing to all alike by means of Thy servant and apostle Thomas.

And being in good health, and rejoicing, we pray Thee that we may be of Thy flock, and be numbered among Thy sheep; receive us, therefore, O Lord, and consider not our transgressions and former offences which we did, being in ignorance.

And the apostle said:

Glory to the only-begotten from the Father; [14] glory to the first-born of many brethren; [15] Glory to Thee, the defender and helper of those who come to Thy place of refuge; Thou that sleepest not, and raisest those that are asleep; that livest and bringest to life those that are lying in death; O God Jesus Christ, Son of the living God, redeemer and helper, refuge and rest of all that labour in Thy work, who affordest health to those who for Thy name's sake bear the burden of the day, and the icy coldness of the night; we give thanks for the gracious gifts that have been given us by Thee, and for the help from Thee bestowed upon us, and Thy providential care that has come upon us from Thee.

Perfect these things upon us, therefore, unto the end, that we may have confidence in Thee; look upon us, because for Thy sake we have left our homes, and for Thy sake have become strangers gladly and willingly; look upon us, O Lord, because for Thy sake we have abandoned our possessions, that we may have Thee for a possession that shall not be taken away; look upon us, O Lord, because we have left those related to us by ties of kindred in order that we may be united in relationship to Thee; look upon us, O Lord, who have left our fathers and mothers, and those that nourished us, that we may behold Thy Father, and be satisfied with His divine nourishment:

look upon us, O Lord, because for Thy sake we have left our bodily yoke-fellows, [16] and our earthly fruit, in order that we may share in that intercourse which is lasting and true, and bring forth true fruits, whose nature is from above, the enjoyment of which no one can take away from us, with which we abide, and they abide with us.

Footnotes:
1. Or, stand in awe of no one.
2. 1 Cor. vi. 9.
3. Matt. vii. 7; Luke xi. 9.
4. Matt. vi. 9; Luke xi. 2.
5. Matt. vii. 7.
6. Or, having our sins in view.
7. Lit., with iron.
8. Lit., days of number.
9. Obviously omitted either in the mss. or in the text.
10. Eph. iv. 28.
11. Or, deacons.
12. Comp. Luke xxiv. 46.
13. Comp. Acts v. 15.
14. John i. 14.
15. Rom. viii. 29.
16. i.e., wives.

Consummation of Thomas the Apostle [1]

At the command of King Misdeus [2] the blessed Apostle Thomas was cast into prison; and he said:

I glorify God, and I shall preach the word to the prisoners, so that all rejoiced at his presence.

When, therefore, Juzanes the king's son, and Tertia his mother, and Mygdonia, and Markia, had become believers, but were not yet thought worthy of baptism, they took it exceedingly ill that the blessed one had been shut up.

And having come to the prison, and given much money to the jailor,[3] they went in to him.

And he, seeing them, was glad, and glorified the Lord, and blessed them.

And they entreated and begged the seal in the Lord, a beautiful young man having appeared to them in a dream, and ordered the apostle into the house of Juzanes.

And again the beautiful young man coming to them and Thomas, bade them do this on the coming night.

And he ran before them, and gave them light on the way, and without noise opened the doors that had been secured, until all the mystery was completed.

And having made them communicate in the Eucharist, and having talked much with them, and confirmed them in the faith, and commended them to the Lord, he went forth thence, leaving the women, and again went to be shut up. [4] And they grieved and wept because Misdeus the king was to kill him.

And Thomas went and found the jailors fighting, and saying:

What wrong have we done to that sorcerer, that, availing himself of his magic art, he has opened the doors of the prison, and wishes to set all the prisoners free?

But let us go and let the king know about his wife and his son.[5] And when he came they stripped him, and girded him with a girdle; and thus they stood before the king.

And Misdeus said to him:

Art thou a slave, or a freeman?

And Thomas answered and said to him:

I am not [6] a slave, and thou hast no power against me at all.

And how, said Misdeus, hast thou run away and come to this country?

And Thomas said:

I came here that I might save many, and that I might by thy hands depart from this body.

Misdeus says to him:

Who is thy master? and what is his name? and of what country, and of whom is he?

My Lord, says Thomas, is my Master and thine, being the Lord of heaven and earth.

And Misdeus said:

What is he called?

And Thomas said:

Thou canst not know His true name at this time; but I tell thee the name that has been given Him for a season--Jesus the Christ.

And Misdeus said:

I have not been in a hurry [7] to destroy thee, but have restrained myself; but thou hast made a display of works, so that thy sorceries have been heard of in all the country.

But now this will I do, [8] that thy sorceries may also perish with thee, that our nation may be purified from them.

And Thomas said:

Dost thou call these things which will follow me sorceries?

They shall never be removed from the people here.

And while these things were saying, Misdeus was considering in what manner he should put him to death; for he was afraid of the multitude standing round, many, even some of the chief men, having believed in him.

And he arose, and took Thomas outside of the city; and a few soldiers accompanied him with their arms.

And the rest of the multitude thought that the king was wishing to learn something from him;

and they stood and observed him closely.

And when they had gone forth three stadia, he delivered him to four soldiers, and to one of the chief officers, [9] and ordered them to take him up into the mountain and spear him; but he himself returned to the city.

And those present ran to Thomas, eager to rescue him; but he was led away by the soldiers who were with him.

For there were two on each side having hold of him, because of sorcery.

And the chief officer held him by the hand, and led him with honour.

And at the same time the blessed apostle said:

O the hidden mysteries of Thee, O Lord! for even to the close of life is fulfilled in us the riches of Thy grace, which does not allow us to be without feeling as to the body.

For, behold, four have laid hold of me, and one leads me, since I belong to One, to whom I am going always invisibly.

But now I learn that my Lord also, since He was a stranger, to whom I am going, who also is always present with me invisibly, was struck by one; but I am struck by four. [10]

And when they came to that place where they were to spear him, Thomas spoke thus to those spearing him:

Hear me now, at least, when I am departing from my body; and let not your eyes be darkened in understanding, nor your ears shut up so as not to hear those things in which you have believed the God whom I preach, after being delivered in your souls from rashness; and behave in a manner becoming those who are free, being void of human glory, and live the life towards God.

And he said to Juzanes:

Son of an earthly king, but servant of Jesus Christ, give what is due to those who are to fulfil the command [11] of Misdeus, in order that I may go apart from them and pray.

And Juzanes having paid the soldiers, the apostle betook himself to prayer; and it was as follows:--

My Lord, and my God, and hope, and leader, and guide in all countries, I follow Thee along with all that serve Thee, and do Thou guide me this day on my way to Thee.

Let no one take my soul, which Thou hast given to me.

Let not publicans and beggars look upon me, nor let serpents slander me, and let not the children of the dragon hiss at me.

Behold, I have fulfilled Thy work, and accomplished what Thou gavest me to do. I have become a slave, that I might receive freedom from Thee; do then give it to me, and make me perfect.

And this I say not wavering, but that they may hear who need to hear.

I glorify Thee in all, Lord and Master; for to Thee is due glory for ever.

Amen.

And when he had prayed, he said to the soldiers:

Come and finish the work of him that sent you.

And the four struck him at once, and killed him.

And all the brethren wept, and wrapped him up in beautiful shawls, and many linen cloths, and laid him in the tomb in which of old the kings used to be buried.

And Syphor and Juzanes did not go to the city, but spent the whole day there, and waited during the night.

And Thomas appeared to them, and said:

I am not there; why do you sit watching? for I have gone up, and received the things I hoped for; but rise up and walk, and after no long time you shall be brought beside me.

And Misdeus and Charisius [12] greatly afflicted Tertia and Mygdonia, but did not persuade them to abandon their opinions.

And Thomas appeared, and said to them: Forget not the former things, for the holy and sanctifying Jesus Himself will aid you.

And Misdeus and Charisius, when they could not persuade them not to be of this opinion, granted them their own will. And all the brethren assembled together, for the blessed one had made Syphorus [13] a presbyter in the mountain, and Juzanius [14] a deacon, when he was led away to die.

And the Lord helped them, and increased the faith by means of them.

And after a long time, it happened that one of the sons of Misdeus was a demoniac; and the demon being stubborn, no one was able to heal him. And Misdeus considered, and said:

I shall go and open the tomb, and take a bone of the apostle's body, and touch my son with it, and I know that he will be healed.

And he went to do what he had thought of.

And the blessed apostle appeared to him, and said:

Thou didst not believe in me when alive; how wilt thou believe in me when I am dead?

Fear not.

Jesus Christ is kindly disposed to thee, through His great clemency.

And Misdeus, when he did not find the bones (for one of the brethren had taken them, and carried them into the regions of the West[15]), took some dust from where the bones had lain, and touched his son with it, and said:

I believe in Thee, Jesus, now when he has left me who always afflicts men, that they may not look to Thy light which giveth understanding, O Lord, kind to men.

And his son being healed in this manner, he met with the rest of the brethren who were under the rule of Syphorus, and entreated the brethren to pray for him, that he might obtain mercy from our Lord Jesus Christ; to whom be glory for ever and ever.

Amen.

Footnotes:

1. The following translation of a ms. in the Bodleian Library, transcribed by Tischendorf (Apocal. Apocr., p. 158), gives a fuller account of the martyrdom of St. Thomas:-- MARTYRDOM OF THE HOLY AND ALL-RENOWNED APOSTLE THOMAS. After the apostle had gone forth, according to the command of our Lord, and God, and Saviour Jesus Christ, the Lord appeared to him, saying:

Peace to thee, my disciple and apostle!

And the apostle fell on his face on the ground, and prayed the Lord to reveal to him the circumstances of his precious departure.

And the Lord said to him:

Misdaeus is contriving a plan to destroy thee very soon; but, behold, he will come to me.

And after having sealed him, He ascended into the heavens.

And the apostle taught the people, and there was added unto the flock of Christ.

But some men who hated Christ accused him before King Misdeus, saying: Destroy this sorcerer, who corrupts and deceives the people in this new one God whom he proclaims.

Moreover, he has deceived thy lady and thy son.

On hearing this, Misdeus, without inquiry, ordered him to be laid hold of, and shut up in prison.

And they quickly did what they were ordered, and threw him into the prison, and sealed it.

And when the women who believed in God had heard that Judas was shut up, they gave a great sum of money to the warders, and went in to him in the prison. And the apostle says to them:

My daughters, handmaidens of Jesus Christ, listen to me.

In my last day I address you, because I shall no more speak in the body; for, lo, I am taken up to my Lord Jesus Christ, who has had pity upon me, who humbled Himself even to my littleness. And I rejoice that the time is at hand for my change from this, that I may depart and receive my reward in the end; for my Lord is just.

And at the end of his discourse to them, he said:

O my Saviour, who hast endured much for our sake, let Thy mercies be upon us.

And he sent them away, saying:

The grace of the Holy Spirit be with you!

And they grieved and wept, knowing that King Misdeus was going to put him to death.

And Judas heard the warders contending with each other, and saying:

Let us go and tell the king, Thy wife and thy son are going to the prison to this sorcerer, and for their sakes thou shouldst put him to death soon.

And at dawn they arose and went to King Misdeus, and said:

My Lord, release that sorcerer, or cause him to be shut up elsewhere; for though we shut in the prisoners, and secure the doors, when we rise we find them opened.

Nay, more:

thy wife and son will not keep away from the man any more than the rest of them.

And when the king heard this, he went to look at the seals.

And he looked all about them on the doors, and found them as they were.

Then he said to the jailors:

What are you telling lies about? for certainly these seals are quite safe:

and how do you say that Tertia, and Mygdonia, and my son go within the prison?

And the warders said:

We have told thee the truth, O king.

And after this the king went into the prison, and sent for the apostle.

And when he came, they took off his girdle, and set him before the tribunal.

And the king said:

Art thou a slave, or free?

And Thomas said:

I am One's slave.

Thou hast no power over me whatever.

And Misdaeus says:

Didst thou run away and come to this country?

Thomas:

I came here to save many, and I am to depart from my body by thy hands.

Misdaeus says to him:

Who is thy master? and what is his name? and what country dost thou belong to?

Thomas:

Thou canst not hear His true name at this time; but I tell thee the name that has been given Him for the time:

it is Jesus the Christ.

And Misdaeus says:

I have been in no hurry to put thee to death, but have restrained myself; but thou hast made a display of thy works, so that thy sorceries have been heard of in every country.

But no; I shall bring thee to an end, that thy sorceries may be destroyed, and our nation purified.

And Thomas said:

What thou callest sorceries shall abound in me, and never be removed from the people here.

And after this was said, Misdeus reflected in what manner he should put the apostle to death, for he was afraid of the people standing by who believed.

And he arose and took Thomas outside of the city; and he was accompanied by a few armed soldiers.

And the multitude suspected that the king was plotting about him, and stood and addressed themselves to him.

And when they had gone forth three stadia, he delivered him to four soldiers and one of the polemarchs, and ordered them to spear him on the mountain; and he returned to the city.

And those who were present ran to Thomas, eager to rescue him.

And he was led away, accompanied by the soldiers, two on each side....And Thomas, walking along, said:

O Thy secret mysteries, O Jesus! for even unto the end of life are they fulfilled in us.

O the riches of Thy grace!...for, lo, how four have laid hold of me, since of four elements...(Here the fragment ends.)

[Thems. in which this occurs is not that one which has been so frequently cited in the preceding Apocryphal Acts.--R.]

2. Pseudo-Abdias, in his Histories of the Apostles, has as follows: Wherefore, in a rage, Mesdeus king of India thrust into prison the Apostle Thomas, and Zuganes his son, and several others.

3. Abdias: Treptia, who was the king's wife, and Mygdonia the wife of Charisius, one of the king's friends, and Narchia the nurse, gave the jailor 360 pieces of silver, and were let in to the apostle.

4. Abdias: Thomas stood in the prison, and said: Lord Jesus, who didst endure very much for us, let the gates be shut as they were before, and the seals be made again on the same doors.

5. Abdias gives an account of the king going to the prison, and disbelieving the report of the warders, because he found the seals on the doors as he had left them.

6. The not should, by the context, be omitted. [So Pseudo-Abdias.--R.]

7. Reading epeichthen for apechthen.

8. i.e., I will so act.

9. Lit., polemarchs, who in the early times of Athens combined the duties of Foreign Secretary and War Secretary, and sometimes took the command in the field.

10. Abdias: The apostle said that great and divine mysteries were revealed in his death, since he was led by four soldiers, because he consisted of four elements; and the Lord Jesus had been struck by one man, because He knew that one Father had begotten Him.

11. Lit., the servants of the order.

12. The husband of Mygdonia.

13. These names are slightly different in form in this paragraph.

14. These names are slightly different in form in this paragraph.

15. Abdias: and buried them in the city of Edessa. [The translator cites the readings of Pseudo-Abdias, as given by Tischendorf (from Fabricius), as those of "Abdias." The same form of citation appears in the footnotes to the Martyrdom of Bartholomew, pp. 553-557.--R.]

Martyrdom of the Holy and Glorious Apostle Bartholomew

Historians declare that India is divided into three parts; and the first is said to end at Ethiopia, and the second at Media, and the third completes the country; and the one portion of it ends in the dark, and the other in the ocean.

To this India, then, the holy Bartholomew the apostle of Christ went, and took up his quarters in the temple of Astaruth, and lived there as one of the pilgrims and the poor.

In this temple, then, there was an idol called Astaruth, which was supposed to heal the infirm, but rather the more injured all.

And the people were in entire ignorance of the true God; and from want of knowledge, but rather from the difficulty of going to any other, they all fled for refuge to the false god.

And he brought upon them troubles, infirmities, damage, violence, and much affliction; and when any one sacrificed to him, the demon, retiring, appeared to give a cure to the person in trouble; and the foolish people, seeing this, believed in him.

But the demons retired, not because they wished to cure men, but that they might the more assail them, and rather have them altogether in their power; and thinking that they were cured bodily, those that sacrificed to them were the more diseased in soul.

And it came to pass, that while the holy apostle of Christ, Bartholomew, stayed there, Astaruth gave no response, and was not able for curing.

And when the temple was full of sick persons, who sacrificed to him daily, Astaruth could give no response; and sick persons who had come from far countries were lying there.

When, therefore, in that temple not even one of the idols was able to give a response, and was of benefit neither to those that sacrificed to them nor to those who were in the agonies of death on their account, they were compelled to go to another city, where there was a temple of idols, where their great and most eminent god was called Becher. [1]

And having there sacrificed, they demanded, asking why their god Astaruth had not responded to them.

And the demon Becher answered and said to them:

From the day and hour that the true God, who dwelleth in the heavens, sent his apostle Bartholomew into the regions here, your god Astaruth is held fast by chains of fire, and can no longer either speak or breathe.

They said to him:

And who is this Bartholomew?

He answered:

He is the friend of the Almighty God, and has just come into these parts, that he may take away all the worship of the idols in the name of his God.

And the servants of the Greeks said to him:

Tell us what he is like, that we may be able to find him.

And the demon answered and said:

He has black hair, a shaggy head, a fair skin, [2] large eyes, beautiful nostrils, his ears hidden by the hair of his head, with a yellow beard, a few grey hairs, of middle height, and neither tall nor stunted, but middling, clothed with a white undercloak bordered with purple, and upon his shoulders a very white cloak; and his clothes have been worn twenty-six years, but neither are they dirty, nor have they waxed old.

Seven times [3] a day he bends the knee to the Lord, and seven times [4] a night does he pray to God.

His voice is like the sound of a strong trumpet; there go along with him angels of God, who allow him neither to be weary, nor to hunger, nor to thirst; his face, and his soul, and his heart are always glad and rejoicing; he foresees everything, he knows and speaks every tongue of every nation.

And behold now, as soon as you ask me, and I answer you about him, behold, he knows; for the angels of the Lord tell him; and if you wish to seek him, if he is willing he will appear to you;

but if he shall not be willing, you will not be able to find him.

I entreat you, therefore, if you shall find him, entreat him not to come here, lest his angels do to me as they have done to my brother Astaruth.

And when the demon had said this, he held his peace.

And they returned, and set to work to look into every face of the pilgrims and poor men, and for two days they could find him nowhere.

And it came to pass, that one who was a demoniac set to work to cry out:

Apostle of the Lord, Bartholomew, thy prayers are burning me up.

Then said the apostle to him:

Hold thy peace, and come out of him.

And that very hour, the man who had suffered from the demon for many years was set free.

And Polymius, the king of that country, happened to be standing opposite the apostle; and he had a daughter a demoniac, that is to say, a lunatic.

And he heard about the demoniac that had been healed, and sent messengers to the apostle, saying:

My daughter is grievously torn; I implore thee, therefore, as thou hast delivered him [5] who suffered for many years, so also to order my daughter to be set free. And the apostle rose up, and went with them.

And he sees the king's daughter bound with chains, for she used to tear in pieces all her limbs; and if any one came near her, she used to bite, and no one dared to come near her.

The servants say to him:

And who is it that dares to touch her?

The apostle answered them:

Loose her, and let her go. They say to him again:

We have her in our power when she is bound with all our force, and dost thou bid us loose her?

The apostle says to them:

Behold, I keep her enemy bound, and are you even now afraid of her?

Go and loose her; and when she has partaken of food, let her rest, and early to-morrow bring her to me.

And they went and did as the apostle had commanded them; and thereafter the demon was not able to come near her.

Then the king loaded camels with gold and silver, precious stones, pearls, and clothing, and sought to see the apostle; and having made many efforts, and not found him, he brought everything back to his palace.

And it happened, when the night had passed, and the following day was dawning, the sun having risen, the apostle appeared alone with the king in his bed-chamber, and said to him:

Why didst thou seek me yesterday the whole day with gold and silver, and precious stones, pearls, and raiment?

For these gifts those persons long for who seek earthly things; but I seek nothing earthly, nothing carnal.

Wherefore I wish to teach thee that the Son of God deigned to be born as a man out of a virgin's womb.

He was conceived in the womb of the virgin; He took to Himself her who was always a virgin, having within herself Him who made the heaven and the earth, the sea, and all that therein is.

He, born of a virgin, like mankind, took to Himself a beginning in time, He who has a beginning neither of times nor days; but He Himself made every beginning, and everything created, whether in things visible or invisible.

And as this virgin did not know man, so she, preserving her virginity, vowed a vow [6] to the Lord God.

And she was the first who did so.

For, from the time that man existed from the beginning of the world, no woman made a vow of this mode of life; but she, as she was the first among women who loved this in her heart, said, I offer to Thee, O Lord, my virginity.

And, as I have said to thee, none of mankind dared to speak this word; but she being called for the salvation of many, observed this--that she might remain a virgin through the love of God, pure and undefiled.

And suddenly, when she was shut up in her chamber, the archangel Gabriel appeared, gleaming like the sun; and when she was terrified at the sight, the angel said to her, Fear not, Mary; for thou hast found favour in the sight of the Lord, and thou shalt conceive.

And she cast off fear, and stood up, and said, How shall this be to me, since I know not man?

The angel answered her, The Holy Ghost shall come upon thee, and the power of the Most High shall overshadow thee; wherefore also that holy thing which is born of thee shall be called Son of God. [7]Thus, therefore, when the angel had departed from her, she escaped the temptation of the devil, who deceived the first man when at rest.

For, having tasted of the tree of disobedience, when the woman said to him, Eat, he ate; and thus the first man was cast out of paradise, and banished to this life.

From him have been born the whole human race.

Then the Son of God having been born of the virgin, and having become perfect man, and having been baptized, and after His baptism having fasted forty days, the tempter came and said to Him:

If thou art the Son of God, tell these stones to become loaves.

And He answered:

Not on bread alone shall man live, but by every word of God.[8]Thus therefore the devil, who through eating had conquered the first man, was conquered through the fasting of the second man; and as he through want of self-restraint had conquered the first man, the son of the virgin earth, so we shall conquer through the fasting of the second Adam, the Son of the Virgin Mary.

The king says to him:

And how is it that thou saidst just now that she was the first virgin of whom was born God and man?

And the apostle answered:

I give thanks to the Lord that thou hearest me gladly.

The first man, then, was called Adam; he was formed out of the earth.

And the earth, his mother out of which he was, was virgin, because it had neither been polluted by the blood of man nor opened for the burial of any one.

The earth, then, was like the virgin, in order that he who conquered the son of the virgin earth might be conquered by the Son of the Virgin Mary.

And, behold, he did conquer; for his wicked craft, through the eating of the tree by which man, being deceived, came forth from paradise, kept paradise shut.

Thereafter this Son of the virgin conquered all the craft of the devil.

And his craft was such, that when he saw the Son of the virgin fasting forty days, he knew in truth that He was the true God.

The true God and man, therefore, hath not given Himself out to be known, except to those who are pure in heart, [9] and who serve Him by good works.

The devil himself, therefore, when he saw that after the forty days He was again hungry, was deceived into thinking that He was not God, and said to Him, Why hast thou been hungry? tell these stones to become loaves, and eat.

And the Lord answered him, Listen, devil; although thou mayst lord it over man, because he has not kept the commandment of God.

I have fulfilled the righteousness of God in having fasted, and shall destroy thy power, so that thou shalt no longer lord it over man.

And when he saw himself conquered, he again takes Jesus to an exceeding high mountain, and shows Him all the kingdoms of the world, and says, All these will I give thee, if thou wilt fall down and worship me.

The Lord says to him, Get thee behind me, Satan; for it is written, Thou shalt worship the Lord thy God, and Him only shalt thou serve.

And there was a third temptation for the Lord; for he takes Him up to the pinnacle of the temple, and says, If thou art the Son of God, cast thyself down.

The Lord says to him, Thou shalt not tempt the Lord thy God.

And the devil disappeared.

And he indeed that once conquered Adam, the son of the virgin earth, was thrice conquered by Christ, the Son of the Virgin Mary.

And when the Lord had conquered the tyrant, He sent His apostles into all the world, that He might redeem His people from the deception of the devil; and one of these I am, an apostle of Christ.

On this account we seek not after gold and silver, but rather despise them, because we labour to be rich in that place where the kingdom of Him alone endureth [10] for ever, where neither trouble, nor grief, nor groaning, nor death, has place; where there is eternal blessedness, and ineffable joy, and everlasting exultation, and perpetual repose. Wherefore also the demon sitting in your temple, who makes responses to you, is kept in chains through the angel of the Lord who has sent me. Because if thou shalt be baptized, and wishest thyself to be enlightened, I will make thee behold Him, and learn from how great evils thou hast been redeemed.

At the same time hear also by what means he injures all those who are lying sick in the temple. The devil himself by his own art causes the men to be sick, and again to be healed, in order that they may the more believe in the idols, and in order that he may have place the more in their souls, in order that they may say to the stock and the stone, Thou art our God. [11]But that demon who dwells in the idol is held in subjection, conquered by me, and is able to give no response to those who sacrifice and pray there.

And if thou wishest to prove that it is so, I order him to return into the idol, and I will make him confess with his own mouth that he is bound, and able to give no response.

The king says to him:

To-morrow, at the first hour of the day, the priests are ready to sacrifice in the temple, and I shall come there, and shall be able to see this wonderful work.

And it came to pass on the following day, as they were sacrificing, the devil began to cry out:

Refrain, ye wretched ones, from sacrificing to me, lest ye suffer worse for my sake; because I am bound in fiery chains, and kept in subjection by an angel of the Lord Jesus Christ, the Son of God, whom the Jews crucified:

for, being afraid of him, they condemned him to death.

And he put to death Death himself, our king, and he bound our prince in chains of fire; and on the third day, having conquered death and the devil, rose in glory, and gave the sign of the cross to his apostles, and sent them out into the four quarters of the world; and one of them is here just now, who has bound me, and keeps me in subjection.

I implore you, therefore, supplicate him on my account, that he may set me free to go into other habitations.

Then the apostle answered:

Confess, unclean demon, who is it that has injured all those that are lying here from heavy diseases?

The demon answered:

The devil, our ruler, he who is bound, he sends us against men, that, having first injured their bodies, we may thus also make an assault upon their souls when they sacrifice to us.

For then we have complete power over them, when they believe in us and sacrifice to us. And when, on account of the mischief done to them, we retire, we appear curing them, and are worshipped by them as gods; but in truth we are demons, and the servants of him who was crucified, the Son of the virgin, have bound us.

For from that day on which the Apostle Bartholomew came I am punished, kept bound in chains of fire.

And for this reason I speak, because he has commanded me.

At the same time, I dare not utter more when the apostle is present, neither I nor our rulers.

The apostle says to him:

Why dost thou not save all that have come to thee?

The demon says to him:

When we injure their bodies, unless we first injure their souls, we do not let their bodies go.

The apostle says to him:

And how do you injure their souls?

The demon answered him:

When they believe that we are gods, and sacrifice to us, God withdraws from those who sacrifice, and we do not take away the sufferings of their bodies, but retire into their souls.

Then the apostle says to the people:

Behold, the god whom you thought to cure you, does the more mischief to your souls and bodies.

Hear even now your Maker who dwells in the heavens, and do not believe in lifeless stones and stocks.

And if you wish that I should pray for you, and that all these may receive health, take down this idol, and break it to pieces; and when you have done this, I will sanctify this temple in the name of our Lord Jesus Christ; and having baptized all of you who are in it in the baptism of the Lord, and sanctified you, I will save all.

Then the king gave orders, and all the people brought ropes and crowbars, and were not at all able to take down the idol.

Then the apostle says to them:

Unfasten the ropes.

And when they had unfastened them, he said to the demon dwelling in it:

In the name of our Lord Jesus Christ, come out of this idol, and go into a desert place, where neither winged creature utters a cry, nor voice of man has ever been heard.

And straightway he arose at the word of the apostle, and lifted it up from its foundations; and in that same hour all the idols that were in that place were broken to pieces.

Then all cried out with one voice, saying:

He alone is God Almighty whom Bartholomew the apostle proclaims.

Then the holy Bartholomew, having spread forth his hands to heaven, said:

God of Abraham, God of Isaac, God of Jacob, who for the salvation of men hast sent forth Thine only begotten Son, our Lord Jesus Christ, in order that He might redeem by His own blood all of us enslaved by sin, and declare us to be Thy sons, that we may know Thee, the true God, that Thou existest always to eternity God without end:

one God, the Father, acknowledged in Son and Holy Spirit; one God, the Son, glorified in Father and Holy Spirit; one God, the Holy Spirit, worshipped in Father and Son; and acknowledged to be truly one, [12] the Father unbegotten, the Son begotten, the Holy Spirit proceeding; and in Thee the Father, and in the Holy Spirit, Thine only begotten Son our Lord Jesus Christ is, in whose name Thou hast given us power to heal the sick, to cure paralytics, to expel demons, and raise the dead:

for He said to us, Verily I say unto you, that whatever ye shall ask in my name ye shall receive. [13] I entreat, then, that in His name all this multitude may be saved, that all may know that Thou alone art God in heaven, and in the earth, and in the sea, who seekest the salvation of men through that same Jesus Christ our Lord, with whom Thou livest and reignest in unity of the Holy Spirit for ever and ever.

And when all responded to the Amen, suddenly there appeared an angel of the Lord, shining brighter than the sun, winged, and other four angels holding up the four corners of the temple; and with his finger the one sealed the temple and the people, and said:

Thus saith the Lord who hath sent me, As you have all been purified from all your infirmity, so also this temple shall be purified from all uncleanness, and from the demons dwelling in it, whom the apostle of God has ordered to go into a desert place; for so hath God commanded me, that I may manifest Him to you.

And when ye behold Him, fear nothing; but when I make the sign of the cross, so also do ye with your finger seal your faces, and these evil things will flee from you.

Then he showed them the demon who dwelt in the temple, like an Ethiopian, black as soot; his face sharp like a dog's, thin-cheeked, with hair down to his feet, eyes like fire, sparks coming out of his mouth; and out of his nostrils came forth smoke like sulphur, with wings spined like a porcupine; and his hands were bound with fiery chains, and he was firmly kept in.

And the angel of the Lord said to him:

As also the apostle hath commanded, I let thee go; go where voice of man is not heard, and be there until the great day of judgment.

And when he let him go, he flew away, groaning and weeping, and disappeared.

And the angel of the Lord went up into heaven in the sight of all.

Then the king, and also the queen, with their two sons, and with all his people, and with all the multitude of the city, and every city round about, and country, and whatever land his kingdom ruled over, were saved, and believed, and were baptized in the name of the Father, and the Son, and the Holy Spirit.

And the king laid aside his diadem, and followed Bartholomew the apostle of Christ.

And after these things the unbelievers of the Greeks, having come together to Astreges [14] the king, who was the elder brother of the king who had been baptized, say to him:

O king, thy brother Polymius has become disciple to a certain magician, who has taken down our temples, and broken our gods to pieces.

And while they were thus speaking and weeping, behold, again there came also some others from the cities round about, both priests [15] and people; and they set about weeping and making accusations [16] before the king.

Then King Astreges in a rage sent a thousand armed men along with those priests, in order that, wherever they should find the apostle, they might bring him to him bound.

And when they had done so, and found him, and brought him, he says to him:

Art thou he who has perverted my brother from the gods?

To whom the apostle answered:

I have not perverted him, but have converted him to God.

The king says to him:

Art thou he who caused our gods to be broken in pieces?

The apostle says to him: I gave power to the demons who were in them, and they broke in pieces the dumb and senseless idols, that all men might believe in God Almighty, who dwelleth in the heavens.

The king says to him:

As thou hast made my brother deny his gods, and believe in thy God, so I also will make you reject thy God and believe in my gods.

The apostle says to him:

If I have bound and kept in subjection the god which thy brother worshipped, and at my order the idols were broken in pieces, if thou also art able to do the same to my God, thou canst persuade me also to sacrifice to thy gods; but if thou canst do nothing to my God, I will break all thy gods in pieces; but do thou believe in my God.

And when he had thus spoken, the king was informed that this god Baldad [17] and all the other idols had fallen down, and were broken in pieces.

Then the king rent the purple in which he was clothed, and ordered the holy apostle Bartholomew to be beaten with rods; and after having been thus scourged, to be beheaded.

And innumerable multitudes came from all the cities, to the number of twelve thousand, who had believed in him along with the king; and they took up the remains of the apostle with singing of praise and with all glory, and they laid them in the royal tomb, and glorified God.

And the king Astreges having heard of this, ordered him to be thrown into the sea; and his remains were carried into the island of Liparis.

And it came to pass on the thirtieth day after the apostle was carried away, that the king Astreges was overpowered by a demon and miserably strangled; and all the priests were strangled by demons, and perished on account of their rising against [18] the apostle, and thus died by an evil fate.

And there was great fear and trembling, and all came to the Lord, and were baptized by the presbyters who had been ordained by the holy apostle Bartholomew.

And according to the commandment of the apostle, all the clergy of the people made King Polymius bishop; and in the name of our Lord Jesus Christ he received the grace of healing, and began to do signs.

And he remained in the bishopric twenty years; and having prospered in all things, and governed the church well, and guided it in right opinions, [19] he fell asleep in peace, and went to the Lord: to whom be glory and strength for ever and ever.

Amen.

Footnotes:

1. The history of Abdias gives the name as Berith, after Judg. ix. 46.
2. Lit., white flesh.
3. Pseudo-Abdias says: a hundred times.
4. Pseudo-Abdias says: a hundred times.
5. Abdias calls him Pseustius.
6. Or, prayed a prayer.
7. Comp. Luke i. 26-38.   Abdias goes on: He then, after His birth, suffered Himself to be tempted by that devil who had overcome the first man, persuading him to eat of the tree forbidden by God.
8. Comp. Luke iv. 1-13.
9. Matt. v. 8.
10. Lit., reigneth.
11. Jer. ii. 27.
12. Or, unity.
13. Matt. xxi. 22.
14. Abdias calls him Astyages; elsewhere he is called Sanathrugus.
15. Lit., no-priests--miereis for me hiereis--a name given in scorn to heathen priests by Christian writers.
16. Lit., calling out.
17. Abdias calls him Vualdath.
18. Or it may mean: that the apostle might be established.
19. Or, in orthodoxy.

Acts of the Holy Apostle Thaddaeus,
One of the Twelve. [1]

Lebbaeus, who also is Thaddaeus, was of the city of Edessa--and it is the metropolis of Osroene, in the interior of the Armenosyrians--an Hebrew by race, accomplished and most learned in the divine writings. He came to Jerusalem to worship in the days of John the Baptist; and having heard his preaching and seen his angelic life, he was baptized, and his name was called Thaddaeus.

And having seen the appearing of Christ, and His teaching, and His wonderful works, he followed Him, and became His disciple; and He chose him as one of the twelve, the tenth apostle according to the Evangelists Matthew and Mark.

In those times there was a governor of the city of Edessa, Abgarus by name.

And there having gone abroad the fame of Christ, of the wonders which He did, and of His teaching, Abgarus having heard of it, was astonished, and desired to see Christ, and could not leave his city and government.

And about the days of the Passion and the plots of the Jews, Abgarus, being seized by an incurable disease, sent a letter to Christ by Ananias the courier, [2] to the following effect:--To Jesus [3] called Christ, Abgarus the governor of the country of the Edessenes, an unworthy slave.

The multitude of the wonders done by thee has been heard of by me, that thou healest the blind, the lame, and the paralytic, and curest all the demoniacs; and on this account I entreat thy goodness to come even to us, and escape from the plottings of the wicked Jews, which through envy they set in motion against thee.

My city is small, but large enough for both.

Abgarus enjoined Ananias to take accurate account of Christ, of what appearance He was, and His stature, and His hair, and in a word everything.

And Ananias, having gone and given the letter, was carefully looking at Christ, but was unable to fix Him in his mind.

And He knew as knowing the heart, and asked to wash Himself; and a towel [4] was given Him; and when He had washed Himself, He wiped His face with it.

And His image having been imprinted upon the linen, He gave it to Ananias, saying:

Give this, and take back this message, to him that sent thee: Peace to thee and thy city!

For because of this I am come, to suffer for the world, and to rise again, and to raise up the forefathers.

And after I have been taken up into the heavens I shall send thee my disciple Thaddaeus, who shall enlighten thee, and guide thee into all the truth, both thee and thy city.

And having received Ananias, and fallen down and adored the likeness, Abgarus was cured of his disease before Thaddaeus came.

And after the passion, and the resurrection, and the ascension, Thaddaeus went to Abgarus; and having found him in health, he gave him an account of the incarnation of Christ, and baptized him, with all his house.

And having instructed great multitudes, both of Hebrews and Greeks, Syrians and Armenians, he baptized them in the name of the Father, and Son, and Holy Spirit, having anointed them with the holy perfume; and he communicated to them of the undefiled mysteries of the sacred body and blood of our Lord Jesus Christ, and delivered to them to keep and observe the law of Moses, and to give close heed to the things that had been said by the apostles in Jerusalem.

For year by year they came together to the passover, and again he imparted to them the Holy Spirit.

And Thaddaeus along with Abgarus destroyed idol-temples and built churches; ordained as bishop one of his disciples, and presbyters, and deacons, and gave them the rule of the psalmody and the holy liturgy. And having left them, he went to the city of Amis, great metropolis of the Mesechaldeans and Syrians, that is, of Mesopotamia-Syria, beside the river Tigris.

And he having gone into the synagogue of the Jews along with his disciples on the Sabbath-day, after the reading of the law the high priest said to Thaddaeus and his disciples:

Men, whence are you? and why are you here?

And Thaddaeus said:

The Forgotten Bible

No doubt you have heard of what has taken place in Jerusalem about Jesus Christ, and we are His disciples, and witnesses of the wonderful things which He did and taught, and how through hatred the chief priests delivered Him to Pilate the procurator of Judaea. And Pilate, having examined Him and found no case, [5] wished to let Him go; but they cried out, If thou let him go, thou art not Caesar's friend, because he proclaims himself king.

And he being afraid, washed his hands in the sight of the multitude, and said, I am innocent of the blood of this man; see ye to it.

And the chief priests answered and said, His blood be upon us and our children.

And Pilate gave him up to them.

And they took Him, and spit upon Him, with the soldiers, and made a great mock of Him, and crucified Him, and laid Him in the tomb, and secured it well, having also set guards upon Him.

And on the third day before dawn He rose, leaving His burial-clothes in the tomb.

And He was seen first by His mother and other women, and by Peter and John first of my fellow disciples, and thereafter to us the twelve, who ate and drank with Him after His resurrection for many days.

And He sent us in His name to proclaim repentance and remission of sins to all the nations, that those who were baptized, having had the kingdom of the heavens preached to them, would rise up incorruptible at the end of this age; and He gave us power to expel demons, and heal every disease and every malady, and raise the dead.

And the multitudes having heard this, brought together their sick and demoniacs.

And Thaddaeus, having gone forth along with his disciples, laid his hand upon each one of them, and healed them all by calling upon the name of Christ.

And the demoniacs were healed before Thaddaeus came near them, the spirits going out of them.

And for many days the people ran together from different places, and beheld what was done by Thaddaeus.

And hearing his teaching, many believed, and were baptized, confessing their sins.

Having therefore remained with them for five years, he built a church; and having appointed as bishop one of his disciples, and presbyters, and deacons, and prayed for them, he went away, going round the cities of Syria, and teaching, and healing all the sick; whence he brought many cities and countries to Christ through His teaching.

Teaching, therefore, and evangelizing along with the disciples, and healing the sick, he went to Berytus, a city of Phoenicia by the sea; [6] and there, having taught and enlightened many, he fell asleep on the twenty-first [7] of the month of August.

And the disciples having come together, buried him with great honour; and many sick were healed, and they gave glory to the Father, and the Son, and the Holy Spirit, for ever and ever.

Amen.

Footnotes:

1. [Curiously enough, the Vienna ms. has in the title: "one of the seventy," instead of "one of the twelve." The same confusion exists in the writings of Eusebius and Jerome.--R.]

2. Lit., the swift runner.

3. [Compare with this letter that found in Eusebius (Hist. Eccl., i. 13), where the reply is also given. Eusebius claims that he had seen the original documents.--R.]

4. Lit., doubled in four.

5. Or, fault.

6. The other [Vienna] ms. here adds: And having gone into it, he preached Christ, saying to them all with tears, Ye men who have ears to hear, hear from me the word of life; hear attentively, and understand. Cast off your many opinions, and believe and come to the one living and true God, the God of the Hebrews. For He only is the true God and Maker of the whole creation, searching the hearts of mankind, and knowing all about each one before their birth, as being the Maker of them all. To Him alone, fixing your eyes upon heaven, fall down evening and morning, and at noon, and to Him alone offer the sacrifice of praise, and give thanks always, refraining from what you yourselves hate; because God is compassionate and benevolent, and recompenses to each one according to his works.

7. The Parisms. has 20th.

Acts of the Holy Apostle and Evangelist John the Theologian.

About His Exile and Departure.

When Agrippa, whom, on account of his plotting against Peace, they stoned and put to death, was king of the Jews, Vespasian Caesar, coming with a great army, invested Jerusalem; and some prisoners of war he took and slew, others he destroyed by famine in the siege, and most he banished, and at length scattered up and down.

And having destroyed the temple, and put the holy vessels on board a ship, he sent them to Rome, to make for himself a temple of peace, and adorned it with the spoils of war.

And when Vespasian was dead, his son Domitian, having got possession of the kingdom, along with his other wrongful acts, set himself also to make a persecution against the righteous men.

For, having learned that the city was filled with Jews, remembering the orders given by his father about them, he purposed casting them all out of the city of the Romans.

And some of the Jews took courage, and gave Domitian a book, in which was written as follows:--

O Domitian, Caesar and king of all the world, as many of us as are Jews entreat thee, as suppliants we beseech of thy power not to banish us from thy divine and benignant countenance; for we are obedient to thee, and the customs, and laws, and practices, and policy, doing wrong in nothing, but being of the same mind with the Romans.

But there is a new and strange nation, neither agreeing with other nations nor consenting to the religious observances of the Jews, uncircumcised, inhuman, lawless, subverting whole houses, proclaiming a man as God, all assembling together [1] under a strange name, that of Christian.

These men reject God, paying no heed to the law given by Him, and proclaim to be the Son of God a man born of ourselves, Jesus by name, whose parents and brothers and all his family have been connected with the Hebrews; whom on account of his great blasphemy and his wicked fooleries we gave up to the cross.

And they add another blasphemous lie to their first one: him that was nailed up and buried, they glorify as having risen from the dead; and, more than this, they falsely assert that he has been taken up by [2] clouds into the heavens.

At all this the king, being affected with rage, ordered the senate to publish a decree that they should put to death all who confessed themselves to be Christians.

Those, then, who were found in the time of his rage, and who reaped the fruit of patience, and were crowned in the triumphant contest against the works of the devil, received the repose of incorruption.

And the fame of the teaching of John was spread abroad in Rome; and it came to the ears of Domitian that there was a certain Hebrew in Ephesus, John by name, who spread a report about the seat of empire of the Romans, saying that it would quickly be rooted out, and that the kingdom of the Romans would be given over to another.

And Domitian, troubled by what was said, sent a centurion with soldiers to seize John, and bring him.

And having gone to Ephesus, they asked where John lived.

And having come up to his gate, they found him standing before the door; and, thinking that he was the porter, they inquired of him where John lived.

And he answered and said:

I am he.

And they, despising his common, and low, and poor appearance, were filled with threats, and said:

Tell us the truth.

And when he declared again that he was the man they sought, the neighbours moreover bearing witness to it, they said that he was to go with them at once to the king in Rome. And, urging them to take provisions for the journey, he turned and took a few dates, and straightway

The Forgotten Bible
went forth.

And the soldiers, having taken the public conveyances, travelled fast, having seated him in the midst of them.

And when they came to the first change, it being the hour of breakfast, they entreated him to be of good courage, and to take bread, and eat with them.

And John said: I rejoice in soul indeed, but in the meantime I do not wish to take any food.

And they started, and were carried along quickly.

And when it was evening they stopped at a certain inn; and as, besides, it was the hour of supper, the centurion and the soldiers being most kindly disposed, entreated John to make use of what was set before them.

But he said that he was very tired, and in want of sleep more than any food.

And as he did this each day, all the soldiers were struck with amazement, and were afraid lest John should die, and involve them in danger.

But the Holy Spirit showed him to them as more cheerful.

And on the seventh day, it being the Lord's day, he said to them:

Now it is time for me also to partake of food.

And having washed his hands and face, he prayed, and brought out the linen cloth, and took one of the dates, and ate it in the sight of all.

And when they had ridden a long time they came to the end of their journey, John thus fasting.

And they brought him before the king, and said:

Worshipful king, we bring to thee John, a god, not a man; for, from the hour in which we apprehended him, to the present, he has not tasted bread.

At this Domitian being amazed, stretched out his mouth on account of the wonder, wishing to salute him with a kiss; but John bent down his head, and kissed his breast.

And Domitian said:

Why hast thou done this?

Didst thou not think me worthy to kiss thee?

And John said to him:

It is right to adore the hand of God first of all, and in this way to kiss the mouth of the king; for it is written in the holy books, The heart of a king is in the hand of God. [3]

And the king said to him:

Art thou John, who said that my kingdom would speedily be uprooted, and that another king, Jesus, was going to reign instead of me?

And John answered and said to him:

Thou also shalt reign for many years given thee by God, and after thee very many others; and when the times of the things upon earth have been fulfilled, out of heaven shall come a King, eternal, true, Judge of living and dead, to whom every nation and tribe shall confess, through whom every earthly power and dominion shall be brought to nothing, and every mouth speaking great things shall be shut.

This is the mighty Lord and King of everything that hath breath and flesh, [4] the Word and Son of the living One, who is Jesus Christ.

At this Domitian said to him:

What is the proof of these things?

I am not persuaded by words only; words are a sight of the unseen.[5] What canst thou show in earth or heaven by the power of him who is destined to reign, as thou sayest?

For he will do it, if he is the Son of God.

And immediately John asked for a deadly poison.

And the king having ordered poison to be given to him, they brought it on the instant.

John therefore, having taken it, put it into a large cup, and filled it with water, and mixed it, and cried out with a loud voice, and said:

In Thy name, Jesus Christ, Son of God, I drink the cup which Thou wilt sweeten; and the poison in it do Thou mingle with Thy Holy Spirit, and make it become a draught of life and salvation, for the healing of soul and body, for digestion and harmless assimilation, for faith not to be repented of, for an undeniable testimony of death as the cup of thanksgiving. [6] And when he had drunk the cup, those standing beside Domitian expected that he was going to fall to the ground in convulsions.

And when John stood, cheerful, and talked with them safe, Domitian was enraged against those who had given the poison, as having spared John.

But they swore by the fortune and health of the king, and said that there could not be a stronger poison than this. And John, understanding what they were whispering to one another, said to the king:

Do not take it ill, O king, but let a trial be made, ⁷ and thou shalt learn the power of the poison.

Make some condemned criminal be brought from the prison.

And when he had come, John put water into the cup, and swirled it round, and gave it with all the dregs to the condemned criminal.

And he, having taken it and drunk, immediately fell down and died.

And when all wondered at the signs that had been done, and when Domitian had retired and gone to his palace, John said to him:

O Domitian, king of the Romans, didst thou contrive this, that, thou being present and bearing witness, I might to-day become a murderer? What is to be done about the dead body which is lying?

And he ordered it to be taken and thrown away.

But John, going up to the dead body, said:

O God, Maker of the heavens, Lord and Master of angels, of glories, of powers, in the name of Jesus Christ, Thine only begotten Son, give to this man who has died for this occasion a renewal of life, and restore him his soul, that Domitian may learn that the Word is much more powerful than poison, and is the ruler of life.

And having taken him by the hand, he raised him up alive.

And when all were glorifying God, and wondering at the faith of John, Domitian said to him:

I have put forth a decree of the senate, that all such persons should be summarily dealt with, without trial; but since I find from thee that they are innocent, and that their religion is rather beneficial, I banish thee to an island, that I may not seem myself to do away with my own decrees.

He asked then that the condemned criminal should be let go; and when he was let go, John said:

Depart, give thanks to God, who has this day delivered thee from prison and from death.

And while they were standing, a certain home-born slave of Domitian's, of those in the bed-chamber, was suddenly seized by the unclean demon, and lay dead; and word was brought to the king.

And the king was moved, and entreated John to help her.

And John said:

It is not in man to do this; but since thou knowest how to reign, but dost not know from whom thou hast received it, learn who has the power over both thee and thy kingdom.

And he prayed thus:

O Lord, the God of every kingdom, and master of every creature, give to this maiden the breath of life.

And having prayed, he raised her up.

And Domitian, astonished at all the wonders, sent him away to an island, appointing for him a set time.

And straightway John sailed to Patmos, where also he was deemed worthy to see the revelation of the end.

And when Domitian was dead, Nerva succeeded to the kingdom, and recalled all who had been banished; and having kept the kingdom for a year, he made Trajan his successor in the kingdom.

And when he was king over the Romans, John went to Ephesus, and regulated all the teaching of the church, holding many conferences, and reminding them of what the Lord had said to them, and what duty he had assigned to each.

And when he was old and changed, he ordered Polycarp to be bishop over the church.

And what like his end was, or his departure from men, who cannot give an account of?

For on the following day, which was the Lord's day, and in the presence of the brethren, he began to say to them:

Brethren, and fellow-servants, and co-heirs, and copartners of the kingdom of the Lord, know the Lord what miracles He hath shown you through me, what wonders, what cures, what signs, what gracious gifts, teachings, rulings, rests, services, glories, graces, gifts, faiths, communions; how many things you have seen with your eyes, that ear hath not heard. Be strong, therefore, in Him, remembering Him in all your doings, knowing the mystery of the dispensation that has come to men, for the sake of which the Lord has worked.

He then, through me, exhorts you: Brethren, I wish to remain without grief, without insult, without treachery, without punishment.

For He also knows insult from you, He knows also dishonour, He knows also treachery, He knows also punishment from those that disobey His commandments.

Let not therefore our God be grieved, the good, the compassionate, the merciful, the holy, the pure, the undefiled, the only, the one, the immutable, the sincere, the guileless, the slow to anger,

The Forgotten Bible

He that is higher and more exalted than every name that we speak or think of--our God, Jesus Christ.

Let Him rejoice along with us because we conduct ourselves well; let Him be glad because we live in purity; let Him rest because we behave reverently; let Him be pleased because we live in fellowship; let Him smile because we are sober-minded; let Him be delighted because we love.

These things, brethren, I communicate to you, pressing on to the work set before me, already perfected for me by the Lord.

For what else have I to say to you?

Keep the sureties of your God; keep His presence, that shall not be taken away from you.

And if then ye sin no more, He will forgive you what ye have done in ignorance; but if, after ye have known Him, and He has had compassion upon you, you return to the like courses, even your former offences will be laid to your charge, and ye shall have no portion or compassion before His face. [8]

And when he had said this to them, he thus prayed:

Jesus, who didst wreathe this crown by Thy twining, who hast inserted these many flowers into the everlasting flower of Thy countenance, who hast sown these words among them, be Thou Thyself the protector and healer of Thy people.

Thou alone art benignant and not haughty, alone merciful and kind, alone a Saviour, and just; Thou who always seest what belongs to all, and art in all, and everywhere present, God Lord Jesus Christ; who with Thy gifts and Thy compassion coverest those that hope in Thee; who knowest intimately those that everywhere speak against us, and blaspheme Thy holy name, do Thou alone, O Lord, help Thy servants with Thy watchful care.

So be it, Lord.

And having asked bread, he gave thanks thus, saying:

What praise, or what sort of offering, or what thanksgiving, shall we, breaking the bread, invoke, but Thee only?

We glorify the name by which Thou hast been called by the Father; we glorify the name by which Thou hast been called through the Son; we glorify the resurrection which has been manifested to us through Thee; of Thee we glorify the seed, [9] the word, the grace, the true pearl, the treasure, the plough, the net, [10] the majesty, the diadem, Him called Son of man for our sakes, the truth, the rest, the knowledge, the freedom, the place of refuge in Thee.

For Thou alone art Lord, the root of immortality, and the fountain of incorruption, and the seat of the ages; Thou who hast been called all these for our sakes, that now we, calling upon Thee through these, may recognise Thine illimitable majesty, presented to us by Thy presence, that can be seen only by the pure, seen in Thine only Son.

And having broken the bread, he gave it to us, praying for each of the brethren, that he might be worthy of the Eucharist of the Lord.

He also therefore, having likewise tasted it, said:

To me also let there be a portion with you, and peace, O beloved.

And having thus spoken, and confirmed the brethren, he said to Eutyches, also named Verus: Behold, I appoint thee a minister [11] of the Church of Christ, and I entrust to thee the flock of Christ.

Be mindful, therefore, of the commandments of the Lord; and if thou shouldst fall into trials or dangers, be not afraid:

for thou shalt fall under many troubles, and thou shalt be shown to be an eminent witness [12] of the Lord.

Thus, then, Verus, attend to the flock as a servant of God, until the time appointed for thy testimony.

And when John had spoken this, and more than this, having entrusted to him the flock of Christ, he says to him:

Take some brethren, with baskets and vessels, and follow me.

And Eutyches, without considering, [13] did what he was bid.

And the blessed John having gone forth from the house, went outside of the gates, having told the multitude to stand off from him.

And having come to the tomb of one of our brethren, he told them to dig.

And they dug.

And he says:

Let the trench be deeper.

And as they dug, he conversed with those who had come out of the house with him, building them up, and furnishing them thoroughly into the majesty of the Lord.

And when the young men had finished the trench, as he had wished, while we knew [14] nothing, he takes off the clothes he had on, and throws them, as if they were some bedding, into the depth of the trench; and, standing in only his drawers, [15] stretched forth his hands, and prayed.

O God, who hast chosen us for the mission [16] of the Gentiles, who hast sent us out into the world, who hast declared Thyself through the apostles; who hast never rested, but always savest from the foundation of the world; who hast made Thyself known through all nature; who hast made our wild and savage nature quiet and peaceable; who hast given Thyself to it when thirsting after knowledge; [17] who hast put to death its adversary, when it took refuge in Thee; who hast given it Thy hand, and raised it from the things done in Hades; who hast shown it its own enemy; who hast in purity turned its thoughts upon Thee, O Christ Jesus, Lord of things in heaven, and law of things on earth, the course of things aerial, and guardian of things etherial, the fear of those under the earth, and grace of Thine own people, receive also the soul of Thy John, which has been certainly deemed worthy by Thee, Thou who hast preserved me also till the present hour pure to Thyself, and free from intercourse with woman; who, when I wished in my youth to marry, didst appear to me, and say, I am in need of thee, John; who didst strengthen for me beforehand my bodily weakness; who, when a third time I wished to marry, didst say to me at the third hour, in the sea, John, if thou wert not mine, I would let thee marry; who hast opened up the sight of my mind, and hast favoured my bodily [18] eyes; who, when I was looking about me, didst call even the gazing upon a woman hateful; who didst deliver me from temporary show, and preserve me for that which endureth for ever; who didst separate me from the filthy madness of the flesh; who didst stop up [19] the secret disease of the soul, and cut out its open actions; who didst afflict and banish him who rebelled in me; who didst establish my love to Thee spotless and unimpaired; who didst give me undoubting faith in Thee; who hast drawn out for me pure thoughts towards Thee; who hast given me the due reward of my works; who hast set it in my soul to have no other possession than Thee alone:

for what is more precious than Thou?

Now, O Lord, when I have accomplished Thy stewardship with which I was entrusted, make me worthy of Thy repose, having wrought that which is perfect in Thee, which is ineffable salvation.

And as I go to Thee, let the fire withdraw, let darkness be overcome, let the furnace be slackened, let Gehenna be extinguished, let the angels follow, let the demons be afraid, let the princes be broken in pieces, let the powers of darkness fall, let the places on the right hand stand firm, let those on the left abide not, let the devil be muzzled, let Satan be laughed to scorn, let his madness be tamed, let his wrath be broken, let his children be trodden under foot, and let all his root be uprooted; and grant to me to accomplish the journey to Thee, not insulted, not despitefully treated, and to receive what Thou hast promised to those that live in purity, and that have loved a holy life.

And gazing towards heaven, he glorified God; and having sealed himself altogether, he stood and said to us, Peace and grace be with you, brethren! and sent the brethren away.

And when they went on the morrow they did not find him, but his sandals, and a fountain welling up.

And after that they remembered what had been said to Peter by the Lord about him:

For what does it concern thee if I should wish him to remain until I come? [20] And they glorified God for the miracle that had happened.

And having thus believed, they retired praising and blessing the benignant God; because to Him is due glory now and ever, and to ages of ages.

Amen.

Footnotes:

1. Tischendorf gives a conjectural reading: who is present to them when they assemble; but the mss. reading will bear the interpretation given above.
2. Or, in.
3. Prov. xxi. 1.
4. Lit., of all breath and flesh.
5. Equal to our proverb, Seeing is believing.
6. i.e., the Eucharist.
7. Tischendorf conjectures this clause, as the original is illegible.
8. Comp. Heb. x. 26.
9. Or, sowing.
10. Comp. Matt. xiii.
11. Or, deacon.
12. i.e., martyr.
13. The othermss. has: not without concern.
14. Or, saw.
15. The word digrosio is not to be found in any of the dictionaries. Perhaps it is a misreading of diazostra.

16. Or, apostleship.
17. Lit., words or reasons.
18. Or, visible.
19. Or, muzzle.
20. John xxi. 22.

Revelation of Moses

Account and life of Adam and Eve, the first-created, revealed by God to His servant Moses, when he received from the hand of the Lord the tables of the law of the covenant, instructed by the archangel Michael.

This is the account of Adam and Eve.

After they went forth out of paradise, Adam took Eve his wife, and went up into the east.

And he remained there eighteen years and two months; and Eve conceived and brought forth two sons, Diaphotus called Cain, and Amilabes [1] called Abel.

And after this, Adam and Eve were with one another; and when they lay down, Eve said to Adam her lord:

My lord, I have seen in a dream this night the blood of my son Amilabes, who is called Abel, thrown into the mouth of Cain his brother, and he drank it without pity.

And he entreated him to grant him a little of it, but he did not listen to him, but drank it all up; and it did not remain in his belly, but came forth out of his mouth.

And Adam said to Eve:

Let us arise, and go and see what has happened to them, lest perchance the enemy should be in any way warring against them.

And having both gone, they found Abel killed by the hand of Cain his brother.

And God says to the archangel Michael:

Say to Adam, Do not relate the mystery which thou knowest to thy son Cain, for he is a son of wrath.

But grieve thyself not; for I will give thee instead of him another son, who shall show thee all things, as many as thou shalt do to him; but do thou tell him nothing.

This God said to His angel; and Adam kept the word in his heart, and with him Eve also, having grief about Abel their son.

And after this, Adam knew his wife Eve, and she conceived and brought forth Seth.

And Adam says to Eve:

Behold, we have brought forth a son instead of Abel whom Cain slew; let us give glory and sacrifice to God.

And Adam had [2] thirty sons and thirty daughters. [3] And he fell into disease, and cried with a loud voice, and said:

Let all my sons come to me, that I may see them before I die.

And they were all brought together, for the earth was inhabited in three parts; and they all came to the door of the house into which he had entered to pray to God.

And his son Seth said:

Father Adam, what is thy disease?

And he says:

My children, great trouble has hold of me.

And they say:

What is the trouble and disease?

And Seth answered and said to him:

Is it that thou rememberest the fruits of paradise of which thou didst eat, and grievest thyself because of the desire of them?

If it is so, tell me, and I will go and bring thee fruit from paradise.

For I will put dung upon my head, and weep and pray, and the Lord will hearken to me, and send his angel; and I shall bring it to thee, [4] that thy trouble may cease from thee.

Adam says to him:

No, my son Seth; but I have disease and trouble.

Seth says to him:

And how have they come upon thee?

Adam said to him:

When God made us, me and your mother, for whose sake also I die, He gave us every plant in paradise; but about one he commanded us not to eat of it, because on account of it we should die.

And the hour was at hand for the angels who guarded your mother to go up and worship the Lord; and the enemy gave to her, and she ate of the tree, knowing that I was not near her, nor the holy angels; then she gave me also to eat.

And when we had both eaten, God was angry with us.

And the Lord, coming into paradise, set His throne, and called with a dreadful voice, saying, Adam, where art thou? and why art thou hidden from my face? shall the house be hidden from him that built it?

And He says, Since thou hast forsaken my covenant, I have brought upon thy body seventy strokes. [5]The trouble of the first stroke is the injury of the eyes; the trouble of the second stroke, of the hearing; and so in succession, all the strokes shall overtake thee.

And Adam thus speaking to his sons, groaned out loud, and said:

What shall I do?

I am in great grief.

And Eve also wept, saying:

My lord Adam, arise, give me the half of thy disease, and let me bear it, because through me this has happened to thee; through me thou art in distresses and troubles.

And Adam said to Eve:

Arise, and go with our son Seth near paradise, and put earth upon your heads, and weep, beseeching the Lord that He may have compassion upon me, and send His angel to paradise, and give me of the tree in which flows the oil out of it, and that thou mayest bring it to me; and I shall anoint myself, and have rest, and show thee the manner in which we were deceived at first.

And Seth and Eve went into the regions of paradise.

And as they were going along, Eve saw her son, and a wild beast fighting with him.

And Eye wept, saying:

Woe's me, woe's me; for if I come to the day of the resurrection, all who have sinned will curse me, saying, Eve did not keep the commandment of God.

And Eve cried out to the wild beast, saying:

O thou evil wild beast, wilt thou not be afraid to fight with the image of God?

How has thy mouth been opened? how have thy teeth been strengthened? how hast thou not been mindful of thy subjection, that thou wast formerly subject to the image of God?

Then the wild beast cried out, saying:

O Eve, not against us thy upbraiding nor thy weeping, but against thyself, since the beginning of the wild beasts was from thee.

How was thy mouth opened to eat of the tree about which God had commanded thee not to eat of it?

For this reason also our nature has been changed.

Now, therefore, thou shalt not be able to bear up, if I begin to reproach thee.

And Seth says to the wild beast:

Shut thy mouth and be silent, and stand off from the image of God till the day of judgment.

Then the wild beast says to Seth: Behold, I stand off, Seth, from the image of God.

Then the wild beast fled, and left him wounded, and went to his covert.

And Seth went with his mother Eve near paradise:

and they wept there, beseeching God to send His angel, to give [6] them the oil of compassion.

And God sent to them the archangel Michael, and he said to them these words:

Seth, man of God, do not weary thyself praying in this supplication about the tree in which flows the oil to anoint thy father Adam; for it will not happen to thee now, but at the last times.

Then shall arise all flesh from Adam even to that great day, as many as shall be a holy people; then shall be given to them all the delight of paradise, and God shall be in the midst of them; and there shall not any more be sinners before Him, because the wicked heart shall be taken from them, and there shall be given to them a heart made to understand what is good, and to worship God only.

Do thou again go to thy father, since the measure of his life has been fulfilled, equal to [7] three days.

And when his soul goes out, thou wilt behold its dreadful passage.

And the angel, having said this, went away from them.

And Seth and Eve came to the tent where Adam was lying.

And Adam says to Eve:

Why didst thou work mischief against us, and bring upon us great wrath, which is death, holding sway over all our race?

And he says to her: Call all our children, and our children's children, and relate to them the manner of our transgression.

Then Eve says to them:

Listen, all my children, and my children's children, and I shall relate to you how our enemy deceived us.

It came to pass, while we were keeping paradise, that we kept each the portion allotted to him by God.

And I was keeping in my lot the south and west.

And the devil went into the lot of Adam where were the male wild beasts; since God parted to us the wild beasts, and had given all the males to your father, and all the females He gave to me, and each of us watched his own.

And the devil spoke to the serpent, saying, Arise, come to me, and I shall tell you a thing in which thou mayst be of service.

Then the serpent came to him, and the devil says to him, I hear that thou art more sagacious than all the wild beasts, and I have come to make thy acquaintance; [8] and I have found thee greater than all the wild beasts, and they associate with thee; notwithstanding, thou doest reverence to one far inferior.

Why eatest thou of the tares [9] of Adam and his wife, and not of the fruit of paradise?

Arise and come hither, and we shall make him be cast out of paradise through his wife, as we also were cast out through him.

The serpent says to him, I am afraid lest the Lord be angry with me.

The devil says to him, Be not afraid; only become my instrument, and I will speak through thy mouth a word by which thou shalt be able to deceive him.

Then straightway he hung by the walls of paradise about the hour when the angels of God went up to worship.

Then Satan came in the form of an angel, and praised God as did the angels; and looking out from the wall, I saw him like an angel.

And says he to me, Art thou Eve? And I said to him, I am.

And says he to me, What doest thou in paradise?

And I said to him, God has set us to keep it, and to eat of it.

The devil answered me through the mouth of the serpent, Ye do well, but you do not eat of every plant.

And I say to him, Yes, of every plant we eat, but one only which is in the midst of paradise, about which God has commanded us not to eat of it, since you will die the death.

Then says the serpent to me, As God liveth, I am grieved for you, because you are like cattle.

For I do not wish you to be ignorant of this; but rise, come hither, listen to me, and eat, and perceive the value of the tree, as He told us.

But I said to him, I am afraid lest God be angry with me.

And he says to me, Be not afraid; for as soon as thou eatest, thine eyes shall be opened, and ye shall be as gods in knowing what is good and what is evil.

And God, knowing this, that ye shall be like Him, has had a grudge against you, and said, Ye shall not eat of it.

But do thou observe the plant, and thou shalt see great glory about it.

And I observed the plant, and saw great glory about it.

And I said to him, It is beautiful to the eyes to perceive; and I was afraid to take of the fruit.

And he says to me, Come, I will give to thee: follow me.

And I opened to him, and he came inside into paradise, and went through it before me.

And having walked a little, he turned, and says to me, I have changed my mind, and will not give thee to eat.

And this he said, wishing at last to entice and destroy me.

And he says to me, Swear to me that thou wilt give also to thy husband.

And I said to him, I know not by what oath I shall swear to thee; but what I know I say to thee, By the throne of the Lord, and the cherubim, and the tree of life, I will give also to my husband to eat.

And when he had taken the oath from me, then he went and ascended upon it.

And he put upon the fruit which he gave me to eat the poison of his wickedness, that is, of his desire; for desire is the head [10] of all sin.

And I bent down the branch to the ground, and took of the fruit, and ate.

And in that very hour mine eyes were opened. and I knew that I was stripped [11] of the righteousness with which I had been clothed; and I wept, saying, What is this thou hast done to me, because I have been deprived of the glory with which I was clothed?

And I wept too about the oath.

And he came down out of the tree, and went out of sight.

And I sought leaves in my portion, [12] that I might cover my shame; and I did not find them from the plants of paradise, since, at the time that I ate, the leaves of all the plants in my portion fell, except of the fig alone.

And having taken leaves off it, I made myself a girdle, and it is from those plants of which I ate.

And I cried out with a loud voice, saying, Adam, Adam, where art thou?

Arise, come to me, and I shall show thee a great mystery.

And when your father came, I said to him words of wickedness, which brought us down from great glory.

For as soon as he came I opened my mouth, and the devil spoke; and I began to advise him, saying, Come hither, my lord Adam, listen to me, and eat of the fruit of the tree of which God said to us not to eat of it, and thou shalt be as God.

And your father answered and said, I am afraid lest God be angry with me.

And I said to him, Be not afraid, for as soon as thou shalt eat thou shalt know good and evil.

And then I quickly persuaded him, and he ate; and his eyes were opened, and he was aware, he also, of his nakedness.

And he says to me, O wicked woman, why hast thou wrought mischief in us?

Thou hast alienated me from the glory of God.

And that same hour we heard the archangel Michael sounding his trumpet, calling the angels, saying, Thus saith the Lord, Come with me to paradise, and hear the word in which I judge Adam.

And when we heard the archangel sounding, we said, Behold, God is coming into paradise to judge us.

And we were afraid, and hid ourselves.

And God came up into paradise, riding upon a chariot of cherubim, and the angels praising Him.

When God came into paradise, the plants both of Adam's lot and of my lot bloomed, and all lifted themselves up; and the throne of God was made ready where the tree of life was.

And God called Adam, saying, Adam, where art thou hidden, thinking that I shall not find thee?

Shall the house be hidden from him that built it?

Then your father answered and said, Not, Lord, did we hide ourselves as thinking that we should not be found by Thee; but I am afraid, because I am naked, and stand in awe of Thy power, O Lord.

God says to him, Who hath shown thee that thou art naked, unless it be that thou hast forsaken my commandment which I gave thee to keep it?

Then Adam remembered the word which I spake to him when I wished to deceive him, I will put thee out of danger from God.

And he turned and said to me, Why hast thou done this?

And I also remembered the word of the serpent, and said, The serpent deceived me.

God says to Adam, Since thou hast disobeyed my commandment, and obeyed thy wife, cursed is the ground in thy labours.

For whenever thou labourest it, and it will not give its strength, thorns and thistles shall it raise for thee; and in the sweat of thy face shalt thou eat thy bread.

And thou shalt be in distresses of many kinds.

Thou shalt weary thyself, and rest not; thou shalt be afflicted by bitterness, and shall not taste of sweetness; thou shalt be afflicted by heat, and oppressed by cold; and thou shalt toil much, and not grow rich; and thou shalt make haste, [13] and not attain thine end; and the wild beasts, of which thou wast lord, shall rise up against thee in rebellion, because thou hast not kept my commandment.

And having turned to me, the Lord says to me, Since thou hast obeyed the serpent, and disobeyed my commandment, thou shalt be in distresses [14] and unbearable pains; thou shalt bring forth children with great tremblings; and in one hour shalt thou come to bring them forth, [15] and lose thy life in consequence of thy great straits and pangs.

And thou shalt confess, and say, Lord, Lord, save me; and I shall not return to the sin of the flesh.

And on this account in thine own words I shall judge thee, on account of the enmity which the enemy hath put in thee; and thou shalt turn again to thy husband, and he shall be thy lord. [16]And after speaking thus to me, He spoke to the serpent in great wrath, saying to him, Since thou hast done this, and hast become an ungracious instrument until thou shouldst deceive those that were remiss in heart, cursed art thou of all the beasts. Thou shalt be deprived of the food which thou eatest; and dust shalt thou eat all the days of thy life; upon thy breast and belly shalt thou go, and thou shalt be deprived both of thy hands and feet; there shall not be granted thee ear, nor wing, nor one limb of all which those have whom thou hast enticed by thy wickedness, and hast caused them to be cast out of paradise.

And I shall put enmity between thee and between his seed.

He shall lie in wait for [17] thy head, and thou for his heel, until the day of judgment.

And having thus said, He commands His angels that we be cast out of paradise.

And as we were being driven along, and were lamenting, your father Adam entreated the angels, saying, Allow me a little, that I may entreat God, and that He may have compassion upon me, and pity me, for I only have sinned.

And they stopped driving him.

And Adam cried out with weeping, saying, Pardon me, Lord, what I have done.

Then says the Lord to His angels, Why have you stopped driving Adam out of paradise?

It is not that the sin is mine, or that I have judged ill?

Then the angels, falling to the ground, worshipped the Lord, saying, Just art Thou, Lord, and judgest what is right.

And turning to Adam, the Lord said, I will not permit thee henceforth to be in paradise.

And Adam answered and said, Lord, give me of the tree of life, that I may eat before I am cast out.

Then the Lord said to Adam, Thou shalt not now take of it, for it has been assigned to the cherubim and the flaming sword, which turneth to guard it on account of thee, that thou mayst not taste of it and be free from death for ever, but that thou mayst have the war which the enemy has set in thee.

But when thou art gone out of paradise, if thou shalt keep thyself from all evil, as being destined to die, I will again raise thee up when the resurrection comes, and then there shall be given thee of the tree of life, and thou shalt be free from death for ever.

And having thus said, the Lord commanded us to be cast out of paradise.

And your father wept before the angels over against paradise.

And the angels say to him, What dost thou wish that we should do for thee, Adam?

And your father answered and said to the angels, Behold, you cast me out.

I beseech you, allow me to take sweet odours out of paradise, in order that, after I go out, I may offer sacrifice to God, that God may listen to me.

And the angels, advancing, said to God, Jael, eternal King, order to be given to Adam sacrifices [18] of sweet odour out of paradise.

And God ordered Adam to go, that he might take perfumes of sweet odour out of paradise for his food.

And the angels let him go, and he gathered both kinds--saffron and spikenard, and calamus [19] and cinnamon, and other seeds for his food; and having taken them, he went forth out of paradise.

And we came to the earth. [20]

Now, then, my children, I have shown you the manner in which we were deceived.

But do ye watch over yourselves, so as not to forsake what is good.

And when she had thus spoken in the midst of her sons, and Adam was lying in his disease, and he had one other day before going out of the body, Eve says to Adam:

Why is it that thou diest, and I live? or how long time have I to spend after thou diest? tell me.

Then says Adam to Eve:

Do not trouble thyself about matters; for thou wilt not be long after me, but we shall both die alike, and thou wilt be laid into my place. [21] And when I am dead you will leave [22] me, and let no one touch me, until the angel of the Lord shall say something about me; for God will not forget me, but will seek His own vessel which He fashioned.

Arise, rather, pray to God until I restore my spirit into the hands of Him who has given it; because we know not how we shall meet Him who made us, whether He shall be angry with us, or turn and have mercy upon us.

Then arose Eve, and went outside; and falling to the ground, she said:

I have sinned, O God; I have sinned, O Father of all; I have sinned to Thee, I have sinned against Thy chosen angels, I have sinned against the cherubim, I have sinned against Thine unshaken throne; I have sinned, O Lord, I have sinned much, I have sinned before Thee, and every sin [23] through me has come upon the creation.

And while Eve was still praying, being on her knees, behold, there came to her the angel of humanity, and raised her up, saying:

Arise, Eve, from thy repentance; for, behold, Adam thy husband has gone forth from his body; arise and see his spirit carried up to Him that made [24] it, to meet Him.

And Eve arose, and covered her face with her hand; and the angel says to her:

Raise thyself from the things of earth.

And Eve gazed up into heaven, and she saw a chariot of light going along under four shining eagles--and it was not possible for any one born of woman [25] to tell the glory of them, or to see the face of them--and angels going before the chariot.

And when they came to the place where your father Adam was lying, the chariot stood still, and the seraphim between your father and the chariot.

And I saw golden censers, and three vials; and, behold, all the angels with incense, and the censers, and the vials, came to the altar, and blew them up, and the smoke of the incense covered the firmaments.

And the angels fell down and worshipped God, crying out and saying:

Holy Jael, forgive; for he is Thine image, and the work of Thine holy hands.

And again, I Eve saw two great and awful mysteries standing before God.

And I wept for fear, and cried out to my son Seth, saying: Arise, Seth, from the body of thy father Adam, and come to me, that thou mayst see what the eye of no one hath ever seen; and they are praying for thy father Adam. [26]

Then Seth arose and went to his mother, and said to her:

What has befallen thee? and why weepest thou?

She says to him:

Look up with thine eyes, and see the seven firmaments opened, and see with thine eyes how the body of thy father lies upon its face, and all the holy angels with him, praying for him, and saying:

Pardon him, O Father of the universe; for he is Thine image.

What then, my child Seth, will this be? and when will he be delivered into the hands of our invisible Father and God?

And who are the two dark-faced ones who stand by at the prayer of thy father?

And Seth says to his mother:

These are the sun and the moon, and they are falling down and praying for my father Adam.

Eve says to him:

And where is their light, and why have they become black-looking?

And Seth says to her:

They cannot shine in the presence of the Light of the universe, [27] and for this reason the light from them has been hidden.

And while Seth was speaking to his mother, the angels lying upon their faces sounded their trumpets, and cried out with an awful voice, saying, Blessed be the glory of the Lord upon what He has made, for He has had compassion upon Adam, the work of His hands.

When the angels had sounded this forth, there came one of the six-winged seraphim, and hurried Adam to the Acherusian lake, and washed him in presence of God.

And he spent three hours [28] lying, and thus the Lord of the universe, sitting upon His holy throne, stretched forth His hands, and raised Adam, and delivered him to the archangel Michael, saying to him:

Raise him into paradise, even to the third heaven, and let him be there until that great and dreadful day which I am to bring upon the world.

And the archangel Michael, having taken Adam, led him away, and anointed him, as God said to him at the pardoning of Adam.

After all these things, therefore, the archangel asked about the funeral rites of the remains; and God commanded that all the angels should come together into His presence, each according to his rank. And all the angels were assembled, some with censers, some with trumpets.

And the Lord of Hosts went up, [29] and the winds drew Him, and cherubim riding upon the winds, and the angels of heaven went before Him; and they came to where the body of Adam was, and took it. And they came to paradise, and all the trees of paradise were moved so that all begotten from Adam hung their heads in sleep at the sweet smell, except Seth, because he had been begotten according to the appointment of God.

The body of Adam, then, was lying on the ground in paradise, and Seth was grieved exceedingly about him.

And the Lord God says:

Adam, why hast thou done this?

If thou hadst kept my commandment, those that brought thee down to this place would not have rejoiced.

Nevertheless I say unto thee, that I will turn their joy into grief, but I will turn thy grief into joy; and having turned, I will set thee in thy kingdom, on the throne of him that deceived thee; and he shall be cast into this place, that thou mayst sit upon him.

Then shall be condemned, he and those who hear him; and they shall be much grieved, and shall weep, seeing thee sitting upon his glorious throne.

And then He said to the archangel Michael:

Go into paradise, into the third heaven, and bring me three cloths of fine linen and silk.

And God said to Michael, Gabriel, Uriel, and Raphael: [30]Cover Adam's body with the cloths, and bring olive oil of sweet odour, and pour upon him.

And having thus done, they prepared his body for burial.
And the Lord said:
Let also the body of Abel be brought.
And having brought other cloths, they prepared it also for burial, since it had not been prepared for burial since the day on which his brother Cain slew him. For the wicked Cain, having taken great pains to hide it, had not been able; for the earth did not receive it, saying:
I will not receive a body into companionship [31] until that dust which was taken up and fashioned upon me come to me.
And then the angels took it up, and laid it on the rock until his father died.
And both were buried, according to the commandment of God, in the regions of paradise, in the place in which God found the dust. [32] And God sent seven angels into paradise, and they brought many sweet-smelling herbs, and laid them in the earth; and thus they took the two bodies, and buried them in the place which they had dug and built.
And God called Adam, and said:
Adam, Adam.
And the body answered out of the ground, and said:
Here am I, Lord.
And the Lord says to him: I said to thee, Dust [33] thou art, and unto dust thou shalt return. Again I promise thee the resurrection.
I will raise thee up in the last day in the resurrection, with every man who is of thy seed.
And after these words God made a three-cornered seal, and sealed the tomb, that no one should do anything to him in the six days, until his rib should return to him.
And the beneficent God and the holy angels having laid him in his place, after the six days Eve also died.
And while she lived she wept about her falling asleep, because she knew not where her body was to be laid.
For when the Lord was present in paradise when they buried Adam, both she and her children fell asleep, except Seth, as I said.
And Eve, in the hour of her death, besought that she might be buried where Adam her husband was, saying thus:
My Lord, Lord and God of all virtue, do not separate me, Thy servant, from the body of Adam, for of his members Thou madest me; but grant to me, even me, the unworthy and the sinner, to be buried by his body.
And as I was along with him in paradise, and not separated from him after the transgression, so also let no one separate us.
After having prayed, therefore, she looked up into heaven, and stood up, and said, beating her breast:
God of all, receive my spirit.
And straightway she gave up her spirit to God.
And when she was dead, the archangel Michael stood beside her; and there came three angels, and took her body, and buried it where the body of Abel was.
And the archangel Michael said to Seth:
Thus bury every man that dies, until the day of the resurrection.
And after having given this law, he said to him:
Do not mourn beyond six days. And on the seventh day, rest, and rejoice in it, because in it God and we the angels rejoice in the righteous soul that has departed from earth.
Having thus spoken, the archangel Michael went up into heaven, glorifying, and saying the Alleluia: [34] Holy, holy, holy Lord, to the glory of God the Father, because to Him is due glory, honour, and adoration, with His unbeginning and life-giving Spirit, now and ever, and to ages of ages.
Amen.

Footnotes:

1. There is great variety as to these names in the mss. The true reading was probably diaphutor or diaphuteutes, a planter, and melatas or melobotes, a keeper of sheep.
2. Lit., made.
3. One ms. adds: And Adam lived 930 years; and when he came to his end he cried, etc.
4. One ms. has: and he will bring to me of the tree in which compassion flows, and thy trouble shall cease from thee.
5. Or, plagues.
6. Lit., and he will give.
7. Perhaps for ison we should read eiso, within. Another reading is: for the days of his life

The Forgotten Bible

have been fulfilled, and he will live from today three days, and he will die.

8. C has: I take counsel with thee. [C is a Vienna manuscript of the twelfth century; see p. 358, and Tischendorf, Apocalypses Apocryphae, pp. xi., xii.--R.]

9. It seems to be settled that the zizania of the Greeks, the zawan of the Arabs, was darnel; but, from the associations connected with the word, it is better to keep the common translation.

10. C has, root and origin.

11. Lit, naked.

12. i.e., of the garden.

13. I have read tachunthesei for pachunthesei, thou shalt grow fat.

14. The text has mataiois, vain; the true reading is probably kamatois or mochthois.

15. Inserted fromms. C.

16. ms. B. inserts: And Eve was twelve years old when the demon deceived her, and gave her evil desires. For night and day he ceased not to bear hatred against them, because he himself was formerly in paradise; and therefore he supplanted them, because he could not bear to see them in paradise. [B is a Viennams. of the thirteenth or fourteenth century; see Tischendorf, Apocal. Apocr., p. xi.--R.]

17. This is after the version of the LXX., and it is also the interpretation of Gesenius of the Hebrew shuph, Gen. iii. 15.

18. Or, incense.

19. This is the "sweet cane" of Isa. xliii. 24; Jer. vi. 20. See also Ex. xxx. 23; Cant. iv. 14; Ezek. xxvii. 19.

20. Or, and we were upon the earth.

21. Perhaps taphon, tomb, would be better than topon.

22. Or, anoint.

23. Or, all sin.

24. The text has ponesanta, a misprint for poiesanta.

25. Lit., of a womb.

26. The last clause is not in C.

27. ms. A here ends thus: the Father, and the Son, and the Holy Spirit, now and ever, and to ages of ages. Amen. [A is the Venice ms. "of about the thirteenth century;" Tischendorf, Apocal. Apocr., p. xi.--R.]

28. The mss. originally had days, and hours is substituted in another hand.

29. i.e., mounted His chariot.

30. According to a Jewish tradition, these were the four angels who stood round the throne of God.

31. Probably the reading should be heteron, another, and not hetairon. Or it may mean: I will not receive a friendly body, i.e., one upon which I have no claims.

32. i.e., of which Adam was made.

33. Lit., earth.

34. ms. D ends here with: To whom be glory and strength to ages of ages. Amen. [D is the Milan manuscript which Tischendorf assigns to "About the eleventh century," Apocalypses Apocryphae, p. xi.--R.]

Revelation of Esdras

Word and Revelation of Esdras, the Holy Prophet and Beloved of God.

It came to pass in the thirtieth year, on the twenty-second of the month, I was in my house.

And I cried out and said to the Most High: Lord, give the glory, [1] in order that I may see Thy mysteries. And when it was night, there came an angel, Michael the archangel, and says to me:

O Prophet Esdras, refrain from bread for seventy weeks. [2] And I fasted as he told me.

And there came Raphael the commander of the host, and gave me a storax rod.

And I fasted twice sixty [3] weeks.

And I saw the mysteries of God and His angels. And I said to them:

I wish to plead before God about the race of the Christians.

It is good for a man not to be born rather than to come into the world.

I was therefore taken up into heaven, and I saw in the first heaven a great army of angels; and they took me to the judgments.

And I heard a voice saying to me:

Have mercy on us, O thou chosen of God, Esdras.

Then began I to say:

Woe to sinners when they see one who is just more than the angels, and they themselves are in the Gehenna of fire!

And Esdras said:

Have mercy on the works of Thine hands, Thou who art compassionate, and of great mercy.

Judge me rather than the souls of the sinners; for it is better that one soul should be punished, and that the whole world should not come to destruction.

And God said:

I will give rest in paradise to the righteous, and I have become [4] merciful.

And Esdras said:

Lord, why dost Thou confer benefits on the righteous? for just as one who has been hired out, and has served out his time, goes and again works as a slave when he come to his masters, so also the righteous has received his reward in the heavens.

But have mercy on the sinners, for we know that Thou art merciful.

And God said:

I do not see how I can have mercy upon them.

And Esdras said:

They cannot endure Thy wrath.

And God said:

This is the fate of such.

And God said:

I wish to have thee like Paul and John, as thou hast given me uncorrupted the treasure that cannot be stolen, the treasure of virginity, the bulwark [5] of men.

And Esdras said:

It is good for a man not to be born.

It is good not to be in life.

The irrational creatures are better than man, because they have no punishment; but Thou hast taken us, and given us up to judgment.

Woe to the sinners in the world to come! because their judgment is endless, and the flame unquenchable.

And while I was thus speaking to him, there came Michael and Gabriel, and all the apostles; and they said:

Rejoice, O faithful man of God!

And Esdras said: [6] Arise, and come hither with me, O Lord, to judgment.

And the Lord said:

Behold, I give thee my covenant between me and thee, that you may receive it.

And Esdras said:

Let us plead in Thy hearing. [7] And God said:

Ask Abraham your father how a son pleads with his father, [8] and come plead with us.

And Esdras said:

As the Lord liveth, I will not cease pleading with Thee in behalf of the race of the Christians.

Where are Thine ancient compassions, O Lord?

Where is Thy long-suffering?

And God said:

As I have made night and day, I have made the righteous and the sinner; and he should have lived like the righteous.

And the prophet said:

Who made Adam the first-formed? And God said:

My undefiled hands.

And I put him in paradise to guard the food of the tree of life; and thereafter he became disobedient, and did this in transgression.

And the prophet said:

Was he not protected by an angel? and was not his life guarded by the cherubim to endless ages? and how was he deceived who was guarded by angels? for Thou didst command all to be present, and to attend to what was said by Thee. [9]But if Thou hadst not given him Eve, the serpent would not have deceived her; [10] but whom Thou wilt Thou savest, and whom Thou wilt Thou destroyest. [11]And the prophet said:

Let us come, my Lord, to a second judgment.

And God said:

I cast fire upon Sodom and Gomorrah.

And the prophet said:

Lord, Thou dealest with us according to our deserts.

And God said:

Your sins transcend my clemency.

And the prophet said:

Call to mind the Scriptures, my Father, who hast measured out Jerusalem, and set her up again.

Have mercy, O Lord, upon sinners; have mercy upon Thine own creatures; [12] have pity upon Thy works.

Then God remembered those whom He had made, and said to the prophet:

How can I have mercy upon them?

Vinegar and gall did they give me to drink, [13] and not even then did they repent.

And the prophet said:

Reveal Thy cherubim, and let us go together to judgment; and show me the day of judgment, what like it is.

And God said:

Thou hast been deceived, Esdras; for such is the day of judgment as that in which there is no rain upon the earth; for it is a merciful tribunal as compared with that day.

And the prophet said:

I will not cease to plead with Thee, unless I see the day of the consummation.

And God said: [14]Number the stars and the sand of the sea; and if thou shalt be able to number this, thou art also able to plead with me.

And the prophet said:

Lord, Thou knowest that I wear human flesh; and how can I count the stars of the heaven, and the sand of the sea?

And God said:

My chosen prophet, no man will know that great day and the appearing [15] that comes to judge the world.

For thy sake, my prophet, I have told thee the day; but the hour have I not told thee. And the prophet said:

Lord, tell me also the years.

And God said:

If I see the righteousness of the world, that it has abounded, I will have patience with them; but if not, I will stretch forth my hand, and lay hold of the world by the four quarters, and bring them all together into the valley of Jehoshaphat, [16] and I will wipe out the race of men, so that the world shall be no more.

And the prophet said:

And how can Thy right hand be glorified?

And God said:

I shall be glorified by my angels.

And the prophet said:
Lord, if Thou hast resolved to do this, why didst Thou make man?
Thou didst say to our father Abraham, [17] Multiplying I will multiply thy seed as the stars of the heaven, and as the sand that is by the sea-shore; [18] and where is Thy promise?
And God said:
First will I make an earthquake for the fall of four-footed beasts and of men; and when you see that brother gives up brother to death, and that children shall rise up against their parents, and that a woman forsakes her own husband, and when nation shall rise up against nation in war, then will you know that the end is near. [19]
For then neither brother pities brother, nor man wife, nor children parents, nor friends friends, nor a slave his master; for he who is the adversary of men shall come up from Tartarus, and shall show men many things.
What shall I make of thee, Esdras? and wilt thou yet plead with me?
And the prophet said:
Lord, I shall not cease to plead with Thee.
And God said:
Number the flowers of the earth.
If thou shalt be able to number them, thou art able also to plead with me.
And the prophet said:
Lord, I cannot number them.
I wear human flesh; but I shall not cease to plead with Thee.
I wish, Lord, to see also the under parts of Tartarus.
And God said:
Come down and see.
And He gave me Michael, and Gabriel, and other thirty-four angels; and I went down eighty-five steps, and they brought me down five hundred steps, and I saw a fiery throne, and an old man sitting upon it; and his judgment was merciless.
And I said to the angels:
Who is this? and what is his sin?
And they said to me:
This is Herod, who for a time was a king, and ordered to put to death the children from two years old and under. [20] And I said:
Woe to his soul!
And again they took me down thirty steps, and I there saw boilings up of fire, and in them there was a multitude of sinners; and I heard their voice, but saw not their forms.
And they took me down lower many steps, which I could not measure.
And I there saw old men, and fiery pivots turning in their ears.
And I said:
Who are these? and what is their sin?
And they said to me:
These are they who would not listen. [21] And they took me down again other five hundred steps, and I there saw the worm that sleeps not, and fire burning up the sinners.
And they took me down to the lowest part of destruction, and I saw there the twelve plagues of the abyss.
And they took me away to the south, and I saw there a man hanging by the eyelids; and the angels kept scourging him. And I asked:
Who is this? and what is his sin?
And Michael the commander said to me:
This is one who lay with his mother; for having put into practice a small wish, he has been ordered to be hanged.
And they took me away to the north, and I saw there a man bound with iron chains.
And I asked:
Who is this?
And he said to me:
This is he who said, I am the Son of God, that made stones bread, and water wine.
And the prophet said:
My lord, let me know what is his form, and I shall tell the race of men, that they may not believe in him.
And he said to me:
The form of his countenance is like that of a wild beast; his right eye like the star that rises in the morning, and the other without motion; his mouth one cubit; his teeth span long; his fingers like scythes; the track of his feet of two spans; and in his face an inscription, Antichrist.

He has been exalted to heaven; he shall go down to Hades. [22] At one time he shall become a child; at another, an old man.

And the prophet said:

Lord, and how dost Thou permit him, and he deceives the race of men?

And God said:

Listen, my prophet.

He becomes both child and old man, and no one believes him that he is my beloved Son.

And after this a trumpet, and the tombs shall be opened, and the dead shall be raised incorruptible. [23] Then the adversary, hearing the dreadful threatening, shall be hidden in outer darkness.

Then the heaven, and the earth, and the sea shall be destroyed.

Then shall I burn the heaven eighty cubits, and the earth eight hundred cubits.

And the prophet said:

And how has the heaven sinned?

And God said:

Since [24] ...there is evil.

And the prophet said:

Lord, and the earth, how has it sinned?

And God said: Since the adversary, having heard the dreadful threatening, shall be hidden, even on account of this will I melt the earth, and with it the opponent of the race of men.

And the prophet said:

Have mercy, Lord, upon the race of the Christians.

And I saw a woman hanging, and four wild beasts sucking her breasts.

And the angels said to me:

She grudged to give her milk, but even threw her infants into the rivers. And I saw a dreadful darkness, and a night that had no stars nor moon; nor is there there young or old, nor brother with brother, nor mother with child, nor wife with husband.

And I wept, and said:

O Lord God, have mercy upon the sinners.

And as I said this, there came a cloud and snatched me up, and carried me away again into the heavens.

And I saw there many judgments; and I wept bitterly, and said:

It is good for a man not to have come out of his mother's womb.

And those who were in torment cried out, saying:

Since thou hast come hither, O holy one of God, we have found a little remission.

And the prophet said: Blessed are they that weep for their sins.

And God said:

Hear, O beloved Esdras.

As a husbandman casts the seed of the corn into the ground, so also the man casts his seed into the parts of the woman. The first month it is all together; the second it increases in size; the third it gets hair; the fourth it gets nails; the fifth it is turned into milk; [25] and the sixth it is made ready, and receives life; [26] the seventh it is completely furnished; the ninth the barriers of the gate of the woman are opened; and it is born safe and sound into the earth.

And the prophet said:

Lord, it is good for man not to have been born.

Woe to the human race then, when Thou shalt come to judgment!

And I said to the Lord:

Lord, why hast Thou created man, and delivered him up to judgment?

And God said, with a lofty proclamation:

I will not by any means have mercy on those who transgress my covenant.

And the prophet said:

Lord, where is Thy goodness?

And God said:

I have prepared all things for man's sake, and man does not keep my commandments.

And the prophet said:

Lord, reveal to me the judgments and paradise.

And the angels took me away towards the east, and I saw the tree of life.

And I saw there Enoch, and Elias, and Moses, and Peter, and Paul, and Luke, and Matthias, and all the righteous, and the patriarchs.

And I saw there the keeping of the air within bounds, and the blowing of the winds, and the storehouses of the ice, and the eternal judgments.

And I saw there a man hanging by the skull.

And they said to me:

This man removed landmarks.

And I saw there great judgments. [27]And I said to the Lord:

O Lord God, and what man, then, who has been born has not sinned?

And they took me lower down into Tartarus, and I saw all the sinners lamenting and weeping and mourning bitterly.

And I also wept, seeing the race of men thus tormented.

Then God says to me:

Knowest thou, Esdras, the names of the angels at the end of the world? Michael, Gabriel, Uriel, Raphael, Gabuthelon, Aker, Arphugitonos, Beburos, Zebuleon.

Then there came a voice to me:

Come hither and die, Esdras, my beloved; give that which hath been entrusted to thee. [28]And the prophet said:

And whence can you bring forth my soul?

And the angels said:

We can put it forth through the mouth.

And the prophet said: Mouth to mouth have I spoken with God, [29] and it comes not forth thence.

And the angels said:

Let us bring it out through thy nostrils.

And the prophet said:

My nostrils have smelled the sweet savour of the glory of God.

And the angels said:

We can bring it out through thine eyes.

And the prophet said:

Mine eyes have seen the back parts of God. [30]And the angels said:

We can bring it out through the crown of thy head.

And the prophet said:

I walked about with Moses also on the mountain, and it comes not forth thence.

And the angels said:

We can put it forth through the points of thy nails. And the prophet said:

My feet also have walked about on the altar. And the angels went away without having done anything, saying:

Lord, we cannot get his soul.

Then He says to His only begotten Son:

Go down, my beloved Son, with a great host of angels, and take the soul of my beloved Esdras.

For the Lord, having taken a great host of angels, says to the prophet:

Give me the trust which I entrusted to thee; the crown has been prepared for thee. [31]And the prophet said:

Lord, if Thou take my soul from me, who will be left to plead with Thee for the race of men?

And God said:

As thou art mortal, and of the earth, do not plead with me.

And the prophet said:

I will not cease to plead.

And God said:

Give up just now the trust; the crown has been prepared for thee.

Come and die, that thou mayst obtain it.

Then the prophet began to say with tears:

O Lord, what good have I done pleading with Thee, and I am going to fall down into the earth?

Woe's me, woe's me, that I am going to be eaten up by worms!

Weep, all ye saints and ye righteous, for me, who have pleaded much, and who am delivered up to death.

Weep for me, all ye saints and ye righteous, because I have gone to the pit of Hades.

And God said to him:

Hear, Esdras, my beloved.

I, who am immortal, endured a cross; I tasted vinegar and gall; I was laid in a tomb, and I raised up my chosen ones; I called Adam up out of Hades, that I might save [32] the race of men.

Do not therefore be afraid of death:

for that which is from me--that is to say, the soul--goes to heaven; and that which is from the earth--that is to say, the body--goes to the earth, from which it was taken. [33]And the prophet said:

The Forgotten Bible

Woe's me! woe's me! what shall I set about? what shall I do? I know not.

And then the blessed Esdras began to say:

O eternal God, the Maker of the whole creation, who hast measured the heaven with a span, and who holdest the earth as a handful, [34] who ridest upon the cherubim, who didst take the prophet Elias to the heavens in a chariot of fire, [35] who givest food to all flesh, whom all things dread and tremble at from the face of Thy power,--listen to me, who have pleaded much, and give to all who transcribe this book, and have it, and remember my name, and honour my memory, give them a blessing from heaven; and bless him [36] in all things, as Thou didst bless Joseph at last, and remember not his former wickedness in the day of his judgment.

And as many as have not believed this book shall be burnt up like Sodom and Gomorrah.

And there came to him a voice, saying:

Esdras, my beloved, all things whatever thou hast asked will I give to each one.

And immediately he gave up his precious soul with much honour, in the month of October, on the twenty-eighth.

And they prepared him for burial with incense and psalms; and his precious and sacred body dispenses strength of soul and body perpetually to those who have recourse to him from a longing desire.

To whom is due glory, strength, honour, and adoration,--to the Father, and to the Son, and to the Holy Spirit, now and ever, and to ages of ages.

Amen.

Footnotes:

1. i.e., reveal.
2. Supplied by Tischendorf.   Perhaps it should be days.
3. Perhaps this should be five--e instead of x--which would make seventy days, as above.
4. Or, I am.
5. Lit., wall.
6. Tischendorf supplies this clause from conjecture, and adds that some more seems to have fallen out.
7. Lit., to Thine ear.
8. This seems to be the meaning of the text, which is somewhat corrupt. It obviously refers to Abraham pleading for Sodom.
9. This passage is very corrupt in the text; but a few emendations bring out the meaning above.
10. Better, him.
11. Comp. Ex. xxxiii. 19; Rom. ix. 18.
12. Lit., framing, or fashioning.
13. Matt. xxvii. 34.
14. This is inserted by Tischendorf.
15. Comp. 2 Tim. iv. 1, 8; Tit. ii. 13.
16. Joel iii. 2, 12.
17. Gen. xxii. 17.
18. Lit., the lip of the sea.
19. Comp. Matt. xxiv.
20. Matt. ii. 16.
21. Or, who heard wrong.
22. Comp. Matt. xi. 23.
23. 1 Cor. xv. 52.
24. There is something wanting here in the text.
25. So in the text.
26. Or, the soul.
27. Or, tribunals.
28. Or, thy trust, or pledge. Comp. 1 Tim. vi. 20; 2 Tim. i. 14, in Textus Receptus.
29. Comp. Deut. xxxiv. 10.
30. Comp. Ex. xxxiii. 23.
31. Comp. 2 Tim. iv. 8.
32. The word is wanting in the ms.
33. Eccles. xii. 7.
34. Or, in a measure. Draken in the text should be draka. Comp. Isa. xl. 12 in the LXX.
35. Comp. 1 Kings ii. 11; Ecclus. xlviii. 9.
36. So the ms. Perhaps them would be better.

Revelation of Paul

Revelation of the holy Apostle Paul:
the things which were revealed to him when he went up even to the third heaven, and was caught up into paradise, and heard unspeakable words. [1]

There dwelt a certain nobleman in the city of Tarsus, in the house of St. Paul the apostle, in the government of Theodosius the worshipful king, and of the most illustrious Gratianus; [2] and there was revealed to him an angel of the Lord, saying:

Upturn the foundation of this house, and lift up what thou shalt find.

But he thought that he had had a dream.

And the angel having persisted even to a third vision, the nobleman was compelled to upturn the foundation; and having dug, he found a marble [3] box containing this revelation; and having taken it, he showed it to the ruler of the city.

And the ruler, seeing it sealed up with lead, sent it to the King Theodosius, thinking that it was something else. [4] And the king having received it, and transcribed it, sent the original writing to Jerusalem.

And there was written in it thus:--

The word of the Lord came to me, saying:

Say to this people, Till when do you sin, and add to your sin, and provoke to anger the God who made you, saying that you are children to Abraham, [5] but doing the works of Satan, going on in speaking against God, boasting only in your addressing of God, but poor on account of the substance of sin?

Know, ye sons of men, that the whole creation has been made subject to God; but the human race alone, by sinning, provokes God to anger.

For often the great light, the sun, has come before God, saying against men: Lord God Almighty, how long dost Thou endure all the sin of men? Command me, and I will burn them up.

And there came a voice to him: My long-suffering endures them all, that they may repent; but if not, they shall come to me, and I will judge them.

And often also the moon and the stars have come before God, saying:

Lord God Almighty, Thou hast given us the dominion of the night, and we no longer cover the thefts, and adulteries, and blood-sheddings of men; command us, and we shall do marvels against them.

And there came a voice:

My long-suffering bears with them, that they may turn to me; but if not, they shall come to me, and I will judge them.

And in like manner also the sea cried out, saying:

Lord God Almighty, the sons of men have profaned Thy holy name; command me, and I shall rise up and cover the earth, and wipe out from it [6] the sons of men.

And there came a voice, saying:

My long-suffering bears with them, that they may repent; but if not, they shall come to me, and I will judge them.

You see, ye sons of men, that the whole creation has been made subject to God, but the human race alone sins before God.

On account of all these things, bless God without ceasing, and yet more when the sun is setting.

For at this hour all the angels come to God to adore Him, and they bring before Him the works of men, of each what he has done from morning even to evening, whether good or evil.

And one angel goes rejoicing on account of man when he behaves well, and another goes with a sad countenance.

All the angels at the appointed hour meet for the worship of God, to bring each day's works of men.

But do ye men bless God without ceasing.

Whenever, therefore, at the appointed hour the angels of pious men come, rejoicing and singing psalms, they meet for the worship of the Lord; and, behold, the Spirit of God says to them:

Whence do ye come rejoicing?

And they answered and said:

We are here from the pious men, who in all piety spend their life, fearing the name of God.

Command them, Lord, to abide even to the end in Thy righteousness.

And there came to them a voice:

I have both kept and will keep them void of offence in my kingdom.

And when it came to pass that they went away, there came other angels with a cheerful countenance, shining like the sun.

And behold a voice to them:

Whence have ye come?

And they answered and said:

We have come from those who have held themselves aloof from the world and the things in the world for Thy holy name's sake, who in deserts, and mountains, and caves, and the dens of the earth, in beds on the ground, and in fastings, spend their life. [7]Command us to be with them.

And there came a voice:

Go with them in peace, guarding them.

Moreover, when they went away, behold, there came other angels to worship before God, mourning and weeping.

And the Spirit went forth to meet them, and there came a voice to them:

Whence have ye come?

And they answered and said:

We have come from those who have been called by Thy name, and are slaves to the matter of sin. [8]Why, then, is it necessary to minister unto them?

And there came a voice to them:

Do not cease to minister unto them; perhaps they will turn; but if not, they shall come to me, and I will judge them.

Know, sons of men, that all that is done by you day by day, the angels write in the heavens.

Do you therefore cease not to bless God.

And I was in the Holy Spirit, and an angel says to me:

Come, follow me, that I may show thee the place of the just, where they go after their end.

And I went along with the angel, and he brought me up into the heavens under the firmament; and I perceived and saw powers great and dreadful, full of wrath, and through the mouth of them a flame of fire coming out, and clothed in garments of fire.

And I asked the angel:

Who are these?

And he said to me:

These are they who are sent away to the souls of the sinners in the hour of necessity; for they have not believed that there is judgment and retribution.

And I looked up into the heaven, and saw angels, whose faces shone like the sun, girded with golden girdles, having in their hands prizes, on which the name of the Lord was inscribed, full of all meekness and compassion. And I asked the angel:

Who are these?

And he answered and said to me:

These are they who are sent forth in the day of the resurrection to bring the souls of the righteous, [9] who intrepidly walk according to God. [10]And I said to the angel:

I wish to see the souls of the righteous and of the sinners, how they go out of the world.

And the angel said to me:

Look to the earth.

And I looked, and saw the whole world as nothing disappearing before me.

And I said to the angel:

Is this the greatness of men?

And he said to me:

Yes; for thus every unjust man disappears.

And I looked, and saw a cloud of fire wrapped over all the world; and I said:

What is this, my lord? And he said to me:

This is the unrighteousness mingled with the destruction of the sinners.

And I wept, and said to the angel:

I wished to see the departures of the righteous and of the sinners, in what manner they go out of the world.

And the angel says to me:

Paul, look down, and see what thou hast asked.

And I looked, and saw one of the sons of men falling near death.

And the angel says to me:

This is a righteous man, and, behold, all his works stand beside him in the hour of his necessity. [11]And there were beside him good angels, and along with them also evil angels.

And the evil angels indeed found no place in him, but the good took possession of [12] the soul of the righteous man, and said to it:

Take note of the body whence thou art coming out; for it is necessary for thee again to return to it in the day of the resurrection, that thou mayst receive what God hath promised to the righteous.

And the good angels who had received the soul of the righteous man, saluted it, as being well known to them.

And it went with them; and the Spirit came forth to meet them, saying:

Come, soul, enter into the place of the resurrection, which God hath prepared for His righteous ones.

And the angel said to me:

Look down to the earth, and behold the soul of the impious, how it goes forth from its tabernacle, which has provoked God to anger, saying, Let us eat and drink; [13] for who is it that has gone down to Hades, and come up and announced that there is judgment and retribution?

And take heed, and see all his works which he has done standing before him.

And the evil angels came and the good.

The good therefore found no place of rest in it, but the evil took possession of it, saying:

O wretched soul, pay heed to thy flesh; take note of that whence thou art coming forth, for thou must return into thy flesh in the day of the resurrection, that thou mayst receive the recompense of thy sins.

And when it had gone forth from its tabernacle, the angel who had lived along with it ran up to it, saying to it:

O wretched soul, whither goest thou?

I am he who each day wrote down thy sins.

Thou hast destroyed the time of repentance; be exceedingly ashamed.

And when it came, all the angels saw it, and cried out with one voice, saying:

Woe to thee, wretched soul! what excuse hast thou come to give to God?

And the angel of that soul said:

Weep for it, all of you, along with me. And the angel came up, and worshipped the Lord, saying:

Lord, behold the soul which has dwelt in wickedness in its time, and in its temporary life; do to it according to Thy decision.

And there came a voice to that soul, saying:

Where is the fruit of thy righteousness? And it was silent, [14] not being able to give an answer.

And again there came a voice to it:

He who has shown mercy will have mercy shown to him; [15] he who has not shown mercy will not have mercy shown to him.

Let this soul be delivered to the merciless angel Temeluch, and let it be cast into outer darkness, where there is weeping and gnashing of teeth.

And there was a voice as of tens of thousands, saying: Righteous art Thou, O Lord, and righteous is Thy judgment. [16]And moreover I saw, and, behold, another soul was led by an angel; and it wept, saying:

Have mercy upon me, O righteous Judge, and deliver me from the hand of this angel, because he is dreadful and merciless.

And a voice came to it, saying:

Thou wast altogether merciless, and for this reason thou hast been delivered up to such an angel.

Confess thy sins which thou hast done in the world.

And that soul said:

I have not sinned, O righteous Judge.

And the Lord said to that soul:

Verily thou seemest as if thou wert in the world, and wert hiding thy deeds from men.

Knowest thou not that whensoever any one dies, his deeds run before him, whether they are good or evil?

And when it heard this, it was silent.

And I heard the Judge saying:

Let the angel come, having in his hands the record of thy sins.

And the Judge says to the angel: I say to thee the angel, Disclose all.

Say what he has done five years before his death.

By myself I swear to thee, that in the first period of his life there was forgetfulness of all his former sins.

And the angel answered and said:

Lord, command the souls to stand beside their angels; and that same hour they stood beside them.

And the lord of that soul said:

Take note of these souls, and whether thou hast in any way sinned against them.

And it answered and said:

Lord, a year has not been completed since I killed the one and lived with the other. And not only this, but I also wronged it.

And the Lord said to it: Knowest thou not that he who wrongs any one in the world is kept, as soon as he dies, in the place until he whom he has wronged come, and both shall be judged before me, and each receive according to his works?

And I heard a voice saying:

Let this soul be delivered to the angel Tartaruch, and guarded till the great day of judgment.

And I heard a voice as of tens of thousands saying:

Righteous art Thou, O Lord, and righteous Thy judgment.

And the angel says to me:

Hast thou seen all these things?

And I answered:

Yes my lord.

And again he said to me:

Come, follow me, and I shall show thee the place of the righteous.

And I followed him, and he set me before the doors of the city.

And I saw a golden gate, and two golden pillars before it, and two golden plates upon it full of inscriptions.

And the angel said to me:

Blessed is he who shall enter into these doors; because not every one goeth in, but only those who have single-mindedness, and guiltlessness, and a pure heart. [17] And I asked the angel:

For what purpose have the inscriptions been graven on these plates?

And he said to me:

These are the names of the righteous, and of those who serve God.

And I said to him:

Is it so that their names have been inscribed in heaven itself while they are yet alive?

And the angel said to me:... [18] of the angels, such as serve Him well are acknowledged by God.

And straightway the gate was opened, and there came forth a hoary-headed man to meet us; and he said to me:

Welcome, Paul, beloved of God! and, with a joyful countenance, he kissed me with tears.

And I said to him:

Father, why weepest thou?

And he said to me:

Because God hath prepared many good things for men, and they do not His will in order that they may enjoy them. And I asked the angel:

My lord, who is this?

And he said to me:

This is Enoch, the witness of the last day. [19] And the angel says to me:

See that whatever I show thee in this place thou do not announce, except what I tell thee.

And he set me upon [20] the river whose source springs up in the circle of heaven; and it is this river which encircleth the whole earth.

And he says to me:

This river is Ocean. And there was then a great light.

And I said:

My lord, what is this? And he said to me:

This is the land of the meek.

Knowest thou not that it is written, Blessed are the meek, for they shall inherit the earth? [21] The souls of the righteous, therefore, are kept in this place.

And I said to the angel:

When, then, will they be made manifest?

And he said to me:

When the Judge shall come in the day of the resurrection, and sit down.

Then, accordingly, shall he command, and shall reveal the earth, and it shall be lighted up; and the saints shall appear in it, and shall delight themselves in the good [22] that have been reserved from the foundation of the world.

And there were by the bank of the river, trees planted, full of different fruits.

And I looked towards the rising of the sun, and I saw there trees of great size full of fruits; and that land was more brilliant than silver and gold; and there were vines growing on those date-palms, and myriads of shoots, and myriads of clusters on each branch.

And I said to the archangel:

What is this, my lord?

And he says to me: This is the Acherusian lake, and within it the city of God.

All are not permitted to enter into it, except whosoever shall repent of his sins; and as soon as he shall repent, and alter his life, he is delivered to Michael, and they cast him into the Acherusian lake, and then he brings him in the city of God, near the righteous.

And I wondered and blessed God at all that I saw.

And the angel said to me: Follow me, that I may bring thee into the city of God, and into its light.

And its light was greater than the light of the world, and greater than gold, and walls encircled it.

And the length and the breadth of it were a hundred stadia.

And I saw twelve gates, exceedingly ornamented, leading into the city; and four rivers encircled it, flowing with milk, and honey, and oil, and wine.

And I said to the angel:

My lord, what are these rivers?

And he said to me:

These are the righteous who, when in the world, did not make use of these things, but humbled themselves for the sake of God; and here they receive a recompense ten thousand fold.

And I, going into the city, saw a very lofty tree before the doors of the city, having no fruit, and a few men under it; and they wept exceedingly, and the trees bent down to them.

And I, seeing them, wept, and asked the angel:

Who are these, that they have not turned to go into the city?

And he said to me:

Yes, the root of all evils is vainglory.

And I said:

And these trees, why have they thus humbled themselves?

And the angel answered and said to me:

For this reason the trees are not fruit-bearing, because they have not withheld themselves from vaunting.

And I asked the angel:

My lord, for what reason have they been put aside before the doors of the city?

And he answered and said to me:

On account of the great goodness of God, since by this way Christ is going to come into the city, and that those who go along with Him may plead for these men, and that they may be brought in along with them.

And I was going along, guided by the angel, and he set me upon the river.

And I saw there all the prophets; and they came and saluted me, saying:

Welcome, Paul, beloved of God. And I said to the angel:

My lord, who are these?

And he said to me: These are all the prophets, and these are the songs of all the prophecies, [23] and of whoever hath grieved his soul, not doing its will, for God's sake.

Having departed, then, he comes here, and the prophets salute him.

And the angel brought me to the south of the city, where the river of milk is.

And I saw there all the infants that King Herod slew for the Lord's name's sake.

And the angel took me again to the east of the city, and I saw there Abraham, Isaac, Jacob. And I asked the angel:

My lord, what place is this?

And he said to me:

Every one who is hospitable to men comes hither when he comes out of the world, and they salute him as a friend of God on account of his love to strangers.

And again he took me away to another place, and I saw there a river like oil on the north of the city, and I saw people there rejoicing and singing praises.

And I asked:

Who are these, my lord?

And he said to me:

These are they who have given themselves up to God; for they are brought into this city.

The Forgotten Bible

And I looked, and saw in the midst of the city an altar, great and very lofty; and there was one standing near the altar, whose face shone like the sun, and he had in his hands a psaltery and a harp, and he sung the Alleluia delightfully, and his voice filled all the city.

And all with one consent accompanied him, so that the city was shaken by their shouting.

And I asked the angel:

Who is this that singeth delightfully, whom all accompany?

And he said to me:

This is the prophet David; this is the heavenly Jerusalem.

When, therefore, Christ shall come in His second appearing, David himself goes forth with all the saints.

For as it is in the heavens, so also upon earth:

for it is not permitted without David to offer sacrifice even in the day of the sacrifice of the precious body and blood of Christ; but it is necessary for David to sing the Alleluia.

And I asked the angel:

My lord, what is the meaning of Alleluia?

It is called in Hebrew, thebel, marematha--speech to God who founded all things:

let us glorify Him in the same.

So that every one who sings the Alleluia glorifies God.

When these things, therefore, had been thus said to me by the angel, he led me outside of the city, and the Acherusian lake, and the good land, and set me upon the river of the ocean that supports the firmament of the heaven, and said to me:

Knowest thou where I am going?

And I said:

No, my lord.

And he said to me:

Follow me, that I may show thee where the souls of the impious and the sinners are.

And he took me to the setting of the sun, and where the beginning of the heaven had been founded upon the river of the ocean.

And I saw beyond the river, and there was no light there, but darkness, and grief, and groaning; and I saw a bubbling river, and a great multitude both of men and women who had been cast into it, some up to the knees, others up to the navel, and many even up to the crown of the head.

And I asked:

Who are these?

And he said to me:

These are they who lived unrepenting in fornications and adulteries.

And I saw at the south-west of the river another river, where there flowed a river of fire, and there was there a multitude of many souls.

And I asked the angel:

Who are these, my lord?

And he said to me:

These are the thieves, and slanderers, and flatterers, who did not set up God as their help, but hoped in the vanity of their riches.

And I said to him:

What is the depth of this river?

And he said to me:

Its depth has no measure, but it is immeasurable.

And I groaned and wept because of mankind.

And the angel said to me:

Why weepest thou?

Art thou more merciful than God? for, being holy, God, repenting over men, waits for their conversion and repentance; but they, deceived by their own will, come here, and are eternally punished.

And I looked into the fiery river, and saw an old man dragged along by two, and they pulled him in up to the knee. And the angel Temeluch coming, laid hold of an iron with his hand, and with it drew up the entrails of that old man through his mouth.

And I asked the angel:

My lord, who is this that suffers this punishment? And he said to me:

This old man whom thou seest was a presbyter; and when he had eaten and drunk, then he performed the service of God.

And I saw there another old man carried in haste by four angels; and they threw him into the fiery river up to the girdle, and he was frightfully burnt by the lightnings.

And I said to the angel:
Who is this, my lord?
And he said to me:
This whom thou seest was a bishop, and that name indeed he was well pleased to have; but in the goodness of God he did not walk, righteous judgment he did not judge, the widow and the orphan he did not pity, he was neither affectionate nor hospitable; [24] but now he has been recompensed according to his works.

And I looked, and saw in the middle of the river another man up to the navel, having his hands all bloody, and worms were coming up through his mouth.

And I asked the angel:
Who is this, my lord?
And he said to me:
This whom thou seest was a deacon, who ate and drank, and ministered to God.

And I looked to another place where there was a brazen wall in flames, and within it men and women eating up their own tongues, dreadfully judged.

And I asked the angel:
Who are these, my lord?
And he said to me:
These are they who in the church speak against their neighbours, and do not attend to the word of God.

And I looked, and saw a bloody pit.
And I said:
What is this pit?
And he said to me:
This is the place where are cast the wizards, and sorcerers, and the whoremongers, and the adulterers, and those that oppress widows and orphans.

And I saw in another place women wearing black, and led away into a dark place.
And I asked:
Who are these, my lord?
And he said to me:
These are they who did not listen to their parents, but before their marriage defiled their virginity.

And I saw women wearing white robes, being blind, and standing upon obelisks of fire; and an angel was mercilessly beating them, saying:
Now you know where you are; you did not attend when the Scriptures were read to you.
And the angel said to me:
These are they who corrupted themselves and killed their infants.
Their infants therefore came crying out:
Avenge us of our mothers.
And they were given to an angel to be carried away into a spacious place, but their parents into everlasting fire.

And the angel took me up from these torments, and set me above a well, which had seven seals upon its mouth.

And the angel who was with me said to the angel at the well of that place:
Open the well, that Paul the beloved of God may see, because there has been given to him authority to see the torments.

And the angel of the place said to me: Stand afar off, until I open the seals.

And when he had opened them, there came forth a stench which it was impossible to bear.

And having come near the place, I saw that well filled with darkness and gloom, and great narrowness of space in it.

And the angel who was with me said to me:
This place of the well which thou seest is cast off from the glory of God, and none of the angels is importunate in behalf of them; and as many as have professed that the holy Mary is not the mother of God, and that the Lord did not become man out of her, and that the bread of the thanksgiving and the cup of blessing are not His flesh and blood, [25] are cast into this well:
and as I said before no angel is importunate in their behalf.

And I saw towards the setting of the sun, where there is weeping and gnashing of teeth, many men and women there tormented.

And I said to the angel:
Who are these, my lord?
And he said to me:
These are they who say that there is no resurrection of the dead; and to them mercy never

comes.

Having heard this, I wept bitterly; and looking up into the firmament, I saw the heaven opened, and the archangel Gabriel coming down with hosts of angels, who were going round about all the torments.

And they who were judged in the torments seeing them, all cried out with one loud voice:

Have mercy upon us, Gabriel, who standest in the presence of God; for we heard that there was a judgment:

behold, we know it. And the archangel Gabriel answered and said:

As the Lord liveth, beside whom I stand, night and day without ceasing I plead in behalf of the race of men; but they did not do any good when in life, but spent the period of their life in vanity.

And now I shall weep, even I, along with the beloved Paul; perhaps the good Lord may have compassion, and grant you remission.

And they assented with one voice:

Have mercy upon us, O Lord.

And they fell down before God, and supplicated, saying:

Have mercy, O Lord, upon the sons of men whom Thou hast made after Thine image.

And the heaven was shaken like a leaf, and I saw the four and twenty elders lying on their face; and I saw the altar, and the throne, and the veil; and all of them entreated the glory of God; [26] and I saw the Son of God with glory and great power coming down to the earth. [27] And when the sound of the trumpet took place, all who were in the torments cried out, saying:

Have mercy upon us Son of God; for to Thee has been given power over things in heaven, and things on earth, and things under the earth.

And there came a voice saying:

What good work have you done, that you are asking for rest?

For you have done as you wished, and have not repented, but you have spent your life in profligacy.

But now for the sake of Gabriel, the angel of my righteousness and for the sake of Paul my beloved, I give you a night and the day of the holy Lord's day, on which I rose from the dead, for rest.

And all who were in the torments cried out, saying:

We bless Thee, O Son of the living God; better for us is such rest than the life which we lived when spending our time in the world.

And after these things the angel says to me:

Behold, thou hast seen all the torments:

come, follow me, that I may lead thee away to paradise, and that thou mayst change thy soul by the sight of the righteous; for many desire to salute thee.

And he took me by an impulse of the Spirit, and brought me into paradise.

And he says to me:

This is paradise, where Adam and Eve transgressed.

And I saw there a beautiful tree of great size, on which the Holy Spirit rested; and from the root of it there came forth all manner of most sweet-smelling water, parting into four channels.

And I said to the angel:

My lord, what is this tree, that there comes forth from it a great abundance of this water, and where does it go?

And he answered and said to me:

Before the heaven and the earth existed, He divided them into four kingdoms and heads, of which the names are Phison, Gehon, Tigris, Euphrates.

And having again taken hold of me by the hand, he led me near the tree of the knowledge of good and evil.

And he says to me:

This is the tree by means of which death came into the world, and Adam took of the fruit of it from his wife, and ate; and thereafter they were cast out hence.

And he showed me another, the tree of life, and said to me:

This the cherubim and the flaming sword guard.

And when I was closely observing the tree, and wondering, I saw a woman coming from afar off, and a multitude of angels singing praises to her.

And I asked the angel:

Who is this, my lord, who is in so great honour and beauty?

And the angel says to me:

This is the holy Mary, the mother of the Lord.

And she came and saluted me, saying: Welcome, Paul, beloved of God, and angels, and men;

thou hast proclaimed the word of God in the world, and established churches, and all bear testimony to thee who have been saved by means of thee:

for, having been delivered from the deception of idols through thy teaching, they come here.

While they were yet speaking to me, I gazed, and saw other three men coming.

And I asked the angel:

Who are these, my lord?

And he said to me:

These are Abraham, Isaac, and Jacob, the righteous forefathers.

And they came and saluted me, saying:

Welcome, Paul, beloved of God....God did not grieve us.

But we know thee in the flesh, before thou camest forth out of the world.

And in succession they told me their names from Abraham to Manasseh.

And one of them, Joseph who was sold in Egypt, says to me:

Hear me, Paul, friend of God:

I did not requite my brethren who cursed me.

For blessed is he who is able to endure trial, because the Lord will give him in requital sevenfold reward in the world to come. [28] And while he was yet speaking with me, I saw another coming afar off, and the appearance of him was as the appearance of an angel.

And I asked the angel, saying: My lord, who is this?

And he said to me:

This is Moses the lawgiver, by whom God led forth the children of Israel out of the slavery of Egypt.

And when he came near me, he saluted me weeping.

And I said to him:

Father, why weepest thou, being righteous and meek? [29] And he answered and said to me:

I must weep for every man, because I brought trouble upon a people that does not understand, and they have not borne fruit; and I see the sheep of which I was shepherd scattered, and the toil which I toiled for the children of Israel has been counted for nothing; and they saw powers [30] and hosts in the midst of them, and they did not understand; and I see the Gentiles worshipping, and believing through thy word, and being converted, and coming here, and out of my people that was so great not one has understood.

For, when the Jews hanged the Son of God upon the cross, all the angels and archangels, and the righteous, and the whole creation of things in heaven, and things in earth, and things under the earth, lamented and mourned with a great lamentation, but the impious and insensate Jews did not understand; wherefore there has been prepared for them the fire everlasting, and the worm that dies not.

While he was yet speaking, there came other three, and saluted me, saying:

Welcome, Paul, beloved of God, the boast of the churches, and model of angels.

And I asked:

Who are you?

And the first said:

I am Isaiah, whom Manasseh sawed with a wood saw. [31] And the second said:

I am Jeremiah, whom the Jews stoned, but they remained burnt up with everlasting fire.

And the third said:

I am Ezekiel, whom the slayers of the Messiah pierced; all these things have we endured, and we have not been able to turn the stony heart of the Jews.

And I threw myself on my face, entreating the goodness of God, because He had had mercy upon me, and had delivered me from the race of the Hebrews.

And there came a voice saying:

Blessed art thou, Paul, beloved of God; and blessed are those who through thee have believed in the name of our Lord Jesus Christ, because for them has been prepared everlasting life.

While this voice was yet speaking, there came another, crying:

Blessed art thou, Paul.

And I asked the angel:

Who is this, my lord?

And he said to me:

This is Noah, who lived in the time of the deluge.

And when we had saluted each other, I asked him:

Who art thou?

And he said to me:

I am Noah, who in a hundred years built the ark, and without putting off the coat which I wore, or shaving my head; moreover, I practised continence, and did not come near my wife; and in the hundred years my coat was not dirtied, and the hair of my head was not diminished.

And I ceased not to proclaim to men, Repent, for, behold, a deluge is coming.

And no one paid heed; but all derided me, not refraining from their lawless deeds, until the water of the deluge came and destroyed them all.

And looking away, I saw other two from afar off.

And I asked the angel:

Who are these, my lord?

And he said to me:

These are Enoch and Elias.

And they came and saluted me, saying:

Welcome, Paul, beloved of God!

And I said to them:

Who are you?

And Elias the prophet answered and said to me:

I am Elias the prophet, who prayed to God, and He caused that no rain should come down upon the earth for three years and six months, on account of the unrighteousness of the sons of men.

For often, of a truth, even the angel besought God on account of the rain; and I heard, Be patient until Elias my beloved shall pray, and I send rain upon the earth. [32]

Footnotes:

1. 2 Cor. xii. 4.
2. The mss. have Kontianus.
3. Or, according to the primary meaning of the word, shining, sparkling. The translation of the Syriac version has, "a box of white glass."
4. Syr., Thinking that there was something of gold within it.
5. Syr., of the living God.
6. Or, sweep off it.
7. Comp. Heb. xi. 38.
8. i.e., to sinful matter--hule--the source of the soma in the Gnostic doctrine.
9. Comp. Matt. xiii. 41.
10. Or, come to God.
11. Comp. Rev. xiv. 13.
12. Or, bare rule over.
13. Isa. xxii. 13; 1 Cor. xv. 32.
14. Lit., shut up.
15. Matt. v. 7.
16. Ps. cxix. 137.
17. Comp. Ps. xxiv. 3.
18. The hiatus is thus filled up in the Syriac: Yes, not only are their names written, but their works from day to day: the angel their minister brings tidings of their works every day from morning to morning; they are known to God by their hearts and their works. And after they are recorded, if there happen to them a matter of sin or deficiency, it is purified by chastisement according to their sin, that there be not unto them any defect in their strivings.
19. Rev. xi. 3-12. Enoch and Elijah were supposed to be the two witnesses there mentioned.
20. Or, above.
21. Matt. v. 5.
22. Or, the good things.
23. Syr., This is the place of the prophets. A very slight change in the Greek text would give this reading.
24. Comp. 1 Tim. iii. 1-4.
25. The Syriac has: Those who do not confess Jesus Christ, nor His resurrection, nor His humanity, but consider Him as all mortal, and who say that the sacrament of the body of our Lord is bread. The word theotokos in the text was the occasion of the three years' struggle between Nestorius and Cyril of Alexandria, which ended by the condemnation of the former by the Council of Ephesus, a.d. 431. The view of the Eucharist in the text is not inconsistent with an early date, though it must be remembered that the idea of a substantial presence became the orthodox doctrine only after the Second Council of Nicaea in a.d. 787.
26. Rev. iv. 4.
27. Matt. xxiv. 30.
28. Comp. Matt. xix. 29.
29. Num. xii. 3.
30. Or, miracles.

31. For this tradition, see the Bible Dictionaries under Manasseh. Comp. Heb. xi. 37.

32. Here the [Greek]ms. abruptly ends. The Syriac thus continues:--And He gave not until I called upon Him again; then He gave unto them. But blessed art thou, O Paul, that thy generation and those thou teachest are the sons of the kingdom. And know thou, O Paul, that every man who believes through thee hath a great blessing, and a blessing is reserved for him. Then he departed from me. And the angel who was with me led me forth, and said unto me: Lo, unto thee is given this mystery and revelation. As thou pleasest, make it known unto the sons of men.--And then follow details of the depositing of the revelation under the foundation of the house in Tarsus,--details which Tischendorf says the translator of the Syriac did not find in his original. [The close of the English translation of the Syriac version is given in full by Tischendorf (pp. 68, 69). It varies greatly from the above paragraph in the text, besides the addition of the details which Tischendorf regards as spurious.--R.]

Revelation of John

Revelation of Saint John the Theologian.

After the taking up of our Lord Jesus Christ, I John was alone upon Mount Tabor, [1] where also He showed us His undefiled Godhead; and as I was not able to stand, I fell upon the ground, and prayed to the Lord, and said:

O Lord my God, who hast deemed me worthy to be Thy servant, hear my voice, and teach me about Thy coming.

When Thou shalt come to the earth, what will happen?

The heaven and the earth, and the sun and the moon, what will happen to them in those times? Reveal to me all; for I am emboldened, because Thou listenest to Thy servant.

And I spent seven days praying; and after this a cloud of light caught me up from the mountain, and set me before the face of the heaven.

And I heard a voice saying to me:

Look up, John, servant of God, and know.

And having looked up, I saw the heaven opened, and there came forth from within the heaven a smell of perfumes of much sweet odour; and I saw an exceeding great flood of light, more resplendent than the sun.

And again I heard a voice saying to me:

Behold, righteous John. And I directed my sight, and saw a book lying, of the thickness, methought, of seven mountains; [2] and the length of it the mind of man cannot comprehend, having seven seals.

And I said:

O Lord my God, reveal to me what is written in this book.

And I heard a voice saying to me:

Hear, righteous John.

In this book which thou seest there have been written the things in the heaven, and the things in the earth, and the things in the abyss, and the judgments and righteousness of all the human race. [3]And I said:

Lord, when shall these things come to pass? and what do those times bring?

And I heard a voice saying to me:

Hear, righteous John. [4]There shall be in that time abundance of corn and wine, such as there hath never been upon the earth, nor shall ever be until those times come.

Then the ear of corn shall produce a half choenix, [5] and the bend of the branch shall produce a thousand clusters, and the cluster shall produce a half jar of wine; and in the following year there shall not be found upon the face of all the earth a half choenix of corn or a half jar of wine.

And again I said:

Lord, thereafter what wilt Thou do?

And I heard a voice saying to me:

Hear, righteous John.

Then shall appear the denier, and he who is set apart in the darkness, who is called Antichrist. And again I said:

Lord, reveal to me what he is like. And I heard a voice saying to me:

The appearance of his face is dusky; [6] the hairs of his head are sharp, like darts; his eyebrows like a wild beast's; his right eye like the star which rises in the morning, and the other like a lion's; his mouth about one cubit; his teeth span long; his fingers like scythes; the print of his feet of two spans; and on his face an inscription, Antichrist; he shall be exalted even to heaven, and shall be cast down even to Hades, making false displays. [7]And then will I make the heaven brazen, so that it shall not give moisture [8] upon the earth; and I will hide the clouds in secret places, so that they shall not bring moisture upon the earth; and I will command the horns of the wind, so that the wind shall not blow upon the earth. [9]

And again I said:

Lord, and how many years will he do this upon the earth?

And I heard a voice saying to me:

Hear, righteous John.

Three years shall those times be; and I will make the three years like three months, and the three months like three weeks, and the three weeks like three days, and the three days like three hours, and the three hours like three seconds, as said the prophet David, His throne hast Thou broken down to the ground; Thou hast shortened the days of his time; Thou hast poured shame upon him. [10]And then I shall send forth Enoch and Elias to convict him; and they shall show him to be a liar and a deceiver; and he shall kill them at the altar, as said the prophet, Then shall they offer calves upon Thine altar. [11]

And again I said:

Lord, and after that what will come to pass?

And I heard a voice saying to me:

Hear, righteous John.

Then all the human race shall die, and there shall not be a living man upon all the earth.

And again I said:

Lord, after that what wilt Thou do?

And I heard a voice saying to me:

Hear, righteous John.

Then will I send forth mine angels, and they shall take the ram's horns that lie upon the cloud; and Michael and Gabriel shall go forth out of the heaven and sound with those horns, as the prophet David foretold, With the voice of a trumpet of horn. [12]And the voice of the trumpet shall be heard from the one quarter of the world to the other; [13] and from the voice of that trumpet all the earth shall be shaken, as the prophet foretold, And at the voice of the bird every plant shall arise; [14] that is, at the voice of the archangel all the human race shall arise. [15]

And again I said:

Lord, those who are dead from Adam even to this day, and who dwell in Hades from the beginning of the world, and who die at the last ages, what like shall they arise?

And I heard a voice saying to me:

Hear, righteous John.

All the human race shall arise thirty years old.

And again I said:

Lord, they die male and female, and some old, and some young, and some infants.

In the resurrection what like shall they arise?

And I heard a voice saying to me:

Hear, righteous John.

Just as the bees are, and differ not one from another, but are all of one appearance and one size, so also shall every man be in the resurrection.

There is neither fair, nor ruddy, nor black, neither Ethiopian nor different countenances; but they shall all arise of one appearance and one stature.

All the human race shall arise without bodies, as I told you that in the resurrection they neither marry nor are given in marriage, but are as the angels of God. [16]

And again I said:

Lord, is it possible in that world to recognise each other, a brother his brother, or a friend his friend, or a father his own children, or the children their own parents?

And I heard a voice saying to me:

Hear, John.

To the righteous there is recognition, but to the sinners not at all; they cannot in the resurrection recognise each other.

And again I John said:

Lord, is there there recollection of the things that are here, either fields or vineyards, or other things here?

And I heard a voice saying to me:

Hear, righteous John. The prophet David speaks, saying, I remembered that we are dust:

as for man, his days are as grass; as a flower of the field, so he shall flourish:

for a wind hath passed over it, and it shall be no more, and it shall not any longer know its place. [17]And again the same said:

His spirit [18] shall go forth, and he returns to his earth; in that day all his thoughts shall perish. [19]

And again I said:

Lord, and after that what wilt Thou do?

And I heard a voice saying to me:

Hear, righteous John.

Then will I send forth mine angels over the face of all the earth, and they shall lift off the earth everything honourable, and everything precious, and the venerable and holy images, and the glorious and precious crosses, and the sacred vessels of the churches, and the divine and sacred books; and all the precious and holy things shall be lifted up by clouds into the air. And then will I order to be lifted up the great and venerable sceptre, [20] on which I stretched forth my hands, and all the orders of my angels shall do reverence to it.

And then shall be lifted up all the race of men upon clouds, as the Apostle Paul foretold. [21]Along with them we shall be snatched up in[22] clouds to meet the Lord in the air.

And then shall come forth every evil spirit, both in the earth and in the abyss, wherever they are on the face of all the earth, from the rising of the sun even to the setting, and they shall be united to him that is served by the devil, that is, Antichrist, and they shall be lifted up upon the clouds.

And again I said:

Lord, and after that what wilt Thou do?

And I heard a voice saying to me:

Hear, righteous John.

Then shall I send forth mine angels over the face of all the earth, and they shall burn up the earth eight thousand five hundred [23] cubits, and the great mountains shall be burnt up, and all the rocks shall be melted and shall become as dust, and every tree shall be burnt up, and every beast, and every creeping thing creeping upon the earth, and every thing moving upon the face of the earth, and every flying thing flying in the air; and there shall no longer be upon the face of all the earth anything moving, and the earth shall be without motion.

And again I said:

Lord, and after that what wilt Thou do?

And I heard a voice saying to me:

Hear, righteous John.

Then shall I uncover the four parts of the east, and there shall come forth four great winds, and they shall sweep [24] all the face of the earth from the one end of the earth to the other; and the Lord shall sweep sin from off the earth, and the earth shall be made white like snow, and it shall become as a leaf of paper, without cave, or mountain, or hill, or rock; but the face of the earth from the rising even to the setting of the sun shall be like a table, and white as snow; and the reins of the earth shall be consumed by fire, and it shall cry unto me, saying, I am a virgin before thee, O Lord, and there is no sin in me; as the prophet David said aforetime, Thou shalt sprinkle me with hyssop, and I shall be made pure; Thou shalt wash me, and I shall be made whiter than snow. [25]And again he [26] said:

Every chasm shall be filled up, and every mountain and hill brought low, and the crooked places shall be made straight, and the rough ways into smooth; and all flesh shall see the salvation of God. [27]

And again I said:

Lord, and after that what wilt Thou do?

And I heard a voice saying to me:

Hear, righteous John.

Then shall the earth be cleansed from sin, and all the earth shall be filled with a sweet smell, because I am about to come down upon the earth; and then shall come forth the great and venerable sceptre, with thousands of angels worshipping it, as I said before; and then shall appear the sign of the Son of man from the heaven with power and great glory.[28]And then the worker of iniquity with his servants shall behold it, and gnash his teeth exceedingly, and all the unclean spirits shall be turned to flight.

And then, seized by invisible power, having no means of flight, they shall gnash their teeth against him, saying to him: Where is thy power?

How hast thou led us astray? and we have fled away, and have fallen away from the glory which we had beside Him who is coming to judge us, and the whole human race.

Woe to us! because He banishes us into outer darkness.

And again I said:

Lord, and after that what wilt Thou do?

And I heard a voice saying to me:

Then will I send an angel out of heaven, and he shall cry with a loud voice, saying, Hear, O earth, and be strong, saith the Lord; for I am coming down to thee.

And the voice of the angel shall be heard from the one end of the world even to the other, and even to the remotest part of the abyss.

And then shall be shaken all the power of the angels and of the many-eyed ones, and there shall be a great noise in the heavens, and the nine regions of the heaven shall be shaken, and there shall be fear and astonishment upon all the angels.

And then the heavens shall be rent from the rising of the sun even to the setting, and an innumerable multitude of angels shall come down to the earth; and then the treasures of the heavens shall be opened, and they shall bring down every precious thing, and the perfume of incense, and they shall bring down to the earth Jerusalem robed like a bride. [29] And then there shall go before me myriads of angels and archangels, bearing my throne, crying out, Holy, holy, holy, Lord of Sabaoth; heaven and earth are full of Thy glory. [30] And then will I come forth with power and great glory, and every eye in [31] the clouds shall see me; and then every knee shall bend, of things in heaven, and things on earth, and things under the earth. [32] And then the heaven shall remain empty; and I will come down upon the earth, and all that is in the air shall be brought down upon the earth, and all the human race and every evil spirit along with Antichrist, and they shall all be set before me naked, and chained by the neck.

And again I said:

Lord, what will become of the heavens, and the sun, and the moon, along with the stars?

And I heard a voice saying to me: Behold, righteous John.

And I looked, and saw a Lamb having seven eyes and seven horns.[33] And again I heard a voice saying to me:

I will bid the Lamb come before me, and will say, Who will open this book?

And all the multitudes of the angels will answer, Give this book to the Lamb to open it.

And then will I order the book to be opened. And when He shall open the first seal, the stars of the heaven shall fall, from the one end of it to the other.

And when He shall open the second seal, the moon shall be hidden, and there shall be no light in her.

And when He shall open the third seal, the light of the sun shall be withheld, and there shall not be light upon the earth.

And when He shall open the fourth seal, the heavens shall be dissolved, and the air shall be thrown into utter confusion, as saith the prophet:

And the heavens are the works of Thy hands; they shall perish, but Thou endurest, and they shall all wax old as a garment. [34] And when He shall open the fifth seal, the earth shall be rent, and all the tribunals upon the face of all the earth shall be revealed.

And when He shall open the sixth seal, the half of the sea shall disappear.

And when He shall open the seventh seal, Hades shall be uncovered.

And I said:

Lord, who will be the first to be questioned, and to receive judgment?

And I heard a voice saying to me, The unclean spirits, along with the adversary.

I bid them go into outer darkness, where the depths [35] are.

And I said:

Lord, and in what place does it lie?

And I heard a voice saying to me:

Hear, righteous John.

As big a stone as a man of thirty years old can roll, and let go down into the depth, even falling down for twenty years will not arrive at the bottom of Hades; as the prophet David said before, And He made darkness His secret place. [36]

And I said:

Lord, and after them what nation [37] will be questioned?

And I heard a voice saying to me:

Hear, righteous John. There will be questioned of Adam's race those nations, both the Greek and those who have believed in idols, and in the sun, and in the stars, and those who have defiled the faith by heresy, and who have not believed the holy [38] resurrection, and who have not confessed the Father, and the Son, and the Holy Ghost:

then will I send them away into Hades, as the prophet David foretold, Let the sinners be turned into Hades, and all the nations that forget God. [39] And again he said:

They were put in Hades like sheep; death shall be their shepherd.[40]

And again I said:

Lord, and after them whom wilt Thou judge?

And I heard a voice saying to me:

Hear, righteous John.

Then the race of the Hebrews shall be examined, who nailed me to the tree like a malefactor.

And I said:

And what punishment will these get, and in what place, seeing that they did such things to Thee?

And I heard a voice saying to me:

They shall go away into Tartarus, as the prophet David foretold, They cried out, and there was none to save; to the Lord, and He did not hearken to them. [41]And again the Apostle Paul said:

As many as have sinned without law shall also perish without law, and as many as have sinned in law shall be judged by means of law. [42]

And again I said:

Lord, and what of those who have received baptism? And I heard a voice saying to me:

Then the race of the Christians shall be examined, who have received baptism; and then the righteous shall come at my command, and the angels shall go and collect [43] them from among the sinners, as the prophet David foretold:

The Lord will not suffer the rod of the sinners in the lot of the righteous; [44] and all the righteous shall be placed on my right hand, [45] and shall shine like the sun. [46]As thou seest, John, the stars of heaven, that they were all made together, but differ in light, [47] so shall it be with the righteous and the sinners; for the righteous shall shine as lights and as the sun, but the sinners shall stand in darkness.

And again I said:

Lord, and do all the Christians go into one punishment?--kings, high priests, priests, patriarchs, rich and poor, bond and free?

And I heard a voice saying to me:

Hear, righteous John.

As the prophet David foretold, The expectation of the poor shall not perish for ever. [48]Now about kings:

they shall be driven like slaves, and shall weep like infants; and about patriarchs, and priests, and Levites, of those that have sinned, they shall be separated in their punishments, according to the nature [49] of the peculiar transgression of each,--some in the river of fire, and some to the worm that dieth not, and others in the seven-mouthed pit of punishment.

To these punishments the sinners will be apportioned.

And again I said:

Lord, and where will the righteous dwell?

And I heard a voice saying to me:

Then shall paradise be revealed; and the whole world and paradise shall be made one, and the righteous shall be on the face of all the earth with my angels, as the Holy Spirit foretold through the prophet David:

The righteous shall inherit the earth, and dwell therein for ever and ever. [50]

And again I said:

Lord, how great is the multitude of the angels? and which is the greater, that of angels or of men?

And I heard a voice saying to me:

As great as is the multitude of the angels, so great is the race of men, as the prophet has said, He set bounds to the nations according to the number of the angels of God. [51]

And again I said:

Lord, and after that what wilt Thou do? and what is to become of the world?

Reveal to me all.

And I heard a voice saying to me:

Hear, righteous John.

After that there is no pain, there is no grief, there is no groaning; there is no recollection of evils, there are no tears, there is no envy, there is no hatred of brethren, there is no unrighteousness, there is no arrogance, there is no slander, there is no bitterness, there are none of the cares of life, there is no pain from parents or children, there is no pain from gold, there are no wicked thoughts, there is no devil, there is no death, there is no night, but all is day. [52]As I said before, And other sheep I have, which are not of this fold, that is, men who have been made like the angels through their excellent course of life; them also must I bring, and they will hear my voice, and there shall be one fold, one shepherd. [53]

And again I heard a voice saying to me:

Behold, thou hast heard all these things, righteous John; deliver them to faithful men, that they also may teach others, and not think lightly of them, [54] nor cast our pearls before swine, lest perchance they should trample them with their feet. [55]

And while I was still hearing this voice, the cloud brought me down, and put me on Mount Thabor.

And there came a voice to me, saying: Blessed are those who keep judgment and do righteousness in all time. [56]And blessed is the house where this description lies, as the Lord said, He that loveth me keepeth my sayings [57] in Christ Jesus our Lord; to Him be glory for ever.

Amen. [58]

Footnotes:

1. For the history of the tradition that the transfiguration occurred on Mount Tabor, see Robinson's Researches, ii. 358.
2. One ms. has: 700 cubits.
3. ms. B adds: And they shall be manifested at the consummation of the age, in the judgment to come. Just as the prophet Daniel saw the judgment, I sat, and the books were opened. Then also shall the twelve apostles sit, judging the twelve tribes of Israel. And when I heard this from my Lord, I again asked: Show me, my Lord, when these things shall come to pass, etc. [B is the designation of a Paris manuscript dated 1523. All the manuscripts are comparatively recent; see Tischendorf, pp. xviii., xix.--R.]
4. ms. B. here inserts Luke xxi. 11.
5. The choenix of corn was a man's daily allowance. It was equal to two points according to some, a pint and a half according to others.
6. Or, gloomy.
7. ms. B. adds: And he will love most of all the nation of the Hebrews; and the righteous shall hide themselves, and flee to mountains and caves. And he shall take vengeance on many of the righteous; and blessed is he who shall not believe in him.
8. Or, dew.
9. To the description of Antichrist, ms. E adds: He holds in his hand a cup of death; and all that worship him drink of it. His right eye is like the morning star, and his left like a lion's; because he was taken prisoner by the archangel Michael, and he took his godhead from him. And I was sent from the bosom of my Father, and I drew up the head of the polluted one, and his eye was consumed. And when they worship him, he writes on their right hands, that they may sit with him in the outer fire; and for all who have not been baptized, and have not believed, have been reserved all anger and wrath. And I said: My Lord, and what miracles does he do? Hear, righteous John: He shall remove mountains and hills, and he shall beckon with his polluted hand, Come all to me; and through his displays and deceits they will be brought together to his own place. He will raise the dead, and show in everything like God. [E is one of the Venice manuscripts.--R.]
10. Ps. lxxxix. 44, 45.
11. Ps. li. 19.
12. Ps. xcviii. 6 according to the LXX.
13. Lit., from quarters even to quarters of the world.
14. Adapted from Eccles. xii. 4.
15. To this sectionms. E adds many details: They that have gold and silver shall throw them into the streets, and into every place in the world, and no one will heed them. They shall throw into the streets ivory vessels, and robes adorned with stones and pearls; kings and rulers wasting away with hunger, patriarchs and governors (or abbots), elders and peoples. Where is the fine wine, and the tables, and the pomp of the world? They shall not be found in all the world; and men shall die in the mountains and in the streets, and in every place of the world. And the living shall die from the stink of the dead, etc. Whosoever shall not worship the beast and his pomp shall be called a witness (or martyr) in the kingdom of heaven, and shall inherit eternal life with my holy ones.
16. Comp. Matt. xxii. 30, and parallel passages.
17. Ps. ciii. 14-16 according to LXX.
18. Or, breath.
19. Ps. cxlvi. 4 according to LXX.
20. Another reading is cross.
21. 1 Thess. iv. 17.
22. Or, by.
23. Two mss. have this number; the other four have 500, 1800, 30, 60-100ths.
24. Or, winnow.
25. Ps. li. 7.
26. ms. D has: Again another prophet has said. [D is another Paris manuscript of the fifteenth century.--R.]
27. Isa. xl. 4.
28. Comp. Matt. xxiv. 30.
29. Rev. xxi. 2.
30. Comp. Isa. vi. 3.
31. Or, upon.
32. Phil. ii. 10.
33. Rev. v. 6.
34. Ps. cii. 26.
35. Or, regions sunk in water.

36. Ps. xviii. 11.
37. Lit., tongue.
38. ms. D inserts, Trinity and.
39. Ps. ix. 17.
40. Ps. xlix. 14.
41. Ps. xviii. 41.
42. Rom. ii. 12.
43. Lit., heap up.
44. Ps. cxxv. 3.
45. Matt. xxv. 33.
46. Matt. xiii. 43.
47. 1 Cor. xv. 41.
48. Ps. ix. 18.
49. Lit., proportion or analogy.
50. Ps. xxxvii. 29.
51. Deut. xxxii. 8 according to the LXX.
52. Rev. vii. 17, xxi. 4.
53. John x. 16. [The correct text of John x. 16 is: "one flock, one shepherd," but it was altered quite early.--R.]
54. i.e., the things heard.
55. Matt. vii. 6.
56. Ps. cvi. 3.
57. John xiv. 23.
58. As a specimen of the eschatology of these documents, Tischendorf gives the following extracts from the termination of ms. E:-- Hear, righteous John:

All these shall be assembled, and they shall be in the pit of lamentation:

and I shall set my throne in the place, and shall sit with the twelve apostles and the four and twenty elders, and thou thyself an elder on account of thy blameless life; and to finish three services thou shalt receive a white robe and an unfading crown from the hand of the Lord, and thou shalt sit with the four and twenty elders, etc.

And after this the angels shall come forth, having a golden censer and shining lamps; and they shall gather together on the Lord's right hand those who have lived well, and done His will, and He shall make them to dwell for ever and ever in light and joy, and they shall obtain life everlasting.

And when He shall separate the sheep from the goats, that is, the righteous from the sinners, the righteous on the right, and the sinners on the left; then shall He send the angel Raguel, saying:

Go and sound the trumpet for the angels of cold and snow and ice, and bring together every kind of wrath upon those that stand on the left.

Because I will not pardon them when they see the glory of God, the impious and unrepentant, and the priests who did not what was commanded.

You who have tears, weep for the sinners.

And Temeluch shall call out to Taruch:

Open the punishments, thou keeper of the keys; open the judgments; open the worm that dieth not, and the wicked dragon; make ready Hades; open the darkness; let loose the fiery river, and the frightful darkness in the depths of Hades.

Then the pitiful sinners, seeing their works, and having no consolation, shall go down weeping into streams as it were of blood.

And there is none to pity them, neither father to help, nor mother to compassionate, but rather the angels going against them, and saying:

Ye poor wretches, why are you weeping?

In the world you had no compassion on the weak, you did not help them.

And these go away into everlasting punishment. There you will not be able to bear the sight of Him who was born of the virgin; you lived unrepenting in the world, and you will get no pity, but everlasting punishment.

And Temeluch says to Taruch:

Rouse up the fat three-headed serpent; sound the trumpet for the frightful wild beasts to gather them together to feed upon them (i.e., the sinners); to open the twelve plagues, that all the creeping things may be brought together against the impious and unrepenting.

And Temeluch will gather together the multitude of the sinners, and will kick the earth; and the earth will be split up in diverse places, and the sinners will be melted in frightful punishments.

Then shall God send Michael, the leader of His hosts; and having sealed the place, Temeluch shall strike them with the previous cross, and the earth shall be brought together as before.

Then their angels lamented exceedingly, then the all-holy Virgin and all the saints wept for

them, and they shall do them no good.
    And John says:
    Why are the sinners thus punished?
    And I heard a voice saying to me:
    They walked in the world each other after his own will, and therefore are they thus punished.
Blessed is the man who reads the writing:
    blessed is he who has transcribed it, and given it to other Catholic churches:
    blessed are all who fear God.
    Hear ye priests, and ye readers; hear ye people, etc.

The Book of John Concerning the Falling Asleep of Mary

The Account of St. John the Theologian [1] of the Falling Asleep of the Holy Mother of God.

As the all-holy glorious mother of God and ever-virgin Mary, as was her wont, was going to the holy tomb of our Lord to burn incense, and bending her holy knees, she was importunate that Christ our God who had been born of her should return to her.

And the Jews, seeing her lingering by the divine sepulchre, came to the chief priests, saying: Mary goes every day to the tomb.

And the chief priests, having summoned the guards set by them not to allow any one to pray at the holy sepulchre, inquired about her, whether in truth it were so.

And the guards answered and said that they had seen no such thing, God having not allowed them to see her when there.

And on one of the days, it being the preparation, the holy Mary, as was her wont, came to the sepulchre; and while she was praying, it came to pass that the heavens were opened, and the archangel Gabriel came down to her and said: Hail, thou that didst bring forth Christ our God!

Thy prayer having come through to the heavens to Him who was born of thee, has been accepted; and from this time, according to thy request, thou having left the world, shall go to the heavenly places to thy Son, into the true and everlasting life.

And having heard this from the holy archangel, she returned to holy Bethlehem, having along with her three virgins who ministered unto her.

And after having rested a short time, she sat up and said to the virgins:

Bring me a censer, that I may pray.

And they brought it, as they had been commanded.

And she prayed, saying:

My Lord Jesus Christ, who didst deign through Thy supreme goodness to be born of me, hear my voice, and send me Thy apostle John, in order that, seeing him, I may partake of joy; and send me also the rest of Thy apostles, both those who have already gone to Thee, and those in the world that now is, in whatever country they may be, through Thy holy commandment, in order that, having beheld them, I may bless Thy name much to be praised; for I am confident that Thou hearest Thy servant in everything.

And while she was praying, I John came, the Holy Spirit having snatched me up by a cloud from Ephesus, and set me in the place where the mother of my Lord was lying.

And having gone in beside her, and glorified Him who had been born of her, I said:

Hail, mother of my Lord, who didst bring forth Christ our God, rejoice that in great glory thou art going out of this life.

And the holy mother of God glorified God, because I John had come to her, remembering the voice of the Lord, saying: Behold thy mother, and, Behold thy son. [2] And the three virgins came and worshipped.

And the holy mother of God says to me:

Pray, and cast incense.

And I prayed thus:

Lord Jesus Christ, who hast done wonderful things, now also do wonderful things before her who brought Thee forth; and let Thy mother depart from this life; and let those who crucified Thee, and who have not believed in Thee, be confounded.

And after I had ended the prayer, holy Mary said to me:

Bring me the censer.

And having cast incense, she said, Glory to Thee, my God and my Lord, because there has been fulfilled in me whatsoever Thou didst promise to me before thou didst ascend into the heavens, that when I should depart from this world Thou wouldst come to me, and the multitude of Thine angels, with glory.

And I John say to her:

Jesus Christ our Lord and our God is coming, and thou seest [3] Him, as He promised to thee.

And the holy mother of God answered and said to me: The Jews have sworn that after I have died they will burn my body.

And I answered and said to her:

Thy holy and precious body will by no means see corruption.

And she answered and said to me:

Bring a censer, and cast incense, and pray.

And there came a voice out of the heavens saying the Amen.

And I John heard this voice; and the Holy Spirit said to me:

John, hast thou heard this voice that spoke in the heaven after the prayer was ended?

And I answered and said:

Yes, I heard.

And the Holy Spirit said to me:

This voice which thou didst hear denotes that the appearance of thy brethren the apostles is at hand, and of the holy powers that they are coming hither to-day.

And at this I John prayed.

And the Holy Spirit said to the apostles:

Let all of you together, having come by the clouds from the ends of the world, be assembled to holy Bethlehem by a whirlwind, on account of the mother of our Lord Jesus Christ; Peter from Rome, Paul from Tiberia,[4] Thomas from Hither India, James from Jerusalem.

Andrew, Peter's brother, and Philip, Luke, and Simon the Cananaean, and Thaddaeus who had fallen asleep, were raised by the Holy Spirit out of their tombs; to whom the Holy Spirit said:

Do not think that it is now the resurrection; but on this account you have risen out of your tombs, that you may go to give greeting to the honour and wonder-working of the mother of our Lord and Saviour Jesus Christ, because the day of her departure is at hand, of her going up into the heavens.

And Mark likewise coming round, was present from Alexandria; he also with the rest, as has been said before, from each country.

And Peter being lifted up by a cloud, stood between heaven and earth, the Holy Spirit keeping him steady.

And at the same time, the rest of the apostles also, having been snatched up in clouds, were found along with Peter.

And thus by the Holy Spirit, as has been said, they all came together.

And having gone in beside the mother of our Lord and God, and having adored, we said:

Fear not, nor grieve; God the Lord, who was born of thee, will take thee out of this world with glory.

And rejoicing in God her Saviour, she sat up in the bed, and says to the apostles:

Now have I believed that our Master and God is coming from heaven, and I shall behold Him, and thus depart from this life, as I have seen that you have come.

And I wish you to tell me how you knew that I was departing and came to me, and from what countries and through what distance you have come hither, that you have thus made haste to visit me.

For neither has He who was born of me, our Lord Jesus Christ, the God of the universe, concealed it; for I am persuaded even now that He is the Son of the Most High.

And Peter answered and said to the apostles:

Let us each, according to what the Holy Spirit announced and commanded us, give full information to the mother of our Lord.

And I John answered and said:

Just as I was going in to the holy altar in Ephesus to perform divine service, the Holy Spirit says to me, The time of the departure of the mother of thy Lord is at hand; go to Bethlehem to salute her.

And a cloud of light snatched me up, and set me down in the door where thou art lying.

Peter also answered:

And I, living in Rome, about dawn heard a voice through the Holy Spirit saying to me, The mother of thy Lord is to depart, as the time is at hand; go to Bethlehem to salute her.

And, behold, a cloud of light snatched me up; and I beheld also the other apostles coming to me on clouds, and a voice saying to me, Go all to Bethlehem.

And Paul also answered and said:

And I, living in a city at no great distance from Rome, called the country of Tiberia, heard the Holy Spirit saying to me, The mother of thy Lord, having left this world, is making her course to the celestial regions through her departure;[5] but go thou also to Bethlehem to salute her.

And, behold, a cloud of light having snatched me up, set me down in the same place as you.

And Thomas also answered and said:

And I, traversing the country of the Indians, when the preaching was prevailing by the grace of Christ, and the king's sister's son Labdanus by name, was about to be sealed by me in the palace, on a sudden the Holy Spirit says to me, Do thou also, Thomas, go to Bethlehem to salute the mother of thy Lord, because she is taking her departure to the heavens.

And a cloud of light having snatched me up, set me down beside you.

And Mark also answered and said:

And when I was finishing the canon [6] of the third day in the city of Alexandria, just as I was praying, the Holy Spirit snatched me up, and brought me to you.

And James also answered and said:

While I was in Jerusalem, the Holy Spirit commanded me, saying, Go to Bethlehem, because the mother of thy Lord is taking her departure.

And, behold, a cloud of light having snatched me up, set me beside you.

And Matthew also answered and said:

I have glorified and do glorify God, because when I was in a boat and overtaken by a storm, the sea raging with its waves, on a sudden a cloud of light overshadowing the stormy billow, changed it to a calm, and having snatched me up, set me down beside you.

And those who had come before likewise answered, and gave an account of how they had come.

And Bartholomew said:

I was in the Thebais proclaiming the word, and behold the Holy Spirit says to me, The mother of thy Lord is taking her departure; go, then, to salute her in Bethlehem.

And, behold, a cloud of light having snatched me up, brought me to you.

The apostles said all these things to the holy mother of God, why they had come, and in what way; and she stretched her hands to heaven and prayed, saying:

I adore, and praise, and glorify Thy much to be praised name, O Lord, because Thou hast looked upon the lowliness of Thine handmaiden, and because Thou that art mighty hast done great things for me; and, behold, all generations shall count me blessed. [7]And after the prayer she said to the apostles:

Cast incense, and pray.

And when they had prayed, there was thunder from heaven, and there came a fearful voice, as if of chariots; and, behold, a multitude of a host of angels and powers, and a voice, as if of the Son of man, was heard, and the seraphim in a circle round the house where the holy, spotless mother of God and virgin was lying, so that all who were in Bethlehem beheld all the wonderful things, and came to Jerusalem and reported all the wonderful things that had come to pass.

And it came to pass, when the voice was heard, that the sun and the moon suddenly appeared about the house; and an assembly [8] of the first-born saints stood beside the house where the mother of the Lord was lying, for her honour and glory.

And I beheld also that many signs came to pass, the blind seeing, the deaf hearing, the lame walking, lepers cleansed, and those possessed by unclean spirits cured; and every one who was under disease and sickness, touching the outside of the wall of the house where she was lying, cried out:

Holy Mary, who didst bring forth Christ our God, have mercy upon us.

And they were straightway cured.

And great multitudes out of every country living in Jerusalem for the sake of prayer, having heard of the signs that had come to pass in Bethlehem through the mother of the Lord, came to the place seeking the cure of various diseases, which also they obtained.

And there was joy unspeakable on that day among the multitude of those who had been cured, as well as of those who looked on, glorifying Christ our God and His mother.

And all Jerusalem from Bethlehem kept festival with psalms and spiritual songs.

And the priests of the Jews, along with their people, were astonished at the things which had come to pass; and being moved [9] with the heaviest hatred, and again with frivolous reasoning, having made an assembly, they determine to send against the holy mother of God and the holy apostles who were there in Bethlehem.

And accordingly the multitude of the Jews, having directed their course to Bethlehem, when at the distance of one mile it came to pass that they beheld a frightful vision, and their feet were held fast; and after this they returned to their fellow-countrymen, and reported all the frightful vision to the chief priests.

And they, still more boiling with rage, go to the procurator, crying out and saying:

The nation of the Jews has been ruined by this woman; chase her from Bethlehem and the province of Jerusalem.

And the procurator, astonished at the wonderful things, said to them:

I will chase her neither from Bethlehem nor from any other place.

And the Jews continued crying out, and adjuring him by the health of Tiberius Caesar to bring the apostles out of Bethlehem.

And if you do not do so, we shall report it to the Caesar. Accordingly, being compelled, he sends a tribune of the soldiers [10] against the apostles to Bethlehem.

And the Holy Spirit says to the apostles and the mother of the Lord:

Behold, the procurator has sent a tribune against you, the Jews having made an uproar.

Go forth therefore from Bethlehem, and fear not:

for, behold, by a cloud I shall bring you to Jerusalem; for the power of the Father, and the Son, and the Holy Spirit is with you.

The apostles therefore rose up immediately, and went forth from the house, carrying the bed of the Lady the mother of God, and directed their course to Jerusalem; and immediately, as the Holy Spirit had said, being lifted up by a cloud, they were found in Jerusalem in the house of the Lady.

And they stood up, and for five days made an unceasing singing of praise.

And when the tribune came to Bethlehem, and found there neither the mother of the Lord nor the apostles, he laid hold of the Bethlehemites, saying to them:

Did you not come telling the procurator and the priests all the signs and wonders that had come to pass, and how the apostles had come out of every country?

Where are they, then?

Come, go to the procurator at Jerusalem.

For the tribune did not know of the departure of the apostles and the Lord's mother to Jerusalem.

The tribune then, having taken the Bethlehemites, went in to the procurator, saying that he had found no one.

And after five days it was known to the procurator, and the priests, and all the city, that the Lord's mother was in her own house in Jerusalem, along with the apostles, from the signs and wonders that came to pass there.

And a multitude of men and women and virgins came together, and cried out:

Holy virgin, that didst bring forth Christ our God, do not forget the generation of men. And when these things came to pass, the people of the Jews, with the priests also, being the more moved with hatred, took wood and fire, and came up, wishing to burn the house where the Lord's mother was living with the apostles.

And the procurator stood looking at the sight from afar off.

And when the people of the Jews came to the door of the house, behold, suddenly a power of fire coming forth from within, by means of an angel, burnt up a great multitude of the Jews.

And there was great fear throughout all the city; and they glorified God, who had been born of her.

And when the procurator saw what had come to pass, he cried out to all the people, saying:

Truly he who was born of the virgin, whom you have thought of driving away, is the Son of God; for these signs are those of the true God.

And there was a division among the Jews; and many believed in the name of our Lord Jesus Christ, in consequence of the signs that had come to pass.

And after all these wonderful things had come to pass through the mother of God, and ever-virgin Mary the mother of the Lord, while we the apostles were with her in Jerusalem, the Holy Spirit said to us: You know that on the Lord's day the good news was brought to the Virgin Mary by the archangel Gabriel; and on the Lord's day the Saviour was born in Bethlehem; and on the Lord's day the children of Jerusalem came forth with palm branches to meet him, saying, Hosanna in the highest, blessed is [11] He that cometh in the name of the Lord; [12] and on the Lord's day He rose from the dead; and on the Lord's day He will come to judge the living and the dead; and on the Lord's day He will come out of heaven, to the glory and honour of the departure of the holy glorious virgin who brought Him forth.

And on the same [13] Lord's day the mother of the Lord says to the apostles:

Cast incense, because Christ is coming with a host of angels; and, behold, Christ is at hand, sitting on a throne of cherubim.

And while we were all praying, there appeared innumerable multitudes of angels, and the Lord mounted upon cherubim in great power; and, behold, a stream of light [14] coming to the holy virgin, because of the presence of her only-begotten Son, and all the powers of the heavens fell down and adored Him.

And the Lord, speaking to His mother, said:

Mary.

And she answered and said:

Here am I, Lord.

And the Lord said to her: Grieve not, but let thy heart rejoice and be glad; for thou hast found grace to behold the glory given to me by my Father.

And the holy mother of God looked up, and saw in Him a glory which it is impossible for the mouth of man to speak of, or to apprehend.

And the Lord remained beside her, saying:

Behold, from the present time thy precious body will be transferred to paradise, and thy holy soul to the heavens to the treasures of my Father in exceeding brightness, where there is peace and joy of the holy angels,--and other things besides. [15]And the mother of the Lord answered and said to him:

Lay Thy right hand upon me, O Lord, and bless me.

And the Lord stretched forth His undefiled right hand, and blessed her.

And she laid hold of His undefiled right hand, and kissed it, saying:

I adore this right hand, which created the heaven and the earth; and I call upon Thy much to be praised name Christ, O God, the King of the ages, the only-begotten of the Father, to receive Thine handmaid, Thou who didst deign to be brought forth by me, in a low estate, to save the race of men through Thine ineffable dispensation; do Thou bestow Thine aid upon every man calling upon, or praying to, or naming the name of, Thine handmaid. And while she is saying this, the apostles, having gone up to her feet and adored, say:

O mother of the Lord, leave a blessing to the world, since thou art going away from it.

For thou hast blessed it, and raised it up when it was ruined, by bringing forth the Light of the world.

And the mother of the Lord prayed, and in her prayer spoke thus:

O God, who through Thy great goodness hast sent from the heavens Thine only-begotten Son to dwell in my humble body, who hast deigned to be born of me, humble as I am, have mercy upon the world, and every soul that calls upon Thy name.

And again she prayed, and said:

O Lord, King of the heavens, Son of the living God, accept every man who calls upon Thy name, that Thy birth may be glorified.

And again she prayed, and said:

O Lord Jesus Christ, who art all-powerful in heaven and on earth, in this appeal I implore Thy holy name; in every time and place where there is made mention of my name, make that place holy, and glorify those that glorify Thee through my name, accepting of such persons all their offering, and all their supplication, and all their prayer.

And when she had thus prayed, the Lord said to His mother: Let thy heart rejoice and be glad; for every favour [16] and every gift has been given to thee from my Father in heaven, and from me, and from the Holy Spirit:

every soul that calls upon thy name shall not be ashamed, but shall find mercy, and comfort, and support, and confidence, both in the world that now is, and in that which is to come, in the presence of my Father in the heavens.

And the Lord turned and said to Peter:

The time has come to begin the singing of the hymn.

And Peter having begun the singing of the hymn, all the powers of the heavens responded with the Alleluiah.

And then the face of the mother of the Lord shone brighter than the light, and she rose up and blessed each of the apostles with her own hand, and all gave glory to God; and the Lord stretched forth His undefiled hands, and received her holy and blameless soul.

And with the departure of her blameless soul the place was filled with perfume and ineffable light; and, behold, a voice out of the heaven was heard, saying:

Blessed art thou among women.

And Peter, and I John, and Paul, and Thomas, ran and wrapped up her precious feet for the consecration; and the twelve apostles put her precious and holy body upon a couch, and carried it.

And, behold, while they were carrying her, a certain well-born Hebrew, Jephonias by name, running against the body, put his hands upon the couch; and, behold, an angel of the Lord by invisible power, with a sword of fire, cut off his two hands from his shoulders, and made them hang about the couch, lifted up in the air.

And at this miracle which had come to pass all the people of the Jews who beheld it cried out:

Verily, He that was brought forth by thee is the true God, O mother of God, ever-virgin Mary.

And Jephonias himself, when Peter ordered him, that the wonderful things of God might be showed forth, stood up behind the couch, and cried out:

Holy Mary, who broughtest forth Christ who is God, have mercy upon me.

And Peter turned and said to him:

In the name of Him who was born of her, thy hands which have been taken away from thee, will be fixed on again.

And immediately, at the word of Peter, the hands hanging by the couch of the Lady came, and were fixed on Jephonias.

And he believed, and glorified Christ, God who had been born of her.

And when this miracle had been done, the apostles carried [17] the couch, and laid down her precious and holy body in Gethsemane in a new tomb.

And, behold, a perfume of sweet savour came forth out of the holy sepulchre of our Lady the mother of God; and for three days the voices of invisible angels were heard glorifying Christ our God, who had been born of her.

And when the third day was ended, the voices were no longer heard; and from that time forth all knew that her spotless and precious body had been transferred to paradise.

And after it had been transferred, behold, we see Elisabeth the mother of St. John the Baptist, and Anna the mother of the Lady, and Abraham, and Isaac, and Jacob, and David, singing the Alleluiah, and all the choirs of the saints adoring the holy relics of the mother of the Lord, and the place full of light, than which light nothing could be more brilliant, and an abundance of perfume in that place to which her precious and holy body had been transferred in paradise, and the melody of those praising Him who had been born of her--sweet melody, of which there is no satiety, such as is given to virgins, and them only, to hear.

We apostles, therefore, having beheld the sudden precious translation of her holy body, glorified God, who had shown us His wonders at the departure of the mother of our Lord Jesus Christ, whose[18] prayers and good offices may we all be deemed worthy to receive, [19] under her shelter, and support, and protection, both in the world that now is and in that which is to come, glorifying in every time and place her only-begotten Son, along with the Father and the Holy Spirit, for ever and ever.

Amen.

Footnotes:

1. The titles vary considerably. In two mss. the author is said to be James the Lord's brother; in one, John Archbishop of Thessalonica, who lived in the seventh century.

2. John xix. 26, 27.

3. i.e., wilt see.

4. A place near Rome; one ms. calls it Tiberis.

5. Or, dissolution.

6. A canon is a part of the Church service consisting of nine odes. The canon of the third day is the canon for Tuesday.

7. Luke i. 48.

8. Or, a church.

9. Burning--ms. B. [Thisms. is in Venice; see Tischendorf, Apocalypses Apocryphae, p. xliii., for designations of mss.--R.]

10. Lit., chiliarch, i.e., commander of a thousand.

11. Or, be.

12. Matt. xxi. 9; Luke xix. 38; Ps. cxviii. 26.

13. The holy--ms. A.

14. Lit., a going forth of illumination.

15. Perhaps the true reading is: thou shalt dwell where there is peace and joy of the holy angels.

16. Or, grace.

17. Four of themss. give a different account here: While the apostles were going forth from the city of Jerusalem carrying the couch, suddenly twelve clouds of light snatched up the apostles, with the body of our Lady, and translated them to paradise.

18. i.e., the mother's.

19. One ms. has: To find mercy and remission of sins from our Lord Jesus Christ.

The Passing of Mary

First Latin Form

Concerning the Passing [1] of the Blessed Virgin Mary.

In that time before the Lord came to His passion, and among many words which the mother asked of the Son, she began to ask Him about her own departure, addressing Him as follows:--O most dear Son, I pray Thy holiness, that when my soul goes out of my body, Thou let me know on the third day before; and do Thou, beloved Son, with Thy angels, receive it. [2]Then He received the prayer of His beloved mother, and said to her:

O palace and temple of the living God, O blessed mother, [3] O queen of all saints, and blessed above all women, before thou carriedst me in thy womb, I always guarded thee, and caused thee to be fed daily with my angelic food, [4] as thou knowest:

how can I desert thee, after thou hast carried me, and nourished me, and brought me down in flight into Egypt, and endured many hardships for me?

Know, then, that my angels have always guarded thee, and will guard thee even until thy departure.

But after I undergo suffering for men, as it is written, and rise again on the third day, and after forty days ascend into heaven, when thou shalt see me coming to thee [5] with angels and archangels, with saints and with virgins, and with my disciples, know for certain that thy soul will be separated from the body, and I shall carry it into heaven, where it shall never at all have tribulation or anguish.

Then she joyed and gloried, and kissed the knees of her Son, and blessed the Creator of heaven and earth, who gave her such a gift through Jesus Christ her Son.

In the second year, therefore, after the ascension of our Lord Jesus Christ, the most blessed Virgin Mary continued always in prayer day and night.

And on the third day before she passed away, an angel of the Lord came to her, and saluted her, saying:

Hail, Mary, full of grace! the Lord be with thee.

And she answered, saying:

Thanks to God. Again he said to her:

Receive this palm which the Lord promised to thee.

And she, giving thanks to God, with great joy received from the hand of the angel the palm sent to her.

The angel of the Lord said to her:

Thy assumption will be after three days.

And she answered: Thanks to God. [6]

Then she called Joseph of the city of Arimathaea, and the other [7] disciples of the Lord; and when they, both relations and acquaintances, were assembled, she announced her departure to all standing there. Then the blessed Mary washed [8] herself, and dressed herself like a queen, and waited the advent of her Son, as He had promised to her. And she asked all her relations to keep beside [9] her, and give her comfort.

And she had along with her three virgins, Sepphora, Abigea, and Zael; but the disciples of our Lord Jesus Christ had been already dispersed throughout the whole world to preach to the people of God.

Then at the third hour [10] there were great thunders, and rains, and lightnings, and tribulation, and an earthquake, [11] while queen Mary was standing in her chamber.

John the evangelist and apostle was suddenly brought from Ephesus, and entered the chamber of the blessed Mary, and saluted her, and said to her:

Hail, Mary, full of grace! the Lord be with thee.

And she answered:

Thanks to God.

And raising herself up, she kissed Saint John.

And the blessed Mary said to him: O my dearest son, why hast thou left me at such a time, and hast not paid heed to the commands of thy Master, to take care of me, as He commanded thee while He was hanging on the cross?

And he asked pardon with bended knee.

Then the blessed Mary gave him her benediction, and again kissed him.

And when she meant to ask him whence he came, and for what reason he had come to Jerusalem, behold, all the disciples of the Lord, except Thomas who is called Didymus, were brought by a cloud to the door of the chamber of the blessed Mary.

They stood and went in, and saluted the queen with the following words, and adored her: Hail, Mary, full of grace! the Lord be with thee.

And she eagerly rose quickly, and bowed herself, and kissed them, and gave thanks to God. These are the names of the disciples of the Lord who were brought thither in the cloud:

John the evangelist and James his brother, Peter and Paul, Andrew, Philip, Luke, Barnabas, Bartholomew and Matthew, Matthias who is called Justus, [12] Simon the Chananaean, Judas and his brother, Nicodemus and Maximianus, and many others who cannot be numbered.

Then the blessed Mary said to her brethren:

What is this, that you have all come to Jerusalem?

Peter, answering, said to her: We had need to ask this of thee, and dost thou question us? Certainly, as I think, none of us knows why we have come here to-day with such rapidity. I was at Antioch, and now I am here.

All declared plainly the place where they had been that day.

And they all wondered that they were there when they heard these things.

The blessed Mary said to them:

I asked my Son, before He endured the passion, that He and you should be at my death; and He granted me this gift.

Whence you may know that my departure will be to-morrow.[13] Watch and pray with me, that when the Lord comes to receive my soul, He may find you watching.

Then all promised that they would watch.

And they watched and prayed the whole night, with psalms and chants, with great illuminations.

And when the Lord's day came, at the third hour, just as the Holy Spirit descended upon the apostles in a cloud, [14] so Christ descended with a multitude of angels, and received the soul of His beloved mother.

For there was such splendour and perfume of sweetness, and angels singing the songs of songs, where the Lord says, As a lily among thorns, so is my love among the daughters, [15] that all who were there present fell on their faces, as the apostles fell when Christ transfigured Himself before them on Mount Thabor, and for a whole hour and a half no one was able to rise.

But when the light went away, and at the same time with the light itself, the soul of the blessed virgin Mary was taken up into heaven with psalms, and hymns, and songs of songs.

And as the cloud went up the whole earth shook, and in one moment all the inhabitants of Jerusalem openly saw the departure of St. Mary.

And that same hour Satan entered into them, and they began to consider what they were to do with her body.

And they took up weapons, that they might burn her body and kill the apostles, because from her had gone forth the dispersions of Israel, on account of their sins and the gathering together of the Gentiles.

But they were struck with blindness, striking their heads against the walls, and striking each other. [16] Then the apostles, alarmed by so much brightness, arose, and with psalms carried the holy body down from Mount Zion to the valley of Jehoshaphat.

But as they were going in the middle of the road, behold, a certain Jew, [17] Reuben by name, wishing to throw to the ground the holy bier with the body of the blessed Mary.

But his hands dried up, even to the elbow; whether he would or not, he went down even to the Valley of Jehoshaphat, weeping and lamenting because his hands were raised to the bier, and he was not able to draw back his hands to himself.

And he began to ask the apostles [18] that by their prayer he might be saved and made a Christian.

Then the apostles, bending their knees, asked the Lord to let him loose.

And he, being healed that same hour, giving thanks to God and kissing the feet of the queen of all the saints and apostles, was baptized in that same place, and began to preach the name of our God Jesus Christ.

Then the apostles with great honour laid the body in the tomb, weeping and singing through exceeding love and sweetness.

And suddenly there shone round them a light from heaven, and they fell to the ground, and the holy body was taken up by angels into heaven.

Then the most blessed Thomas was suddenly brought to the Mount of Olivet, and saw the most blessed body going up to heaven, and began to cry out and say:

O holy mother, blessed mother, spotless mother, if I have now found grace because I see thee, make thy servant joyful through thy compassion, because thou art going to heaven.

Then the girdle with which the apostles had encircled the most holy body was thrown down from heaven to the blessed Thomas.

And taking it, and kissing it, and giving thanks to God, he came again into the Valley of Jehoshaphat.

He found all the apostles and another great crowd there beating their breasts on account of the brightness which they had seen.

And seeing and kissing each other, the blessed Peter said to him:

Truly thou hast always been obdurate and unbelieving, because for thine unbelief it was not pleasing to God that thou shouldst be along with us at the burial of the mother of the Saviour.

And he, beating his breast, said:

I know and firmly believe that I have always been a bad and an unbelieving man; therefore I ask pardon of all of you for my obduracy and unbelief.

And they all prayed for him.

Then the blessed Thomas said:

Where have you laid her body?

And they pointed out the sepulchre with their finger.

And he said:

The body which is called most holy is not there.

Then the blessed Peter said to him:

Already on another occasion thou wouldst not believe the resurrection of our Master and Lord at our word, unless thou went to touch Him with thy fingers, and see Him; how wilt thou believe us that the holy body is here?

Still he persists saying:

It is not here.

Then, as it were in a rage, they went to the sepulchre, which was a new one hollowed out in the rock, and took up the stone; but they did not find the body, not knowing what to say, because they had been convicted by the words of Thomas.

Then the blessed Thomas told them how he was singing mass in India--he still had on his sacerdotal robes.

He, not knowing the word of God, had been brought to the Mount of Olivet, and saw the most holy body of the blessed Mary going up into heaven, and prayed her to give him a blessing.

She heard his prayer, and threw him her girdle which she had about her.

And the apostles seeing the belt which they had put about her, glorifying God, all asked pardon of the blessed Thomas, on account of the benediction which the blessed Mary had given him, and because he had seen the most holy body going up into heaven.

And the blessed Thomas gave them his benediction, and said:

Behold how good and how pleasant it is for brethren to dwell together in unity! [19]

And the same cloud by which they had been brought carried them back each to his own place, just like Philip when he baptized the eunuch, as is read in the Acts of the Apostles; [20] and as Habakkuk the prophet carried food to Daniel, who was in the lions' den, and quickly returned to Judaea. [21] And so also the apostles quickly returned to where they had at first been, to preach to the people of God.

Nor is it to be wondered at that He should do such things, who went into the virgin and came out of her though her womb was closed; who, though the gates were shut, went in to His disciples; [22] who made the deaf to hear, raised the dead, cleansed the lepers, gave sight to the blind, [23] and did many other wonderful things.

To believe this is no doubtful matter.

I am Joseph who laid the Lord's body in my sepulchre, and saw Him rising again; and who, before the ascension and after the ascension of the Lord, always kept his most sacred temple the blessed ever-virgin Mary, and who have kept in writing and in my breast the things which came forth from the mouth of God, and how the things mentioned above were done by the judgment of God.

And I have made known to all, Jews and Gentiles, those things which I saw with my eyes, and heard with my ears; and as long as I live I shall not cease to declare them.

And her, whose assumption is at this day venerated and worshipped throughout the whole world, let us assiduously entreat that she be mindful of us in the presence of her most pious Son in heaven, to whom is praise and glory through endless ages of ages.

Amen.[24]

Footnotes:

1. ms. B, the assumption. [For the list of mss. used by Tischendorf, see his Apocal. Apocr., p. xliii.--R.]
2. ms. C adds: And cause all the apostles to be present at my departure.
3. Puerpera.
4. Protevangelium of James, ch. 8, p. 363.
5. ms. C has: When, therefore, thou shalt see my archangel Gabriel coming to thee with a palm which I shall send to thee from heaven, know that I shall soon come to thee, my disciples, and angels, etc.
6. ms. C: And she began to give great thanks to God in these words: My soul doth magnify the Lord, and my spirit hath rejoiced in God my Saviour.
7. Or, other.
8. ms. A, raised. Levavit instead of lavit.
9. Lit., guard.
10. ms. C inserts: of the second day after the angel had come to her with the palm.
11. Or, earthquakes.
12. It was Joseph, the other candidate for the apostleship, who was called Justus (Acts i. 23).
13. ms. C adds: And she showed them the palm which the Lord had sent her from heaven by His angel.
14. ms. C has: just as the Holy Spirit appeared in a cloud to His disciples, viz., Peter, James, and John, when He was transfigured, so, etc.
15. Cant. ii. 2.
16. ms. C: By the divine vengeance, at that very instant they began to strike and slay each other with their weapons, and struck their heads against the walls like madmen.
17. ms. C inserts: a scribe of the tribe of Dan.
18. ms. C adds: and firmly to promise that, if he were made whole by their prayers, he would become a Christian.
19. Ps. cxxxiii. 1.
20. Acts viii. 39.
21. Bel and the Dragon, vers. 33-39.
22. John xx. 19.
23. ms. C adds: and in Cana of Galilee made wine out of water.
24. ms. C has this last section as follows:

For I am Joseph, who laid the body of our Lord Jesus Christ in my sepulchre, and saw Him and spoke with Him after His resurrection; who afterwards kept His most pious mother in my house until her assumption into the heavens, and served her according to my power; who also was deemed worthy to hear and see from her holy mouth many secrets, which I have written and keep in my heart.

That which I saw with mine eyes, and heard with mine ears, of her holy and glorious assumption, I have written for faithful Christians, and those that fear God; and while I live I shall not cease to preach, speak, and write them to all nations.

And let every Christian know, that if he keep this writing by him, even in his house, whether he be cleric, or lay, or a woman, the devil will not hurt him; his son will not be lunatic, or demoniac, or deaf, or blind; no one will die suddenly in his house; in whatever tribulation he cries to her, he will be heard; and in the day of his death he will have her with her holy virgins for his help.

I beseech continually that the same most pious and merciful queen may be always mindful of me, and all who believe in her and hope before her most pious Son, or Lord Jesus Christ, who with the Father and the Holy Spirit, lives and reigns God through endless ages of ages.

Amen.

The Forgotten Bible
Second Latin Form

Here Beginneth the Passing of the Blessed Virgin Mary.

1. [1]Therefore, when the Lord and Saviour Jesus Christ was hanging on the tree fastened by the nails of the cross for the life of the whole world, He saw about the cross His mother standing, and John the evangelist, whom He peculiarly loved above the rest of the apostles, because he alone of them was a virgin in the body.

He gave him, therefore, the charge of holy Mary, saying to him:

Behold thy mother! and saying, to her:

Behold thy son! [2]From that hour the holy mother of God remained specially in the care of John, as long as she had her habitation in this life.

And when the apostles had divided the world by lot for preaching, she settled in the house of his parents near Mount Olivet.

2.

In the second year, therefore, after Christ had vanquished death, and ascended up into heaven, on a certain day, Mary, burning with a longing for Christ, began to weep alone, within the shelter of her abode.

And, behold, an angel, shining in a dress of great light, stood before her and gave utterance to [3] the words of salutation saying:

Hail! thou blessed by the Lord, receive the salutation of Him who commanded safety to Jacob by His prophets.

Behold, said He, a palm branch--I have brought it to thee from the paradise of the Lord-- which thou wilt cause to be carried before thy bier, when on the third day thou shalt be taken up from the body.

For, lo, thy Son awaits thee with thrones and angels, and all the powers of heaven.

Then Mary said to the angel:

I beg that all the apostles of the Lord Jesus Christ be assembled to me.

To whom the angel said:

Behold, to-day, by the power of my Lord Jesus Christ, all the apostles will come to thee.

And Mary says to him:

I ask that thou send upon me thy blessing, that no power of the lower world may withstand me in that hour in which my soul shall go out of my body, and that I may not see the prince of darkness.

And the angel said:

No power indeed of the lower world will hurt thee; and thy Lord God, whose servant and messenger I am, hath given thee eternal blessing; but do not think that the privilege of not seeing the prince of darkness is to be given thee by me, but by Him whom thou hast carried in thy womb; for to Him belongeth power over all for ever and ever.

Thus saying, the angel departed with great splendour.

And that palm shone with exceeding great light.

Then Mary, undressing herself, put on better garments.

And, taking the palm which she had received from the hands of the angel, she went out to the mount of Olivet, and began to pray, and say:

I had not been worthy, O Lord, to bear Thee, unless Thou hadst had compassion on me; but nevertheless I have kept the treasure which Thou entrustedst to me.

Therefore I ask of Thee, O King of glory, that the power of Gehenna hurt me not.

For if the heavens and the angels daily tremble before Thee, how much more man who is made from the ground, who possesses no good thing, except as much as he has received from Thy benignant bounty!

Thou art, O Lord, God always blessed for ever.

And thus saying, she went back to her dwelling.

3.

And, behold, suddenly, while St. John was preaching in Ephesus, on the Lord's day, at the third hour of the day, there was a great earthquake, and a cloud raised him and took him up from the eyes of all, and brought him before the door of the house where Mary was.

And knocking at the door, he immediately went in.

And when Mary saw him, she exulted in joy, and said:

I beg of thee, my son John, be mindful of the words of my Lord Jesus Christ, in which He entrusted me to thee.

For, behold, on the third day, when I am to depart from the body, [4] I have heard the plans of the Jews, saying, Let us wait for the day when she who bore that seducer shall die, and let us burn her body with fire.

She therefore called St. John, and led him into the secret chamber of the house, and showed him the robe of her burial, and that palm of light which she had received from the angel, instructing him that he should cause it to be carried before her couch when she was going to her tomb.

4.

And St. John said to her:

How shall I alone perform thy funeral rites, unless my brethren and fellow-apostles of my Lord Jesus Christ come to pay honour to thy body?

And, behold, on a sudden, by the command of God, all the apostles were snatched up, raised on a cloud, from the places in which they were preaching the word of God, and set down before the door of the house in which Mary dwelt.

And, saluting each other, they wondered, saying:

What is the cause for which the Lord hath assembled us here? [5]

5.

Then all the apostles, rejoicing [6] with one mind, finished their prayer.

And when they had said the Amen, behold, on a sudden, there came the blessed John, and told them all these things.

The apostles then, having entered the house, found Mary, and saluted her, saying:

Blessed art thou by the Lord, who hath made heaven and earth. And she said to them:

Peace be with you, most beloved brethren!

How have you come hither?

And they recounted to her how they had come, each one raised on a cloud by the Spirit of God, and set down in the same place.

And she said to them:

God hath not deprived me of the sight of you.

Behold, I shall go the way of all the earth, and I doubt not that the Lord hath now conducted you hither to bring me consolation for the anguish which is just coming upon me.

Now therefore I implore you, that without intermission you all with one mind watch, even till that hour in which the Lord will come, and I shall depart from the body.

6.

And when they had sat down in a circle consoling her, when they had spent three days in the praises of God, behold, on the third day, about the third hour of the day, a deep sleep seized upon all who were in that house, and no one was at all able to keep awake but the apostles alone, and only the three virgins who were there.

And, behold, suddenly the Lord Jesus Christ came with a great multitude of angels; and a great brightness came down upon that place, and the angels were singing a hymn, and praising God together.

Then the Saviour spoke, saying:

Come, most precious pearl, within the receptacle of life eternal.

7.

Then Mary prostrated herself on the pavement, adoring God, and said:

Blessed be the name of Thy glory, O Lord my God, who hast deigned to choose me Thine handmaid, and to entrust to me Thy hidden mystery.

Be mindful of me, therefore, O King of glory, for Thou knowest that I have loved Thee with all my heart, and kept the treasure committed to me.

Therefore receive me, Thy servant, and free me from the power of darkness, that no onset of Satan may oppose me, and that I may not see filthy spirits standing in my way.

And the Saviour answered her:

When I, sent by my Father for the salvation of the world, was hanging on the cross, the prince of darkness came to me; but when he was able to find in me no trace of his work, [7] he went off vanquished and trodden under foot.

But when thou shalt see him, thou shalt see him indeed by the law of the human race, in accordance with which thou hast come to the end of thy life; but he cannot hurt thee, because I am with thee to help thee.

Go in security, because the heavenly host is waiting for thee to lead thee in to the joys of paradise.

And when the Lord had thus spoken, Mary, rising from the pavement, reclined upon her couch, and giving thanks to God, gave up the ghost.

And the apostles saw that her soul was of such whiteness, that no tongue of mortals can worthily utter it; for it surpassed all the whiteness of snow, and of every metal, and of gleaming silver, by the great brightness of its light.

8.

Then the Saviour spoke, saying:

Rise, Peter, and take the body of Mary, and send it to the right hand side of the city towards the east, and thou wilt find there a new tomb, in which you will lay her, and wait until I come to you.

And thus saying, the Lord delivered the soul of St. Mary to Michael, who was the ruler of paradise, and the prince of the nation of the Jews; [8] and Gabriel went with them.

And immediately the Saviour was received up into heaven along with the angels.

9.

And the three virgins, who were in the same place, and were watching, took up the body of the blessed Mary, that they might wash it after the manner of funeral rites.

And when they had taken off her clothes, that sacred body shone with so much brightness, that it could be touched indeed for preparation for burial, but the form of it could not be seen for the excessive flashing light:

except that the splendour of the Lord appeared great, and nothing was perceived, the body, when it was washed, was perfectly clean, and stained by no moisture of filth. [9] And when they had put the dead-clothes on her, that light was gradually obscured.

And the body of the blessed Mary was like lily flowers; and an odour of great sweetness came forth from it, so that no sweetness could be found like it.

10.

Then, accordingly, the apostles laid the holy body on the bier, and said to each other:

Who is to carry this palm before her bier? Then John said to Peter:

Thou, who hast precedence of us in the apostleship, shouldst carry this palm before her couch.

And Peter answered him:

Thou wast the only virgin among us chosen by the Lord, and thou didst find so great favour that thou didst recline upon His breast. [10] And He, when for our salvation He was hanging upon the stem of the cross, entrusted her to thee with His own mouth.

Thou therefore oughtest to carry this palm, and let us take up that body to carry it even to the place of sepulture. [11] After this, Peter, raising it, and saying, Take the body, began to sing and say:

Israel hath gone forth out of Egypt.

Alleluiah.

And the other apostles along with him carried the body of the blessed Mary, and John bore the palm of light before the bier.

And the other apostles sang with a most sweet voice.

11.

And, behold, a new miracle.

There appeared above the bier a cloud exceeding great, like the great circle which is wont to appear beside the splendour of the moon; and there was in the clouds an army of angels sending forth a sweet song, [12] and from the sound of the great sweetness the earth resounded.

Then the people, having gone forth from the city, about fifteen thousand, wondered, saying:

What is that sound of so great sweetness?

Then there stood up one who said to them:

Mary has departed from the body, and the disciples of Jesus are singing [13] praises around her.

And looking, they saw the couch crowned with great glory, and the apostles singing with a loud voice. And, behold, one of them, who was chief of the priests of the Jews in his rank, filled with fury and rage, said to the rest:

Behold, the tabernacle of him who disturbed us and all our race, what glory has it received?

And going up, he wished to overturn the bier, and throw the body down to the ground.

And immediately his hands dried up from his elbows, and stuck to the couch.

And when the apostles raised the bier, part of him hung, and part of him adhered to the couch; and he was vehemently tormented with pain, while the apostles were walking and singing.

And the angels who were in the clouds smote the people with blindness.

12.

Then that chief cried out, saying:

I implore thee, Saint Peter, do not despise me, I beseech thee, in so great an extremity, because I am exceedingly tortured by great torments.

Bear in mind that when, in the praetorium, the maid that kept the door [14] recognised thee, and told the others to revile thee, then I spoke good words in thy behalf. Then Peter answering, said:

It is not for me to give other to thee; but if thou believest with thy whole heart on the Lord Jesus Christ, whom she carried in her womb, and remained a virgin after the birth, the compassion of the Lord, which with profuse benignity saves [15] the unworthy, will give thee salvation. [16]

To this he replied:

Do we not believe?

But what shall we do?

The enemy of the human race has blinded our hearts, and confusion has covered our face, lest we should confess the great things of God, especially when we ourselves uttered maledictions against Christ, shouting:

His blood be upon us, and upon our children. [17] Then Peter said:

Behold, this malediction will hurt him who has remained unfaithful to Him; but to those who turn themselves to God mercy is not denied.

And he said:

I believe all that thou sayest to me; only I implore, have mercy upon me, lest I die.

13.

Then Peter made the couch stand still, and said to him:

If thou believest with all thy heart upon the Lord Jesus Christ, thy hands will be released from the bier.

And when he had said this [18] his hands were immediately released from the bier, and he began to stand on his feet; but his arms were dried up, and the torture did not go away from him.

Then Peter said to him:

Go up to the body, and kiss the couch, and say:

I believe in God, and in the Son of God, Jesus Christ, whom she bore, and I believe all whatsoever Peter the apostle of God has said to me.

And going up, he kissed the couch, and immediately all pain went away from him, and his hands were healed.

Then he began greatly to bless God, and from the books of Moses to render testimony to the praises of Christ, so that even the apostles themselves wondered, and wept for joy, praising the name of the Lord.

14.

And Peter said to him:

Take this palm from the hand of our brother John, and going into the city thou wilt find much people blinded, and declare to them the great things of God; and whosoever shall believe in the Lord Jesus Christ, thou shalt put this palm upon their eyes, and they shall see; but those who will not believe shall remain blind.

And when he had done so, he found much people blinded, lamenting thus:

Woe unto us, because we have been made like the Sodomites struck with blindness. [19] Nothing now is left to us but to perish.

But when they heard the words of the chief who had been cured speaking, they believed in the Lord Jesus Christ; and when he put the palm over their eyes, they recovered sight.

Five of them remaining in hardness of heart died.

And the chief of the priests going forth, carried back the palm to the apostles, reporting all things whatsoever had been done.

15.

And the apostles, carrying Mary, came to the place of the Valley of Jehoshaphat which the Lord had showed them; and they laid her in a new tomb, and closed the sepulchre.

And they themselves sat down at the door of the tomb, as the Lord had commanded them; and, behold, suddenly the Lord Jesus Christ came with a great multitude of angels, with a halo of great brightness gleaming, and said to the apostles: Peace be with you!

And they answered and said:

Let Thy mercy, O Lord, be upon us, as we have hoped in Thee. [20] Then the Saviour spoke to them, saying:

Before I ascended to my Father I promised to you, saying that you who have followed me in the regeneration, when the Son of man shall sit upon the throne of His majesty, will sit, you also, upon twelve thrones, judging the twelve tribes of Israel. [21]Her, therefore, did I choose out of the tribes of Israel by the command of my Father, that I should dwell in her.

What, therefore, do you wish that I should do to her?

Then Peter and the other apostles said: Lord, Thou didst choose beforehand this Thine handmaid to become a spotless chamber for Thyself, and us Thy servants to minister unto Thee.

Before the ages Thou didst foreknow all things along with the Father, with whom to Thee and the Holy Spirit there is one Godhead, equal and infinite power.

If, therefore, it were possible to be done in the presence of the power of Thy grace, it had seemed to us Thy servants to be right that, just as Thou, having vanquished death, reignest in glory, so, raising up again the body of Thy mother, Thou shouldst take her with Thee in joy into heaven.

16.

Then the Saviour said:

Let it be according to your opinion.

And He ordered the archangel Michael to bring the soul of St. Mary.

And, behold, the archangel Michael [22] rolled back the stone from the door of the tomb; and the Lord said:

Arise, my beloved and my nearest relation; thou who hast not put on corruption by intercourse with man, suffer not destruction of the body in the sepulchre.

And immediately Mary rose from the tomb, and blessed the Lord, and falling forward at the feet of the Lord, adored Him, saying:

I cannot render sufficient thanks to Thee, O Lord, for Thy boundless benefits which Thou hast deigned to bestow upon me Thine handmaiden.

May Thy name, O Redeemer of the world, God of Israel, be blessed for ever.

17.

And kissing her, the Lord went back, and delivered her soul to the angels, that they should carry it into paradise.

And He said to the apostles:

Come up to me.

And when they had come up He kissed them, and said:

Peace be to you! as I have always been with you, so will I be even to the end of the world.

And immediately, when the Lord had said this, He was lifted up on a cloud, and taken back into heaven, and the angels along with Him, carrying the blessed Mary into the paradise of God.

And the apostles being taken up in the clouds, returned each into the place allotted [23] for his preaching, telling the great things of God, and praising our Lord Jesus Christ, who liveth and reigneth with the Father and the Holy Spirit, in perfect unity, and in one substance of Godhead, for ever and ever.

Amen.

Footnotes:

1. The other ms. has the following introductory chapter: Melito, servant of Christ, bishop of the church of Sardis, to the venerable brethren in the Lord appointed at Laodicea, in peace greeting. I remember that I have often written of one Leucius, who, having along with ourselves associated with the apostles, turned aside through alienated feelings and a rash soul from the path of rectitude, and inserted very many things in his books about the acts of the apostles. Of their powers, indeed, he said many and diverse things; but of their teaching he gave a very false account, affirming that they taught otherwise than they did, and establishing his own impious statements, as it were, by their words. Nor did he think this to be enough; but he even vitiated, by his impious writing, the assumption of the blessed ever-virgin Mary, the mother of God, to such a degree that it would be impious not only to read it in the church of God, but even to hear it. When you ask us, therefore, what we heard from the Apostle John, we simply write this, and have directed it to your brotherhood; believing, not the strange dogmas hatched by heretics, but the Father in the Son, the Son in the Father, while the threefold person of the Godhead and undivided substance remains; believing not that two human natures were created by a good God, which by the craft of the serpent was vitiated through sin, and restored through the grace of Christ. [Tischendorf gives this from Maxima Bibliotheca vet. patr , ii. 2, pp. 212 sqq. (ed. Sugdun).--R.]

2. John xix. 26, 27.

3. Lit., sprung forward to.

4. The otherms. has a better reading: For, behold, on the third day I am to depart from the body; and I have heard, etc.

5. The otherms. here adds: And there came with them Paul, converted from the circumcision, who had been selected along with Barnabas for the ministry of the Gentiles. And when there was a pious contention among them as to which of them should be the first to pray to the Lord to show them the reason, and Peter was urging Paul to pray first, Paul answered and said: That is thy duty, to begin first, especially seeing that thou hast been chosen by God a pillar (Gal. ii. 9) of the Church, and thou hast precedence of all in the apostleship; but it is by no means mine, for I am the least of you all, and Christ was seen by me as one born out of due time (1 Cor. xv. 8); nor do I presume to make myself equal to you: nevertheless by the grace of God I am what I am (1 Cor. xv. 10).

6. The otherms. adds: at the humility of Paul.
7. Comp. John xiv. 30.
8. Comp. Dan. x. 21, xii. 1.
9. This does not seem to make very good sense. Another reading is: And the splendour appeared great, and nothing was perceived, while the body, perfectly clean, and unstained by any horror of filth, was being washed.
10. John xiii. 23.
11. The otherms. inserts: And Paul said to him: And I, who am younger than any of you, will carry along with thee. And when all had agreed, Peter, raising the bier at the head, began to sing and say.
12. Lit., a song of sweetness.
13. Lit., saying.
14. John xviii. 17.
15. Or, heals.
16. Or, health.
17. Matt. xxvii. 25.
18. The otherms. has: And when he had said this, "I believe."
19. Gen. xix. 11; Wisd. xix. 17.
20. Ps. xxxiii. 22.
21. Matt. xix. 28.
22. The otherms. has Gabriel.
23. Lit., the lot.

The Gospel of Peter

by Professor J. Armitage Robinson.
Editor of the Cambridge Texts and Studies
Introduction by Andrew Rutherfurd, B.D.

Introduction

The important fragment of which Mr. J. Armitage Robinson's translation here follows was discovered by the French Archaeological Mission, Cairo, in a grave (supposed to be a monk's) in an ancient cemetery at Akhmim (Panopolis), in Upper Egypt, in 1886.

It was published in 1892 under the care of M. Bouriant in vol. ix., fasc. i., of the Memoirs of the French Archaeological Mission at Cairo.

The same parchment which contained this fragment also contained a fragment of the Revelation of Peter and a fragment of the Book of Enoch in Greek.

The parchment codex is assigned to a date between the eighth and the twelfth century.

Before this discovery the following is all that was known of the Gospel of Peter:

1.

Serapion, Bishop of Antioch 190-203, writing to the church at Rhossus, says (Eusebius, H. E., vi., 12, 2):

"We, brethren, receive Peter and the other Apostles even as Christ; but the writings that go falsely by their names we, in our experience, reject, knowing that such things as these we never received.

When I was with you I supposed you all to be attached to the right faith; and so without going through the gospel put forward under Peter's name, I said, If this is all that makes your petty quarrel, [1] why then let it be read.'

But now that I have learned from information given me that their mind was lurking in some hole of heresy, I will make a point of coming to you again:

so, brethren, expect me speedily.

Knowing then, brethren, of what kind of heresy was Marcion--[Here follows a sentence where the text is faulty.]...From others who used this very gospel--I mean from the successors of those who started it, whom we call Docetae; for most of its ideas are of their school--from them, I say, I borrowed it, and was able to go through it, and to find that most of it belonged to the right teaching of the Saviour, but some things were additions." From this we learn that a Gospel of Peter was in use in the church of Rhossus in the end of the second century, but that controversy had arisen as to its character, which, on a careful examination, Serapion condemned.

2.

Origen (253 a.d.), in commenting on Matthew x. 17, says:

"But, proceeding on the tradition that is recorded in the Gospel according to Peter or in the Book of James, they say that there are certain brothers of Jesus, the sons of Joseph by a former wife, who lived with him before Mary."

3.

Eusebius (H. E., iii., 3, 2) says:

"As to that work, however, which is ascribed to him, called The Acts,' and The Gospel according to Peter,' and that called The Preaching and the Revelations of Peter,' we know nothing of their being handed down as Catholic writings; since neither among the ancient nor the ecclesiastical writers of our own day has there been one that has appealed to testimony taken from them." And in H. E., iii., 25, 6 sq., he includes the Gospel of Peter among the forged heretical gospels--"those that are adduced by the heretics under the name of the apostles,...of which no one of those writers in the ecclesiastical succession has condescended to make any mention in his works; and, indeed, the character of the style itself is very different from that of the apostles; and the sentiments, and the purport of those things that are advanced in them, deviating as far as possible from sound orthodoxy, evidently proves they are the fictions of heretical men; whence they are not only to be ranked among the spurious writings, but are to be rejected as altogether absurd and impious."

It is, however, uncertain whether Eusebius himself was acquainted with the Gospel of Peter.

4.

Theodoret (c. 455), in his Religious History, ii., 2, says that the Nazarenes used "the gospel called according to Peter.'"

Later references in Western literature, e.g., Jerome, De vir. ill., i., and the Decretum Gelasianum, condemning the book, are based upon the judgement of Eusebius, and not upon direct knowledge (cf. Harnack, Geschichte der altchristl. Lit., I. Th., p. 11).

This was all that was known of the Gospel of Peter till the publication of the Akhmim fragment.

The latter extends to about 174 stichi, counting 32 words to the stichus.

It begins in the middle of the history of the Passion, just after Pilate has washed his hands of all responsibility, and ends in the middle of a sentence, with the departure of the disciples into Galilee at the end of the Feast of Unleavened Bread, exactly a week after the crucifixion, the ostensible author, Peter, and Andrew, his brother, taking their nets and going to the sea; "and there was with us Levi the son of Alphaeus, whom the Lord..."

The accompanying Synoptical Table shows where the Petrine narrative agrees with and where it varies from those supplied by the canonical gospels.

Of that part of the Passion history which it narrates, it gives an account which follows the main lines of the canonical tradition, but with important variations in detail.

Of the events between the burial and the resurrection of our Lord, its account is much more ample and detailed than anything in the canonical tradition.

Harnack (Texte und Untersuchungen, ix., 2, 2d ed., p. 76) gives the following list of new traits contained in the Petrine account of the history of the Passion and burial:

1.
Herod was the judge who condemned Jesus, and to him application had to be made for the body.

2.
The Jews, Herod, and the judges would not wash their hands, and Pilate then raised the sitting.

3.
Joseph was the friend of Pilate (sec. 2).

4.
Joseph begged for the body before the crucifixion, and Pilate sent for permission from Herod.

5.
The soldiers "pushed him as they ran," and their speech (sec. 3).

6.
The mockery of the soldiers.

7.
Mocking speech.

8.
"As though having no pain" (sec. 4).

9.
"Having placed his garments before him."

10.
One of the malefactors blamed the multitude, and his speech.

11. The legs of either the malefactor or Jesus were not broken, in order that he might die in torment.

12. The gall and vinegar (sec. 5).

13. In the darkness many went about with lamps, and fell down.

14. The cry, "My power, my power."

15. The fact that when he had so cried Christ was taken up.

16. Mention of the nails in the hands at the taking down from the cross (sec. 6).

17. The earthquake when the body touched the ground.

18. The joy of the Jews when the sun shone again.

19. Joseph "had seen all the good things" that the Lord had done.

20. Joseph washed the body.

21. The cries of woe of the Jews and their leaders over their sins, and their expectation of the judgement on Jerusalem (sec. 7).

22. The disciples remained in concealment, full of grief, and fasted and wept till the Sabbath.

23. They were searched for as malefactors and as anxious to burn the temple.

24. The name of the centurion of the watch--Petronius (sec. 8).

25. The centurion, the soldiers, and the elders rolled up the stone.

26. The elders also watched at the grave.

27. Seven seals were placed on the stone.

28. A tent pitched for the watch.

29. The gathering of the multitude on the morning of the Sabbath to view the sealed grave (sec. 9).

The whole narrative of the resurrection is so different from that of the canonical gospels that it would be useless to go into details; but it is important to notice the prominence assigned to Mary

Magdalene, and:

1.
That the women fled from the grave and did not see the Lord (sec. 12).

2.
That there is no account of any appearance of Christ for the first eight days after his death (sec. 13).

3.
That the disciples, along with the rest of those who had taken part in the feast, returned home to Galilee on the seventh day of unleavened bread.

4.
That they were then sad, and wept.

5.
That the first appearance of Jesus must have taken place on the Lake of Gennesaret, either to Peter alone, or to Peter, Andrew, and Levi (Matthew), while fishing.

Moreover, according to section 13 (see sec. 5), the author puts the resurrection and ascension on the same day, or, rather, did not know of the latter as a separate event.

He makes the angel say, "He is risen and gone away thither whence he was sent."

Whether the author used any other sources than the canonical gospels is a matter still in doubt.

He is certainly influenced by views which are foreign to these gospels, and which are known from other quarters in early Christian literature.

As between the Synoptists and the Fourth Gospel, the narrator is generally more closely akin both in matter and in manner to the Synoptists, but he agrees with the author of the Fourth Gospel in regard to the chronology of the crucifixion and several of the events at the cross, and in his general attitude towards the Jews and Pilate.

With regard to the last two points, the Petrine Gospel seems to present a later and more exaggerated form of the tendency perceptible in the Johannine, and fully worked out in the Acts of Pilate, to blame the Jews and exculpate Pilate.

Of the new features in this fragment some are at least liable to a Docetic interpretation, e.g., the silence on the cross "as though he had no pain" (sec. 4), the cry, "My power, my power" (sec. 5), and "he was taken up" (sec. 5).

This fact was recognised in subsequent times and condemned this gospel in the eye of the church.

The date of the work is variously fixed by different scholars; Harnack assigns it to the first quarter of the second century, while Mr. Armitage Robinson and other scholars place it later.

Footnote:

1. Parechein mikropsuchian, perhaps "causes you ill-feeling."

The translation of Serapion's letter with this note is taken from Mr. Armitage Robinson's edition of the gospel.

The Gospel According to Peter [1]

1.

But of the Jews none washed his hands, neither Herod nor any one of his judges.

And when they had refused to wash them, Pilate rose up. And then Herod the king commandeth that the Lord be taken, [2] saying to them, What things soever I commanded you to do unto him, do.

2.

And there was standing there Joseph the friend of Pilate and of the Lord; and, knowing that they were about to crucify [3] him, he came to Pilate and asked the body of the Lord for burial.

And Pilate sent to Herod and asked his body.

And Herod said, Brother Pilate, even if no one had asked for him, we purposed to bury him, especially as the sabbath draweth on: [4]for it is written in the law, that the sun set not upon one that hath been put to death.

3.

And he delivered him to the people on the day before the unleavened bread, their feast.

And they took the Lord and pushed him as they ran, and said, Let us drag away the Son of God, having obtained power over him.

And they clothed him with purple, and set him on the seat of judgment, saying, Judge righteously, O king of Israel.

And one of them brought a crown of thorns and put it on the head of the Lord.

And others stood and spat in his eyes, and others smote his cheeks:

others pricked him with a reed; and some scourged him, saying, With this honour let us honour the Son of God.

4.

And they brought two malefactors, and they crucified the Lord between them.

But he held his peace, as though having no pain.

And when they had raised the cross, they wrote the title:

This is the king of Israel.

And having set his garments before him they parted them among them, and cast lots for them.

And one of those malefactors reproached them, saying, We for the evils that we have done have suffered thus, but this man, who hath become the Saviour of men, what wrong hath he done to you?

And they, being angered at him, commanded that his legs should not be broken, that he might die in torment.

5.

And it was noon, and darkness came over all Judaea:

and they were troubled and distressed, lest the sun had set, whilst he was yet alive:

[for] it is written for them, that the sun set not on him that hath been put to death.

And one of them said, Give him to drink gall with vinegar.

And they mixed and gave him to drink, and fulfilled all things, and accomplished their sins against their own head.

And many went about with lamps, supposing that it was night, and fell down. [5]

And the Lord cried out, saying, My power, my power, thou hast forsaken me.

And when he had said it he was taken up.

And in that hour the vail of the temple of Jerusalem was rent in twain. [6]

6.
And then they drew out the nails from the hands of the Lord, and laid him upon the earth, and the whole earth quaked, and great fear arose.

Then the sun shone, and it was found the ninth hour:

and the Jews rejoiced, and gave his body to Joseph that he might bury it, since he had seen what good things he had done.

And he took the Lord, and washed him, and rolled him in a linen cloth, and brought him into his own tomb, which was called the Garden of Joseph.

7.
Then the Jews and the elders and the priests, perceiving what evil they had done to themselves, began to lament and to say, Woe for our sins:

the judgement hath drawn nigh, and the end of Jerusalem.

And I with my companions was grieved; and being wounded in mind we hid ourselves:

for we were being sought for by them as malefactors, and as wishing to set fire to the temple.

And upon all these things we fasted and sat mourning and weeping night and day until the sabbath.

8.
But the scribes and Pharisees and elders being gathered together one with another, when they heard that all the people murmured and beat their breasts saying, If by his death these most mighty signs have come to pass, see how righteous he is,--the elders were afraid and came to Pilate, beseeching him and saying, Give us soldiers, that we may guard his sepulchre for three days, lest his disciples come and steal him away, and the people suppose that he is risen from the dead and do us evil.

And Pilate gave them Petronius the centurion with soldiers to guard the tomb.

And with them came elders and scribes to the sepulchre, and having rolled a great stone together with [7] the centurion and the soldiers, they all together who were there set it at the door of the sepulchre; and they affixed seven seals, and they pitched a tent there and guarded it.

And early in the morning as the sabbath was drawing on, there came a multitude from Jerusalem and the region round about, that they might see the sepulchre that was sealed.

9.
And in the night in which the Lord's day was drawing on, as the soldiers kept guard two by two in a watch, there was a great voice in the heaven; and they saw the heavens opened, and two men descend from thence with great light and approach the tomb.

And that stone which was put at the door rolled of itself and made way in part; and the tomb was opened, and both the young men entered in.

10.
When therefore those soldiers saw it, they awakened the centurion and the elders; for they too were hard by keeping guard.

And, as they declared what things they had seen, again they see three men come forth from the tomb, and two of them supporting one, and a cross following them:

and of the two the head reached unto the heaven, but the head of him that was led by them overpassed the heavens.

And they heard a voice from the heavens, saying, Thou hast preached to them that sleep. And a response was heard from the cross, Yea.

11.
They therefore considered one with another whether to go away and shew these things to Pilate.

And while they yet thought thereon, the heavens again are seen to open, and a certain man to descend and enter into the sepulchre.

When the centurion and they that were with him saw these things, they hastened in the night to Pilate, leaving the tomb which they were watching, and declared all things which they had seen, being greatly distressed and saying, Truly he was the Son of God. Pilate answered and said, I am pure from the blood of the Son of God: but it was ye who determined this.

Then they all drew near and besought him and entreated him to command the centurion and the soldiers to say nothing of the things which they had seen:

For it is better, say they, for us to be guilty of the greatest sin before God, and not to fall into the hands of the people of the Jews and to be stoned.

The Forgotten Bible

Pilate therefore commanded the centurion and the soldiers to say nothing.

12.

And at dawn upon the Lord's day Mary Magdalen, a disciple of the Lord, fearing because of the Jews, since they were burning with wrath, had not done at the Lord's sepulchre the things which women are wont to do for those that die and for those that are beloved by them--she took her friends with her and came to the sepulchre where he was laid.

And they feared lest the Jews should see them, and they said, Although on that day on which he was crucified we could not weep and lament, yet now let us do these things at his sepulchre.

But who shall roll away for us the stone that was laid at the door of the sepulchre, that we may enter in and sit by him and do the things that are due?

For the stone was great, and we fear lest some one see us.

And if we cannot, yet if we but set at the door the things which we bring for a memorial of him, we will weep and lament, until we come unto our home.

13.

And they went and found the tomb opened, and coming near they looked in there; and they see there a certain young man sitting in the midst of the tomb, beautiful and clothed in a robe exceeding bright: who said to them, Wherefore are ye come?

Whom seek ye?

Him that was crucified? [8]He is risen and gone.

But if ye believe not, look in and see the place where he lay, that he is not [here]; for he is risen and gone thither, whence he was sent.

Then the women feared and fled.

14.

Now it was the last day of the unleavened bread, and many were going forth, returning to their homes, as the feast was ended.

But we, the twelve disciples of the Lord, wept and were grieved:

and each one, being grieved for that which was come to pass, departed to his home. But I Simon Peter and Andrew my brother took our nets and went to the sea; and there was with us Levi the son of Alphaeus, whom the Lord...

Footnotes:

1. This translation is based on that which I published in The Gospel and Apocalypse of Peter: Two Lectures, etc. (Camb., 1892). It is now carefully revised in accordance with the photographic facsimile. A corrected Greek text will be found in Dr. Swete's edition (1893).

2. Par[alem]phthenai is perhaps supported by paralabontes, Matt. xxiv. 27.

3. I know no other instance of stauriskein.

4. cf. John xix. 31, where Syr. Pesch. reads: "They say, These bodies shall not remain on the cross, because the sabbath dawneth."

5. The text here is corrupt: for epesanto I have provisionally read epesan te.

6. For autos horas we must read autes horas (cf. Clem., Hom., xx., 16); aute is the equivalent in later Greek literature of ekeine, as in the modern tongue (cf. Lc. x. 7, 21, and xii. 12; || ekeine, Mt., Mc.)

7. I have ventured to substitute meta, "together with" (cf. Matt. xxvii. 66), for kata, "down upon." Dr. Swete, however, keeps kata, and interprets it as "against," i.e., to guard the sepulchre against.

8. The form of the question in the Greek suggests a negative answer.

The Revelation of Peter
by Andrew Rutherford, B.D.

Introduction

The fragment here translated was discovered in 1886 by the French Archaeological Mission in an ancient burying place at Akhmim in Upper Egypt.

It was published at Paris in 1892 (Bouriant, Memoires publies par les membres de la Mission Archeologique Franc,aise au Caire, T. ix., fasc. 1, 1892).

The ms. is now in the Gizeh Museum and has been held to be of a date between the eighth and twelfth centuries.

Until the discovery of the fragment, the following was all that was known about the Revelation of Peter.

1.

The so-called Muratorian Fragment, a list of sacred writings, first published by Muratori in 1740, and found by him in a seventh or eighth century ms. belonging to the Ambrosian Library in Milan, but which had previously belonged to the Columban Monastery of Bobbio, is assigned on internal evidence to the third quarter of the second century.

(Vide Westcott, Canon of the N.T., p. 514.)

At line 69 it says:

"the Apocalypses also of John and Peter only do we receive, which (latter) some among us would not have read in church."

2.

Clement of Alexandria (fl. c. 200 a.d.) in his Hypotoposes, according to the testimony of Eusebius, H. E., vi., 14, gave "abridged accounts of all the canonical Scriptures, not even omitting those that are disputed, I mean the book of Jude and the other general epistles. Also the Epistle of Barnabas and that called the Revelation of Peter." Also in his Eclogae Prophetiae, chapters 41, 48 and 49, he gives three, or as some think, four quotations from the Revelation of Peter, mentioning it twice by name.

3.

The Catalogus Claromontanus, an Eastern list of Holy Scriptures, belonging to the third century, gives at the end the Revelation of Peter (v. Westcott, Canon, p. 555).

This catalogue gives the length of the various books it enumerates measured in stichoi.

Our book is said to have two hundred and seventy, which makes it rather longer than the Epistle to the Colossians which has two hundred and fifty-one.

4.

Methodius, bishop of Olympus in Lycia in the beginning of the fourth century, in his Symposium, ii., 6, says, "wherefore we have also learned from divinely inspired Scriptures that untimely births even if they are the offspring of adultery are delivered to caretaking angels."

Though Peter is not here mentioned, the purport of the passage is the same as that of one of the quotations given by Clement of Alexandria.

5.

Eusebius (c. 339 a.d.), in his Ecclesiastical History, iii., 25, expressly mentions the Revelation of Peter along with the Acts of Paul and the Pastor as spurious books, while at iii., 3, he says:

"as to that which is called the Preaching and that called the Apocalypse of Peter, we know nothing of their being handed down as Catholic writings.

Since neither among the ancients nor among the ecclesiastical writers of our own day, has

The Forgotten Bible

there been anyone that has appealed to testimony taken from them."

6.

Macarius Magnes (beginning of fifth century) in his Apocritica, iv., 6, quotes as from a heathen opponent of Christianity the following:

"Let us by way of superfluity cite also that saying in the Apocalypse of Peter.

It thus introduces the heaven as being about to undergo judgment along with the earth.

The earth,' it says, shall present all men before God at the day of judgment, being itself also to be judged along with the heaven also which encompasses it.'"

And at iv., 16, he examines this passage again, naming the revelation of Peter, and supporting the doctrine of the passage by the authority of prophecy (Isaiah xxxiv. 4) and the Gospel (Matt. xxiv. 35).

7.

Sozomen (middle of fifth century), H. E., vii., 19, says:

"For instance, the so-called Apocalypse of Peter which was esteemed as entirely spurious by the ancients, we have discovered to be read in certain churches of Palestine up to the present day, once a year, on the day of preparation, during which the people most religiously fast in commemoration of the Saviour's Passion" (i.e., on Good Friday).

It is to be noted that Sozomen himself belonged to Palestine.

8.

In the list of the Sixty Books which is assigned to the fifth or sixth century the Revelation of Peter is mentioned among the Apocrypha (v. Westcott, Canon, p. 551).

9.

The so-called Stichometry of Nicephorus, a list of scriptures with notes of their extent, ascribed to Nicephorus, Patriarch of Constantinople, 806-814 a.d., includes the Revelation of Peter among the antilegomena or disputed writings of the New Testament, and gives it three hundred stichoi or thirty more than the above-mentioned Catalogus Claromontanas.

10.

The Armenian annalist Mkhitan (thirteenth century) in a list of the New Testament antilegomena mentions the Revelation of Peter, after the Gospel of Thomas and before the Periodoi Pauli, and remarks that he has himself copied these books.

(Cf. Harnack, Geschichte der altchristlichen Literatur.)

Up till lately these facts represented all that was positively known of the Revelation of Peter.

From them we gather that it must have been written before the middle of the second century (so as to be known at Rome and included in the Muratorian Canon), that it had a wide circulation, that it was for some time very popular, so that it would appear to have run a considerable chance of achieving a place in the canon, but that it was ultimately rejected and in the long run dropped out of knowledge altogether.

But even previously to the discovery at Akhmim, the general character of the book had been inferred from the scanty fragments preserved in ancient writers and from the common elements contained in other and later apocalyptic writings which seemed to require some such book as the Revelation of Peter as their ultimate source.

Such writings are the (Christian) Apocalypse of Esdras, the Vision of Paul, the Passion of S. Perpetua and the visions contained in the History of Barlaam and Josaphat.

(Cf. Robinson, Texts and Studies, i., 2, p. 37-43, and Robinson and James, The Gospel according to Peter and the Revelation of Peter, 1892.)

The Revelation of Peter affords the earliest embodiment in Christian literature of those pictorial presentations of heaven and hell which have exercised so widespread and enduring an influence.

It has, in its imagery, little or no kinship with the Book of Daniel, the Book of Enoch, or the Revelation of S. John.

Its only parallels in canonical scripture, with the notable exception of the Second Epistle of Peter, are to be found in Isaiah lxvi. 24, Mark ix. 44, 48, and the parable of Dives and Lazarus in Luke xvi. 19.

It is indeed Judaic in the severity of its morality and even in its phraseology (cf. the frequent use of the word righteous, and the idea that God and not Christ will come to judge sinners).

But the true parallels for, if not the sources of, its imagery of the rewards and punishments which await men after death are to be found in Greek beliefs which have left their traces in such passages as the Vision of Er at the end of Plato's Republic.

The heaven of the Petrine Apocalypse is akin to the Elysian Fields and the Islands of the Blest.

In it the saints are crowned as with flowers and beautiful of countenance, singing songs of praise in the fragrant air, in a land all lighted up with the light of the sun. [1]We are reminded of "the Elysian Fields and the world's end where is Rhadamanthus of the fair hair, where life is easiest for men.

No snow is there, nor yet great storm, nor any rain; but alway Ocean sendeth forth the breeze of the shrill West to blow cool on men" (Odyssey, iv., 563), and of the garden of the gods on Olympus, which "is not shaken by winds, or ever wet with rain, nor doth the snow come nigh thereto, but most clear air is spread about it cloudless, and the white light floats over it" (Odyssey, vi., 43, Butcher and Lang's transl.).

Perhaps the most striking parallel of all is afforded by the fragment of a dirge of Pindar:

"For them shineth below the strength of the sun, while in our world it is night, and the space of crimson-flowered meadow before their city is full of the shade of frankincense trees, and of fruits of gold.

And some in horses, and in bodily feats, and some in dice, and some in harp-playing have delight; and among them thriveth all fair-flowering bliss; and fragrance streameth ever through the lovely land, as they mingle incense of every kind upon the altars of the gods" (Pindar, E. Myer's transl., p. 176).

Beside this heaven the New Jerusalem of the canonical Apocalypse is austere.

But it is the spiritual city.

"For the city had no need of the sun, neither of the moon to shine on it, for the Lord God Almighty and the Lamb were in the midst of it and the Lamb was the light thereof."

So likewise in the case of the torments of the wicked as presented in the Revelation of Peter.

We are not here in the Jewish Sheol, or among the fires of the valley of Hinnom, so much as among the tortures of Tartarus and the boiling mud of the Acherusian Lake (cf. Plato, Phaedo, p. 113; Aristophanes, Frogs, line 145), or where "wild men of fiery aspect...seized and carried off several of them, and Ardiaeus and others, they bound head and foot and hand, and threw them down and flayed them with scourges, and dragged them along the road at the side, carding them on thorns like wool, and declaring to the passers-by what were their crimes, and that they were being taken away to be cast into hell" (Republic, x., p. 616, Jowett's transl.).

It is not surprising that in later visions of the same kind the very names of the Greek underworld are ascribed to localities of hell.

It is across the river Oceanus.

It is called Tartarus.

In it is the Acherusian Lake.

Notice in this connection that the souls of innocent victims are present along with their murderers to accuse them.

The Revelation of Peter shows remarkable kinship in ideas with the Second Epistle of Peter.

The parallels will be noted in the margin of the translation.

It also presents notable parallels to the Sibylline Oracles (cf. Orac. Sib., ii., 225 sqq.), while its influence has been conjectured, almost with certainty, in the Acts of Perpetua and the visions narrated in the Acts of Thomas and the History of Barlaam and Josaphat.

It certainly was one of the sources from which the writer of the Vision of Paul drew.

And directly or indirectly it may be regarded as the parent of all the mediaeval visions of the other world.

The fragment begins in the middle of an eschatological discourse of Jesus, probably represented as delivered after the resurrection, for verse 5 implies that the disciples had begun to preach the Gospel.

It ends abruptly in the course of a catalogue of sinners in hell and their punishments.

The fragments preserved in the writings of Clement of Alexandria and Methodius probably belonged to the lost end of the book; that preserved by Macarius Magnes may have belonged to the eschatological discourse at the beginning.

Taking the length of the whole at from two hundred and seventy to three hundred stichoi, the Akhmim fragment contains about the half.

The present translation is made from Harnack's edition of the text, 2d ed., Leipzig, 1893.

There is another and later Apocalypse of Peter in Arabic, of which mss. exist in Rome and Oxford.

It is called the Apocalypse of Peter, or the narrative of things revealed to him by Jesus Christ which had taken place from the beginning of the world and which shall take place till the end of the world or the second coming of Christ.

The Forgotten Bible

The book is said to have been written by Clement, to whom Peter had communicated the secrets revealed to him.

The writer himself calls the book Librum Perfectionis or Librum Completum.

Judging from the analysis of its contents quoted by Tischendorf (Apocalypses Apocr.) it has no connection with the present work.

Footnote:

1. Cf. "...the island valley of Avilion; Where falls not rain or hail or any snow, Nor ever wind blows loudly; but it lies Deep-meadowed, happy, fair with orchard lawns And bowery hollows crowned with summer seas." Tennyson, Passing of Arthur.

The Apocalypse of Peter

1.
...many of them will be false prophets, [1] and will teach divers ways and doctrines of perdition: but these will become sons of perdition. [2]3.
And then God will come unto my faithful ones who hunger and thirst and are afflicted and purify their souls in this life; and he will judge the sons of lawlessness. [3]

4.
And furthermore the Lord said:
Let us go into the mountain: [4]
Let us pray.

5.
And going with him, we, the twelve disciples, begged that he would show us one of our brethren, the righteous who are gone forth out of the world, in order that we might see of what manner of form they are, and having taken courage, might also encourage [5] the men who hear us.

6.
And as we prayed, suddenly there appeared two men standing before the Lord towards the East, on whom we were not able to look; [6] 7, for there came forth from their countenance a ray as of the sun, and their raiment was shining, such as eye of man [7] never saw; for no mouth is able to express or heart to conceive the glory with which they were endued, and the beauty of their appearance.

8.
And as we looked upon them, we were astounded; for their bodies were whiter than any snow and ruddier than any rose; [8] 9, and the red thereof was mingled with the white, and I am utterly unable to express their beauty; 10, for their hair was curly and bright and seemly both on their face and shoulders, as it were a wreath [9] woven of spikenard and divers-coloured flowers, or like a rainbow in the sky, such was their seemliness.

11.
Seeing therefore their beauty we became astounded at them, since they appeared suddenly.

12.
And I approached the Lord and said:
Who are these?

13.
He saith to me:
These are your brethren the righteous, whose forms ye desired to see.

14.
And I said to him:
And where are all the righteous ones and what is the aeon in which they are and have this glory?

15.
And the Lord showed me [10] a very great country outside of this world, exceeding bright with light, and the air there lighted with the rays of the sun, and the earth itself blooming with unfading flowers and full of spices and plants, fair-flowering and incorruptible and bearing blessed fruit.

16.
And so great was the perfume that it [11] was borne thence even unto us.

17.
And the dwellers in that place were clad in the raiment of shining angels and their raiment was like unto their country; and angels hovered about them there.

18.
And the glory of the dwellers there was equal, and with one voice they sang praises alternately to the Lord God, rejoicing in that place.

19.
The Lord saith to us:
This is the place of your high-priests, [12] the righteous men.

20.
And over against that place I saw another, squalid, and it was the place of punishment; and those who were punished there and the punishing angels had their raiment dark [13] like the air of the place.

21.
And there were certain there hanging by the tongue:
and these were the blasphemers of the way of righteousness; and under them lay fire, [14] burning and punishing them.

22.
And there was a great lake, full of flaming mire, in which were certain men that pervert righteousness, [15] and tormenting angels afflicted them.

23.
And there were also others, women, hanged by their hair over that mire that bubbled up:
and these were they who adorned themselves for adultery; and the men who mingled with them in the defilement [16] of adultery, were hanging by the feet and their heads in that mire.
And I said:
I did not believe that I should come into this place.

24.
And I saw the murderers and those who conspired with them, cast into a certain strait place, full of evil snakes, and smitten by those beasts, and thus turning to and fro in that punishment; and worms, [17] as it were clouds of darkness, afflicted them.
And the souls of the murdered stood and looked upon the punishment of those murderers and said:
O God, thy judgment is just.

25.
And near that place I saw another strait place into which the gore and the filth of those who were being punished ran down and became there as it were a lake:
and there sat women having the gore up to their necks, and over against them sat many children who were born to them out of due time, crying; and there came forth from them sparks of fire and smote the women in the eyes:
and these were the accursed who conceived and caused abortion.

26.
And other men and women were burning up to the middle and were cast into a dark place and were beaten by evil spirits, and their inwards were eaten by restless worms: [18] and these were they who persecuted the righteous and delivered them up.

27.
And near those there were again women and men gnawing their own lips, and being punished and receiving a red-hot iron in their eyes: and these were they who blasphemed and slandered [19] the way of righteousness.

28.
And over against these again other men and women gnawing their tongues and having flaming fire in their mouths:
and these were the false witnesses. [20]

29.
And in a certain other place there were pebbles sharper than swords or any spit, red-hot, and women and men in tattered and filthy raiment rolled about on them in punishment:
and these were the rich who trusted in their riches and had no pity for orphans and widows, and despised the commandment [21] of God.

30.
And in another great lake, full of pitch and blood and mire bubbling up, there stood men and women up to their knees:
and these were the usurers and those who take interest on interest.

31.
And other men and women were being hurled down from a great cliff and reached the bottom, and again were driven by those who were set over them to climb up upon the cliff, and thence were hurled down again, and had no rest from this punishment:
and these were they who defiled [22] their bodies acting as women; and the women who were with them were those who lay with one another as a man with a woman.

32.
And alongside of that cliff there was a place full of much fire, and there stood men who with their own hands had made for themselves carven images instead of God.
And alongside of these were other men and women, having rods and striking each other and never ceasing from such punishment.

33.
And others again near them, women and men, burning and turning themselves and roasting:
and these were they that leaving the way of God [23] ...

Footnotes:

1. False prophets. Cf. Matt. vii. 15; xxiv. 5, 11. Cf. Pastor of Hermas, Mand. xi.
2. Sons of perdition. Cf. 2 Peter ii. 1-3; iii. 7, 16; 2 Thess. ii. 3, and Ep. of Lyons and Vienne, Euseb. H. E. v. 1.
3. Purify their souls. Cf. 2 Peter i. 18. Sons of lawlessness. Cf. Pastor Herm. Vis. iii. 6.
4. Mountain. Cf. 2 Peter i. 18.
5. The righteous. Cf. 2 Peter i. 1; iii. 19. What manner of. Cf. 2 Peter iii. 11. Encourage. Cf. Pastor Herm. Vis. iii. 3.
6. Not able to look. Cf. 2 Cor. iii. 7 ff.
7. Eye of man, etc. Cf. 1 Cor. ii. 9.
8. Snow and rose. Cf. Bk. of Enoch cvi. 2.
9. Wreath. Cf. Ep. of Lyons and Vienne, ap. Euseb. H. E. v. 1, 36.
10. Apparently all the disciples are supposed to have had the vision of heaven, but Peter alone that of hell. Unfading. Cf. 1 Peter i. 4.
11. Odour. Cf. Ep. of Lyons and Vienne, l. c., and Passion of S. Perpetua, ch. xiii.
12. High priests. Cf. Didache 13, 3.
13. Squalid. Cf. 2 Peter i. 19. Punishment. Cf. 2 Peter ii. 9. Punishing angels. Cf. Pastor Herm. Sim. vi. 3. Dark. Cf. Jude, vv. 6 and 13.
14. Blasphemers. Cf. 2 Peter ii. 12; Pastor Herm. Sim. viii. 6; ix. 18. Fire. Cf. 2 Peter iii. 7.
15. Mire. Cf. 2 Peter ii. 22. Pervert righteousness. Cf. Pastor Herm. Sim. viii. 6. Cf. Titus i. 14.
16. Cf. Jude 7. Defilement. Cf. 2 Peter ii. 10, 14, 17, 20; Jude 8. Cf. Pastor Herm. Sim. vi. 5.
17. Darkness. Cf. 2 Peter ii. 17. Worms. Cf. Isaiah lxvi. 24; Mark ix. 48.
18. Restless worms. Cf. Isaiah lxvi. 24; Mark ix. 48. Cf. Esdras, Ante-Nicene Lib., vol. xvi., p. 47; Pastor Herm. Sim. ix. 19; viii. 6.
19. Slandered. Cf. 2 Peter ii. 2; Jude 8, 10.
20. False witnesses. Cf. Hermas. Mand. viii. 5.

21. The rich, etc. Cf. 2 Peter ii. 14. Cf. Pastor Herm. Vis. iii. 9; Sim. ix. 20; Sim. i. 8, and Mand. viii. 5. Commandment. Cf. 2 Peter ii. 21; iii. 2.
22. Defiled. 2 Peter ii. 10. Cf. Rom. i. 26 ff.; Jude 8.
23. Way of God. 2 Peter ii. 2. Pastor Herm. Vis. iii. 7; viii. 6; ix. 19, 22.

Fragments of the Apocalypse of Peter

1.
Clemens Alexandrinus, Eclog. 48.
For instance, Peter in the Apocalypse says that the children who are born out of due time shall be of the better part:
and that these are delivered over to a care-taking angel that they may attain a share of knowledge and gain the better abode [after suffering what they would have suffered if they had been in the body:
but the others shall merely obtain salvation as injured beings to whom mercy is shown, and remain without punishment, receiving this as a reward]. [1]

2.
Clem. Alex. Eclog. 49.
But the milk of the women running down from their breasts and congealing shall engender small flesh-eating beasts: and these run up upon them and devour them. [2]

3.
Macarius Magnes, Apocritica iv., 6 cf. 16.
The earth, it (sc. the Apoc. of Peter) says, "shall present all men before God at the day of judgment, being itself also to be judged, with the heaven also which encompasses it."

4.
Clem. Alex. Eclog. 41.
The scripture says that infants that have been exposed are delivered to a care-taking angel, by whom they are educated and so grow up, and they will be, it says, as the faithful of a hundred years old are here.

5.
Methodius, Conviv. ii., 6.
Whence also we have received in divinely-inspired scriptures that untimely births are delivered to care-taking angels, even if they are the offspring of adultery.

Footnotes:

1. The part of the quotation between square brackets is assigned by Harnack to Clement himself and not to the Apocalypse.
2. Cf. Esdras, Ante-Nicene Lib., vol. xvi., p. 473.

The Vision of Paul

Introduction

The present translation of the Vision of Paul is made from the text of a Latin version, edited by Mr. M. R. James in the Cambridge Texts and Studies, ii., 3, p. 11 ff.--from a ms. of the eighth century now in the Bibliotheque Nationale at Paris.

Tischendorf's Greek text was based on two mss., the earliest of which is at Munich and is of the thirteenth century.

This version has already been translated in the Ante-Nicene Library, vol. xvi.

A translation into English from a Syriac version (date unknown) was published by the Rev. J. Perkins, D.D., in the Journal of Sacred Literature, N. S., vol. vi., 1865, and republished by Tischendorf alongside of the Greek version in his Apocalypses Apocryphae.

The Revelation of Paul was known to S. Augustine, who thus refers to it in his Tractate 98 on the Gospel of John, S: 8:

"...There have been some vain individuals, who, with a presumption that betrays the grossest folly, have forged a Revelation of Paul, crammed with all manner of fables, which has been rejected by the Orthodox Church; affirming it to be that whereof he had said that he was caught up into the third heavens, and there heard unspeakable words which it is not lawful for a man to utter.'

Nevertheless, the audacity of such might be tolerable, had he said that he heard words which it is not as yet lawful for a man to utter; but when he said which it is not lawful for a man to utter,' who are they that dare to utter them with such impudence and non-success?"

Sozomen, H. E., vii., 19, after speaking of the Apocalypse of Peter, continues:

"So the work entitled The Apocalypse of the Apostle Paul,' though rejected by the ancients, is still esteemed by most of the monks.

Some persons affirm that the book was found during this reign (i.e., of Theodosius) by divine revelation, in a marble box, buried beneath the soil, in the house of Paul, at Tarsus, in Cilicia.

I have been informed that this report is false, by a presbyter of Tarsus, a man of very advanced age, as is indicated by his grey hairs."

The book was probably composed, or rather compiled, for it is largely indebted to previous Apocalyptic writings, about the time when it purports to have been discovered at Tarsus, i.e., 388 a.d., the year of the consulship of Theodosius the Less and Cynegius.

The alleged sending of a copy of the original to Jerusalem probably indicates the place where it was composed, or, at least, first found currency.

The Vision of Paul seems to have enjoyed great popularity during the Middle Ages.

Brandes (Halle, 1885), in his edition of two shorter Latin versions, enumerates twenty-two different mss. of the Latin and "gives particulars of French, English, Danish, and Slavonic forms of the legend."

Of the three main versions, the Latin and Syriac are longer and fuller than the Greek, which in its present form has been abbreviated.

Taking advantage of the excellent comparative table presented by Mr. M. R. James in his edition of the text, the translator has endeavoured to point out to the reader, by notes in the margin, the passages where the Latin varies from the Greek, and, to a less extent, from the Syriac. Parallel passages in other and earlier Apocalyptic writings are also indicated in the notes.

The Vision of Paul

Here Begins the Vision of Saint Paul the Apostle.
"But I will come to visions and revelations of the Lord:
I know a man in Christ fourteen years ago (whether in the body, I know not; or out of the body, I know not, God knoweth) snatched up in this manner to the third heaven:
and I know such a man, whether in the body or out of the body I know not, God knoweth; how that he was snatched up into Paradise and heard secret words which it is not lawful for men to speak; on behalf of such a one will I glory; but on mine own behalf I will not glory, save in my infirmities."--2 Cor. xii. 1-5.

1.
At what time was this revelation made?
In the consulship of Theodosius Augustus the Younger and Cynegius, [1] a certain nobleman then living in Tharsus, in the house which was that of Saint Paul, an angel appearing in the night revealed to him, saying that he should open the foundations of the house and should publish what he found, but he thought that these things were dreams.

2.
But the angel coming for the third time beat him and forced him to open the foundation.
And digging he found a marble box, inscribed on the sides; there was the revelation of Saint Paul, and his shoes in which he walked teaching the word of God.
But he feared to open that box and brought it to the judge; when he had received it, the judge, because it was sealed with lead, sent it to the Emperor Theodosius, fearing lest it might be something else; which when he had received the emperor opened it, and found the revelation of Saint Paul; a copy of it he sent to Jerusalem, and retained the original himself.

3.
While I was in the body in which I was snatched up to the third heaven, the word of the Lord came to me saying:
speak to the people: until when will ye transgress, and heap sin upon sin, and tempt the Lord who made you?
Ye are the sons of God, doing the works of the devil in the faith of Christ, on account of the impediments of the world.
Remember therefore and know that while every creature serves God, the human race alone sins.
But it reigns over every creature and sins more than all nature.

4.
For indeed the sun, the great light, often addressed the Lord saying:
Lord God Almighty, I look out upon the impieties and injustices of men; permit me and I shall do unto them what are my powers, that they may know that thou art God alone.
And there came a voice saying to him:
I know all these things, for mine eye sees and ear hears, but my patience bears them until they shall be converted and repent.
But if they do not return to me I will judge them all.

5.
For sometimes the moon and stars addressed the Lord saying:
Lord God Almighty, to us thou hast given the power of the night; till when shall we look down upon the impieties and fornications and homicides done by the sons of men?
Permit us to do unto them according to our powers, that they may know that thou art God alone.
And there came a voice unto them saying:
I know all these things, and mine eye looks forth and ear hears, but my patience bears with

The Forgotten Bible

them until they shall be converted and repent.

But if they do not return unto me I will judge them.

6.

And frequently also the sea exclaimed saying:

Lord God Almighty, men have defiled thy holy name in me; permit me to arise and cover every wood and orchard and the whole world, until I blot out all the sons of men from before thy face, that they may know that thou art God alone.

And the voice came again and said:

I know all things; mine eye seeth everything, and mine ear heareth, but my patience bears with them until they be converted and repent.

But if they do not return, I will judge them.

Sometimes the waters [2] also spoke against the sins of men saying:

Lord God Almighty, all the sons of men have defiled thy holy name.

And there came a voice saying:

I know all things before they come to pass, for mine eye seeth and mine ear heareth all things, but my patience bears with them until they be converted.

But if not I will judge them.

Frequently also the earth [3] too exclaimed to the Lord against the sons of men saying:

Lord God Almighty, I above every other creature of thine am harmed, supporting the fornications, adulteries, homicides, thefts, perjuries and magic and ill-doings of men and all the evil they do, so that the father rises up against the son, and the son upon the father, the alien against the alien, so that each one defiles his neighbour's wife.

The father ascends upon the bed of his own son, and the son likewise ascends the couch of his own father; and in all these evils, they who offer the sacrifice to thy name have defiled thy holy place.

Therefore I am injured above every creature, desiring not to shew my power to myself, and my fruits to the sons of men.

Permit me and I will destroy the virtue of my fruits. And there came a voice and said:

I know all things, and there is none who can hide himself from his sin.

Moreover I know their impieties, but my holiness suffers them until they be converted and repent.

But if they do not return unto me I will judge them.

7.

Behold, ye sons of men, the creature is subject to God, but the human race alone sins.

For this cause, therefore, ye sons of men, bless the Lord God unceasingly, every hour and every day: but more especially when the sun has set: [4]for at that hour all the angels proceed to the Lord to worship him and to present the works of men, which every man has wrought from the morning till the evening, whether good or evil.

And there is a certain angel who proceeds rejoicing concerning the man in whom he dwells.

When therefore the sun [5] has set in the first hour of night, in the same hour the angel of every people and every man and woman, who protect and preserve them, because man is the image of God:

similarly also in the matin hour which is the twelfth of the night, all the angels of men and women, go up to God to worship God, and present every work which each man has wrought, whether good or evil.

Moreover every day and night the angels show to God an account [6] of all the acts of the human race.

To you, therefore, I say, ye sons of men, bless the Lord God without fail all the days of your life.

8.

Therefore at the appointed hour all the angels whatever, rejoicing at once together, proceed before God that they may meet to worship at the hour determined.

And behold suddenly it became the hour of meeting, and the angels came to worship in the presence of God, and the spirit proceeded to meet them:

and there came a voice and said: Whence come ye, our angels, bearing the burdens of tidings?

9.

They answered and said:

We come from those who have renounced this world for the sake of thy holy name, wandering as pilgrims, and in caves of the rocks, and weeping every hour in which they inhabited the earth, and hungering and thirsting because of thy name, with their loins girded, having in their hands the incense of their hearts, and praying and blessing every hour, and restraining and overcoming themselves, weeping and wailing above the rest that inhabit the earth. And we indeed, their angels, mourn along with them:

whither therefore it shall please thee, command us to go and minister, lest others also do it, but the destitute above the rest who are on earth.

And there came the voice of God to them saying:

Know ye that now henceforward my grace is appointed unto you, and my help, who is my well-beloved Son, shall be present with them, guiding them every hour; ministering also to them, never deserting them, since their place is his habitation.

10.

When therefore these angels had retired, behold other angels came to adore in the presence of honour, in the assembly, who wept; and the spirit of God proceeded to meet them, and there came the voice of God and said:

Whence come ye, our angels, bearing the burdens of the ministry of the tidings of the world?

They answered and said in the presence of God:

We have arrived from those who called upon thy name, and the impediments of the world made them wretched, devising many occasions every hour, not even making one pure prayer, nor out of their whole heart, in all the time of their life; what need, therefore, is there to be present with men who are sinners?

And there came the voice of God to them:

It is necessary that ye should minister to them, until they be converted and repent:

but if they do not return to me I will judge them.

Know therefore, sons of men, that whatever things are wrought by you, these angels relate to God, whether good or evil.

11.

And the angel answered and said unto me:

Follow me, and I will show you the place of the just where they are led when they are deceased, and after these things taking thee into the abyss, I will show thee the souls of sinners and what sort of place they are led into when they have deceased.

And I proceeded back after the angel, and he led me into heaven, and I looked back upon the firmament, and I saw in the same place power, and there was there oblivion which deceives and draws down to itself the hearts of men, and the spirit of detraction, and the spirit of fornication, and the spirit of madness, and the spirit of insolence, and there were there the princes of vices:

these I saw under the firmament of heaven:

and again I looked back, and I saw angels without mercy, having no pity, whose countenance was full of madness, and their teeth sticking out beyond the mouth:

their eyes shone like the morning star of the east, and from the hairs of their head sparks of fire went out, or from their mouth.

And I asked the angel saying:

Sir, who are those?

And the angel answered and said unto me:

These are those who are destined to the souls of the impious in the hour of need, who did not believe that they had the Lord for their helper, nor hoped in him.

12.

And I looked on high and I saw other angels whose countenance shone as the sun, their loins girded with golden girdles, having palms in their hands, and the sign of God, clothed with garments in which was written the name of the Son of God, filled moreover with all meekness and pity; and I asked the angels saying:

Who are these, Lord, in so great beauty and pity?

And the angel answered and said unto me:

These are the angels of justice who are sent to lead up the souls of the just, in the hour of need, who believed that they had the Lord for their helper.

And I said to him:

Do the just and sinners necessarily meet witnesses when they have died?

And the angel answered and said to me:
There is one way by which all pass over to God, but the just having their helper with them are not confounded when they go to appear in the sight of God.

13.

And I said to the angel:
I wished to see the souls of the just and of sinners going out of the world.
And the angel answered and said unto me:
Look down upon the earth.
And I looked down from heaven upon the earth, and saw the whole world, and it was nothing in my sight and I saw the sons of men as though they were naught, and a-wanting, and I wondered and said to the angel:
Is this the greatness of men?
And the angel answered and said unto me:
It is, and these are they who do evil from morning till evening.
And I looked and saw a great cloud of fire spread over the whole world, and I said to the angel:
What is this, my Lord? and he said to me:
This is injustice stirred up by the princes of sinners.

14.

I indeed when I had heard this sighed and wept, and said to the angel:
I wished to see the souls of the just and of sinners, and to see in what manner they go out of the body.
And the angel answered and said unto me:
Look again upon the earth.
And I looked and saw all the world, and men were as naught and a-wanting:
and I looked carefully and saw a certain man about to die, and the angel said to me:
This one whom thou seest is a just man.
And I looked again and saw all his works, whatever he had done for the sake of God's name, and all his desires, both what he remembered, and what he did not remember; they all stood in his sight in the hour of need; and I saw the just man advance and find refreshment and confidence, and before he went out of the world the holy and the impious angels both attended:
and I saw them all, but the impious found no place of habitation in him, but the holy took possession of his soul, guiding it till it went out of the body:
and they roused the soul saying:
Soul, know thy body whence thou goest out, for it is necessary that thou shouldst return to the same body on the day of the resurrection, that thou mayest receive the things promised to all the just.
Receiving therefore the soul from the body, they immediately kissed it as familiarly known to them, saying to it:
Do manfully, for thou hast done the will of God while placed in the earth.
And there came to meet him the angel who watched him every day, and said to him:
Do manfully, soul; for I rejoice in thee, because thou hast done the will of God on earth:
for I related to God all thy works, such as they were.
Similarly also the spirit proceeded to meet him and said:
Soul, fear not, nor be disturbed, until thou comest into a place which thou hast never known, but I will be a helper unto thee:
for I found in thee a place of refreshment in the time when I dwelt in thee, while I was on earth.
And his spirit strengthened him, and his angel received him, and led him into heaven:
and an angel said:
Whither runnest thou, O soul, and dost thou dare to enter into heaven?
Wait and let us see if there is anything of ours in thee:
and behold we find nothing in thee.
I see also thy divine helper and angel, and the spirit is rejoicing along with thee, because thou hast done the will of God on earth.
And they led him along till he should worship in the sight of God.
And when they had ceased, immediately Michael and all the army of angels, with one voice, adored the footstool of his feet, and his doom, saying at the same time to the soul:
This is your God of all things, who made you in his own image and likeness.
Moreover the angel returns and points him out saying: God, remember his labours:

for this is the soul, whose works I related to thee, doing according to thy judgment.

And the spirit said likewise:

I am the spirit of vivification inspiring him:

for I had refreshment in him, in the time when I dwelt in him, doing according to thy judgment.

And there came the voice of God and said:

In as much as this man did not vex me, neither will I vex him; for according as he had pity, I also will have pity.

Let him therefore be handed over to Michael, the angel of the Covenant, and let him lead him into the Paradise of joy, that he himself may become co-heir with all the saints.

And after these things I heard the voices of a thousand thousand angels, and archangels, and cherubim, and twenty-four elders saying hymns, and glorifying the Lord and crying:

thou art just, O Lord, and just are thy judgments, and there is no acceptance of persons with thee, but thou rewardest unto every man according to thy judgment.

And the angel answered and said unto me:

Hast thou believed and known, that whatever each man of you has done, he sees in the hour of need?

And I said:

Yes, sir.

15.

And he saith to me:

Look again down on the earth, and watch the soul of an impious man going out of the body, which vexed the Lord day and night, saying:

I know nothing else in this world, I eat and drink, and enjoy what is in the world; for who is there who has descended into hell, and ascending has declared to us that there is judgment there! And again I looked carefully, and saw all the scorn of the sinner, and all that he did, and they stood together before him in the hour of need:

and it was done to him in that hour, in which he was threatened about his body at the judgment, and I said:

It were better for him if he had not been born.

And after these things, there came at the same time, the holy angels, and the malign, and the soul of the sinner and the holy angels did not find a place in it.

Moreover the malign angels cursed it; and when they had drawn it out of the body, the angels admonished it a third time, saying:

O wretched soul, look upon thy flesh, whence thou camest out:

for it is necessary that thou shouldst return to thy flesh in the day of resurrection, that thou mayest receive the due for thy sins and thy impieties.

16.

And when they had led it forth, the customary angel preceded it, and said to it:

O wretched soul, I am the angel belonging to thee, relating daily to the Lord thy malign works, whatever thou didst by night or day:

and if it were in my power, not for one day would I minister to thee, but none of these things was I able to do:

the judge is pitiful and just, and he himself commanded us that we should not cease to minister to the soul, till you should repent, but thou hast lost the time of repentance.

I indeed was strange to thee and thou to me.

Let us go on then to the just judge:

I will not dismiss thee, before I know from to-day why I was strange to thee.

And the spirit confounded him, and the angel troubled him.

When, therefore, they had arrived at the power, when he started to enter heaven, a labour was imposed upon him, above all other labour:

error and oblivion and murmuring met him, and the spirit of fornication, and the rest of the powers, and said to him:

Whither goest thou, wretched soul, and darest thou to rush into heaven? hold, that we may see if we have our qualities in thee, since we do not see that thou hast a holy helper. And after that I heard voices in the height of heaven saying:

Present that wretched soul to God, that it may know that it is God that it despised.

When, therefore, it had entered heaven, all the angels saw it, a thousand thousand exclaimed with one voice, all saying:

Woe to thee, wretched soul, for the sake of thy works which thou didst on earth; what answer art thou about to give to God when thou shalt have approached to adore him?

The angel who was with it answered and said: Weep with me, my beloved, for I have not found rest in this soul.

And the angels answered him and said:

Let such a soul be taken away from the midst of ours, for from the time he entered, the stink of him crosses to us angels.

And after these things it was presented, that it might worship in the sight of God, and an angel of God showed him God who made him after his own image and likeness.

Moreover his angel ran before him saying:

Lord God Almighty, I am the angel of this soul, whose works I presented to thee day and night, not doing according to thy judgment.

And the spirit likewise said:

I am the spirit who dwelt in it from the time it was made, in itself moreover I know it, and it has not followed my will:

judge it, Lord, according to thy judgment. And there came the voice of God to it and said:

Where is thy fruit which thou has made worthy of the goods which thou hast received?

Have I put a distance of one day between thee and the just man?

Did I not make the sun to arise upon thee as upon the just?

But the soul was silent, having nothing to answer:

and again there came a voice saying:

Just is the judgment of God, and there is no acceptance of persons with God, for whoever shall have done mercy, on them shall he have mercy, and whoever shall not have pitied neither shall God pity him.

Let him therefore be handed over to the angel Tartaruch, who is set over the punishments, and let him place him in outer darkness, where there is weeping and gnashing of teeth, and let him be there till the great day of judgment.

And after these things I heard the voice of angels and archangels saying:

Thou art just, Lord, and thy judgment is just.

17.

And again I saw, and behold a soul which was led forward by two angels, weeping and saying:

Have pity on me, just God, God the judge, for to-day is seven days since I went out of my body, and I was handed over to these two angels, and they led me through to those places, which I had never seen.

And God, the just judge, saith to him:

What hast thou done? for thou never didst mercy, wherefore thou wast handed over to such angels as have no mercy, and because thou didst not do uprightly, so neither did they act piously with thee in the hour of thy need.

Confess therefore thy sins which thou didst commit when placed in the world.

And he answered and said:

Lord, I did not sin.

And the Lord, the just Lord, was angered in fury when it said:

I did not sin, because it lied; and God said:

Dost thou think thou art still in the world? if any one of you, sinning there, conceal and hide his sin from his neighbour, here indeed nothing whatever shall be hid:

for when the souls come to adore in sight of the throne, both the good works and the sins of each one are made manifest.

And hearing these things the soul was silent, having no answer.

And I heard the Lord God, the just judge, again saying:

Come, angel of this soul, and stand in the midst.

And the angel of the sinful soul came, having in his hands a manuscript, and said:

These, Lord, in my hands, are all the sins of this soul from his youth till to-day, from the tenth year of his birth:

and if thou command, Lord, I will also relate his acts from the beginning of his fifteenth year.

And the Lord God, the just judge, said:

I say unto thee, angel, I do not expect of thee an account of him since he began to be fifteen years old, but state his sins for five years before he died and before he came hither.

And again God, the just judge, said:

For by myself I swear, and by my holy angels, and by my virtue, that if he had repented five years before he died, on account of one year's life, oblivion would now be thrown over all the evils which he sinned before, and he would have indulgence and remission of sins:

now indeed he shall perish.
And the angel of the sinful soul answered and said:
Lord, command that angel to exhibit those souls.

18.
And in that same hour the souls were exhibited in the midst, and the soul of the sinner knew them; and the Lord said to the soul of the sinner:
I say unto thee, soul, confess thy work which thou wroughtest in these souls, whom thou seest, when they were in the world.
And he answered and said:
Lord, it is not yet a full year since I slew this one and poured his blood upon the ground, and with another (a woman) I committed fornication:
not this alone, but I also greatly harmed her in taking away her goods.
And the Lord God, the just judge, said: Either thou didst not know that he who does violence to another, if he dies first who sustains the violence, is kept in this place until the doer of hurt dies, and then both stand in the presence of the judge, and now each receives according to his deed.
And I heard a voice of one saying:
Let that soul be delivered into the hands of Tartarus, and led down into hell:
he shall lead him into the lower prison and he shall be put in torments, and left there till the great day of judgment.
And again I heard a thousand thousand angels saying hymns to the Lord, and crying:
Thou art just, O Lord, and just are thy judgments.

19.
The angel answered and said unto me:
Hast thou perceived all these things? and I said, Yes, sir.
And he said to me:
Follow me again, and I will take thee, and show thee the places of the just.
And I followed the angel, and he raised me to the third heaven, and placed me at the entry of the door:
and looking carefully I saw, and the door was of gold, and two columns of gold, full above of golden letters, and the angel tuned again to me and said:
Blessed wert thou, if thou hadst entered into these doors, for it is not allowed to any to enter except only to those who have goodness and innocence of body in all things. And I asked the angel about everything and said:
Sir, tell me on what account these letters are put upon those tables?
The angel answered and said unto me:
These are the names of the just, serving God with their whole heart, who dwell on the earth.
And again I said:
Sir, therefore their names and countenance and the likeness of these who serve God are in heaven, and are known to the angels:
for they know who are the servants of God with all their heart, before they go out of the world.

20.
And when I had entered the interior of the gate of Paradise, [7] there came out to meet me an old man whose countenance shone as the sun; and when he had embraced me he said:
Hail, Paul, beloved of God.
And he kissed me with a cheerful countenance.
He wept, and I said to him:
Brother, why dost thou weep?
And again sighing and lamenting he said:
We are hurt by men, and they vex us greatly; for many are the good things which the Lord has prepared, and great is his promise, but many do not perceive them.
And I asked the angel, and said:
Sir, who is this?
And he said to me:
This is Enoch, the scribe of righteousness.
And I entered into the interior of that place, and immediately I saw the sun, [8] and coming it saluted me laughing and rejoicing.
And when it had seen (me), it turned away and wept, and said to me:
Paul, would that thou shouldst receive thy labours which thou hast done in the human race.

For me, indeed, I have seen the great and many good things, which God has prepared for the just, and the promises of God are great, but many do not perceive them; but even by many labours scarcely one or two enters into these places.

21.

And the angel answered and said to me, [9] Whatever I now show thee here, and whatever thou shalt hear, tell it not to any one in the earth.

And he led me and shewed me:

and there I heard words which it is not lawful for a man to speak.

And again he said, For now follow me, and I will shew thee what thou oughtest to narrate in public and relate.

And he took me down from the third heaven, and led me into the second heaven, and again he led me on to the firmament and from the firmament he led me over the doors of heaven:

the beginning of its foundation was on the river which waters all the earth.

And I asked the angel and said, Lord, what is this river of water? and he said to me, This is Oceanus!

And suddenly I went out of heaven, and I understood that it is the light of heaven which lightens all the earth.

For the land there is seven times brighter [10] than silver.

And I said, Lord, what is this place?

And he said to me, This is the land of promise. Hast thou never heard what is written:

Blessed are the meek:

for they shall inherit the earth?

The souls therefore of the just, when they have gone out of the body, are meanwhile dismissed to this place.

And I said to the angel, Then this land will be manifested before the time?

The angel answered and said to me, When Christ, whom thou preachest, shall come to reign, then, by the sentence of God, [11] the first earth will be dissolved and this land of promise will then be revealed, and it will be like dew or cloud, and then the Lord Jesus Christ, the King Eternal, will be manifested and will come with all his saints to dwell in it, and he will reign over them a thousand years, and they will eat of the good things which I shall now show unto thee.

22.

And I looked around upon that land and I saw a river flowing of milk and honey, and there were trees planted by the bank of that river, full of fruit:

moreover each single tree bore twelve fruits in the year, having various and diverse fruits:

and I saw the created things which are in that place and all the work of God, and I saw there palms of twenty cubits, but others of ten cubits:

and that land was seven times brighter than silver.

And there were trees full of fruits from the roots to the highest branches, of ten thousand fruits of palms upon ten thousand fruits.

The grape-vines moreover had ten thousand plants. [12]Moreover in the single vines there were ten thousand thousand bunches and in each of these a thousand single grapes:

moreover these single trees bore a thousand fruits.

And I said to the angel, Why does each tree bear a thousand fruits?

The angel answered and said unto me, Because the Lord God gives an abounding flood of gifts to the worthy, because they also of their own will afflicted themselves when they were placed in the world doing all things on account of his holy name.

And again I said to the angel, Sir, are these the only promises which the Most Holy God makes?

And he answered and said to me:

No! there are seven times greater than these.

But I say unto thee that when the just go out of the body they shall see the promises and the good things which God has prepared for them.

Till then, they shall sigh, and lament saying:

Have we emitted any word from our mouth to vex our neighbour even on one day?

I asked and said again:

Are these alone the promises of God?

And the angel answered and said unto me:

These whom you now see are the souls of the married [13] and those who kept the chastity of their nuptials, containing themselves.

But to the virgins and those who hunger and thirst after righteousness and those who afflicted themselves for the sake of the name of God, God will give seven times greater than these, which I shall now show thee.

And then he took me up from that place where I saw these things and behold, a river, and its waters were greatly whiter than milk, and I said to the angel, What is this?

And he said to me:

This is the Acherousian Lake where is the City of Christ, but not every man is permitted to enter that city; for this is the journey which leads to God, and if anyone is a fornicator and impious, and is converted and shall repent and do fruits worthy of repentance, at first indeed when he shall have gone out of the body, he is led and adores God, and thence by command of the Lord he is delivered to the angel Michael and he baptizes him in the Acherousian Lake--thus he leads them into the City of Christ alongside of those who have never sinned.

But I wondered and blessed the Lord God for all the things which I saw.

23.

And the angel answered and said unto me:
Follow me and I will lead thee into the City of Christ.

And he was standing on the Acherousian Lake and he put me into a golden ship [14] and angels as it were three thousand were saying hymns before me till I arrived at the City of Christ.

Moreover those who inhabited the City of Christ greatly rejoiced over me as I went to them, and I entered and saw the City of Christ, and it was all of gold, and twelve walls encircled it, and twelve interior towers, and each wall had between them single stadia in the circuit:

And I said to the angel, Sir, how much is a stadium?

The angel answered and said to me:

As much as there is between the Lord God and the men who are on the earth, for the City of Christ is alone great.

And there were twelve gates in the circuit of the city, of great beauty, and four rivers which encircled it.

There was, moreover, a river of honey and a river of milk, and a river of wine and a river of oil.

And I said to the angel:
What are these rivers surrounding that city?

And he saith to me:

These are the four rivers which flow sufficiently for those who are in this land of promise, of which the names [15] are:

the river of honey is called Fison, and the river of milk Euphrates, and the river of oil Gion, and the river of wine Tigris, such therefore they are for those who when placed in the world did not use the power of these things, but they hungered for these things and afflicted themselves for the sake of the Lord God:

so that when these enter into this city, the Lord will assign them these things on high above all measure.

24.

I indeed entering the gates saw trees great and very high before the doors of the city, having no fruit but leaves only, and I saw a few men scattered in the midst of the trees, and they lamented greatly when they saw anyone enter the city.

And those trees were sorry for them and humbled themselves and bowed down and again erected themselves. And I saw and wept with them and I asked the angel and said:

Sir, who are these who are not admitted to enter into the City of Christ?

And he said to me:

These are they who zealously abstained day and night in fasts, but they had a proud heart above other men, glorifying and praising themselves and doing nothing for their neighbours.

For they gave some friendly greeting, but to others they did not even say hail! and indeed they shewed hospitality to those only whom they wished, and if they did anything whatever for their neighbour they were immoderately puffed up.

And I said:
What then, Sir?

Did their pride prevent them from entering into the City of Christ?

And the angel answered and said unto me:

Pride is the root of all evils.

Are they better than the Son of God who came to the Jews with much humility? And I asked him and said:

Why is it that the trees humble themselves and erect themselves again?

And the angel answered and said to me: The whole time which these men passed on earth zealously serving God, on account of the confusion and reproaches of men at the time, they blushed and humiliated themselves, but they were not saddened. nor did they repent that they should recede from their pride which was in them.

This is why the trees humble themselves, and again are raised up.

And I asked and said:

For what cause were they admitted to the doors of the city?

The angel answered and said unto me:

Because of the great goodness of God, and because there is the entry of his holy men entering into this city:

for this cause they are left in this place, but when Christ the King Eternal enters with his saints, as he enters just men may pray for these, and then they may enter into the city along with them:

but yet none of them is able to have assurance such as they have who humbled themselves, serving the Lord God all their lives.

25.

But I went on while the angel instructed me, and he carried me to the river of honey, and I saw there Isaiah and Jeremiah [16] and Ezekiel and Amos, and Micah and Zechariah, the minor and major prophets, and they saluted me in the city.

I said to the angel:

What way is this?

And he said to me:

This is the way of the prophets, every one who shall have afflicted his soul and not done his own will because of God, when he shall have gone out of the world and have been led to the Lord God and adored him, then by the command of God he is handed over to Michael, and he leads him into the city to this place of the prophets, and they salute him as their friend and neighbour because he did the will of God.

26.

Again he led me where there is a river of milk, and I saw in that place all the infants whom Herod slew because of the name of Christ, and they saluted me, and the angel said to me:

All who keep their chastity with purity, when they shall have come out of the body, after they adore the Lord God are delivered to Michael and are led to the infants and they salute them, saying that they are our brothers and friends and members; in themselves they shall inherit the promises of God.

27.

Again he took me up and carried me to the north of the city and led me where there was a river of wine, and there I saw Abraham and Isaac and Jacob, Lot and Job and other saints, [17] and they saluted me:

and I asked and said:

What is this place, my Lord?

The angel answered and said to me:

All who are receivers of pilgrims, when they go out of the world, first adore the Lord God, and are delivered to Michael and by this way are led into the city, and all the just salute him as son and brother, and say unto him:

Because thou hast observed humanity and the receiving of pilgrims, come, have an inheritance in the city of the Lord our God:

every just man shall receive good things of God in the city, according to his own action.

28.

And again he carried me near the river of oil on the east of the city.

And I saw there men rejoicing and singing psalms, and I said: Who are those, my Lord?

And the angel saith to me:

Those are they who devoted themselves to God with their whole heart and had no pride in themselves.

For all those who rejoice in the Lord God and sing psalms to the Lord with their whole heart are here led into this city.

29.

And he carried me into the midst of the city near the twelve walls. [18]But there was in this place a higher wall, and I asked and said:

Is there in the City of Christ a wall which in honour exceeds this place?

And the angel answering said to me:

There is a second better than the first, and similarly a third than the second, as each exceeds the other, unto the twelfth wall.

And I said:

Tell me, Sir, why one exceeds another in glory?

And the angel answered and said unto me:

All who have in themselves even a little detraction or zeal or pride, something of his glory would be made void even if he were in the city of Christ:

look backward!

And turning round I saw golden thrones placed in each gate, and on them men having golden diadems and gems: [19]and I looked carefully and I saw inside between the twelve men thrones placed in another rank which appeared of much glory, so that no one is able to recount their praise.

And I asked the angel and said:

My lord, who is on the throne?

And the angel answered and said unto me:

Those thrones belong to those who had goodness and understanding of heart and made themselves fools for the sake of the Lord God, nor knew new Scriptures nor psalms, but, mindful of one chapter of the commands of God, and hearing what it contained they wrought thereby in much diligence and had a right zeal before the Lord God, and the admiration of them will seize all the saints in presence of the Lord God, for talking with one another they say, Wait and see the unlearned who know nothing more:

by which means they merited so great and such a garment and so great glory on account of their innocence.

And I saw in the midst of this city a great altar, very high, and there was one standing near the altar whose countenance shone as the sun, and he held in his hands a psaltery and harp, and he sang psalms, saying Halleluia!

And his voice filled the whole city:

at the same time when all they who were on the towers and gates heard him they responded Halleluia! so that the foundations of the city were shaken:

and I asked the angel and said, Sir, who is this of so great power?

And the angel said to me:

This is David:

this is the city of Jerusalem, for when Christ the King of Eternity shall come with the assurance of His kingdom, he again shall go before him that he may sing psalms, and all the just at the same time shall sing psalms responding Halleluia!

And I said, Sir, how did David alone above the other saints make a beginning of psalm-singing?

And the angel answered and said unto me: Because Christ the Son of God sits at the right hand of His Father, and this David sings psalms before him in the seventh heaven, and as is done in the heavens so also below, because the host may not be offered to God without David, but it is necessary that David should sing psalms in the hour of the oblation of the body and blood of Christ:

as it is performed in heaven so also on earth.

30.

And I said to the angel:

Sir, what is Alleluia?

And the angel answered and said to me:

You ask questions about everything.

And he said to me, Alleluia is said in the Hebrew language of God and angels, for the meaning of Alleluia is this:

tecel cat. marith macha. [20] And I said, Sir, what is tecel cat. marith macha?

And the angel answered and said unto me:

Tecel cat. marith macha is:

Let us all bless him together.

I asked the angel and said, Sir, do all who say Alleluia bless the Lord?

And the angel answered and said to me:

It is so, and again, therefore, if any one sing Alleluia and those who are present do not sing at the same time, they commit sin because they do not sing along with him.

The Forgotten Bible

And I said:

My lord, does he also sin if he be hesitating or very old?

The angel answered and said unto me:

Not so, but he who is able and does not join in the singing, know such as a despiser of the Word, and it would be proud and unworthy that he should not bless the Lord God his maker.

31.

Moreover when he had ceased speaking to me, he led me outside the city through the midst of the trees and far from the places of the land of the good, and put me across the river of milk and honey:

and after that he led me over the ocean which supports the foundations of heaven.

The angel answered and said unto me:

Dost thou understand why thou goest hence?

And I said:

Yes, sir.

And he said to me:

Come and follow me, and I will show thee the souls of the impious and sinners, that thou mayest know what manner of place it is.

And I proceeded with the angel and he carried me by the setting of the sun, and I saw the beginning of heaven founded on a great river of water, and I asked: What is this river of water?

And he said to me:

This is Ocean which surrounds all the Earth.

And when I was at the outer limit of Ocean I looked, and there was no light in that place, but darkness and sorrow and sadness:

and I sighed.

And I saw there a fervent river of fire, and in it a multitude of men and women immersed up to the knees, and other men up to the navel, others even up to the lips, others moreover up to the hair.

And I asked the angel and said:

Sir, who are those in the fiery river?

And the angel answered and said to me:

They are neither hot nor cold, because they were found neither in the number of the just nor in the number of the impious. [21]For those spent the time of their life on earth passing some days in prayer, but others in sins and fornications, until their death.

And I asked him and said:

Who are these, Sir, immersed up to their knees in fire?

He answered and said to me:

These are they who when they have gone out of church throw themselves into strange conversations to dispute.

Those indeed who are immersed up to the navel are those who, when they have taken the body and blood of Christ go and fornicate and did not cease from their sins till they died.

Those who are immersed up to the lips are the detractors of each other when they assemble in the church of God: those up to the eyebrows are those who nod approval of themselves and plot spite against their neighbour. [22]

32.

And I saw on the north a place of various and diverse punishments full of men and women,[23] and a river of fire ran down into it. Moreover I observed and I saw pits great in depth, and in them several souls together, and the depth of that place was as it were three thousand cubits, and I saw them groaning and weeping and saying:

Have pity on us, O Lord! and none had pity on them.

And I asked the angel and said:

Who are these, Sir?

And the angel answered and said unto me:

These are they who did not hope in the Lord, that they would be able to have him as their helper.

And I asked and said:

Sir, if these souls remain for thirty or forty generations thus one upon another, if they were sent deeper, the pits I believe would not hold them.

And he said to me:

The Abyss has no measure, for beyond [24] this it stretches down below him who is down in it: and so it is, that if perchance anyone should take a stone and throw it into a very deep well and after many hours it should reach the bottom, such is the abyss. For when the souls are thrown in there, they hardly reach the bottom in fifty years.

33.

I, indeed, when I heard this, wept and groaned over the human race.
The angel answered and said unto me:
Why dost thou weep?
Art thou more pitiful than God?
For though God is good, He knows also that there are punishments, and He patiently bears with the human race, dismissing each one to work his own will in the time in which he dwells on the earth.

34.

I further observed the fiery river and saw there a man being tortured by Tartaruchian angels having in their hands an iron with three hooks with which they pierced the bowels of that old man:
and I asked the angel, and said:
Sir, who is that old man on whom such torments are imposed?
And the angel answered and said to me:
He whom you see was a presbyter who did not perform well his ministry:
when he had been eating and drinking and committing fornication he offered the host to the Lord at his holy altar.

35.

And I saw not far away another old man led on by malign angels running with speed, and they pushed him into the fire up to his knees, and they struck him with stones and wounded his face like a storm, and did not allow him to say:
Have pity on me!
And I asked the angel and he said to me:
He whom you see was a bishop, and did not perform well his episcopate, who indeed accepted the great name but did not enter into the witness of him who gave him the name in all his life, seeing that he did not do just judgment, and did not pity widows and orphans, but now he receives retribution according to his iniquity and his works.

36.

And I saw another man in the fiery river up to his knees. Moreover his hands were stretched out and bloody, and worms proceeded from his mouth and nostrils and he was groaning and weeping, and crying he said:
Have pity on me! for I am hurt above the rest who are in this punishment.
And I asked, Sir, who is this?
And he said to me:
This man whom thou seest, was a deacon who devoured the oblations and committed fornications and did not right in the sight of God, for this cause he unceasingly pays this penalty.
And I looked closely and saw alongside of him another [25] man whom they delivered up with haste and cast into the fiery river, and he was (in it) up to the knees:
and there came the angel who was set over the punishments having a great fiery razor, and with it he cut the lips of that man and the tongue likewise.
And sighing, I lamented and asked: Who is that, sir.
And he said to me, He whom thou seest was a reader and read to the people, but he himself did not keep the precepts of God:
now he also pays the proper penalty.

37.

And I saw another multitude of pits in the same place, and in the midst of it a river full of a multitude of men and women, [26] and worms [27] consumed them.
But I lamented and sighing asked the angel and said:
Sir, who are these?
And he said to me:
These are those who exacted interest [28] on interest and trusted in their riches and did not hope in God that He was their helper.
And after that I looked and saw another place, very narrow, and it was like a wall, and fire round about it.
And I saw inside men and women gnawing [29] their tongues, and I asked:

The Forgotten Bible

Sir, who are these.

And he said to me:

These are they who in church disparage the Word of God, not attending to it, but as it were make naught of God and His angels: for that cause they now likewise pay the proper penalty.

38.

And I observed and saw another old man down in a pit and his countenance was like blood, and I asked and said, Sir, what is this place?

And he said to me:

Into that pit stream all the punishments. And I saw men and women immersed up to the lips and I asked, Sir, who are these?

And he said to me:

These are the magicians who prepared for men and women evil magic arts and did not find how to stop them till they died.

And again I saw men and women with very black faces in a pit of fire, [30] and I sighed and lamented and asked, Sir, who are these?

And he said to me:

These are fornicators and adulterers who committed adultery having wives of their own: likewise also the women committed adultery having husbands of their own: therefore they unceasingly suffer penalties.

39.

And I saw there girls having black [31] raiment, and four terrible angels having in their hands burning chains, and they put them on the necks of the girls and led them into darkness:

and I, again weeping, asked the angel:

Who are these, Sir?

And he said to me: These are they who, when they were virgins, defiled their virginity unknown to their parents; for which cause they unceasingly pay the proper penalties.

And again I observed there men and women with hands cut and their feet placed naked in a place of ice and snow, and worms devoured them.

But seeing them I lamented and asked:

Sir, who are these?

And he said to me:

These are they who harmed orphans and widows and the poor, [32] and did not hope in the Lord, for which cause they unceasingly pay the proper penalties.

And I observed and saw others hanging over a channel of water, and their tongues were very dry, and many fruits were placed in their sight, and they were not permitted to take of them, and I asked:

Sir, who are these?

And he said to me:

These are they who break their fast [33] before the appointed hour, for this cause they unceasingly pay these penalties.

And I saw other men and women hanging by their eyebrows and their hair, [34] and a fiery river drew them, and I said:

Who are these, my Lord?

And he said to me: [35]These are they who join themselves not to their own husbands and wives but to whores, and therefore they unceasingly pay the proper penalties.

And I saw other men and women covered with dust, and their countenance was like blood, and they were in a pit of pitch and sulphur and running down into a fiery river, and I asked:

Sir, who are these? [36]And he said to me:

These are they who committed the iniquity of Sodom and Gomorrah, the male with the male, for which reason they unceasingly pay the penalties.

40.

And [37] I observed and saw men and women clothed in bright garments, having their eyes blind, placed in a pit, and I asked:

Sir, who are these?

And he said to me:

These are of the people who did alms, and knew not the Lord God, for which reason they unceasingly pay the proper penalties.

And I observed and saw other men and women on an obelisk of fire, and beasts tearing them in pieces, and they were not allowed to say, Lord have pity on us!

And I saw the angel [38] of penalties putting heavy punishments on them and saying:

Acknowledge the Son of God; for this was predicted to you, when the divine Scriptures were read to you, and you did not attend; for which cause God's judgment is just, for your actions have apprehended you and brought you into these penalties.

But I sighed and wept, and I asked and said:

Who are these men and women who are strangled in fire and pay their penalties?

And he answered me:

These are women who defiled the image of God when bringing forth infants out of the womb, and these are the men who lay with them.

And their infants addressed the Lord God and the angels who were set over the punishments, saying: [39] Cursed be the hour to our parents, for they defiled the image of God, having the name of God but not observing His precepts:

they gave us for food to dogs and to be trodden down of swine:

others they threw into the river.

But their infants [40] were handed over to the angels of Tartarus who were set over the punishments, that they might lead them to a wide place of mercy:

but their fathers and mothers were tortured in a perpetual punishment.

And after that I saw men and women clothed with rags full of pitch and fiery sulphur, and dragons were coiled about their necks and shoulders and feet, and angels having fiery horns restrained them and smote them, and closed their nostrils, saying to them:

Why did ye not know the time in which it was right to repent and serve God, and did not do it? And I asked:

Sir, who are these?

And he said to me:

These are they who seem to give up the world for God, [41] putting on our garb, but the impediments of the world made them wretched, not maintaining agapae, and they did not pity widows and orphans:

they did not receive the stranger and the pilgrim, nor did they offer the oblations, and they did not pity their neighbour.

Moreover their prayer did not even on one day ascend pure to the Lord God, but many impediments of the world detained them, and they were not able to do right in the sight of God, and the angels enclosed them in the place of punishments. Moreover they saw those who were in punishments and said to them:

We indeed when we lived in the world neglected God, and ye also did likewise:

as we also truly when we were in the world knew that ye were sinners.

But ye said:

These are just and servants of God, now we know why ye were called by the name of the Lord:

for which cause they also pay their own penalties.

And sighing I wept and said:

Woe unto men, woe unto sinners! why were they born?

And the angel answered and said unto me:

Why dost thou lament? [42] Art thou more pitiful than the Lord God who is blessed forever, who established judgment and sent forth every man to choose good and evil in his own will and do what pleases him?

Then I lamented again very greatly, and he said to me:

Dost thou lament when as yet thou hast not seen greater punishments?

Follow me and thou shalt see seven times greater than these.

41.

And he carried me south and placed me above a well, and I found it sealed with seven seals:

and answering, the angel who was with me said to the angel of that place:

Open the mouth of the well that Paul, the well-beloved of God, may see, for authority is given him that he may see all the pains of hell.

And the angel said to me:

Stand afar off that thou mayest be able to bear the stench of this place.

When therefore the well was opened, immediately there arose from it a certain hard and malign stench, which surpasses all punishments:

and I looked into the well and I saw fiery masses glowing in every part, and narrow places, and the mouth of the well was narrow so as to admit one man only.

And the angel answered and said unto me:

If any man shall have been put into this well of the abyss and it shall have been sealed over him, no remembrance of him shall ever be made in the sight of the Father and His Son and the holy angels.

And I said:

Who are these, Sir, who are put into this well?

And he said to me:

They are whoever shall not confess that Christ has come in the flesh and that the Virgin Mary brought him forth, and whoever says that the bread and cup of the Eucharist of blessing are not this body and blood of Christ.

42.

And I looked to the south in the west and I saw there a [43] restless worm and in that place there was gnashing of teeth:

moreover the worms were one cubit long, and had two heads, and there I saw men and women in cold and gnashing of teeth.

And I asked and said, Sir, who are these in this place?

And he said to me:

These are they who say that Christ did not rise from the dead and that this flesh will not rise again.

And I asked and said:

Sir, is there no fire nor heat in this place?

And he said to me:

In this place there is nothing else but cold and snow: [44] and again he said to me:

Even if the sun should rise upon them, they do not become warm on account of the superabundant cold of that place and the snow.

But hearing these things I stretched out my hands and wept, and sighing again, I said:

It were better for us if we had not been born, [45] all of us who are sinners.

43.

But when those who were in the same place saw me weeping with the angel, they themselves cried out and wept saying, Lord God have mercy upon us!

And after these things I saw the heavens open, and Michael [46] the archangel descending from heaven, and with him was the whole army of angels, and they came to those who were placed in punishment and seeing him, again weeping, they cried out and said, Have pity on us!

Michael the archangel, have pity on us and on the human race, for on account of thy prayers the earth standeth.

We now see the judgment and acknowledge the Son of God!

It was impossible for us before these things to pray for this, before we entered into this place:

for we heard that there was a judgment before we went out of the world, but impediments and the life of the world did not allow us to repent.

And Michael answered and said:

Hear Michael speaking!

I am he who stands in the sight of God every hour:

As the Lord liveth, in whose sight I stand, I do not intermit one day or one night praying incessantly for the human race, and I indeed pray for those who are on the earth:

but they do not cease doing iniquity and fornications, and they do not bring to me any good while they are placed on earth:

and ye have consumed in vanity the time in which ye ought to have repented.

But I have always prayed thus and I now beseech that God may send dew and send forth rains upon the earth, and now I desire until the earth produce its fruits and verily I say, that if any have done but a little good, I will agonise for him, protecting him till he have escaped the judgment of penalties.

Where therefore are your prayers?

Where are your penances?

Ye have lost your time contemptuously.

But now weep and I will weep with you and the angels who are with me with the well-beloved Paul, if perchance the merciful God will have pity and give you refreshment.

But hearing these words they cried out and wept greatly, and all said with one voice:

Have pity on us, Son of God! And I, Paul, sighed and said:

O Lord God! have pity on thy creature, have pity on the sons of men, have pity on thine image.

44.
And I looked and saw the heaven move like a tree shaken by the wind.
Suddenly, moreover, they threw themselves on their faces in the sight of the throne.
And I saw twenty-four elders and twenty-four thousand adoring God, and I saw an altar and veil and throne, and all were rejoicing; and the smoke of a good odour was raised near the altar of the throne of God, and I heard the voice of one saying:
For the sake of what do ye our angels and ministers intercede?
And they cried out saying:
We intercede seeing thy many kindnesses to the human race.
And after these things I saw the Son of God descending from heaven, and a diadem was on his head.
And seeing him those who were placed in punishment exclaimed all with one voice saying:
Have pity, Son of the High God!
Thou art He who shewest refreshment for all in the heavens and on earth, and on us likewise have pity, for since we have seen Thee, we have refreshment.
And a voice went out from the Son of God through all the punishments saying:
And what work have ye done that ye demand refreshment from me?
My blood was poured out for your sakes, and not even so did ye repent:
for your sakes I wore the crown of thorns on my head:
for you I received buffets on my cheeks, and not even so did ye repent.
I asked water when hanging on the cross and they gave me vinegar mixed with gall, with a spear they opened my right side, for my name's sake they slew my prophets and just men, and in all these things I gave you a place of repentance and ye would not.
Now, however, for the sake of Michael the archangel of my covenant and the angels who are with him, and because of Paul the well-beloved, whom I would not vex, for the sake of your brethren who are in the world and offer oblations, and for the sake of your sons, because my precepts are in them, and more for the sake of mine own kindness, on the day on which I rose from the dead, I give to you all who are in punishment a night and a day of refreshment forever.
And they all cried out and said, We bless thee, Son of God, that Thou hast given us a night and a day of respite.
For better to us is a refreshment of one day above all the time of our life which we were on earth, and if we had plainly known that this was intended for those who sin, we would have worked no other work, we would have done no business, and we would have done no iniquity:
what need had we for pride in the world?
For here our pride is crushed which ascended from our mouth against our neighbour:
our plagues and excessive straitness and the tears and the worms which are under us, these are much worse to us than the pains which we have left behind us.
When they said thus, the malign angels of the penalties were angered with them, saying:
How long do ye lament and sigh? for ye had no pity.
For this is the judgment of God who had no pity.
But ye received this great grace of a day and a night's refreshment on the Lord's Day for the sake of Paul the well-beloved of God who descended to you.

45.
And after that the angel said to me:
Hast thou seen all these things?
And I said:
Yes, Sir.
And he said to me:
Follow me and I will lead thee into Paradise, that the just who are there may see thee, for lo! they hope to see thee, and they are ready to come to meet thee in joy and gladness.
And I followed the angel by the impulse of the Holy Spirit, and he placed me in Paradise and said to me:
This is Paradise in which Adam and his wife erred.
Moreover I entered Paradise and saw the beginning of waters, and there was an angel making a sign to me and he said to me:
Observe, said he, the waters, for this is the river of Physon which surrounds all the land of Evilla, and the second is Geon which surrounds all the land of Egypt and Ethiopia, and the third is Thigris which is over against the Assyrians, and another is Eufrates which waters all the land of Mesopotamia.
And when I had gone inside I saw a tree planted from whose roots water flowed out, and from this beginning there were four rivers.

And the spirit of God rested on that tree, and when the Spirit blew, the waters flowed forth, and I said:

My Lord, is it this tree itself which makes the waters flow? And he said to me:

That from the beginning, before the heavens and earth were manifested, and all things here invisible, the Spirit of God was borne upon the waters, but from the time when the command of God made the heavens and earth to appear, the Spirit rested upon this tree:

wherefore whenever the Spirit blows, the waters flow forth from the tree.

And he held me by the hand and led me near the tree of knowledge of good and evil, and he said:

This is the tree by which death entered into the world, and receiving of it through his wife Adam ate and death entered into the world.

And he shewed me another tree in the midst of Paradise, and saith to me:

This is the tree of life.

46.

While I was yet looking upon the tree, I saw a virgin coming from afar and two hundred angels before her saying hymns, and I asked and said:

Sir, who is she who comes in so great glory?

And he said to me:

This is Mary the Virgin, the Mother of the Lord.

And coming near she saluted me and said:

Hail, Paul! well-beloved of God and angels and men.

For all the saints prayed my Son Jesus who is my Lord that thou mightest come hither in the body that they might see thee before thou goest out of the world.

And the Lord said to them:

Bear and be patient:

yet a little and ye shall see him and he shall be with you for ever:

and again they all said to him together:

Do not vex us, for we desire to see him in the flesh, for by him Thy name was greatly glorified in the world, and we have seen that he endured all the labours whether of the greater or of the less.

This we learn from those who come hither.

For when we say:

Who is he who directed you in the world? they reply to us:

There is one in the world whose name is Paul, he preaches and announces Christ, and we believe that many have entered into the kingdom through the virtue and sweetness of his speeches.

Behold all the just men are behind me coming to meet thee, Paul, and I first come for this cause to meet them who did the will of my Son and my Lord Jesus Christ, I first advance to meet them and do not send them away to be as wanderers until they meet in peace.

47.

When she had thus spoken, I saw three coming from afar, very beautiful in the likeness of Christ, and their forms were shining, and their angels, and I asked:

Sir, who are these?

And he said to me: Dost thou not know those?

And I said:

No, Sir.

And he answered: These are the fathers of the people, Abraham, Isaac, and Jacob.

And coming near they saluted me, and said:

Hail, Paul, well-beloved of God and men; blessed is he who suffers violence for the Lord's sake.

And Abraham answered me and said:

This is my son Isaac, and Jacob my well-beloved, and we have known the Lord and followed him; blessed are all they who believed in thy word, that they may be able to inherit the Kingdom of God by labour, by renunciation, and sanctification, and humility, and charity, and meekness, and right faith in the Lord; and we also have had devotion to the Lord whom thou preachest in the testament, that we might assist those who believed in him with their whole soul, and might minister unto them as fathers minister to their children.

When they had thus spoken, I saw other twelve coming from afar in honour, and I asked:

Sir, who are these?

And he said:

These are the patriarchs.

And coming near they saluted me and said:

Hail, Paul, well-beloved of God and men:

the Lord did not vex us, that we might see thee yet in the body, before thou goest out of the world.

And each one of them reminded me of his name in order, from Ruben to Benjamin: and Joseph said to me:

I am he who was sold; but I say to thee, Paul, that all the things, whatever my brothers did to me, in nothing did I act maliciously with them, nor in all the labour which they imposed on me, nor in any point was I hurt by them on that account from morning till evening:

blessed is he who receives some hurt on account of the Lord, and bears it, for the Lord will repay it to him manifold, when he shall have gone out of the world.

48.

When he had spoken thus far, I saw another beautiful one coming from afar, and his angels saying hymns, and I asked:

Sir, who is this that is beautiful of countenance?

And he saith to me:

Dost thou not know him?

And I said:

No, Sir.

And he said to me:

This is Moses the law-giver, to whom God gave the law.

And when he had come near me, he immediately wept, and after that he saluted me:

and I said to him: What dost thou lament? for I have heard that thou excellest every man in meekness.

And he answered saying:

I weep for those whom I planted with toil, because they did not bear fruit, nor did any profit by them; and I saw all the sheep whom I fed, that they were scattered and become as if they had no shepherd, and because all the toils which I endured for the sake of the sons of Israel were accounted as naught, and how greatsoever virtues I did in the midst of them these they did not understand, and I wonder that strangers and uncircumcised and idol-worshippers have been converted and have entered into the promises of God, but Israel has not entered; and now I say unto thee, brother Paul, that in that hour when the people hanged Jesus whom thou preachest, that the Father, the God of all, who gave me the law, and Michael and all the angels and archangels, and Abraham and Isaac, and Jacob, and all the just wept over the Son of God hanging on the cross. In that hour all the saints attended on me looking (upon me) and they said to me:

See, Moses, what men of thy people have done to the Son of God.

Wherefore thou art blessed, Paul, and blessed the generation and race which believed in thy word.

49.

When he had spoken thus far, there came other twelve, and seeing me said:

Art thou Paul the glorified in heaven and on earth?

And I answered and said:

What are ye?

The first answered and said:

I am Esaias whom Manasses cut asunder with a wooden saw.

And the second said likewise:

I am Jeremias who was stoned by the children of Israel and slain.

And the third said:

I am Ezekiel whom the children of Israel dragged by the feet over a rock in a mountain till they knocked out my brains, and we endured all these toils, wishing to save the children of Israel:

and I say unto thee that after the toils which they laid upon me, I cast myself on my face in the sight of the Lord praying for them, bending my knees until the second hour of the Lord's day, till Michael came and lifted me up from the earth.

Blessed art thou, Paul, and blessed the nation which believed through thee.

And as these passed by, I saw another, beautiful of countenance, and I asked:

Sir, Who is this?

Who when he had seen me, rejoiced and said to me:

This is Lot [47] who was found just in Sodom.

And approaching [48] he saluted me and said:

Blessed art thou, Paul, and blessed the generation to which thou didst minister.

The Forgotten Bible

And I answered and said to him:

Art thou Lot who wast found just in Sodom?

And he said:

I entertained angels, as travellers, and when they of the city wished to violate them, I offered them my two virgin daughters who had not yet known men, and gave them to them saying:

use them as ye will, but only to these men ye shall do no evil; for this cause they entered under the roof of my house.

For this cause, therefore, we ought to be confident and know that if anyone shall have done anything, God shall repay him manifold when they shall come to him.

Blessed art thou, Paul, and blessed the nation which believed in thy word.

When, therefore, he had ceased talking to me, I saw another coming from a distance, very beautiful of countenance, and smiling, and his angels saying hymns:

and I said to the angel who was with me:

Has then each of the just an angel for companion?

And he said to me:

Each one of the saints has his own (angel) assisting him, and saying a hymn, and the one does not depart from the other.

And I said:

Who is this, Sir?

And he said:

This is Job.

And approaching, he saluted me and said:

Brother Paul, thou hast great praise with God and men.

And I am Job, who laboured much for a period of thirty years from a plague in the blood; and verily in the beginning, the wounds which went forth from my body were like grains of wheat.

But on the third day, they became as the foot of an ass; worms moreover which fell four digits in length:

and on the third (day) the devil appeared and said to me:

Say something against God and die.

I said to him:

If such be the will of God that I should remain under a plague all the time of my life till I die, I shall not cease from blessing the Lord, and I shall receive more reward.

For I know that the labours of that world are nothing to the refreshment which is afterwards:

for which cause blessed art thou, Paul, and blessed the nation which believed through thee.

50.

When he had spoken thus far, another came calling from afar and saying:

Blessed art thou, Paul, and blessed am I because I saw thee, the beloved of the Lord.

And I asked the angel:

Sir, who is this? And he answered and said unto me:

This is Noe in the time of the deluge.

And immediately we saluted each other:

and greatly rejoicing he said to me:

Thou art Paul the most beloved of God.

And I asked him:

Who art thou?

And he said:

I am Noe, who was in the time of the deluge.

And I say to thee, Paul, that working for a hundred years, I made the ark, not putting off the tunic with which I was clad, nor did I cut the hair of my head.

Till then also I cherished continence, not approaching my own wife:

in those hundred years not a hair of my head grew in length, nor did my garments become soiled:

and I besought men at all times saying:

Repent, for a deluge of waters will come upon you.

But they laughed at me, and mocked my words; and again they said to me:

But this is the time of those who are able to play and sin freely, desiring her with whom it is possible to commit fornication frequently:

for God does not regard this, and does not know what things are done by us men, and there is no flood of waters straightway coming upon this world.

And they did not cease from their sins, till God destroyed all flesh which had the breath of life in it.

Know then that God loveth one just man more than all the world of the impious. Wherefore, blessed art thou, Paul, and blessed is the nation which believes through thee.

51.

And turning round, I saw other just ones coming from afar, and I asked the angel:
Sir, who are those?
And he answered me:
These are Elias and Eliseus. [49] And they saluted me:
and I said to them: Who are ye?
And one of them answered and said:
I am Elias, the prophet of God; I am Elias who prayed, and because of my word, the heaven did not rain for three years and six months, on account of the unrighteousness of men.
God is just and true, who doeth the will of his servants:
for the angels often besought the Lord for rain, and he said:
Be patient till my servant Elias shall pray and petition for this and I will send rain on the earth. [50]
The End of the Vision of Saint Paul.

Footnotes:

1. Theodosius the younger and Cynegius, Consuls, 388 a.d.
2. The waters (not in Greek version); rivers in Syriac.
3. The earth (not in Greek version, but in Syriac).
4. Cf. Test. of Abraham, Rec. B, iv.
5. Cf. Test. of Abraham, Rec. B, S: 4.
6. Cf. Test. of Abraham, Rec. A, S: 12.
7. Cf. Ascension of Isaiah ix. 9.
8. And the sun. Not in Greek: Elias in Syriac.
9. (Not in Syriac.)
10. Cf. Rev. of Peter. 15.
11. Cf. Enoch.
12. Cf.Papias. ap. Iren. Haer. v. 33. 3, 4.
13. (In Syriac, but not in Greek version.)
14. The Greek has not the golden ship, the angels or the walls. They are given in the Syriac.
15. Not in the Greek, but given in the Syriac. Cf. Genesis ii. 11 ff.
16. Names not in the Greek. Isaiah, Jeremiah, Ezekiel, Moses and all the Prophets in the Syriac.
17. Names not in the Greek or Syriac.
18. Not in Greek, which here has the altar in the city and David. The Syriac is the same as the Latin.
19. Not in the Greek. Cf. Ascension of Isaiah viii. 36.
20. These letters are unintelligible. In the Greek version, the interpretation of Alleluia is given as thebel marematha, which is also unintelligible. In the Syriac the interpretation of Alleluia is correctly given.
21. Not in Greek or Syriac.
22. Not in the Greek or Syriac.
23. The Greek has here thieves and slanderers.
24. Passage probably corrupt.
25. Not in the Greek but in the Syriac.
26. Not in the Greek. The Syriac has simply those who trusted in their riches.
27. Cf. Rev. of Peter, 27.
28. Cf. Rev. of Peter, 31.
29. Cf. Rev. of Peter, 29.
30. Cf. Rev. of Peter, 24. Not in the Greek. The Syriac has darkness the torment of patriarchs, bishops, etc.
31. Cf. Rev. of Peter xxi. 30. Not in Syriac.
32. Cf. Rev. of Peter, 30. Not in the Greek.
33. Not in the Greek.
34. Not in the Greek.
35. Cf. Rev. of Peter, 24.
36. Cf. Rev. of Peter, 32. Not in the Greek.
37. Not in the Greek. Whole section omitted in the Syriac.
38. Cf. Rev. of Peter xxi. 23.

39. Cf. Rev. of Peter, 26.
40. Cf. Rev. of Peter. Fragments 4, 5.
41. Not in the Greek.
42. Not in the Greek.
43. Cf. Rev. of Peter, 27.
44. Not in the Greek.
45. Cf. Esdras, Ante-Nicene Lib., vol. xvi., p. 469.
46. Gabriel in the Greek version.
47. Lot and Job, in the Syriac but not in the Greek.
48. For adproprians read adpropinquans.
49. Elias and Eliseus. Latin and Syriac. The Greek has Enoch and Elijah.

50. The Latin version here breaks off abruptly, as does also the Greek. In the Syriac as translated by the Rev. J. Perkins, D.D. (cf. Journal of Sacred Literature, N. S., vi., 1865, p. 399), the narrative runs as follows: "And often the angels asked that he would give them rain, and he gave not, until I called upon him again; then he gave unto them. But blessed art thou, O Paul, that thy generation, and those thou teachest, are the sons of the Kingdom. And know thou, O Paul, that every man who believes through thee hath a great blessing, and a blessing is reserved for him." Then he departed from me. And the angel who was with me led me forth, and said unto me: "Lo, unto thee is given this mystery and revelation; as thou pleasest, make it known unto the sons of men." And I, Paul, returned unto myself, and I knew all that I had seen; and in life I had not rest that I might reveal this mystery, but I wrote it and deposited it under the ground and the foundation of a certain faithful man with whom I used to be, in Tarsus, a city of Cilicia. And when I was released from this life of time and stood before my Lord, thus said He unto me: "Paul, have we shown all these things unto thee, that thou shouldst deposit them under the foundation of a house? Then send, and disclose, concerning this Revelation that men may read it, and turn to the way of truth, that they also may not come to these bitter torments." Then follows the story of the discovery of the Revelation at Tarsus in the reign of Theodosius as given at the beginning of the Greek and Latin versions.

The Apocalypse of the Virgin

Introduction

The present translation of this Apocalypse [1] is made from the text as published by Mr. M. R. James in Texts and Studies, ii., 3, from a ms. in the Bodleian Library, which he assigns to the eleventh century. The original he conjecturally assigns to the ninth century, and regards it as a late and clumsy compilation based on (1) the Assumption Legends and (2) the Apocalypse of Paul.

Its main feature, intercession for the lost, it has in common with the Testament of Abraham, the Apocalypse of Paul, 4 Esdras, the Apocalypse of Baruch, the Apocalypse of Esdras and the Apocalypse of Sedrach.

Parallels are pointed out in the notes.

Footnote:

1. In this Apocalypse and that of Sedrach which follows, the text is in many places so obviously corrupt that the translator cannot be confident that he has given the correct meaning of the original in all cases.--A.R.

The Apocalypse of the Holy Mother of God Concerning the Chastisements

I.

The all-holy mother of God was about to proceed to the Mount of Olives to pray; and praying to the Lord our God she said:

In the name of the Father and the Son and the Holy Spirit; let the archangel Gabriel descend, that he may tell me concerning the chastisements and concerning things in heaven and on the earth and under the earth.

And as she said the word the archangel Michael descended with the angels of the East and the West and angels of the South and the North, and they saluted the highly favoured one and said to her:

Hail, reflection of the Father, hail dwelling of the Son, hail command of the Holy Spirit, hail firmament of the seven heavens, hail firmament of the eleven strongholds, hail worship of the angels, hail loftier than the prophets unto the throne of God.

And the holy mother of God said to the angel: Hail Michael, commander-in-chief, the minister of the invisible Father, hail Michael, commander-in-chief, associate of my Son, hail Michael, commander-in-chief, most dread of the six-winged, hail Michael, commander-in-chief, who rules through all things and art worthy to stand beside the throne of the Lord, hail Michael, commander-in-chief, who art about to sound the trumpet and awaken those who have been asleep for ages:

hail Michael, commander-in-chief, first of all unto the throne of God.

II.

And having greeted all the angels in like manner, the highly favoured one prayed the commander-in-chief regarding the chastisements, saying:

Tell to me all things on the earth.

And the commander-in-chief said to her:

If thou askest me, highly favoured one, I will tell thee.

And the highly favoured one said to him:

How many are the chastisements with which the race of man is chastised? And the archangel said to her:

The chastisements are innumerable.

And the highly favoured one said to him:

Tell me the things in heaven and on the earth.

III.

Then the commander-in-chief, Michael, commanded the Western angels that revelation should be made, and Hades opened, and she saw those who were chastised [1] in Hades:

and there lay there a multitude of men and women, and there was a great lamentation.

And the highly favoured one asked the commander-in-chief:

Who are these and what is their sin?

And the commander-in-chief said:

These, all holy, are those who did not worship the Father and the Son and the Holy Spirit and for this cause they are thus chastised here.

IV.

And she saw in another place [2] a great darkness:

and the all holy said:

What is this darkness and who are they who are being chastised?

And the commander-in-chief said:

Many souls are lying in this darkness.

And the all holy one said:

Let this darkness be taken away in order that I may see this chastisement also.

And the commander-in-chief said to the highly favoured one:
It is not possible, all holy, that thou shouldst see this chastisement also.
And the angels guarding them answered and said:
We have a command from the invisible Father that they shall not see the light till thy blessed Son shall shine forth.
And plunged in grief the all holy lifted up her eyes to the angels touching the undefiled word of the Father, and said:
In the name of the Father and the Son and the Holy Spirit let the darkness be taken away, that I may see this chastisement also.
And straightway that darkness was lifted up and covered the seven heavens: and there lay a great multitude of both men and women, and there arose a great lamentation and a great cry began.
And seeing them the all holy wept and said to them:
What are ye doing, wretched ones?
Who are ye?
And how are ye found there? and there was no voice or hearkening. And the angels guarding them said:
Why do ye not speak to the highly favoured one?
And those who were under chastisement said to her:
O highly favoured one, from eternity we see not the light, and we are not able to keep off that up there.
And splashing pitch flowed down upon them:
and seeing them the all holy wept.
And again those who were being chastised said to her:
How dost thou ask concerning us, holy lady, Mother of God?
Thy blessed Son came to The earth and did not make enquiry concerning us, neither Abraham the patriarch, nor John the Baptist, nor Moses the great prophet, nor the Apostle Paul, and unto us their light shone not:
and now, all holy Mother of God, the armour of the Christians, the bringer of great comfort on account of the Christians, how dost thou ask concerning us?
Then the all holy Mother of God said to Michael, the commander-in-chief:
What is their sin? And Michael, the commander-in-chief, said:
These are they who did not believe in the Father and the Son and the Holy Spirit, and did not confess thee [3] to be the Mother of God, and that the Lord Jesus Christ was born of thee and took flesh, and for this cause they are chastised there.
And again weeping, the all holy Mother of God said to them:
Why did ye so greatly err, wretched ones?
Did ye not hear that the whole creation names my name?
And having said these words the darkness fell over them as it was from the beginning.

V.

And the commander-in-chief said:
Whither wouldst thou go, highly favoured one? to the West or to the South?
And the highly favoured answered:
Let us go to the South.
And immediately there appeared the cherubim and the seraphim and four hundred angels, and led out the highly favoured one to the South, where came out the river of fire, [4] and there there lay a multitude of men and women, some up to the girdle, others up to the neck, and others up to the crown of the head: and seeing them the all holy Mother of God cried out with a loud voice to the commander-in-chief and said:
Who are these, and what is their sin who stand in the fire up to the girdle?
And the commander-in-chief said:
These, all holy one, are they who inherited the curse of father and mother, and for this cause they are thus chastised here as accursed.

VI.

And the all holy one said:
And who are these standing in the fire up to the breasts?
And the commander-in-chief said:
These are whosoever cast off their wives and defiled them in adultery, and for this cause they are thus chastised here.

The Forgotten Bible

VII.

And the all holy one said to the commander-in-chief:
Who are these standing up to the neck in the flame of the fire?
And the commander-in-chief said:
These, all holy one, are whosoever ate of the flesh of men.
And the all holy one said:
And how is it possible for one man to eat of the flesh of another?
And the commander-in-chief said:
Listen, all holy one, and I will tell thee:
These are they whosoever brought down their own children out of their own wombs and cast them out [5] as food for dogs, and whosoever gave up their brothers in the presence of kings and governors, these ate the flesh of man, and for this cause they are thus chastised.

VIII.

And the all holy one said:
Who are these set in the fire up to the crown?
And the commander-in-chief said:
These, all holy one, are whosoever lay hold of the precious cross and swear to a lie:
by the power of the cross of the Lord.
The angels tremble and worship with fear, and men lay hold of it and swear to a lie and do not know what they testify:
and for this cause they are thus chastised here.

IX.

And in another place the all holy one saw a man hung by the feet, [6] and worms devoured him.
And she asked the commander-in-chief: Who is this and what is his sin?
And the commander-in-chief said: This is he who took usury [7] for his gold, and for this cause he is thus chastised here.

X.

And she saw a woman hanging by her two ears, and all the beasts [8] came out of her mouth and gnawed her in pieces:
and the highly favoured one asked the commander-in-chief:
Who is she, and what is her sin?
And the commander-in-chief said:
She is she who turned aside into strange houses and those of her neighbours and spoke evil words to make strife, and for that cause she is thus chastised here.

XI.

And seeing these things the all holy Mother of God wept and said to the commander-in-chief:
It were well for man that he had not been born.
And the commander-in-chief said:
Verily, all holy one, thou hast not seen the great chastisements.
And the all holy one said to the commander-in-chief:
Come, Michael, great commander-in-chief, and lead me that I may see all the chastisements.
And the commander-in-chief said:
Where dost thou wish, all holy one, that we should go?
And the highly favoured one answered:
To the West:
and straightway the cherubim appeared and led the highly favoured to the West.

XII.

And she saw a cloud full of fire and in it there was a [9] multitude of men and women.
And the all holy one said:
What was their sin?
And the commander-in-chief said:
These, all holy one, are they who on the morning of the Lord's day sleep like the dead, and for that reason they are thus chastised here.
And the all holy one said:
If anyone cannot rise, what shall he do?
And the commander-in-chief said:
Listen, all holy one:

if anyone's house is fastened on the four (sides?) and surrounds him and he cannot come out, he has forgiveness.

XIII.

And she saw in another place burning benches of fire and on them sat a multitude of men and women and burned on them.

And the all holy one asked:

Who are these and what is their sin?

And the commander-in-chief said:

These, all holy one, are they who do not rise up to the presbyter when they enter into the church of God, and for this cause they are thus chastised here.

XIV.

And the all holy one saw in another place an iron tree and it had branches of iron, and on it there hung a multitude of men and women by their tongues. [10]And seeing them the all holy one wept, and asked the commander-in-chief saying:

Who are these and what was their sin?

And the commander-in-chief said:

These are perjurers, blasphemers, slanderers, whosoever divided brothers from brothers.

And the all holy one said:

How is it possible to divide brothers from brothers?

And the commander-in-chief said:

Listen, all holy one, and I will tell thee about this:

When some from among the nations desired to be baptised, he would say to them one word:

Thou foul-feeding, unbelieving Gentile; because he thus blasphemed, he shall receive ceaseless retribution.

XV.

And in another place the all holy one saw a man hanging from his four extremities, and from his nails blood gushed vehemently, and his tongue [11] was tied in a flame of fire, and he was unable to groan and say the Kyrie eleison me.

And when she had seen him the all holy one wept and herself said the Kyrie eleison thrice:

and after the saying of the prayer, came the angel who had authority over the scourge and loosed the man's tongue:

and the all holy one asked the commander-in-chief:

Who is this wretched one who has this chastisement?

And the commander-in-chief said:

This, all holy one, is the steward who did not the will of God, but ate the things of the church and said:

"He who ministers to the altar shall be nourished from the altar": [12]and for this cause he is thus chastised here.

And the all holy one said:

Let it be unto him according to his faith.

And again he tied his tongue.

XVI.

And Michael, the commander-in-chief said:

Come hither, all holy one, and I will show unto thee where the priests are chastised.

And the all holy one came out and saw presbyters hanging by their twenty nails, and fire came out of their heads.

And seeing them the all holy one asked the commander-in-chief:

Who are these and what is their sin?

And the commander-in-chief said:

These, all holy one, are they who stand beside the throne of God, and when they sang of the body of our Lord Jesus Christ, the pearls fell out, and the awful throne of heaven shook and the footstool of our Lord Jesus Christ trembled, and they did not perceive it:

and for this cause they are thus chastised here.

XVII.

And the all holy one saw a man and a winged beast having three heads like flames of fire: the two heads were towards his eyes and the third head towards his mouth.

And seeing him the all holy one asked the commander-in-chief:

Who is this, that he cannot save himself from the mouth of the dragon?

And the commander-in-chief said to her: This, all holy one, is the reader who does not practise in his own habits according to what is worthy of the holy Gospel:

and for this cause he is thus chastised here.

XVIII.

And the commander-in-chief said:

Come hither, all holy one, and I will show thee where the angelic and archangelic form is chastised.

She proceeded and saw [13] them lying in the fire and the sleepless worm gnawed them:

and the all holy one said:

Who are these, and what is their sin?

And the commander-in-chief said:

These, all holy one, are they who possessed the archangelic and apostolic form: hearken, all holy one, concerning this:

on earth they were called patriarchs and bishops, and they were not worthy of their name:

on earth they heard Bless (the Lord) ye saints,' and in heaven they were not called saints, because they did not act as bearers of the archangelic form:

and for this cause they are thus chastised here.

XIX.

And she saw women hanging by their nails, and a flame of fire came out of their mouth and burned them:

and all the beasts [14] coming out of the fire gnawed them to pieces, and groaning they cried out:

Have pity on us, have pity, for we are chastised worse than all those who are under chastisement.

And seeing them the all holy one wept, and asked the commander-in-chief, Michael:

Who are these and what is their sin?

And the commander-in-chief said:

These are the wives of presbyters who did not honour the presbyters, but after the death of the presbyter took husbands, and for this cause they are thus chastised here.

XX.

And the all holy one saw after the same manner also a deaconess hanging from a crag and a beast with two heads devoured her breasts. And the all holy one asked:

What is her sin?

And the commander-in-chief said:

She, all holy one, is an archdeaconess who defiled her body in fornication, and for this cause she is thus chastised here.

XXI.

And she saw other women hanging over the fire, and all the beasts devoured them.

And the all holy one asked the commander-in-chief:

Who are these and what is their sin?

And he said:

These are they who did not do the will of God, lovers of money and those who took interest[15] on accounts, and the immodest.

XXII.

And when she had heard these things the all holy one wept and said:

Woe unto sinners.

And the commander-in-chief said:

Why dost thou lament, all holy one?

Now verily thou hast not seen the great chastisements.

And the highly favoured one said:

Come, Michael, the great commander-in-chief of the powers above, tell me how I may see all the chastisements.

And the commander-in-chief said:
Where dost thou wish that we should go, all holy one? to the East or towards the left parts of Paradise?
And the all holy one said:
To the left parts of Paradise.

XXIII.
And immediately when she had spoken, the cherubim and seraphim stood beside her and led the highly favoured one out to the left parts of Paradise.
And behold, there was a great river, and the appearance of the river was blacker than pitch, and in it there were a multitude [16] of men and women:
it boiled like a furnace of forges, and its waves were like a wild sea over the sinners:
and when the waves rose, they sank the sinners ten thousand cubits and they were unable to keep it off and say:
Have mercy on us, thou just judge:
for the sleepless worm devoured them, and there was no reckoning of the number of those who devoured them.
And seeing the all holy Mother of God the angels [17] who chastised them cried out with one voice:
Holy is God who has compassion on account of the Mother of God:
we give thee thanks, O Son of God, that from eternity we did not see the light, and to-day through the Mother of God we have seen the light:
and again they shouted with one voice, saying:
Hail, highly favoured Mother of God: Hail, lamp of the inaccessible light:
Hail to thee also, Michael, the commander-in-chief, thou that art ambassador from the whole creation: for we, seeing the chastisement of sinners are greatly grieved.
And the all holy one, when she saw the angels humbled on account of the sinners, lamented and said:
Woe to sinners and their neighbours.
And the all holy one said:
Let us see the sinners.
And the highly favoured one, coming with the archangel Michael and all the armies of the angels lifted up one voice saying:
Lord have mercy.
And after the making of the prayer earnestly, the wave of the river rested and the fiery waves grew calm, and the sinners appeared as a grain of mustard-seed:
and seeing them the all holy one lamented and said: What is this river, and what are its waves?
And the commander-in-chief said:
This river is the outer fire, and those who are being tortured are the Jews who crucified our Lord Jesus Christ the Son of God, and who refused holy baptism, and those who commit fornication and sin against the sweet and passionless perfume of marriage, and he who debauches mother and daughter, and the poisoners and those who slay with the sword, and the women who strangle their offspring.
And the all holy one said:
According to their faith so be it unto them.
And straightway the waves rose over the sinners and the darkness covered them.
And the commander-in-chief said:
Hearken, thou highly favoured one:
if anyone shall be cast into this darkness, [18] his remembrance shall never be in the sight of God.
And the all holy Mother of God said:
Woe to sinners, because the flame of the fire is everlasting.

XXIV.
And the commander-in-chief said:
Come hither, all holy one, and I will show unto thee the lake of fire:
and see thou where the race of the Christians is chastised. [19] And the all holy one proceeded and saw:
and some she heard, but others she did not see:
and she asked the commander-in-chief:
Who are these, and what is their sin? And the commander-in-chief said:

These, all holy one, are those who were baptised and arrayed under the oracle of Christ, but worked the works of the devil and wasted the time of their repentance:

and for this cause they are thus chastised here.

XXV.

And she said:

I pray, one request will I make of thee, let me also be chastised with the Christians, because they are the children of my son.

And the commander-in-chief said:

Rest thou in Paradise, holy lady, Mother of God.

And the all holy one said:

I pray thee, move the fourteen firmaments and the seven heavens, and let us pray for the Christians that the Lord our God may hearken unto us and have mercy on them. [20] And the commander-in-chief said:

As the Lord God liveth, the great name, seven times a day and seven times a night, when we lead up the hymn of the Lord, we make remembrance for the sake of sinners, and the Lord accounts us as naught.

XXVI.

And the all holy one said:

I pray thee, commander-in-chief, command the armies of the angels and let them place me on the height of heaven and let me into the presence of the invisible Father.

And immediately the commander-in-chief commanded, and the chariot of the cherubim and seraphim appeared, and they exalted the highly favoured one to the height of heaven and placed her in the presence of the invisible Father:

And she stretched forth her hands to the undefiled throne of the Father and said:

Have mercy, O Lord, on the Christian sinners, for I saw them being chastised and I cannot bear their complaint.

Let me go forth and be chastised myself for the Christians.

I do not pray, O Lord, for the unbelieving Jews, but for the Christians I entreat thy compassion.

And there came a second voice from the invisible Father saying:

How can I have mercy on them, when they did not have mercy on their own brothers?[21] And the all holy one said:

Lord, have mercy on the sinners:

behold the chastisements, for every creature on the earth calls upon my name:

and when the soul comes forth out of the body, it cries saying, "Holy Lady, Mother of God."

Then the Lord said to her:

Hearken, all holy Mother of God, if anyone names and calls upon thy name, I will not forsake him, either in heaven or on earth.

XXVII.

And the all holy one said:

Where is Moses?

Where are all the prophets and fathers who never sinned?

Where art thou, holy Paul of God? where is the holy Lord's Day, the boast of the Christians? where is the power of the precious and life-giving cross, which delivered Adam and Eve from the ancient curse?

Then Michael and all the angels raised one voice saying:

Lord, have mercy on the sinners.

Then Moses also cried:

Have mercy, Lord, on those to whom I gave thy law.

Then John also called:

Have mercy, Lord, on those to whom I gave thy Gospel.

Then Paul cried:

Have mercy, Lord, on those to whom I brought thy epistles in the Church.

And the Lord God said:

Hearken, all ye righteous:

if according to the law which Moses gave, and according to the Gospel which John gave, and according to the epistles which Paul carried, they thus be judged.

And they had nothing to say except, Have mercy, O just judge.

XXVIII.
And the all holy Mother of God said:
Have mercy, Lord, on the Christians, because they kept thy law and gave heed to thy gospel, but they were simple ones.
Then the Lord said to her:
Hearken, all holy one:
if anyone did evil to them and they did not requite him the evil, thou sayest well that they attended to both my law and my gospel, but if he did not do them wrong and they requited him evil, how may I say that these are holy men? now they shall be rewarded according to their wrongdoing.
Then all hearing the voice of the Lord had nothing to answer; and the all holy one, when she saw that the saints were at a loss, and their Lord did not hear, and his mercy was hidden from them, then the all holy one said:
Where is Gabriel, who announced unto me the "Hail, thou that from eternity shalt conceive him who is without beginning like the Father," and now does not look upon sinners?
Where is the great commander-in-chief? come hither, all ye saints whom God justified, and let us fall down in the presence of the invisible Father, in order that the Lord God may hear us, and have mercy on sinners.
Then Michael, the commander-in-chief, and all the saints fell on their faces in the presence of the invisible Father, saying:
Have mercy, Lord, on the Christian sinners.

XXIX.
Then the Lord, seeing the prayer of the saints, had compassion and said:
Go down, my beloved son, and because of the prayer of the saints let thy face shine on earth to sinners.
Then the Lord came down from his undefiled throne:
and when they saw Him, those who were under chastisement raised one voice saying:
Have mercy on us, King of ages. Then the Lord of all things said:
Hearken, all ye sinners and righteous men:
I made paradise and made man after my image:
but he transgressed, and for his own sins was delivered to death:
but I did not suffer the works of my hands to be tyrannized over by the serpent: wherefore I bowed the heavens and came down and was born of Mary, the holy undefiled Mother of God, that I might set you free:
I was baptised in Jordan in order that I might save the creature (nature) which had grown old under sin:
I was nailed to the cross [22] to free you from the ancient curse:
I asked for water and ye gave me vinegar mingled with gall:
I was laid in the grave:
I trampled on the enemy:
I raised up mine elect, and even thus ye would not hear me. But now, because [23] of the prayer of my mother Mary, because she has wept much for your sake, and because of Michael my archangel, and because of the multitude of my saints, I grant you to have rest on the day of Pentecost to glorify the Father and the Son and the Holy Spirit.

XXX.
Then all the angels and archangels, thrones, lordships, authorities, governments, powers, and the many-eyed cherubim and the six-winged seraphim and all the apostles and prophets and martyrs and all the saints raised one voice, saying:
Glory to thee, O Lord:
glory to thee, lover of men:
glory to thee, King of ages:
glory be to thy compassion:
glory be to thy long suffering:
glory be to thy unspeakable justice of judgment, because thou hast been long-suffering with sinners and impious men:
Thine is it to pity and to save.
To him be the glory and the power to the Father and to the Son and to the Holy Spirit for ever and ever.
Amen.

Footnotes:

1. Cf. Vision of Paul, 31.
2. Rev. of Peter, 21. Paul, 37.
3. Cf. Paul, 41.
4. Cf. Paul, 31.
5. Cf. Peter, Frag.; Paul, 40; Peter, 27.
6. Cf. Peter, 24.
7. Cf. Peter, 31; Paul, 37.
8. Cf. Peter, Frag. 2.
9. Cf. Peter, 25.
10. Cf. Peter, 22.
11. Cf. Peter, 29.
12. Cf. Lev. x. 12 ff.; Num. xviii. 7 ff..
13. Cf. Peter, 27.
14. Cf. Peter fr. ap. Clem. Alex.
15. Cf. Peter, 31.
16. Cf. Paul, 31.
17. Cf. Peter, 23.
18. Cf. Paul, 41.
19. Cf. Esdras. Ante-Nicene Lib., vol. xvi., p. 473.
20. Cf. Paul, 43.
21. Cf. Esdras, l. c., pp. 469, 470.
22. Cf. Paul, 44; Esdras, l. c., p. 470.
23. Cf. Paul, 44.

The Apocalypse of Sedrach

Introduction

The translation is from Mr. M. R. James's text in Texts and Studies, ii. 3, p. 130ff., published from a fifteenth century ms. in the Bodleian Library.

The original, Mr. James conjecturally assigns to the tenth or eleventh century.

It is notable for its close resemblance in several passages to 4 Esdras, to the Greek original of which the author seems to have had direct access.

Like the Apocalypse of Esdras it deals with the subject of intercession for sinners and the reluctance of the seer to die.

The parallel passages in 4 Esdras and the Apocalypse of Esdras are pointed out in the margin of the translation.

Chapter I. consists of a few lines from the beginning and end of a homily on love which appears in the ms. at the beginning of the Apocalypse, but which Mr. James regards as "quite unimportant and quite irrelevant."

The Apocalypse of Sedrach

The Word of the holy and blessed Sedrach concerning love and concerning repentance and Orthodox Christians, and concerning the Second Coming of our Lord Jesus Christ.
Lord give thy blessing.

I.

Beloved, let us prefer nothing in honour except sincere love:
for in many things we stumble every day and night and hour.
And for this cause let us gain love, for it covereth a multitude of sins:
for what is the profit, my children, if we have all things, and have not saving love...
O blessed love, supplier of all good things.
Blessed is the man who has gained the true faith and sincere love, according as the Master said, there is no greater love than this that a man should lay down his life for his friend.
Cf. John xv. 13.

II.

And invisibly he received a voice in his ears:
Come hither, Sedrach, since thou wishest and desirest to converse with God and ask of him that he may reveal unto thee whatever thou wishest to ask.
And Sedrach said:
What, Sir?
And the voice said to him:
I was sent to thee to raise thee here into heaven.
And he said:
I desired to speak mouth to mouth with God:
I am not fit, Sir, to come into heaven.
And stretching out his wings he took him up and he came into heaven to the very flame, and he set him as high as the third heaven, and in it stood the flame of the divinity.

III.

And the Lord saith to him:
Welcome, my beloved Sedrach:
What suit hast thou against God who created thee, that thou saidst, I desired to speak face to face with God?
Sedrach saith to him: [1] Yea, verily, the son hath a suit with the Father:
my Lord, why didst thou make the earth?
The Lord saith to him:
For man's sake.
Sedrach saith:
And why didst Thou make the sea?
Why didst Thou scatter every good thing on the earth?
The Lord saith to him:
For man's sake. Sedrach saith to him: [2] If thou didst these things, [3] why wilt Thou destroy him?
And the Lord said:
Man is my work and the creature of my hands, and I discipline him as I find good.

IV.

Sedrach saith to him:
Chastisement and fire are thy discipline: they are bitter, my Lord: [4] it were well for man if he had not been born:
why then didst thou make him, my Lord?
Why didst thou weary thine undefiled hands [5] and create man, since thou didst not intend to have mercy on him?
God saith to him:

I made Adam the first creature and placed him in Paradise in the midst of the tree of life and said to him:

Eat of all the fruits, but beware of the tree of life:

for if thou eat of it, thou shalt die the death.

But he transgressed my commandment, and being beguiled by the devil ate of the tree.

V.

Sedrach saith to him:

Of thy will Adam was beguiled, my Lord: Thou commandest thine [6] angels to make approach to Adam, and the first of the angels himself transgressed thy commandment and did not make approach to him, and Thou didst banish him, because he transgressed thy commandment and did not make any approach to the work of thine hands:

if thou lovedst man, why didst Thou not slay the devil, the worker of unrighteousness?

Who is able to fight an invisible spirit?

And he as a smoke enters into the hearts of men and teaches them every sin:

he fights against thee, the immortal God, and what can wretched man then do to him?

But have mercy, O Lord, and stop the chastisements:

but if not, count me also with the sinners:

if thou wilt have no mercy on the sinners, where are thy mercies, where is thy [7] compassion, O Lord?

VI.

God saith to him:

Be it known unto thee that I ordered all things to be placable to him:

I gave him understanding and made him the heir of heaven and earth, and I subjected all things to him, and every living thing flees from him and from before his face:

but he, having received of mine, became alien, adulterous, and sinful:

tell me, what father, having given his son his portion, when he takes his substance and leaves his father and goes away and becomes an alien and serves an alien, when the father sees that the son has deserted him, does not darken his heart, and does not the father go and take his substance and banish him from his glory because he deserted his father?

And how have I, the wonderful and jealous God, given him everything, and he having received these things has become an adulterer and a sinner?

VII.

Sedrach saith to him:

Thou, O Lord, didst create man.

Thou knewest of what sort of mind he was and of what sort of knowledge we are, and thou makest it a cause for chastisement:

but cast him forth; for shall not I alone fill up the heavenly places?

But if that is not to be so save man too, O Lord.

He failed by thy will, wretched man. Why dost thou waste words on me, Sedrach?

I created Adam and his wife and the sun and said:

Behold each other how bright he is, and the wife of Adam is brighter in the beauty of the moon and he was the giver of her life. [8]Sedrach saith:

but of what profit are beauties if they die away into the earth?

How didst thou say, O Lord, Thou shalt not return evil for evil?

How is it, O Lord? the word of Thy divinity never lies, and why dost Thou retaliate on man? or dost thou not in so doing render evil for evil?

I know that among the quadrupeds there is no other so wily and unreasonable as the mule.

But we strike it with the bridle when we wish:

and thou hast angels:

send them forth to guard them, and when man inclines towards sin, to take hold of his foot and not let him go whither he would.

VIII.

God saith to him:

If I catch him by the foot, he will say, Thou hast given me no joy in the world.

But I have left him to his own will because I loved him.

Wherefore I sent forth my righteous angels to guard him night and day.

Sedrach saith: [9]I know, O Lord, that of all thy creatures Thou chiefly lovedst man, of the quadrupeds the sheep, of woods the olive, of fruits the vine, of flying things the bee, of rivers the

The Forgotten Bible
Jordan, of cities Jerusalem.

And all these man also loves, my Lord.
God saith to Sedrach:
I will ask thee one thing, Sedrach:
if thou answerest me, then I may fitly help thee, even though thou hast tempted thy creator.
Sedrach saith:
Speak. [10]The Lord God saith:

Since I made all things, how many men were born and how many died, and how many are to die and how many hairs have they? Tell me, Sedrach, [11] since the heaven was created and the earth, how many trees grew in the world, and how many fell, and how many are to fall, and how many are to arise, and how many leaves have they? Tell me, Sedrach, since I made the sea, how many waves arose and how many fell, and how many are to arise, and how many winds blow along the margin of the sea?

Tell me, Sedrach, from the creation of the world of the aeons, when the air rained, how many drops fell upon the world, and how many are to fall?
And Sedrach said:
Thou alone knowest all these things, O Lord; thou only understandest all these things:
only, I pray thee, deliver man from chastisement, and I shall not be separated from our race.

IX.

And God said to his only begotten Son:
Go, [12] take the soul of Sedrach my beloved, and place it in Paradise.
The only begotten Son saith to Sedrach:
Give me the trust which our Father deposited in the womb of thy mother in the holy tabernacle of thy body from a child. Sedrach saith:
I will not give thee my soul.
God saith to him:
And wherefore was I sent to come hither, and thou pleadest against me?
For I was commanded by my Father not to take thy soul with violence; but if not, (then) give me thy most greatly desired soul.

X.

And Sedrach saith to God:
And whence dost Thou intend to take my soul, and from which limb?
And God saith to him:
Dost thou not know that it is placed in the midst of thy lungs and thy heart and is dispersed into all thy limbs?

It is brought up through the throat and gullet and the mouth and at whatever hour it is predestined to come forth, it is scattered, and brought together from the points of the nails and from all the limbs, and there is a great necessity that it should be separated from the body and parted from the heart.

When Sedrach had heard all these things and had considered the memory of death he was greatly astounded, and Sedrach said to God:
O Lord, give me a little respite that I may weep, for I have heard that tears are able to do much and much remedy comes to the lowly body of thy creature.

XI.

And weeping and bewailing he began to say:
O marvellous head of heavenly adornment:
O radiant as the sun which shines on heaven and earth:
thy hairs are known from Teman, thine eyes from Bosor, thine ears from thunder, thy tongue from a trumpet, and thy brain is a small creation, thy head the energy of the whole body:
O friendly and most fair beloved by all, and now falling into the earth it must become forgotten.
O hands, mild, fair-fingered, worn with toil by which the body is nourished:
O hands, deftest of all, heaping up from all quarters ye made ready houses.
O fingers adorned and decked with gold and silver (rings):
and great worlds are led by the fingers:
the three joints enfold the palms, and heap up beautiful things:
and now ye must become aliens to the world.
O feet, skilfully walking about, self-running, most swift, unconquerable:
O knees, fitted together, because without you the body does not move:

the feet run along with the sun and the moon in the night and in the day, heaping up all things, foods and drinks, and nourishing the body:

O feet, most swift and fair runners, moving on the face of the earth, getting ready the house with every good thing:

O feet which bear up the whole body, that run up to the temples, making repentance and calling on the saints, and now ye are to remain motionless.

O head and hands and feet, until now I have kept you.

O soul, what sent thee into the humble and wretched body? and now being separated from it, thou art going up where the Lord calleth thee, and the wretched body goes away to judgment.

O body well-adorned, hair clothed with stars, head of heavenly adornment and dress:

O face well-anointed, light-bringing eyes, voice trumpet-like, tongue placable, chin fairly adorned, hairs like the stars, head high as heaven, body decked out, light-bringing eyes that know all things--and now you shall fall into the earth and under the earth your beauty shall disappear.

XII.

Christ saith to him:

Stay, Sedrach; how long dost thou weep and groan?

Paradise is opened to thee, and, dying, thou shalt live. Sedrach saith to him:

Once more I will speak unto thee, O Lord:

How long shall I live before I die? and do not disregard my prayer.

The Lord saith to him:

Speak, O Sedrach.

Sedrach saith:

If a man shall live eighty or ninety or an hundred years, and live these years in sin, and again shall turn, and the man live in repentance, in how many days dost thou forgive him his sins?

God saith to him:

If he shall live an hundred or eighty years and shall turn and repent for three years and do the fruit of righteousness, and death shall overtake him, I will not remember all his sins.

XIII.

Sedrach saith to him:

The three years are a long time, my Lord, lest death overtake him and he fulfil not his repentance:

have mercy, Lord, on thine image and have compassion, for the three years are many.

God saith to him:

If a man live an hundred years and remember his death and confess before men and I find him, after a time I will forgive all his sins.

Sedrach saith again:

I will again beseech thy compassion for thy creature.

The time is long lest death overtake him and snatch him suddenly.

The Saviour saith to him:

I will ask thee one word, Sedrach, my beloved, then thou shalt ask me in turn:

if the man shall repent for forty days I will not remember all his sins which he did.

XIV.

And Sedrach saith [13] to the archangel Michael:

Hearken to me, O powerful chief, and help thou me and be my envoy that God may have mercy on the world.

And falling on their faces, they besought the Lord and said:

O Lord, teach us how and by what sort of repentance and by what labour man shall be saved.

God saith:

By repentances, by intercessions, by liturgies, by tears in streams, in hot groanings. Dost thou not know that my prophet David was saved by tears, and the rest were saved in one moment?

Thou knowest, Sedrach, that there are nations which have not the law and which do the works of the law:

for if they are unbaptized and my divine spirit come unto them and they turn to my baptism, I also receive them with my righteous ones into Abraham's bosom.

And there are some who have been baptized with my baptism and who have shared in my divine part and become reprobate in complete reprobation and will not repent:

and I suffer them with much compassion and much pity and wealth [14] in order that they may repent, but they do the things which my divinity hates, and did not hearken to the wise man asking (them), saying, we by no means justify a sinner.

Dost thou not most certainly know that it is written:
And those who repent never see chastisement?
And they did not hearken to the Apostles or to my word in the Gospels, and they grieve my angels, and verily they do not attend to my messenger in the assemblies (for communion) and in my services, and they do not stand in my holy churches, but they stand and do not fall down and worship in fear and trembling, but boast things which I do not accept, or my holy angels.

XV.

Sedrach saith to God:
O Lord, Thou alone art sinless and very compassionate, having compassion and pity for sinners, but thy divinity said:
I am not come to call the righteous but sinners to repentance. And the Lord said to Sedrach:
Dost thou not know, Sedrach, that the thief was saved in one moment to repent?
Dost thou not know that my apostle and evangelist was saved in one moment?
"Peccatores enim non salvantur," for their hearts are like rotten stone:
these are they who walk in impious ways and who shall be destroyed with Antichrist. Sedrach saith:
O my Lord, Thou also saidst:
My divine spirit entered into the nations which, not having the law, do the things of the law. So also the thief and the apostle and evangelist and the rest of those who have already got into thy Kingdom.
O my Lord; so likewise do Thou pardon those who have sinned to the last:
for life is very toilsome and there is no time for repentance.

XVI.

The Lord saith to Sedrach:
I made man in three stages:
when he is young, I overlooked his stumblings as he was young:
and again when he was a man I considered his purpose:
and again when he grows old, I watch him till he repent.
Sedrach saith:
O Lord, Thou knowest and understandest all these things:
but have sympathy for sinners.
The Lord saith to him:
Sedrach, my beloved, I promise to have sympathy and bring down the forty days to twenty:
and whosoever shall remember thy name shall not see the place of chastisement, but shall be with the just in a place of refreshment and rest:
and if anyone shall record this wonderful word his sins shall not be reckoned against him for ever and ever. [15]And Sedrach saith:
O Lord, and if anyone shall bring enlightenment to thy servant, save him, O Lord, from all evil. And Sedrach, the servant of the Lord, saith:
Now take my soul, O Lord.
And God took him and placed him in Paradise with all the saints.
To whom be the glory and the power for ever and ever.
Amen.

Footnotes:

1. Cf. Esdras. Ante-Nicene Lib., xvi., 469.
2. Cf. 4 Esdras viii. 15 ff.
3. Cf. Esdras, Ante-Nicene Lib., xvi., p. 471.
4. Cf. Esdras, Ante-Nicene Lib., vol. xvi., p. 469.
5. Undefiled hands. Cf. Esdras, p. 469.
6. Angels. Cf. Esdras, p. 470.
7. Compassion. Cf. Esdras, p. 469.
8. Passage corrupt; the above appears to be the best sense it admits of as it stands.
9. Cf. iv. Esdras v. 23 ff.
10. Cf. iv. Esdras iv. 4-11, v. 36.
11. Cf. Esdras, p. 470.
12. Cf.Apoc. of Esdras, in Ante-Nicene Lib., vol. xvi., p. 474, and Testament of Abraham, Rec. A., Chaps. vii. and xvi.

13. Cf. Test. of Abraham, Rec. A. S:S: xiv., xviii.
14. Rom. ii. 4.
15. Cf. Esdras, p. 476.

The Testament of Abraham
By W. A. Craigie, M.A., B.A. (Oxon.)

Introduction

The Greek text of both the recensions of this work is published for the first time in "Texts and Studies," Vol. II., No. 2 (Cambridge, 1892), by Montague Rhodes James, M.A.

None of the manuscripts are older than the thirteenth century; of the six which contain the longer version the best is a Paris ms. written 1315, and the principal ms. of the shorter recension (also in Paris) belongs to the fifteenth century.

There are also versions in Roumanian, Slavonic, Ethiopic, and Arabic.

The work itself has hitherto been little noticed, and it is doubtful how far it was well known in ancient times.

It is perhaps that cited as "Abraham" in early lists of Apocryphal works, and some passages in early Christian writers may indicate their knowledge of such a work. The evidence for this is given in full by the editor of the Greek text in his introduction (pp. 7-29).

The conclusions drawn by him from these notices, and from the work itself, are "that it was written in the second century, that it embodies legends earlier than that century, that it received its present form perhaps in the ninth or tenth century."

Certain features in it also "seem to point to Egypt as its birthplace," such as the conception of Death in the longer recension, which has parallels in the Coptic Apocryphal books, the weighing of souls, and the presence of recording angels at the judgment scene.

Neither of the two versions can be supposed to be true copies of the original work.

They differ from each other not only in length, but in arrangement.

The shorter recension may preserve more of the original language, but it transposes certain sections, thereby confusing the order of the narrative, and in this the Arabic version generally agrees with it.

The most essential discrepancy begins with Chap. X. of the longer recension, where Abraham, after being taken up on the cloud, is first shown the iniquities that take place on earth.

The shorter text places this at the end of his journey, quite destroying the original moral of the writer, who wishes to emphasize the mercy of God, and to show how Abraham's righteous indignation is replaced by feelings of compassion for the sinner.

The vision of judgment is then altered in the shorter version, the doubtful soul being there condemned, instead of being saved by the intercession of Abraham.

In this point the editor thinks that the shorter recension may have been influenced by the Apocalypse of Paul, as would also seem to be the case with Michael's reason for leaving Abraham in Chap. IV, which is quite different from the pretext given in the longer text.

It is also remarkable that in the shorter form there is no word. of Abraham's unwillingness to die, which is so prominent a feature of the other, and is no doubt original, as the idea is not otherwise unknown in Apocryphal literature.

The conclusion of the shorter version is very much curtailed, compared with the longer one.

On account of these many differences between the recensions of this remarkable work, it has been judged best to give both of them entire, and so arranged that the reader can readily discover in what respects the one differs from the other.

The tone of the work is perhaps rather Jewish than Christian, but as phrases and conceptions of a New Testament character appear in it, especially in the judgment scene, it is most probably to be assigned to a Jewish Christian, who for the substance of it drew partly on older legends, and partly on his own imagination.

Some of its features are very striking, and a few of them do not seem to occur elsewhere in literature of this class; it is possible that some of these do not go further back than the medieval editors of the text.

Among the most remarkable points may be noticed the age of Abraham, variously given in different mss., his hospitality, and the sending of Michael to announce his death (Chap. I.):

Michael's refusal to mount a horse (Chap. II.): the tree speaking with a human voice (Chap. III.); the tears of Michael turning into precious stones (ibid.); and the devouring spirit sent to consume the food for him (Chap. IV.).

In Chap. VI. the narrative of Genesis is recalled by Sarah's recognizing Michael as one of the three who came to Abraham at the oak of Mamre, with the added circumstance of the calf rising up whole after being eaten.

The dream of Isaac in Chap. VII. is perhaps remotely suggested by that of Joseph.

The whole vision of judgment, with the presence of Adam and Abel, is very noteworthy, as also the conception of Death, and the explanation of his various forms.

The Testament of Abraham

Version I

I.

Abraham lived the measure of his life, nine hundred and ninety-five years, and having lived all the years of his life in quietness, gentleness, and righteousness, the righteous one was exceeding hospitable; for, pitching his tent in the cross-ways at the oak of Mamre, he received every one, both rich and poor, kings and rulers, the maimed and the helpless, friends and strangers, neighbors and travelers, all alike did the devout, all-holy, righteous, and hospitable Abraham entertain.

Even upon him, however, there came the common, inexorable, bitter lot of death, and the uncertain end of life.

Therefore the Lord God, summoning his archangel Michael, said to him:

Go down, chief-captain [1] Michael, to Abraham and speak to him concerning his death, that he may set his affairs in order, for I have blessed him as the stars of heaven, and as the sand by the sea-shore, and he is in abundance of long life and many possessions, and is becoming exceeding rich.

Beyond all men, moreover, he is righteous in every goodness, hospitable and loving to the end of his life; but do thou, archangel Michael, go to Abraham, my beloved friend, and announce to him his death and assure him thus:

Thou shalt at this time depart from this vain world, and shalt quit the body, and go to thine own Lord among the good.

II.

And the chief-captain departed from before the face of God, and went down to Abraham to the oak of Mamre, and found the righteous Abraham in the field close by, sitting beside yokes of oxen for ploughing, together with the sons of Masek and other servants, to the number of twelve.

And behold the chief-captain came to him, and Abraham, seeing the chief-captain Michael coming from afar, like to a very comely warrior, arose and met him as was his custom, meeting and entertaining all strangers.

And the chief-captain saluted him and said:

Hail, most honored father, righteous soul chosen of God, true son of the heavenly one.

Abraham said to the chief-captain:

Hail, most honored warrior, bright as the sun and most beautiful above all the sons of men; thou art welcome; therefore I beseech thy presence, tell me whence the youth of thy age has come; teach me, thy suppliant, whence and from what army and from what journey thy beauty has come hither.

The chief-captain said:

I, O righteous Abraham, come from the great city.

I have been sent by the great king to take the place of a good friend of his, for the king has summoned him.

And Abraham said, Come, my Lord, go with me as far as my field.

The chief-captain said: I come; and going into the field of the ploughing, they sat down beside the company.

And Abraham said to his servants, the sons of Masek:

Go ye to the herd of horses, and bring two horses, quiet, and gentle and tame, so that I and this stranger may sit thereon.

But the chief-captain said, Nay, my Lord, Abraham, let them not bring horses, for I abstain from ever sitting upon any four-footed beast.

Is not my king rich in much merchandise, having power both over men and all kinds of cattle? but I abstain from ever sitting upon any four-footed beast. Let us go, then, O righteous soul, walking lightly until we reach thy house.

And Abraham said, Amen, be it so.

III.

And as they went on from the field toward his house, beside that way there stood a cypress tree, and by the command of the Lord the tree cried out with a human voice, saying, Holy, holy, holy is the Lord God that calls himself to those that love him; but Abraham hid the mystery, thinking that the chief-captain had not heard the voice of the tree. And coming nigh to the house they sat down in the court, and Isaac seeing the face of the angel said to Sarah his mother, My lady mother, behold, the man sitting with my father Abraham is not a son of the race of those that dwell on the earth.

And Isaac ran, and saluted him, and fell at the feet of the Incorporeal, and the Incorporeal blessed him and said, The Lord God will grant thee his promise that he made to thy father Abraham and to his seed, and will also grant thee the precious prayer of thy father and thy mother.

Abraham said to Isaac his son, My son Isaac, draw water from the well, and bring it me in the vessel, that we may wash the feet of this stranger, for he is tired, having come to us from off a long journey.

And Isaac ran to the well and drew water in the vessel and brought it to them, and Abraham went up and washed the feet of the chief captain Michael, and the heart of Abraham was moved, and he wept over the stranger.

And Isaac, seeing his father weeping, wept also, and the chief captain, seeing them weeping, also wept with them, and the tears of the chief captain fell upon the vessel into the water of the basin and became precious stones.

And Abraham seeing the marvel, and being astonished, took the stones secretly, and hid the mystery, keeping it by himself in his heart.

IV.

And Abraham said to Isaac his son:

Go, my beloved son, into the inner chamber of the house and beautify it.

Spread for us there two couches, one for me and one for this man that is guest with us this day.

Prepare for us there a seat and a candlestick and a table with abundance of every good thing.

Beautify the chamber, my son, and spread under us linen and purple and fine linen.

Burn there every precious and excellent incense, and bring sweet-smelling plants from the garden and fill our house with them.

Kindle seven lamps full of oil, so that we may rejoice, for this man that is our guest this day is more glorious than kings or rulers, and his appearance surpasses all the sons of men.

And Isaac prepared all things well, and Abraham taking the archangel Michael went into the chamber, and they both sat down upon the couches, and between them he placed a table with abundance of every good thing.

Then the chief captain arose and went out, as if by constraint of his belly to make issue of water, and ascended to heaven in the twinkling of an eye, and stood before the Lord, and said to him:

Lord and Master, let thy power know that I am unable to remind that righteous man of his death, for I have not seen upon the earth a man like him, pitiful, hospitable, righteous, truthful, devout, refraining from every evil deed.

And now know, Lord, that I cannot remind him of his death.

And the Lord said:

Go down, chief-captain Michael, to my friend Abraham, and whatever he say to thee, that do thou also, and whatever he eat, eat thou also with him. And I will send my Holy Spirit upon his son Isaac, and will put the remembrance of his death into the heart of Isaac, so that even he in a dream may see the death of his father, and Isaac will relate the dream, and thou shalt interpret it, and he himself will know his end.

And the chief-captain said, Lord, all the heavenly spirits are incorporeal, and neither eat nor drink, and this man has set before me a table with abundance of all good things earthly and corruptible.

Now, Lord, what shall I do?

How shall I escape him, sitting at one table with him? The Lord said:

Go down to him, and take no thought for this, for when thou sittest down with him, I will send upon thee a devouring spirit, and it will consume out of thy hands and through thy mouth all that is on the table.

Rejoice together with him in everything, only thou shalt interpret well the things of the vision, that Abraham may know the sickle of death and the uncertain end of life, and may make disposal of all his possessions, for I have blessed him above the sand of the sea and as the stars of heaven.

V.

Then the chief captain went down to the house of Abraham, and sat down with him at the table, and Isaac served them.

And when the supper was ended, Abraham prayed after his custom, and the chief-captain prayed together with him, and each lay down to sleep upon his couch. And Isaac said to his father, Father, I too would fain sleep with you in this chamber, that I also may hear your discourse, for I love to hear the excellence of the conversation of this virtuous man.

Abraham said, Nay, my son, but go to thy own chamber and sleep on thy own couch, lest we be troublesome to this man.

Then Isaac, having received the prayer from them, and having blessed them, went to his own chamber and lay down upon his couch.

But the Lord cast the thought of death into the heart of Isaac as in a dream, and about the third hour of the night Isaac awoke and rose up from his couch, and came running to the chamber where his father was sleeping together with the archangel. Isaac, therefore, on reaching the door cried out, saying, My father Abraham, arise and open to me quickly, that I may enter and hang upon thy neck, and embrace thee before they take thee away from me.

Abraham therefore arose and opened to him, and Isaac entered and hung upon his neck, and began to weep with a loud voice.

Abraham therefore being moved at heart, also wept with a loud voice, and the chief-captain, seeing them weeping, wept also.

Sarah being in her room, heard their weeping, and came running to them, and found them embracing and weeping.

And Sarah said with weeping, My Lord Abraham, what is this that ye weep?

Tell me, my Lord, has this brother that has been entertained by us this day brought thee tidings of Lot, thy brother's son, that he is dead? is it for this that ye grieve thus?

The chief-captain answered and said to her, Nay, my sister Sarah, it is not as thou sayest, but thy son Isaac, methinks, beheld a dream, and came to us weeping, and we seeing him were moved in our hearts and wept.

VI.

Then Sarah, hearing the excellence of the conversation of the chief-captain, straightway knew that it was an angel of the Lord that spoke.

Sarah therefore signified to Abraham to come out towards the door, and said to him, My Lord Abraham, knowest thou who this man is? Abraham said, I know not.

Sarah said, Thou knowest, my Lord, the three men from heaven that were entertained by us in our tent beside the oak of Mamre, when thou didst kill the kid without blemish, and set a table before them.

After the flesh had been eaten, the kid rose again, and sucked its mother with great joy.

Knowest thou not, my Lord Abraham, that by promise they gave to us Isaac as the fruit of the womb?

Of these three holy men this is one.

Abraham said, O Sarah, in this thou speakest the truth.

Glory and praise from our God and the Father.

For late in the evening when I washed his feet in the basin I said in my heart, These are the feet of one of the three men that I washed then; and his tears that fell into the basin then became precious stones. And shaking them out from his lap he gave them to Sarah, saying, If thou believest me not, look now at these.

And Sarah receiving them bowed down and saluted and said, Glory be to God that showeth us wonderful things.

And now know, my Lord Abraham, that there is among us the revelation of some thing, whether it be evil or good!

VII.

And Abraham left Sarah, and went into the chamber, and said to Isaac, Come hither, my beloved son, tell me the truth, what it was thou sawest and what befell thee that thou camest so hastily to us.

And Isaac answering began to say, I saw, my Lord, in this night the sun and the moon above my head, surrounding me with its rays and giving me light.

As I gazed at this and rejoiced, I saw the heaven opened, and a man bearing light descend from it, shining more than seven suns.

And this man like the sun came and took away the sun from my head, and went up into the heavens from whence he came, but I was greatly grieved that he took away the sun from me.

After a little, as I was still sorrowing and sore troubled, I saw this man come forth from heaven a second time, and he took away from me the moon also from off my head, and I wept greatly and called upon that man of light, and said, Do not, my Lord, take away my glory from me; pity me and hear me, and if thou takest away the sun from me, then leave the moon to me.

He said, Suffer them to be taken up to the king above, for he wishes them there.

And he took them away from me, but he left the rays upon me.

The chief-captain said, Hear, O righteous Abraham; the sun which thy son saw is thou his father, and the moon likewise is Sarah his mother.

The man bearing light who descended from heaven, this is the one sent from God who is to take thy righteous soul from thee.

And now know, O most honored Abraham, that at this time thou shalt leave this worldly life, and remove to God.

Abraham said to the chief captain O strangest of marvels! and now art thou he that shall take my soul from me?

The chief-captain said to him, I am the chief-captain Michael, that stands before the Lord, and I was sent to thee to remind thee of thy death, and then I shall depart to him as I was commanded.

Abraham said, Now I know that thou art an angel of the Lord, and wast sent to take my soul, but I will not go with thee; but do thou whatever thou art commanded.

VIII.

The chief-captain hearing these words immediately vanished, and ascending into heaven stood before God, and told all that he had seen in the house of Abraham; and the chief-captain said this also to his Lord, Thus says thy friend Abraham, I will not go with thee, but do thou whatever thou art commanded; and now, O Lord Almighty, doth thy glory and immortal kingdom order aught?

God said to the chief-captain Michael, Go to my friend Abraham yet once again, and speak to him thus, Thus saith the Lord thy God, he that brought thee into the land of promise, that blessed thee above the sand of the sea and above the stars of heaven, that opened the womb of barrenness of Sarah, and granted thee Isaac as the fruit of the womb in old age, Verily I say unto thee that blessing I will bless thee, and multiplying I will multiply thy seed, and I will give thee all that thou shalt ask from me, for I am the Lord thy God, and besides me there is no other.

Tell me why thou hast rebelled against me, and why there is grief in thee, and why thou rebelled against my archangel Michael?

Knowest thou not that all who have come from Adam and Eve have died, and that none of the prophets has escaped death?

None of those that rule as kings is immortal; none of thy forefathers has escaped the mystery of death. They have all died, they have all departed into Hades, they are all gathered by the sickle of death.

But upon thee I have not sent death, I have not suffered any deadly disease to come upon thee, I have not permitted the sickle of death to meet thee, I have not allowed the nets of Hades to enfold thee, I have never wished thee to meet with any evil.

But for good comfort I have sent my chief-captain Michael to thee, that thou mayst know thy departure from the world, and set thy house in order, and all that belongs to thee, and bless Isaac thy beloved son.

And now know that I have done this not wishing to grieve thee.

Wherefore then hast thou said to my chief-captain, I will not go with thee?

Wherefore hast thou spoken thus?

Knowest thou not that if I give leave to death and he comes upon thee, then I should see whether thou wouldst come or not?

IX.

And the chief-captain receiving the exhortations of the Lord went down to Abraham, and seeing him the righteous one fell upon his face to the ground as one dead, and the chief-captain told him all that he had heard from the Most High.

Then the holy and just Abraham rising with many tears fell at the feet of the Incorporeal, and besought him, saying, I beseech thee, chief-captain of the hosts above, since thou hast wholly deigned to come thyself to me a sinner and in all things thy unworthy servant, I beseech thee even now, O chief-captain, to carry my word yet again to the Most High, and thou shalt say to him, Thus saith Abraham thy servant, Lord, Lord, in every work and word which I have asked of thee thou hast heard me, and hast fulfilled all my counsel.

Now, Lord, I resist not thy power, for I too know that I am not immortal but mortal.

Since therefore to thy command all things yield, and fear and tremble at the face of thy power,

I also fear, but I ask one request of thee, and now, Lord and Master, hear my prayer, for while still in this body I desire to see all the inhabited earth, and all the creations which thou didst establish by one word, and when I see these, then if I shall depart from life I shall be without sorrow.

So the chief-captain went back again, and stood before God, and told him all, saying, Thus saith thy friend Abraham, I desired to behold all the earth in my lifetime before I died.

And the Most High hearing this, again commanded the chief-captain Michael, and said to him, Take a cloud of light, and the angels that have power over the chariots, and go down, take the righteous Abraham upon a chariot of the cherubim, and exalt him into the air of heaven that he may behold all the earth.

X.

And the archangel Michael went down and took Abraham upon a chariot of the cherubim, and exalted him into the air of heaven, and led him upon the cloud together with sixty angels, and Abraham ascended upon the chariot over all the earth.

And Abraham saw the world as it was in that day, some ploughing, others driving wains, in one place men herding flocks, and in another watching them by night, and dancing and playing and harping, in another place men striving and contending at law, elsewhere men weeping and having the dead in remembrance.

He saw also the newly-wedded received with honor, and in a word he saw all things that are done in the world, both good and bad.

Abraham therefore passing over them saw men bearing swords, wielding in their hands sharpened swords, and Abraham asked the chief-captain, Who are these?

The chief-captain said, These are thieves, who intend to commit murder, and to steal and burn and destroy.

Abraham said, Lord, Lord, hear my voice, and command that wild beasts may come out of the wood and devour them.

And even as he spoke there came wild beasts out of the wood and devoured them.

And he saw in another place a man with a woman committing fornication with each other, and said, Lord, Lord, command that the earth may open and swallow them, and straightway the earth was cleft and swallowed them.

And he saw in another place men digging through a house, and carrying away other men's possessions, and he said, Lord, Lord, command that fire may come down from heaven and consume them.

And even as he spoke, fire came down from heaven and consumed them.

And straightway there came a voice from heaven to the chief-captain, saying thus, O chief-captain Michael, command the chariot to stop, and turn Abraham away that he may not see all the earth, for if he behold all that live in wickedness, he will destroy all creation.

For behold, Abraham has not sinned, and has no pity on sinners, but I have made the world, and desire not to destroy any one of them, but wait for the death of the sinner, till he be converted and live.

But take Abraham up to the first gate of heaven, that he may see there the judgments and recompenses, and repent of the souls of the sinners that he has destroyed.

XI.

So Michael turned the chariot and brought Abraham to the east, to the first gate of heaven; and Abraham saw two ways, the one narrow and contracted, the other broad and spacious, and there he saw two gates, the one broad on the broad way, and the other narrow on the narrow way.

And outside the two gates there he saw a man sitting upon a gilded throne, and the appearance of that man was terrible, as of the Lord. ²And they saw many souls driven by angels and led in through the broad gate, and other souls, few in number, that were taken by the angels through the narrow gate.

And when the wonderful one who sat upon the golden throne saw few entering through the narrow gate, and many entering through the broad one, straightway that wonderful one tore the hairs of his head and the sides of his beard, and threw himself on the ground from his throne, weeping and lamenting.

But when he saw many souls entering through the narrow gate, then he arose from the ground and sat upon his throne in great joy, rejoicing and exulting.

And Abraham asked the chief-captain, My Lord chief-captain, who is this most marvelous man, adorned with such glory, and sometimes he weeps and laments, and sometimes he rejoices and exults?

The incorporeal one said:

This is the first-created Adam who is in such glory, and he looks upon the world because all are born from him, and when he sees many souls going through the narrow gate, then he arises and sits upon his throne rejoicing and exulting in joy, because this narrow gate is that of the just, that leads to life, and they that enter through it go into Paradise.

For this, then, the first-created Adam rejoices, because he sees the souls being saved.

But when he sees many souls entering through the broad gate, then he pulls out the hairs of his head, and casts himself on the ground weeping and lamenting bitterly, for the broad gate is that of sinners, which leads to destruction and eternal punishment.

And for this the first-formed Adam falls from his throne weeping and lamenting for the destruction of sinners, for they are many that are lost, and they are few that are saved, for in seven thousand there is scarcely found one soul saved, being righteous and undefiled.

XII.

While he was yet saying these things to me, behold two angels, fiery in aspect, and pitiless in mind, and severe in look, and they drove on thousands of souls, pitilessly lashing them with fiery thongs.

The angel laid hold of one soul, and they drove all the souls in at the broad gate to destruction.

So we also went along with the angels, and came within that broad gate, and between the two gates stood a throne terrible of aspect, of terrible crystal, gleaming as fire, and upon it sat a wondrous man bright as the sun, like to the Son of God.

Before him stood a table like crystal, all of gold and fine linen, and upon the table there was lying a book, the thickness of it six cubits, and the breadth of it ten cubits, and on the right and left of it stood two angels holding paper and ink and pen.

Before the table sat an angel of light, holding in his hand a balance, and on his left sat an angel all fiery, pitiless, and severe, holding in his hand a trumpet, having within it all-consuming fire with which to try the sinners.

The wondrous man who sat upon the throne himself judged and sentenced the souls, and the two angels on the right and on the left wrote down, the one on the right the righteousness and the one on the left the wickedness.

The one before the table, who held the balance, weighed the souls, and the fiery angel, who held the fire, tried the souls.

And Abraham asked the chief-captain Michael, What is this that we behold?

And the chief-captain said, These things that thou seest, holy Abraham, are the judgment and recompense.

And behold the angel holding the soul in his hand, and he brought it before the judge, and the judge said to one of the angels that served him, Open me this book, and find me the sins of this soul.

And opening the book he found its sins and its righteousness equally balanced, and he neither gave it to the tormentors, nor to those that were saved, but set it in the midst.

XIII.

And Abraham said, My Lord chief-captain, who is this most wondrous judge? and who are the angels that write down? and who is the angel like the sun, holding the balance? and who is the fiery angel holding the fire?

The chief-captain said, "Seest thou, most holy Abraham, the terrible man sitting upon the throne?

This is the son of the first created Adam, who is called Abel, whom the wicked Cain killed, and he sits thus to judge all creation, and examines righteous men and sinners.

For God has said, I shall not judge you, but every man born of man shall be judged.

Therefore he has given to him judgment, to judge the world until his great and glorious coming, and then, O righteous Abraham, is the perfect judgment and recompense, eternal and unchangeable, which no one can alter.

For every man has come from the first-created, and therefore they are first judged here by his son, and at the second coming they shall be judged by the twelve tribes of Israel, every breath and every creature.

But the third time they shall be judged by the Lord God of all, and then, indeed, the end of that judgment is near, and the sentence terrible, and there is none to deliver.

And now by three tribunals the judgment of the world and the recompense is made, and for this reason a matter is not finally confirmed by one or two witnesses, but by three witnesses shall everything be established.

The two angels on the right hand and on the left, these are they that write down the sins and the righteousness, the one on the right hand writes down the righteousness, and the one on the left the sins.

The Forgotten Bible

The angel like the sun, holding the balance in his hand, is the archangel, Dokiel the just weigher, and he weighs the righteousnesses and sins with the righteousness of God.

The fiery and pitiless angel, holding the fire in his hand, is the archangel Puruel, who has power over fire, and tries the works of men through fire, and if the fire consume the work of any man, the angel of judgment immediately seizes him, and carries him away to the place of sinners, a most bitter place of punishment.

But if the fire approves the work of anyone, and does not seize upon it, that man is justified, and the angel of righteousness takes him and carries him up to be saved in the lot of the just.

And thus, most righteous Abraham, all things in all men are tried by fire and the balance."

XIV.

And Abraham said to the chief-captain, My Lord the chief-captain, the soul which the angel held in his hand, why was it adjudged to be set in the midst?

The chief-captain said, Listen, righteous Abraham. Because the judge found its sins. and its righteousnesses equal, he neither committed it to judgment nor to be saved, until the judge of all shall come.

Abraham said to the chief-captain, And what yet is wanting for the soul to be saved?

The chief-captain said, If it obtains one righteousness above its sins, it enters into salvation. Abraham said to the chief-captain, Come hither, chief-captain Michael, let us make prayer for this soul, and see whether God will hear us. The chief-captain said, Amen, be it so; and they made prayer and entreaty for the soul, and God heard them, and when they rose up from their prayer they did not see the soul standing there.

And Abraham said to the angel, Where is the soul that thou didst hold in the midst?

And the angel answered, It has been saved by thy righteous prayer, and behold an angel of light has taken it and carried it up into Paradise.

Abraham said, I glorify the name of God, the Most High, and his immeasurable mercy.

And Abraham said to the chief-captain, I beseech thee, archangel, hearken to my prayer, and let us yet call upon the Lord, and supplicate his compassion, and entreat his mercy for the souls of the sinners whom I formerly, in my anger, cursed and destroyed, whom the earth devoured, and the wild beasts tore in pieces, and the fire consumed through my words.

Now I know that I have sinned before the Lord our God.

Come then, O Michael, chief-captain of the hosts above, come, let us call upon God with tears that he may forgive me my sin, and grant them to me.

And the chief-captain heard him, and they made entreaty before the Lord, and when they had called upon him for a long space, there came a voice from heaven saying, Abraham, Abraham, I have hearkened to thy voice and thy prayer, and forgive thee thy sin, and those whom thou thinkest that I destroyed I have called up and brought them into life by my exceeding kindness, because for a season I have requited them in judgment, and those whom I destroy living upon earth, I will not requite in death.

XV.

And the voice of the Lord said also to the chief-captain Michael, Michael, my servant, turn back Abraham to his house, for behold his end has come nigh, and the measure of his life is fulfilled, that he may set all things in order, and then take him and bring him to me.

So the chief-captain, turning the chariot and the cloud, brought Abraham to his house, and going into his chamber he sat upon his couch.

And Sarah his wife came and embraced the feet of the Incorporeal, and spoke humbly, saying, I give thee thanks, my Lord, that thou hast brought my Lord Abraham, for behold we thought he had been taken up from us.

And his son Isaac also came and fell upon his neck, and in the same way all his men-slaves and women-slaves surrounded Abraham and embraced him, glorifying God.

And the Incorporeal one said to them, Hearken, righteous Abraham.

Behold thy wife Sarah, behold also thy beloved son Isaac, behold also all thy men-servants and maid-servants round about thee.

Make disposition of all that thou hast, for the day has come nigh in which thou shalt depart from the body and go to the Lord once for all.

Abraham said, Has the Lord said it, or sayest thou this of thyself?

The chief-captain answered, Hearken, righteous Abraham.

The Lord has commanded, and I tell thee.

Abraham said, I will not go with thee.

The chief-captain, hearing these words, straightway went forth from the presence of Abraham, and went up into the heavens, and stood before God the Most High, and said, Lord Almighty, behold I have hearkened to Thy friend Abraham in all he has said to Thee, and have fulfilled his requests.

I have shown to him Thy power, and all the earth and sea that is under heaven.

I have shown to him judgment and recompense by means of cloud and chariots, and again he says, I will not go with thee.

And the Most High said to the angel, Does my friend Abraham say thus again, I will not go with thee?

The archangel said, Lord Almighty, he says thus, and I refrain from laying hands on him, because from the beginning he is Thy friend, and has done all things pleasing in Thy sight.

There is no man like him on earth, not even Job the wondrous man, and therefore I refrain from laying hands on him. Command, therefore, Immortal King, what shall be done.

XVI.

Then the Most High said, Call me hither Death that is called the shameless countenance and the pitiless look.

And Michael the Incorporeal went and said to Death, Come hither; the Lord of creation, the immortal king, calls thee.

And Death, hearing this, shivered and trembled, being possessed with great terror, and coming with great fear it stood before the invisible father, shivering, groaning and trembling, awaiting the command of the Lord.

Therefore the invisible God said to Death, Come hither, thou bitter and fierce name of the world, hide thy fierceness, cover thy corruption, and cast away thy bitterness from thee, and put on thy beauty and all thy glory, and go down to Abraham my friend, and take him and bring him to me.

But now also I tell thee not to terrify him, but bring him with fair speech, for he is my own friend.

Having heard this, Death went out from the presence of the Most High, and put on a robe of great brightness, and made his appearance like the sun, and became fair and beautiful above the sons of men, assuming the form of an archangel, having his cheeks flaming with fire, and he departed to Abraham.

Now the righteous Abraham went out of his chamber, and sat under the trees of Mamre, holding his chin in his hand, and awaiting the coming of the archangel Michael.

And behold, a smell of sweet odor came to him, and a flashing of light, and Abraham turned and saw Death coming towards him in great glory and beauty.

And Abraham arose and went to meet him, thinking that it was the chief-captain of God, and Death beholding him saluted him, saying, Rejoice, precious Abraham, righteous soul, true friend of the Most High God, and companion of the holy angels.

Abraham said to Death, Hail thou of appearance and form like the sun, most glorious helper, bringer of light, wondrous man, from whence does thy glory come to us, and who art thou, and whence comest thou?

Then Death said, Most righteous Abraham, behold I tell thee the truth.

I am the bitter lot of death.

Abraham said to him, Nay, but thou art the comeliness of the world, thou art the glory and beauty of angels and men, thou art fairer in form than every other, and sayest thou, I am the bitter lot of death, and not rather, I am fairer than every good thing.

Death said, I tell thee the truth.

What the Lord has named me, that also I tell thee.

Abraham said, For what art thou come hither?

Death said, For thy holy soul am I come.

Then Abraham said, I know what thou meanest, but I will not go with thee; and Death was silent and answered him not a word.

XVII.

Then Abraham arose, and went into his house, and Death also accompanied him thither.

And Abraham went up into his chamber, and Death went up with him.

And Abraham lay down upon his couch, and Death came and sat by his feet.

Then Abraham said, Depart, depart from me, for I desire to rest upon my couch.

Death said, I will not depart until I take thy spirit from thee.

Abraham said to him, By the immortal God I charge thee to tell me the truth.

Art thou death? Death said to him, I am Death.

I am the destroyer of the world. Abraham said, I beseech thee, since thou art Death, tell me if thou comest thus to all in such fairness and glory and beauty?

Death said, Nay, my Lord Abraham, for thy righteousnesses, and the boundless sea of thy hospitality, and the greatness of thy love towards God has become a crown upon my head, and in beauty and great peace and gentleness I approach the righteous, but to sinners I come in great corruption and fierceness and the greatest bitterness and with fierce and pitiless look.

Abraham said, I beseech thee, hearken to me, and show me thy fierceness and all thy corruption and bitterness.

And Death said, Thou canst not behold my fierceness, most righteous Abraham.

Abraham said, Yes, I shall be able to behold all thy fierceness by means of the name of the living God, for the might of my God that is in heaven is with me.

Then Death put off all his comeliness and beauty, and all his glory and the form like the sun with which he was clothed, and put upon himself a tyrant's robe, and made his appearance gloomy and fiercer than all kind of wild beasts, and more unclean than all uncleanness. And he showed to Abraham seven fiery heads of serpents and fourteen faces, (one) of flaming fire and of great fierceness, and a face of darkness, and a most gloomy face of a viper, and a face of a most terrible precipice, and a face fiercer than an asp, and a face of a terrible lion, and a face of a cerastes and basilisk.

He showed him also a face of a fiery scimitar, and a sword-bearing face, and a face of lightning, lightening terribly, and a noise of dreadful thunder.

He showed him also another face of a fierce stormy sea, and a fierce rushing river, and a terrible three-headed serpent, and a cup mingled with poisons, and in short he showed to him great fierceness and unendurable bitterness, and every mortal disease as of the odor of Death.

And from the great bitterness and fierceness there died servants and maid-servants in number about seven thousand, and the righteous Abraham came into indifference of death so that his spirit failed him.

XVIII.

And the all-holy Abraham, seeing these things thus, said to Death, I beseech thee, all-destroying Death, hide thy fierceness, and put on thy beauty and the shape which thou hadst before.

And straightway Death hid his fierceness, and put on his beauty which he had before.

And Abraham said to Death, Why hast thou done this, that thou hast slain all my servants and maidservants?

Has God sent thee hither for this end this day?

Death said, Nay, my Lord Abraham, it is not as thou sayest, but on thy account was I sent hither.

Abraham said to Death, How then have these died?

Has the Lord not spoken it?

Death said, Believe thou, most righteous Abraham, that this also is wonderful, that thou also wast not taken away with them.

Nevertheless I tell thee the truth, for if the right hand of God had not been with thee at that time, thou also wouldst have had to depart from this life.

The righteous Abraham said, Now I know that I have come into indifference of death, so that my spirit fails, but I beseech thee, all-destroying Death, since my servants have died before their time, come let us pray to the Lord our God that he may hear us and raise up those who died by thy fierceness before their time.

And Death said, Amen, be it so.

Therefore Abraham arose and fell upon the face of the ground in prayer, and Death together with him, and the Lord sent a spirit of life upon those that were dead and they were made alive again.

Then the righteous Abraham gave glory to God.

XIX.

And going up into his chamber he lay down, and Death came and stood before him.

And Abraham said to him, Depart from me, for I desire to rest, because my spirit is in indifference.

Death said, I will not depart from thee until I take thy soul.

And Abraham with an austere countenance and angry look said to Death, Who has ordered thee to say this?

Thou sayest these words of thyself boastfully, and I will not go with thee until the chief-captain Michael come to me, and I shall go with him.

But this also I tell thee, if thou desirest that I shall accompany thee, explain to me all thy changes, the seven fiery heads of serpents and what the face of the precipice is, and what the sharp sword, and what the loud-roaring river, and what the tempestuous sea that rages so fiercely.

Teach me also the unendurable thunder, and the terrible lightning, and the evil-smelling cup mingled with poisons.

Teach me concerning all these.

And Death answered, Listen, righteous Abraham.

For seven ages I destroy the world and lead all down to Hades, kings and rulers, rich and poor, slaves and free men, I convoy to the bottom of Hades, and for this I showed thee the seven heads of serpents.

The face of fire I showed thee because many die consumed by fire, and behold death through a face of fire.

The face of the precipice I showed thee, because many men die descending from the tops of trees or terrible precipices and losing their life, and see death in the shape of a terrible precipice.

The face of the sword I showed thee because many are slain in wars by the sword, and see death as a sword.

The face of the great rushing river I showed thee because many are drowned and perish snatched away by the crossing of many waters and carried off by great rivers, and see death before their time.

The face of the angry raging sea I showed thee because many in the sea falling into great surges and becoming shipwrecked are swallowed up and behold death as the sea.

The unendurable thunder and the terrible lightning I showed thee because many men in the moment of anger meet with unendurable thunder and terrible lightning coming to seize upon men, and see death thus.

I showed thee also the poisonous wild beasts, asps and basilisks, leopards and lions and lions' whelps, bears and vipers, and in short the face of every wild beast I showed thee, most righteous one, because many men are destroyed by wild beasts, and others by poisonous snakes, serpents and asps and cerastes and basilisks and vipers, breathe out their life and die.

I showed thee also the destroying cups mingled with poison, because many men being given poison to drink by other men straightway depart unexpectedly.

XX.

Abraham said, I beseech thee, is there also an unexpected death? Tell me.

Death said, Verily, verily, I tell thee in the truth of God that there are seventy-two deaths.

One is the just death, buying its fixed time, and many men in one hour enter into death being given over to the grave.

Behold, I have told thee all that thou hast asked, now I tell thee, most righteous Abraham, to dismiss all counsel, and cease from asking anything once for all, and come, go with me, as the God and judge of all has commanded me.

Abraham said to Death, Depart from me yet a little, that I may rest on my couch, for I am very faint at heart, for since I have seen thee with my eyes my strength has failed me, all the limbs of my flesh seem to me a weight as of lead, and my spirit is distressed exceedingly.

Depart for a little; for I have said I cannot bear to see thy shape.

Then Isaac his son came and fell upon his breast weeping, and his wife Sarah came and embraced his feet, lamenting bitterly.

There came also his men slaves and women slaves and surrounded his couch, lamenting greatly.

And Abraham came into indifference of death, and Death said to Abraham, Come, take my right hand, and may cheerfulness and life and strength come to thee.

For Death deceived Abraham, and he took his right hand, and straightway his soul adhered to the hand of Death.

And immediately the archangel Michael came with a multitude of angels and took up his precious soul in his hands in a divinely woven linen cloth, and they tended the body of the just Abraham with divine ointments and perfumes until the third day after his death, and buried him in the land of promise, the oak of Mamre, but the angels received his precious soul, and ascended into heaven, singing the hymn of "thrice holy" to the Lord the God of all, and they set it there to worship the God and Father.

And after great praise and glory had been given to the Lord, and Abraham bowed down to worship, there came the undefiled voice of the God and Father saying thus, Take therefore my friend Abraham into Paradise, where are the tabernacles of my righteous ones, and the abodes of my saints Isaac and Jacob in his bosom, where there is no trouble, nor grief, nor sighing, but peace and rejoicing and life unending.

(And let us, too, my beloved brethren, imitate the hospitality of the patriarch Abraham, and attain to his virtuous way of life, that we may be thought worthy of the life eternal, glorifying the Father, Son and Holy Ghost; to whom be glory and power forever.

The Forgotten Bible
Amen.).

Version II

I.

It came to pass, when the days of the death of Abraham drew near, that the Lord said to Michael:

Arise and go to Abraham, my servant, and say to him, Thou shalt depart from life, for lo! the days of thy temporal life are fulfilled:

so that he may set his house in order before he die.

II.

And Michael went and came to Abraham, and found him sitting before his oxen for ploughing, and he was exceeding old in appearance, and had his son in his arms.

Abraham, therefore, seeing the archangel Michael, rose from the ground and saluted him, not knowing who he was, and said to him:

The Lord preserve thee.

May thy journey be prosperous with thee.

And Michael answered him:

Thou art kind, good father.

Abraham answered and said to him:

Come, draw near to me, brother, and sit down a little while, that I may order a beast to be brought that we may go to my house, and thou mayest rest with me, for it is toward evening, and in the morning arise and go whithersoever thou wilt, lest some evil beast meet thee and do thee hurt.

And Michael enquired of Abraham, saying:

Tell me thy name, before I enter thy house, lest I be burdensome to thee.

Abraham answered and said, My parents called me Abram, and the Lord named me Abraham, saying:

Arise and depart from thy house, and from thy kindred, and go into the land which I shall show unto thee.

And when I went away into the land which the Lord showed me, he said to me:

Thy name shall no more be called Abram, but thy name shall be Abraham.

Michael answered and said to him:

Pardon me, my father, experienced man of God, for I am a stranger, and I have heard of thee that thou didst go forty furlongs and didst bring a goat and slay it, entertaining angels in thy house, that they might rest there.

Thus speaking together, they arose and went towards the house. And Abraham called one of his servants, and said to him:

Go, bring me a beast that the stranger may sit upon it, for he is wearied with his journey.

And Michael said:

Trouble not the youth, but let us go lightly until we reach the house, for I love thy company.

III.

And arising they went on, and as they drew nigh to the city, about three furlongs from it, they found a great tree having three hundred branches, like to a tamarisk tree.

And they heard a voice from its branches singing, "Holy art thou, because thou hast kept the purpose for which thou wast sent."

And Abraham heard the voice, and hid the mystery in his heart, saying within himself, What is the mystery that I have heard?

As he came into the house, Abraham said to his servants, Arise, go out to the flocks, and bring three sheep, and slay them quickly, and make them ready that we may eat and drink, for this day is a feast for us.

And the servants brought the sheep, and Abraham called his son Isaac, and said to him, My son Isaac, arise and put water in the vessel that we may wash the feet of this stranger. And he brought it as he was commanded, and Abraham said, I perceive, and so it shall be, that in this basin I shall never again wash the feet of any man coming to us as a guest.

And Isaac hearing his father say this wept, and said to him, My father what is this that thou sayest, This is my last time to wash the feet of a stranger?

And Abraham seeing his son weeping, also wept exceedingly, and Michael seeing them weeping, wept also, and the tears of Michael fell upon the vessel and became a precious stone.

IV.

When Sarah, being inside in her house, heard their weeping, she came out and said to Abraham, Lord, why is it that ye thus weep? Abraham answered, and said to her, It is no evil.

Go into thy house, and do thy own work, lest we be troublesome to the man.

And Sarah went away, being about to prepare the supper.

And the sun came near to setting, and Michael went out of the house, and was taken up into the heavens to worship before God, for at sunset all the angels worship God and Michael himself is the first of the angels.

And they all worshipped him, and went each to his own place, but Michael spoke before the Lord and said, Lord, command me to be questioned before thy holy glory!

And the Lord said to Michael, Announce whatsoever thou wilt!

And the Archangel answered and said, Lord, thou didst send me to Abraham to say to him, Depart from thy body, and leave this world; the Lord calls thee; and I dare not, Lord, reveal myself to him, for he is thy friend, and a righteous man, and one that receives strangers.

But I beseech thee, Lord, command the remembrance of the death of Abraham to enter into his own heart, and bid not me tell it him, for it is great abruptness to say, Leave the world, and especially to leave one's own body, for thou didst create him from the beginning to have pity on the souls of all men.

Then the Lord said to Michael, Arise and go to Abraham, and lodge with him, and whatever thou seest him eat, eat thou also, and wherever he shall sleep, sleep thou there also.

For I will cast the thought of the death of Abraham into the heart of Isaac his son in a dream.

V.

Then Michael went into the house of Abraham on that evening, and found them preparing the supper, and they ate and drank and were merry.

And Abraham said to his son Isaac, Arise, my son, and spread the man's couch that he may sleep, and set the lamp upon the stand. And Isaac did as his father commanded him, and Isaac said to his father, I too am coming to sleep beside you.

Abraham answered him, Nay, my son, lest we be troublesome to this man, but go to thy own chamber and sleep.

And Isaac not wishing to disobey his father's command, went away and slept in his own chamber.

VI.

And it happened about the seventh hour of the night Isaac awoke, and came to the door of his father's chamber, crying out and saying, Open, father, that I may touch thee before they take thee away from me.

Abraham arose and opened to him, and Isaac entered and hung upon his father's neck weeping, and kissed him with lamentations.

And Abraham wept together with his son, and Michael saw them weeping and wept likewise.

And Sarah hearing them weeping called from her bed-chamber, saying, My Lord Abraham, why is this weeping?

Has the stranger told thee of thy brother's son Lot that he is dead? or has aught else befallen us?

Michael answered and said to Sarah, Nay, Sarah, I have brought no tidings of Lot, but I knew of all your kindness of heart, that therein ye excel all men upon earth, and the Lord has remembered you.

Then Sarah said to Abraham, How durst thou weep when the man of God has come in to thee, and why have thy eyes [3] shed tears for today there is great rejoicing?

Abraham said to her, How knowest thou that this is a man of God?

Sarah answered and said, Because I say and declare that this is one of the three men who were entertained by us at the oak of Mamre, when one of the servants went and brought a kid and thou didst kill it, and didst say to me, Arise, make ready that we may eat with these men in our house.

Abraham answered and said, Thou has perceived well, O woman, for I too, when I washed his feet knew in my heart that these were the feet which I had washed at the oak of Mamre, and when I began to enquire concerning his journey, he said to me, I go to preserve Lot thy brother from the men of Sodom, and then I knew the mystery.

VII.
And Abraham said to Michael, Tell me, man of God, and show to me why thou hast come hither.

And Michael said, Thy son Isaac will show thee.

And Abraham said to his son, My beloved son, tell me what thou hast seen in thy dream today, and wast frightened.

Relate it to me. Isaac answered his father, I saw in my dream the sun and the moon, and there was a crown upon my head, and there came from heaven a man of great size, and shining as the light that is called the father of light.

He took the sun from my head, and yet left the rays behind with me.

And I wept and said, I beseech thee, my Lord, take not away the glory of my head, and the light of my house, and all my glory.

And the sun and the moon and the stars lamented, saying, Take not away the glory of our power.

And that shining man answered and said to me, Weep not that I take the light of thy house, for it is taken up from troubles into rest, from a low estate to a high one; they lift him up from a narrow to a wide place; they raise him from darkness to light. And I said to him, I beseech thee, Lord, take also the rays with it. He said to me, There are twelve hours of the day, and then I shall take all the rays.

As the shining man said this, I saw the sun of my house ascending into heaven, but that crown I saw no more, and that sun was like thee my father.

And Michael said to Abraham, Thy son Isaac has spoken truth, for thou shalt go, and be taken up into the heavens, but thy body shall remain on earth, until seven thousand ages are fulfilled, for then all flesh shall arise.

Now therefore, Abraham, set thy house in order, and thy children, for thou hast heard fully what is decreed concerning thee.

Abraham answered and said to Michael, I beseech thee, Lord, if I shall depart from my body, I have desired to be taken up in my body that I may see the creatures that the Lord my God has created in heaven and on earth.

Michael answered and said, This is not for me to do, but I shall go and tell the Lord of this, and if I am commanded I shall show thee all these things.

VIII.
And Michael went up into heaven, and spoke before the Lord concerning Abraham, and the Lord answered Michael, Go and take up Abraham in the body, and show him all things, and whatsoever he shall say to thee do to him as to my friend.

So Michael went forth and took up Abraham in the body on a cloud, and brought him to the river of Ocean.

XII.
And after Abraham had seen the place of judgment, the cloud took him down upon the firmament below, and Abraham, looking down upon the earth, saw a man committing adultery with a wedded woman.

And Abraham turning said to Michael, Seest thou this wickedness? but, Lord, send fire from heaven to consume them.

And straightway there came down fire and consumed them, for the Lord had said to Michael, Whatsoever Abraham shall ask thee to do for him, do thou.

Abraham looked again, and saw other men railing at their companions, and said, Let the earth open and swallow them, and as he spoke the earth swallowed them alive.

Again the cloud led him to another place, and Abraham saw some going into a desert place to commit murder, and he said to Michael, Seest thou this wickedness? but let wild beasts come out of the desert, and tear them in pieces, and that same hour wild beasts came out of the desert, and devoured them.

Then the Lord God spoke to Michael saying, Turn away Abraham to his own house, and let him not go round all the creation that I have made, because he has no compassion on sinners, but I have compassion on sinners that they may turn and live, and repent of their sins and be saved.

(VIII.)
And Abraham looked and saw two gates, the one small and the other large, and between the two gates sat a man upon a throne of great glory, and a multitude of angels round about him, and he was weeping, and again laughing, but his weeping exceeded his laughter seven-fold. And Abraham said to Michael, Who is this that sits between the two gates in great glory; sometimes he laughs,

and sometimes he weeps, and his weeping exceeds his laughter seven-fold?

And Michael said to Abraham, Knowest thou not who it is?

And he said, No, Lord.

And Michael said to Abraham, Seest thou these two gates, the small and the great?

These are they which lead to life and to destruction.

This man that sits between them is Adam, the first man whom the Lord created, and set him in this place to see every soul that departs from the body, seeing that all are from him.

When, therefore, thou seest him weeping, know that he has seen many souls being led to destruction, but when thou seest him laughing, he has seen many souls being led into life. Seest thou how his weeping exceeds his laughter?

Since he sees the greater part of the world being led away through the broad gate to destruction, therefore his weeping exceeds his laughter seven-fold.

IX.

And Abraham said, And he that cannot enter through the narrow gate, can he not enter into life?

Then Abraham wept, saying, Woe is me, what shall I do? for I am a man broad of body, and how shall I be able to enter by the narrow gate, by which a boy of fifteen years cannot enter?

Michael answered and said to Abraham, Fear not, father, nor grieve, for thou shalt enter by it unhindered, and all those who are like thee.

And as Abraham stood and marveled, behold an angel of the Lord driving sixty thousand souls of sinners to destruction.

And Abraham said to Michael, Do all these go into destruction?

And Michael said to him, Yea, but let us go and search among these souls, if there is among them even one righteous.

And when they went, they found an angel holding in his hand one soul of a woman from among these sixty thousand, because he had found her sins weighing equally with all her works, and they were neither in motion nor at rest, but in a state between; but the other souls he led away to destruction.

Abraham said to Michael, Lord, is this the angel that removes the souls from the body or not?

Michael answered and said, This is death, and he leads them into the place of judgment, that the judge may try them.

X.

And Abraham said, My Lord, I beseech thee to lead me to the place of judgment so that I too may see how they are judged.

Then Michael took Abraham upon a cloud, and led him into Paradise, and when he came to the place where the judge was, the angel came and gave that soul to the judge.

And the soul said, Lord have mercy on me.

And the judge said, How shall I have mercy upon thee, when thou hadst no mercy upon thy daughter which thou hadst, the fruit of thy womb?

Wherefore didst thou slay her?

It answered, Nay, Lord, slaughter has not been done by me, but my daughter has lied upon me.

But the judge commanded him to come that wrote down the records, and behold cherubim carrying two books.

And there was with them a man of exceeding great stature, having on his head three crowns, and the one crown was higher than the other two.

These are called the crowns of witness.

And the man had in his hand a golden pen, and the judge said to him, Exhibit the sin of this soul.

And that man, opening one of the books of the cherubim, sought out the sin of the woman's soul and found it.

And the judge said, O wretched soul, why sayest thou that thou hast not done murder? Didst thou not, after the death of thy husband, go and commit adultery with thy daughter's husband, and kill her?

And he convicted her also of her other sins, whatsoever she had done from her youth.

Hearing these things the woman cried out, saying, Woe is me, all the sins that I did in the world I forgot, but here they were not forgotten.

Then they took her away also and gave her over to the tormentors.

XI.

And Abraham said to Michael, Lord, who is this judge, and who is the other, who convicts the sins?

And Michael said to Abraham, Seest thou the judge?

This is Abel, who first testified, and God brought him hither to judge, and he that bears witness here is the teacher of heaven and earth, and the scribe of righteousness, Enoch, for the Lord sent them hither to write down the sins and righteousnesses of each one.

Abraham said, And how can Enoch bear the weight of the souls, not having seen death? or how can he give sentence to all the souls? Michael said, If he gives sentence concerning the souls, it is not permitted; but Enoch himself does not give sentence, but it is the Lord who does so, and he has no more to do than only to write.

For Enoch prayed to the Lord saying, I desire not, Lord, to give sentence on the souls, lest I be grievous to anyone; and the Lord said to Enoch, I shall command thee to write down the sins of the soul that makes atonement and it shall enter into life, and if the soul make not atonement and repent, thou shalt find its sins written down and it shall be cast into punishment.

And about the ninth hour Michael brought Abraham back to his house.

But Sarah his wife, not seeing what had become of Abraham, was consumed with grief, and gave up the ghost, and after the return of Abraham he found her dead, and buried her.

XIII.

But when the day of the death of Abraham drew nigh, the Lord God said to Michael, Death will not dare to go near to take away the soul of my servant, because he is my friend, but go thou and adorn Death with great beauty, and send him thus to Abraham, that he may see him with his eyes.

And Michael straightway, as he was commanded, adorned Death with great beauty, and sent him thus to Abraham that he might see him.

And he sat down near to Abraham, and Abraham seeing Death sitting near to him was afraid with a great fear.

And Death said to Abraham, Hail, holy soul! hail, friend of the Lord God! hail, consolation and entertainment of travelers!

And Abraham said, Thou art welcome, servant of the Most High. God.

I beseech thee, tell me who thou art; and entering into my house partake of food and drink, and depart from me, for since I have seen thee sitting near to me my soul has been troubled.

For I am not at all worthy to come near thee, for thou art an exalted spirit and I am flesh and blood, and therefore I cannot bear thy glory, for I see that thy beauty is not of this world.

And Death said to Abraham, I tell thee, in all the creation that God has made, there has not been found one like thee, for even the Lord himself by searching has not found such an one upon the whole earth.

And Abraham said to Death, How durst thou lie? for I see that thy beauty is not of this world.

And Death said to Abraham, Think not, Abraham, that this beauty is mine, or that I come thus to every man.

Nay, but if any one is righteous like thee, I thus take crowns and come to him, but if it is a sinner I come in great corruption, and out of their sin I make a crown for my head, and I shake them with great fear, so that they are dismayed.

Abraham therefore said to him, And whence comes thy beauty? And Death said, There is none other more full of corruption than I am. Abraham said to him, And art thou indeed he that is called Death?

He answered him and said, I am the bitter name.

I am weeping....

XIV.

And Abraham said to Death, Show us thy corruption.

And Death made manifest his corruption; and he had two heads, the one had the face of a serpent and by it some die at once by asps, and the other head was like a sword; by it some die by the sword as by bows.

In that day the servants of Abraham died through fear of Death, and Abraham seeing them prayed to the Lord, and he raised them up. But God returned and removed the soul of Abraham as in a dream, and the archangel Michael took it up into the heavens.

And Isaac buried his father beside his mother Sarah, glorifying and praising God, for to him is due glory, honor and worship, of the Father, Son and Holy Ghost, now and always and to all eternity.

Amen.

Footnotes:
1. Literally Commander-in-chief, or Chief-General.
2. Two mss. read, "Of our Lord Jesus Christ."
3. "Eyes of the fountain of light" is apparently what the text has.

The Acts of Xanthippe and Polyxena

Introduction

The original Greek text of this work is edited for the first time in Text and Studies, Vol. II., No. 3 (1893), by Montague Rhodes James, M.A., from the only ms. known to him, a Paris one of the eleventh century.

References to these Acts are not common in works dealing with the saints of the early church, and few writers seem to have known the work itself.

In substance the Acts are a religious novel, similar in form, and to some extent in matter, to the Greek romances by Achilles Tatius, Heliodorus, and others, and based upon the belief that St. Paul actually did visit Spain, according to the intention expressed by him in Romans xv. 24.

The editor of the Greek text is inclined to assign its composition to about the middle of the third century, reasoning from its relations to the Acts of Paul, and those of other apostles, which its author apparently knew and made use of.

Thus a knowledge of the Acts of Paul and Thecla may be inferred from c. xxvi., of the Acts of Peter from c. xxiv., and of those of Andrew from cc. xxviii.-xxxi.

The first and longest part of the story (from c. i. to xxi.) gives an account of the conversion of Xanthippe, wife of Probus, a man of rank in Spain.

In this part the narrative is less prominent than the speeches and prayers, which are numerous, and of considerable length. With c. xxii. a new section of the story begins, of which no previous warning has been given except in the title, containing the adventures of Polyxena, the sister of Xanthippe, who is carried off in the latter's absence.

The rest of the story is much more diversified than the early part, being full of incident and introducing a great variety of persons--the apostles Peter, Philip, and Andrew, an ass-driver, the Jewess Rebecca, a wicked prefect and his kind-hearted son, and finally Onesimus, who brings Polyxena back to Spain.

This difference in the character of the narrative in the two parts causes also some difference in the language, which in the earlier section is more diffuse and more difficult of exact translation than in the later one.

The meaning of some words is also doubtful:

those translated "lamp-stand" and "destroyer," towards the end of c. xxi., are so rendered in accordance with suggestions by his Exc. M. Gennadius, who also characterises the language of the text as full of errors.

Life and Conduct of the Holy Women, Xanthippe, Polyxena, and Rebecca

I.

When the blessed Paul was at Rome through the word of the Lord, it happened that a certain servant of a ruler of Spain came to Rome with letters of his master's, and heard the word of God from Paul, the truly golden and beautiful nightingale.

This servant being greatly touched, and being unable to remain and be filled with the divine word because he was hastened by the letters, returned into Spain in great grief, and being unable to show his desire to any one, because his master was an idolater, he was always pained at heart and sighing greatly.

Now this servant was honoured and faithful to his masters, and as time went past, the servant fell sick and grew lean of flesh, which his master perceiving said to him, What has happened to thee that thou art thus fallen together in countenance?

The servant said, here is a great pain in my heart, and I can in no way find rest.

His master said to him, And what is the pain that cannot receive healing from my chief physician?

The servant said, While I was still in Rome, this pain and its recurring mishap made itself known to me.

His master said, And knowest thou not of any who have fallen into this disease and been healed?

The servant said, Yes, but where that physician is I know not, for I left him in Rome.

So many as have been attended by that physician and have gone through the water m his hands, have received healing immediately.

His master said, I ought not to grudge to send thee yet again to Rome, if perchance thou mightest obtain healing.

II.

And while they spoke thus, behold his mistress, by name Xanthippe, overhearing these words, and learning of the teaching of Paul, said, What is the name of that physician, and what is the healing to ward off such a disease?

The servant said to her, The calling upon a new name, and anointing with oil and washing with water.

By this treatment I have seen many that had incurable pains receive healings.

As he said this, the images of the idols that stood in the house began to be shaken and fall down.

And his mistress beckoned to him, saying, Seest thou, brother, the images of the idols being shaken, how they cannot endure the power of the word?

And his master, by name Probus, arose from his mid-day sleep with a very gloomy countenance, for the Devil had greatly disturbed him, because the knowledge of God had come into his house.

And he questioned the servant of everything in order, and the servant having been seized by sickness by the foreknowledge of God, disclosed to him the life of man, and Xanthippe was incurable in her soul concerning this teaching.

So Probus too was grieved for Xanthippe, because from that time she was wasting herself away with waking and abstinence and other austerities.

III.

And Xanthippe going away to her couch and groaning, said, Woe is me, wretched one, lying in darkness, that I have not learned the name of the new teacher, that I might summon his prayer to help me, and what to say I know not.

Shall I call upon him by the name of his God? but I cannot say, The God that is preached by such a one.

Nevertheless I shall say thus by conjecture, O God, giving light in Hades, and guiding those in darkness, Lord of free men and kings, and preached by worthy servants in all the world, called upon as a brother by sinful men and quick to hear, to whom not even archangels can send up worthy songs of praise, who hast shown to me, humble and unworthy, the ever-living and abiding seed (though my ignorance permits me not to receive it), hasten also the things that concern me, Lord, since by thy will thou hast made thyself heard by me, and in thy compassion show me the proclamation of thy herald, that I may learn of him what is pleasing to thee.

Yea, I beseech thee look upon my ignorance, O God, and enlighten me with the light of thy countenance, thou that never overlookest any of those that call upon thee in truth.

Probus, her husband said to her, Why troublest thou thyself so much, lady, and dost not at all turn to sleep?

Xanthippe said, I cannot sleep, for there is in me an incurable pain.

Probus said to her, And what is thy pain or grief, O lady, that I am not sufficient to comfort thee?

All that thou hast wished unto this day I have served thee in, and now what is it that thou hast, and dost not tell me?

Xanthippe says to him, I beseech thee this thing only, my lord, permit me for a little and for this day only to sleep apart from thee.

And Probus said to her, Be it as thou wilt, lady; only leave off thy groaning.

IV.

Then entering into her bed-chamber alone, she spoke thus with tears, In what way, my God, I shall act, or what counsel I shall take, I know not.

Shall I declare the thought that has come upon me?

I fear the madness and disorder of the city.

Shall I fly from this impious city?

I fear the contrivance of the devil for seizing the sheep. Shall I await the mercy and swiftness of the Lord?

Again I fear the untimely snatching away of life, for the death of sinners has no warning.

Shall I depart and flee away to Rome?

I fear the length of the journey, being unable to go on foot.

But while I say these things by conjecture, constrained by my desire (for I cannot speak with surety), may I find pardon with thee, my God, and do thou fulfil my desire with excess of right words, and think me but worthy to hear thy preacher, for if I say, to see his face, I ask a great thing.

Blessed is he that is found in the company of thy preachers, and is satisfied with their precious countenances.

Blessed are they that are yoked under the preaching of thy commandments.

Blessed are they that keep thy commandments; but where now, Lord, are thy mercies to our fathers, that we also may be their successors in love toward thee and heirs of faith.

But behold now, Lord, I cannot find any one that has love for thee, that communing with him I might even a little refresh my soul. Speed therefore, Lord, to yoke me in desire for thee, and keep me under the shadow of thy wings, for thou alone art God, glorified to all eternity.

Amen.

V.

Therefore Xanthippe saying these words and others like them, groaned continually all the night, and Probus heard her and was greatly distressed, and arising from his couch when the morning came he went in to her, and seeing her eyes inflamed with tears, he said, Wherefore, lady, dost thou thus vex me, and wilt not tell me thy pain?

Tell it me, that I may do whatever is pleasing to thee, and distress me not with thy trouble.

Xanthippe says to him, Be of good cheer rather, my lord, and be not vexed, for my trouble shall not harm thee, but if I have found favour before thee, go forth now to the salutation, and allow me to indulge myself in it as I will, for it is not possible for man to take from me the insatiable pain.

And listening to her he went out immediately to receive the salutations of the men of the city, for he was the great man among them, and was also known to Nero, the Emperor.

And sitting down, great grief appeared in his countenance, and being asked the reason of his grief by the chief men of the city, he said to them that he had fallen into many and unfounded charges.

VI.

And Xanthippe went out into the garden, that she might await there looking closely for certainty of her husband, and she saw the delight of the trees, and the various warbling of the birds, and said, groaning, O beauty of the world! for that which we hitherto thought to come of itself, we know now that all things are beautifully fashioned by the beautiful One.

O power and invention of wisdom! for not only has he placed in men a thousand tongues, but also in birds he has distinguished various voices, as if from anthems and responses to receive sweet-voiced and heart-stirring hymns from his own works.

O delightfulness of the air, declaring the inimitable creator!

Who shall turn my sorrow into rejoicing?

And again she said, God to whom praise is sung by all, give me peace and comfort.

As she said these things, Probus also came up from the street to break his fast, and when he saw her countenance altered by tears, he began to pull out the hairs of his head, but he dared not speak to her then so as not to mingle other trouble with her trouble.

So he went and fell upon his couch, and said, groaning, Alas, that I had not even the consolation of a child from her, but only acquire grief upon grief.

Two years are not yet full since I was wedded to her, and already she meditates divorce.

VII.

But Xanthippe was always keeping watch through the doors into the streets of the city, and the blessed Paul, the preacher and teacher and illuminator of the world, left Rome and came even into Spain by the fore-knowledge of God.

And coming up to the gates of the city he stood and prayed, and crossing himself entered the city.

When Xanthippe saw the blessed Paul walking quietly and equally, and adorned with all virtue and understanding, she was greatly delighted in him and her heart leaped continually, and as possessed with an unexpected joy she said with herself, Why does my heart beat vehemently at the sight of this man?

Why is his walk quiet and equable, as of one who expects to take in his arms one that is pursued?

Why is his countenance kindly, as of one that tends the sick?

Why does he look so lovingly hither and thither, as one who desires to assist those who are seeking to flee from the mouths of dragons?

Who shall tell me that this is one from the flock of preachers?

If it were possible for me, I should wish to touch the hem of his garments, that I may behold his kindness and readiness to receive and sweet odour; for the servant had told her this also, that the hems of his garments had the odour of precious perfumes.

VIII.

Now Probus heard her words, and straightway ran out by himself into the street, and laying hold of Paul's hand said to him, Man, who thou art I know not, but deign to enter into my house; perchance thou mayest be to me a cause of salvation.

Paul said to him, It will be well with thee, son, after thy request!

And they went in together to Xanthippe.

When Xanthippe therefore saw the great Paul, the intellectual eyes of her heart were uncovered, and she read upon his forehead, having as it were golden seals, these words, Paul the Preacher of God.

Then exulting and rejoicing she threw herself at his feet, and twisting her hair together she wiped his feet, saying, Welcome, O man of God, to us humble ones, that live as shadows among shadows.

For thou hast looked upon those who were running into Hades as into something beautiful, who addressed the crooked serpent and destroyer as provider and protector, who were running into the dark Hades as to their father, those that were fashioned with a rational nature but have become like irrational creatures.

Thou hast sought me, lowly one, having the sun of righteousness in my heart.

Now the poison is stayed, when I have seen thy precious face.

Now he that troubled me is flown away, when thy most beautiful counsel has appeared to me.

Now I shall be considered worthy of repentance, when I have received the seal of the preacher of the Lord.

Before now I have deemed many happy who met with you, but I say boldly that from this time forth I myself shall be called happy by others, because I have touched thy hem, because I have received thy prayers, because I have enjoyed thy sweet and honeyed teaching.

Thou hast not hesitated to come to us, thou that fishest the dry land in thy course, and gatherest the fish that fall in thy way into the net of the kingdom of heaven.

IX.

The great Paul said to her, Arise, daughter, and look not upon me as having been sought out of thy ignorance by my foresight.

For Christ, the provider of the world, the searcher out of sinners and the lost, who has not only called to mind those upon earth, but also by his own presence has redeemed those in Hades, he himself has pitied thee, and sent me hither that he might visit and pity many others together with thee.

For this mercy and visitation are not of us, but are his injunction and command, even as we also have received mercy and been saved by him.

Probus hearing this was astonished at their words, for he was altogether ignorant of these things.

But Paul by force raised up Xanthippe from his feet, and she running set a new gilded chair for Paul to sit down upon.

The great Paul said to her, My daughter Xanthippe, do not thus, for ye have not yet accorded to the faith of Christ, but wait a little, till the Lord shall set in order what is necessary!

Xanthippe said to Paul, Sayest thou this to try me, O preacher of God, or hast thou any foreknowledge?

Paul said, No, daughter, but the devil, who hates the servants of God, sows wickedness in the hearts of his own servants, to oppose those that labour for Christ in preaching, for his wickedness has extended to the apostles and even to the Lord himself.

Therefore it is fitting to approach the unbelievers gently and kindly!

Xanthippe said to Paul, I beseech thee, if thou lovest thy servants, make prayer for Probus, and let me see if he that is hated by thee can work in him; let me see if he can even stand against thy prayer.

And Paul rejoiced exceedingly at the words of her faith, and said to her, Believe me, daughter, that by his suggestion and working I have not passed a single hour without chains and blows.

Xanthippe said to him, But thou sufferest these things by thy own free will, since thou hast not neglected thy preaching even to scourging, but this again I tell thee, that thy bonds shall be the defeat of the prompter, and thy humiliation their overthrow.

X.

Now the report of his presence ran through the whole city and the country round about, for some of that city having been at Rome had seen the signs and wonders that were done by the blessed Paul, and came to see if this was he.

Many therefore came into the house of Probus, and he began to be annoyed and to say, I will not suffer my house to be made an inn.

Xanthippe knowing that the face of Probus had begun to be estranged, and that he spoke thus, was greatly distressed, saying, Alas, wretched me, that we are not thought fully worthy to keep this man in our house; for if Paul goes hence, the church also will be held elsewhere.

Then Xanthippe, considering these matters, put her hand on the foot of Paul, and taking dust she called Probus to her, and placing her hand on his breast said, O Lord, my God, who hast sought out me, lowly one and ignorant of thee, send what is fitting into this heart. And Paul perceived her prayer, and made the sign of the cross, and for several days the people entered unhindered, and as many as had sick and vexed by unclean spirits brought them, and all were healed.

XI.

And Xanthippe said to Paul, Teacher, my heart is greatly consumed because I have not as yet received baptism.

And after this Probus being again moved by the devil, cast Paul out of the house and shut up Xanthippe in her chamber.

Then one of the chief men, Philotheus by name, besought the great Paul to come into his house, but the great Paul was unwilling to do so, saying, Lest Probus trouble thy house on my account.

Philotheus said to him, Nay, father, I am not at all subject to him, for in no other thing is he greater than me, except in rank, and that because the parents of Xanthippe are above me.

But if Probus come to me, I am above him in riches and in war.

Then Paul, the great apostle of the Lord, was persuaded, and went into the house of Philotheus the ex-prefect.

All this was done by the Evil one that Xanthippe might receive holy baptism with tribulation, and be faint-hearted concerning the commandments of Christ.

XII.

Xanthippe therefore, with tears, said to her servants, Have ye learned where Paul is gone to?

They said, Yea, in the house of Philotheus the ex-prefect, and Xanthippe rejoiced greatly that Philotheus also believed, being able, as she said, to persuade Probus also.

Then Probus called Xanthippe to supper, and when she consented not, Probus said, Think not that in bed also thou wilt keep away from me.

But when he lay down to supper, Xanthippe bending her knees, prayed to the Lord, saying, Eternal and immortal God, that didst take dust from the ground, and didst not value it according to the nature of its creation, but didst call it the son of immortality, thou who didst come from the heart of the father to the heart of the earth for our sake, on whom the cherubim dare not fix their gaze, and for us wast hidden in the womb that by taking up thy abode in a mother thou mightest make good the offence of Eve.

Thou that didst drink gall and vinegar, and wast pierced in the side by a spear, that thou mightest heal the wound given by the rib to Adam.

For Eve being his rib wrought a blow for Adam, and through him for all the world.

Thou that gavest a sleep without perception to the serpent, so that he might not know thy Incarnation, remember also my groaning and tears, and grant fulfilment to my sleep, [1] and bring sleep upon Probus until I shall be deemed worthy of the gift of holy baptism, for I vehemently desire to obtain this, to the glory and praise of thy holy name.

XIII.

But Probus, while still at supper, commanded the doors of their house to be secured by cruel and wicked soldiers, and having given these orders, he straightway fell asleep upon the couch.

Then the servants came and announced this to Xanthippe that he might be awakened, but she said, Put out the lights, my children, and leave him thus.

And in the first sleep, taking three hundred pieces of gold, she went to the doors, saying with herself, Perchance the porter will be persuaded by the amount of money.

But he, being evil and froward, would not be persuaded to do this, and she, loosing also her girdle, which was set with precious stones and worth two hundred pieces of gold, gave it to him and went out saying, Lord, I win over my own slaves with money, that thy preacher Paul may not be oppressed by Probus.

And Xanthippe went on to the house of Philotheus the ex-prefect, as to a great and incredible work, running and praising God.

As she therefore passed through a certain place, the demons pursued her with fiery torches and lightnings, and she, turning, saw behind her this terrible sight, and being possessed with great fear said, What has happened to thee now, wretched soul?

Thou hast been deprived of thy desire.

Thou wast running to salvation, thou wast running to baptism, and thou hast fallen into the serpent and his ministers, and these things thy sins have prepared for thee.

Speaking thus she was even fainting at heart from great despair, but the great Paul being forewarned by God of the assault of the demons, immediately stood beside her, being also preceded by a beautiful youth.

And straightway the vision of the demons disappeared, and Paul said to her, Arise, daughter Xanthippe, and behold the Lord desired by thee, by whose flame the heavens are shaken and the deep is dried up, coming to thee and pitying and saving thee.

Behold him that accepts thy prayers and straightway gives ear.

See him coming in the shape of a man, and take courage against the demons.

Then she rising from the ground said to him, Master, why hast thou left me solitary?

Even now make haste to seal me, so that if death come upon me I may depart to him who is full of compassion and has no arrogance.

XIV.

Therefore the great Paul straightway taking her hand, went into the house of Philotheus, and baptised her in the name of the Father and of the Son and the Holy Ghost.

Then taking bread also he gave her the eucharist saying, Let this be to thee for a remission of sins and for a renewing of thy soul.

Then the blessed Xanthippe, receiving the divine grace of holy baptism, returned to her own house, rejoicing and praising the Lord.

The porter seeing her complained loudly in violent words, that her going out might be deemed to have been without his will if Probus should notice it; but he that gave her light along with Paul kept the whole house, together with Probus, in a deep sleep, and they did not hear his words at all.

Then she went running into her bed-chamber, saying, What shall I say of thee, searcher out of sinners, who art most present with us in tribulations.

Thy goodness does these things, since for the sake of man whom thou didst make thou didst go down even to death, for, however much man stir thee to anger many times, yet thou, Lord, pourest out thy mercies upon him.

O depth of compassion and wealth of mercy; O immeasurable goodness and incomparable kindness; O treasure of good things, and giver of mercy, and enricher of all that believe in thee!

If, therefore, one who loves thee say, Be near me, Lord, thou hast already anticipated him.

If he say, I give thee thanks; hear my words, before they are spoken, thou understandest.

And as for those that ask of thee, thou givest to each after his asking.

Thy goodness seeks out those that know thee not, and thou runnest to sinners.

O cheerful look, filling the ways of sinners with mercy; O excellent watching and exhortation of the ignorant!

Who shall tell my lord Paul of the salvation that has now befallen me, that he might come and give words of thanksgiving for me to this protector of sinners?

Come many and behold and know the Lord, who hates sin, but has mercy on sinners.

Come, now, O Paul, preacher of God, for with thee even now I sit under instruction, and give words of thanksgiving for me, for I desire to keep silence, since human reason makes me afraid, lest I have not the grace of eloquence.

I desire to keep silence, and am compelled to speak, for some one inflames and sweetens me within.

If I say, I will shut my mouth, there is some one that murmurs in me.

Shall I say a great thing?

Is it not that teacher that is in Paul, without arrogance, filling the heavens, speaking within and waiting without, sitting on the throne with the father and stretched upon the cross by man.

What, therefore, I shall do I know not.

My worthless mind delights me, and is not unfolded to the end.

Thou that hadst thy hands fixed with nails and thy side pierced with the spear, thou star out of Jacob and lion's whelp out of Judah, thou rod out of Jesse, and man and God out of Mary, thou invisible God in the bosom of the Father, and that canst not be looked upon by cherubim, and art mocked in Israel, glory be to thee, who didst appear on the earth and wast taken by the people, hung upon the tree and by the report of the wicked falsely said to be stolen, and that hast bought us all together.

XV.

While she was still speaking thus, there appeared a cross on the eastern wall, and straightway there entered through it a beautiful youth, having round about him trembling rays, and under him an extended light, on which also he walked.

And as he entered within, all the foundations of that house shook and sounded with a great trembling. Xanthippe seeing him cried out and fell to the ground as if dead; but he being pitiful and kind, changing immediately into the shape of Paul, raised her up, saying, Arise, Xanthippe, and fear not, for the servants of God are thus glorified.

Then Xanthippe arising, gazed upon him, and thinking it to be Paul said, How art thou come in hither, preacher of God, seeing that I have given five hundred pieces of gold to the porter, and that although he is my slave, while thou hast no money? The Lord said to her, My servant Paul is richer than all wealth, for whatsoever treasure he acquires here he sends it before him into the kingdom of heaven, that departing thither he may rest in the unending and eternal rest.

This is the treasure of Paul, thou and thy like. Then Xanthippe gazing upon him, desirous to say something, saw his face shining as the light; and being greatly amazed, and putting both her hands over her face she threw herself to the ground, and said, Hide thyself, Lord, from my bodily eyes and enlighten my understanding, for I know now who thou art.

Thou art he whose precursor was the cross, the only begotten son of the Father alone above, and only son of the Virgin alone below.

Thou art he who was pierced in the hands and who rent the rocks.

Thou art he whom none other can carry except the bosom of the Father.

XVI.

And as she spoke thus the Lord was again hidden from her, and Xanthippe, coming to herself, said, Woe is me wretched one, that no one has told me what is the gratitude of slaves towards their master.

If Paul the preacher of the Lord were here, how could he give praise?

But perchance in the face of such favors and gifts they are silent, possessed only with tears, for it is not possible worthily to praise any one according to his favour.

Saying this she was seized with great faintness from lack of food, for having been strongly possessed with desire for Christ she had forgotten to take nourishment.

Therefore, being greatly exhausted by abstinence and the vision and want of sleep and other austerities, she was unable to rise from the ground.

XVII.

And Probus arose from his couch with a very gloomy countenance, for in his sleep he had seen a dream, and was greatly troubled concerning it.

But the porter seeing him about to issue to the market-place, having his countenance thus troubled, was greatly afraid, Lest, said he, he know what has happened, and will miserably destroy me.

Probus, however, having gone forth and signified to those in the market what was fitting for the day and season, speedily returned into the house, and said to his servants, Call me quickly the wise men Barandus and Gnosteas.

When they were summoned he said to them, I have seen a very terrible vision, and what appeared in it is difficult for our power to interpret.

This, however, do ye disclose to me, as being the most excellent of all the world.

Expound it to me when I tell it you.

Barandus says to him, If the vision can be interpreted by our wisdom, we shall explain it to thee, but if it be of the faith that is now spoken of we cannot expound it to thee, for it is of another wisdom and understanding.

However, let our lord and master tell the dream, and let us see if there is any explanation for it.

Probus says to Gnosteas, Wherefore answerest thou nothing?

Gnosteas said, I have not heard the dream, and what can I say but whatever it may be, if it is by reason of Paul?

Tell me now, and thou wilt find it so.

Probus said, I thought I was standing in a certain unknown and strange country, and that there sat there an Ethiop king, who ruled over all the earth and seemed never to have any successor.

There stood beside him multitudes of servants, and all hastened to destruction and had mastery far and wide.

And when that Ethiop seemed to have gained his purpose, there arose a raven and standing above him croaked with a pitiful voice.

And straightway there arose from the eastern parts an eagle, and seized his kingdom, and his power was made vain, and those standing by him fled to the eagle.

Then that king strove against those that fled to the eagle, but the eagle carried it up into heaven, and, behold, there came a helper to those that fled to the eagle and left his staff to them. Then they laying hold of it were not overcome by the violence of that king.

So many as ran to those who had the staff, he washed them in pure water, and they that were washed had power over his kingdom.

And by that staff the enemies of the king were put to flight, therefore capable men laying hold of the staff turned to themselves great multitudes.

And that king strove against them, and had no might at all, but he hindered many from believing in him that sent out the men into the world to bear witness, and for that reason many were grieved. Nevertheless, this one did not constrain any like the other, for he himself was ruler of all light.

This then was the end.

XVIII.

Then the wise Barandus said, By the grace of God I shall tell the things sent into the world by the Lord.

The king whom thou sawest is the Devil, and the multitudes of his servants are the demons, and the throngs about him are they that worship the gods.

Whereas he thought to have no successor, he looked not for the coming of Christ. The raven betokened the weakness of his kingdom, for the raven kept not obedience to the righteous Noah, but loved pitiful things.

The eagle that arose and took away his kingdom and carried it up into heaven, and that there came a protector of those that fled to the eagle, having a staff, that is the Lord Jesus Christ, who left to them his staff, that is, his precious cross; and that he washed those that fled to him signifies the invulnerable breast-plate of baptism, and therefore they were not overcome.

The capable men sent into the world with the cross are the preachers of God like Paul who is now with us, against whom that king has no power.

This was made known to thee because even on those who are hard of belief God has compassion in some way.

See therefore whether even thou wilt be able to injure Paul though thou desirest, for the mighty power that shields him has been shown thee by the Lord.

Therefore, understand what has been said to thee by me, and serve not that king of darkness, for as thou sawest his kingdom vanish away, so shall all his servants perish with him.

Come now, therefore, my Lord, let us go to Paul and receive baptism from him, lest Satan have mastery over us also.

Probus said, Let us first go to Xanthippe and see whether she still lives, for behold there are twenty-nine days since she has tasted anything; for I saw her face in the evening, and it was as of one prepared to depart.

XIX.

And as they went into the chamber, they heard her singing.
Praise the Lord ye sinners also, because he accepts your prayers also. Alleluia.
Praise the Lord ye that have despaired like me, for many are his mercies.
Alleluia.
Praise him ye ungodly, because for you he was crucified.
Alleluia.
Praise him ye that strive for the salvation of sinners, because God loves you.
Alleluia.
Praise him, ye that rejoice at the calling of sinners, because ye are fellow-citizens with the saints.
Alleluia.
As she said these words and more than these with tears, the wise men Barandus and Gnosteas opening the door entered and fell at her feet, saying, Pray for us lowly ones, O servant of Christ, that he may bring us also into thy number.

But she said to them, Brethren, I am not Paul who remits sins, but neither is he far from you.

Therefore fall not before my knees, but go to him, who is also more able to benefit you. Then they came running to the house of Philotheus to Paul, and found him teaching a great multitude.

And Probus also came to hear Paul, and Xanthippe entered along with him to salute him, and coming near to Paul and bending her knees she did him reverence.

Probus seeing this marvelled that her so proud spirit had changed to so great humility, for she sat beside the feet of Paul on the ground humbly and as one of the worthless.

And Probus was greatly grieved, not yet attending to the hearing of the word, but was ever gazing and fixing his attention on Xanthippe.

XX.

The great Paul was teaching thus, Let those that burn in the flesh observe lawful marriage, avoiding fornication, especially that with another's wife, and let those that are united keep to one another. Probus heard this teaching with delight, and said, O Paul, how excellently and wisely thou employest this teaching.

Why then has Xanthippe withdrawn from me?

And Paul said, My son Probus, they that foresee that the works of men shall be tried with fire, and that have always in their mind the inexorableness of death, cast out all desire that cleaves to the flesh.

But woe when the desire shall judge him that desired, then he shall gnash his teeth to no effect and in vain, for the amendment of repentance is past.

Hearing this Probus went up into his house marvelling, and tasted nothing that day, but went and lay down upon his bed.

And about the third hour of the night he arose and said, Alas, how wretched was the day in which I was wedded to Xanthippe.

Would that I had died and not seen her.

Saying this he arose and said, I shall pray to the God of Paul.

Perchance he will do to me also what is fitting, that I may not become a reproach in the world, being rejected by her.

And straightway falling upon the ground he said, O God of Paul, if, as I have heard from Xanthippe, thou dost seek after the ignorant and turn back those that are astray, do to me also what is fitting; for thou art the king of life and death, as I have heard, and hast dominion over things in heaven and on earth and under the earth, and over all the thoughts and desires of men, and to thee alone belongs glory to all eternity.

Amen.

XXI.

Then Probus arising from the ground fell again upon the couch, and arising early he came to Paul, and finding him baptising many in the name of the life-giving Trinity, he said, My lord Paul, if only I were worthy to receive baptism, behold the hour.

Paul said to him, Son, behold the water is ready for the cleansing of those that come to Christ.

Therefore immediately taking off his garments, and Paul laying hold of him, he leapt into the water, saying, Jesus Christ, son of God, and everlasting God, let all my sins be taken away by this water.

And Paul said, We baptise thee in the name of the Father and Son and Holy Ghost.

After this he made him to receive the eucharist of Christ. Then Xanthippe, being greatly rejoiced, began in the house toward evening together with her husband to give good cheer to all those in the house, and to prepare a feast, and when they came, after giving orders for the supper to be magnificent she herself went up to the chamber.

And behold on the stairs a demon coming in the likeness of one of the actors, and standing in a dark corner, was desirous to frighten and terrify Xanthippe.

But she thinking it to be the actor that she ordinarily had, said in anger, Many a time have I said to him that I no longer care for toys, and he despises me as being a woman; and straightway seizing an iron lamp-stand, she hurled it at his face, and crushed all his features.

Then the demon cried out, saying, O violence, from this destroyer even women have received power to strike us.

But Xanthippe was greatly afraid.

XXII.

After supper then Probus went forth to hear the word, but Xanthippe sitting in her bed-chamber was reading the prophets, her sister Polyxena lying upon the couch.

Xanthippe loved Polyxena exceedingly, because she was younger than herself, and beautiful in appearance, and Probus also loved her greatly.

And as Polyxena lay upon the couch she saw this dream, that a dragon, hideous in appearance, came and signified to her to come to him, and when she did not obey him to go to him, he came running and swallowed her.

From fear of this the girl leapt up trembling, and Xanthippe running to her said, What has happened to thee, dearest, that thou hast leapt up thus suddenly?

She for a long time was unable to speak; then coming to herself she said, Alas, my sister Xanthippe, what danger or tribulation awaits me, I know not; for I saw in my dream that a hideous dragon came and signed to me to go to him, and, when I would not go, he came running and swallowed me, beginning at my feet.

While I was terrified at this, there suddenly spoke out of the air, in the light of the sun, a beautiful youth, whom I thought to be the brother of Paul, saying, Verily, thou hast no power.

Who also took me by the hand and straightway drew me out of him, and straightway the dragon disappeared.

And behold his hand was full of sweet odour as of balsam or aught else for fragrance.

Xanthippe said to her, Truly thou must be greatly troubled, my sister Polyxena, but God has thee dear, seeing that he has shown thee strange and marvellous things.

Therefore arise quickly in the morning and receive the holy baptism, and ask in the baptism to be delivered from the snares of the dragon.

XXIII.

Xanthippe, having said this to Polyxena, and having made a cross of wood, went to Paul, but Polyxena remained alone in the bed-chamber, her nurse having gone together with Xanthippe.

And about the middle of the night, a certain man, powerful in wealth and assistance, finding the doors open and using magical arts, entered within, desiring to carry away Polyxena.

She discovering this fled into the mill, but the magicians led by the demons found her.

And she, not finding any door to escape by, said, Alas that I am given over to this destroyer; for she had heard that he was at enmity with her suitor, and he did this to assail and vex him, being a man who was a robber and exceeding cruel.

Therefore seizing her they went out of the city, dragging her to the sea.

She looked round this way and that, but there was none to deliver her, and groaning she said, Alas, my sister Xanthippe, thou didst send seven hundred pieces of gold to Rome and buy books, that through them thou mightest prophesy by me; for this evening thou didst read, I looked to my right hand and beheld, but there was no one that knew me; flight perished from me and there is no one that seeketh out my soul. ²

XXIV.

While she said these words, those that were dragging her away walked in haste, and coming to the shore they hired a ship and sailed for Babylonia, for he that carried her off had a brother there, a ruler of a district.

But the wind blew against them, so that they could not proceed by reason of it, and as they were rowing on the sea, behold the great apostle of the Lord, Peter, was sailing past in a ship, being urged by a dream to go to Rome, because when Paul departed for Spain there had entered into Rome a certain deceiver and magician, Simon by name, and had broken up the church which Paul had established.

And, behold, as he journeyed he heard a voice from heaven saying to him, Peter, to-morrow there will meet thee a ship coming from Spain; arise, therefore, and pray for the soul that is troubled in it.

As soon therefore as Peter saw the ship, remembering the dream, he said, O Jesus, that hast care for the troubled, whom the tribulation of those in a strange land moves to compassion, whom the weeping of those in captivity made to come upon the earth, who givest us at all time whatsoever we desire, and never turnest away from our request, show now also pity and assistance to the soul that is tossed about in that ship, because thou, O Lord, pitiest at all time those in pain.

The demons then, perceiving his prayer, said to the magicians, Avoid ye the course of that ship, for if we meet with it, we cannot move.

XXV.

But the loving God taking care for Polyxena, the vessel arrived in Greece, the blessed Philip being there, and having come down to the shore by a vision, and there accompanied him also great multitudes of those who were being taught by him.

And behold the vessel wherein was Polyxena appeared, terribly tossed about.

And the blessed Philip said, Behold the vessel on account of which we came down here, in which there is a soul in trouble.

When the vessel arrived and all had disembarked upon the dry land, they lay as half dead, because they had been greatly tossed about in the sea.

But the apostle Philip ordered Polyxena to be lifted and taken to the place where he was lodging, and the rest to be looked to.

But he that had carried off Polyxena, recovering from the disorder of the sea, was desirous to take her again, for Philip, having entrusted Polyxena to one of those that were taught by him, went on his way rejoicing.

But he that had her said, She was committed to me by a holy man, and I cannot give her up to thee.

He, however, giving no heed to him and finding there a kinsman of his, a nobleman, prepared for war, gathering eight thousand men.

Polyxena, knowing this, went forth by night and departed, but he that had charge of Polyxena said, Taking the tunic of Philip, I shall go forth alone to meet them; but as he said this it was announced to him that the maid was not there.

Then he, leaving all thought of the war, ran into the bed-chamber, and not finding the maid threw himself on the ground, saying, Woe is me, wretched one, that have become an enemy of Philip.

What shall I answer him, when he asks the maiden from me?

His servants came and said to him, Arise, our lord, from the ground, for the forces have surrounded thy house, and the maid cannot be found.

He said, Leave me thus to die on her account.

Perhaps, even by this, Philip the servant of Christ may be fully satisfied, since I shall be found despising his command. Then the servants, seeing that he heeded them not, took counsel to flee from the enemies, but again after a little, being moved by the foreknowledge of God, they said, It is not right for our master to die.

Come, let us go forth to meet them, raising the sign of the cross.

Then raising the precious cross they went forth, about thirty men, upon the enemy, and slew five thousand, and the rest fled.

And they returned with victory to their master, praising God and saying, What God is so great as our God, who has not suffered his servant to be slain by the wicked?

And coming upon their lord, still weeping, they said to him, Arise, lord, and weep not, for it befits it to be not as we will, but as the Lord wills.

XXVI.

Polyxena, however, going out of the city, and not knowing by what way she should walk, found herself in desert places of the hills, and sitting down said thus with tears, Woe is me, outcast and captive, that I cannot find even a wild beast's den to rest in.

Woe is me, left desolate, that not even Hades, that no one escapes, has devoured me. Woe is me, who at one time showed myself not even to my servants, and now display myself to demons.

Woe is me, that I am now made manifest to all those by whom I disdained to be seen.

Alas for me that was formerly devoted to idols; for this now even the mercy of God has passed me in silence.

Whom, then, shall I call upon to help me?

The God of Paul whom I have constantly offended?

But who shall help me now?

No one sees or heeds or hears my groaning.

Verily I shall beseech Him that sees the hidden things, for who is more pitiful and compassionate than He who always keeps watch over the oppressed?

But because my mouth is unclean and defiled, I dare not ask help from Him. Would that I were as one of the wild beasts that I might not know what captivity is.

Would that I had been drowned in the sea; perhaps having received the divine baptism I should have gone where no one is made captive.

What then shall I do, for death delays, and night has come on, and there is no help anywhere.

Having said thus, she arose and began to walk onwards, and passing through a small defile she fell into a wood very thick and large, and finding there a hollow in a tree, which was the den of a lioness, she sat down there, for the lioness had gone forth for her food.

And sitting down she said, O wretched begetting, O grievous hour in which I, unhappy one, came into this world; O mother that bore me, why, foreseeing my troubles and wanderings, didst thou name me Polyxena?

Has any other ever fallen into such tribulations and misfortunes?

Truly, my sister Xanthippe, didst thou read concerning me, unhappy one, saying, I have suffered affliction and been utterly bowed down (--Psalm xxxviii. 6).

These words thou didst utter with grief, while I lay upon the couch, thinking not at all of my sorrows.

On this account I have now come into the depths of evils, and pass the night in deserts like a wild beast.

But the beasts live with others of their kind, while I am left solitary, as not being of one race with mankind.

XXVII.

And as she was saying these words, and more than these, the morning dawned, and the lioness came from her hunting.

Polyxena, seeing the wild beast, trembled and said, By the God of Paul, O wild beast, have compassion on me and tear me not until I receive baptism. And the wild beast, fearing the adjuration, immediately went away, and standing afar off gazed at her.

And she said, Behold, the beast has obeyed me; I will also retire from its dwelling.

And immediately she began to journey towards the east, and the beast went before her until she was come out of the wood.

Then Polyxena said, What shall I give to thee in return, O beast?

The God of Paul will repay thee this kindness; and the wild beast, hearing her prayer, immediately returned to its place.

Then she, descending, found a public road, and standing on it wept, not knowing whither she should go, and though many went past, she turned to none of them, but said, Perchance the God of Paul will remember me, and whoever shall have pity upon me, to him will I go.

XXVIII.

As she said this, Andrew, the apostle of the Lord, also came journeying to that place, and as he drew near to Polyxena he felt in his heart some commotion arising in himself.

Standing, therefore, to pray, and folding his arms in the shape of the cross, he said, Lord Jesus Christ, partaker of light and knower of things hidden, from whom nothing on earth is hid, do unto me kindness and mercy, and make clear to me this commotion of heart, and calm my reason, thou that makest peace always with those that love peace.

Then Polyxena ran to him, and Andrew, the apostle of the Lord, said to her, Approach me not, daughter, but tell me who and whence thou art.

Polyxena said, My lord, I am a stranger here, but I see thy face is gracious, and thy words as the words of Paul, and I suppose thee to be of the same God.

Andrew understood that she spoke of the apostle Paul, and said to her, And whence dost thou know of Paul?

She said, From my own country, for I left him in Spain.

Andrew said to her, And how happenest thou to be here, the country being far distant?

She said, Because it was thus appointed for me, and came to pass; but I beseech thee and fall at thy feet, seal me, as Paul seals, by the baptism of regeneration, so that even I, lowly one, may be known by our God, for the kind God, seeing my tribulation and distress, sent thee to pity me.

Andrew, the great apostle of the Lord, said to her, Let us go, daughter, where there is water.

XXIX.

And when they had gone no long way, they came to a well most transparent and pure.

And as the blessed Andrew stood to pray beside the well, behold a certain maiden named Rebecca, of the tribe of Israel, brought as a captive to that country, came to draw water at the well, and seeing the blessed Andrew, knew him by his appearance.

For Rebecca said, This is the appearance of a Prophet, and this is one of the apostles.

And bowing down to him she said, Have mercy on me, servant of the true God, who am captive and sold for the third time, who was once honored by prophets, and am now insulted by idolaters, and recall me, lowly one, thou that wast sent to call back many sinners. Andrew, the apostle of Christ, said, God will care for thee also, daughter, as well as for this stranger.

Therefore, receive ye now baptism, and be ye as of one people, glorifying God always.

XXX.

Therefore the apostle standing prayed, and, behold, the lioness came running, and stood gazing upon him.

And Andrew the apostle of the Lord said, What then does this beast wish?

The lioness opening her mouth spoke with a human voice, Andrew, apostle of Christ, the prayer of her, that stands on thy right hand, has overtaken me.

Therefore confirm thou and instruct and admonish them in the right and true faith of Christ, for they greatly desire the name of the Lord.

And, behold, the wonderful condescension of God, that even on irrational and untamable beasts he has poured out his mercy.

The blessed Andrew weeping said, What shall I say or what shall I speak concerning thy mercy, O God, that thus thou at all times cleavest to the lowly, and takest care for those in ignorance, being without arrogance and full of mercy?

And having completed the prayer he baptised the maidens in the name of the Father, Son and Holy Ghost.

Then the lioness immediately set off to the mountain, and the Apostle Andrew said to the maidens, Be zealous, daughters, to be of good repute before God by living well in a strange land, and separate not from each other, and God, that is always present to those that call upon him, keep you in holiness, driving away from you the Evil One.

And pray ye also for me.

Polyxena said, We will follow thee whithersoever thou goest.

The Apostle Andrew said, This was not made known to me by the Lord, daughters; therefore remain with peace, hoping in the Lord, and he will preserve you to the end.

XXXI.

And Andrew went his way rejoicing and glorifying God.

Then said Polyxena, Whither shall we go, sister?

Rebecca said, Let us depart whither thou wilt, lest my mistress send and separate us.

Polyxena said, Come, let us depart into the mountain to the lioness.

Rebecca said, It is indeed better for us to live with wild beasts and perish of hunger than to be compelled by Greeks and idolaters to fall into the filth of marriage.

So they began to journey, and, behold, by the providence of God, they met a man driving asses, who seeing them said, Ye are not of this country, and, as I see, ye wear not its dress. Command therefore of your servant to eat bread and receive one piece of silver that ye may remember your servant when ye buy bread.

And he made haste and took the sacks off his asses and spread them on the ground, and made the maidens to sit upon them and said to them, Seeing that the wine which your servant carries is gathered by Greeks, tell me of what faith ye are, that thus we may taste of it.

Polyxena said, We, brother, taste no wine, and are of the God of Paul.

The ass-driver said. Is this God upon earth?

Polyxena said to him, God is everywhere, both in heaven and on earth.

The ass-driver, being desirous to learn clearly, said, Does this Paul then have the same God that is preached by Philip?

Polyxena, learning that he was a Christian, said, Yea, brother, this is the God of all, whom Paul and Philip preach.

XXXII.

The ass-driver hearing this wept unceasingly, and Polyxena said, Has then the providence of God overtaken thee, that thou weepest thus?

The ass-driver said, If thou art desirous to learn wherefore I weep, hear the truth, for one ought not to grudge to tell the things of Christ.

I was a disciple of Philip, the apostle of Christ, and seeing how all his thought was towards the poor, I took all that I had and sold it.

And taking the price, I bought bread and wine, and divided them throughout the cities to those that had need, when therefore I had done this for some time in the neighbouring city, a certain maimed person cried out, saying (though it was not himself that spoke, but Satan through his mouth), I desire nothing, I take nothing from thee, because thou art a Christian.

Then the whole city arose against me and sought to take me, but some ran one way and some another, while I go through their midst and no one sees me.

And issuing from the city I gave praise and glory to God that thus I had been rewarded, and I prayed to my God that I should meet some one who knew his all-holy name, so that relating these things I might obtain relief.

For the men of this country will not hear at all concerning Christ, being full of impiety and filled with wickedness.

I exhort you therefore, take ye also one coin from me, and if it seem good, take ye rest also upon the asses.

Polyxena said, Mayest thou obtain mercy from God, brother.

But if thou wilt receive a full reward, save us as far as the sea, so that, if God wills, we may sail for Spain.

XXXIII.

The ass-driver, as if commanded by the voice of God, eagerly receiving the maidens, went on his way rejoicing in the Lord.

And he said to Polyxena, Alter thy appearance to that of a man, lest for thy beauty's sake some one snatch thee away from us.

And coming to an inn, they stayed there, and on the morrow they went forward taking heed to the way.

And behold there came past a certain prefect journeying to Greece, who seeing the maidens ordered Polyxena to be carried off on his chariot.

Then the ass-driver followed, crying and saying, A prefect does violence to none.

Why do ye this?

Then they beat him and drove him away.

XXXIV.

And he going on his way lamented, saying, Woe is me, wretched and abominable one.

Woe is me that thought to do good, but now I have wrought mischief.

Woe is me that my trouble and my running were unacceptable.

Would that I had died before yesterday, that I might not have met with these maidens at all.

But why troublest thou me, O wretched soul?

Let us go to Philip the apostle of God.

If there is not forgiveness for me, it is better for me to choose death in whatsoever fashion than to live with such evil and bitter conscience. So he went and found Philip the apostle of Christ, and said to him, O disciple and preacher of Christ, thus and thus it has happened to me and befallen me.

Has my soul salvation?

Philip the apostle of Christ said, Be not distressed concerning this, my son, it is impossible for them to be dishonoured, seeing that no one ever overcomes God; for this same Polyxena, when she first came from the sea, I entrusted to a certain brother, who also was greatly distressed because of her running away secretly from his house.

Him also I persuaded not to grieve, for through her tribulation and wanderings many shall know God.

XXXV.

The prefect therefore carried Polyxena to the city where he stayed, and ordered her to be shut up in a chamber.

And one of the soldiers seized Rebecca, but the maid secretly escaping fled into the house of an old woman, who received the maiden kindly and entreated her well.

And sitting down she wept, saying, Alas, my sister Polyxena, I wretched one did not think that anyone was oppressed like myself, but now I am persuaded and know that all my misfortunes and tribulations do not compare with one day of thine.

And most grievous of all, behold I have been separated from thee and am again a captive, but do thou search for me even into the next world, my sister Polyxena.

The old woman said to her, What ails thee, daughter, that thou weepest thus bitterly?

Rebecca said, Suffer me, mother, to be distressed and to lament the great and incurable pain of my heart.

The old woman greatly compassionating her wept exceedingly, for the maid had told her all that had happened to her, and how through Polyxena she had believed in Christ.

So too Polyxena, shut up in the chamber, said, Woe is me, wretched one; alas for me miserable one; now I know clearly how the devil hates virginity, but O Lord Jesus Christ, God of all, since I dare not beseech thee of myself, I bring to thee the prayers of thy holy preacher Paul, that thou mayst not suffer my virginity to be destroyed by any one.

XXXVI.

And as she was yet praying, the attendants came to lead her to the couch of the prefect.

But Polyxena said to them, Brethren, make not haste to any one's destruction, for this time shall quickly pass away, and they that work together with the destroyers shall perish with them.

Rather assist strangers, that ye be not found strangers to the angels of God.

The men, being shamed by these words, went to the prefect and said, The maid from fear is seized with a violent fever. And the prefect said, Let her alone.

And, behold, the son of the prefect came to Polyxena by night, and she seeing him was afraid, but the youth said to her, Fear not, girl.

I seek not to be wedded with thee as the bridegroom of destruction, for I know from thy prayer that thou art the bride of the God of heaven.

I know this God who is never overcome by any one, for a certain man of glorious countenance lately in Antioch preached this God, and a certain maid, whose name was Thecla, believing him followed him, and encountered dangers on account of her beauty, of whom I have heard that she was condemned to the wild beasts.

I therefore continually gazed upon the man, and he having observed me said to me, God give heed to thee, my son.

From that time therefore by the grace of Christ I have not gone into the sacrifices of idols, but sometimes feigning illness and sometimes involving myself in some business, my father said to me, Because thou hast no zeal for the sacrifices of the gods, therefore neither art thou in health, not being worthy of the gods.

But I rejoiced, hearing that I was not worthy of the sacrifices to idols; and, by the grace of God, art thou come hither as a providence to me.

Polyxena said, And what is the name of that man?

The youth said, Paul is his name.

Polyxena said, He is in my city.

The youth said, Come then, girl, put on my appearance, and go down to the shore and wait me there; I having taken money will come quickly.

XXXVII.

And one of the servants overhearing them told all this to the prefect, who being filled with great anger condemned them to be cast to the wild beasts.

And when they were cast into the arena, a fierce lioness was let loose upon them, which ran and embraced the feet of Polyxena, and licked the soles of her feet.

Then the prefect and all the city, seeing this fearful and wonderful sight, gave praise and glory to the merciful God, saying, Of a truth thou art, and he, that is named by Polyxena, alone is God, for the gods of the heathen are the works of men's hands, unable to save or assist any one.

Let them perish now, both themselves and their makers.

And the prefect straightway taking his son and Polyxena into the palace, heard from them in order the faith and religion in Christ without omission, and he and all in the city believed, and there was great joy and giving of glory to God.

And Polyxena said to the prefect, Be of good cheer, my lord, for the man of God will quickly come, who will perfectly teach, exhort, instruct, and enlighten you in the knowledge of Christ.

She however prepared in all haste to depart into Spain.

XXXVIII.

And as I, Onesimus, was sailing into Spain to Paul, I received from the Lord a revelation saying to me, Onesimus, the vessel in which thou now art will land in the parts of Greece, and thou wilt find on the shore of the harbour two maids and one youth.

Assist them and take them to Paul.

When we reached this place according to the command of the Lord, we found the maids together with the youth seeking a vessel.

When the maids saw us therefore, they knew that we were of the hope of Christ, and Polyxena running to us said, Verily the man of God cannot be concealed, for the grace and kindliness of his countenance makes him manifest.

And when we sought to sail away, the sea was troubled by the providence of God.

And there was with us a disciple of Paul, by name Lucius, capable in word to teach the city. Therefore we remained seven days, and God opened to that place a great door of faith, and twenty thousand believed, and there was great joy and rejoicing in all the city.

And when the season was favourable for us to sail the prefect again constrained us, and we stayed another seven days, until all believed and rejoiced in the Lord.

XXXIX.

Thus now by the foreknowledge of Christ, the prefect sent us away with supplies for the voyage, sending also his son with us.

And when we had sailed twenty days, Polyxena was greatly exhausted, and we touched at a certain island for the sake of rest.

And behold, certain fierce and hardened men, coming down to us and seeing Polyxena, prepared for battle; but by the grace of Christ our men defended Polyxena and vanquished them, although the strangers were more numerous and more powerful.

Polyxena therefore fearing again to become a captive threw herself into the sea; but the pilot dragged her out, having suffered no harm.

Then we embarked in the vessel and fled, for the places were rough and wooded, and we were afraid to remain, and in twelve days we arrived in Spain, by the grace of God.

XL.

And Paul seeing us rejoiced greatly, and said, Welcome ye that have been troubled.

And Polyxena, laying hold of his feet, said, It may be that this trouble came upon me because I would have blasphemed thee, but now I beseech and entreat that I may not again be delivered into such troubles and misfortunes.

And Paul said, weeping, Thus must we be troubled, my daughter, that we may know our defender, Jesus Christ.

XLI.

And while we were giving the letters of the brethren to Paul, one ran and told Xanthippe of the arrival of Polyxena.

And she made haste and came to us, and seeing Polyxena, was overcome by an unspeakable joy and fell to the ground; but Polyxena embracing her and caressing her for a long time brought her back to life.

Then Xanthippe said to her, I, my true sister Polyxena, went not forth at all for forty days, praying much for thee to the loving God, that thy virginity might not be taken away.

And Paul, the preacher of God, said to me, Her virginity will not be taken away, and she will come quickly.

And Probus said to me, It was assigned to her by God to be thus afflicted. Seest thou how by many devices God saves many?

But now, my beloved sister, having unexpectedly seen thy face, now I shall willingly die.

XLII.

Then he who had carried her away came up again and sought for Polyxena, but the great Paul persuaded him to refrain from her, and he also believed and was baptised by Paul, as also the suitor of Polyxena believed, and there was great joy in all that city of Spain for the recovery of Polyxena.

From that time forward she left not at all the blessed Paul in her fear of temptations.

These things then being thus, all rejoiced in the Lord, glorifying Father, Son and Holy Ghost, one God, to whom is glory and power, now and ever and to all eternity. Amen.

The Forgotten Bible
Footnotes:
1. So the text; perhaps "prayer" ought to be read.
2. Psalm 142. 4.

The Narrative of Zosimus

Introduction

The Greek text of this work is printed for the first time in the same part of "Texts and Studies" as the Acts of Xanthippe and Polyxena.

The sources for it are two manuscripts--one in Paris, belonging to the twelfth century, and the other in Oxford, dating from the fifteenth or sixteenth.

The latter, however, only extends to the close of c. viii., the copy used by the scribe having been imperfect.

There are versions of the work in Slavonic, Syriac, Ethiopic, and Arabic; in the former of these the Blessed Ones are called the Brachmani.

From two passages in the poems of Commodian (c. 250 a.d.) it would seem that the work was known in his day, and the canon of Nicephoras (c. 850 a.d.) places it among certain apocryphal books which are to be rejected.

At the same time, it is doubtful whether, in its present form, it can be put as far back as the earlier of these dates.

It professes to be the account of a visit to the Makares, or Blessed Ones, given by a hermit, Zosimus, who was privileged to visit them. For forty years he had abstained from bread and wine and from seeing the face of man, always praying to be permitted to see the life of the Blessed.

With the second chapter the narrative begins in the first person, and is continued in this up to c. xxi., just where the angels come to receive the soul of Zosimus, and the work is then finished off by one of the hermits who were present at his last moments.

While the style is inelegant and sometimes obscure, the matter of the book is very interesting, and shows considerable powers of imagination.

The land of the Blessed is reached by means of a camel, which comes from the desert, and then by a storm of wind, which carries Zosimus along with it.

He is addressed by the river to which he comes, as well as by the wall of cloud which rises above it, and is finally lifted across it by two trees.

The origin of the Blessed Ones is noteworthy, as connecting the story with early literature on the Lost Tribes.

They are the descendants of Rechab in the days of Jeremiah the prophet, who, for refusing to give up their observances, are cast into prison by the king.

From this they are delivered by an angel, and brought to the place they now inhabit,--a level land covered with flowers,--a view of Paradise which continues all through the Middle Ages.

The chapters (x.-xv.) in which the Blessed describe their life and death are of special merit, and form the best part of the whole. In striking contrast to its lofty tone is the appearance of Satan with his 1360 demons, whom Zosimus finally overcomes and drives away.

To the various accounts of the Earthly Paradise, the story of Zosimus forms an important addition; on these it may, either directly or indirectly, have had considerable influence, although the difficulty of assigning a definite date to it makes this very uncertain.

The Narrative of Zosimus Concerning the Life of the Blessed

I.

About that time there was in the desert a certain man named Zosimus, who for forty years ate no bread, and drank no wine, and saw not the face of man.

This man was entreating God that he might see the way of life of the blessed, and behold an angel of the Lord was sent saying to him, Zosimus, man of God, behold I am sent by the Most High, the God of all, to tell thee that thou shalt journey to the blessed, but shalt not dwell with them.

But exalt not thy heart, saying, For forty years I have not eaten bread, for the word of God is more than bread, and the spirit of God is more than wine.

And as for thy saying, I have not seen the face of man, behold the face of the great king is nigh thee.

Zosimus said, I know that the Lord can do whatsoever he will.

The angel said to him, Know this also, that thou art not worthy of one of their delights, but arise and set out.

II.

And I, Zosimus, issuing from my cave with God leading me, set out not knowing which way I went, and after I had travelled forty days my spirit grew faint and my body failed, and being exhausted I sat down, and continued praying in that place for three days.

And, behold, there came a beast from the desert, whose name is the camel, and placing its knees on the ground, it received me upon its neck and went into the desert and set me down.

There there was much howling of wild beasts, and gnashing of teeth, and deadly poison.

And becoming afraid, I prayed to the Lord, and there came in that place a great earthquake with noise, and a storm of wind blew and lifted me from the earth, and exalted me on its wing, and I was praying and journeying till it set me upon a place beside a river, and the name of the river is Eumeles.

And behold when I desired to cross the river, some one cried as if from the water, saying, Zosimus, man of God, thou canst not pass through me, for no man can divide my waters:

but look up from the waters to the heaven.

And looking up I saw a wall of cloud stretching from the waters to the heaven, and the cloud said, Zosimus, man of God, through me no bird passes out of this world, nor breath of wind, nor the sun itself, nor can the tempter in this world pass through me.

III.

And I was astonished at these words, and at the voice that spake these things to me.

And as I prayed, behold two trees sprang up out of the earth, fair and beautiful, laden with fragrant fruits.

And the tree on this side bent down and received me on its top, and was lifted up exceedingly above the middle of the river, and the other tree met me and received me in its branches and bending down set me on the ground; and both trees were lifted up and set me away from the river on the other side.

In that place I rested three days, and arising again I went forward, whither I knew not, and that place was filled with much fragrance, and there was no mountain on either hand, but the place was level and flowery, all crowned with garlands, and all the land beautiful.

IV.

And I saw there a naked man sitting, and said in myself, Surely this is not the tempter.

And I remembered the voice of the cloud that it said to me, Not even the tempter in this world passes through me. And thus taking courage I said to him, Hail, brother.

And he answering said to me, The grace of my God be with thee.

Again I said to him, Tell me, man of God, who thou art?

He answered and said to me, Who art thou rather?

And I answered and told him all concerning myself, and that I had prayed to God and he had brought me into that place.

He answered and said to me, I also know that thou art a man of God, for if not, thou couldst not have passed through the cloud and the river and the air.

For the breadth of the river is about thirty thousand paces, and the cloud reaches to heaven, and the depth of the river to the abyss.

V.

And having ended this discourse the man spoke again, Hast thou come hither out of the vanity of the world?

I said to him, Wherefore art thou naked?

He said, How knowest thou that I am naked?

Thou wearest skins of the cattle of the earth, that decay together with thy body, but look up to the height of heaven and behold of what nature my clothing is.

And looking up into heaven I saw his face as the face of an angel, and his clothing as lightning, which passes from the east to the west, and I was greatly afraid, thinking that it was the son of God, and trembled, falling upon the ground.

And giving me his hand he raised me up, saying, Arise, I also am one of the blessed.

Come with me, that I may lead thee to the elders.

And laying hold of my hand he walked about with me and led me toward a certain crowd, and there were in that crowd elders like sons of God, and young men were standing beside the elders.

And as I came near to them, they said, This man has come hither out of the vanity of the world; come, let us beseech the Lord and he will reveal to us this mystery.

Surely the end is not at hand, that the man of vanity is come hither?

Then they arose and besought the Lord with one accord, and behold two angels came down from heaven and said, Fear not the man, for God has sent him, that he may remain seven days and learn your ways of life, and then he shall go forth and depart to his own place.

The angels of God having said this ascended into heaven before our eyes.

VI.

Then the elders of the blessed gave me over to one of the attendants, saying, Keep him for seven days.

So the attendant receiving me led me to his cave, and we sat under a tree partaking of food.

For from the sixth hour even to the sixth, then we ate, and the water came out from the root of the tree sweeter than honey, and we drank our fill, and again the water sank down into its place.

And all the country of those there heard of me, that there had come thither a man out of the vanity of the world, and all the country was stirred up, and they came to see me because it seemed strange to them.

Therefore they were asking me all things and I was answering them, and I became faint in spirit and in body, and besought the man of God that served me, and said, I beseech thee, brother, if any come to see me, tell them He is not here, so that I may rest a little.

And the man of God cried out saying, Woe is me, that the story of Adam is summed up in me, for Satan deceived him through Eve, and this man by his flattery desires to make me a liar while he is here.

Take me away from hence, for I shall flee from the place.

For behold he wishes to sow in me seeds of the world of vanity.

And all the multitude and the elders rose up against me, and said, Depart from us, man; we know not whence thou art come to us.

But I lamented with great lamentation, and my senses left me, and I cried out to the elders, saying, Forgive me, my lords, and the elders stilled them and made quietness.

Then I related to them all from the beginning till that time, and said, I besought the Lord to come to you, and he deemed me worthy.

And the elders said, And now what wilt thou we should do to thee?

I said to them, I desire to learn of you your way of life.

VII.

And they rejoiced with great joy, and taking up tables of stone they wrote on them with their nails, thus, Hear, ye sons of men, hear ye us who are become blessed, that we also are of you; for when the prophet Jeremiah proclaimed that the city of Jerusalem should be delivered into the hands of the destroyers, he rent his garments, and put sackcloth upon his loins, and sprinkled dust upon his head, and took earth upon his bed, and told all the people to turn from their wicked way.

And our father Rechab, the son of Aminadab, heard him and said to us, Ye sons and daughters of Rechab, hearken to your father, and put off your garments from your body, and drink no vessel of wine, and eat no bread from the fire, and drink not strong drink and honey until the Lord hear your entreaty.

And we said, All that he has commanded us we shall do and hearken.

So we cast away our clothing from our bodies, and we ate no bread from the fire, and drank no vessel of wine nor honey nor strong drink, and we lamented with a great lamentation and besought the Lord, and he heard our prayer and turned away his anger from the city of Jerusalem, and there came to the city of Jerusalem mercy from the Lord, and he pitied its people, and turned away his deadly anger.

VIII.

And after these things the king of the city of Jerusalem died, and there arose another king.

And all the people gathered to him and informed him concerning us, and said, There are certain of thy people, who have changed their way from us.

Therefore the king summoned them, and asked them wherefore they had done this; and he sent for us and asked, Who are ye and of what worship and of what country?

And we said to him, We are the sons of thy servant, and our father is Rechab the son of Jonadab, and when Jeremiah the prophet preached in the days of thy father the king, he proclaimed death to the city of Jerusalem, saying, Yet three days and all the city shall be put to death.

And the king thy father hearing this repented of his sins, and issued a command to all to turn aside from their wicked way.

And our father thy servant hearing it charged us, saying, Drink no vessel of wine, and eat no bread from the fire, until the Lord shall hear your entreaty.

And we hearkened to the commandment of our father, and made naked our bodies, we drank no wine and ate no bread, and we prayed to the Lord for the city of Jerusalem, and the Lord pitied his people and turned away his anger, and we saw it and our soul was rejoiced, and we said, It is good for us to be so.

IX.

And the king said to us, Ye have done well.

Now therefore mingle with my people, and eat bread and drink wine, and glorify your Lord, and ye shall be serving God and the king.

But we said, We will not disobey God.

Then the king was enraged and set us in prison, and we passed that night there.

And behold a light shone in the building, and an angel uncovered the prison and laid hold of the crowns of our heads, and took us out of the prison, and set us beside the water of the river, and said to us, Whithersoever the water goes, go ye also.

And we travelled with the water and with the angel.

When therefore he had brought us to this place, the river was dried up and the water was swallowed up by the abyss, and he made a wall round this country, and there came a wall of cloud, and shadowed above the water; and he did not scatter us over all the earth, but gave to us this country.

X.

Hear, ye sons of men, hear the way of life of the blessed.

For God placed us in this land, for we are holy but not immortal.

For the earth produces most fragrant fruit, and out of the trunks of the trees comes water sweeter than honey, and these are our food and drink.

We are also praying night and day, and this is all our occupation.

Hear, ye sons of men; with us there is no vine, nor ploughed field, nor works of wood or iron, nor have we any house or building, nor fire nor sword, nor iron wrought or unwrought, nor silver nor gold, nor air too heavy or too keen.

Neither do any of us take to themselves wives, except for so long as to beget two children, and after they have produced two children they withdraw from each other and continue in chastity, not knowing that they were ever in the intercourse of marriage, but being in virginity as from the beginning.

And the one child remains for marriage, and the other for virginity.

XI.

And there is no count of time, neither weeks nor months nor years, for all our day is one day. In our caves lie the leaves of trees, and this is our couch under the trees.

But we are not naked of body, as ye wrongly imagine, for we have the garment of immortality and are not ashamed of each other.

At the sixth hour of every day we eat, for the fruit of the tree falls of itself at the sixth hour, and we eat and drink our fill, and again the water sinks into its place.

We also know you who are there in the world, and who are in sins, and your works, for every day the angels of the Lord come and tell them to us, and the number of your years.

But we pray for you to the Lord, because we also are of you and of your race, except that God has chosen us, and has set us in this place without sin.

And the angels of God dwell with us every day, and tell us all things concerning you, and we rejoice with the angels over the works of the just, but over the works of sinners we mourn and lament, praying to the Lord that he may cease from his anger and spare your offences.

XII.

But when the time of the forty days comes, all the trees cease from their fruits, and the manna that he gave to our fathers rains down from heaven, and the manna is sweeter than honey.

Thus we know that the season of the year is changed.

But when the time of the holy passover comes, then again the trees put forth fragrant fruit, and thus we know that it is the beginning of the year.

But the feast of the resurrection of the Lord is performed with much watching, for we continue watching for three days and three nights.

XIII.

We know also the time of our end, for we have no torment nor disease nor pain in our bodies, nor exhaustion nor weakness, but peace and great patience and love.

For our soul is not troubled by the angels to go forth, for the angels rejoice when they receive our souls, and the souls also rejoice with the angels when they behold them; as a bride receives the bridegroom, so our soul receives the announcement of the holy angels, saying nothing more than only this, The Lord calls thee.

Then the soul quits the body and goes to the angels, and the angels seeing the soul coming forth spotless rejoice, and spreading out their robes receive it.

Then the angels call it blessed, saying, Blessed art then, O soul, because the will of the Lord is fulfilled in thee.

XIV.

The time of our life is this.

If one quits the body in his youth, the days of his life here are three hundred and sixty years, and he that quits the body in old age, the days of his life here are six hundred and eighty-eight years.

And the day of our completion is made known to us by the angels, and when the angels of God come to take us, we go with them, and the elders, seeing the angels, gather together all the people and we depart together with the angels, singing psalms, until the angels arrive at the place of our abode.

And because we have no tools, the angels of God themselves make the grave for our body, and thus he that is called by God goes down, and all salute him from small to great, sending him on his way and bidding him farewell.

Then the soul quits the body and the angels receive it, but we see the shape of the soul as a shape of light, perfect in all the body apart from the distinction of male and female.

XV.

Then the angels taking it up sing a song and hymn, making melody to God, and again other troops of angels come in haste to meet them, saluting the soul that is coming and entering into the firmaments.

And when it has come to the place where it is to worship God, the son of God himself, together with the angels, receives the soul of the blessed one and bears it to the undefiled father of the ages, and again, when the angels sing above, we being below listen to them, and again we sing and they listen in heaven above, and thus between us and the angels there arises a giving of praise in hymns.

But when the soul of the blessed one, falling upon its face, worships the Lord, then we also falling down worship the Lord in that same hour, and when the Lord raises it up then we also arise;

and when it goes to its appointed place, we also go into the church, fulfilling the eucharist of the Lord.

Having written these things, and all the life of the blessed, we gave them to our brother Zosimus, and escorted him as far as the place of trees beside the river Eumeles.

XVI.

And I, Zosimus, besought again the blessed ones to make entreaty for me to the Lord that the trees might receive me to take me across. And they all cried to the Lord and said, O God that hast shown us thy marvels and hast made thy servant Zosimus to come to us out of the world of vanity, set him again in his own place with peace, and command these trees to bow down and take up thy servant and set him on the further side.

And as they finished their prayer, the trees straightway bent down before them, and received me as on the second day before; and being set on the other side of the river I cried with a loud voice and said, Men of righteousness, who are brothers of the holy angels, grant me your prayer in peace, for behold I depart from you.

And making prayer they all cried out, saying, Peace, peace be with you, brother.

XVII.

Then I prayed to the Lord, and there came to me a storm of wind, and received me upon its wings, and carried me to the place where it found me sitting, and left me there in peace.

And raising its voice the wind said to me, Blessed art thou, Zosimus, that thou hast been numbered with the blessed.

And the beast from the desert, whose name is the camel, came and received me upon its neck and carried me eighty and five stations, and set me in the place where it found me praying, and left me in peace, crying and saying, Blessed art thou, Zosimus, that thou hast been numbered with the blessed.

XVIII.

But seeing me thus praised, Satan desired to tempt me and throw his dart at me from his station, but an angel of God came and said to me, Zosimus, behold Satan is coming to tempt thee, but the Lord will fight for thee, for the glory of thy faith must bind [1] Satan.

And an angel of God appeared, crying and saying, Welcome, blessed one of Christ.

Come and I shall lead thee to the cave that is the dwelling-place of thy body, for thy cave shall be a testimony of the desert, a healing of the sick that come to it, a place of trial and touchstone of demons.

And laying hold of my hand he strengthened me, and led me for forty days to the cave where I had dwelt.

And there was there a table of righteousness, and I spent the night with the angels of God.

And I placed the tablets that were given me by the holy blessed ones on the step of the altar in my cave.

XIX.

And, behold, when the angels of God ascended, the Devil came, having a fierce shape, and possessed with anger and gall, and said to me, I knew that God would do with thee as with the blessed ones, and that they shall be free from sin and be above the angels, and therefore I brought in an evil design, and entered into the vessel of the serpent, an evil-doer added to evil-doer.

And by this I made the first man Adam to transgress and taste of the tree of life, since God had commanded him not to eat of it, that he might remain equal in glory to God and the holy angels; and thou again hast gone and brought this commandment, but now that they may not be without sin, I shall show thee how I shall destroy thee and all those that receive this commandment, so that they may not be without sin, and the book that thou hast brought.

XX.

Saying these things the Devil departed from me, and after eight days he brought with him one thousand three hundred and sixty demons, and dragged me from the cave as I prayed, and they beat me, tossing me about between them, for forty days.

And after the forty days the devil lamented before me and said, Woe is me that through one man I have lost the world, for he has vanquished me by his prayer.

And he began to run from me, but I laying hold of him stayed him and said, Thou shalt not run away and flee from me until thou swearest to me never again to tempt man.

And lamenting with great and violent lamentation he swore to me by the firmament of heaven, So long as thy dwelling is here, and after thee, I will not come upon this place.

Then I let him go, sending him and the demons with him into eternal fire.

Then the angel came, who had companied with me at the table, and led me into my cave with great glory.

XXI.

After this I lived thirty-six years, and communicated the way of life of the blessed to the fathers in the desert.

But the Devil wept because of the tables of the life of the blessed, saying, If this get abroad in the world, I shall be mocked, and these will remain without sin and I alone in folly.

And after the completion of the thirty-six years, the angels of God came to me as to the blessed.

And all the monks were gathered together and all who heard it, and this testament was read to all of them, and in such life he gave up his soul to God.

XXII.

And I, Cryseos, [2] being one of those in the desert, spread it abroad and gave it to all that were willing to learn it and profit by it.

Therefore the angels of God helped to bury the body of Zosimus as a precious gift, and we saw the soul of the blessed one shining seven times brighter than the sun.

And straightway upon that place there came up seven palm-trees and overshadowed the cave.

There came up also a fountain of water in that place, holy water, and unto this day a healing and salvation to all the sick that come to it.

Peace be to all that have heard the memorial of the holy Zosimus; the Lord is the advocate and helper of all to the endless ages of ages.

Amen.

Footnotes:

1. Text corrupt; "bind" is conjectural.
2. The name is corrupt.

www.ingramcontent.com/pod-product-compliance
Lightning Source LLC
Chambersburg PA
CBHW021132230426
43667CB00005B/92